Faking It!

Intersections

INTERDISCIPLINARY STUDIES IN EARLY MODERN CULTURE

VOLUME 84 – 2023

The titles published in this series are listed at *brill.com/inte*

Faking It!

The Performance of Forgery in Late Medieval and Early Modern Culture

Edited by

Philip Lavender
Matilda Amundsen Bergström

BRILL

LEIDEN | BOSTON

European Research Council
Established by the European Commission

Funding for this volume was received from the European Research Council (ERC) under the European Union's Horizon 2020 research and innovation program under grant agreement No 707946.

The Introduction and the chapter *Sailing and Sinking on the Sea of Forgery: The Tradition of Fake Sagas in Seventeenth- and Eighteenth-Century Sweden and Denmark* by Philip Lavender are available in Open Access, made possible by the University of Gothenburg.

Cover illustration: Thomas Barrett, *The Charlotte Medal*, 1788. Silver, 74 mm (diameter). Sydney, Australian National Maritime Museum Collection purchased with the assistance of the Australian Government through the National Cultural Heritage Account. Image © Australian National Maritime Museum Collection.

The Library of Congress Cataloging-in-Publication Data is available online at https://catalog.loc.gov
LC record available at https://lccn.loc.gov/2022043625

Typeface for the Latin, Greek, and Cyrillic scripts: "Brill". See and download: brill.com/brill-typeface.

ISSN 1568-1181
ISBN 978-90-04-44948-0 (hardback)
ISBN 978-90-04-10690-1 (e-book)

This book is printed on acid-free paper and produced in a sustainable manner.

Contents

Acknowledgements

The present volume originates from the international conference 'Faking It!: Forgery and Fabrication in Late Medieval and Early Modern Culture'. The conference marked the culmination of research carried out on a Marie Skłodowska-Curie Individual Fellowship (Grant Agreement No. 707946) entitled 'Forging Ahead: Faking Sagas and Developing Concepts of Cultural Authenticity and National Identity', funded by the European Research Council under the European Union's Horizon 2020 research and innovation program. The conference took place in August 2019 at the University of Gothenburg, Sweden. It was made possible by generous funding from the Wenner-Gren Foundations and Riksbankens Jubileumsfond. In addition, we are very grateful to the Early Modern Seminar at the University of Gothenburg for continuous support throughout the process of preparing this volume. We also thank Johan Sunegård for valuable assistance with proof-reading and formatting.

We also wish to thank Karl A.E. Enenkel, General Editor of the Intersections series, Jan L. de Jong, Series Editor responsible for this volume, and Ivo Romein, Arjan van Dijk and Gera van Bedaf at Brill for their help throughout the various stages of putting together this volume.

Figures

Notes on the Editors

Matilda Amundsen Bergström

Ph.D. (2019), University of Gothenburg, is a researcher in comparative literature at the Department of Literature, History of Ideas and Religion at that university. She previously held a postdoc in philosophy at the University of Copenhagen. Her dissertation explored authorial self-presentation in the works of Louise Labé, Katherine Philips and Hedvig Charlotta Nordenflycht. Her area of expertise is early modern women's philosophical writing, primarily in Scandinavia but also in England and France. Her current research project investigates Scandinavian women's writing on happiness in the seventeenth and eighteenth centuries. She has published many articles on early modern women's writing. She is the coordinator of Philosophy in Other Words – Nordic Research Network for Early Modern Women and Philosophy, and secretary of European Society for Early Modern Philosophy.

Philip Lavender

Ph.D. (2015), University of Copenhagen, is a researcher in comparative literature and Nordic philology at the University of Gothenburg. His area of expertise is medieval and early modern Nordic literature, in particular Icelandic, and its reception. One strand of this is the forgery of supposedly ancient Scandinavian texts during the antiquarian revival of the seventeenth and eighteenth centuries. He is the author of *Long Lives of Short Sagas: The Irrepressibility of Narrative and the Case of Illuga saga Gríðarfóstra* (2020). He has also published a number of articles on the genres of legendary sagas and Icelandic *riddarasögur* ('sagas of knights', 'chivalric sagas') as well as on long narrative poetry from the post-medieval period in Iceland (*rímur*). He is on the editorial board of the journal *Viking and Medieval Scandinavia* and is the coordinator of the Early Modern Seminar at the University of Gothenburg.

Notes on the Contributors

Brian J. Boeck
obtained his Ph.D. in Russian History from Harvard University and is Professor of Russian History at DePaul University. He is the author of *Imperial Boundaries: Cossack Communities and Empire Building in the Age of Peter the Great* (2010) and *Stalin's Scribe: Literature, Ambition, and Survival: The Life of Mikhail Sholokhov* (2019).

Federica Boldrini
is a researcher in medieval and modern legal history at the University of Parma. Her research interests include Franciscan legal literature and law and theology in the romano-canonical system of law.

Patricia Pires Boulhosa
is Honorary Research Associate at the Department of Anglo-Saxon, Norse and Celtic at the University of Cambridge. She specialises in medieval Icelandic law. Her publications include *Gamli sáttmáli: Tilurð og tilgangur* (2006) and *Icelanders and the Kings of Norway: Mediaeval Sagas and Legal Texts* (2005).

Laurent Curelly
is Professor of English at the Université de Haute Alsace in Mulhouse, France. He specialises in the literature and the history of the British Civil Wars. He is especially interested in the Civil War press, sectarian radicalism and devotional poetry. He has written extensively on all these topics. His key-publications include *An Anatomy of an English Radical Newspaper – The Moderate* (1648–9) (2017) and a collection of essays that he co-edited with Nigel Smith, *Radical Voices, Radical Ways – Articulating and Disseminating Radicalism in Seventeenth- and Eighteenth-Century Britain* (2016). Forthcoming is a joint French translation of some of the Digger leader Gerrard Winstanley's political pamphlets. He is also the editor of two online scientific journals, *XVII–XVIII* and *Revue française de civilisation britannique*, as well as the reviews editor of *Marvell Studies*.

Helen Hughes
is a Senior Lecturer in Art History, Theory and Curatorial Practice at Monash University in Melbourne, Australia. She was a 2019–20 Getty/ACLS Postdoctoral Fellow in the History of Art. Her research focuses on Australian art, both historical and contemporary. She is currently writing a book on late eighteenth- and early nineteenth-century convict art of Australia. Recent publications

include: *Double Displacement: Rex Butler on Queensland Art* (co-edited with Francis Plagne, 2019); *Tom Nicholson: Lines towards Another* (co-edited with Amelia Barikin, 2019); and *Mutlu Çerkez: 1988–2065* (co-edited with Charlotte Day and Hannah Mathews, 2018).

Jacqueline Hylkema
is Assistant Professor of Cultural History and History of Art at Leiden University, the Netherlands. Her research focuses on different kinds of forgery in seventeenth- and early eighteenth-century print, and their cultural, social and political implications. She has published widely on this subject, in terms of individual forgery cases as well as the general role and perception of faked texts and images in early modern societies. In 2014, she curated an exhibition on the dynamics of print in early modern forgery at Leiden University Library, *Books, Crooks and Readers: The Seduction of Forgery (1600–1800)*.

Lorenzo Paoli
is a Ph.D. student at the Centre d'Études Supérieures de la Renaissance of Tours, under the direction of Florence Alazard, and at the University of Bologna, under the direction of Isabella Lazzarini. He is currently working on the fortune of Annius of Viterbo in French historiography with his thesis, *Annius de Viterbe et les historiens français du XVIe siècle: les vrais usages d'un faux*, expected to be defended in 2023.

Ingrid Rowland
is Professor at the University of Notre Dame's School of Architecture in Rome. She is also Associate Professor of Art History at the University of Chicago. As well as being a frequent contributor to the *New York Review of Books* she is author of numerous articles and monographs on classical, early modern and baroque culture, among which can be mentioned *The Culture of the High Renaissance: Ancients and Moderns in Sixteenth-Century Rome* (1998), *The Scarith of Scornello: A Tale of Renaissance Forgery* (2004), *The Collector of Lives: Giorgio Vasari and the Invention of Art* (2017), co-written with Noah Charney, and *The Divine Spark of Syracuse* (2018).

Camilla Russo
is a post-doctoral researcher at the University of Trento, working on the PRIN (Research Projects of National Relevance) project 'Charte vulgares antiquiores'. She is the author of a monograph, *Firenze Nuova Roma: Arte retorica e impegno civile nelle miscellanee di prosa del primo Rinascimento* (2019), on the rhetorical miscellanies of speeches and letters in the vernacular produced in Florence in

the Quattrocento. At the University of Trento, she has collaborated on the creation of the *Archivio dei falsi letterari Italiani* (ArFLI), the first digital database of Italian literary forgeries in the vernacular, and has contributed particularly with regard to those forgeries attributed to the earlier centuries.

Ksenija Tschetschik-Hammerl
is Assistant Curator at the Department of Prints and Drawings, Hessisches Landesmuseum Darmstadt. She completed her Ph.D. in History of Art at Humboldt-University in Berlin. In her dissertation, *Die Originalität der Nachahmung um 1600: Kunst begegnet Natur bei Hans Hoffmann und Daniel Fröschel*, she examined, by focusing on two artists from the Rudolfine court in Prague, the interplay of illusion of nature and imitation of art in the Early Modern period.

CHAPTER 1

Introduction: The Performance of Forgery

Philip Lavender and Matilda Amundsen Bergström

What is a forgery? This straightforward question is a fitting jumping-off point for a volume on that very subject, but for those with some experience within the study of this phenomenon, it should come as no surprise that there is no readily forthcoming answer. K.K. Ruthven provides a working definition of literary forgery as 'any text whose actual provenance differs from what it is made out to be'.[1] For this volume, which dares to juxtapose studies of forgeries not only literary but also of other kinds, a slight modification provides us with 'any *created object* whose actual provenance differs from what it is made out to be'.[2] If we mistake a painting by an unknown artist for the work of a master, our confusion regarding the origin of the painting is not sufficient to make it a forgery: this is a pure misinterpretation and has nothing to do with the work of art being 'made out to be' anything other than what it is. An agent with an intention would thus seem to be required, in spite of Ruthven's evasive use of the passive tense (*who* has been making it out to be other than it is?).[3]

Forgery, too, is often defined or delimited in relation to adjacent phenomena and practices or can itself end up being used to distinguish a subgroup of what is popularly understood as forgery. For example in philatelic circles a postage stamp can be called a forgery if it is a copy of an existing stamp

1 Ruthven K.K., *Faking Literature* (Cambridge: 2001) 39. In Speyer W., *Die literarische Fälschung im heidnischen und christlichen Altertum* (Munich: 1975) 13, an extra qualification is asserted, in addition to the intentional misrepresentation regarding provenance, for a work to qualify as a literary forgery. The qualification is that the motivation for misrepresentation cannot derive from literary or aesthetic concerns.

2 Referring to 'created' objects raises the question of whether naturally occurring objects can be forgeries. The many medieval examples of random bones passed off as saints' relics would suggest otherwise. Nevertheless, a natural object like a bone would normally require a created context, be it a reliquary, a shrine or even a speech by a salesperson, which would serve to convince an observer of a provenance beyond the ordinary. Thus an alternative would be to refer to 'created or curated objects'.

3 It is only this particular definition which is evasively phrased, as elsewhere Ruthven discusses in detail the many complexities involved in pinning down forgery. Evasion can be seen as necessary in such minimal definitions due to the slippery nature of the concept under discussion.

DOI:10.1163/9789004106901_002

used to trick collectors, but it is designated a counterfeit if put into circulation (on a letter, for example) and used to defraud the government. A fake stamp, on the other hand, is a real stamp which has been modified to make it seem more valuable. William Casement, considering the ways in which writers in specialised fields, such as philately, have tried to distinguish forgeries from fakes points out that, regardless, 'a number of twentieth- and twenty-first-century commentators, including respected scholars, have treated the terms synonymously'.[4] In calling this volume *Faking It!* and supplying the subtitle referring to the 'Performance of Forgery', we follow such respected scholars and Casement himself in seeing no inevitable difference between faking and forgery: in fact we accept Casement's assessment that 'differentiating forgeries from fakes makes for an exercise in semantics that, while sometimes offering helpful explications, on the whole bodes difficulty'.[5]

Casement also draws attention to the fraught exercise that is the transdisciplinary study of forgery. In addition to stamp collectors' idiosyncrasies, literary historians sometimes propose and adopt distinctions which differ from those used by art historians, or even end up using terminology which is the direct inverse of that used by them. Umberto Eco, for example, delineated a theory of forgery applicable to the Middle Ages in which various types of false identification were outlined. While mentioning artworks, it seems literary texts and documents were foremost in his mind. Thus Eco describes a category of pseudo-identification which is said often to be accompanied by 'historical forgery', exemplified by a case 'when somebody writes a letter bearing false witness, a report that misrepresents the results of a scientific experiment, a dispatch or communiqué issued by a government that lies about the results of an election'.[6] It seems that in focussing so much on the duplication and identification processes of medieval charters and the like, Eco relegates forgery to a very specialised role not at all compatible in wider discussions: it is just fabricated supporting documentation. Another example is Wolfgang Speyer's distinction that a true literary forgery misleads the reader concerning the provenance of the text, but must do so for extra-literary and extra-aesthetic reasons. This poses questions, one of which is how we distinguish aesthetic intentions from other kinds (are they always discrete?) and whether, particularly when ancient artefacts are involved, it is practically possible. Any attempt

4 Casement W., "Is It a Forgery? Ask a Semanticist", *Journal of Aesthetic Education* 54:1 (2020) 51–68: 61.

5 Casement, "Is It a Forgery?" 52.

6 Eco U., "Fake and Forgeries in the Middle Ages", in Eco U., *From the Tree to the Labyrinth* (Cambridge MA: 2014) 222–249: 228.

to do so may result even more problematic when dealing with a more directly aesthetic form of culture production, such as painting.[7] One may forge a painting in the hope of economic gain, but does that empty the act of producing the forged painting of any aesthetic element?

This brings us back to the tricky question of intention and Ruthven's definition involving the misrepresentation of provenance. In the process of making something out to have a different provenance than it actually has, a number of complications arise. Presumably in most cases it is the forger who is involved in misdirecting the viewer, reader etc. Nevertheless, this volume touches on cases where the intention to deceive – to mislead a person or people as to the provenance of a cultural artefact – has been unstable or dispersed. Ingrid Rowland, for example, in her work *The Scarith of Scornello*, a study of Curzio Inghirami's seventeenth-century pseudo-Etruscan forgeries (a scarith is a type of cocoon containing an inscription), suggests that Inghirami's manservant's account of seeing his young master laughing at the moment when the first scarith was discovered points towards Inghirami's initial intention being more akin to that of playing a practical joke.[8] It was only when people took the scarith seriously that their creator was cornered into defending them and adopting the role of a serious forger. Intentions are not monolithic, but rather shifting and at times self-contradictory. In Inghirami's case it may have been more the act of reception that locked in a trajectory whereby the artefacts were made out to have a different provenance than they actually had (and thus made them forgeries). This misinterpretation may have subsequently been imposed upon the creator of the objects.

A more common critique of the assumption of an intention to deceive in forgery is quite simply that many forgeries have been created to enlighten their intended audiences with what their creators believed was in fact the truth. Alfred Hiatt has referred to this as the 'sympathetic' approach to forgery, whereby faking a document (or some such) is salvaged from any criminal or underhand taint if the intentions were noble or a greater truth was being served.[9] A fake charter may not be fake if the forger believes that it simply stands in for a charter which should exist because the benefice alluded to is genuine (or at least believed to be). Hiatt is not won over by such arguments,

---

7 It may simply be that Speyer's definition of literary forgery is too specialised to work for forgery in a more general sense. Hence our decision to favour Ruthven's broader definition.

8 Rowland I., *The Scarith of Scornello: A Tale of Renaissance Forgery* (Chicago – London: 2004) 3, 130.

9 Hiatt A., *The Making of Medieval Forgeries: False Documents in Fifteenth-Century England* (London – Toronto: 2004) 7.

pointing out that good and lofty intentions have abounded among forgers throughout history, but these have rarely spared them from the criticism of their contemporaries for their methods. Regardless it is worth keeping in mind that truth and lies can be inexorably entangled and one can deceive at the same time as one reveals truths.

If this brief foray into the nature of forgery remains inconclusive, what can be said with regard to our juxtaposition of it with 'performance'? The renowned anthropologist Victor Turner, reflecting on his experiences with Richard Schechner's company, The Performance Group, described their method of understanding anthropological fieldwork through performance as 'making, not faking'. This catchphrase seems to put performance at odds with forgery, while at the same time hinting at a (contested) perception that the two are kin.[10] Moreover, in a somewhat polemical essay from 1964 entitled "What Is Wrong with a Forgery?", Alfred Lessing made the observation that 'the concept of forgery applies only to the creative and not to the performing arts'.[11] He expands upon this idea by noting that the performing arts place emphasis on reproduction and technique, while the creative arts place greater emphasis on creativity or originality. If somebody copies a world-renowned painting there are situations in which the resulting work might be seen as a forgery, but it is very hard to imagine a situation – Lessing argues – in which a new performance of *Hamlet* might be considered a forgery. If we accept Turner's statement and Lessing's proposition concerning the opposition of creative and performing arts then our choice to produce an edited volume on the performance of forgery may raise some eyebrows. Nevertheless, we hope to show that performance, conceived in the broad sense, is an integral part of many forgeries.

To come to this realisation it is worthwhile considering the various meanings that 'performance' can have. Paul Allain and Jen Harvie in *The Routledge Companion to Theatre and Performance* identify 'at least five relevant meanings'.[12] The first is 'the live event of presenting something usually pre-prepared before an audience'. Other meanings are as a synonym for 'success' or 'quality' (e.g. in the phrase 'high-performance motor vehicle'), as a synonym for 'performance art' and as another way of talking about 'deconstructive performance'. The

10 Turner V., *From Ritual to Theatre: The Human Seriousness of Play* (New York: 1982) 93. See also Hylkema's chapter in this volume for an exploration of the conceptual relationship between stage performance and hoaxes.

11 Lessing A., "What Is Wrong with a Forgery?", in *The Forger's Art: Forgery and the Philosophy of Art* (Berkeley – Los Angeles – London: 1983) 58–76: 67.

12 Allain P. – Harvie J., *The Routledge Companion to Theatre and Performance* (Abingdon, Oxon – New York: 2006) 181.

meaning which is most relevant here is the second of those which Allain and Harvie present: 'performance describes all social behaviour', since 'scholars from philosophy to anthropology and sociology identified in social behaviour and ritual the repetitive or restored behaviour that Richard Schechner saw as essential to performance'.[13]

We will come back to this second meaning, but it is worth pointing out first that the contributions to this volume on occasion refer to moments when forged objects were presented in a way which chimes with the first meaning ennumerated by Allain and Harvie. In her chapter Ingrid Rowland, for example, points out that Annius of Viterbo's Dominican training in preaching, rhetoric and scholastic argumentation would have provided him with a performative edge when presenting and defending his renowned forgery, the *Antiquities* (*Antiquitates*). An individual's powers of verbal persuasion, presented before a live audience, are more elusive to modern scholars than the material artefacts which have endured and can therefore still be subjected to scrutiny. But in many cases, verbal gymnastics accompanied by gestures and stagecraft may provide a partial explanation for why a forged object received the acceptance it did. We would do well to factor the possibility of such performances into our analyses.

The complex entanglement of, on the one hand, performance, including verbal and gestural elements, and, on the other, artefactual methods of authentication also surfaces in Patricia Pires Boulhosa's contribution to this volume. In discussing Iceland in the fifteenth century she evokes a culture that was moving from a stage in which agreements relied on 'memory, ritual, [and] oral testimony' to one in which the physical artefact of the written document had greater weight. We do not want reductively to affirm that the authentication processes of oral cultures are equivalent to performances used to bolster forgeries. But this period of transition can be informative as regards the ways in which performances and material objects can interact. In such a period one might justifiably seek ways to materialise ephemeral knowledge in more substantial modes of dissemination. One might desire to create artefacts which embody known truths from a recent past in which such artefacts were not the preferred vector of transmission. The ritual performance which accompanies a charter in a culture which has not fully transitioned from oral to literate might provide clues and inspiration for other types of performance which seek to give credence to objects of more dubious origin.

Moreover, when one looks at forgeries from the perspective of performance, more attention can be paid to the timeframes or temporalities which they

13 Ibidem.

inhabit. We may occasionally overlook the fact that forged objects exist in and through time, treating them rather as static and fixed, created at a point in time and petrified in that moment for future generations to ponder. But when we consider forgeries as part of a performance their vicissitudes across a duration must be reckoned with. With this in mind, Allain and Harvie's first meaning of performance as a 'live event [...] before an audience', can be applied to the public event that any forgery implies. In order for the provenance of an object to be made out to be something it is not, an audience is obligatory: a forgery never presented before an audience is perhaps not worthy of the name. The audience (be they an individual or a multitude) may not realise that they are part of a live event, but it does not require too great a stretch of the imagination to see the series of moments when an object enters into and circulates within the public sphere as just that (and the clandestine preparation as a prehistory to this public event phase, much like the rehearsals of a play). The timeframe of the typical forgery-performance then continues with the discussions, debates, circulation and eventual exposure of the object as inauthentic.[14] This may take days, decades or centuries, but is usually longer than the couple of hours of a more familiar performance, such as a speech, concert or play.

Even with this new twist, accounts of forgeries as performances remain bound up with an oft-repeated normative conception of forgery, as the central axis in a detective story is presented during which the deceptive creation appears on the scene and is ultimately uncovered. But alternatives to this standard narrative can also be imagined. One such might arise through the compression of a performance into what we might call a micro-forgery. Ksenija Tschetschik-Hammerl's contribution to this volume presents an example of such. She analyses cases where the viewer is expected to be deceived and uncover the deception in a short amount of time (in this case false monograms which upon closer inspection give up their secrets). In her words 'the artist intended the deception through his works to be an inevitable but temporary situation'. This resembles what Julia Abramson discusses as 'mystification'.[15] Abramson talks of how the *philosophes* in Paris in the 1750s produced works which lay midway on the spectrum between fiction and forgery, since the intention was never permanently to deceive, only temporarily to confound. The problem with making a clear distinction between temporary mystification and permanent forgery is that it assumes too much of the forger and their intentions. Is it not naïve

14 If the object is never exposed as a forgery, then there is little that we can say about it. It has been pointed out that the history of forgeries is the history of failures, although this may be overestimating the long-term goals of forgers.

15 Abramson J.L., *Learning from Lying: Paradoxes of the Literary Mystification* (Newark: 2005).

to assume that all forgers imagined their works going forever unquestioned? Most forgeries are produced at a specific time and with a specific audience in mind: we should not assume that forgers have planned out the eternal lifespan of their works. And thus whether a forgery is micro or macro merely ends up being a question of the scale upon which the object in question is considered.

With the idea of the public forgery performance we find ourselves on the border between the first and the second meanings of 'performance', the latter embracing all social behaviour and ritual. Allain and Harvey emphasise the repetitive behaviour which is crucial to social ritual as performance. This might lead us to think of how, in certain cases, forgery is an act of repetition or duplication through the making of a kind of facsimile of an original (a direct forgery as opposed to a stylistic forgery). But when we look at the normative narratives of how forgeries are acted out, repetition seems to be for the most part absent: the item appears once, hangs around for a while and then is discredited once and for all. In reality, however, forgeries can live much more extended lifetimes with many appearances and many refutations. Textual forgeries, for example, were often widely disseminated within a short time after publication. Even if the original forgery came to be exposed and discredited, this was no safeguard against copies, derivative works, re-editions or translations continuing to circulate without coming under scrutiny. Discussion of this process of 're-forgery', as Walter Stephens has called it, is taken up in Lorenzo Paoli's chapter in this collection, which highlights how Annius' *Antiquities* could continue to circulate in new contexts – an example of a forgery being repeated numerous times, albeit with variations.[16] A curious additional example of the transplantation of the *Antiquities*, despite Annius' forgeries having been discredited by the end of the sixteenth century, is a seventeenth-century Icelandic poem on Cyrus the Great which refers to Metasthenes, one of Annius' spurious authors, alongside Herodotus and Plutarch.[17] Somebody in Iceland had 'not received the memo', so to speak, that Metasthenes was a confabulated creation of a debunked inventor.

It is not just the repetitions and reiterations of a single forged work which can lend a performance aspect to fabrications. Each individual forgery can also serve as a model for subsequent ones. Anthony Grafton's groundbreaking

16 Stephens originally discussed 'reforging' in the context of the work of Jean Lemaire de Belge's *Illustrations de Gaule et Singularitez de Troyes* (1510–1514), based on Annius' *Antiquities*. See Stephens W.E., *Berosus Chaldaeus: Counterfeit and Fictive Editors of the Early Sixteenth Century* (Ph.D. dissertation, Cornell University: 1979) 210.

17 The author of the *Rímur af Cyrus Persakonungi*, which have not been edited, was Jón Sigmundsson (*c.*1637–1725). See Lavender P., "Herodotus in Iceland", in *Gott skálkaskjól veitt Gottskálki Jenssyni sextugum 4. apríl 2018* (Reykjavik: 2018) 72–74: 73.

work, *Forgers and Critics*, made a strong case for forgery as an ongoing tradition, intimately intertwined with the parallel work of critics who are constantly developing methods to continue exposing the products of said tradition.[18] This sounds antagonistic, but the polarisation is mitigated by the fact that many of the key figures were playing on both teams, both fabricating and discrediting. Following this line of thought, different forged objects can be seen as ritual repetitions within a broader superstructure of cultural production including the negotiation of wider cultural authenticity. Despite Grafton's work, the many highly focused case studies of individual forgeries or forgers can sometimes miss the bigger picture. This can result in the many similarities and interconnections between various fabricated works remaining obscure. Philip Lavender's contribution to this volume is, however, an example of how works by different individuals and produced over several decades – in seventeenth- and eighteenth-century Sweden and Denmark – could be said to form a tradition which takes up similar themes and then subjects them to similar debates.

The value of performativity and its potential for engaging with the repetitive, recursive and drawn-out nature of forgery also becomes clear when we consider the historical context of this volume.[19] The examples discussed in the various chapters are rooted in the Late Medieval and Early Modern periods. Discussions of forgery have, however, a tendency to strain normative concepts of periodisation. Does one discuss early modern forgeries of antique statuary in the context of antique culture or early modern culture? If fragments of medieval charters are incorporated into a nineteenth-century spuriosity does this fit into a discussion of medieval charters and their reception or into one of fraudsters in the industrial age? The answer is probably 'both', but in many cases the options may not be so binary, with forgeries based on forgeries and responding to forgeries spanning several conventional periods. How do we approach, for example, forged political prophecies – as discussed in Brian J. Boeck's contribution to this volume – made at one point in time, made out to be from another point of time, and making predictions about a third point of time? If anything, these examples invite us to think more in terms of the types

18 Grafton A., *Forgers and Critics, New Edition: Creativity and Duplicity in Western Scholarship* (Princeton – Oxford: 2019).

19 The term 'performativity' may invoke Judith Butler's influential work on performativity and gender in *Gender Trouble: Feminism and the Subversion of Identity* (New York: 1990) and *Bodies that Matter: On the Discursive Limits of 'Sex'* (New York: 1993). Issues of body, gender, normativity and power structures are certainly relevant to many of the case studies presented in this volume, and in her chapter Tschetschik-Hammerl, like Butler, builds on J.L. Austin's speech act theory. But as the type of critical analysis explored by Butler is generally beyond the scope of this book, the concept 'performance' will consistently be used in the more limited meaning discussed above.

of multiple temporalities proposed by Reinhart Koselleck.[20] Nevertheless, while accepting that Late Medieval and Early Modern may be insufficient as neat temporal designations for containing the protean cultural artefacts under consideration here, there are reasons why this particular historical context is worthy of greater scrutiny.

The (approximate) period from the fifteenth century until the end of the eighteenth saw a number of developments which had a significant impact upon ways of conceiving forgery. One such development, as Alfred Hiatt has pointed out in *The Making of Medieval Forgeries*, is that 'in the Middle Ages the "producer" of the forgery is usually an anonymous figure, partly because forgeries [...] are frequently corporate in nature'.[21] This perceived shift from corporate forgeries to individual forgeries is what led up to the later focus on forgery as a question of individual motivations. However, one of the observations that arises from this book is that even at the end of the Middle Ages and into the Early Modern period, and beyond, forgeries continue to involve multiple agents, albeit in different constellations. The individual forger/author who arises in the Renaissance is just as embedded in networks of influence as his or her fraudulent predecessors.

In *Forgery, Replica, Fiction*, Christopher Wood too has argued for a paradigm-shift emerging around the end of the Medieval and start of the Early Modern periods in connection with technological developments such as printing. He makes the claim that 'over the course of the fifteenth and sixteenth centuries substitution (which is basically a system of forgery without criminality) was replaced by fictionality (which is basically a system of lying without dishonesty)'.[22] If substitution was the 'sympathetic approach' form which forgery took in the Middle Ages, more attention ought to be paid to how alternative, less sympathetic, forms of forgery arose alongside the fictional boom of the Early Modern period. These shifts concerning the roles of individual authors and their capacity to disseminate and have access to information mark the start of the period covered in this volume.

That period ends in the eighteenth century, when legal changes transformed forgery. Albrecht Dürer (discussed by Tschetschik-Hammerl in this volume) was responsible for the 'first-known case of art-specific intellectual property

20 Jordheim H., "Against Periodization: Koselleck's Theory of Multiple Temporalities", *History and Theory* 51 (2012) 151–171.

21 Hiatt, *The Making of Medieval Forgeries* 14–15.

22 Wood C.S., *Forgery, Replica, Fiction: Temporalities of German Renaissance Art* (Chicago – London: 2008) 107.

law being brought to trial' in 1506.[23] But it was in eighteenth-century Great Britain that intellectual property law, approximating the concept as we know it in the modern world, really took off. The Statute of Anne (also known as the Copyright Act), appearing in 1709–1710, was introduced to restrict which stationers and printing houses had the right to reprint which works. The juridical formulation of intellectual property continued apace from that point onwards. Likewise, with the gradual decline of aristocratic patronage, commercial authors became ever more involved in the process of regulating how their works were disseminated. The public discourse on forgery in the arts became symbolically connected with a new emphasis on financial forgery: new economic developments such as paper money, credit and promissory notes, and international trading companies led to an anxiety regarding signatures and authentication, which pervaded the popular consciousness. Paul Baines has pointed out that while the highwayman was the iconic rogue at the start of the eighteenth century, he gradually gave way to the forger, as '[n]ew possibilities in the analysis of forgers' biographies became increasingly dominant in the 1770s and in the end squeezed out the picaresque style'.[24] Forgers became associated with poets as solitary geniuses – criminals, yes, but also alluring. It is this shift which gave birth to the modern narrative which revels in the trickery of the forgery and the joy of the 'whodunnit' aspect. Our volume challenges such narratives, but also accepts that they play an important role in the performance of forgery. It is at the end of the period under discussion that this trope falls firmly into place.

This volume also casts a wide geographical net, bringing together discussions of cultural production from diverse parts of Europe, and the odd exception from even further afield (see Helen Hughes' contribution which ends in the Antipodes). This spread provides yet another challenge to neat periodisation, since ambiguities proliferate and multiple temporalities emerge when Italy, France, Germany, England, Russia, Sweden, Iceland and, indeed, Australia start jostling up against one another. To give just one example, the end of the Middle Ages in Iceland is often and quite precisely dated to 1550, the year in which the last Catholic bishop was deposed (and beheaded) and the Lutheran Reformation came into effect. In Italy, on the other hand, the Renaissance and Early Modern period seem to be in the offing already by the end of the fourteenth century.

23 Charney N., *The Art of Forgery: The Minds, Motives and Methods of Master Forgers* (London – New York: 2015) 12.

24 Baines P., *The House of Forgery in Eighteenth-Century Britain* (Aldershot: 1999) 129.

Italy, as is common in discussions of early modern culture, surfaces in several of the chapters in this volume, from guilds in Rome, Milan and Venice, to the court in Ferrara and academic disputes with their roots in Volterra and Viterbo. Italy in the fifteenth century also provides us with some noteworthy developments in the history of forgery which can be enlightening with regard to why this period deserves closer investigation. Over fifty years before Annius' *Antiquities* was published in Rome in 1498,[25] a work appeared which dramatically refuted the authenticity of an important document of Western Christianity which had been for the most part unquestioned for over 500 years. Grafton, in an afterword to a new edition of *Forgers and Critics*, written thirty years after the original was released, refers to this work stating that 'no demonstration of forgery is more famous, none captures the imagination of students and readers more powerfully, than Lorenzo Valla's demolition of the Donation of Constantine'.[26] As a grandstanding example of the exposure of a forgery lying at the cusp of the Medieval and Early Modern periods, Valla's *De falso credita et ementita Constantini donatione declamatio*, written in 1439–1440, thus deserves closer attention.[27]

The basic story of the Donation (the document itself also called the *Constitutum Constantini*, to distinguish it from the act it supposedly describes) is well known. Constantine I (also the Great) was the Roman emperor in the early fourth century known for presiding over the empire's conversion to Christianity and the move of the imperial capital to Byzantium in the east. The Donation is a text which describes how Constantine professes Christianity and hands the western empire over into the possession of Pope (at that time called Bishop of Rome) Sylvester I. Constantine's gift is connected to events described in the life of Sylvester (*Actus Silvestri*), in which Sylvester had cured Constantine of an illness thus convincing him of the Christian faith. This text was passed down through the generations until in the fifteenth century Lorenzo Valla proved that it was in fact a forgery. Constantine had, quite simply, never given the western empire to the Church.

Above we used the words 'for the most part' to qualify the unquestioned status of the Donation. This is because Valla was not the only sceptic. The German

25 See Paoli's and Rowland's contributions for more in-depth discussion of Annius' work.
26 Grafton, *Forgers and Critics* 130.
27 As G.W. Bowersock points out ("Introduction", in Lorenzo Valla, *On The Donation of Constantine* (Cambridge MA – London: 2007) viii), Valla's work is more accurately referred to as an 'oratio' than a 'declamatio', since a declamation presents both sides of an argument. It was Ulrich von Hutten who first attached the word 'declamatio' to the title of the work in his editions from 1518 and 1519.

humanist Nicolas of Cusa had also presented a refutation of the Donation prior to Valla in his *De concordantia catholica* (1433) and the Welsh bishop Reginald Pecock presented arguments against its validity in his work *Repressor of Overmuch Blaming the Clergy* (*c.* 1445).[28] Prior to this flurry of attention, there seems to have been little objection to the Donation for centuries. What distinguishes Valla's refutation, however, is that, as well as the typical rhetorical objections, he uses a completely new method to discredit the Donation, namely philological argumentation. As Glen W. Bowersock puts it, 'Valla rips apart the Latinity of the text of the Donation to prove, brilliantly and decisively, that Constantine could not have written it'.[29] Valla's refutation thus serves to remind us that not all attempts to expose a forgery are treated equally: it is not enough merely to have truth on one's side. In the Donation and its refutation, moreover, we have a performance of forgery which establishes the relative positions of Antiquity, the Middle Ages and the Renaissance. This because, as Robert Black has pointed out, Constantine's Donation to the church was seen by some as the end of the greatness of Antiquity, when the primitive church became corrupted by worldly concerns and thus entered into a dark age of Catholic venality.[30] And likewise because Valla's philological method introduced the defining methodology of Renaissance humanism which would reshape western culture and put an end to medieval scholasticism.

Valla's work is destructive rather than constructive: while rejecting the Donation's authenticity it makes no attempt to determine who was responsible for this document or why. It remained for scholars much later, in the twentieth and twenty-first centuries, to ponder and provide answers to these questions. Its origins seem to be connected to a revival of the cult of Sylvester in eighth-century Rome (i.e. four centuries after Constantine). Umberto Eco has pointed out that it may have been produced 'with no intention to deceive, as an exercise, a joke, or by mere chance'.[31] The manuscript tradition, dating back to the ninth century, may also be connected to a papal power play at that time, and seems to have arisen from the same Frankish environment as

28 On Nicolas of Cusa's refutation see Fubini R., "Humanism and Truth: Valla Writes against the Donation of Constantine", *Journal of the History of Ideas* 57 (1996) 79–86. On Pecock's refutation see Levine J.M., "Reginald Pecock and Lorenzo Valla on the *Donation of Constantine*", *Studies in the Renaissance* 20 (1973) 118–143: esp. 120–134.

29 Bowersock, "Introduction" vii.

30 Black R., "The Donation of Constantine: A New Source for the Concept of the Renaissance", in Brown A. (ed.), *Language and Images of Renaissance Italy* (Oxford: 1995) 51–85.

31 Eco, "Fake and Forgeries in the Middle Ages" 228.

a number of forgeries attributed to Pseudo-Isidore.[32] In the twelfth century the *Decretals* of Gratian gained the status of the principal collection of canon law of the Roman Catholic church and the Donation came to be attached to the *Decretals* as an additional interpolation (one of the so-called 'Paleae') by Gratian's student Paucapalea. Having made it into the manuscript traditions of the *Decretals* the Donation's wide dissemination throughout the medieval period was ensured. This complex transmission history also exemplifies a situation where numerous individuals, some intentionally and others innocently, were responsible for propagating a spurious text over a period of centuries.

This dispersed transmission history also meant that no single refutation, no matter how convincing, would suffice to do away with the Donation of Constantine, if not in the form of the *Constitutum Constantini* then at least in the popular legend attached to it. Johannes Fried has discussed how important cultural figures of the Middle Ages such as Walter von der Vogelweide and Giraldus Cambrensis discuss the Donation of Constantine without ever having seen the document in question.[33] The forgery was successful enough to render itself unnecessary, since the narrative that it put forward became part of cultural memory. After Valla's refutation the story also continued. Valla's work, as well as being epoch-making scholarship, can be seen as a targeted intervention in disputes between the papacy and secular leaders, specifically between, on the one hand, Valla's employer, Alfonso, King of Aragon and Sicily, and, on the other, Pope Eugene and papal clients in the House of Anjou, over the possession of Naples. Although Valla's work can be seen as highly damaging to the church, the dispute over Naples was solved and by 1455 Valla had been made papal secretary by one of Eugene's successors, Pope Calixtus III. The Donation had done its work, but when it came to be printed, first in 1506 and then in 1518 and 1519 by Ulrich von Hutten, times had changed and the onset of the Reformation meant that critiques of popish avarice had taken on a new valency. Valla's work formed the basis of Protestant critiques, while Catholic scholars took a variety of positions, among which was accepting the document as forged but insisting on the validity of the events described.

At the end of the sixteenth century, Cesare Baronio, the Italian cardinal responsible for the twelve-volume *Annales Ecclesiastici*, was forging new archaeological evidence from the original basilica of St Peter's in Rome to back

---

32 See Fried J., *Donation of Constantine and Constitutum Constantini: The Misinterpretation of a Fiction and its Original Meaning. With a Contribution by Wolfram Brandes, "The Satraps of Constantine"* (Berlin – New York: 2007).

33 Ibidem, 8.

up the claims made in the Donation.[34] He used real ancient bricks with real brick stamps but wrote about them in a way which made them out to have a different provenance than they actually had: in his description of them he silently expanded the abbreviation 'CONSTANT.' so that it gave the name of Constantine, when in fact it gives 'CONSTANT(IS)', the genitive form of Constans, Constantine's son. By misleadingly associating the building of St. Peter's with Constantine, Baronio lent credence to the idea that Constantine had acted as patron to the papacy and thus could credibly have made the donation. The case shows how literary forgeries can easily spin off into more artefactual modes.

Alfred Hiatt has posed the question of whether the fact that the Donation of Constantine was a forgery has been of benefit to its continued existence. Has it, we might ask, remained relevant in scholarly discussions in a way inconceivable had it been an authentic document?[35] This turns conventional wisdom on its head: if you want a work to really have a long-lasting impact then perhaps the scandal of the inauthentic is an expedient route to take (inasmuch as 'all publicity is good publicity'). That said, not all forgeries can aspire to the heights to which the Donation in combination with Valla's refutation has risen. Valla's own success lies in the fact that his work is not merely a skillful refutation of a forgery but also an exposition of the art of forgery exposure in general. By representing a new step in the application of techniques for uncovering forgeries, it gains a place not just in the history of papal tergiversation but in the history of forgery and its exposure in a more abstract sense. The potential for forgeries and those who uncover them to be actors in a history all of their own is one strand of this volume which we wish to emphasise.

Another example of a monumental forgery, this time from the end of the period which is the focus of this book, is James MacPherson's *Fragments of Ancient Poetry* (1760), one of the most famous literary forgeries of

34 Bowersock G.W., "Peter and Constantine", in Tronzo W. (ed.), *St. Peter's in the Vatican* (Cambridge: 2005) 5–15. Interestingly enough Baronio seems to have played a role in inspiring the extensive spurious works of another forger, Jerónimo Román de la Higuera. See Olds K.B., *Forging the Past: Invented Histories in Counter-Reformation Spain* (New Haven – London: 2015) 193–197.

35 The comment was made at the conference "Fake Blues: The Exposure of Forgeries and Their Aftermaths" (18th June 2021), organised by Stephan Bauer. Hiatt's paper was entitled "The Donation of Constantine in 1439". A similar idea seems to be suggested by Walter Stephens and Earle A. Havens when they remark that 'the importance of a forgery may derive even more from the broader cultural ramifications of its reception', in "Introduction: Forgery's Valhalla", in Stephens W. – Havens E.A. (eds.), *Literary Forgery in Early Modern Europe 1450–1800* (Baltimore: 2018) 1–14: 12.

eighteenth-century Europe. Suspicions concerning the authenticity of this work, supposedly composed by the Gaelic bard Ossian in the legendary past, were voiced already in several of the earliest reviews. As MacPherson went on to publish the Ossianic epics *Fingal* (1762) and *Temora* (1763), finishing off with *The Works of Ossian* (1765), debates over the authenticity of the works raged.[36] More often than not, defenders and skeptics alike based their opinions on external concerns having to do with Scottish-Irish-English relations. The debates over Ossian were brought to an end in 1805, as what may be considered the definitive arguments on both sides were published. Henry MacKenzie's 50-page *Report of the Committee of the Highland Society of Scotland, Appointed to Enquire Into the Nature and Authenticity of the Poems of Ossian* concluded that the poems of Ossian were not forged. MacPherson had, however, emended and edited them considerably, creating a form of hybrid, semi-authentic text.[37] Malcolm Laing's *Poems of Ossian*, on the other hand, presented the poems as MacPherson's work. Yet interestingly, Laing did not want to give MacPherson credit as author of the celebrated poetry. Instead, his argument was that MacPherson had stolen every line of Ossian from other poems, making him a plagiariser as well as a forger.[38] When Walter Scott reviewed the two works in the *Edinburgh Review*, he came down decisively in favour of Laing.[39] The show, it seemed, was over.

It was, however, not. Between 1805 and 1825, over 100 editions of Ossian's poems were published in more than ten European languages – an impressive

36 MacPherson James, *Fragments of Ancient Poetry, Collected in the Highlands of Scotland and Translated from the Galic or Erse Language* (Edinburgh: 1760); MacPherson James, *Fingal, an Ancient Epic Poem in Six Books, Together with Several Other Poems Composed by Ossian, the Son of Fingal, Translated from the Galic Language by James MacPherson* (London: 1762); MacPherson James, *Temora, an Ancient Epic Poem in Eight Books, Together with Several Other Poems Composed by Ossian, the Son of Fingal, Translated from the Galic Language by James MacPherson* (London: 1763); MacPherson James, *The Works of Ossian, the Son of Fingal* (London: 1765). See also MacPherson James, *Poems of Ossian and Related Works*, ed. H. Gaskill (Edinburgh: 1996).

37 MacKenzie H., *Report of the Committee of the Highland Society of Scotland, Appointed to Enquire Into the Nature and Authenticity of the Poems of Ossian* (Edinburgh: 1805). MacKenzie's report is explored in Manning S., "Henry MacKenzie's Report on Ossian: Cultural Authority in Transition", *Modern Language Quarterly* 68:4 (2007) 517–539.

38 Laing M., *The Poems of Ossian etc., Containing the Poetical Works of James MacPherson in Prose and Rhyme* (Edinburgh: 1805) vi–vii.

39 Scott W., "Report of the Committee of the Highland Society on the Poems of Ossian. Drawn up by Henry Mackenzie Esq. And The Poetical Works of James Macpherson Esq.; with Notes and Illustrations, by Malcolm Laing Esq", *Edinburgh Review* 6:12 (1805) 429–462: 462.

publication rate that would continue throughout the century.[40] The discussions about the authenticity of the poems also continued, in several European languages, even though the matter seemed to have been settled. Moreover, Ossian was given new life in poems, novels and paintings, becoming something of a cult figure in the budding romanticist movement (at least outside of England). Werther's feverish love for Ossian in Goethe's 1774 *Sturm und Drang* novel *Die Leiden des jungen Werthers* is just one early example.[41]

Ossian's continued appeal for a variety of readers throughout Europe and throughout the nineteenth century, despite – or perhaps because of – his acknowledged inauthenticity, profoundly challenges the notion that a forgery once revealed 'fails'. Moreover, MacPherson's Ossianic poetry brings to the fore several of the performative aspects of forgery that we explore in this book.

First, MacPherson's forgery demonstrates our previously discussed point that a forgery is always enacted, bound up in a story that is presented to the audience together with the forged objects. This story often concerns the origin of the objects in question – where they have been found and how – but also serves to create the fictions necessary for the objects to become plausible. In MacPherson's case, the existence of the Gaelic bard Ossian [Fig. 1.1], whose poetry had been passed down orally for a thousand years in the Scottish Highlands, is such a fiction. The forged poems are thus entangled in a web of fakery, a fact that seems to have made it difficult, if not impossible, to draw any clear line between authentic and inauthentic. In the decades following MacPherson's publication several other agents expanded this web of fakery by means of a number of material objects. In *A Tour in Scotland, and Voyage to the Hebrides* (1774), readers could learn of naturalist Sir Joseph Banks' 'discovery' of Fingal's cave on the remote Scottish Isle of Staffa.[42] In 1807, Sir John Sinclair included in his edition of Ossian's poetry both a one-page score presented as 'A Specimen of Ossianic Music' and a map of 'the residence of Fingal'.[43]

As Dafydd Moore has pointed out, in nineteenth-century debates concerning *The Poems of Ossian* critics defended multiple positions between wholesale

40 Barnaby P., "Timeline: European Reception of Ossian", in Gaskill H. (ed.), *The Reception of Ossian in Europe* (London: 2004) xxi–lxviii.

41 Lamport F.J., "Goethe, Ossian and Werther", in Stafford F.J. – Gaskill H. (eds.), *From Gaelic to Romantic: Ossianic Translations* (Amsterdam: 1998) 97–106.

42 Pennant Thomas, *A Tour in Scotland, and Voyage to the Hebrides* vol. 1 (Chester: 1774) 301–303. On Fingal's cave, see Gidal E., *Ossianic Unconformities: Bardic Poetry in the Industrial Age* (Charlottesville – London: 2015) 8–10.

43 Sinclair J. (ed.), *Poems of Ossian, in the Original Gaelic, with a Literal Translation into Latin* (London: 1807). On this, see Gidal, *Ossianic Unconformities* 55–59.

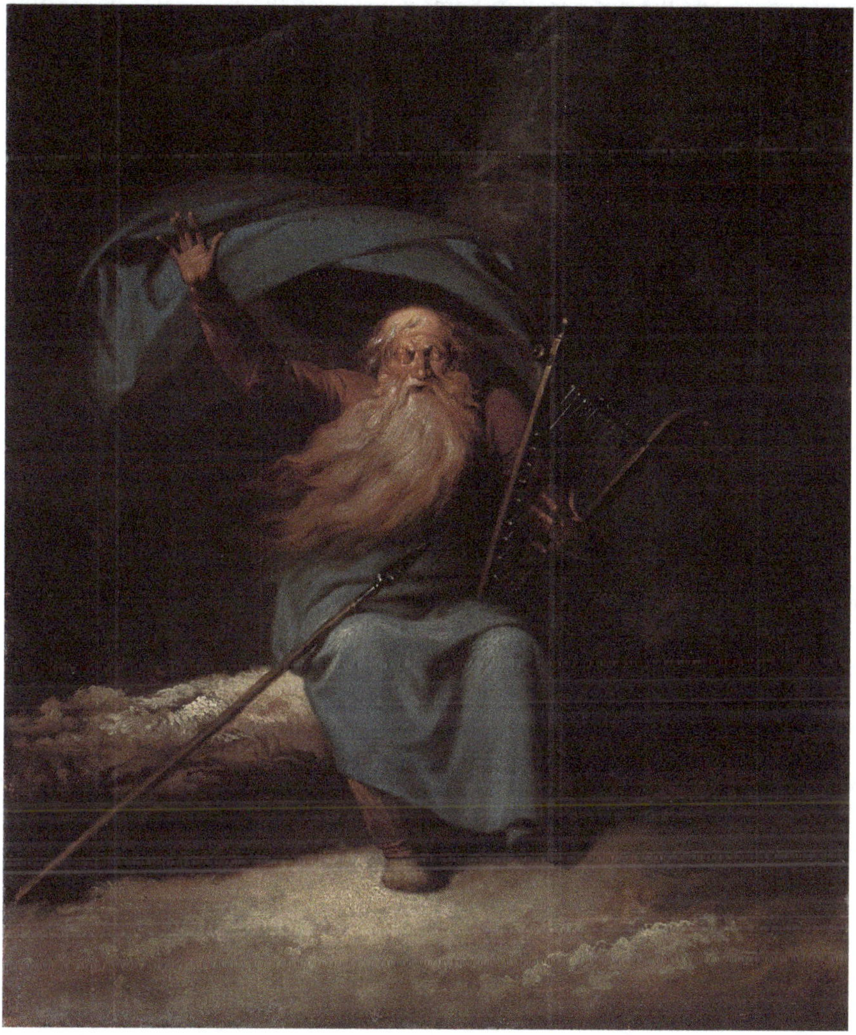

FIGURE 1.1 Nicolai Abildgaard, *Ossian. Den gamle blinde skotske barde synger til harpen sin svanesang* (Ossian Singing His Swan Song), 1780–1782. Oil on canvas. 42 × 35.5 cm
COPENHAGEN, STATENS MUSEUM FOR KUNST. OPEN ACCESS.
[https://open.smk.dk/artwork/image/KMS395]

acceptance and flat-out rejection. Some considered the material to be genuine but believed that MacPherson had arranged fragments into an epic. They perceived *The Poems of Ossian* as textually authentic but generically inauthentic. Others assumed that MacPherson had added to Ossian's text to enlarge the corpus, seeing the poems as an authentic/inauthentic hybrid. Yet other critics accepted the explanation MacPherson himself offered as to why he could not produce any Gaelic manuscripts: *The Poems of Ossian* had not been preserved in written records but in oral tradition. This would make *The Poems of Ossian* an inauthentic 'translation', as it was first claimed to be, but still an authentic report of Gaelic lyrical tradition. And lastly, some critics regarded *The Poems of Ossian* as a forgery, but one that was based on authentic cultural content if not a concrete oral tradition.[44]

MacPherson's enactment of his forged poems meant that the issue of authenticity could be regarded from many angles and did not necessarily rest on the existence of a Gaelic manuscript. Moreover, readers and critics shifted back and forth between these and other positions over the years, making it impossible to locate a point in history when *The Poems of Ossian* became accepted as inauthentic or any linear progression towards such a point. Instead, MacPherson's Ossianic poems appeared simultaneously as fake and real, depending on who was looking for what.

Second, *The Poems of Ossian* demonstrate that a forgery can continue to perform a host of functions even after it is revealed as such. As Moore points out, in the eighteenth and nineteenth centuries MacPherson's poems gave rise to creative and adaptational activities that appear unaffected by, and often unconcerned with, debates over the text's authenticity. Fake as the work was, *The Poems of Ossian*'s immense influence on the romantic literary movement is certainly very real.[45] So is its importance in the history of translation and in relation to Scottish nationalism. In the early nineteenth century, British essayist William Hazlitt went so far as to claim that the doubt surrounding *The Poems of Ossian* was more productive than any certainty concerning Ossian's existence could ever be:

> [I]f it were indeed possible to show that this writer [Ossian] was nothing, it would only be another instance of mutability, another blank made,

44 Moore D., "The Reception of the Poems of Ossian in England and Scotland", in Gaskill H. (ed.), *The Reception of Ossian in Europe* (London: 2004) 21–39.

45 This is comprehensively established in Schmidt W.G., *"Homer des Nordens" und "Mutter der Romantik": James Macphersons 'Ossian' und seine Rezeption in der deutschsprachigen Literatur* (Berlin – New York: 2003–2004).

> another voice left in the heart, another confirmation of that feeling which makes him so often complain, roll on ye dark brown years, ye bring no joy on your wing to Ossian![46]

As the case of Ossian amply demonstrates, forgeries can continue to perform, sometimes even perform better, when they are revealed to be such. This is the reason why we strive in this volume to get past a narrow focus on deception and revelation, exploring instead the continued life of forgeries, be they ambiguous, questioned or debunked.

A third way in which Ossianic poetry brings to the fore performative aspects of forgery relates to audience. Both the early critical discussions and the continued life of MacPherson's Ossianic poems show that a forgery can have different functions for different audiences, and that an old forgery may acquire new meaning as it reaches a new audience. Originally, *The Poems of Ossian* was a political performance intrinsically connected to Scottish nationalism. Demonstrating the antiquity and eminence of Gaelic epic tradition in Scotland, the poems can be considered to be an attempt to bolster the Scottish self-image in opposition to English oppression. The fact that the poems were fiercely defended by Scottish intellectuals, and just as fiercely contested by British and Irish Gaelic critics, indicates that this function was clearly perceivable to audiences in all countries.[47] But as new audiences in other European countries encountered *The Poems of Ossian*, the forgeries began to perform differently. For Goethe, Ossian's works provided a powerful expression of *Sturm und Drang*.[48] For tourists of the Scottish Highlands the books functioned as evocative guidebooks.[49] These shifting uses of *The Poems of Ossian* – and there were many more – show that forgeries are always put to work in the service of certain functions. This means that a forgery is not, as critics often suppose, simply the creation of a forger. Rather, it is the joint product of the forger who fashions it and the audiences who use it, in the process constantly creating the forgery anew.

This brings us to a fourth and final point: the complex relationship between forger and forgery. In 1773, MacPherson published a new edition of *The Poems*

46 Hazlitt W., *Lectures on the English Poets: Delivered at the Surrey Institution* (London: 1818) 37–38.

47 Manning S., "Ossian, Scott and Nineteenth-Century Scottish Literary Nationalism", *Studies in Scottish Literature* 17:1 (1982) 39–54.

48 Ó Dochartaigh C., "Goethe's Translation from the Gaelic Ossian", in Gaskill H. (ed.), *The Reception of Ossian in Europe* (London: 2004) 156–175: 156.

49 Leask N., "Fingalian Topographies: Ossian and the Highland Tour, 1760–1805", *Journal for Eighteenth-Century Studies* 39:2 (2016) 183–196.

of Ossian. By then, critical debates concerning authenticity notwithstanding, the poems had enjoyed enormous success. Ossian was repeatedly hailed as one of the greatest literary geniuses of European history, on a par with Homer. As Howard Gaskill has pointed out, this seems to have sparked some professional jealousy in MacPherson. In the 1773 edition, he chose to revise the text extensively to downplay Ossian's role as narrator. Apparently, MacPherson was not comfortable with having produced a work that was hailed as the product of genius without being able to lay claim to that prodigious title. Instead, he was prepared to risk exposing his own forgery to receive praise for his literary product. Yet interestingly, the plan backfired. Readers were horrified by the changes and rumors began circulating that the revisions did not prove MacPherson's role in creating the literary masterpiece, but rather his poor command of Gaelic.[50]

Instead of being praised as creator, MacPherson became criticised as translator. In addition, Macpherson, in Edmund von Harold and John Smith, got competition from other Ossians. In 1787 and 1780 respectively, they published their own forged Ossianic poetry, claiming to have found it in similar ways to MacPherson.[51] In several European countries, these later Ossians became at least as successful as the original Ossian, and they were sometimes bound together.[52] Twenty years after his first Ossianic forgeries, MacPherson had lost control of his own fiction. This highlights the central insight that, though most forgers have motives for creating their forgeries, once created forgeries take on lives of their own.

Between (and around) Valla's refutation and MacPherson's bestseller there are numerous other stories. Some of these have been presented in a recent volume edited by Walter Stephens and Earle A. Havens on literary forgery in early modern Europe.[53] That collection focusses exclusively on literary forgery, however, and moreover on state-centred ideologically-motivated and mythopoetic works whose 'entire purpose [...] has been to antedate and invalidate another

---

50 Gaskill H., "Genuine Poetry ... Like Gold", in Gaskill H. (ed.), *The Reception of Ossian in Europe* (London: 2004) 1–20.

51 Harold Edmund von, *Poems of Ossian Lately Discover'd by Edmond Baron De Harold* (Dusseldorf: 1787); Smith John., *Galic Antiquities: Consisting of a History of the Druids, Particularly of Those of Caledonia, a Dissertation on the Authenticity of the Poems of Ossian, and a Collection of Ancient Poems Translated from the Galic of Ullin, Ossian, Orran, Etc* (Edinburgh: 1780).

52 Gaskill, "Genuine Poetry ... Like Gold" 15–17.

53 Stephens W. – Havens E.A. (eds.), *Literary Forgery in Early Modern Europe 1450–1800*.

presumed claim to legitimacy'.[54] Thus the eleven chapters of this book offer additional stories which broaden the scope of that collection and represent a wider array of motivations. They appear in roughly chronological order, though the complex multiple temporalities already discussed mean that alternative arrangements could be imagined. The reader should feel free to approach them in any order they see fit. And while each chapter can stand alone, we do hope that readers will explore the material in ways which juxtapose contributions that might not normally be traditional bed-partners. In doing so, we see the greatest potential for provoking new and unexpected understandings, an outcome thoroughly in line with the ethos of the Intersections series.

Appearing first is Patricia Pires Boulhosa's chapter, "Forgery, Audience and Authentication: Icelandic Agreements of the Fifteenth Century", which evaluates the role of audiences in shaping forgeries. Boulhosa takes as her focus agreements found in fifteenth-century manuscripts which supposedly have their origins in the late thirteenth century when the Icelandic commonwealth submitted to the Norwegian crown. Arguing that in the making of these agreements forgers and audience were in a symbiotic relationship, Boulhosa places the appearance of the documents in the context of a culture which was gradually shifting from oral to literate forms of authentication. In so doing, she demonstrates how, as a forger understands the audience's expectations and shares these expectations with them, a forgery is also shaped by what its audience wants it to be.

In the chapter "All that Glitters is not Gold: False Jewellery and its Juridical Regulation in Italy between the Late Middle Ages and the Early Modern Period", Federica Boldrini unpacks the economic, moral and social dimensions of a classic forgery: fake gold. She demonstrates how early modern legal ideas about counterfeit gold and gemstones developed out of medieval discourses which questioned the moral and theological implications of creating gold by means of alchemical processes. Boldrini then draws on guild statutes to show how shifting fashion and sumptuary laws gradually led to changed attitudes regarding jewellery that looked like something that, in reality, it was not.

Lorenzo Paoli's chapter, "Re-Forging a Forgery: The French Editions of Annius' *Antiquitates*", shows how forgeries take on new functions as they are transplanted into new contexts. Surveying all French sixteenth-century editions of Annius' iconic forgery, the *Antiquities*, Paoli demonstrates how editors, printers and commentators continuously repurposed Annius' work. Paoli argues that such repurposing contributed significantly to the acceptance

54 Stephens – Havens, "Introduction: Forgery's Valhalla" 2.

and survival of the *Antiquities*, and that as a result of this process the *Antiquities* came to play an important political role in the consolidation of the French state.

In the chapter "Prenatal Prophecies and Linguistic Ciphers: A Russian Political Forgery Devoted to the Autocratic Evil of Ivan the Terrible", Brian J. Boeck analyses a forged prophecy from late sixteenth-century Russia which appears to foretell the violence of Ivan the Terrible's rule. Placing the text in the context of international orthodoxy, Boeck demonstrates that the forgery functioned as a cipher through which it became possible to discuss the violence of Ivan's *oprichnina* despite censorship. Resisting the notion that forgeries must fool all, Boeck argues that the forged prophecy performed a political function because it was identifiable as a forgery by a specific group of readers.

Camilla Russo's chapter, entitled "Girolamo Baruffaldi as a Forger: The Case of Barbara Torrelli", outlines the ideological dimensions of forgery and how these can contribute to a forgery's continued performative power. The forgery in question is a sonnet appearing in the Ferraran 'archpriest' Baruffaldi's eighteenth-century *Rime scelte* and attributed to Barbara Torrelli, a woman who had a dramatic life but whose literary output is restricted to this one dubious poem. Russo considers the motivation behind this forgery, making the argument that Baruffaldi wanted to promote a tradition of Ferraran female poetry, one which captured the hearts of later generations of literary scholars and thus led to the sonnet being reproduced well into the twentieth century.

In the chapter "The Deceptive Power of a Monogram: Appropriating Dürer's Identity in the Sixteenth and Early Seventeenth Centuries", Ksenija Tschetschik-Hammerl investigates fake signatures as a type of speech act. Focusing on sixteenth- and seventeenth-century artists' creative incorporation of the hugely influential Albrecht Dürer's monogram into their own paintings, Tschetschik-Hammerl questions the notion that forgeries 'fail' when they are revealed. Instead, she argues that the possibility of revelation was essential to the performative power of the fake Dürer monograms. This suggests that a more nuanced approach to the imitation of monograms can change our understanding of the meta-pictorial functions of fake signatures.

In the chapter "Mind your *U*'s and *V*'s!: Counterfeiting Newspapers in Civil War Britain", Laurent Curelly studies the forms and functions of the many counterfeited newspapers that circulated in England during the civil wars of the 1640s. In addition to considering them as a forum for expression, Curelly draws attention to the physical and material aspects of Civil War newsbooks. Highlighting the economic, socio-cultural and political aspects of these products, he demonstrates how forged newspapers fulfilled multiple purposes –

not least economic – causing them to affect the whole news market in ways that prefigure twenty-first-century 'fake news'.

Ingrid Rowland's chapter, "The Theatre of Forgery: Curzio Inghirami (Volterra, 1614–1655) and Giorgio Grognet de Vassé (Malta, 1774–1862)", highlights public performance as a significant aspect of textual and material forgeries. Rowland anchors her case in studies of the seventeenth-century Volterran Curzio Inghirami and the eighteenth-century Maltese Giorgio Grognet de Vassé. Inghirami was a skilled orator and used his gift to promote his 'ancient' Etruscan scarith. Rowland also discusses these scarith as a continuation of Inghirami's earlier comic writing. Grognet de Vassé, on the other hand, used his social network to spread knowledge of his forged manuscript of Eumalos of Cyrene – which identified Malta as Atlantis – and reinforced his ideas by creating Atlantean-inspired architecture in his homeland.

Philip Lavender, in the chapter "Sailing and Sinking on the Sea of Forgery: The Tradition of Fake Sagas in Seventeenth- and Eighteenth-Century Sweden and Denmark", uses the theme of sailing and sea-travel as a lens through which to draw together reflections on a tradition of saga forgery in early modern Scandinavia. A runic manuscript hinting at ancient Swedish connections with Mediterranean cultures, a saga which tells of the Cimbrian migrations originating in Sweden and leading to war with Rome and Danish eighteenth-century forgeries which came to be expatriated to independent Iceland in the twentieth century as cultural patrimony are all considered. Previously only treated in isolation by scholars, an argument is made that each forgery has had an impact beyond that of merely its own closed circuit of appearance, exposure and oblivion.

Jacqueline Hylkema's contribution, "Of Theatrical Illusion and Fake Advertisements: George Bickham the Younger, Samuel Foote and the Great Bottle Hoax of 1749", draws attention to an eighteenth-century discussion about the relationship between theatrical deception and forgery. The Great Bottle Hoax of 1749, in which a newspaper advertisement lured spectators to a London theatre to see a man in a bottle, inspired a print by George Bickham the Younger in which these intellectual currents collide. Bickham reveals whom he considered to be the author of the hoax and provides grounds for comparing the perpetrator's actions to the illusionist theatre of London of the time.

Last but certainly not least comes Helen Hughes' chapter, "Counterfeiting Coins and Convict Transportation from England to Australia in the Eighteenth Century", which links forgery, craftsmanship and colonialism. Hughes highlights the roles played by convicted forgers in the development of settler art in eighteenth-century Australia. Taking as her point of departure the fact that what was a capital offence in England became the basis for Western art on the Australian continent, Hughes demonstrates how forgery performed differently in the old and new worlds. These differences had profound effects on Australian art history, especially so in the settler tradition of Australian art history, where anxieties over cultural authenticity and originality have been dominant for decades.

In closing we wish to mention a comment which appeared in a recent newspaper article about an artefact conclusively proven to be a forgery. The Vinland Map was a document which surfaced in 1957 and was believed to be a fifteenth-century map of the world testifying to the advanced seafaring and cartographical knowledge of Nordic peoples in the North Atlantic [Fig. 1.2]. Speculation about its origins raged for decades but in recent years a study of the ink used proved conclusively, due to the presence of an artificial pigment, that it must have been made in the twentieth century. Raymond Clemens, curator of early books and manuscripts at the Beinecke Rare Book and Manuscript Library at Yale, commenting on this said that 'objects like the

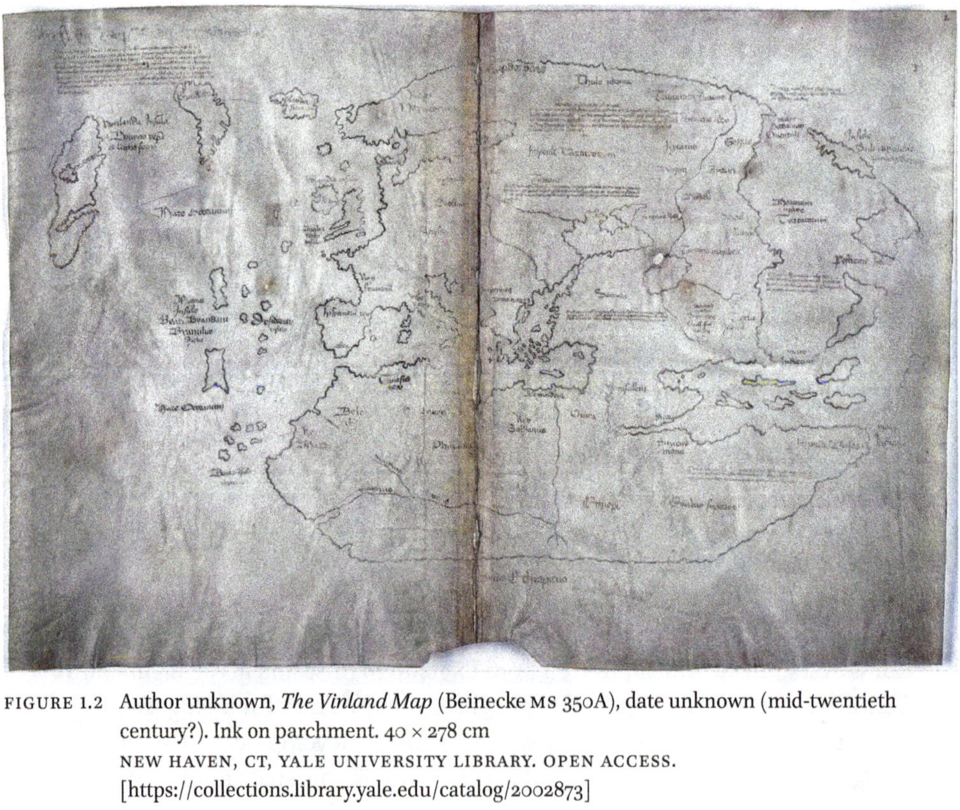

FIGURE 1.2 Author unknown, *The Vinland Map* (Beinecke MS 350A), date unknown (mid-twentieth century?). Ink on parchment. 40 × 278 cm
NEW HAVEN, CT, YALE UNIVERSITY LIBRARY. OPEN ACCESS. [https://collections.library.yale.edu/catalog/2002873]

Vinland Map soak up a lot of intellectual air space'.[55] It is certainly true that the debates which surround objects of dubious authenticity can sometimes appear to overshadow other potential discussions. But research should not be seen as a zero-sum game, where the inauthentic must be put aside so that we can focus on the authentic. And the implication that the Vinland Map will cease to 'soak up' intellectual air space once it is discredited, remains to be seen. The contributions to this book show that even once an artefact – be it a book, a painting or a gemstone – is proven to be a fake, much remains to be said about it. Forgeries are not just dead ends, but fruitful avenues for contemplation. Perhaps it is our duty to ensure that questions of authenticity are not blinkered and disconnected from the vast array of contiguous questions which embed such items in social and cultural history.

Bringing various forgeries together, moreover, allows for even more holistic forms of contemplation. One such observation regarding this volume might be in response to the absence of contributions concerning female forgers. Were women not engaged in forgery in the Late Medieval and Early Modern periods or have they merely been neglected by researchers working within the history of forgery? The discussions gathered here – in particular Russo's chapter – indicate that women could well be evoked by forgers but perhaps rarely adopted the role of active forger themselves.[56] Much more research would, however, be required to substantiate such hunches. This volume has its limits and has not been able to delve into these questions. But we present the eleven contributions of this book in the hope that they will inspire more consideration of this and other fascinating topics which, we affirm, should continue to take their rightful place in the intellectual air space.

---

55 Yuhas A., "Yale Says Its Vinland Map, Once Called a Medieval Treasure, Is Fake", in *The New York Times* (30 September 2021, updated 5 October 2021).

56 Perhaps the most well-known example of this is the controversy regarding French sixteenth-century poet Louise Labé. In her 2006 book *Louise Labé: Une creature de papier*, Mireille Huchon argues that the 1555 volume *Euvres de Louïze Labé Lïonnoize* is not, as it has long been considered, one of the most prominent examples of French women's writing in the Early Modern period. Instead, Huchon claims that the book is a forgery created by a group of Lyonnaise male poets – a suggestion that has given rise to intense scholarly debate that continues to rage. For arguments from both sides, see Huchon M., *Louise Labé: Une créature de papier* (Geneva: 2006); Huchon M., *Le Labérynthe* (Geneva: 2020); Martin D., "Louise Labé est-elle 'une créature de papier'?", *Réforme, Humanisme, Renaissance* 63 (2006) 7–37.

Bibliography

Abramson J.L., *Learning from Lying: Paradoxes of the Literary Mystification* (Newark: 2005).

Allain P. – Harvie J., *The Routledge Companion to Theatre and Performance* (Abingdon, Oxon – New York: 2006).

Baines P., *The House of Forgery in Eighteenth-Century Britain* (Aldershot: 1999).

Barnaby P., "Timeline: European Reception of Ossian", in Gaskill H. (ed.), *The Reception of Ossian in Europe* (London: 2004) xxi–lxviii.

Black R., "The Donation of Constantine: A New Source for the Concept of the Renaissance", in Brown A. (ed.), *Language and Images of Renaissance Italy* (Oxford: 1995) 51–85.

Bowersock G.W., "Peter and Constantine", in Tronzo W. (ed.), *St. Peter's in the Vatican* (Cambridge: 2005) 5–15.

Butler J., *Gender Trouble: Feminism and the Subversion of Identity* (New York: 1990).

Butler J., *Bodies that Matter: On the Discursive Limits of 'Sex'* (New York: 1993).

Casement W., "Is It a Forgery? Ask a Semanticist", *Journal of Aesthetic Education* 54:1 (2020) 51–68.

Charney N., *The Art of Forgery: The Minds, Motives and Methods of Master Forgers* (London – New York: 2015).

Eco U., "Fake and Forgeries in the Middle Ages", in Eco U., *From the Tree to the Labyrinth* (Cambridge MA: 2014) 222–249.

Fried J., *Donation of Constantine and Constitutum Constantini: The Misinterpretation of a Fiction and its Original Meaning. With a Contribution by Wolfram Brandes, "The Satraps of Constantine"* (Berlin – New York: 2007).

Fubini R., "Humanism and Truth: Valla Writes against the Donation of Constantine", *Journal of the History of Ideas* 57 (1996) 79–86.

Gaskill H., "Genuine Poetry … Like Gold", in Gaskill H. (ed.), *The Reception of Ossian in Europe* (London: 2004) 1–20.

Gidal E., *Ossianic Unconformities: Bardic Poetry in the Industrial Age* (Charlottesville – London: 2015).

Grafton A., *Forgers and Critics, New Edition: Creativity and Duplicity in Western Scholarship* (Princeton – Oxford: 2019).

Harold Edmond von, *Poems of Ossian Lately Discover'd by Edmond Baron De Harold* (Dusseldorf: 1787).

Hazlitt W., *Lectures on the English Poets: Delivered at the Surrey Institution* (London: 1818).

Hiatt A., *The Making of Medieval Forgeries: False Documents in Fifteenth-Century England* (London – Toronto: 2004).

Huchon M., *Louise Labé: Une créature de papier* (Geneva: 2006).
Huchon M., *Le Labérynthe* (Geneva: 2020).
Jordheim H., "Against Periodization: Koselleck's Theory of Multiple Temporalities", *History and Theory* 51 (2012) 151–171.
Laing M., *The Poems of Ossian etc., Containing the Poetical Works of James MacPherson in Prose and Rhyme* (Edinburgh: 1805).
Lamport F.J., "Goethe, Ossian and Werther", in Stafford F.J. – Gaskill H. (eds.), *From Gaelic to Romantic: Ossianic Translations* (Amsterdam: 1998) 97–106.
Lavender P., "Herodotus in Iceland", in *Gott skálkaskjól veitt Gottskálki Jenssyni sextugum 4. apríl 2018* (Reykjavik: 2018) 72–74.
Leask N., "Fingalian Topographies: Ossian and the Highland Tour, 1760–1805", *Journal for Eighteenth-Century Studies* 39:2 (2016) 183–196.
Lessing A., "What Is Wrong with a Forgery?", in *The Forger's Art: Forgery and the Philosophy of Art* (Berkeley – Los Angeles – London: 1983) 58–76.
Levine J.M., "Reginald Pecock and Lorenzo Valla on the *Donation of Constantine*", *Studies in the Renaissance* 20 (1973) 118–143.
MacKenzie H., *Report of the Committee of the Highland Society of Scotland, Appointed to Enquire Into the Nature and Authenticity of the Poems of Ossian* (Edinburgh: 1805).
MacPherson James, *Fingal, an Ancient Epic Poem in Six Books, Together with Several Other Poems Composed by Ossian, the Son of Fingal, Translated from the Galic Language by James MacPherson* (London: 1762).
MacPherson James, *Fragments of Ancient Poetry, Collected in the Highlands of Scotland and Translated from the Galic or Erse Language* (Edinburgh: 1760).
MacPherson James, *Poems of Ossian and Related Works*, ed. H. Gaskill (Edinburgh: 1996).
MacPherson James, *Temora, an Ancient Epic Poem in Eight Books, Together with Several Other Poems Composed by Ossian, the Son of Fingal, Translated from the Galic Language by James MacPherson* (London: 1763).
MacPherson James, *The Works of Ossian, the Son of Fingal* (London: 1765).
Manning S., "Henry MacKenzie's Report on Ossian: Cultural Authority in Transition", *Modern Language Quarterly* 68:4 (2007) 517–539.
Manning S., "Ossian, Scott and Nineteenth-Century Scottish Literary Nationalism", *Studies in Scottish Literature* 17:1 (1982) 39–54.
Martin D., "Louise Labé est-elle 'une créature de papier'?", *Réforme, Humanisme, Renaissance* 63 (2006) 7–37.
Moore D., "The Reception of the Poems of Ossian in England and Scotland", in Gaskill H. (ed.), *The Reception of Ossian in Europe* (London: 2004) 21–39.
Ó Dochartaigh C., "Goethe's Translation from the Gaelic Ossian", in Gaskill H. (ed.), *The Reception of Ossian in Europe* (London: 2004) 156–175.

Olds K.B., *Forging the Past: Invented Histories in Counter-Reformation Spain* (New Haven – London: 2015).

Pennant Thomas, *A Tour in Scotland, and Voyage to the Hebrides* vol. 1 (Chester: 1774).

Rowland I., *The Scarith of Scornello: A Tale of Renaissance Forgery* (Chicago – London: 2004).

Ruthven K.K., *Faking Literature* (Cambridge: 2001).

Schmidt W.G., *"Homer des Nordens" und "Mutter der Romantik": James Macphersons 'Ossian' und seine Rezeption in der deutschsprachigen Literatur* (Berlin – New York: 2003–2004).

Scott W., "Report of the Committee of the Highland Society on the Poems of Ossian. Drawn up by Henry Mackenzie Esq. And The Poetical Works of James Macpherson Esq.; with Notes and Illustrations, by Malcolm Laing Esq", *Edinburgh Review* 6:12 (1805) 429–462.

Sinclair J. (ed.), *Poems of Ossian, in the Original Gaelic, with a Literal Translation into Latin* (London: 1807).

Smith J., *Galic Antiquities: Consisting of a History of the Druids, Particularly of Those of Caledonia, a Dissertation on the Authenticity of the Poems of Ossian, and a Collection of Ancient Poems Translated from the Galic of Ullin, Ossian, Orran, Etc* (Edinburgh: 1780).

Speyer W., *Die literarische Fälschung im heidnischen und christlichen Altertum* (Munich: 1971).

Stephens W.E., *Berosus Chaldaeus: Counterfeit and Fictive Editors of the Early Sixteenth Century* (Ph.D. dissertation, Cornell University: 1979).

Stephens W. – Havens E.A. (eds.), *Literary Forgery in Early Modern Europe 1450–1800* (Baltimore: 2018).

Stephens W. – Havens E.A, "Introduction: Forgery's Valhalla", in Stephens W. – Havens E.A. (eds.), *Literary Forgery in Early Modern Europe 1450–1800* (Baltimore: 2018) 1–14.

Turner V., *From Ritual to Theatre: The Human Seriousness of Play* (New York: 1982).

Valla Lorenzo, *On The Donation of Constantine*, ed. G.W. Bowersock (Cambridge, MA – London: 2007).

Wood C.S., *Forgery, Replica, Fiction: Temporalities of German Renaissance Art* (Chicago – London: 2008).

Yuhas A., "Yale Says Its Vinland Map, Once Called a Medieval Treasure, Is Fake", in *The New York Times* (30 September 2021, updated 5 October 2021).

CHAPTER 2

Forgery, Audience and Authentication: Icelandic Agreements of the Fifteenth Century

Patricia Pires Boulhosa

Studies of forgeries tend to focus on their agents, the forgers. As with legal definitions of forgery, the forger's intention plays an essential part in our understanding of what a forged object is: a fake, a counterfeit, even if semantic nuances may set these terms apart. This paper places its emphasis on the role of the audience of forgeries, and on the historical and cultural circumstances that enable the forgers; it will reflect on the agency of both forger and the forgery's audience. The forgeries discussed here were produced in the last half of the fifteenth century in Iceland and are believed to be copies of an agreement (or agreements) made between Icelanders and King Haakon IV of Norway in the mid thirteenth century. These copies are short texts containing eight or ten clauses that lay down the conditions upon which Icelanders submitted to the king.[1]

The Icelanders' submission to the king is well documented in Icelandic sagas and annals, which tell how Icelanders, kingless from the time of settlement in *c.* 870 albeit not entirely impervious to the Norwegian king's influence,[2] finally swore allegiance and payment of tribute to the king in *c.* 1262–1264 after negotiations that lasted for more than a decade. Some of these sources mention that the king sent letters or documents during the negotiations, but they don't mention a formal agreement with rights and obligations in the model of the Magna Carta, to which the agreements are often compared.

I want to argue that in the making of these agreements, forgers and audience were in a symbiotic relationship; that is to say, the audience was no less the faker than the forger was. As no 'original' document exists – and perhaps never

1 The texts vary and contain between 251 and 336 words. A detailed classification and discussion of these documents is found in Boulhosa P.P., *Icelanders and the Kings of Norway: Sagas and Legal Texts* (Leiden: 2005). I would like to thank the Árni Magnússon Institute for Icelandic Studies for their continuous support and hospitality and for permission to display pictures of their manuscripts. Special thanks to the institute's photographer, Sigurður Stefán Jónsson.

2 See, for example, Long A., *Iceland's Relationship with Norway c. 870–c. 1100: Memory, History and Identity* (Leiden: 2017) 158.

 | DOI:10.1163/9789004106901_003

existed – these agreements cannot be strictly classified as fraudulent 'copies' of an original, but they can be understood through our own expectations – as we are their latest audience – of what a truthful agreement would be.

As the forger understands the audience's expectations and shares these expectations with it, a forgery is also what its audience wants it to be. A forgery's power to endure will depend on the expectations of its successive audiences. A forgery is perpetually shifting; it has no fixed meaning on its own. In the context of the Icelandic forgeries, I will first investigate the material means through which such expectations were articulated and how they were historically shaped.

1 A Historiographical Phenomenon

Iceland had a solid legal manuscript tradition from the thirteenth to the sixteenth century. Table 2.1 below shows that twenty-two per cent of all extant Icelandic manuscripts and fragments from 1201 to 1600 are legal manuscripts, the majority of which contain, in some form, the law-code issued by King Magnus VI of Norway in *c.* 1281 and known as Jónsbók.[3] It was only in the middle of the fifteenth century that twelve copies of the agreement were recorded in ten legal manuscripts. There are textual variations among these twelve texts, and so the numbers in the right-hand column of Table 2.1 conflate documents that are textually diverse.

TABLE 2.1 Distribution of manuscripts containing the submission agreements

	Icelandic manuscripts	**Legal manuscripts**	**Submission agreements**
1201–1300	111	8	–
1301–1400	332	55	–
1401–1500	241	54	12
1501–1600	210	82	14

3 Már Jónsson, "The Size of Medieval Icelandic Legal Manuscripts", in Rohrbach L. (ed.), *The Power of the Book: Medial Approaches to Medieval Nordic Legal Manuscripts* (Berlin: 2014) 25–38: 30. Boulhosa, *Icelanders* 109–111. The name Jónsbók, the 'Book of John', derives from one of its earliest compilers, the Icelander Jón Einarsson (d. 1306). The earliest mention of the name Jónsbók is found in the manuscript GKS 1005 fol., dated *c.* 1387–1395.

Leaving aside the hypothesis that the agreements themselves and all of their oldest recordings have been lost, these numbers show that the sudden simultaneous emergence of these recordings in the mid-fifteenth century, a hundred and fifty years after the event they purport to document, is a historiographical phenomenon that deserves closer attention.

Scholars of Icelandic history have accepted, by tradition, that these fifteenth- and sixteenth-century copies are fairly faithful reproductions of an original, now-lost document. This is not unusual in Icelandic scholarship: several of the most cherished texts, from sagas to law-books, are thought to be copies of older texts.[4] Only in 2005 was it proposed that the agreements were fabrications because they do not stand the scrutiny of historical, historiographical and codicological analysis. The historical problems are mainly anachronisms and other factual inaccuracies which have generated scholarly discussion, but for the present analysis the focus will be on the historiographical phenomenon itself.[5] The twelve fifteenth-century copies appear after a century-old manuscript tradition that allows us to investigate their origins within a solid historiographical and codicological context.

As noted above, the legal manuscripts that were made after the submission almost always contained the new law-code, Jónsbók, followed by royal amendments (*réttarbœtr*).[6] These amendments could be adjustments, corrections or additions to the law-code. The earliest amendments to the law were recorded in the manuscripts in two ways: they were either recorded after the text of the law-code and were marked by dedicated illuminated initials or were recorded within the body of the law-code marked by small red capitals. That is, the amendments were worked into the text and the clauses that had been repealed were not copied. The legal manuscripts also contained church laws, statutes and other texts with a legal nature or tone, from legal formulas to biblical passages, but also agreements between bishops and the Norwegian kings, and so

4 The most notorious example is *Íslendingabók*, a text that deals with the early history of Iceland, that is preserved in three manuscripts dated *c.* 1650–1600; see Hreinn Benediktsson, *Early Icelandic Script: As Illustrated in Vernacular Texts from the Twelfth and Thirteenth Centuries* (Reykjavik: 1965) 23–24. For a discussion on the numbers of lost Icelandic manuscripts, see Guðvarður Már Gunnlaugsson, "Manuscripts and Palaeography", in McTurk R. (ed.), *A Companion to Old Norse-Icelandic Literature and Culture* (Oxford: 2005) 245–264; also Már Jónsson, "The Size" 26.

5 For a summary and references concerning this debate, see Rohrbach L., "Construction, Organization, Stabilization. Administrative Literacy in the Realm of Norway: The Case of Iceland", in Imsen S. (ed.), *Rex Insularum: The King of Norway and His 'Skattlands' as a Political System c. 1260–c. 1450* (Bergen: 2014) 227–263: 231 and 259, note 35.

6 The terms 'law-books' and 'legal manuscripts' are used interchangeably but law-code always refers to the codified laws issued by the king and known as Jónsbók.

on. The makers of these law-books did not set out to record a fixed body of texts in a strict chronological order – rather, the texts were transcribed subject to taste and the availability of copies.

The contents of AM 135 4to, for example, a mid-fourteenth-century law-book, are typical of a fourteenth-century legal manuscript.[7] It is complete with an intact beginning and ending and written in a single hand throughout. The first folios were originally left blank but on folio 4v the opening words come from John 1.1–15: 'In principio erat Verbum et Verbum erat apud Deum et Deus erat Verbum' ('In the beginning was the Word, and the Word was with God, and the Word was God'). On folio 105v, the closing words are: 'Svá enda ok bók hér sem byrjaðisk í Guðs nafni. Christus scribentem custodiat atque legentem' ('So also ends here this book, as it began, in God's name. May Christ protect writer and reader') [Figs. 2.1–2.2].[8]

We may consider AM 135 4to as a finished project and understand its creators' purpose in making the book, even if their choice and order of texts seems higgledy-piggledy. Following the quotation from St John's Gospel comes a prayer and then a paraphrased narrative of the ten commandments from Exodus. Then comes Jónsbók, followed by amendments dated from the thirteenth and fourteenth centuries, then a single article on the king's land, followed by the Christian Laws, and then the old pre-submission Christian laws, and then a string of statutes on priests' pay, the tithe and so on.

The choice of old and new laws, framed by a Christian perspective of law and history, shows, on the part of the law-book's makers, a preoccupation with recording a history of Icelandic law. The higgledy-piggledy appearance of the book makes sense as we understand that its makers were trying to amass as much material as possible, old and new. Lena Rohrbach, who has studied the Icelandic legal manuscripts in greater detail, explains:

7 See, for example, Agnes S. Arnórsdottir, "Cultural Memory and Gender in Iceland from Medieval to Early Modern Times", *Scandinavian Studies* 85 (2013) 378–399: 380–382.

8 On the dating of all hands in AM 135 4to, see Schnall J.E., "Recht und Heil: Zu Kompilationsmustern in Handschriften der Jónsbók", *Gripla* 16 (2005) 75–114: 77; and Kålund K., *Katalog over den Arnamagnæanske håndskriftsamling I* (Copenhagen: 1889) 422–425. But the digital directory of the manuscripts of the National and University Library of Iceland (Landsbókasafn Íslands) and the Árni Magnússon Institute for Icelandic Studies (Stofnun Árna Magnússonar í íslenskum fræðum) give a slightly later date for folio 4v (handrit.is/en/manuscript/view/is/AM04-0135).

> There are no two medieval Icelandic legal manuscripts that are identical in terms of their inclusion of texts and the material presentation. Every manuscript is unique and tells a story about the social context of their commissioners and scribes.[9]

Rohrbach calls the law-books 'archives'. It is a fitting term, as several administrative texts were 'copied time and again in [these] comprehensive legal manuscripts'.[10] These law-books were not reference tools for easy, handy consultation. Even if the compilation of texts varies from manuscript to manuscript, almost all of the Icelandic legal manuscripts of the fourteenth century share this archival characteristic with AM 135 4to, and despite visual markers or their makers' declarations that the books end on such or such a folio, the law-books were not 'ready' or 'finished' forever. They were passed from generation to generation, among the administrative, legal, and ecclesiastical elites, who added to them according to their own liking. Each new owner added other texts.

In the fifteenth century, new owners added contemporary fifteenth-century material but also fourteenth-century material that was left out or was not issued by the time the law-books were first made. It is among these later added texts that the forged agreements appear. In AM 135 4to, a hand from the end of the fifteenth century wrote down legal formulas and other pieces of legislation across two pages, including a text of the agreement on folio 107r. [Fig. 2.3].

The same hand wrote down some amendments at the beginning of the manuscript on the pages that had been left blank in the fourteenth century. Later hands added text in the sixteenth and seventeenth centuries, perhaps through the addition of new pages.[11] The texts have been crammed onto their pages and it is visually possible to detect that they were written in different hands at different times.

The agreement also appears at the end of manuscript GKS 3269 b 4to, the earliest parts of which are dated to the middle of the fourteenth century; it was written on the last page of the manuscript by a fifteenth-century hand. In another mid-fourteenth-century manuscript, AM 168 b 4to, the agreement is

9 Rohrbach, "Construction" 246.

10 Ibidem.

11 A physical check of the manuscripts mentioned in this article was not possible due to the COVID19 pandemic, so information on the manuscripts' original pages or quires may contain inaccuracies. See Schnall, "Recht" 77–80.

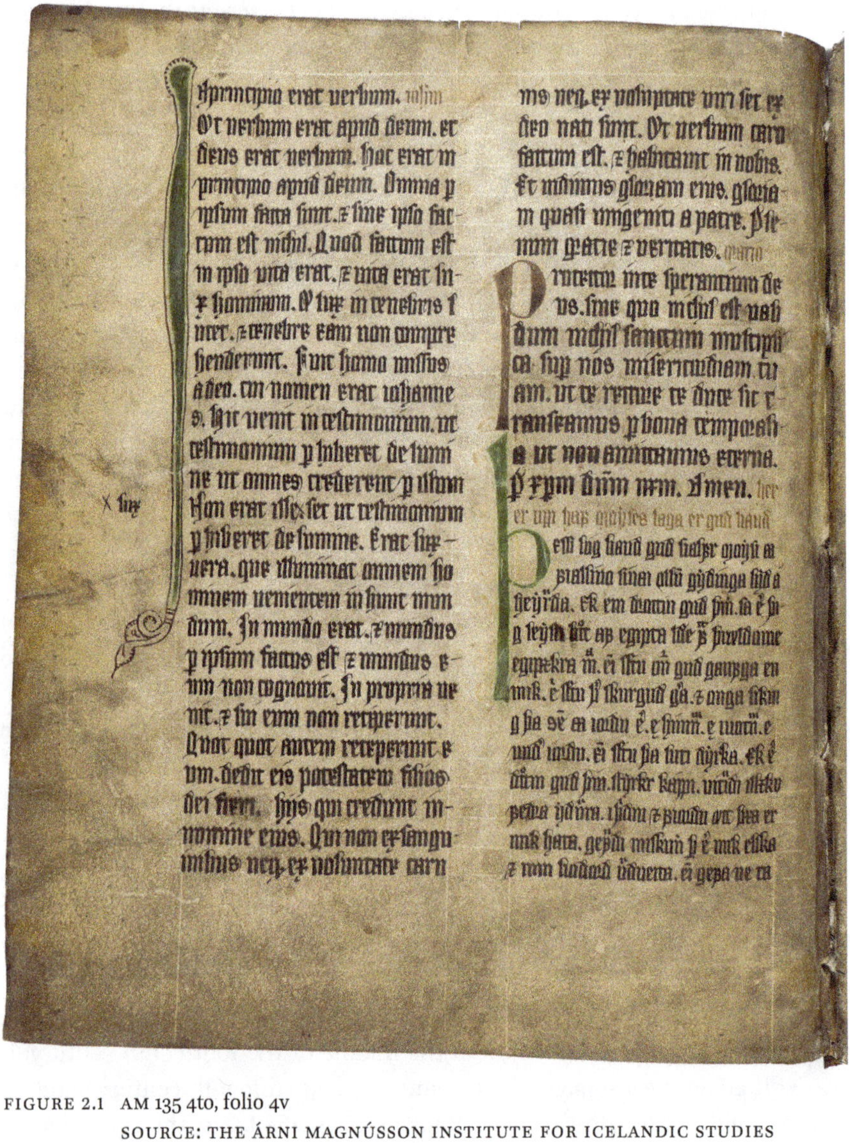

FIGURE 2.1 AM 135 4to, folio 4v
SOURCE: THE ÁRNI MAGNÚSSON INSTITUTE FOR ICELANDIC STUDIES

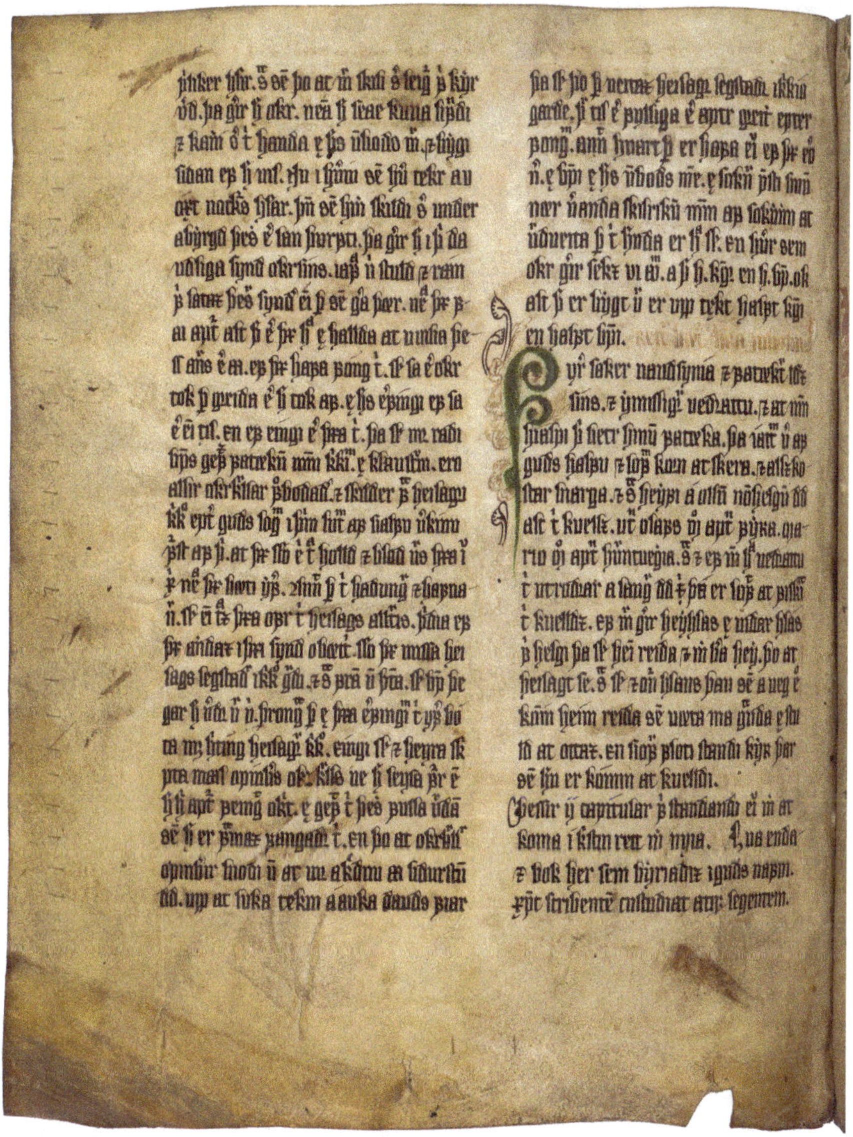

FIGURE 2.2 AM 135 4to, folio 105v
SOURCE: THE ÁRNI MAGNÚSSON INSTITUTE FOR ICELANDIC STUDIES

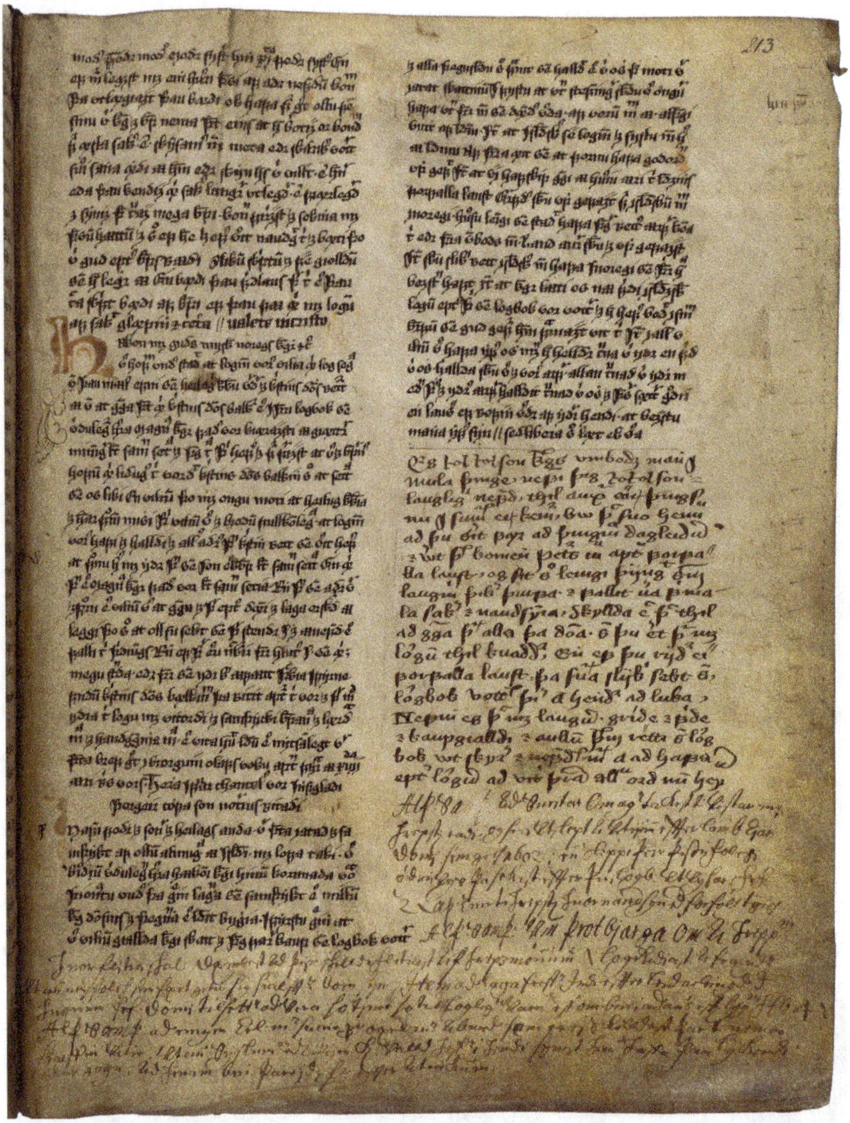

FIGURE 2.3 AM 135 4to, folio 107r. The agreement starts at line 35 in the inner column and ends on line 18 of the outer column

SOURCE: THE ÁRNI MAGNÚSSON INSTITUTE FOR ICELANDIC STUDIES

written in a hand from the end of the fifteenth-century on a single leaf that was inserted among other added texts [Figs. 2.4–2.6].[12]

This filling in of older manuscripts may be explained, in part, by the same desire for completeness displayed by the fourteenth-century owners. But it also reveals a desire for authentication – by being recorded between older texts, the newly-entered texts were being legitimised. The added texts, with their blatantly different scripts, jump off the pages – no attempt has been made to emulate the original script, as the act of recording the texts in the old law-books was enough to lend them authentication. When it was not possible to cram text onto existing pages, new folios were inserted between the older ones. The manuscripts, as objects, were used to authenticate the texts.

The other seven manuscripts that contain the agreements are law-books made in the fifteenth century, and two of them contain different texts of the agreement. Manuscript AM 137 4to, for example, has an agreement at the beginning, on folios 3v–4r, but a slightly later hand has added a variant version of the agreement at the end of the manuscript on folio 101r. The proper making of these law-books legitimises and authenticates the texts – they were created on the expectation of what a law-book contained and should contain, that is, that they should contain, at the time of writing, the complete legal history of Iceland, imagined or not [Figs. 2.7–2.9].

2 Culture, Memory and the Written Document

So should we see the use of old and new manuscripts to legitimise and authenticate the texts as intentional deceit? And if there *was* deceitful intention, why did Icelanders not forge a document proper, rather than making copies? There exist forged documents from fifteenth-century Iceland: forging documents was not beyond their capacity. But the forging of a document of such a nature and importance would require the attachment of seals – of all Icelandic participants and/or the king. To forge a king's writ or his seal was a crime with no

12 This is the list of the manuscripts and folio numbers on which the agreements are recorded: AM 137 4to, fol. 101r; AM 148 4to, fols 107r–107v; AM 135 4to, fol. 107r; AM 151 4to, fol. 139v; AM 157 b 4to, fol. 27r; AM 168 b 4to, fols 12r–12v; AM 175 a 4to, fol. 19r; AM 456 12mo, fols 41v–42r; GKS 3269 b 4to, fol. 67v; AM 136 4to, fols 105r–105v; AM 137 4to, fols 3v–4r; AM 456 12mo, fols 36r–37r. Details and transcriptions of all the extant agreements can be found in Boulhosa, *Icelanders* 216–226.

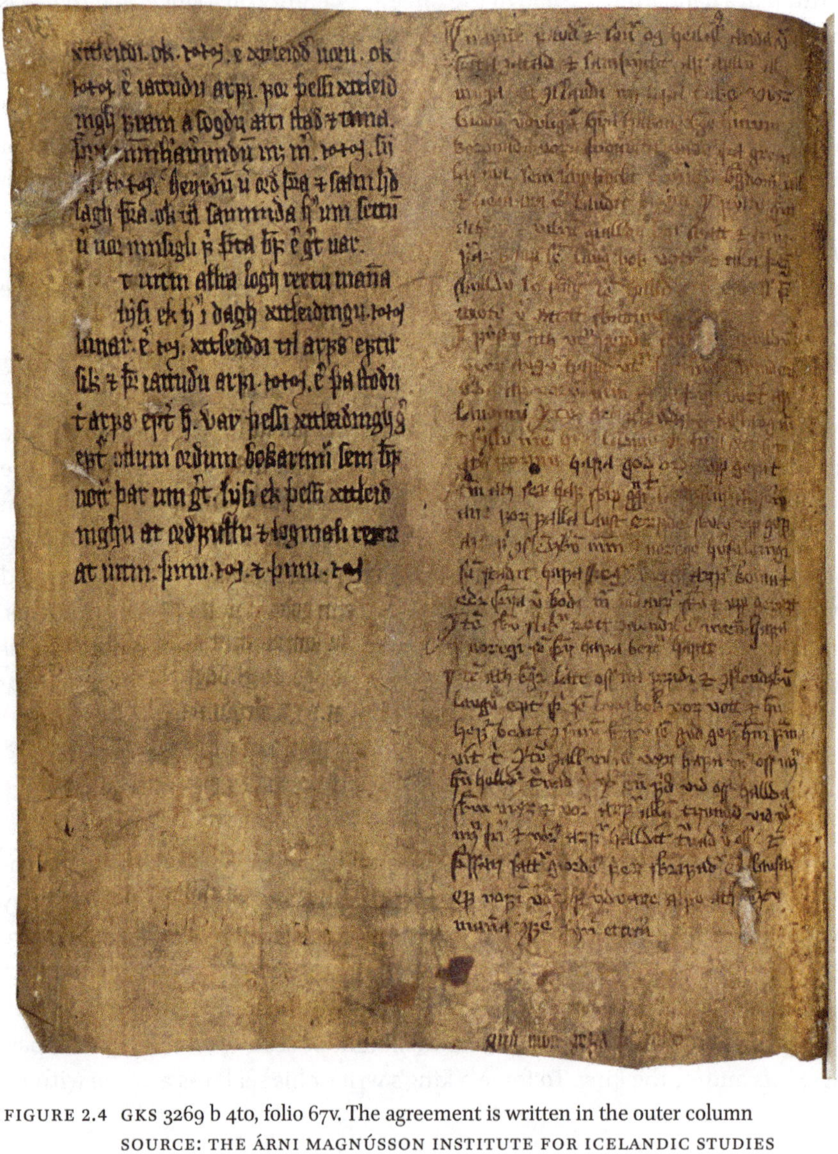

FIGURE 2.4 GKS 3269 b 4to, folio 67v. The agreement is written in the outer column
SOURCE: THE ÁRNI MAGNÚSSON INSTITUTE FOR ICELANDIC STUDIES

chance of monetary atonement.[13] There would be other material constraints, such as the appearance of the parchment, the script, the witnesses and their seals.

The documents are referred to as agreements because that is how they are known in Icelandic, *sáttmáli*.[14] As has been said, these documents are traditionally understood as a letter of conditions, a charter of rights, in the vein of Magna Carta, but a charter of rights would be granted by the king whereas the agreements are issued by the Icelanders. The language in these documents is also peculiar: they read more as law amendments and ordinances, *skipani* in Icelandic, which are relatively common in the fifteenth century. They make constant use of the conditional subjunctive ('we would like', 'we would expect'), which makes them look more like a wish list than a legally binding document. The contents, the language and the words of the agreements present problems, in particular anachronisms. What makes them 'good forgeries' is the fact that they were copied in the law-books and thus within traditional expectations that these books would record truthful historical legal texts. The documents were forged, as copies, on the strength of the legal manuscript tradition, that is, because their makers knew that the agreements, had they existed, would have been copied in law-books, the Icelanders' legal archives.

But it is also worth reflecting on the role of documents in fifteenth-century Iceland. Documents were rare in Iceland, even in the fifteenth century. Even if we allow for the number of lost documents – estimated at the highest percentage – we can see from the extant documents from the fourteenth and fifteenth centuries that they still relied on non-written traditions, that they were made from memory into record.[15] Only a few of the surviving original documents were based on older written documents or mention written records as evidence.[16] From the end of the thirteenth century and well into the fifteenth, legal affairs in Iceland relied on memory, ritual and oral testimony.

13 *Jónsbók: The Laws of Later Iceland*, ed. J.K. Schulman (Saarbrücken: 2010) 39. The law does not clearly specify the forger's punishment but forfeiture of property would be included.

14 Even though there are several variant texts, the agreements are collectively known as 'gamli sáttmáli' ('old agreement'); a variant that was recorded in the sixteenth century is known as 'Gizurarsáttmáli' ('Gizurr's agreement', in reference to the Icelander Gizurr Þorvaldsson, 1208–1268).

15 See footnote 4 above on lost manuscripts.

16 On the intersections between oral and written culture in Iceland, see Boulhosa P.P., "Narratives and Documents", in Ármann Jakobsson – Sverrir Jakobsson (eds.), *The Routledge Research Companion to the Medieval Icelandic Sagas* (London: 2017) 164–174 and the references given there, as well as Hermann P., "Literacy", in Ármann Jakobsson – Sverrir

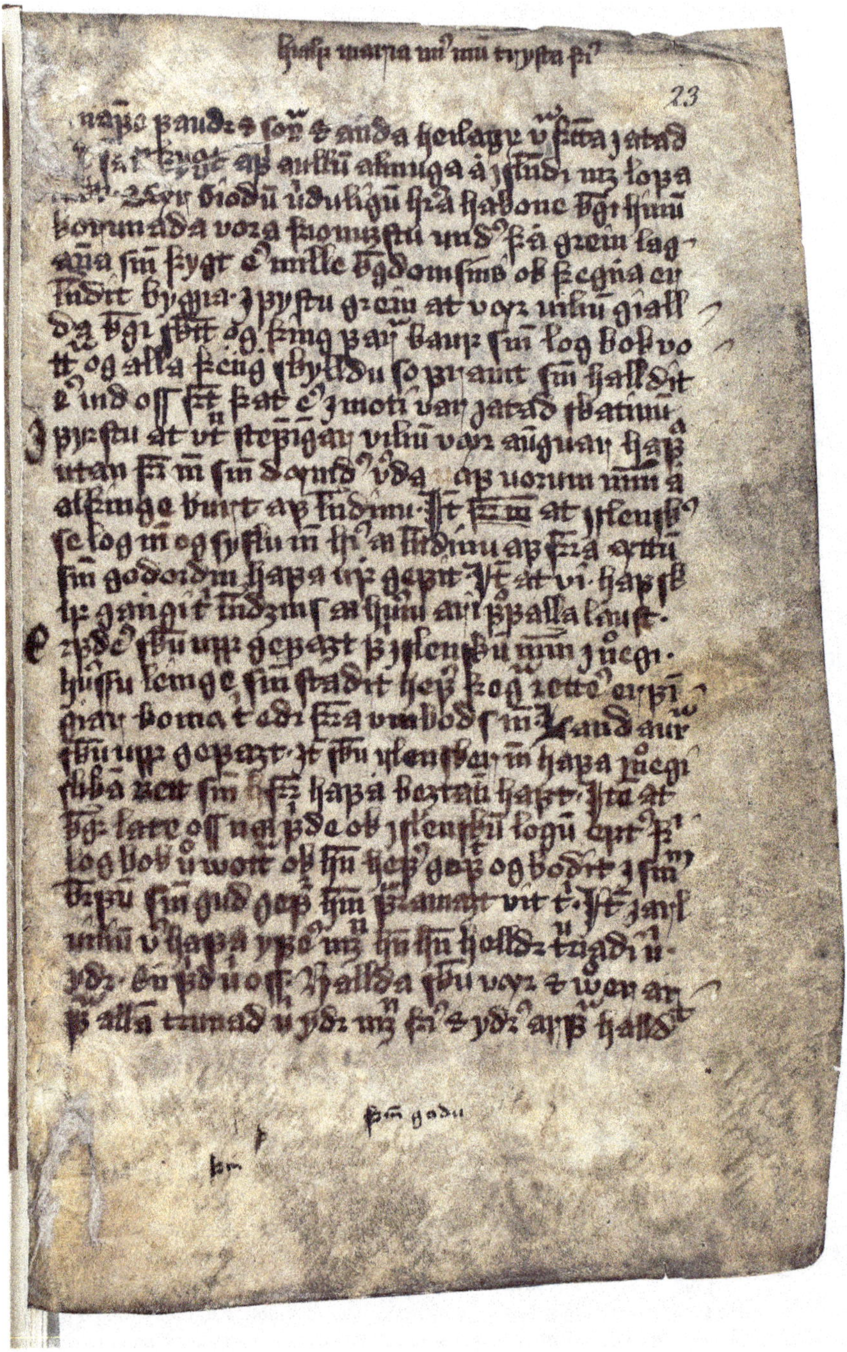

FIGURE 2.5 AM 168 b 4to, folio 12r
SOURCE: THE ÁRNI MAGNÚSSON INSTITUTE FOR ICELANDIC STUDIES

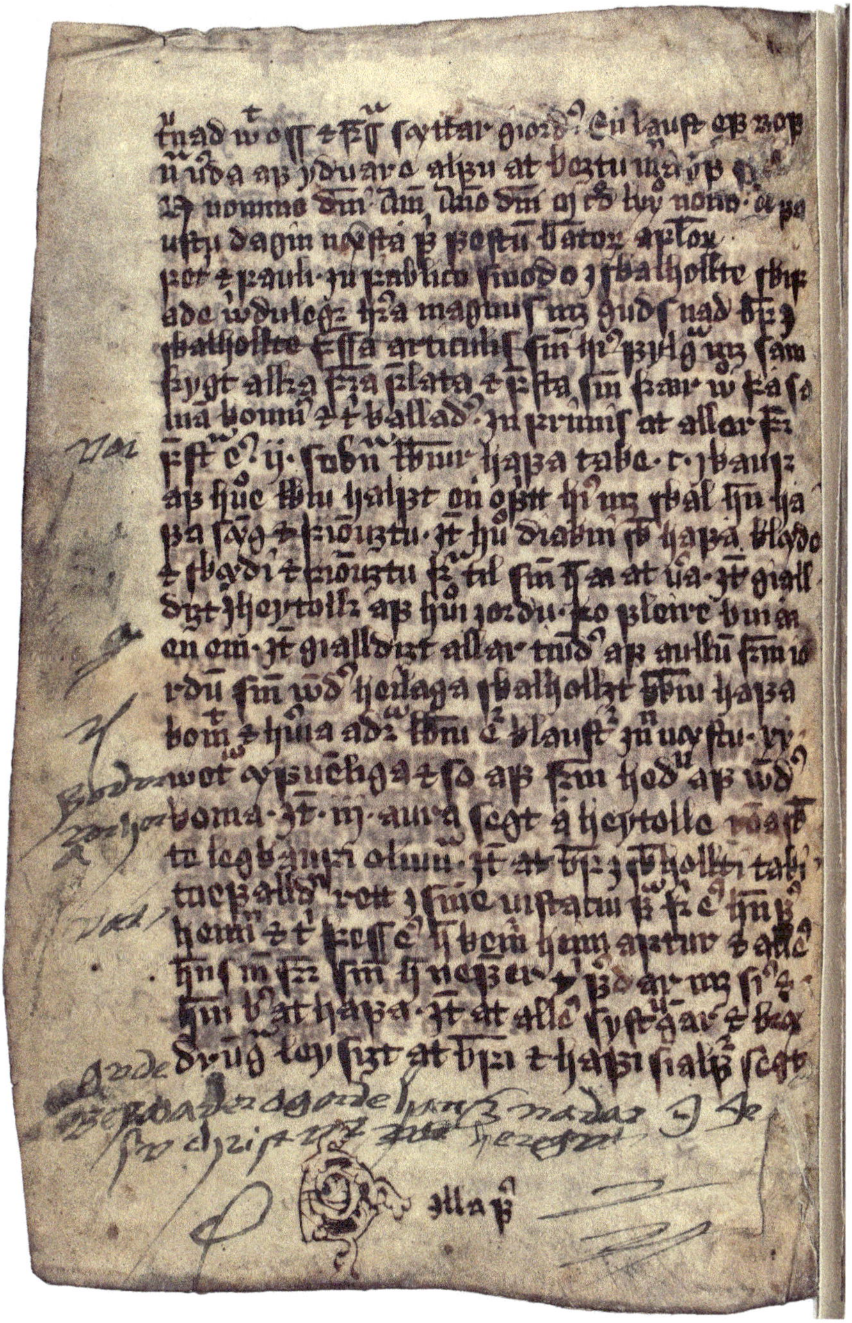

FIGURE 2.6 AM 168 b 4to, folio 12v
SOURCE: THE ÁRNI MAGNÚSSON INSTITUTE FOR ICELANDIC STUDIES

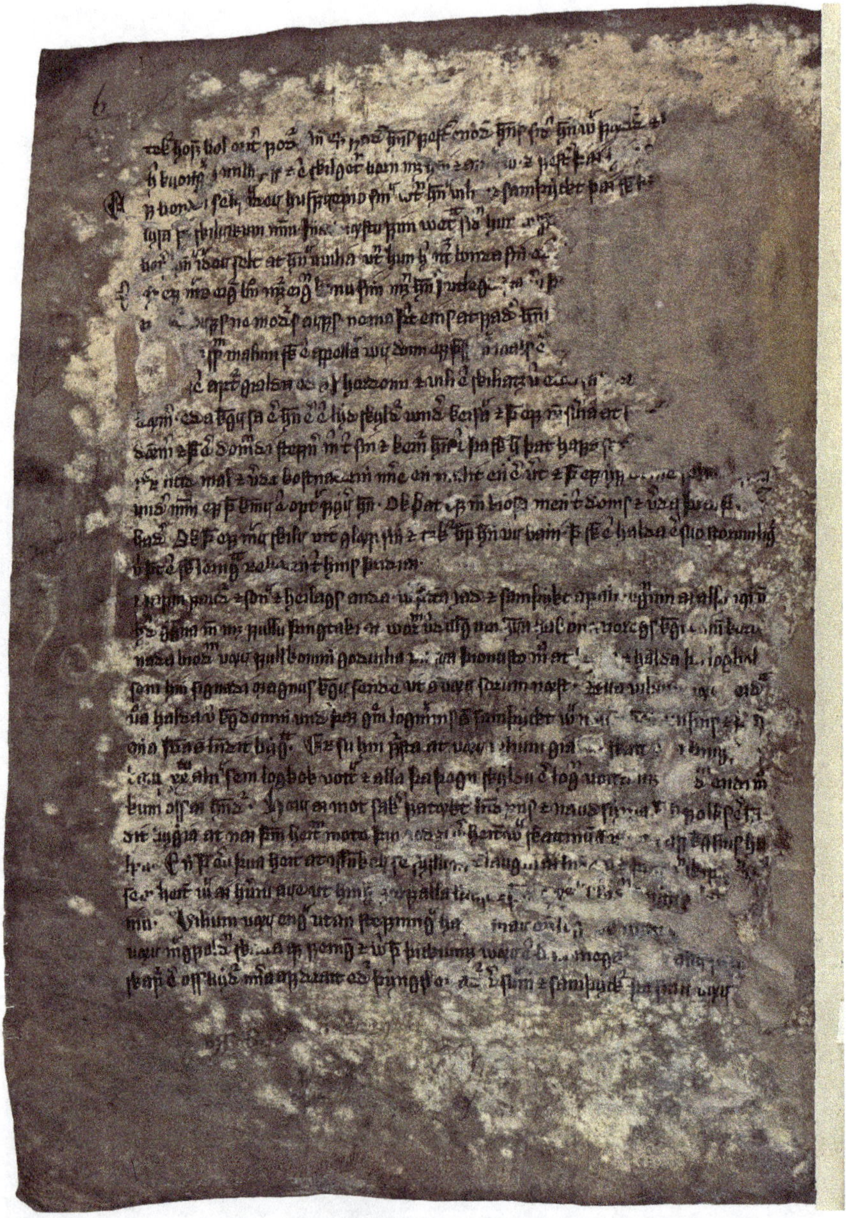

FIGURE 2.7 AM 137 4to, folio 3v. The agreement starts at line 16 on folio 3v and ends at line 6 on folio 4r

SOURCE: THE ÁRNI MAGNÚSSON INSTITUTE FOR ICELANDIC STUDIES

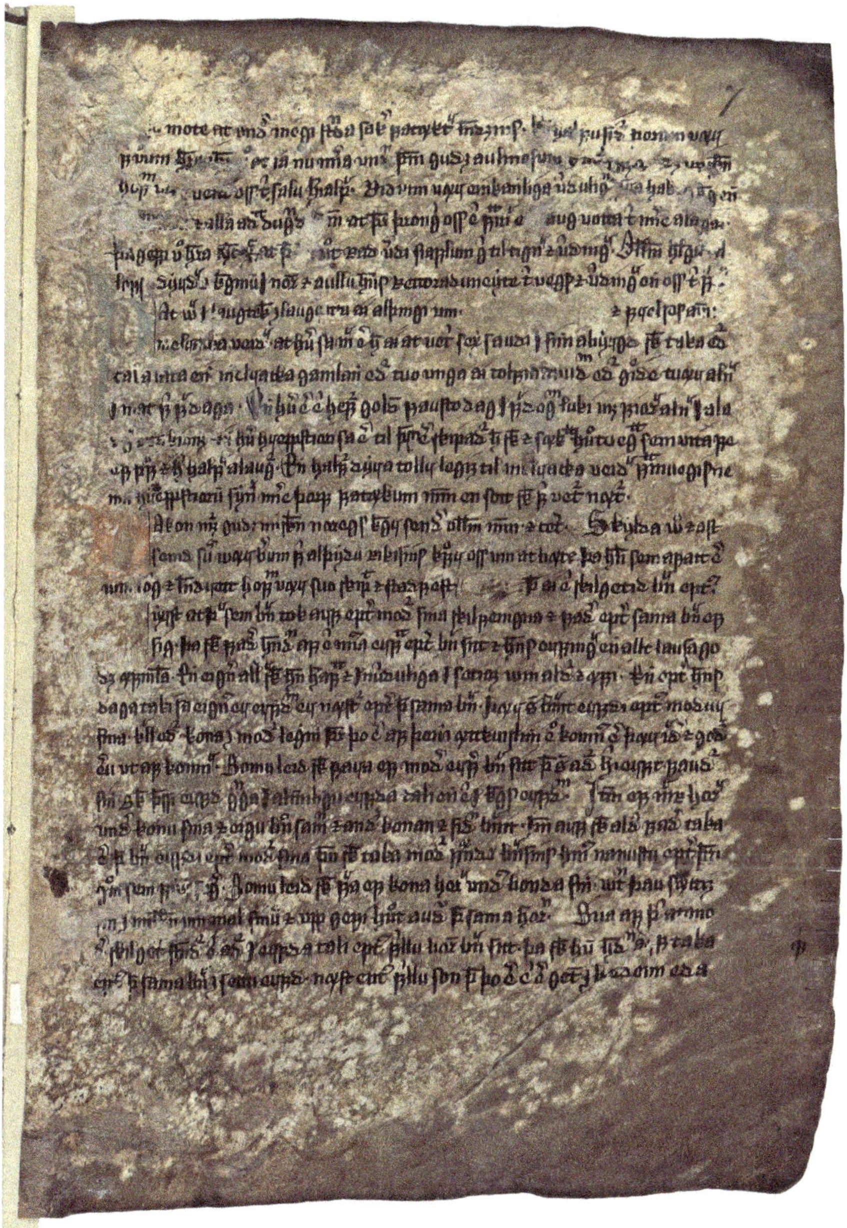

FIGURE 2.8 AM 137 4to, folio 4r. The agreement starts at line 16 on folio 3v and ends at line 6 on folio 4r

SOURCE: SOURCE: THE ÁRNI MAGNÚSSON INSTITUTE FOR ICELANDIC STUDIES

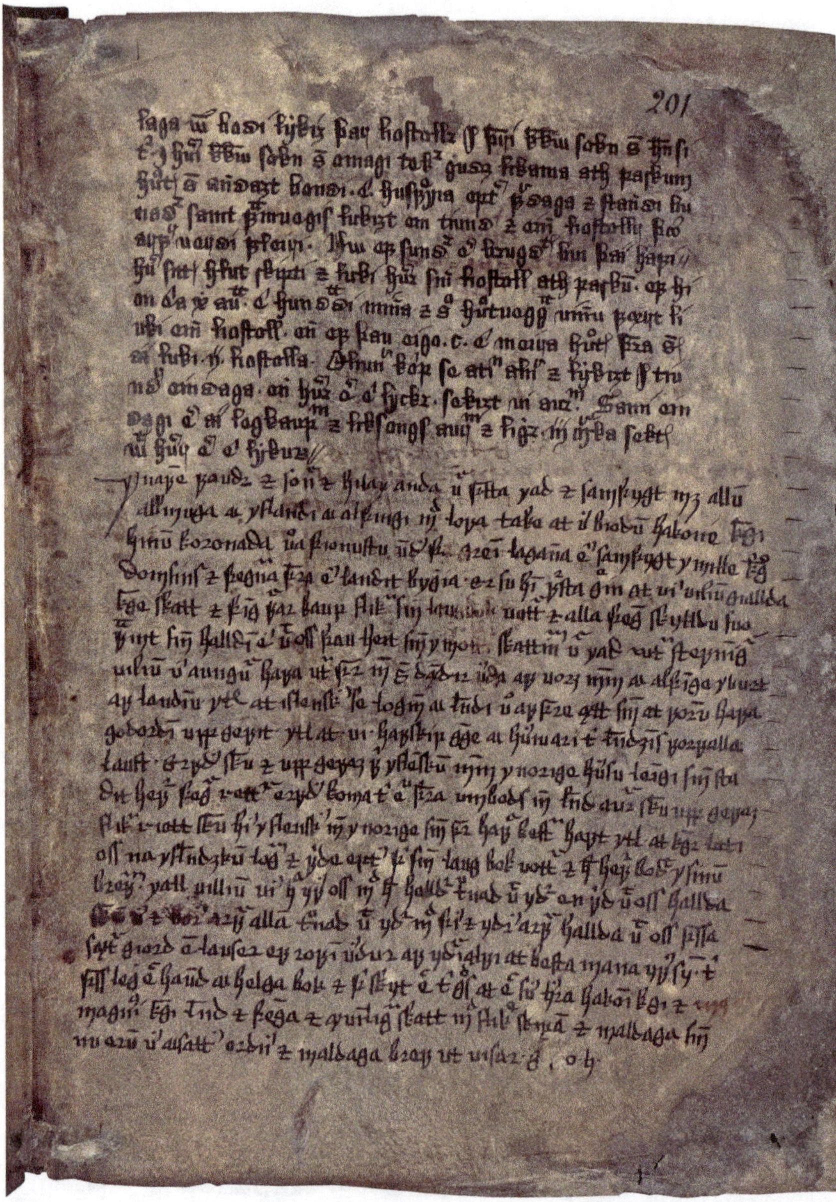

FIGURE 2.9 AM 137 4to, folio 101r. The agreement starts at line 13
SOURCE: THE ÁRNI MAGNÚSSON INSTITUTE FOR ICELANDIC STUDIES

In thirteenth-century Iceland, written documents were only required for ecclesiastical affairs, and only on two occasions: when land was donated to the church and when foreign priests wanted to minister in Iceland. In both cases, the documents were mediated through oral traditions. Donations were written down but had to be recited aloud to the congregation. Foreign priests had to produce a letter and a seal from the bishop, but they also had to produce two witnesses who were present at their ordination and could repeat the bishop's words in the letter.[17] These oral traditions mediated the written document to the non-literate and also dispelled suspicions of the written medium.

Suspicion and distrust of the written word stemmed from the strength of oral tradition, memory and ritual in Icelandic legal affairs. This can be seen in the way land deals were made before and after the new law-code. Until *c.* 1280 (when the king issued Jónsbók), the selling of land was done without the need for a single written document. When a person wanted to sell his land, seller and buyer had to say to each other what the boundaries of the land were and all the natural resources that went with that land. Then they would walk the boundaries together, inviting the owners of neighbouring land to walk with them.[18] This ritual not only imprinted the legal transaction in the memory of the participants but also marked their agency in the procedures. With Jónsbók, the royal law required the production of a written document in land deals of a certain value. Even if this requirement did not affect the whole population, the change had the potential to create tension – people with land but no written document found their ownership suddenly less secure. Owners of land with small value still had to seal their deals through a traditional, non-written medium.[19]

The walking of boundaries and other rituals prescribed in Icelandic law allowed for a more concrete relation between man and law. Witnesses could relate directly and concretely with the space in which events, such as land deals, took place. The written document robs people of this physical and material participation in the law. It creates a distance that enables the participants

---

Jakobsson (eds.), *The Routledge Research Companion to the Medieval Icelandic Sagas* (London: 2017) 34–47.

17 *Laws of Early Iceland*, ed. A. Dennis – P. Foote – R. Perkins, 2 vols. (Winnipeg: 1980–2000) v. 1, §4 32, §6 36. Boulhosa, "Narratives" 166.

18 Boulhosa, "Narratives" 167. *Laws of Early Iceland* v. 2, §174 101–103.

19 There are no court records in Iceland that can exemplify the conflict between parties in land disputes, but Clanchy M.T., "Remembering the Past and the Good Old Law", *History* 55 (1970) 165–176: 173–174, while discussing a shire court in Norfolk and Suffolk in the mid-thirteenth century, shows how the arbitrary requirement for written records in what were once pre-literate transactions presented difficulties (and opportunities) for the involved parties.

to project a narrative onto parchment or paper. The written document even creates masks for the participants to enact this narrative: after an initial mention of the names of those involved, documents speak of 'the vendor', 'the buyer', 'the defendant'. When legal rituals were replaced, people lost control and agency over the law, but they gained that power of projection.[20]

In his sketch of the semiotics of forgery, Umberto Eco exemplifies diplomatic forgery with the creation of a document 'to assert privileges that may in fact have really been conceded but whose original documentation has been lost'.[21] Diplomatic forgery, Eco explains, belongs to the category of false identification, the occurrence of which demands a culture that is able 'to establish indiscernibility or equivalence between objects, and therefore criteria for establishing the authenticity of an object'.[22] Eco explains that our modern European concepts of identification and authentication, which support his model of classification, cannot be simply transported to past cultures. Medieval culture, via Christianity, knew the past through information transmitted by tradition; hence a monk who would forge a foundation charter for his abbey believed it had been founded in the circumstances he laid out, on the basis of tradition, in the 'false' document.[23] Could these be the circumstances in fifteenth-century Iceland?

As has been shown, the cultural context in Iceland was different. In Iceland documents were being produced from memory into writing even in the fifteenth century. These were circumstances that offered great potential for forgery, and forgeries were made. There are documents about land ownership and

20 Other rituals were only gradually replaced by the written medium, such as the handshake to seal agreements; the passing of a cross-token around to summon people to a meeting; the demarcation of the 'place of action', the physical area within which a crime took place and determined which witnesses were called to testify. *Laws of Early Iceland* v. 1, §221 160, §234, 187. See Boulhosa, "Narratives" 165–167.

21 Eco U., *From the Tree to the Labyrinth* (Cambridge MA: 2014) 239. On the concept of diplomatic forgeries, see Hiatt A., *The Making of Medieval Forgeries: False Documents in Fifteenth-Century England* (London – Toronto: 2004) 14.

22 Ibidem, 229. According to Eco, historical forgery belongs to another category, as it 'concerns a formally genuine document that contains inexact or invented information'. Ibidem, 239.

23 It is worth pointing out that Eco moves from traditional associations of medieval forgery with criminality to one of naivety. Even Anthony Grafton, while recognizing the importance of forgery in the development of early modern philological scholarship, calls the former 'the criminal sibling' of the latter. Grafton A., *Forgers and Critics, New Edition: Creativity and Duplicity in Western Scholarship* (Princeton – Oxford: 2019) 127. For traditional associations of medieval forgery with criminality, see Tout T.F., "Mediaeval Forgers and Forgeries", *Bulletin of the John Rylands Library* 5 (1919) 208–234 and Mcgurk J.J., "Forgery in the Middle Ages", *History Today* 20 (1970) 47–53.

boundaries that pretend to be fourteenth-century deeds with an attached old seal that gives them an appearance of legitimacy.[24] But those who committed memorial records into writing were not merely forging documents, even if they were not creating documents in the modern sense. They were translating the old memorial record into the new medium, and when doing so they kept part of the agency that their old rituals conferred on them: by controlling the narrative, by exercising their power of projection. There was a greater understanding of the nature and power of the written record: the awareness of its contradictions within the oral-ritual legal culture allowed Icelanders to work with the new medium to their own advantage.

It is in this context that the creation of the submission agreements is situated – in Icelanders' power to retain their agency by controlling the narrative of the documents. Wider historical contexts rendered the forgeries more feasible, such as the Union of Kalmar, which temporarily moved the administrative axis to Denmark and the Danish king. In the first two decades of the fifteenth century, Erik of Pomerania started restricting all direct trade between Icelanders and foreign merchants, a strategy that harmed Iceland more than most, and thus it was a good time to invoke conditions and privileges that were agreed, or not, with the Norwegian king.[25] In a letter from 1419, Icelanders greet the king and promise their allegiance and tribute as their ancestors had promised the kings of Norway. But with respect to the prohibition on trade with foreigners, they imply that the crown has not fulfilled a condition to send the poverty-stricken country six ships every year – such a condition, the letter continues, was set in a law amendment (*réttarbœtr*).[26]

No such amendment was ever recorded in law-books; the mention of six ships and other conditions only ever appears in the agreements. Icelanders gambled with the new administration and, as was customary, invoked an old

24 Stefán Karlsson (ed.), *Islandske originaldiplomer indtil 1450: Tekst* (Copenhagen: 1963) xxvii–xxxvi.

25 Many conflicts around the 1420–1430s arose because of administrative policies; see Groshe I.P., "Fremmede i forvaltningen: Rakkestad og Orknøyene 1424/25", *Historisk tidsskrift* 99 (2020) 97–111. See also Schott R., "Marguerite, ses officiers et la lettre d'instructions à Erik de Poméranie (1405)", *Médiévales* 50 (2006) 103–120; Helgi Þorláksson, "King and Commerce: The Foreign Trade of Iceland in Medieval Times and the Impact of Royal Authority", in Imsen S. (ed.), *The Norwegian Domination and the Norse World c. 1100–c. 1400* (Trondheim: 2010) 149–174; Holterman B., *The Fish Lands: German Trade with Iceland, Shetland and the Faroe Islands in the Late 15th and 16th Century* (Berlin – Boston: 2020) 77–79.

26 Boulhosa, *Icelanders* 136. It is mentioned in some of the agreements that these ships would be laden with goods needed by the country; Boulhosa, *Icelanders* 136–137.

right in an old document.[27] Some years later, they recorded the first documents of the submission in their law-books, their archives of law and history. They were exerting control over the narrative.

3 The Forgeries' Audience: Then and Now

It is possible that an agreement similar to one or another of the surviving texts was written down at a time contemporary with the submission to Norway. It is possible that copies were made shortly after the submission, from the thirteenth century onwards, the words only slightly changed over the centuries as Icelanders renewed their vows of allegiance. It is also possible that all fourteenth-century manuscripts which recorded the agreements have been lost and that the surviving manuscripts are all part of a sample that did not record the agreement. This may still be the canonical view, which is based on the possibility of all of these hypotheses and the historical plausibility of the clauses of the agreements. Similar arguments of possibility and probability are also extended to agreements that were first recorded in the mid-sixteenth century and which are still regarded as copies of an older agreement.[28]

To raise a charge of forgery against one of the most precious documents of a country was never going to be free of challenges. The agreements have acquired totemic value in Iceland: they have come to signify the submission to the king. They had a prominent role in the struggle for Icelandic independence from Denmark during the nineteenth and twentieth centuries as scholars and politicians placed them at the centre of the discussion about the legal status of Iceland in relation to Denmark.[29] As noted by the Icelandic scholar Ármann Jakobsson, most of what twentieth-century scholarship has written about the submission comes down to this document.[30] The agreements are thought to be a charter of rights, the Icelanders' Magna Carta, and a reason for them to

27 See, for example, Gustafsson H., "The Eighth Argument: Identity, Ethnicity and Political Culture in Sixteenth-Century Scandinavia", *Scandinavian Journal of History* 27 (2002) 91–114: 97; and Clanchy M.T., *From Memory to Written Record: England 1066–1307* (Oxford: 1993) 148.

28 This mid-sixteenth-century document is known as 'Gizurarsáttmáli'; see footnote 14 above. Some historians believe that its contents reflect that of an original submission agreement; see Jón Viðar Sigurðsson, "The Making of a 'Skattland': Iceland 1247–1450", in Imsen S. (ed.), *Rex Insularum: The King of Norway and His 'Skattlands' as a Political System c. 1260–c. 1450* (Bergen: 2014) 181–225: 184–185.

29 See Boulhosa, *Icelanders* 151–153.

30 Ármann Jakobsson, "Hákon Hákonarson: friðarkonungur eða fúlmenni?", *Saga* 33 (1995) 166–185.

be proud even if the submission itself is not regarded by many as Iceland's finest hour.[31]

Despite the original intentions of the forgers, a forgery is what its audience wants it to be. A forgery's power to endure depends on the expectations of its successive audiences. The submission documents endure as they are nourished by contemporary expectations and helped by scholars' efforts to adjust the forgeries' narrative when new theories come to light: there was an original agreement but it was lost; at first the agreement wasn't copied in manuscripts because it had special status; at each new king, Icelanders would make a new document, hence the different versions; all manuscripts from the thirteenth and fourteenth centuries, which may have contained copies of the agreements, have been lost; the agreements 'make sense' within their historical context and their contents are plausible.[32] The agreements endure because they respond to contemporary expectations of Icelanders' agency in the history of submission.

Those who wrote down the agreements understood the manuscript tradition of which they were part. They were lawyers, clerks, and officials of the king's administration who were responsible for the production, transmission, and use of law-books. They were both maker and audience of the forgeries. They circulated their manuscripts among themselves, they copied each other's texts, checked them against each other. The documents reflect their expectation that Icelanders would have been cunning enough to get privileges from the king in exchange for their allegiance. They were not forging documents to show the king, but to control and authenticate their own narrative of the submission. They were seeking to authenticate their texts, there and then, but they also knew that the manuscripts would authenticate them for future generations. Up to a point, it has worked.

---

31 Prominent Icelandic scholars have at different times compared the agreements to the Magna Carta, for example, Sigurður Líndal in Gunnar Hrafn Jónsson, "Legg ek hönd á helga bók", *Lesbók Morgunblaðsins* (30 September 2006) 10 and Björn Þorsteinsson, "Sáttmáli Hákonar gamla og Íslendinga 100 ára", *Þjóðviljinn Blað II* (17 June 1962) 14–17.

32 These theories are discussed in Boulhosa, *Icelanders* 87–153; Boulhosa P.P., "A Response to 'Gamli sáttmáli: Hvað næst?'", *Saga* 49 (2011) 137–151; Boulhosa P.P., *Gamli sáttmáli: Tilurð og tilgangur* (Reykjavik: 2006); Már Jónsson, "Gamli sáttmáli: Er hann ekki til?", *Lesbók Morgunblaðsins* (9 September 2006) 10; Már Jónsson, "Efasemdir um sáttmála Íslendinga og Noregskonungs árið 1262", in Benedikt Eyþórsson – Hrafnkell Lárusson (eds.), *Þriðja íslenska söguþingið: Ráðstefnurit* (Reykjavik: 2007) 399–406; Helgi Skúli Kjartansson, "Gamli sáttmáli: Hvað næst?", *Saga* 49 (2011) 53–88; Helgi Þorláksson, "Er Gamli sáttmáli tómur tilbúningur?", in Benedikt Eyþórsson – Hrafnkell Lárusson (eds.), *Þriðja íslenska söguþingið: Ráðstefnurit* (Reykjavik: 2007) 392–398. See also references in footnote 28 and Helgi Þorláksson's article in footnote 25.

Bibliography

Agnes S. Arnórsdóttir, "Cultural Memory and Gender in Iceland from Medieval to Early Modern Times", *Scandinavian Studies* 85 (2013) 378–399.

Ármann Jakobsson, "Hákon Hákonarson: friðarkonungur eða fúlmenni?", *Saga* 33 (1995) 166–185.

Björn Þorsteinsson, "Sáttmáli Hákonar gamla og Íslendinga 100 ára", *Þjóðviljinn Blað II* (17 June 1962) 14–17.

Boulhosa P.P., *Icelanders and the Kings of Norway: Sagas and Legal Texts* (Leiden: 2005).

Boulhosa P.P., *Gamli sáttmáli: Tilurð og tilgangur* (Reykjavik: 2006).

Boulhosa P.P., "A Response to 'Gamli sáttmáli: Hvað næst?'", *Saga* 49 (2011) 137–151.

Boulhosa P.P., "Narratives and Documents", in Ármann Jakobsson – Sverrir Jakobsson (eds.), *The Routledge Research Companion to the Medieval Icelandic Sagas* (London: 2017) 164–174.

Clanchy M.T., "Remembering the Past and the Good Old Law", *History* 55 (1970) 165–176.

Clanchy M.T., *From Memory to Written Record: England 1066–1307* (Oxford: 1993).

Eco U., *From the Tree to the Labyrinth* (Cambridge MA: 2014).

Grafton A., *Forgers and Critics, New Edition: Creativity and Duplicity in Western Scholarship* (Princeton – Oxford: 2019).

Grohse I.P., "Fremmede i forvaltningen: Rakkestad og Orknøyene 1424/25", *Historisk tidsskrift* 99 (2020) 97–111.

Guðvarður Már Gunnlaugsson, "Manuscripts and Palaeography", in McTurk R. (ed.), *A Companion to Old Norse-Icelandic Literature and Culture* (Oxford: 2005) 245–264.

Gunnar Hrafn Jónsson, "Legg ek hönd á helga bók", *Lesbók Morgunblaðsins* (30 September 2006).

Gustafsson H., "The Eighth Argument: Identity, Ethnicity and Political Culture in Sixteenth-Century Scandinavia", *Scandinavian Journal of History* 27 (2002) 91–114.

Helgi Skúli Kjartansson, "Gamli sáttmáli: Hvað næst?", *Saga* 49 (2011) 53–88.

Helgi Þorláksson, "Er Gamli sáttmáli tómur tilbúningur?", in Benedikt Eyþórsson – Hrafnkell Lárusson (eds.), *Þriðja íslenska söguþingið: Ráðstefnurit* (Reykjavik: 2007) 392–398.

Helgi Þorláksson, "King and Commerce: The Foreign Trade of Iceland in Medieval Times and the Impact of Royal Authority", in Imsen S. (ed.), *The Norwegian Domination and the Norse World c. 1100–c.1400* (Trondheim: 2010) 149–174.

Hermann P., "Literacy", in Ármann Jakobsson – Sverrir Jakobsson (eds.), *The Routledge Research Companion to the Medieval Icelandic Sagas* (London: 2017) 34–47.

Hiatt A., *The Making of Medieval Forgeries: False Documents in Fifteenth-Century England* (London – Toronto: 2004).

Holterman B., *The Fish Lands: German Trade with Iceland, Shetland and the Faroe Islands in the Late 15th and 16th Century* (Berlin – Boston: 2020).

Hreinn Benediktsson, *Early Icelandic Script: As Illustrated in Vernacular Texts from the Twelfth and Thirteenth Centuries* (Reykjavik: 1965).

Jón Viðar Sigurðsson, "The Making of a 'Skattland': Iceland 1247–1450", in Imsen S. (ed.), *Rex Insularum: The King of Norway and His 'Skattlands' as a Political System c. 1260–c. 1450* (Bergen: 2014) 181–225.

Jónsbók: The Laws of Later Iceland, ed. J.K. Schulman (Saarbrücken: 2010).

Kålund K., *Katalog over den Arnamagnœanske håndskriftsamling I* (Copenhagen: 1889).

Laws of Early Iceland, ed. A. Dennis – P. Foote – R. Perkins, 2 vols. (Winnipeg: 1980–2000).

Long A., *Iceland's Relationship with Norway c. 870–c. 1100: Memory, History and Identity* (Leiden: 2017).

Már Jónsson, "Gamli sáttmáli: Er hann ekki til?", *Lesbók Morgunblaðsins* (9 September 2006).

Már Jónsson, "Efasemdir um sáttmála Íslendinga og Noregskonungs árið 1262", in Benedikt Eyþórsson – Hrafnkell Lárusson (eds.), *Þriðja íslenska söguþingið: Ráðstefnurit* (Reykjavik: 2007) 399–406.

Már Jónsson, "The Size of Medieval Icelandic Legal Manuscripts", in Rohrbach L. (ed.), *The Power of the Book: Medial Approaches to Medieval Nordic Legal Manuscripts* (Berlin: 2014) 25–38.

Mcgurk J.J., "Forgery in the Middle Ages", *History Today* 20 (1970) 47–53.

Rohrbach L., "Construction, Organization, Stabilization. Administrative Literacy in the Realm of Norway: The Case of Iceland", in Imsen S. (ed.), *Rex Insularum: The King of Norway and His 'Skattlands' as a Political System c. 1260–c. 1450* (Bergen: 2014) 227–263.

Schnall J.E., "Recht und Heil: Zu Kompilationsmustern in Handschriften der Jónsbók", *Gripla* 16 (2005) 75–114.

Schott R., "Marguerite, ses officiers et la lettre d'instructions à Erik de Poméranie (1405)", *Médiévales* 50 (2006) 103–120.

Stefán Karlsson (ed.), *Islandske originaldiplomer indtil 1450: Tekst* (Copenhagen: 1963).

Tout T.F., "Mediaeval Forgers and Forgeries", *Bulletin of the John Rylands Library* 5 (1919) 208–234.

CHAPTER 3

All That Glitters Is Not Gold: False Jewellery and Its Juridical Regulation in Italy between the Late Middle Ages and the Early Modern Period

Federica Boldrini

The great socio-economical changes set in motion by the commercial revolution of the eleventh century led to the establishment of an increasingly consumerist mindset among the urban population of Italy.[1] From the late Middle Ages on merchant families, who had gladly resorted to luxury in order to demonstrate their financial success, started using dress and ornaments as a fundamental instrument of social self-representation.[2]

This evolution in mentality gave new juridical relevance to the problem of counterfeit jewellery, whose marketing appeared to be not only a commercial fraud, but also an act that could undermine the hierarchy of appearances that made the articulations of urban societies universally visible. It is thus not surprising that between the late Middle Ages and the Early Modern period both legal scholarship and local legislators (municipal as well as corporative) repeatedly addressed the juridical issues raised by counterfeit gold and imitation gemstones.

Theologians usually discussed this problem in the context of a wider reflection on the matter of commercial fraud. The economic ethics devised during the late Middle Ages devoted much effort to elaborating a precise definition of this crime. Writing around 1267 Bonaventura di Bagnoregio for example distinguished three kinds of fraud: the first concerning the weight of goods, the second concerning their number and the third concerning their measure. It was rare – he disconsolately concluded – for merchants to be able to completely avoid every kind of fraudulent practice.[3]

In the same years, Thomas Aquinas, the most influential among all scholastic thinkers, clarified that commercial fraud could pertain to the nature, the

1 Hunt A., *Governance of the Consuming Passions: A History of Sumptuary Law* (New York: 1996) 136.

2 Kovesi Killerby C., *Sumptuary Law in Italy 1200–1500* (Oxford: 2002) 116.

3 Bonaventura di Bagnoregio, *De decem praeceptis collatio*, VI.18.

 | DOI:10.1163/9789004106901_004

quantity and the quality of the goods involved: in the first of these cases frauds were realised through counterfeiting.[4] Gold forgery was thus to be considered a form of fraud pertaining to the nature of things that were sold.

Notwithstanding the frequent theological reflection upon this matter, during the late Middle Ages the problem of gold forgery was discussed by legal scholarship almost exclusively in relation to alchemy. Debating this subject, most jurists and moralists demonstrated little interest in the social and commercial implications of such practices, aiming first of all to verify the effectiveness of alchemical techniques and to question the morality of producing artificial gold by manipulating natural elements. The conclusions of various *ius commune* scholars who tackled this topic, aiming to define the legal status of alchemy, are discussed in the second section of this chapter.

At the same time some authors, influenced by the wide ranging legal and theological reflection on trade frauds that flourished in late medieval Italy as a consequence of commercial development, started discussing the lawfulness of selling artificial gold, as illustrated in the third section. Was it legal to market the product of alchemical processes as if it was real gold? Was this, on the contrary, to be considered a fraud?

While debating these issues *ius commune* doctors demonstrated that they had little, if any, knowledge of the techniques that were used, by alchemists and goldsmiths alike, for the production of artificial gold ('aurifaction'), or at least to create objects that had the exterior appearance of gold ('aurifiction'). More detailed information about such techniques and their juridical implications could be found in a different kind of legal source: the statutes of the Guilds of Goldsmiths (and of other groups of artisans involved in the production of luxury goods) that were enacted in various Italian cities between the late Middle Ages and the Early Modern period, as discussed in the fourth section.

As a whole, these statutes reveal a changing perception of imitation precious materials, that will be analysed in the fifth and final section of this chapter: at first simply outlawed as commercial fraud, during the Early Modern period their use started to be seen as a way to produce original craft creations, that soon became fashionable among the upper classes, up to the point of supplanting more traditional forms of jewellery.

4 Thomas Aquinas, *Summa Theologiae*, II^{a}–II^{ae} q. 77 a. 2 co.

1 Effectiveness and Morality of Alchemy: A Long Debated Juridical Problem

As mentioned, during the late Middle Ages the problem of gold forgery was discussed by legal scholarship almost exclusively in relation to alchemy, whose moral legitimacy and validity as a science was subjected to extensive debate among jurists. Roman law did not provide any specific regulation of this practice: those who approached the *Corpus Iuris Civilis* in search of an answer on this point could thus find very few useful guidelines.

The canon law sources apparently offered more pertinent norms. The *Decretum Gratiani* – the most important canon law collection of the twelfth century – included in fact a chapter of dubious origin, known as '*Canon Episcopi*',[5] in which bishops were invited to do everything in their power to extirpate sorcery and other magical arts from their dioceses.[6] The chapter ended with a strong statement that could easily be read as an affirmation of the fraudulent nature of alchemy: since the power to transmute the substance of things resided exclusively with God, those who believed in the possibility of making similar transformations with human means had to be regarded as pagans and unbelievers.[7]

Notwithstanding this firm condemnation, jurists continued questioning for several centuries both the moral legitimacy and the credibility of alchemy.[8]

5 Throughout the Middle Ages this text was erroneously presented as a canon of the Late Antique Council of Ancyra (AD 314). Included by Abbot Regino of Prüm in his *Libellus de ecclesiasticis disciplinis et religione christiana* (n. 364), it constantly appeared in the most important canon law collections of the subsequent centuries, including the *Decretum* of Burchard of Worms, as well as in the works of Yves of Chartres. Its later insertion in the *Decretum Gratiani* made this chapter one of the fundamental sources in the canon law discussion on witchcraft and magic. On this matter see Kors A.C. – Peters E. (eds.), *Witchcraft in Europe 400–1700: A Documentary History* (Philadelphia: 2001) 60–63.

6 C. 26 q. 5 c. 12.

7 *Corpus iuris canonici. Pars prior: Decretum magistri Gratiani*, ed. E. Friedberg (Leipzig: 1879) 1030–1031.

8 A review of the different opinions expressed on these points by legal scholars between the late Middle Ages and the Early Modern period was first presented in the sixteenth-century pamphlet *De iure artis Alchemiae*, attributed to the obscure Giovanni Crisippo Faniani, which was widely circulated after being included in the *Theatrum Chemicum*, a comprehensive collection of alchemical writings published in six volumes during the seventeenth century: *Theatrum Chemicum: Præcipuos selectorum auctorum tractatus de chemiæ et lapidis philosophici*, vol. 1 (Strasbourg, Heredes Eberhardi Zetzneri: 1659) 48–63. On this collection see Gilly C., "On the Genesis of L. Zetzner's *Theatrum Chemicum* in Strasbourg", in Gilly C. – Heertum C.v. (eds.), *Magia, alchimia, scienza dal '400 al '700: l'influsso di Ermete Trismegisto /*

In apparent contradiction with the principle established in the *Decretum Gratiani*, some *ius commune* scholars explicitly stated their belief in the alchemists' power of 'aurifaction', that is in their capacity to turn tin, lead and other base metals into gold or silver. This was the case, for example, for one of the most influential canon lawyers of the fourteenth century, Giovanni D'Andrea (d. 1348), who had discussed this subject in his commentary on the chapter *De falso* ('On counterfeiting') of Guillaume Durand's great work on procedural law, the *Speculum iudiciale* ('the Judiciary Mirror').[9] In a rather long passage Giovanni D'Andrea expressed his faith in the alchemical production of gold, explaining that the transmutation operated by alchemists did not imply the unnatural conversion of one substance into another, but simply consisted in the refinement of a non-valuable metal into a precious one, thanks to the properties of herbs, minerals or other natural elements. If done in this way, by virtue of the sole forces of nature and without using magic powers or any other illegal technique, such an operation had to be considered licit.[10]

After this lengthy explanation on the nature and lawfulness of alchemic processes, Giovanni D'Andrea, in order to dispel all doubts on their effectiveness, concluded his exposition by mentioning the controversial figure of his contemporary, Arnau de Vilanova (*c.* 1240–*c.* 1312). Physician, theologian and astrologer, Arnau was also famous for his alchemical work; according to D'Andrea he had been able to produce sticks of artificial gold, which he did not hesitate to submit to the curious and skeptics for examination.[11]

Giovanni D'Andrea was not the only author to be convinced of the plausibility of alchemy. Along the same lines was the opinion expressed a few decades later by Oldrado da Ponte (*c.* 1270–*c.* 1335), a famous doctor *in utroque iure* who taught Roman law for some years in Padua, before working as an *advocatus consistorialis* in the Papal Curia at Avignon. The issue of alchemy was extensively discussed in one of the legal opinions included in his collection of *Consilia*

Magic, Alchemy and Science, 15th–18th Centuries: The Influence of Hermes Trismegistus, vol. 1 (Florence: 2002) 451–467.

9 This text can be read in Durand Guillaume, *Speculum iudiciale* (Venice, Battista Torti: 1499) fol. 521r.

10 Ibidem. In general, on Giovanni D'Andrea's opinion on alchemy see Hallebeek J., "Artificial Gold, Sold as Natural: Francisco de Vitoria on a Latent Defect in the Merchandise", in Dondorp J.H. – Hallebeek J. – Wallinga T. – Winkel L. (eds.), *Ius Romanum – Ius Commune – Ius Hodiernum: Studies in Honour of Eltjo J.H. Schrage on the Occasion of His 65th Birthday* (Amsterdam – Aalen: 2010) 163–165.

11 Durand, *Speculum iudiciale* fol. 521r.

seu responsa,[12] which was circulated widely in manuscript form, before being printed on multiple occasions throughout the Early Modern period.

This text, which reprises most of Giovanni D'Andrea's arguments for the credibility of alchemy, exerted a significant influence on subsequent legal scholarship, being quoted by many later authors, who reprised its conclusions: this was the case, for example, of one of the main exponents of the study of Roman law in the Middle Ages, Baldo Degli Ubaldi (1327–1400), who considered alchemy 'an art discovered with insightful intelligence',[13] as well as of the great fifteenth-century canon lawyer Nicolò De' Tedeschi (d. 1445),[14] and of many others.[15]

Not all legal scholars shared the same confidence in the alchemists' ability to produce artificial gold by lawfully manipulating the forces of nature. While late medieval inquisitorial law denounced the way in which such operations, just like astrology, could often lead to the invocation of demons and should thus arouse the suspicion of the inquisitors,[16] later jurists seemed inclined, instead, to dismiss alchemy as nothing more than a fraud. Such was the opinion expressed in one of the most famous handbooks for confessors of the late fifteenth century, the *Summa Angelica*, written by the Franciscan Angelo da Chivasso (1410–1495),[17] as well as in the works of many contemporary canon lawyers.[18]

---

12 It was the *consilium* 74, that can be read in Da Ponte Oldrado, *Consilia seu responsa et quaestiones aureae* (Venice, Francesco Ziletti: 1570) fol. 29r. On this text see Migliorino F., "Alchimia lecita e illecita nel Trecento. Oldrado da Ponte", *Quaderni medievali* 11 (1981) 6–41; Hallebeek, "Artificial Gold, Sold as Natural" 165–166.

13 'Ars perspicaci ingenio inventa': Degli Ubaldi Baldo, *Super feudis* (Venice, Bernardino Benali: 1500) fol. 82v.

14 Commenting on a passage of the Decretals, Nicolò de' Tedeschi summarised Oldrado's *consilium* and reaffirmed his conclusions: De' Tedeschi Nicolò, *Super quarto et quinto decretalium* (Lyon, Johannes Moylin alias de Cambray: 1513) fol. 67v.

15 The authors who reprised Oldrado's *consilium* 74 include prominent jurists of the fourteenth and fifteenth centuries like Alberico da Rosciate (d. 1360) and Guy Pape (d. *c.* 1487): see Alberico da Rosciate, *Dictionarium iuris tam civilis quam canonici* (Venice, Guerrei fratres et socii: 1572), s.v. *Alchimia*; Pape Guy, *Singularia iuris*, n. 388 (Lyon, Jean de Jonvelle: 1516) fol. 22r.

16 This was the opinion expressed in one of the most famous handbooks for inquisitors of the fourteenth century, the *Directorium inquisitorum* by Nicolas Eymerich (1320–1399): Eymerich Nicolas, *Directorium inquisitorum* (Venice, Marc'Antonio Zaltieri: 1607) 443.

17 Chivasso Angelo da, *Summa Angelica* (Nuremberg, Anton Koberger: 1492) fol. 8r–v.

18 In the second half of the sixteenth century, in his commentary on Eymerich's *Directorium inquisitorum*, the Aragonese canon lawyer Francisco Peña (d. 1612), for example, concluded that it was safer and more truthful to conclude that alchemy was useless and harmful for the State: Eymerich, *Directorium inquisitorum* 444.

Some of the clearest assertions of the fraudulent nature of alchemy were in any case formulated not by exponents of the Church, but by experts of secular law. For example, in his treatise on monetary obligations, *De monetarum augmento, variatione et diminutione* ('On the increase, variation and decrease of money'), written in the first half of the sixteenth century and later included in the famous collection *Tractatus universi iuris* ('Treatises on the whole of law'), the Piemontese feudal law scholar Alberto Bruno (1467–1541) presented an extensive refutation of the alchemists' capacity to produce gold.

In a long passage Bruno described in detail a failed alchemical experiment, that was attempted in his presence by an alchemy-enthusiast fellow lawyer and a certain unidentified 'old alchemist':

> Arnaldus de Villa Nova [...] fecit in illa scientia librum unum, qui mille homines depauperavit, aut quia non verum, aut quia non intelligitur. Et cum haberem quendam socium in legibus multum insudantem in illa arte, volui videre verum mirabile experimentum ad effectum, ut plura scirem. Nam habuimus nobiscum unum antiquum alchymistam pauperrimum tamen, et me praesente ille meus collega reduci fecit unciam unam argenti preciosissimi ad instar auri in pondere, fusione et malleatione salvo colore, quia non erat croceus, sed mutatus ad instar quasi plumbei coloris. Et ille collega meus habebat modum dandi colorem et croceum. Et in illa materia patiebatur et substinebat aliqua experimenta, sed non extremum experimentum et admixta cum tantundem auri praeciosi videbatur auri 20 characterum, et plus et minus secundum quod illa materia erat melius disposita. Et quidam magnus praelatus ac multi antiqui alchymistae mirati fuerunt de illo experimento, et unus antiquus alchymista putans se divitem, putabat reducere illam materiam ad veram speciem auri, et non potuit, putavitque tunc ipsam artem illusoriam maxime, ex quo tot viri in 40 et ultra annis non viderant tam mirabile experimentum, quod nihilo minus erat sophisticum, ita ut aliud experimentum videre noluerim.[19]
>
> (Arnau de Vilanova [...] wrote a book on that science that led a thousand men to poverty, either because it was false or because it could not be understood. And since I had a certain colleague in legal practice who

19 This passage from the treatise *De monetarum augmento, variatione et diminutione* can be read in the collection *Tractatus illustrium in utraque tum pontificii tum caesarei iuris facultate Iurisconsultorum. XII. De fisco et eius privilegiis* (Venice, Francesco Ziletti: 1584), fol. 208r.

> was extremely passionate about that art, I wanted to see in real life some awe-inspiring experiment, to learn more. We had with us a very old alchemist, who was very poor, though, and in my presence that colleague of mine treated one ounce of the most precious silver, giving it the characteristics of gold in weight, melting temperature and malleability, not in the colour though, since it was not golden, but was changed, becoming almost lead-coloured. But the colleague of mine also knew the way to give it the colour of gold. And that material was subjected to some experiments, and passed them all, but not the final one, and was alloyed with a small quantity of precious gold and it appeared to be 20-karat gold, more or less, on the basis of how that matter was positioned. And some important prelate and many old alchemists were in awe at that experiment, and one old alchemist thinking to be rich, tried to transmute that material into real gold, but he couldn't, and so he concluded that this art was deceptive, since a good number of men did not see such an awe-inspiring experiment in 40 years or more, and yet it was deceitful, and therefore I never wanted to see another experiment again.)[20]

This passage was destined to exert a certain influence on subsequent legal scholarship, being quoted almost verbatim in the great *Tractatus de commerciis et de cambio* ('Treatise on trades and on the exchange contract') by Sigismondo Scaccia (1564–1634), one of the foundational works of commercial law, written around 1618. After reporting the unsuccessful outcome of the experiment witnessed by Alberto Bruno, Scaccia concluded his discourse on this matter by unambiguously affirming the deceptive nature of alchemical knowledge.[21]

2 Alchemical Practices and the Morality of Contracts: Artificial Gold as a Commercial Fraud

While the moral legitimacy of alchemy and the reliability of the results claimed by its practitioners were repeatedly discussed by legal scholarship, most of the jurists who approached this issue between the fourteenth and seventeenth centuries were, in any case, primarily interested in answering a more practical question: did the alchemists who sold artificial gold commit forgery?

---

20 My translation.

21 Scaccia Sigismondo, *Tractatus de commerciis et de cambio*, § 2 gl. 3 n. 66 (Cologne, Anton Boetzer: 1620) 321.

Roman law offered no clear solution to this problem, merely determining – in a passage of the Pandects – that pawning an object of bronze as if it were made of gold had to be punished as a *crimen stellionatus*.[22] This, according to *ius commune* jurists, actually led to the application of a particularly mild penalty.[23] In the *Corpus iuris civilis*, on the contrary, nothing was said about the legal status of artificial gold and the lawfulness of its sale. This was in any case perceived to be a problem of significant moral relevance. For this reason, the juridical discourse on the matter was heavily influenced by scholastic theology. Particularly important, in this sense, was the opinion expressed in the second half of the thirteenth century by Thomas Aquinas (1225–1274).[24]

Aquinas dealt with this issue in a *quaestio* of his *Summa Theologiae*, number 77 of the *Secunda Secundae* ('second part of the second part'), headed 'De fraudolentia quae committitur in emptionibus et venditionibus' ('Concerning the frauds that are committed by buying and selling') and devoted to the discussion of the moral difficulties raised by commercial frauds. To avoid taking an explicit position on the credibility of alchemy, in this text Aquinas concluded that if alchemists were able to produce authentic gold by transmuting base metals without violating the laws of nature, it would not be illicit to sell that gold as true. Selling alchemical gold or silver that differed in substance and properties from the natural materials had on the contrary to be considered a fraud against justice.[25]

The *quaestio* 77 would have a wide resonance in legal scholarship. First mentioned, with a minor misquote, in the commentaries on feudal law of Andrea d'Isernia (d. 1316),[26] throughout the fourteenth and the fifteenth centuries this text would gain relevance in the legal debate about commercial frauds. Alberico da Rosciate (d. 1360), for example, provided a clear account

22 The passage in the Pandects is Dig. 13.7.1.2. *Stellionatus* was used to refer to a general category of offence elaborated by Roman jurisprudence in order to prosecute wilful misconduct that was not punishable as any other crime. It was often used in relation to commercial fraud. On this matter see Robinson O.F., *The Criminal Law of Ancient Rome* (London: 1995) 32.

23 This was, for example, Giovanni D'Andrea's opinion (Durand, *Speculum iudiciale* fol. 521r). Oldrado was of the same opinion, repeating almost to the letter D'Andrea's words (Da Ponte, *Consilia seu responsa* fol. 29r).

24 In general on Aquinas' opinion on alchemy see Crisciani C., "I Domenicani e la tradizione alchemica nel Duecento", in *Atti del Congresso Internazionale 'Tommaso d'Aquino nel suo settimo centenario'*, vol. 2 (Naples: 1976) 39–40; Hallebeek, "Artificial Gold, Sold as Natural" 162–163.

25 Aquinas, *Summa Theologiae* II^{a}–II^{ae} q. 77 a. 2 ad 1.

26 See Andrea d'Isernia, *In usus feudorum commentaria* (Frankfurt, Heredes Andreæ Wecheli: 1598) 743.

of Aquinas' thought on this matter, reporting the main arguments of the *quaestio* 77 in the entry 'emptio' ('purchase') of his famous *Dictionarium iuris* ('Dictionary of Law').[27]

In the subsequent decades, the reception of this text in a wide range of works that dealt, from different perspectives, with the problems of contract law substantially made Aquinas the leading *auctoritas* in the debate on the lawfulness of selling artificial gold.[28] Even if Aquinas himself expressed his conclusions on this point in fairly hypothetical terms – having actually manifested in previous work a highly skeptical opinion on the reliability of the results claimed by alchemists[29] – by the last decades of the fifteenth century a legal scholar such as the *doctor in utroque* Girolamo Zanetini (1457–1493) could explicitly mention the *quaestio* 77 as one of the main sources of the *communis opinio* which acknowledged the lawfulness of alchemy and allowed the sale of artificial gold.[30]

This doctrinal development asserted itself in opposition not only to rigorist positions like the one – explicitly refuted by the same Zanetini – that had been expressed by Angelo da Chivasso in his *Summa Angelica*, but also to one particularly important act of pontifical legislation, that intervened on the issue of alchemy at the beginning of the fourteenth century.

27 Alberico da Rosciate, *Dictionarium iuris*, s.v. *Emptio*.

28 Between the last decades of the Middle Ages and the beginning of the Early Modern period express quotations of Aquinas' *quaestio* 77 appear with a certain frequency both in legal treatises on contract law and in theological works on the morality of trades. For a fifteenth-century example of theological scholarship dealing with the subject of alchemy on the basis of Aquinas' doctrines see the treatise *Compendiosus tractatus de contractibus mercatorum* by the Dominican friar Johannes Nider (1380–1438), which could be read in the collection *De mercatura decisiones, et tractatus varii et de rebus ad eam pertinentibus* (Lyon, Claude Landry: 1621) 534. The same source was used in a legal context in works like the monograph on the contract of trade, *De emptione et venditione et quae ad eandem materiam pertinent*, by jurist Fabiano Ciocchi del Monte (d. 1498), which could be read in the collection *Tractatus de emptione et venditione eorumque omnium quae ad eandem materiam pertinent* (Venice, ad signum iurisconsulti: 1575) 157–158.

29 In his Commentary on Peter Lombard's *Libri sententiarum*, written around 1254–1256, Aquinas actually concluded that alchemists were able to produce something that was similar to gold only in exterior appearance and in other accidental aspects, but did not possess the true substance of gold: 'Sed quaedam formae substantiales sunt quas nullo modo ars inducere potest, quia propria activa et passiva invenire non potest, sed in his potest aliquid simile facere; sicut alchimistae faciunt aliquid simile auro quantum ad accidentia exteriora; sed tamen non faciunt verum aurum' (Thomas Aquinas, *Super Sententiarum* II, dist. 7 quaestio 3 art. 1 ad 5).

30 *Contrarietates seu diversitates inter ius civile et canonicum* (Lyon, Constantine Fradin: 1515), fol. 62r.

In 1317 Pope John XXII issued the decretal *Spondent*, which conveyed a strong condemnation of alchemy, described as a deceptive pseudoscience which impoverished its practitioners. Accordingly, those who under the pretext of alchemy produced and put into circulation counterfeited gold were sanctioned with a fine. The same penalty was imposed on those who asked for artificial gold to be made or assisted alchemists in their operations. For those that were unable to pay, the fine was commuted into some other penalty determined by the judges according to the circumstances of the case. All those that were condemned for illicit alchemical practices were tainted also with perpetual infamy. If they were clerics, they, furthermore, lost their ecclesiastical benefices and were at the same time prevented from acquiring other benefices for the future. Additional penalties, including the confiscation of properties, were applied to those who used alchemical gold to coin counterfeit money.

The decretal was later included in the title on forgery ('de crimine falsi') of the *Decretales communes*,[31] a collection of late medieval pontifical legislation which remained in force in the Church until 1917. Notwithstanding its continued validity for six centuries, this act had surprisingly little influence on subsequent legal scholarship: *ius commune* jurists virtually ignored it, and the few later authors that acknowledged its existence strived to reduce its impact on the *ius commune* legal system.[32] The silence of legal scholars around the *Spondent* decretal is most probably due to the very nature of this text, which in general appeared to be more an ideological declaration against alchemy, than a legal regulation against gold forgeries.

This approach appeared to be in line with the fundamental nature of the debate about alchemical gold carried on by *ius commune* jurists. If the lawfulness of selling metals produced through alchemical processes was often discussed in the context of the wider late medieval debate about the morality of contracts, the answer to this question was always strictly dependent on the ethical-epistemological evaluation of alchemy itself. For this reason *ius commune* jurists appeared first of all interested in determining the nature of alchemical operations, trying to assess, for example, whether alchemists actually attempted to transmute the substance of the matter or merely refined base metals into precious ones without changing their substance, whether they acted in accordance to the laws of nature or illicitly resorted to demonic forces,

---

31 *Corpus juris canonici emendatum et notis illustratum* (Rome, in aedibus Populi Romani: 1582) 84–86.

32 This is the case, for example, of the *De iure alchimiae responsum* ('Legal Opinion on the Legal Regulation of Alchemy') by the *doctor in utroque* Tommaso Arsoncini, as can be read in the collection Faniani Giovanni Crisippo, *De arte metallicae metamorphoseos* (Basel, Pietro Perna: 1576) 112.

and whether the artificial gold they produced shared or not the same nature and properties as the natural element.

Much less was the interest demonstrated by *ius commune* scholars in the description and regulation of the specific techniques used by alchemists and other forgers to produce artificial gold. With the relevant exception of the long passage included by Alberto Bruno in his treatise *De monetarum augmento, variatione et diminutione*, almost nothing is said in *ius commune* legal sources about the processes used to manufacture counterfeit gold. Detailed information on this subject is however available in contemporary sources pertaining to a different level of legislation: the corporative statutes of the Guilds of Goldsmiths.

3 Fake Gold as an Artisanal Product: Gold Counterfeiting in the Statutes of the Guilds of Goldsmiths

Ever since their appearance in the middle of the twelfth century, the Guilds of arts and crafts had among their main functions to control the quality of the raw materials used by their members and to protect customers against commercial frauds. Due to the preciousness of the materials they worked on, goldsmiths – who had exclusive rights to sell gold artefacts in the Italian cities – seem to have made a particular effort to prevent forgeries: many of the statutes enacted by their Guilds throughout Italy, especially at the beginning of the modern age, stressed the urgency of intervening in response to the rapid spread of this crime.

The 1572 'statuti et ordenationi' ('statutes and orders') of the Goldsmiths of Bologna for example, after extensively describing how many local artisans had amassed great fortunes selling counterfeit artefacts as true, at the expense 'of idiotic people, with much damage for them and great dishonor for the Guild',[33] forbade the sale of a long list of such items.[34]

Just a few decades before, the 1509 statute of the *Università degli Orefici* of Rome prohibited the sale of 'cose [...] contrafacte sotto velamento de vetro

33 'Dalle mani delle persone idiote, con loro gran danno e pocha reputacione di dett'Arte': Biblioteca del Senato, Statut, ms. 315, fol. 46v.

34 'Anelle di ramo, ottone e alchimia, colane, collanine, medaglie, bottoni per collo o corone et altri simili lavori di ramo finti, dorrati o scolorati' ('rings in copper or brass or artificial gold, necklaces, chains, medals, buttons, rosaries and other copper artefacts, counterfeit, gilded or decoloured'): Biblioteca del Senato, Statuti, ms. 315, fol. 47v.

de archimia',[35] that is to say, fraudulent products manufactured by dipping objects of base metals into an alchemical substance – most probably to be identified as antimony oxide – in order to give them a gold-like colour.[36] This kind of conduct must already have been widespread in the late Middle Ages, as demonstrated by the inclusion, in the 1310 statute of the Goldsmiths of Mantua, of a norm that banned the dipping of metal rings into baths of sulphur to give them a brighter yellowish colour, closer to the shades of gold.[37]

Realistically reproducing the colour of gold was one of the biggest challenges for alchemists. This was not perceived as a mere problem of appearance, since according to alchemical doctrines the changes in colour that matter could undergo implied and made evident a correspondent development in its spiritual nature: base metals taking a golden tint after a refining process manifested in particular the attainment of perfection which was the main goal of all alchemical practices.[38]

Totally uninterested in these spiritual implications, most forgers simply aimed for 'aurifiction', that is to say in the production of objects which had the exterior appearance of gold. This goal was often achieved by simply gold-plating products, a practice that, unlike chemical baths and other alchemic procedures, was usually tolerated by the Guilds.[39] The commercial importance of this technique and the high risks of forgery it naturally implied, however, caught the attention of both corporative authorities and local rulers, inducing the respective legislators repeatedly to intervene on this matter.

35 Archivio dell'Università e Nobil Collegio degli Orefici, Gioiellieri, Argentieri dell'alma città di Roma, Statuti, ms. 1, fol. 20r.

36 On the alchemical uses of antimony oxide see Fumagalli M., *Dizionario di alchimia e di chimica farmaceutica antiquaria dalla ricerca dell'oro filosofale all'arte spagirica di Paracelso* (Rome: 2000) 218.

37 Ferrari D. – Venturelli P. (eds.), *Gli statuti dell'arte degli orefici di Mantova (1310–1694)* (Mantua: 2008) 81. This provision prohibited the dipping of rings of gold (most probably of lesser purity, which gave it an excessively pale shade of colour) or of gold-plated silver in a bath of sulphur.

38 On this doctrine and its roots in Greek philosophy see Hopkins A.J., "Transmutation by Color: A Study of Earliest Alchemy", in Ruska J. (ed.), *Studien zur Geschichte der Chemie: Festgabe Edmund O. v. Lippmann* (Berlin: 1927) 9–14.

39 Rather emblematic, in this sense, is a chapter from a 1335 statute of the Goldsmiths of Florence, which at the same time allowed objects to be plated in pure gold and prohibited the dipping of products in baths of sulphur to give them the colour of gold. The only kind of products that could lawfully undergo this treatment were threads of gilded silver and garlands: Dorini U. (ed.), *Statuti dell'Arte di Por Santa Maria del tempo della Repubblica* (Florence: 1934) 147.

A provision (n. 244) included in the title *De fabricis et aurificibus et circa eorum artem spectantibus* ('On blacksmiths, goldsmiths and things pertaining to their profession') of the 1396 statutes of the city of Milan, for example, allowed only a very limited range of products to be gold-plated, among which ecclesiastical furnishings ('cruces, terribuli'), horse harnesses ('freni, speroni et fornimenta pro equis') and other minor artefacts ('alia opera minuta').[40] The following chapter (n. 245) in any case prohibited, under the double penalty of a fine and of a perpetual ban from the Guild of Goldsmiths, the deceitful passing off of any gilded product as made of solid gold.[41] Nothing was said in the statute about the lawfulness of gilding items other than those listed in chapter 244.

This legislative gap would not be closed until more than a century later, by a subsequent piece of Milanese municipal legislation: the revised statute enacted in 1502 by the will of King Louis XII of France, Duke of the city at the time. Chapter 133 of this text explicitly allowed for jewels made of brass or copper to be gold-plated, on the sole condition that the original material would still be clearly visible in the lower part or on the reverse side of the objects.[42] The rather obvious aim of this prescription was to protect consumers, guaranteeing them the possibility of recognising gold-plated items. Substantially reprising the statute of 1396, a following provision sanctioned in any case with a fine of 200 liras and with expulsion from the Guild for those individuals who sold, pawned or appraised gold-plated or silver-plated items as if they were entirely made of gold or silver.[43]

The constant inclusion of such prescriptions in the fundamental body of the Milanese municipal legislation demonstrates that in the Duchy of Milan countering commercial frauds of this kind was considered an issue of public relevance since the last decades of the Middle Ages. As the regulation of this matter in any case fell within the competence of the Guild of Goldsmiths, chapters of the same content were included also in the statutes that regulated the life of this institution into the Early Modern period and beyond.[44] Similar

40 *Statuta iurisdictionum Mediolani saeculo XIV lata* (Turin: 1869) 158, ch. 244.

41 Ibidem, ch. 245.

42 As can be read in the commentary: Carpani Orazio, *Commentaria absolutissima in alteram iuris municipalis partem* (Milan, Giovanni Battista Bidelli: 1616) 45, ch. 133.

43 Ibidem, ch. 134.

44 The statute of the local Guild of Goldsmiths, that was promulgated by a diploma of Emperor Charles V in 1554, included three chapters (34–36) on this matter, respectively prohibiting the production of gold-plated or silver-plated items that did not show their original material in the lower part or on the reverse side, the selling, pawning or appraising

norms, however, appeared with a certain frequency in the guild statutes of Goldsmiths, and especially in those dating back to the last century of the *Ancien Régime*.[45]

Gold-plating in any case was not the only stratagem used to give metal objects the colour of gold. As the procedure followed in the failed experiment described by Alberto Bruno eloquently confirms, both alchemists and simple forgers in fact often used to add small percentages of real gold to alloys of base metals.[46]

In order to protect consumers from this kind of fraud, the statutes of almost all Guilds of Goldsmiths outlawed the selling of gold that did not respect legally-established purity standards. In many early modern statutes the standards appeared to be established by the Guild itself, as part of its duty of control on the materials used by its members; more recent texts, on the contrary, make reference to standards established outside the Guilds, by the holders of public authority.[47]

---

of gold-plated or silver-plated items as if they were entirely made of gold or silver and the gold-plating of silver, bronze or copper coins: *Statuti, ordini et privilegi dell'Arte et università de gl'Orefici della Città e Ducato di Milano* (Milan, Paolo Gottardo Pontio: 1554) 26–27. These chapters had a long validity, still appearing in a subsequent version of the statutes that was printed in 1730: *Statuti della camera degl'Orefici di Milano* (Milan, Giuseppe Vigoni: 1730) 22–23.

45 A similar provision from the 1743 statute of the Guild of the Goldsmiths and the Silversmiths of Lucca in the same way prescribed that metal products could be gold-plated or silver-plated only making sure that the original material was still visible in some part of the object. Only one kind of product could be gilded in its entirety, without leaving any space uncovered: the sacred vessels used for the Catholic mass: see *Capitoli ed ordini della matricola degli Orefici ed Argentieri eretta in Lucca* (Lucca, Domenico Ciuffetti e Filippo Maria Benedini: 1743) 21, ch. 36.

46 Bruno described the two alchemists he knew alloying the lead-coloured metal they were working on 'cum tantundem auri praeciosi' ('with a small amount of precious gold'), obtaining some 20-karat gold (*Tractatus illustrium*, fol. 208r).

47 This evolution, that manifested itself as an effect of the progressive centralisation of public functions, is well visible, for example, in the statutes of the Guild of the Goldsmiths of Rome. While a provision added at the end of the statute of 1509 defined a precise purity standard, prescribing that only 22-karat gold should be worked with (Archivio dell'Università e Nobil Collegio degli Orefici, Gioiellieri, Argentieri dell'alma città di Roma, Statuti, ms. 1, fols. <23>r–<24>r), the subsequent statute of 1739 made clear that any decision on this matter was reserved for the supreme political authority ('supremi commandi del Principe': Archivio dell'Università e Nobil Collegio degli Orefici, Gioiellieri, Argentieri dell'alma città di Roma, Statuti, ms. 3, fol. 12r, ch. 14).

4 Fake Gems and Their Role in the Establishment of a New Conception of Luxury

Besides the various forms of gold counterfeiting, another fraudulent conduct which was often mentioned in the corporative legislation of Goldsmiths was the use of imitation gems. Such creation of artificial gemstones had a long tradition in Italy, already being a common practice in ancient Rome.[48]

In some cities the Guilds of Goldsmiths had opted for a complete prohibition on this practice: this was the case, for example, with the 1672 *Statuti della Compagnia degli orefici di Bologna* which, in order to avoid the frequent deceits deriving from the circulation of fake rubies and sapphires, prescribed a total ban on the production of false gemstones, punishing as forgers not only those who manufactured such gems, but also all the jewelers and goldsmiths that were caught keeping them in their workshops.[49]

The Guilds of other cities adopted a more relaxed attitude towards the use of fake gemstones. The 1509 statute of the Goldsmiths of Parma, for example, punished under the penalty of a permanent ban from the Guild only those who sold fake gems as authentic, as well as those who after receiving from their customers some authentic gems to be mounted in gold, substituted them with fake ones.[50] In both cases it was not the use of artificial gems in itself that was sanctioned, but the willingness to deceive consumers by presenting false stones as authentic ones. A similar attitude is revealed also in the contemporary statutes of the Goldsmiths of Rome.[51]

In order to avoid fraud, many early modern statutes prohibited the mounting of false gems in gold. This was the case, for example, with a norm included in the already mentioned municipal statutes of Milan of 1502, that introduced a general prohibition against mounting in gold any piece of glass, crystal or artificial gem under penalty of a fine of 50 liras.[52] The penalty was doubled if the perpetrator was a member of the Guild of Goldsmiths. Both these norms

48 In his *Naturalis Historia*, written around AD 77, Pliny the Elder, for example, mentioned the creation of artificial emeralds and sardonyxes, concluding that there was no fraud in the world as profitable as this (*Naturalis Historia* XXXVII.75).

49 *Riforma delli statuti della compagnia degli Orefici della Città di Bologna* (Bologna, Giacomo Monti: 1672) 21, ch. 27.

50 *Statuti et ordini dell'Arte delli orefici della Magnifica città di Parma e suo territorio*: Archivio di Stato di Parma, Comune, b. 1876, chs. 17–18.

51 This provision allowed for the sale of artificial gems mounted in gold on the condition that the customers were made aware of the real nature of the product: Archivio dell'Università e Nobil Collegio degli Orefici, Gioiellieri, Argentieri dell'alma città di Roma, *Statuti*, ms. 1, fol. 20v.

52 Carpani, *Commentaria absolutissima* 46, ch. 139 and 45, ch. 131.

were transposed and repeated in the statutes of the local Guild of Goldsmiths,[53] together with other ancillary norms, like the one which forbade artisans from producing rings unless they already possessed the gems that had to be mounted in them.[54] Other norms of the same statutes punished the mere possession of fake stones mounted in gold by both retailers and consumers.[55]

The existence of such a far-reaching regulation in Milan was made necessary by the fact that this city was one of the main centers in Europe for the production of false gems. This craft must have already been prosperous in 1488, when a small group of artisans specialising in this profession asked the Duke of the City, Gian Galeazzo Sforza (1469–1494), to establish a Guild of artificial gem makers.[56] The request was granted on the 19th of November of the same year, with the formal approval of the statutes of the new Guild.[57]

The recognition of the production of artificial gems as a licit profession, legitimately inserted in the Milanese corporative system, may seem surprising. This fact, just like the relatively tolerant attitude towards the production of false gemstones that was manifested in the Parmesan and Roman statutes we have mentioned before, is explained by the increased importance of costume jewellery in early modern fashion.

Beginning with the last decades of the Middles Ages, in fact, a profound change occurred in the idea itself of luxury. The traditional conception, denominated by costume historians as 'Old Luxury',[58] revolved around long-lasting conspicuous commodities made in precious materials. These goods were

---

53 The provision was repeated, in the vernacular, in the already mentioned statutes of 1554: *Statuti, ordini et privilegi dell'Arte et università de gl'Orefici della Città e Ducato di Milano* 29, ch. 40. The norm was still included in the subsequent version of the statutes printed in 1730: *Statuti della camera degl'Orefici di Milano* 21, ch. 32.

54 This norm was included both in the municipal statutes of 1502 (Carpani, *Commentaria absolutissima* 45, ch. 132) and in the two versions of the guild statutes of the Goldsmiths (1554: *Statuti, ordini et privilegi dell'Arte et università de gl'Orefici della Città e Ducato di Milano* 25, ch. 33; 1730: *Statuti della camera degl'Orefici di Milano* 22, ch. 33).

55 As with the provisions mentioned before, these norms appeared both in the municipal statutes of 1502 (Carpani, *Commentaria absolutissima* 46, chs. 140–142) and in the two versions of the guild statutes of the Goldsmiths (1554: *Statuti, ordini et privilegi dell'Arte et università de gl'Orefici della Città e Ducato di Milano* 30–31, chs. 41–43; 1730: *Statuti della camera degl'Orefici di Milano* 25–26, chs. 41–43).

56 On this matter see Zanoboni M.P., "« Non c'è inganno a questo mondo che renda maggior guadagno »: La corporazione milanese dei fabbricanti di pietre false", in Lenti L. (ed.), *Gioielli in Italia. Il gioiello e l'artefice: Materiali, opere, committenze* (Venice: 2005) 39–48.

57 This statute can be read in *Annali della Fabbrica del Duomo*, vol. 3 (Milan: 1880) 43–44.

58 This category is used in the sense illustrated in De Vries J., "Luxury in the Dutch Golden Age in Theory and Practice", in Berg M. – Eger E. (eds.), *Luxury in the Eighteenth Century: Debates, Desires and Delectable Goods* (London: 2003) 41–43.

destined to be passed down through generations with little or no changes; their attributes of preciousness and endurance were guaranteed by the high-quality standards prescribed in corporative legislation.

While this conception had been predominant ever since the early Middle Ages, with the beginning of modernity things began to change, and conspicuous consumption started being directed to a new kind of object, made in lesser materials and destined for a much shorter lifespan. The reasons behind this significant shift in consumption habits were multiple. Firstly, the phenomenon of fashion, which established itself in the late Middle Ages, prescribed more rapid changes in attire and accessories, in order to avoid falling out of style. Moreover, in various contexts the members of the leisure class were induced to prefer jewels made in non-precious materials by the effects of sumptuary legislation, that is of laws aiming to curb luxurious consumption.[59]

Since, according to the paradigm of 'Old Luxury', non-precious jewels were not considered luxurious, the sumptuary norms enacted in great number in the Italian cities during the late Middle Ages did not apply to costume jewellery. This is eloquently confirmed by the opinion expressed on the subject of fake pearls by the most famous and influential of all the late medieval *ius commune* jurists, Bartolo di Sassoferrato (1314–1357), who clarified that counterfeit jewels were not affected by sumptuary legislation and, for this reason, people could freely make use of them.[60]

At the same time, the rise of costume jewellery was supported by the influence of foreign fashion, and above all, the new French styles. The new models coming from France, made in lesser metals, but with more fashionable designs, started rapidly spreading in Italy, as confirmed by the frequent reference to them in corporative legislation. A 1730 chapter from Rome, for example, explicitly allowed the sale of French-style rings with fake gemstones, on the sole condition that they were not sold by weight.[61]

The rise of costume jewellery is confirmed by many other norms of the seventeenth and the eighteenth centuries. A prescription of the 1702 *Statuti, Ordini e Privilegi dell'Arte ed Università degli Orefici* ('Statutes, Orders and Privileges of

59 On late medieval and early modern Italian sumptuary legislation see Kovesi Killerby, *Sumptuary Law in Italy*; Hughes D.O., "Sumptuary Law and Social Relations in Renaissance Italy", in Findlen P. (ed.), *The Italian Renaissance: The Essential Readings* (Oxford: 2002) 124–150.

60 Bartolo di Sassoferrato, *Super prima Digesti novi* (Venice, Andrea Torresano: 1493), fol. 183r. On this passage see Sheedy A.T., *Bartolus on Social Conditions in the Fourteenth Century* (New York: 1967) 67.

61 Archivio dell'Università e Nobil Collegio degli Orefici, Gioiellieri, Argentieri dell'alma città di Roma, *Statuti*, ms. 3, fol. 11v, ch. 13.

the Guild of Goldsmiths') of Turin, for example, allowed the sale of false gems, both loose or mounted in jewels, on the sole condition that the customer was made aware that the stones he or she was purchasing were artificial.[62]

In the same way, the regulations enacted around the middle of the eighteenth century by the Goldsmiths of Parma permitted the mounting of fake gems in gold or silver of good quality, a conduct which had been strictly prohibited in most early modern statutes.[63] Another norm of the same regulations went even further, allowing the production of jewellery in which authentic stones were mounted together with fake ones if this was the customer's wish.[64] These norms are hardly surprising, as one of the innovative features of the new styles was the conscious mixing of precious and non-precious materials.

Over the course of a few centuries a thriving costume jewellery industry was established in different Italian cities. The artisans involved came from different professions: not only goldsmiths who chose to produce non-precious commodities in order to diversify their offer, but also glass makers and workers of lesser metals (for example the so called *Ramaioli*, that is the copper makers).

The products of these artisans started being widely used, at first by members of the middle classes who could not afford the lavish 'Old Luxury' commodities, and then by the upper classes themselves, constituting at last what historians ended up calling 'New Luxury'.[65] This change in perception is confirmed by the fact that fake jewels started being included in the prohibitions of sumptuary laws.[66]

The shift from Old Luxury to New Luxury determined a significant change in the conception itself of the falsification of jewels, as illustrated by the history of one of the most important manufacturing industries of non-precious jewellery operating in early modern Italy: the production of glass pearls in the city of Venice. According to historians, the production of false pearls started in Venice as early as the beginning of the thirteenth century, flourishing throughout the

62 *Statuti, Ordini e privilegi dell'Arte ed Università degli Orefici della città di Torino, e Stati di S.A.R. di qua da' Monti,* (Turin, Melchior Garimberti: 1708) 24, ch. 8.

63 Archivio di Stato di Parma, Zecca borbonica, b. 2, serie 4, fasc. 1, ch. 20.

64 Jewellers were prohibited from mounting in the same piece of jewellery artificial and authentic gemstones 'quando non avesse l'ordine da qualche Persona, la quale desiderasse avere cosi quel cappo' ('unless they received an order from some consumer who desired to have a jewel made in that way'): Ibidem, ch. 21.

65 On this category see De Vries, *Luxury in the Dutch Golden Age* 43–44.

66 To give an example, the sumptuary law headed *Nova provisione et riforma sopra le pompe et superfluità,* enacted in Perugia in 1582, prohibited citizens or foreigners from wearing on their clothes ornaments made partially or totally of gold or silver, real or fake, as well as real or fake pearls, gems and precious stones: Nico Ottaviani M.G. (ed.), *La legislazione suntuaria. Secoli XIII–XVI. Umbria* (Rome: 2005) 227.

Early Modern period under the control of the Guild of the *Paternosteri*, that is of the producers of rosary grains.[67] The creation of artificial gems and crystals to be used in the production of semi-precious rosaries is confirmed by the fact that in 1501 this Guild adopted the official denomination of *Arte de' Christaleri et Paternosteri* (that is, 'Guild of Crystal-Makers and Rosary-Makers').

Around 1647, a group of artisans who were experts in the new techniques of blown-glass production left this union to establish a new Guild of '*Supialume*', denominated with a dialect term which is roughly translatable as 'lamp blowers'. The main business of these artisans was the production of imitation pearls made in blown glass, as indicated in the official denomination adopted by the Guild after 1672, that of 'Arte dei Supialume sive perle false' (that is 'Guild of the Lampblowers or of the False Pearls').[68]

The production realised under the strict control of this Guild reached high levels of refinement, becoming a quintessential item of New Luxury, commercialised all around Europe and beyond. The very success of this product led to many attempts at imitation both by Venetian artisans who were not enrolled in the Guild and by foreign workers. This created a secondary market of counterfeited products that the Guild tried in every way to counteract: for example exerting a tight control on the supply of both the raw materials and the work equipment which were needed to produce fake pearls with the blown glass technique.[69]

The concern of the *Supialume* in opposition to these imitation products provoked attempts to contrast them as a different kind of counterfeiting, no longer based on the use of fake precious materials, but implying on the contrary the use of authentic non-precious materials by unauthorised persons, who worked out of the control of the Guild, to realise products that did not respect the quality standards prescribed in the statutes.

This new kind of counterfeiting reflected the distinguishing features of the new kind of luxury, which gave more importance to fashionable designs and to high quality craftsmanship than to the use of precious materials: in this way it ended up being much closer to modern-day brand infringement than to the various forms of forgery which had been prohibited in the early modern statutes of Goldsmiths.

67 On the origin and the subsequent development of this Guild see Zecchin P., "La nascita delle conterie veneziane", *Journal of Glass Studies* 47 (2005) 77–92.

68 Bettoni B., *Perle di vetro e gioie false: Produzioni e cultura del gioiello non prezioso nell'Italia moderna* (Venice: 2017) 57.

69 On this problem and the various solutions implemented both by the Guild and by the city rulers of Venice see Bettoni, *Perle di vetro e gioie false* 117–122.

5 Conclusion

Confirmed also by the universal success of the *Supialume*, the newfound appreciation for imitation materials that is apparent in many statutes of Goldsmiths of the seventeenth and eighteenth centuries highlights an important evolution in the way counterfeiting was conceived in relation to jewellery and other precious commodities.

As we have seen, during the late Middle Ages the attention of jurists and theologians interested in such issues was almost exclusively focused on questioning the lawfulness of producing and selling artificial metals created through alchemical processes. The reasons behind this way of setting out the problem are perfectly clear: on the one hand the doubts about the moral legitimacy of manipulating natural elements had still not been dispelled; on the other the first important reflections on commercial law and business ethics stimulated debate on the legality of marketing fake materials.

While *ius commune* scholars carried on a discussion in those same terms well into the Early Modern period, the legal regulation of the production and marketing of fake gold was substantially developed at different levels of legislation, by the corporative statutes of the Guilds of arts and crafts, and in particular those of the Guilds of Goldsmiths.

A diachronic analysis of such statutes reveals, as we have seen, the progressive diffusion of a more favorable perception of imitation precious materials among the public of consumers. This conclusion seems to be confirmed also by the establishment, specifically in economically well-developed contexts like Venice and Milan, of Guilds of artisans legally producing fake luxury commodities like glass pearls or imitation gems.

These Guilds, which had exclusive rights to sell such commodities on local markets, developed rigorous strategies to avoid the commercialisation of imitation products, made by other artisans with the same raw materials and applying the same techniques as the original ones. This highlights how the diffusion of new conceptions of luxury, which privileged the reputation and the artistic originality of the manufacturer over the sheer preciousness of raw materials, led to the establishment of a new notion of commercial counterfeiting in relation to luxury crafts: a notion which considered as fake not only products made of counterfeit materials and sold to consumers as original, but also imitation products, made by unauthorised artisans and deceptively marketed under the name of the most successful manufacturing industries.

Bibliography

Alberico da Rosciate, *Dictionarium iuris tam civilis quam canonici* (Venice, Guerrei fratres et socii: 1572).

Andrea d'Isernia, *In usus feudorum commentaria* (Frankfurt, Heredes Andreæ Wecheli: 1598).

Annali della Fabbrica del Duomo, vol. 3 (Milan: 1880).

Bettoni B., *Perle di vetro e gioie false: Produzioni e cultura del gioiello non prezioso nell'Italia moderna* (Venice: 2017).

Capitoli ed ordini della matricola degli Orefici ed Argentieri eretta in Lucca (Lucca, Domenico Ciuffetti e Filippo Maria Benedini: 1743).

Carpani Orazio, *Commentaria absolutissima in alteram iuris municipalis partem* (Milan, Giovan Battista Bidelli: 1616).

Chivasso Angelo da, *Summa Angelica* (Nuremberg, Anton Koberger: 1492).

Contrarietates seu diversitates inter ius civile et canonicum (Lyon, Constantine Fradin: 1515).

Corpus iuris canonici. Pars prior: Decretum magistri Gratiani, ed. E. Friedberg (Leipzig: 1879).

Crisciani C., "I Domenicani e la tradizione alchemica nel Duecento", in *Atti del Congresso Internazionale 'Tommaso d'Aquino nel suo settimo centenario'*, vol. 2 (Naples: 1976) 35–42.

Da Ponte Oldrado, *Consilia seu responsa et quaestiones aureae* (Venice, Francesco Ziletti: 1570).

De mercatura decisiones, et tractatus varii et de rebus ad eam pertinentibus (Lyon, Claude Landry: 1621).

De Vries J., "Luxury in the Dutch Golden Age in Theory and Practice", in Berg M. – Eger E. (eds.), *Luxury in the Eighteenth Century: Debates, Desires and Delectable Goods* (London: 2003) 41–56.

De' Tedeschi Nicolò, *Super quarto et quinto decretalium* (Lyon, Johannes Moylin alias de Cambray: 1513).

Degli Ubaldi Baldo, *Super feudis* (Venice, Bernardino Benali: 1500).

Dorini U. (ed.), *Statuti dell'Arte di Por Santa Maria del tempo della Repubblica* (Florence: 1934).

Durand Guillaume, *Speculum iudiciale* (Venice, Battista Torti: 1499).

Eymerich Nicolas, *Directorium inquisitorum* (Venice, Marc'Antonio Zaltieri: 1607).

Faniani Giovanni Crisippo, *De arte metallicae metamorphoseos* (Basel, Pietro Perna: 1576).

Ferrari D. – Venturelli P. (eds.), *Gli statuti dell'arte degli orefici di Mantova (1310–1694)* (Mantua: 2008).

Fumagalli M., *Dizionario di alchimia e di chimica farmaceutica antiquaria dalla ricerca dell'oro filosofale all'arte spagirica di Paracelso* (Rome: 2000).
Gilly C., "On the Genesis of L. Zetzner's *Theatrum Chemicum* in Strasbourg", in Gilly C. – Heertum C.v. (eds.), *Magia, alchimia, scienza dal '400 al '700: l'influsso di Ermete Trismegisto / Magic, Alchemy and Science, 15th–18th Centuries: The Influence of Hermes Trismegistus*, vol. 1 (Florence: 2002) 451–467.
Hallebeek J., "Artificial Gold, Sold as Natural: Francisco de Vitoria on a Latent Defect in the Merchandise", in Dondorp J.H. – Hallebeek J. – Wallinga T. – Winkel L. (eds.), *Ius Romanum – Ius Commune – Ius Hodiernum: Studies in Honour of Eltjo J.H. Schrage on the Occasion of His 65th Birthday* (Amsterdam – Aalen: 2010) 163–165.
Hopkins A.J., "Transmutation by Color: A Study of Earliest Alchemy", in Ruska J. (ed.), *Studien zur Geschichte der Chemie: Festgabe Edmund O. v. Lippmann* (Berlin: 1927) 9–14.
Hughes D.O., "Sumptuary Law and Social Relations in Renaissance Italy", in Findlen P. (ed.), *The Italian Renaissance: The Essential Readings* (Oxford: 2002) 124–150.
Hunt A., *Governance of the Consuming Passions: A History of Sumptuary Law* (New York: 1996).
Kors A.C. – Peters E. (eds.), *Witchcraft in Europe 400–1700: A Documentary History* (Philadelphia: 2001).
Kovesi Killerby C., *Sumptuary Law in Italy 1200–1500* (Oxford: 2002).
Migliorino F., "Alchimia lecita e illecita nel Trecento. Oldrado da Ponte", *Quaderni medievali* 11 (1981) 6–41.
Nico Ottaviani M.G. (ed.), *La legislazione suntuaria. Secoli XIII–XVI. Umbria* (Rome: 2005).
Pape Guy, *Singularia iuris* (Lyon, Jean de Jonvelle: 1516).
Riforma delli statuti della compagnia degli Orefici della Città di Bologna (Bologna, Giacomo Monti: 1672).
Robinson O.F., *The Criminal Law of Ancient Rome* (London: 1995).
Scaccia Sigismondo, *Tractatus de commerciis et de cambio* (Cologne, Anton Boetzer: 1620).
Sheedy A.T., *Bartolus on Social Conditions in the Fourteenth Century* (New York: 1967).
Statuta iurisdictionum Mediolani saeculo XIV lata (Turin: 1869).
Statuti della camera degl'Orefici di Milano (Milan, Giuseppe Vigoni: 1730).
Statuti, Ordini e privilegi dell'Arte ed Università degli Orefici della città di Torino, e Stati di S.A.R. di qua da' Monti, (Turin, Melchior Garimberti: 1708).
Statuti, ordini et privilegi dell'Arte et università de gl'Orefici della Città e Ducato di Milano (Milan, Paolo Gottardo Pontio: 1554).
Theatrum Chemicum: Præcipuos selectorum auctorum tractatus de chemiæ et lapidis philosophici, vol. 1 (Strasbourg, Heredes Eberhardi Zetzneri: 1659).

Tractatus de emptione et venditione eorumque omnium quae ad eandem materiam pertinent (Venice, ad signum iurisconsulti: 1575).

Tractatus illustrium in utraque tum pontificii tum caesarei iuris facultate Iurisconsultorum. XII. De fisco et eius privilegiis (Venice, Francesco Ziletti: 1584).

Zanoboni M.P., "« Non c'è inganno a questo mondo che renda maggior guadagno »: La corporazione milanese dei fabbricanti di pietre false", in Lenti L. (ed.), *Gioielli in Italia. Il gioiello e l'artefice: Materiali, opere, committenze* (Venice: 2005) 39–48.

Zecchin P., "La nascita delle conterie veneziane", *Journal of Glass Studies* 47 (2005) 77–92.

CHAPTER 4

Re-Forging a Forgery: The French Editions of Annius of Viterbo's *Antiquitates*

Lorenzo Paoli

The most acknowledged work of the Dominican friar Giovanni Nanni, better known by his pseudonym Annius of Viterbo,[1] is surely his large-scale forgery of antique texts attributed to eleven ancient authors,[2] commonly referred to as the *Antiquities* (*Antiquitates*) by both modern critics and their Renaissance owners. Yet, the folio format incunable printed in Rome between July and August 1498 does not bear any frontispiece with such a title. Thanks to its two colophons we know that it was titled *Commentaria fratris Ioannis Annii Viterbensis ordinis predicatorum Theologiae professoris super opera diversorum auctorum de Antiquitatibus loquentium*,[3] or alternatively, as it is named in the dedicatory epistle to the Catholic Monarchs of Spain Ferdinand and Isabella, the *De commentariis Antiquitatum* [Fig. 4.1].[4] Either way, the main focus does not seem to be on the *opera diversorum auctorum*, the antiquities themselves, but on the commentaries and their author, Annius of Viterbo. In fact, it is the coordinative action of his erudite commentary that bestowed the meaning he desired upon his concocted *auctores*: each page being an intricate tangle of forty-three lines of quoted authorities and complex linguistic and historical

1 For Annius' biography, Fubini R., "Nanni, Giovanni (Annio da Viterbo)", *Dizionario Biografico degli Italiani* 77 (2012); Weiss R., "Traccia per una biografia di Annio da Viterbo", *Italia medioevale e umanistica* 5 (1962) 425–441.

2 Berosus the Chaldean, Manethon the Egyptian, Mathastenes the Persian, Myrilius of Lesbos, Philo, Archilocus, Xenophon, Sempronius, Cato, Fabius Pictor and Antoninus Pius. A twelfth being the authentic elegy 4.2 of Propertius. Concerning Annian *auctores* see Stephens W.E., *Berosus Chaldaeus: Counterfeit and Fictive Editors of the Early Sixteenth Century* (Ph.D. dissertation, Cornell University: 1979) 57–88.

3 Annius of Viterbo, *Commentaria fratris Ioannis Annii Viterbensis ordinis predicatorum Theologiae professoris super opera diversorum auctorum de Antiquitatibus loquentium* (Rome, Eucharius Silber: 1498), fol. & ii <3> r., fol. i iii <5> r.

4 Ibidem, fol. a ii. For an analysis of the dedicatory epistle, see Olivé M.M., "El prefacio de las *Antiquitates* de Juan Annio de Viterbo: opotunidad e intencion politica", in Maestre J.M. (ed.), *Humanismo y Pervivencia del Mundo Clásico. V. Homenaje al profesor Juan Gil* (Madrid: 2015).

 | DOI:10.1163/9789004106901_005

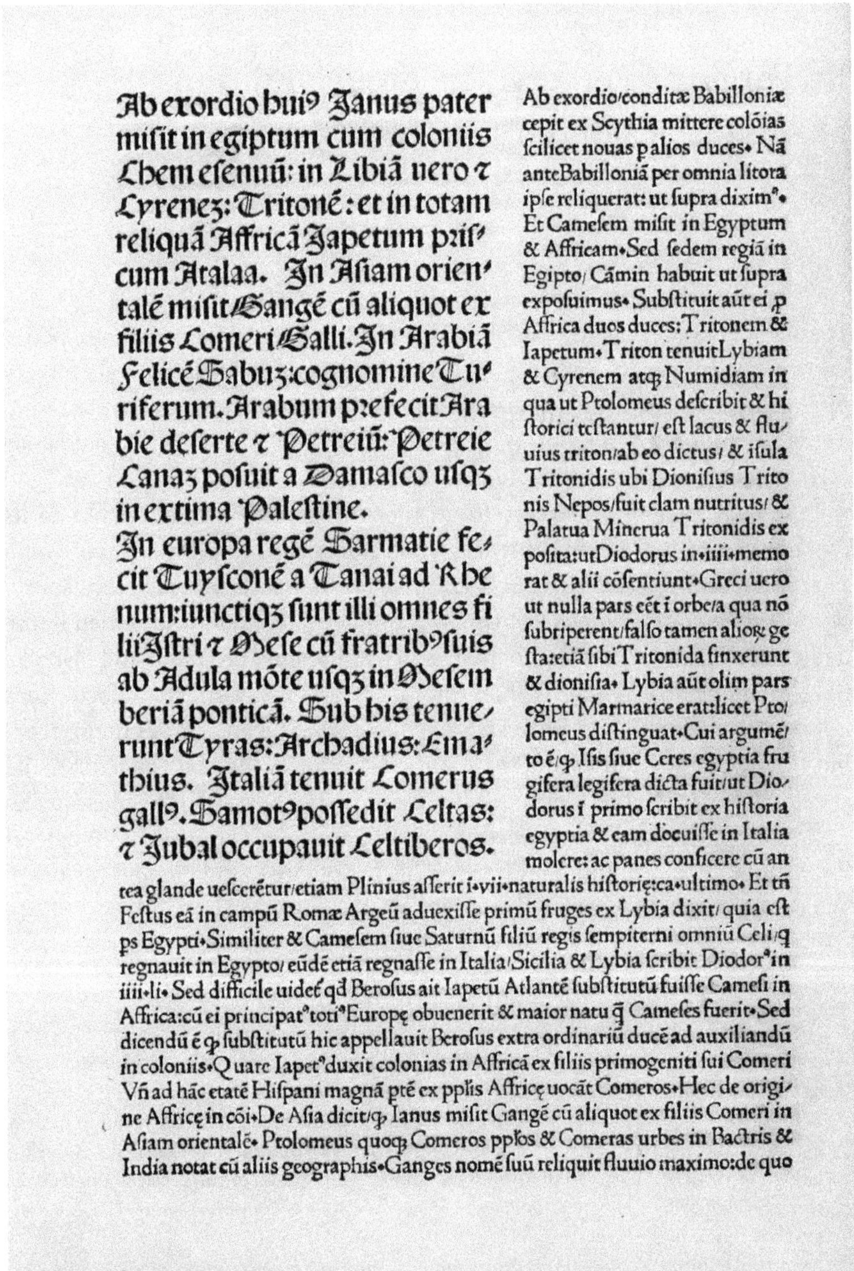

Ab exordio huiꝰ Janus pater misit in egiptum cum coloniis Chem esenuũ: in Libiã uero ⁊ Cyrenez: Tritoné: et in totam reliquã Affricã Japetum pris-cum Atalaa. Jn Asiam orien-talé misit Gangé cũ aliquot ex filiis Comeri Galli. Jn Arabiã Felicé Sabuz: cognomine Tu-riferum. Arabum prefecit Ara-bie deserte ⁊ Petreiũ: Petreie Canaz posuit a Damasco usqz in extima Palestine.

Jn europa regé Sarmatie fe-cit Tuysconé a Tanai ad Rhe-num: iunctiqz sunt illi omnes fi-lii Jstri ⁊ Mese cũ fratribꝰ suis ab Adula mõte usqz in Mesem-beriã ponticã. Sub his tenue-runt Tyras: Archadius: Ema-thius. Jtaliã tenuit Comerus gallꝰ. Samotꝰ possedit Celtas: ⁊ Jubal occupauit Celtiberos.

Ab exordio/conditæ Babilloniæ cepit ex Scythia mittere colõias scilicet nouas p alios duces. Nã ante Babilloniã per omnia litora ipse reliquerat: ut supra diximꝰ. Et Camesem misit in Egyptum & Affricam. Sed sedem regiã in Egipto/ Cãmin habuit ut supra exposuimus. Substituit aũt ei p Affrica duos duces: Tritonem & Iapetum. Triton tenuit Lybiam & Cyrenem atqꝫ Numidiam in qua ut Ptolomeus describit & hi-storici testantur/ est lacus & flu-uius triton/ab eo dictus/ & isula Tritonidis ubi Dionisius Trito-nis Nepos/fuit clam nutritus/ & Palatua Minerua Tritonidis ex-posita: ut Diodorus in. iiii. memo-rat & alii cõsentiunt. Greci uero ut nulla pars eẽt i orbe/a qua nõ subriperent/falso tamen alioꝝ ge-sta: etiã sibi Tritonida finxerunt & dionisia. Lybia aũt olim pars egipti Marmarice erat: licet Pto-lomeus distinguat. Cui argumẽ-to é/ꝙ Isis siue Ceres egyptia fru-gifera legifera dicta fuit/ut Dio-dorus i primo scribit ex historia egyptia & eam docuisse in Italia molere: ac panes conficere cũ an-tea glande uescerẽtur/etiam Plinius asserit i. vii. naturalis historię: ca. ultimo. Et tñ Festus eã in campũ Romæ Argeũ aduexisse primũ fruges ex Lybia dixit/ quia est ps Egypti. Similiter & Camesem siue Saturnũ filiũ regis sempiterni omniũ Celi/q regnauit in Egypto/ eũdẽ etiã regnasse in Italia/Sicilia & Lybia scribit Diodorꝰ in iiii. li. Sed difficile uidet qđ Berosus ait Iapetũ Atlantẽ substitutũ fuisse Camesi in Affrica: cũ ei principatꝰ totiꝰ Europę obuenerit & maior natu q̃ Cameses fuerit. Sed dicendũ é ꝙ substitutũ hic appellauit Berosus extra ordinariũ ducẽ ad auxiliandũ in coloniis. Quare Iapetꝰ duxit colonias in Affricã ex filiis primogeniti sui Comeri Vñ ad hãc etatẽ Hispani magnã ptẽ ex pplis Affricę uocãt Comeros. Hec de origi-ne Affricę in cõi. De Asia dicit/ꝙ Ianus misit Gangẽ cũ aliquot ex filiis Comeri in Asiam orientalẽ. Ptolomeus quoqꝫ Comeros pplos & Comeras urbes in Bactris & India notat cũ aliis geographis. Ganges nomẽ suũ reliquit fluuio maximo: de quo

FIGURE 4.1 Annius of Viterbo, *Commentaria fratris Ioannis Annii Viterbensis ordinis predicatorum Theologiae professoris super opera diversorum auctorum de Antiquitatibus loquentium* (Rome, Eucharius Silber: 1498), fol. Qiii (2) r. BnF RES-G-173

analysis of ancient texts and archaeological findings,[5] all printed in a roman typeface that encircled the main gothic rotunda of the transcribed sources.[6]

As a result, with this combination of scholarly glosses and pseudo-antique materials Annius was able to demonstrate the most illustrious antiquity of his town, Viterbo, the Etruscan origin of civilisation as well as of the Papacy, the Noahic genealogy of most of the European provinces of Annius' time, and the existence of giants after the universal flood.[7]

Curiously however, most of the following editions containing the entirety (or part) of the *opera diversorum auctorum* do not have such commentaries, and sometime do not even mention Annius – including those impressions printed while he was still alive. The Venetian edition printed the same year as the *princeps*, 1498, was in fact titled *Auctores vetustissimi nuper in lucem editi*: just the *auctores* without commentaries. It contains only thirteen books out of seventeen and the Dominican friar is never cited.[8]

Even if we commonly refer to them as editions of Annius' work, succeeding publications of the *Antiquities* often bore miscellaneous materials that at first glance may not seem to be related to the antiquities themselves, nor to Annius' commentaries. Furthermore, as Annius may have been known merely as the *indagator* and *illustrator* of the authorities he was publishing,[9] and not their creator, the editors and typographers did not always feel the need to make the seemingly obvious connection that we do between the friar and his frauds. As Thomas Lehr puts it, 'Auf der anderen Seite lag es nahe, dass die in

5 Concerning Annius' methodology see Goez W., "Die Anfänge der historischen Methoden-Reflexion im italienischen Humanismus", in Heinen H. (ed.), *Geschichte in der Gegenwart. Festschrift fuer Kurt Kluxen* (Paderborn: 1972) 3–21; Idem, "Die Anfange der historischen Methoden-Reflexion in der italienischen Renaissance und ihre Aufnahme in der Geschichtsschreibung des deutschen Humanismus", *Archiv für Kulturgeschichte* 56 (Wien: 1974) 25–48; Guenée B., *Histoire et culture dans l'occident medieval* (Paris: 1980) 130–147; Ligota C.R., "Annius of Viterbo and Historical Method", *Journal of the Warburg and Courtauld Institutes*, 50 (1987) 44–56; Grafton A., *Forgers and Critics: Creativity and Duplicity in Western Scholarship* (Princeton: 1990); Ferraù G., "Riflessioni teoriche e prassi storiografica in Annio da Viterbo", in Canfora D. – Chiabò M. – Nichilo M. (eds.), *Principato ecclesiastico e riuso dei classici. Gli umanisti e Alessandro VI* (Bari-Monte Sant'Angelo: 2002) 151–193.

6 Concerning the *editio princeps*: Baffoni G., "Notarella Anniana", *Studi Urbinati* 1 (1978) 61–74; Fumagalli E., "Un falso tardoquattrocentesco: lo pseudo-Catone di Annio da Viterbo", in Avesani E. – Ferrari M. – Foffano T. – Frasso G. – Sottili A. (eds.), *Vestigia. Studi in onore di Giuseppe Billanovich* (Roma: 1984) 337–363.

7 Stephens, *Berosus Chaldaeus*; Stephens W., "When Pope Noah Ruled the Etruscans: Annius of Viterbo and His Forged *Antiquities*", *Italian Issue Supplement: Studia Humanitatis: Essays in Honor of Salvatore Camporeale*, 119:1 (2004) 201–223.

8 *Auctores Vetustissimi Nuper in lucem editi* (Venice, Bernardino de Vitali: 1498).

9 Those are the adjectives used in the preface of the 1512–1515 edition written by Josse Badius.

den *Antiquitates* enthaltenen pseudoantiken Texte ein Eigenleben gewinnen würden' [On the other hand, it was obvious that the pseudo-ancient texts contained in the *Antiquities* would take on a life of their own].[10] As a complement to the *Eigenleben* of the texts, I would also stress how the authorial meaning of the commentaries that we can infer from the *editio princeps* are not valid for other editions, even those that try to imitate or correct the Roman edition. These sources and commentaries lived a life of their own as long as there were printers and readers ready to bestow upon them new use and meaning, for economical or ideological reasons.

A clear example of this *Eigenleben* is an edition of the comprehensive works of Xenophon, possibly dated 1501 or 1502, maybe printed in the French occupied Duchy of Milan or perhaps by the same Venetian printer of the *Auctores vetustissimi*.[11] Inside this folio, the reader finds works like the *Cyropaedia*, the *Constitution of the Lacedaemonians* translated by the humanist Francesco Filelfo and the *Apology of Socrates* translated by Leonardo Bruni. Amongst these works, presented in the table of contents, one also discovers the *Xenophontis libellus de Aequivocis*, an Annian forgery. In this case, the authentic and the spurious are brought together, thanks to the work of an unknown editor and typographer.[12]

Obviously, there is no falsehood until someone declares it, convincing others while helping to shape a hostile interpretative community. Until that happened, the *Antiquities* were authentic (or suspicious) ancient texts, reemployed and reprinted by a public who believed them and reshaped them to suit their needs. The subject of this study is some of these Annian re-forgeries. With re-forgery I mean the act of reusing a literary forgery,[13] knowingly or not, in order to create a new textual and material object, in this case a book. As Renaissance architects were reusing ancient construction materials for their buildings,[14] editors and typographers recycled textual units that suited their needs. However, in this case most of these components were not what they pretended to be. The idea of a re-forger of Annius was first put forward by

10 Lehr T., *Was nach den Sintflut wirklich geschah. Die* Antiquitates *des Annius von Viterbo und ihre Rezeption in Deutschland im 16. Jahrhundert* (Lausanne: 2012) 194.

11 Ibidem, 350.

12 *Xenophontis opera in hoc volumine impressa* (Milan? Venice?, Alessandro Minuziano? Guillaume Le Signerre? Bernardino de Vitali?: 1501–1502); Lehr, *Was nach den Sintflut* 195–196.

13 Concerning an analysis of the *Antiquitates* as literary forgery, see Stephens W., "Complex Pseudonymity: Annius of Viterbo's Multiple Persona Disorder", *MLN* 126 (2011) 691–694.

14 For this reemployment of *réemploi*, Callard C. – Crouzet-Pavane É. – Tallon A. (eds.), *La politique de l'histoire en Italie* (Paris: 2014) 9.

Walter Stephens in order to describe the *Illustrations des Gaules et Singularitez de Troye* by Jean Lemaire des Belges.[15] In fact, while discussing the presence of Annian sources in the *Illustrations*, he pointed out how the Walloon historiographer did not only reuse Annian material and commentaries, but reshaped them in order to suit his own conclusions. He re-falsified them: 'the fiction of editing justifies and underpins the misrepresentation or falsification'.[16]

Though the three books of the *Illustrations* are a work by themselves, not entirely dependent on Annius' forgeries, the same concept of re-forgery can be applied to understand sixteenth- and seventeenth-century editions containing Annian material. Every printer, typographer or publisher wanting to put these sensational antiquities on the market had to perform a similar, yet more transparent, operation of re-forging. As has been shown by D.F. McKenzie and Roger Chartier amongst others, the workers in the *métier du livre* were not passive receivers of texts, but re-appropriators and adapters of them.[17] The secondary editors of the antiquities are thus primary editors of new books and, as we have seen in Xenophon's case, can actively contribute to reinforcing the authenticity of these forgeries, giving them a new shape and use, sometimes even defending them against critics. Accordingly, every edition of Annius is not really an edition of him, but a different work made with its peculiar contingencies by new editors, typographers, booksellers or others, for different reasons, for a different public, in a different context: 'The "same" work is in fact not the same when it changes its language, its text, or its punctuation'.[18] Hence, we may conjecture that the format, layout, changing corpus of sources, alterations in chapters' order and paratext are all interdependent, with new meaning given to the texts by their editors and readers, so that 'each reading is peculiar to its occasion, each can be at least partially recovered from the physical forms of the text, and the differences in readings constitute an informative history'.[19] After these considerations, we can ask ourselves what the implications are for the reading and understanding of Annius' sources and commentaries detached from their original text units and the narration of which they were a part?[20]

---

15 Stephens, *Berosus Chaldaeus* 216–253.

16 Ibidem, 216.

17 McKenzie D.F., *Bibliography and the Sociology of Texts* (Cambridge: 1999); Chartier R., *The Author's Hand and the Printer's Mind: Transformations of the Written Word in Early Modern Europe* (Cambridge: 2014).

18 Chartier, *The Author's Hand and the Printer's Mind* ix.

19 McKenzie, *Bibliography and the Sociology of Texts* 19.

20 I reformulate here for my purpose R. Chartier's considerations about digital textuality, *The Author's Hand and the Printer's Mind* xi.

There are at least twenty-nine editions of Annian material from the *Antiquities*, the *princeps* excluded, printed between 1498 and 1659, from the first Venetian reforgery to the last printing in Leipzig, at a time when most European learned men considered the sources to be spurious. Of these editions, twenty-six are in Latin, three are translated into Italian and one into English. Not only could there be more, but there are also numerous manuscript transcriptions and translations from the printing process that have not been studied at all. Moreover, the six epigraphical findings presented in the fourth of the Annian *Institutiones*,[21] one of seventeen books of the first edition, may have been republished separately in various epigraphical treaties.[22]

Several academic publications provide various incomplete lists of Annian editions, without which this study would not be possible. A first catalogue was published in 1721 by the historians and Dominican friars Jacques Quétif and Jacques Échard in their *Scriptores Ordinis Prœdicatorum recensiti*, with a list of the main critics and apologists of Annius.[23] More recently than the eighteenth century, general catalogues of editions have been compiled by Walter Stephens in 1989,[24] Fausto Parente in 1994,[25] and lastly Thomas Lehr in 2012.[26]

Of approximately thirty known editions, at least eleven were printed in Paris or Lyon. These two cities were, respectively, the location of one of the

21 Annius of Viterbo, *Commentaria fratris Ioannis Annii Viterbensis*, fol. ciiii (5) r. 'Quarta institutio de excisiis memoris' '(The fourth institution concerning forgotten memories). These forged epigraphies are the *Libyscillae tablets*, the *Cybellarie tablets*, the *Decretum Desiderii* and the *Osirian marble*, all testifying to various significant historical events in viterbian history.

22 I will not directly consider here the performance of these forged epigraphies, which would deserve a study of their own. Concerning Annius' epigraphies: Weiss, "An Unknown Epigraphic Tract by Annius of Viterbo", in Brand C. – Foster K. – Limentani U. (eds.), *Italian Studies Presented to E.R. Vincent* (Cambridge: 1962) 101–120; Collins A., "Renaissance Epigraphy and its Legitimizing Potential: Annius of Viterbo, Etruscan Inscriptions and the Origins of Civilization", in Cooley A. (ed.), *The Afterlife of Inscriptions: Bulletin of the Institute of Classical Studies. Supplement* 75 (2000) 57–76; Stenhouse W., "Reading Inscriptions and Writing Ancient History: Historical Scholarship in the Late Renaissance", *Bulletin of the Institute of Classical Studies. Supplement* 86 (2005). Concerning the *Decretum Desiderii*, see Stephens W., "Discovering the Past: The Renaissance Arch-Forger and His Legacy", in Havens E. (ed.), *Fakes, Lies, and Forgeries: Rare Books and Manuscripts from the Arthur and Janet Freeman Bibliotheca Fictiva Collection* (Baltimore: 2014) 72–73.

23 Quétif Jacques – Échard Jacques, *Scriptores Ordinis Prœdicatorum recensiti*, vol. 2 (Paris, J.B. Christophe Ballard – Nicoles Simart: 1721) 4–7.

24 Stephens W., *Giants in those Days: Folklore, Ancient History and Nationalism* (Lincoln NE – London: 1989) 344–346.

25 Parente F., "Il 'Liber Antiquitatum Biblicarum' e I falsi di Annio da Viterbo", in *Paideia Cristiana. Studi in onore di Mario Naldini* (Rome: 1994) 165–172.

26 Lehr, *Was nach den Sintflut* 348–367.

main European universities and one of the major European centres of book production in the sixteenth century. Consequently, the circulation and reuse of Annian material inside the Kingdom of France is highly interesting, as France provides a clear political, cultural, geographical and historical frame through which to understand the performance of Annian re-forgeries and their reception in the long term on both the French and European stages. The evolving attitude of French printers and both French and international readers towards the *Antiquities* mirrors local and European political and cultural shifts, making it a good case study in order to comprehend the performance of Annius' fabrications.

In fact, the reception of Annius' antiquities in France has been widely studied, especially in relation to figures such as the aforementioned Jean Lemaire de Belges, Guillaume Postel, François Rabelais or in relation to recurrent motives in French Renaissance culture, like the 'Hercule de Lybie'.[27] Additionally, the *Antiquities*' reception in France has been studied with reference to the so called 'celtic myth'. Indeed, as Annius explained through his pseudo-Berosus: 'Celtas sive Gallos Francigenas condidit Samotes' [Samothes founded the Celts or French Gauls].[28] Providing a complete genealogy of Gallic kings of Noahic origin, Annius' forgeries offered the French Monarchs suitable ancestors, and a suitable pre-Roman past for the Kingdom itself.[29]

In a recent essay, Marian Rothstein synthetised and retraced 'the career of Annius' spuria in France, the claims and connections they made possible, and the nature of their sturdy resistance to learned attacks'.[30] However, the editorial and material reception was almost entirely ignored. In this study I will focus on the *Antiquities* editions printed in Paris and Lyon from 1509 to 1604, respectively the first and the last known French reforgeries of Annian material, trying to understand the contingencies of their publication and the possible meanings given to them by their editors and readers, as a key point for the antiquities' French reception. The editions as material objects, being the

27 Stephens, *Berosus Chaldaeus*; Idem, *Giants in those Days*; Biondi A., "Annio da Viterbo e un aspetto dell'orientalismo di Guillaume Postel", in Donattini M. (ed.), *Umanisti, eretici, streghe: Saggi di storia moderna* (Modena: 2008) 217–235.; Jung M.R., *Hercule dans la littérature française du XVIe siècle* (Geneva: 1966) 4–72.

28 Nanni Giovanni, *Commentaria fratris Ioannis*, fol. R v.

29 Concerning this subject: Dubois C.G., *Celtes et Gaulois aux XVIe siècle: Le développement littéraire d'un mythe nationaliste* (Paris: 1972); Asher R.E., *National Myths in Renaissance France: Francus, Samothes and the Druids* (Edinburgh: 1993).

30 Rothstein M., "The Reception of Annius of Viterbo's Forgeries: The Antiquities in Renaissance France", *Renaissance Quarterly* 71:2 (2018) 580–609.

media of this reception, are essential in order to comprehend how these now recognised forgeries were understood and reused in the Francophone sphere.[31]

1 From Rome to Paris 1509–1515

While pretending to be an expert in Hebrew,[32] Annius complained in his commentaries about the corruption of Hebrew names in Latin translations of printed books: 'Nec mirum de Hebreis dictionibus, cum Latina vocabula impressores in immensum corruperint, ut aliquantulum ostendimus in questione anniana XXI' [As we briefly discuss in the Annian *questione* XXI, since printers immensely corrupted Latin words, it is not surprising [that they did the same] to expressions in Hebrew].[33] However, Annius' critique of printers and the printing press was just a strategy, widespread in his time, to put forward his own etymologies. In fact, Annius saw the potential of this new technology, as he made use of it already in 1480 when he published his prophecies against the Turks.[34] In his *Antiquities*, he even made extensive use of incunabula of ancient authors in order to realise his forgery.[35]

The 1498 Roman edition, the *princeps*, is a carefully planned book, created to convince its learned reader about the value of its content. Eucharius Silber, the book's printer, was already known to have published the works of Pomponio Leto and other humanists, as well as the controversies around Pico della Mirandola, but rarely printed expensive in-folio codices such as the

31 In this respect I seek to expand on the forty-year-old article by R. Crahay, the studies of W. Stephens and the more recent work of T. Lehr, all concerning Annius' editions and reception. Crahay R., "Réflexions sur le faux historique: le cas d'Annius de Viterbe", *Bulletin de la Classe des lettres et des sciences morales et politiques* 69 (1983) 241–267.

32 Concerning Annius' real Hebrew knowledge: Grafton A., "Annius of Viterbo as a Student of the Jews: The Sources of His Information", in Stephens W. – Havens E.A. (eds.), *Literary Forgery in Early Modern Europe 1450–1800* (Baltimore: 2018) 147–169.

33 Annius of Viterbo, *Commentaria fratris Ioannis*, fol. P ii v., h ii r. Concerning Annius and his use of printed works, Fumagalli, "Un falso tardo-quattrocentesco" 354; Grafton A., "Traditions of Invention and Inventions of Traditions in Renaissance Europe: The Strange Case of Annius of Viterbo", in Blair A. – Grafton A. (eds.), *The Transmission of Culture in Early Modern Europe* (Philadelphia: 1990) 88–89, 273; Ferraù, "Riflessioni teoriche e prassi storiografica in Annio da Viterbo" 159–160; Idem, "Nota sulla 'filologia' di Annio da Viterbo", in Nichilo M. – Distaso G. – Iurilli A. (eds.), *Confini dell'umanesimo letterario: Studi in onore di Francesco Tateo* 2 (Rome: 2003) 631–647: 633–634.

34 Concerning Annius' prophecies: Vasoli C., *I miti e gli astri* (Naples: 1977) 17–49; Schnapp J.E., *Prophetie de fin du monde et peur des Turcs: Othoman, Antichrist, Apocalypse* (Paris: 2017).

35 Fumagalli E., "Un falso tardoquattrocentesco", 354; Fubini R., *Storiografia dell'Umanesimo in Italia: Da Leonardo Bruni ad Annio da Viterbo* (Rome: 2003) 308–309.

antiquities.[36] There is a particular oddity in the *editio princeps*. The first of the seventeen books is an index *pliniano more*, presenting the subjects and the authorial references of the other sixteen books. Surprisingly, this order is not respected. Moreover, the final printed work presents two colophons and two different signatures. This has been explained by Giovanni Baffioni as a modification made by Annius during the printing process, in order to please the main financial investor of his printed work, Garcilaso de la Vega, the Spanish ambassador at the court of Pope Alexander VI. Baffioni makes this assumption based on the substitution of the *capitula ex Chronologia quattuor monarchiarum* announced in the first book with a more Spanish oriented *De primis temporibus et quattuor ac viginti regibus primis Hispaniae et eius antiquitate*. Moreover, the financial aid of Garcilaso is confirmed by the previously mentioned preface to the monarchs of Spain and by the privilege printed in a variant of this first edition.[37] Such an evident problem in book order has puzzled not only modern researchers, but, as will be shown, Renaissance editors as well.

In Paris, Annius of Viterbo was known before his forgeries, with his title and the Latin version of his real name, *Magister Johannes*. In fact, in 1495, before the first edition of the antiquities, the Parisian typographer and publisher Etienne Jehannot printed Annius' prophecies against the Turks, *De Futuris Christianorum triumphis in Saracenos*.[38] Annius' prophecies were already well known when the antiquities were printed, and the Dominican friar was already renowned as a professor in theology, an astrologer and a commentator and interpreter of the Apocalypse.

Interestingly, the name Annius and his antiquities were probably even known by the French king Charles VIII himself and by the scholars in his following a year before Jehannot's edition. It is known that the king passed by Viterbo in 1494 during his journey down to Naples, and there was met by the local notary Tommaso Veltrellini, who publicly expressed in a learned speech the antiquity of Viterbo, its privileges and its historical relationship with the Kingdom of France: all based on the still unprinted Annius' theories.[39] Besides this, the first mention of the main Annian pseudo-authority, Berosus, in France precedes the first edition of Annius' work. In 1506, Jacques Lefèvre d'Etaples

36 Farenga P., "Le edizioni di Eucario Silber", in Chiabò M. – Maddalo S. – Miglio M. – Oliva A.M., *Roma di fronte all'Europa al tempo di Alessandro VI* (Rome: 2001) 409–439.

37 Baffioni, "Notarella Anniana".

38 Annius of Viterbo, *De Futuris Christianorum triumphis in Saracenos* (Paris, Etienne Jehannot: 1495).

39 Pinzi C., "Carlo VIII a Viterbo", in *Bollettino Storico Archeologico Viterbese* (Viterbo: 1908) 25–39. Annius began developing his theories already in the early 1490s, Baffioni G. – Mattiangeli P., *Annio da Viterbo: Documenti e ricerche* (Rome: 1981).

in his commented edition of the *Politics* of Aristotle, mentions the Chaldean priest twice, together with Metasthenes and Myrsilius, while doubting their authenticity.[40] There is no mention of Annius of Viterbo. Similarily, amongst previous critics of the *Antiquities* the Dominican forger was rarely mentioned, even when they were referring to his glosses. The humanists Sabellicus and Crinitus in 1504, and Volaterranus in 1506, all criticised some pseudo-authors or just some paragraphs of the commentaries. Only Crinitus clearly states *Annius Viterbiensis*.[41] Significantly, these critics were re-edited and reprinted in Paris earlier than or contemporaneously with the first French editions of the *Antiquities*. The very same work of Crinitus which dedicated an entire chapter to emending a specific Annian commentary on pseudo-Cato was printed by Josse Badius and Jean Petit already in 1508.[42] In France, as a result, Annius' *Antiquities* should already have been known from their critics.

However, the detractors appear to have been totally ignored when Jean de Gourmont edited and printed the *Defloratio Berosi Chaldaica*, attributed to Berosus the Chaldean. This history, written from the most primeval annals of the Babylonian priests, dealt with the genealogies of the rulers of the world from Noah to the founding of Troy.[43] By 1509, de Gourmont had already printed some works by Boccaccio and Lorenzo Valla, and some ancient texts such as the *Descriptione* of Pomponius Mela and the *Dictorum ac factorum memorabilium* of Valerius Maximus, all in a quarto format and printed in a humanist typeface. His publication of Berosus seems to fit the trend of this learned line of publishing. The volume is presented in its title as being 'geneseos perutilis' [Fig. 4.2][44] and on the book's first page, the notice to the reader is addressed 'ad lectorem sacris dicatum'.[45] To give context to his theologically-inclined reader de Gourmont even presented a biography of Berosus, entirely patchworked from Annius' 1498 preface.[46] After a table of contents of the *Defloratio*'s five books, he even felt it necessary to explain such a title to the reader, quoting a passage from Flavius Josephus that should be understood as a certificate of authenticity. It is the very same passage from the *Against Apion* that Annius had

40 Jung, *Hercule dans la litterature française* 44.
41 Ibidem.
42 Crinitus Petrus, *De honesta disciplina libri XXV; de poetis Latinis liber V; et poematum liber II; cum indicibus* (Paris, Josse Badius – Jean Petit: 1508) fol. LXXXIX r.
43 Stephens, *Berosus Chaldaeus*; Idem, *From Berossos to Berosus*; Bizzocchi R., *Genealogie incredibili: Scritti di storia nell'Europa moderna* (Bologna: 1995) 25–47.
44 *Berosus babillonicus de antiquitatibus Seu defloratio berosi Caldaica Cum figuris et ipsius eleganti vita Libris Geneseos perutilis* (Paris, Jean de Gourmont: 1509); Lehr, *Was nach den Sintflut* 196.
45 *Berosus babillonicus*, fol. A i v.
46 Ibidem, fol. A ii r.; Nanni, *Commentaria*, fol. N iiii <8> r.

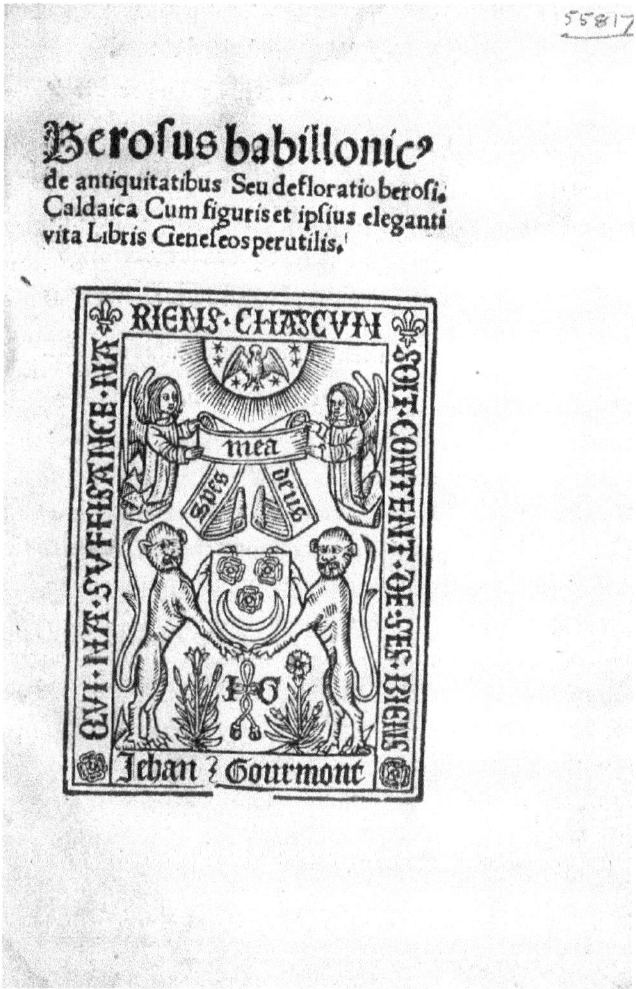

FIGURE 4.2
Frontispiece from *Berosus babillonicus de antiquitatibus Seu defloratio berosi Caldaica Cum figuris et ipsius eleganti vita Libris Geneseos perutilis* (Paris, Jean de Gourmont: 1509)

used to forge Berosus' pseudo-source.[47] Jean de Gourmont also gave another annotation to guide his reader through the *Defloratio*. Understanding that the Annian sources were interconnected in the original Roman printing, he printed a digest of the *De equivocis* by pseudo-Xenophon, which we previously encountered, thus explaining the existence of five ancient floods: the first of them was the universal and biblical one of which Berosus talks.[48] Jean de Gourmont was clearly using the 1498 Rome edition as the basis for his book, even inviting the

47 *Berosus babillonicus*, fol. A ii v.; Cf. Stephens, *Berosus Chaldaeus*.
48 Ibidem, fol. A iii r.

reader to search for more in Annius' commentary.[49] Curiously, the *Defloratio* ends here with a spurious Latin poem, admonishing the possibly envious readers to drop their mortal poison: an early and cryptic defence against critics? Moreover, the poem itself seems a patchwork, with two verses from a *carmen* written by the humanist Michele Ferno to Pietro Sabino in the Eucharius Silber 1495 edition of the works of Giovanni Antonio Campano.[50]

Only one year later, a quarto *Berosus* was edited again, this time together with ten more Annian sources, by the humanist Geoffroy Tory.[51] Tory was working for the Marnef brothers, among the most successful publishers of the time, and this *Berosus Babilonicus* is the result of a collaboration between Tory, the Marnefs and printer Jean Marchant [Fig. 4.3]. The contribution of the latter is known thanks to a variant of this edition containing a colophon.[52] Tory's 1510 *Berosus* is still based on Silber's 1498 edition. This is confirmed by the presence of a woodcut representing the original topography of ancient Rome, as described by pseudo-Fabius Pictor.[53] This woodcut is absent in Bernardino de Vitali's *Auctores Vetustissimi*, and was imitated from the *editio princeps*. Moreover, even though it is absent in the table of contents, Tory inserted the *F. Iohannis Annii Berosi Commentatoris Chronographia Etrusca digesta*, the Etruscan chronography realised by Annius using his own pseudo-authors, in the volume.[54] It is interesting to note that the presumably incorrect author order of the *editio princeps* is preserved by Tory, who otherwise chose to move Berosus and Manetho, the Egyptian priest who supposedly continued the Chaldean history, to the beginning of the volume. In fact, *Berosus* is the centrepiece of this edition, and Annius appears only as Berosus' commentator. In his dedicatory epistle to his friend and protector Philibert Babou, Tory explains how much pressure he was under from his friends who wanted him to edit and publish Berosus and the others' *Antiquities*.[55] Moreover, Tory declares that he had known about Berosus since he printed the cosmography of Pope Pius II for the printer Henri I Estienne, in 1509, the same year as Jean de Gourmont's

49 Ibidem, fol. B iiii v ; Lehr, *Was nach den Sintflut* 196.

50 Ferno Michele – Campano Giovanni Antonio, *Opera Omnia* (Rome, Eucharius Silber: 1495) fol. I r.

51 *Berosus babilonicus: De his quae praecesserunt inundationem terrarum* (Paris, Marnef: 1510); Jimenes R. (ed.), *Geoffroy Tory de Bourges: Humanisme et arts du livre à la Renaissance* (Bourges: 2019) 63.

52 Lehr, *Was nach den Sintflut* 196–197.

53 *Berosus babilonicus*, fol. 24 v.

54 Ibidem, fol. 12 r.

55 Ibidem, fol. 1 v.

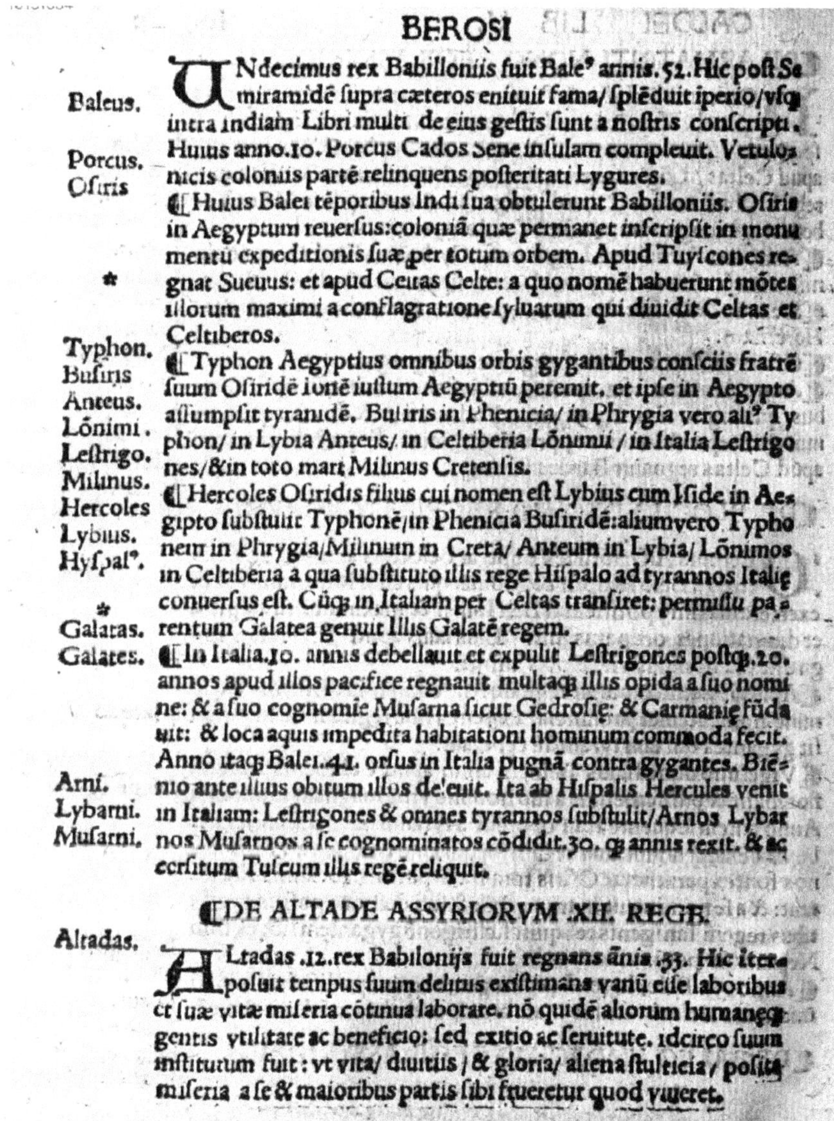

BEROSI

Baleus. UNdecimus rex Babilloniis fuit Bale⁹ annis. 52. Hic post Semiramidē supra cæteros enituit fama/ splēduit iperio/ vsq intra Indiam Libri multi de eius gestis sunt a nostris conscripti. Huius anno. 10. Porcus Cados sene insulam compleuit. Vetulonicis coloniis partē relinquens posteritati Lygures.

Porcus. Osiris ℂ Huius Balei tēporibus Indi sua obtulerunt Babilloniis. Osiris in Aegyptum reuersus: coloniā quæ permanet inscripsit in monumentū expeditionis suæ per totum orbem. Apud Tuyscones regnat Sueuus: et apud Celtas Celte: a quo nomē habuerunt mōtes illorum maximi a conflagratione syluarum qui diuidit Celtas et Celtiberos.

Typhon. Busiris Anteus. Lōnimi. Lestrigo. Milinus. ℂ Typhon Aegyptius omnibus orbis gygantibus consciis fratrē suum Osiridē Iouē iustum Aegyptiū peremit. et ipse in Aegypto assumpsit tyranidē. Busiris in Phenicia/ in Phrygia vero ali⁹ Typhon/ in Lybia Anteus/ in Celtiberia Lōnimii / in Italia Lestrigones/ & in toto mari Milinus Cretensis.

Hercoles Lybius. Hyspal⁹. ℂ Hercoles Osiridis filius cui nomen est Lybius cum Iside in Aegipto substituit Typhonē/ in Phenicia Busiridē: aliumvero Typhonem in Phrygia/ Milinum in Creta/ Anteum in Lybia/ Lōnimos in Celtiberia a qua substituto illis rege Hispalo ad tyrannos Italię conuersus est. Cūq in Italiam per Celtas transiret: permissu parentum Galatea genuit Illis Galatē regem.

Galatas. Galates. ℂ In Italia. 10. annis debellauit et expulit Lestrigones postq. 20. annos apud illos pacifice regnauit multaq illis opida a suo nomine: & a suo cognomie Musarna sicut Gedrosię: & Carmanię fūdauit: & loca aquis impedita habitationi hominum commoda fecit. Anno itaq Balei. 41. orsus in Italia pugnā contra gygantes. Biēnio ante illius obitum illos deleuit. Ita ab Hispalis Hercules venit in Italiam: Lestrigones & omnes tyrannos substulit/ Arnos Lybarnos Musarnos a se cognominatos cōdidit. 30. q annis rexit. & accersitum Tuscum illis regē reliquit.

Arni. Lybarni. Musarni.

ℂ DE ALTADE ASSYRIORVM. XII. REGE.

Altadas. ALtadas. 12. rex Babiloniis fuit regnans ānis. 33. Hic iterū posuit tempus suum delitiis existimans variū esse laboribus et suæ vitæ miseria cōtinua laborare. nō quidē aliorum humanęq gentis vtilitate ac beneficio: sed exitio ac seruitute. idcirco suum institutum fuit: vt vita/ diuitiis / & gloria/ aliena stulticia / posita miseria a se & maioribus partis sibi frueretur quod viueret.

FIGURE 4.3 *Berosus babilonicus: De his quae praecesserunt inundationem terrarum* (Paris, Marnef: 1510) fol 8v, BnF NUMM-8703559

edition.[56] He waited, however, as he did not want to print this 'bellissime' collection of antiquities 'immature', before it was ready.

The Marnef brothers' *Berosus* has other peculiarities. The reader could approach these presumably venerable antiquities with the help of a detailed *index nominum* and rich marginalia running along the borders of the text. Through a closer look at them, we may understand that the focus here is not only Berosus' relation to Genesis and consequently his importance to sacred history, but also his importance to French national history. The index has at least a dozen entries concerning Gauls and Celts and allows the reader to find every single mention of a Gallic King inside the book. In addition, an asterisk has been printed on the margin for any occurrence of the words Gaul, Celt or again of a Gallic King, allowing the reader to immediately track the Gallic references. Tory, his humanist friends and the intended audience of this edition clearly wanted to know more about the antiquity of France, something that the previous de Gourmont *Berosus* could not properly offer. Through this paratextual analysis we can also reach another conclusion. For Tory and his contemporaries there was no longer a distinction between *Galli prisci* and *Galli Celtae* – a division that can be found throughout Annius' commentaries. Annius clearly distinguishes between the former who were the original people settled in Italy after the flood, with no relation to France, and the latter who were the Gallic ancestors of the Frenchmen.[57] With the 1510 *Berosus* they all become ancient Frenchmen! In fact, asterisks pointing out the presumed ancestors of the French can be found beside any occurrence of the words *Galli* and *Celtae*, as well as for every mention of the ancient Gallic kings, showing how Tory was totally unconcerned with the aforementioned distinction.

Finally, the editor adds an *Altercatio Adriani Augusti et Epicteti philosophi* inside his reforging of the *Antiquities*.[58] It is difficult to identify the reason behind this insertion. This stoic dialogue from late antiquity concerning the philosopher Epictetus and Emperor Hadrian was probably selected due to its being an unedited ancient source.

However, Geoffroy Tory worked with Annius' material more than once. In fact, the Annian *Fragmentum Itinerari Antonini Pii* was reprinted by him together with the authentic *Itinerarium Provinciarium Antonini* in 1512, in a small sextodecimo format for the printer Henri I Estienne.[59] In fact, the last

56 Silvio Piccolomini Enea (Pius II), *Cosmographia in Asiae et Europae eleganti descriptione* (Paris, Henri I Estienne: 1509).

57 Stephens, *Berosus Chaldaeus* 192–193. The distinction collapses when Berosus is read without the commentaries.

58 Lehr, *Was nach den Sintflut* 197; Jimenes, *Geoffroy Tory* 63.

59 Concerning the original manuscript of the *Itinerarium*: Jimenes, *Geoffroy Tory* 64.

four pages of the itinerary come directly from the 1510 *Berosus* edition.[60] Yet, the absence of a proper foliation in these last two folios suggests that they may have been added by the editor or the typographer later, together with the peritext, when the bulk of the authentic *Itinerarium* was already printed. As for 1501–1502 Xenophon, the text now known to be a forgery reinforces that which is now known to be authentic and vice-versa.

The 1510 Marnef edition was appreciated even beyond French-speaking territories. A pirate copy was printed, possibly in Strasbourg by J. Gruninger, including an approximation of Marnef's device, the *De origine et situ Germanorum* of Tacitus and the *Germania Illustrata* of the imperial poet Conrad Celtes.[61] This pirate edition mixed humanist and gothic typefaces and contained an enormous number of errors without an *errata corrige*. Curiously, the asterisks in the book's margins for every occurrence of Celts or Gauls have disappeared: a lack of characters or an editorial choice? Probably both. The target readers in this case were German, not French.

Meanwhile, the *Defloratio* of Berosus, together with the other authors of the *Antiquities*, were in all probability circulating at the court of King Louis XII. This is testified to by some manuscripts, the work of Jean Lemaire de Belges and the 1512 Josse Badius and Jean Petit *Antiquitatum Variarum Volumina XVII*.[62] Following a statement written in Jean Lemaire de Belges' *Illustrations*, it has been suggested that the Walloon historiographer himself was the French discoverer of the *Antiquities* in Rome.[63] As Stephens has noted, while commenting on a possible link between the *Illustrations* and the publication of the Josse Badius and Jean Petit edition, this seems highly improbable.[64]

The humanist Josse Badius, official printer for the University of Paris,[65] published the *Antiquitatum Variarum* twice. A first edition was printed in 1512 [Fig. 4.4] and a second one, with a few corrections, in 1515.[66] These are the most well-known editions of the *Antiquities*, as they comprise all the Annian sources and his commentaries. They are in fact commonly used and quoted

60 Antoninus Augustus (?), *Itinerarium Provinciarium Antonini* (Paris, Henri I Estienne: 1512) fol. M 4 <2>–M 4 <3>.

61 Lehr, *Was nach den Sintflut* 197–200.

62 Crahay, *Reflexion sur un faux*, 261–263; Stephens, *Giants in those Days* 142–147; Paoli L., "De Bérose aux Bérosistes", *French Studies Bulletin* 41.154 (2020) 26–27.

63 Cf. Rothstein, "The Reception of Annius" 591.

64 Stephens, *Giants in those Days* 143–144.

65 Renouard, P., *Bibliographie des impressions et des œuvres Josse Badius Ascensius, imprimeur et humaniste, 1462–1535* (Paris: 1908); White P., *Jodocus Badius Ascensius: Commentary, Commerce and Print in the Renaissance* (Oxford: 2013).

66 *Antiquitatum Variarium Volumina XVII* (Paris, Josse Badius – Jean Petit: 1512); *Antiquitatum Variarium Volumina XVII* (Paris, Josse Badius – Jean Petit: 1515).

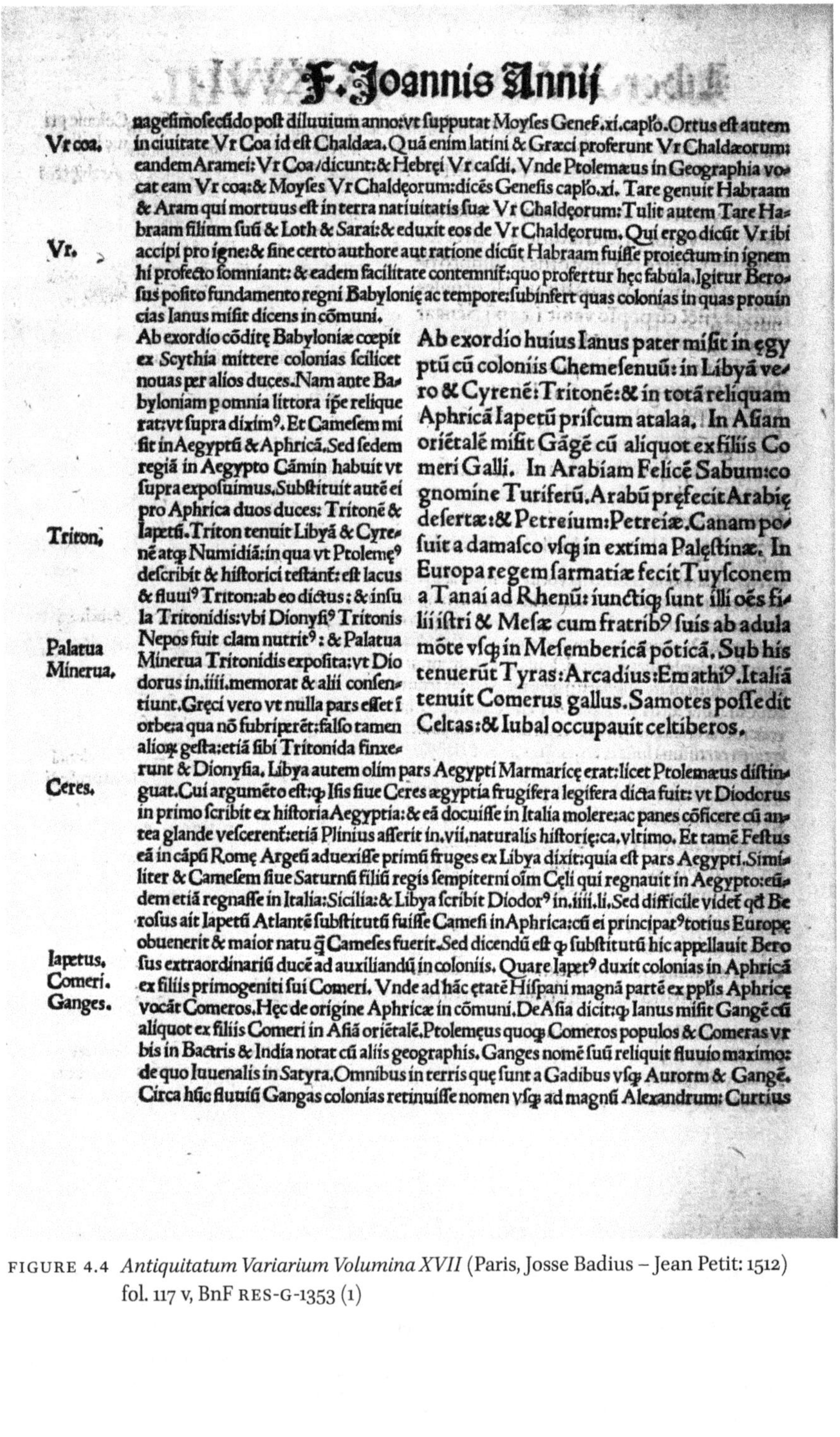

F. Joannis Annij

nageſimoſecūdo poſt diluuium anno:vt ſupputat Moyſes Geneſ.xi.caplõ.Ortus eſt autem
Vr coa. in ciuitate Vr Coa id eſt Chaldæa. Quã enim latini & Græci proferunt Vr Chaldæorum:
eandem Aramei: Vr Coa /dicunt:& Hebręi Vr caſdi. Vnde Ptolemæus in Geographia vo-
cat eam Vr coa:& Moyſes Vr Chaldęorum:dicẽs Geneſis caplõ.xi. Tare genuit Habraam
& Aram qui mortuus eſt in terra natiuitatis ſuæ Vr Chaldęorum:Tulit autem Tare Ha-
braam filium ſuũ & Loth & Sarai:& eduxit eos de Vr Chaldęorum. Qui ergo dicũt Vr ibi
Vr. accipi pro igne:& ſine certo authore aut ratione dicũt Habraam fuiſſe proiectum in ignem
hi profecto ſomniant: & eadem facilitate contemnit:quo profertur hęc fabula.Igitur Bero-
ſus poſito fundamento regni Babylonię ac tempore:ſubinfert quas colonias in quas prouin
cias Ianus miſit dicens in cõmuni.

Ab exordio cõditę Babyloniæ cœpit
ex Scythia mittere colonias ſcilicet
nouas per alios duces.Nam ante Ba-
byloniam p omnia littora ipſe relique
rat:vt ſupra diximꝰ. Et Cameſem mi
ſit in Aegyptũ & Aphricã.Sed ſedem
regiã in Aegypto Cãmin habuit vt
ſupra expoſuimus.Subſtituit autẽ ei
pro Aphrica duos duces: Tritonẽ &
Triton. Iapetũ.Triton tenuit Libyã & Cyre-
nẽ atqꝫ Numidiã:in qua vt Ptolemęꝰ
deſcribit & hiſtorici teſtant: eſt lacus
& fluuiꝰ Triton:ab eo dictus: & inſu
la Tritonidis:vbi Dionyſiꝰ Tritonis
Palatua Nepos fuit clam nutritꝰ: & Palatua
Minerua. Minerua Tritonidis expoſita:vt Dio
dorus in.iiii.memorat & alii conſen-
tiunt.Gręci vero vt nulla pars eſſet i
orbe:a qua nõ ſubriperẽt:falſo tamen
alioꝝ geſta:etiã ſibi Tritonida finxe-

Ab exordio huius Ianus pater miſit in ęgy
ptũ cũ coloniis Chemeſenuũ: in Libyã ve-
ro & Cyrenẽ:Tritonẽ:& in totã reliquam
Aphricã Iapetũ priſcum atalaa. In Aſiam
oriẽtalẽ miſit Gãgẽ cũ aliquot ex filiis Co
meri Galli. In Arabiam Felicẽ Sabum:co
gnomine Turiferũ.Arabũ pręfecit Arabię
deſertæ:& Petreium:Petreiæ.Canam po-
ſuit a damaſco vſqꝫ in extima Palęſtinæ. In
Europa regem ſarmatiæ fecit Tuyſconem
a Tanai ad Rhenũ: iunctiqꝫ ſunt illi oẽs fi-
lii iſtri & Meſæ cum fratribꝰ ſuis ab adula
mõte vſqꝫ in Meſembericã põticã. Sub his
tenuerũt Tyras:Arcadius:Emathiꝰ.Italiã
tenuit Comerus gallus. Samotes poſſedit
Celtas:& Iubal occupauit celtiberos.

runt & Dionyſia. Libya autem olim pars Aegypti Marmaricę erat:licet Ptolemæus diſtin-
Ceres. guat.Cui argumẽto eſt:ꝙ Iſis ſiue Ceres ægyptia frugifera legifera dicta fuit: vt Diodorus
in primo ſcribit ex hiſtoria Aegyptia: & eã docuiſſe in Italia molere:ac panes cõficere cũ an-
tea glande veſcerent:etiã Plinius aſſerit in.vii.naturalis hiſtorię:ca.vltimo. Et tamẽ Feſtus
eã in cãpũ Romę Argeũ aduexiſſe primũ fruges ex Libya dixit:quia eſt pars Aegypti.Simi-
liter & Cameſem ſiue Saturnũ filiũ regis ſempiterni oĩm Cęli qui regnauit in Aegypto:eũ-
dem etiã regnaſſe in Italia:Sicilia: & Libya ſcribit Diodorꝰ in.iiii.li.Sed difficile videt qđ Be
roſus ait Iapetũ Atlantẽ ſubſtitutũ fuiſſe Cameſi in Aphrica:cũ ei principatꝰ totius Europę
obuenerit & maior natu q̃ Cameſes fuerit.Sed dicendũ eſt ꝙ ſubſtitutũ hic appellauit Bero
Iapetus. ſus extraordinariũ ducẽ ad auxiliandũ in coloniis. Quare Iapetꝰ duxit colonias in Aphricã
Comeri. ex filiis primogeniti ſui Comeri. Vnde ad hãc ętatẽ Hiſpani magnã partẽ ex pplis Aphricę
Ganges. vocãt Comeros.Hęc de origine Aphricæ in cõmuni.De Aſia dicit:ꝙ Ianus miſit Gangẽ cũ
aliquot ex filiis Comeri in Aſiã oriẽtalẽ.Ptolemęus quoqꝫ Comeros populos & Comeras vr
bis in Bactris & India notat cũ aliis geographis. Ganges nomẽ ſuũ reliquit fluuio maximo:
de quo Iuuenalis in Satyra.Omnibus in terris quę ſunt a Gadibus vſqꝫ Aurorm & Gangẽ.
Circa hũc fluuiũ Gangas colonias retinuiſſe nomen vſqꝫ ad magnũ Alexandrum: Curtius

FIGURE 4.4 *Antiquitatum Variarium Volumina XVII* (Paris, Josse Badius – Jean Petit: 1512) fol. 117 v, BnF RES-G-1353 (1)

by modern researchers, as Josse Badius inserted proper foliation, a rich index, useful marginal notes, and all the paratexts which had been missing in the *editio princeps*. Badius' edition is an expensive folio conceived to be closer to the Silber edition, while emending the notorious discrepancy between the table of contents of the first book and the order of the subsequent sixteen books. It is in fact declared in the dedicatory epistle by Josse Badius, that he made the effort to rectify the previous confusing order.[67] Nevertheless, it does not use the same combination of roman and gothic rotunda as the Roman edition, preferring simply to employ a roman typeface, with an exception for the title and the foliation, printed in gothic font.

This was in reality the normal appearance of a Josse Badius folio, not exclusive to his Annian editorial reforgery. Actually, it is the very same stylistic choice that Badius and Petit used for their several reprintings of Sabellicus, Crinitus and Volaterranus.[68] Therefore, Josse Badius as a humanist and an editor was surely well informed about the doubts surrounding the antiquities. The layout of these works is so similar to the *Antiquitatum Variarum Volumina XVII* that they seem to be part of the same collection of humanistic historical works. Yet, Badius plainly ignores the critics he edited, making no substantial emendation from the *editio princeps*. This may be part of the editorial policy of Josse Badius, as in a 1514 letter to Jean Lemaire de Belges, he explained his choice not to correct the style or the Latin language of the authors he was printing.[69] Maybe he just believed, as Geoffroy Tory did, that the *Antiquities* were an authentic collection of texts, albeit maybe slightly corrupted, and the Italian humanists were wrong. In any case, he was at least suspicious of Annius' Viterbo-centric commentaries, denouncing such patriotism in the dedicatory epistle.[70] From the same opening epistle, we know that the main interest of his editing is once again Gallic national history, the origin of Christian kingdoms, Sacred History and even the genealogy of Christ himself, as Badius declares.[71]

---

67 Ibidem, fol. 1 v.

68 Crinitus Petrus, *De honesta disciplina*, was reprinted at least eight times by Josse Badius, Jean Petit or both; Sabellicus Marcus Antonius Coccius, *Rapsodie historiarum enneadum* (Paris, Josse Badius – Jean Petit: 1509), was reprinted at least seven times; Raphael Volaterranus, Xenophon, *Commentariorum urbanorum octo et triginta libri. Oeconomicus* (Paris, Josse Badius – Jean Petit: 1511) was reprinted at least twice; Rothstein, "The Reception of Annius" 583.

69 Schoysman A., "Jean Lemaire de Belges et Josse Badius", *Le Moyen Age* CXII, 3 (2006) 575–584.

70 *Antiquitatum Variarium Volumina XVII*, fol. 1 v.

71 The genealogy of Christ is treated by Annius in his *Commentaria super Philonis Breviarium de temporibus*.

As Roland Crahay and Stephens noticed, there is an important patron pushing forward the *Antiquitatum Variarum Volumina XII* both in 1512 and 1515.[72] The previously mentioned dedicatory epistle is addressed to Guillaume Petit, powerful Dominican friar, professor in theology in Paris, personal confessor of Louis XII, and previously general inquisitor of France. Moreover, Guillaume Petit was the librarian of the royal library of Blois and a relative to the bookseller and publisher Jean Petit, Josse Badius' collaborator. Guillaume Petit is behind many publications of ancient and medieval historical works concerning French antiquities and sacred history, as he cooperated with the humanists Jacques Lefevre d'Étaples and Guillaume Budé, and with the editors, printers and publishers Josse Badius, Jean Petit, Henri I Estienne and the Marnef brothers. In fact, G. Petit sponsored, amongst other works, the Estienne and J. Petit *editio princeps* of the *Chronicon* by Sigebert of Gembloux, Badius and J. Petit editions of Aimoin of Fleury and their editions of Paul the Deacon as well, possibly providing the manuscripts to the typographers himself. Even the Badius and J. Petit edition of Gregory of Tours' *History of the Franks* was encouraged by G. Petit, probably as a wider editorial policy in favour of the French King during the dispute against Pope Julius II.[73]

For the buyers and readers of the *Antiquities* the link between these works also seems to have been obvious. At the Bibliothèque Nationale in Paris, there is a sammelband containing the editions of the *Antiquitatum Variarum*, followed by the histories of Aimoin of Fleury and Paul the Deacon.[74] Another owner has bound together the 1512 *Antiquities* with Badius' and Petit's editions of Polybius, Leonardo Bruni and a Latin translation of Plutarch.[75] Both display an expensive Renaissance full leather binding.

However, even in this seemingly successful philological effort to go back to an ideal copy of the *editio princeps*, Josse Badius made changes to the text, intentionally or not, that can be found in both the 1512 and 1515 edition. The tense of some verbs is deliberately changed from the future to the past,[76] and some passages or even entire paragraphs are, perhaps accidentally, omitted.[77] Curiously, in both editions, the woodcut representing Rome is identical to the one used in the 1510 Marnef quarto edition, edited by Tory, attesting again how

---

72 Crahay, *Réflexions sur un faux* 261; Stephens, *Giants in those Days* 236, 383.

73 Stephens, *Giants in those Days* 236; Ibidem, "Discovering the Past" 81.

74 BnF RES-Z-452.

75 BnF RES-G-1353.

76 Fubini, *Storiografia dell'Umanesimo* 328.

77 Stephens, *Giants in those Days* 374; Lehr, *Was nach den Sintflut* 200.

Annian materials and texts were circulating in the same Parisian humanist network related to the printing press.[78]

It is worth noticing that the Silber edition continued to be used in France during these years. The bibliophile Jean Grolier even possessed three copies of the *editio princeps*![79] The one preserved at the Bibliothèque St. Geneviève still retains a majestic binding.[80]

2 The Lyon Editions 1552–1560

As far as we know, after 1515 texts from the *Antiquities* were not reprinted in France until 1552. By that time, the attitude towards Annius' *Antiquities* appears to have slightly changed since the enthusiastic reception during the reign of Louis XII. We can assume that in 1529 Geoffroy Tory no longer believed in Berosus, as in his famous *Champfleury* there are no references to the Chaldean priest, even when Gauls, Hercules or Druids are mentioned.[81] This view is not uncommon, and in France and Europe alike previous devotees of the *Antiquities* became more critical and distrustful. The medic and humanist Symphorien Champier's change of attitude towards Berosus is one example.[82] Even the humanist Beatus Rhenanus, who previously employed Annian sources, became exceptionally skeptical about Berosus and Annius, accusing the first of being an invention and the second a forgerer in his *Rerum Germanicarum libri tres* in 1531.[83] Other serious attacks on the authority of Berosus and the other Annian pseudo-sources were the accusations of falsehood by the Spanish humanist Juan Luis Vives, both in his commentaries to the *City of God* in 1522 and in his *De tradendis disciplinis* in 1531.[84] Other critics followed the authorities, Rhenanus and Vives, often using them as bases for their own refutations of the *Antiquities*.

78 *Antiquitatum Variarum Volumina XVII*, fol. XLIIII r.

79 Gabriel A., *The Library of Jean Grolier: A Preliminary Catalogue* (New York: 1971).

80 Bibliothèque Sainte-Geneviève, OEXV 689 RES; Crahay, *Réflexions sur un faux* 260–261.

81 Especially in the first book. Tory Geoffroy, *Champfleury* (Paris, Geoffroy Tory – Gilles Gourmont: 1529).

82 For Symphorien Champier see Stephens, *Giants in those Days* 171–176.

83 Lehr, *Was nach den Sintflut* 296–318.

84 Tigerstedt E.N., "Ioannes Annius and *Graecia mendax*", in Henderson C. (ed.), *Classical, Medieval and Renaissance Studies in Honor of Berthold Louis Ullman*, 2 vols. (Rome: 1964) 2:293–310: 296; Jung, *Hercule dans la littérature* 44.

However, Jean Lemaire de Belges' *Illustrations*, containing the vulgarisation and re-falsification of the *Antiquities*, continued to be printed until 1549.[85] Moreover, several humanists employed the previously mentioned editions of the *Antiquities* as reliable sources in order to develop and print their own texts, thus reinforcing the *Antiquities*' authenticity. Following Lemaire's example, many French historiographers employed Annian-derived methods and materials for their own theories and purposes, publishing more books partially based on them, hence testifying to the widespread reception of the forgeries.[86]

Outside the Kingdom of France more editions containing Annian material were published. From the perspective of the European book trading network, these non-French reforgeries would often become the basis for new French editions and vice versa. The jurist, historian of law and professor in Rhetoric at the University of Freiburg, Johann Sichard,[87] edited a collection of *Fragmenta vetustissimorum* for the typographer Johannes Bebel in Basel in 1530, confirming once more the reliability of the pseudo-authors.[88] Even more interesting, in Cologne in 1534, the typographer Eucharius Hirtzhorn and the publisher Gottfried Hittorp decided to reprint their previous 1524 folio *opera omnia* of Flavius Josephus, this time with Berosus, Manetho and Metasthenes annexed.[89] In the notice to the reader Hirtzhorn develops the first open defense of Berosus against the criticism of Luis Vives, while avoiding mentioning Annius of Viterbo.[90]

In 1545 an edition 'sub forma enchiridia excusi et castigati' [in a small format corrected and revised] of the *Antiquities* was published in Antwerp by the publisher Johann Steels and the typographer Johannes Grapheus.[91] It is in fact the first edition in a small portable format, an octavo, and the title directly refers, as in the older French editions, to Berosus. Annius of Viterbo is explicitly named in the title and in the notice to the reader. This volume includes all eleven pseudo-authors with commentaries, the Etruscan chronography and the history of the ancient Spanish kings by Annius, all taken from Badius'

85 Abélard J., *Les Illustrations de Gaule et singularités de Troye de Jean Lemaire de Belges: Etudes des éditions, genèse de l'oeuvre* (Geneva: 1976).

86 Stephens, *Giants in those Days* 171–184; Asher, *National Myths* 44–87, 156–183.

87 Kisch G., *Johannes Sichardus als Basler Rechtshistoriker* (Basel: 1952).

88 *Fragmenta Vetustissimorum Autorum* (Basel, Johannes Bebel: 1530).

89 *Flavii Iosephii hebraei, historiographi clarissimus, opera* (Cologne, Eucharius Cervicornus: 1524); *Flavii Iosephii hebraei antiquitatum iudaicarum libri XX* (Cologne, Eucharius Cervicornus: 1534).

90 Ibidem, A ii r.

91 *Berosi sacerdotis chaldaici, antiquitatum libri quinque* (Antwerp, Johannes Steels: 1545); Vervliet H.D., *Post-Incunabula en Hun Uitgevers in de Lage Landen/Post-Incunabula and Their Publishers in the Low Countries* (New York: 1978) 78–79.

edition.[92] Two treatises of the Syracusan Marco Claudio Arezzo were added by Steels, one concerning the chorography of Sicily, the other regarding the topography of Spain: possibly a Spanish-oriented edition for the Spanish-occupied Flanders.[93]

In 1552, while Steels was republishing his *Berosi sacerdotis chaldaici, antiquitatum libri*, the 'prince' of Lyonese typographers, publishers and booksellers Sebastian Gryphius was printing an *Antiquitatum Variarum autores* [Fig. 4.5].[94] It is a thick sextodecimo volume completely printed in an italic roman typeface.[95] The unusual book order chosen by Gryphius and the odd choice of just eight authors from the *Antiquities* comes right from Johannes Bebel's and Johann Sichard's *Fragmenta*.[96] In fact, the jurist Sichard had made the conscious choice to put the three Annian chroniclers, priests and public notaries Berosus, Manetho and Metasthenes one after the other in chronological order, suggesting a linear reading to the public. That was an innovative thematic disposition that would be imitated by other editors. However, Gryphius' *Antiquitatum* lacked a proper paratext: with no notice to the reader, no index, no marginal notes, the buyer could only refer to a lean table of contents, without even a reference to the pagination. It may be understood as an economical choice, not uncommon for one of the most important, active and well-known typographers, editors and publishers of the sixteenth century. In fact, this is the standard appearance of a Gryphius sextodecimo volume from these years. In 1552 Gryphius printed his first sextodecimo edition of the *Historical Library* of Diodorus of Sicily, with a biography by Volaterranus,[97] a collection of Roman historians previously edited by Beatus Rhenanus, again with the same format, paratext and font.[98] During the same year, Gryphius even printed a sextodecimo edition of Dictys of Crete and Dares Phrygius,[99] once again confirming the proximity of the Trojan autoptic chronicles with Annian pseudo-authors.[100]

---

92 Lehr, *Was nach den Sintflut* 358.

93 Zapperi R., "Arezzo, Claudio Mario", *Dizionario Biografico degli Italiani* 4 (1962); Stephens, "Discovering the Past" 81.

94 Febvre L. – Martin H.J., *L'apparition du livre* (Paris: 1958) 219; Zemon Davis N., "Le monde de l'imprimerie humaniste: Lyon", in Martin H.J. – Chartier R., (eds.), *Histoire de l'édition française: Tome 1. Le Livre conquérant, du Moyen Âge au milieu du XVIIe siècle* (Paris: 1989).

95 *Antiquitatum Variarum autores* (Lyon, Sebastian Gryphius: 1552).

96 Lehr has the same opinion, *Was nach den Sintflut* 359.

97 *Bibliothecae historicae libri XVII* (Lyon, Sebastian Gryphius: 1552).

98 *Historiae Romanae autores varii* (Lyon, Sebastian Gryphius: 1552).

99 *De bello Troiano historia. Declamationes tres fere argumenti* (Lyon, Sebastian Gryphius: 1552).

100 Prosperi V., "Veri falsi antichi moderni: le antiquitates di Annio da Viterbo e le Cronache troiane di Ditti Cretese e Darete Frigio", in Martínez J. – Velázquez I., (eds.), *De Falsa et*

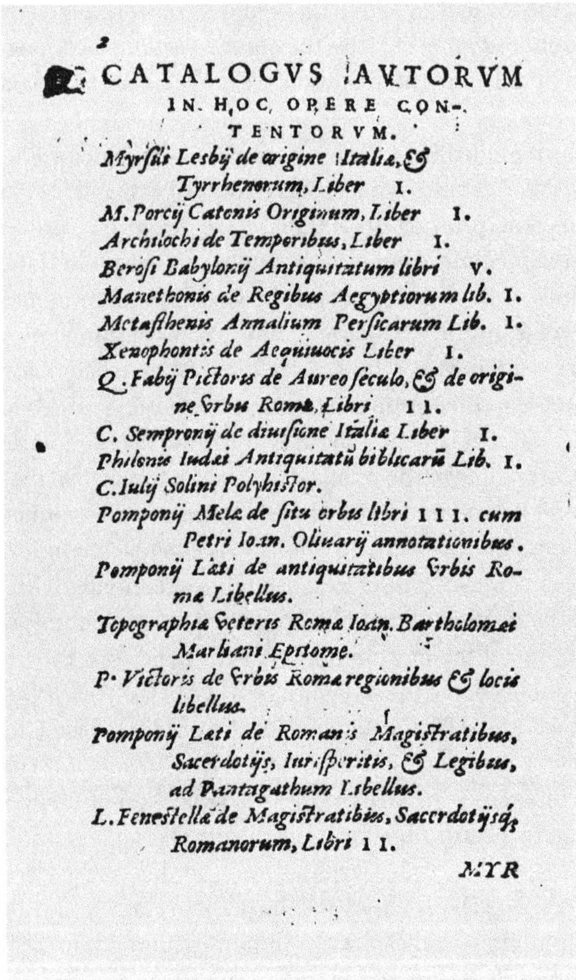

CATALOGVS AVTORVM IN HOC OPERE CONTENTORVM.

Myrsili Lesbij de origine Italiæ, & Tyrrhenorum, Liber I.
M. Porcij Catonis Originum, Liber I.
Archilochi de Temporibus, Liber I.
Berosi Babylonij Antiquitatum libri V.
Manethonis de Regibus Aegyptiorum lib. I.
Metasthenis Annalium Persicarum Lib. I.
Xenophontis de Aequiuocis Liber I.
Q. Fabij Pictoris de Aureo seculo, & de origine Vrbis Romæ, Libri II.
C. Sempronij de diuisione Italiæ Liber I.
Philonis Iudæi Antiquitatū biblicarū Lib. I.
C. Iulij Solini Polyhistor.
Pomponij Melæ de situ orbis libri III. cum Petri Ioan. Oliuarij annotationibus.
Pomponij Læti de antiquitatibus Vrbis Romæ Libellus.
Topographia Veteris Romæ Ioan. Bartholomæi Marliani Epitome.
P. Victoris de Vrbis Romæ regionibus & locis libellus.
Pomponij Læti de Romanis Magistratibus, Sacerdotijs, Iurisperitis, & Legibus, ad Pantagathum Libellus.
L. Fenestellæ de Magistratibus, Sacerdotijsq; Romanorum, Libri II.

MYR

FIGURE 4.5 *Antiquitatum Variarum autores* (Lyon, Sebastian Gryphius: 1552) 2, BnF G-17993

Consequently, we can assume that the *Antiquitatum Variarum autores* was part of a wider project of reprinting already edited and printed ancient historical sources now available in a small portable format. Curiously, the peculiar title *Antiquitatum Variarum autores* and the apparently arbitrary choice of seventeen books also reflect the 1512 and 1515 Badius and Petit editions of the *Antiquities*.

Vera Historia Estudios sobre pseudoepígrafos y falsificaciones textuales antiguas – Studies on Pseudepigrapha and Ancient Text Forgeries (Madrid: 2017); Clark F., *The First Pagan Historian: The Fortunes of a Fraud from Antiquity to the Enlightenment* (Oxford: 2020).

In this small yet copious volume, only nine texts come from the *Antiquities*, the other eight being miscellaneous materials. One of them, *Philonis Iudaei Antiquitatum biblicarum*, comes directly after the Annian pseudo-authors, but it is not Annius' pseudo-Philo. As Fausto Parente has discussed, it is another pseudo-text attributed to Philo of Alexandria that comes from a *Philonis judaei Alexandrini, libri antiquitatum* 1527 edition of Adam Petri, in Basel, edited once again by Johann Sichard, thus reedited and printed again in 1538 and 1550 by Adam' son, Henrich, with some emendations and additions.[101] This text is followed by the *Polyhistor* of Solinus, the *De situ orbis* of Pomponius Mela, the *Antiquitatibus Urbis Romae* of the humanist Pomponius Laeto, the *Topographia veteris Romae* by the humanist Giovanni Bartolomeo Marliani, the *De Urbis Romae* attributed to Publius Victor, then two more works of Leto, indexed as one single text, the *De romanis magistratibus, sacerdotiis, iurisperitis et legibus* and *De sacerdotiis et primo de prima religione apud Latinos*, and finally the *Magistratibus, sacerdotiisque Romanorum*, from yet another pseudo-antique author, Lucius Fenestella, in reality the fifteenth-century Florentine humanist Andrea Fiocchi.

Comparable to the case of the *Antiquitatum biblicarum*, all these texts had already been published by typographers in Basel, by printers in Lyon or by Gryphius himself, usually in other formats. Most of the non-Annian ancient authors in the list are accompanied by a biography or a brief commentary by another ancient or contemporary authority, thus allowing us to understand where the printed books employed by Gryphius come from. As an example, the pseudo-Philo is preceded by a short biography by St. Jerome that can be found in identical form in the Petri and Sichard edition.[102] In the same way the *Polyhistor* of Solinus is introduced with a biography composed by the friar Giovanni Ricuzzi Vellini, known by the humanist name of Ioannes Camers, which had already been published by Gryphius himself in an octavo edition in 1538.[103] Pomponius Mela comes with a dedicatory epistle by the humanist and geographer Pedro Juan Olivar,[104] dedicated to the influential humanist Guillaume du Mayne and dated 1536, as well as a notice to the reader written, once more, by Juan Olivar.[105] This indicates that Gryphius used as a basis the 1536 edition of the *De situ orbis* printed by Robert Winter, once again, in

101 Parente, "Il 'Liber Antiquitatum Biblicarum'".
102 *Antiquitatum variarum autores* 84–85.
103 Ibidem, 245–249; *Polhystor* (Lyon, Sebastian Gryphius: 1538).
104 *Antiquitatum Variarum autores* 440–442.
105 Ibidem, 585–585.

Basel.[106] In fact, Winter's edition of Pomponius Mela also included the previously mentioned work by Solinus edited by Camers. The topography of Rome by Pomponio Leto is no exception. It was published already together with Bartolomeo Marliani and Publius Victor in 1538 by Thomas I Platter in Basel: in the same order that they are found in Gryphius' 1552 *Antiquitatum.*[107] The work of Marliani itself had been edited already in 1534 by François Rabelais for Sebastian Gryphius, with a dedicatory epistle to Rabelais' patron Jean du Bellay.[108] However, in 1552 Gryphius seems to have preferred the Basel edition as a reference. The two works of Pomponio Leto, *De romanis magistratibus* and *De sacerdotiis,* presented as a single text by Gryphius, had often been printed together with Fenestella due to pseudo-Fenestella being one of Leto's inspirations for his treaties. Nevertheless, in 1551 Thibaud Payen, a member of the Grande compagnie des libraires de Lyon, reprinted both authors together, also in a sextodecimo format.[109] Therefore, the *Antiquitatum variorum autores* appears as a collage of three different editions from Basel and a publication from a fellow typographer in Lyon.

Following the various texts, this volume can be divided into several thematic sections, all sharing a common antiquarian interest. The first one running from Myrsilius of Lesbos to Philo is mainly concerned with chronology and ancient history, but also the ancient chorography of Italy and Rome. The second from Solinus to Mela concerns cosmography and topography. A third from *De antiquitatibus Urbis Romae* of Leto to Publius Victor regards the topography and toponyms of ancient Rome. The last one, from Pomponio to Fenestellae concerns Roman jurists and priests, laws and *prisca religio,* ancient public figures and thus ancient constitutions. We can infer that the first section provided a main chronological frame, while the second and the third cover the chorographical and topographical material, starting from general cosmography and ending with the city of Rome. They thus provide a context for understanding the last thematic textual area. Reading these texts together changes the meanings that can be elicited when studying them in isolation. As an example, when speaking of the Temple of Vertumnus in Rome, Marliano states 'sunt qui Vertumnum et Ianum eundem voluerunt' [...],[110] and a learned reader could immediately refer to the pseudo-Berosus in the first thematic area, where Vertumnus and Janus are indeed the same historical figure. Noah, who in fact

106 *De situ et memorabilibus orbis capitula pomponii melae de situ orbis libri tres* (Basel, Robert Winter: 1536).

107 *De urbis Romae regionibus et locis libellus* (Basel, Thomas I Platter: 1538).

108 *Topographia antiquae Romae* (Lyon, Sebastian Gryphius: 1534).

109 *De magistratibus sacerdotiisque Romanorum libellus* (Lyon, Thibaud Payen: 1551).

110 *Antiquitatum Variarum autores,* 680.

died when he was 350, treated as a god was called Vertumnus and a temple was dedicated to him in what would later become Rome. Again, in Leto and pseudo-Fenestella, when checking the Vestal priestesses, a reader would have known from pseudo-Fabius Pictor that they were named thus from Vesta, alias Titea, Noah's wife, queen of sacrifices, who gave the sacred fire to her virgins. The possible combinations are far more numerous.

Gryphius and the humanist circle around him were well aware of critics against Berosus and the other *Antiquities* since the early 1530s. In his *De Gallorum Cisalpinorum antiquitate ac origine* the humanist Gaudenzio Merula quoted a letter from his friend, the eminent jurist Andrea Alciato, in order to dismiss Annius' Etruscan etymologies and Berosus as well.[111] This in 1538 from the press of Gryphius himself.[112] Thus, we also know through Merula that Alciato did not believe that Berosus was authentic. Moreover, Alciato was also a friend of Gryphius and employed the Lyonese typographer to print his own juridical works. Furthermore, it is known that Rabelais worked as a corrector and editor for Gryphius between 1532 and 1549,[113] and he was at least skeptical and ironical about Annius of Viterbo, Jean Lemaire de Belges and the noachid giants.[114] Nonetheless, Gryphius chose to print them anyway, wisely (and cheaply) without commentaries.

Through the editing by the jurist Johann Sichard, the presence of material concerning ancient magistratures, added to the numerous juridical works printed during Gryphius' career and still reprinted in 1552,[115] I may conjecture that the *Antiquitatum Variarum autores* was targeting students in law and jurists, as these figures shared at the time a common interest in antiquarianism.[116] Besides, the three Annian pseudo-authors, Berosus, Manetho and Metasthenes, were known to be ancient public figures, writing with *publica et probata fides*, as well as priests. Annius' commentaries were already deemed suspicious and

111 Jung, *Hercule dans la littérature française* 44.

112 Merula Gaudenzio, *De Gallorum Cisalpinorum antiquitate ac origine* (Lyon, Sebastian Gryphe: 1538) 144.

113 Mireille H., "Rabelais éditeur et auteur chez Gryphe", in Mouren R. (ed.), *Quid novi? Sébastien Gryphe à l'occasion du 450e anniversaire de sa mort, Actes du colloque 23 au 25 novembre 2006*, (Lyon: 2008) 201–218.

114 Stephens, *Giants in those Days* 198–199.

115 Pucci S., "Sébastien Gryphe e la circolazione dei testi di Diritto Comune", in Mouren R. (ed.), *Quid novi? Sébastien Gryphe à l'occasion du 450e anniversaire de sa mort, Actes du colloque 23 au 25 novembre 2006*, (Lyon: 2008) 375–382.

116 Pocock J.G.A., *The Ancient Constitution and the Feudal Law: A Study of English Historical Thought in the Seventeenth Century* (Cambridge: 2009) 1–29; Huppert G., *The Idea of Perfect History: Historical Erudition and Historical Philosophy in Renaissance France* (Urbana: 1970).

not worthy of attention by many, but the sources he edited, even if ambiguous to some readers in 1552, would still be something that was highly interesting for a historian of law at the time.

A renewed interest in the *Antiquities* is confirmed by another edition, once again from a Lyonese editor and publisher. In 1554 and 1555, Jean Temporal printed two imprints of the *Antiquities* in collaboration with the typographer and bookseller Barthélémy Frein. It is a sextodecimo edition, this time edited and sold in two separate volumes, a *tomus prior* and a *tomus alter*, that the buyer would have then bound together or separately.[117] Moreover, the two books also bear linked titles centring on the author Berosus: *Berosi Chaldaei Sacerdotis* and *Berosi et aliorum eius argumenti autorum*. Jean Temporal edited a rich paratext, providing an opening Latin epigram for the first volume, a preface, and an index for both books. The *tomus prior* also provides marginal notes that stop abruptly in the middle of the fifth book of Berosus.

Strikingly, the opening poem is dedicated to 'Berosum et caeteros eiusdem Chronicae Historiae autores' [Fig. 4.6].[118] The poet, possibly Temporal himself, quotes Berosus' biography taken from Pliny and versified for the occasion, then proceeds to elucidate how Berosus, previously forgotten, is now revived thanks to the art of typography, and his chronicle with him.[119] This represents an interesting marketing choice, addressed to erudite readers. The impression is reinforced by Jean Temporal's use of Greek characters and words, both in the poem and in the prefaces. These two volumes were certainly far more expensive to print than Gryphius' 1552 book.

In both prefaces, Jean Temporal explains his editorial choice, namely the authors' and texts' order in his editing. Already in the 'praefatio aetiologica' to the *tomus prior*, Berosus is presented as a certain ancient author, second only to Moses as regards his authority. The editor declares his desire to respect the layout chosen by the original editor, Annius of Viterbo, who is also named in the extended title of the frontispiece.[120] However, facing the impossibility of knowing the true intentions of the commentator Annius, Temporal chose to give a new rational disposition to the texts: a chronological order and a thematic order. Logically for the editor, Berosus should be placed first, as the most ancient, but Temporal prefers to introduce him with pseudo-Archilocus and pseudo-Xenophon, who could give the readers a context in order to better

117 *Berosi Chaldaei Sacerdotis. Reliquorumque consimilis argumenti autorum* (Lyon, Jean Temporal: 1554); *Berosi et aliorum eius argumenti autorum De chronologica priscae memoriae historia* (Lyon, Jean Temporal: 1554).

118 *Berosi Chaldaei Sacerdotis*, fol. a 1 v.

119 Ibidem.

120 Ibidem, fol a 2.

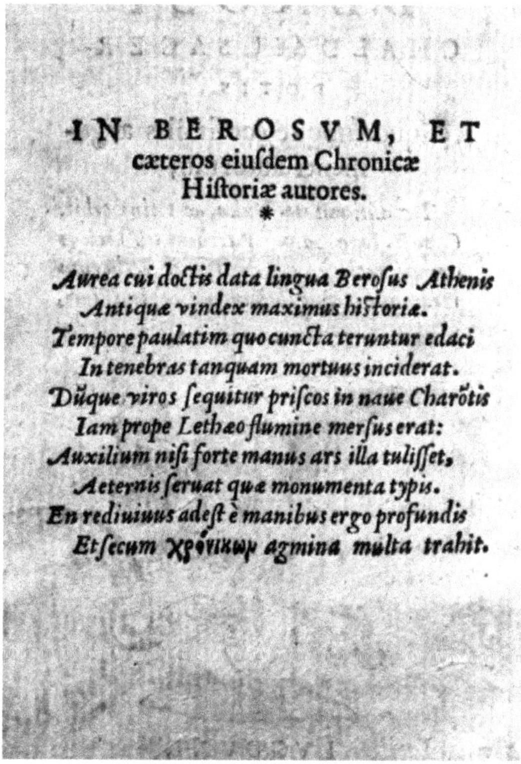

IN BEROSVM, ET
cæteros eiuſdem Chronicæ
Hiſtoriæ autores.
*

Aurea cui doctis data lingua Beroſus Athenis
Antiquæ vindex maximus hiſtoriæ.
Tempore paulatim quo cuncta teruntur edaci
In tenebras tanquam mortuus inciderat.
Dùque viros ſequitur priſcos in naue Charōtis
Iam prope Lethæo flumine merſus erat:
Auxilium niſi forte manus ars illa tuliſſet,
Aeternis ſeruat quæ monumenta typis.
En rediuiuus adeſt è manibus ergo profundis
Et ſecum χρονικῶν agmina multa trahit.

FIGURE 4.6
Berosi Chaldaei Sacerdotis. Reliquorumque consimilis argumenti autorum (Lyon, Jean Temporal: 1554) 1v
PRIVATE COLLECTION

understand the chronicle of the Chaldean priest. It may seem that Temporal did not know about the presumed original order, because he employed as one of his sources the 1545 or the 1552 Antwerp edition. This is confirmed by the fact that, besides Annius' *auctores*, his commentaries, and the Etruscan chronography and chronology of Spanish Kings, Temporal included the two texts by Sicilian historiographer and geographer Mario Claudio Arezzo in the *tomus alter*, possibly considering them to be part of an ideal copy.[121] Yet, the problem is far more complex. He chose deliberately not to include Arezzo in the table of contents, and added Annius' book of *Institutiones iuventutis Etruscae* in the first volume and the comment to the elegy 4.2 of the Latin poet Propertius at the end of the second volume.[122] Now, neither the *Institutiones* nor the *Commentaria super vertumnianam Propertii* had been printed by

121 *Berosi et aliorum eius argumenti autorum* 397–521.

122 Concerning Annius and Propertius see O'Connell S.D., "Fashioning Noah: How a Forger Turned an Etruscan God into a Biblical Figure", in Stephens W. – Havens E.A. (eds.), *Literary Forgery in Early Modern Europe 1450–1800* (Baltimore: 2018) 135–146.

Steels, possibly as they were thought to be too Etruscophile and Italocentric. Moreover, they had not been published since Josse Badius' edition back in 1515. Jean Temporal may have used, together with Steels' edition, Badius' one. Yet, the titles Temporal has chosen for these two Annian texts and their disposition do not match the Parisian edition. That is, unless the *Institutiones* and the commentary to Propertius were reprinted as accessory material in an edition unknown to us, or if Temporal had access to a manuscript copy of both texts. Having the *editio princeps* to hand would explain his anxiety to restore the ideal order and their derivation as well. Nonetheless, the *index pliniano more* of Silber's edition has nothing in common, as regards order, with Temporal's choice. Additionally, the Etruscan Chronography is missing its preface as in every other edition since 1515, thus confirming that Temporal was restoring his own ideal original order without having any real reference for it!

The preface of the *tomus alter* is most interesting. Jean Temporal explains to the reader the practical typographical choice of printing two separate volumes, then proceeds to partially clarify once more the texts' order. Concerning the first point, a single volume comprising all authors and commentaries would simply have been too big.[123] Regarding the texts' disposition, Temporal develops an invective against previous editors of Annius' *Antiquities*. For Temporal, earlier editions confused and threw into disarray the proper authorial order, thus also affecting their meaning. The order of the texts must respect the chronological order of their subjects and the antiquity of the authors, otherwise their content would be confusing to the reader. Temporal admits that Annius' commentaries can be obscure, wrong and open to debate. This due to the friar's ineptitude or forgetfulness. However, for philological reasons, they must be published together with the *auctores* and the order of the latter must be improved, or the price to pay will be to let an already obscure subject become even more complicated.[124] Jean Temporal reveals a rhetorically distrustful attitude towards Annius as a commentator. Hitherto, he shows great respect for the *Antiquities* as sources, and his preface to the *tomus alter* is a carefully planned apology. Annius' commentaries may be erroneous but are considered useful, the pseudo-authors are authentic and the detractors have been misled by the poor editing of previous editions. His marketing strategy involves presenting to the readers the presumed-to-be most accurate edition ever published, moreover in a handy format. This may also attest to direct competition against Gryphius' 1552 edition: one of the editions by a previous publisher which did not respect the proper order. Temporal must have surely had

123 Ibidem, 'In alterum veteris historiae tomum prefatio'.

124 Ibidem.

Gryphius' edition to hand, as he also chooses to replicate Sichard's choice of putting Berosus', Manetho's and Metasthenes' texts one after the other.[125]

In 1560 the heirs of Gryphius reprinted the 1552 edition with no significant variants. The different pagination is probably due to the use of a different italic roman font and different initial letters.[126] This appears to be a marketable choice for the heirs of the Lyonese typographer and bookseller, possibly attesting to the commercial success of the 1552 version.

These three different editions between 1552 and 1560 in Lyon indicate that the French and European public was newly interested in Annian antiquities. Reforgers like Jean Temporal actively contributed to the resilience of the *Antiquities* against detractors. Consequently, it is not surprising to find Berosus and the other pseudo-authors employed in the following years by people like Rabelais' patron Guillaume du Bellay, in 1556,[127] the philosopher Petrus Ramus, in 1559,[128] the famous jurisconsult Charles Dumoulin, in 1561,[129] and even Jean Bodin, in 1566.[130]

3 The Last (?) French Editions 1588–1604

Stephens has convincingly argued that it had to be difficult for critics to properly target an authorial figure like pseudo-Berosus, so closely related to the books of Genesis. An author whose authority was supposedly second only to Moses and who had been employed by both Erasmus and Luther.[131] Furthermore, after half a century of reediting and repurposing of the pseudo-authors, Annius of Viterbo appears to have become detached from the antiquities he created. This happened even when his commentaries were republished. For Jean Temporal, for example, Annius remained mainly known as the *commentator*, an obscure and error-riddled one, yet rich in erudition and (false) linguistic knowledge.

125 There is no mention of Jean Temporal in Maclean I., "Entre concurrence et collaboration? Sébastien Gryphe et ses confrères lyonnais (1528–1556)", in Mouren R. (ed.), *Quid novi? Sébastien Gryphe à l'occasion du 450e anniversaire de sa mort, Actes du colloque 23 au 25 novembre 2006*, (Lyon: 2008).

126 *Antiquitatum Variarum autores* (Lyon, Gryphius' heirs: 1560).

127 Stephens, *Giants in those Days* 180–184.

128 For Petrus Ramus' use of Berosus see Rothstein, "The Reception of Annius" 587.

129 du Moulin Charles, *Traicté de l'origine, progres et excellence du royaume* (Paris, Nicolas Edoard: 1561).

130 For Jean Bodin and Annius: Grafton, *Traditions of Invention and Inventions of Traditions*; Idem, *Forgers and Critics*; Idem, *What Was History? The Art of History in Early Modern Europe* (Cambridge: 2007). For a wider bibliography see Asher, *National Myths*.

131 Stephens, *Giants in those Days*.

Nonetheless, during the second half of the sixteenth century, several learned authorities around Europe questioned Berosus' authenticity. By declaring him to be an invention, they reunited Annius with his *Antiquities*, altering the Dominican friar's authorial function: from *inventor*, editor and patriotic commentator to inventor and counterfeiter. In 1534, Eucharius Hirtzhorn could defend Berosus alone and not his original editor, but the apologists of the second half of the century were often forced to defend Annius too in order to save the truth of the Chaldean *Defloratio*.

The attacks of the Dominican Melchor Cano in 1563, accusing Annius of forgery and heterodoxy just after the Council of Trent, is a good example. Another is the *Censura*, an entire book written against the *Antiquities* by the Jesuit Gaspar Barreiros and published in Latin in 1565.[132] Moreover, the critics of the previous generation, like Luis Vives and Beatus Rhenanus, were still quoted during the late sixteenth century. Especially throughout the French wars of Religion, this ambiguity polarised readers and writers as detractors or apologists of Berosus the Chaldean.

However, when some material from the *Antiquities* was reedited and printed in 1588 there was no *Defloratio* included.[133] The *libraire juré* of the University of Paris Gilles Gilles together with his son Nicolas II Gilles published a thin and elegant octavo titled *Sexti Iulii Frontini De Coloniis*, in collaboration with the typographer and bookseller Jean Charron, *cum privilegio regis* [Fig. 4.7].[134] Together with the work of Frontinus, the volume contains miscellaneous material about Roman laws and Roman *ager*, an extrapolated passage from Velleius Paterculus concerning, again, *De Coloniis*, as well as another extract regarding the same subject from the *De Censibus* of Ulpian. Together with this juridical textual material four Annian authors were printed: pseudo-Cato, pseudo-Fabius Pictor, pseudo-Sempronius and pseudo-Myrsilius. This authorial order does not seem to come from any known previous edition and was chosen by the editor. Another work of Frontinus was already included with part of the *antiquities* by Bebel fifty-eight years earlier, yet Gilles' edition bears no link with it. This volume presents no notice to readers or preface, just a final

132 Tigerstedt, "Ioannes Annius and *Graecia mendax*" 296; Jung, *Hercule dans la littérature* 44; Marocci G., "Contro i falsari: Gaspar Barreiros Censore di Annio da Viterbo", *Rinascimento* 50 (2010) 343–359; Stephens W., "Exposing the Archforger: Annius of Viterbo's First Master Critic", in Stephens W. – Havens E.A. (eds.), *Literary Forgery in Early Modern Europe 1450–1800* (Baltimore: 2018) 170–185.

133 *Sexti Iulii Frontini De Coloniis* (Paris, Gilles Gilles – Nicolas II Gilles: 1588).

134 Renouard P., *Répertoire des imprimeurs parisiens: Libraires, fondeurs de caractères et correcteurs d'imprimerie depuis l'introduction de l'Imprimerie à Paris (1470) jusqu'à la fin deu XVIe siècle* (Paris: 1965) 76, 171.

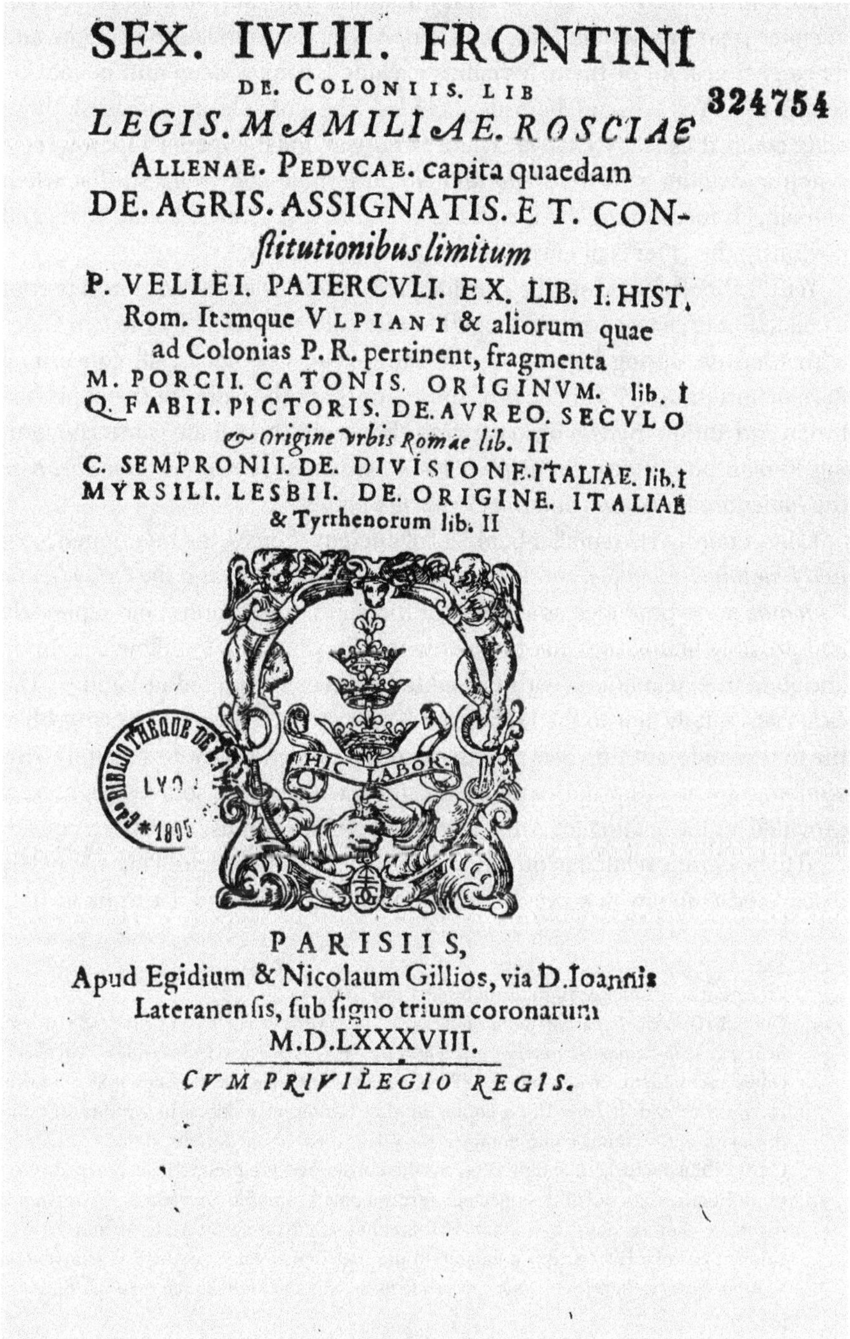
SEX. IVLII. FRONTINI
DE. COLONIIS. LIB
LEGIS. MAMILIAE. ROSCIAE
ALLENAE. PEDVCAE. capita quaedam
DE. AGRIS. ASSIGNATIS. ET. CON-
ſtitutionibus limitum
P. VELLEI. PATERCVLI. EX. LIB. I. HIST.
Rom. Itemque VLPIANI & aliorum quae
ad Colonias P. R. pertinent, fragmenta
M. PORCII. CATONIS. ORIGINVM. lib. I
Q. FABII. PICTORIS. DE. AVREO. SECVLO
& Origine vrbis Romae lib. II
C. SEMPRONII. DE. DIVISIONE. ITALIAE. lib. I
MYRSILI. LESBII. DE. ORIGINE. ITALIAE
& Tyrrhenorum lib. II

PARISIIS,
Apud Egidium & Nicolaum Gillios, via D. Ioannis
Lateranenſis, ſub ſigno trium coronarum
M.D.LXXXVIII.
CVM PRIVILEGIO REGIS.

FIGURE 4.7 Title page from *Sexti Iulii Frontini De Coloniis* (Paris, Gilles Gilles – Nicolas II Gilles: 1588), Bibliothèque Municipale de Lyon, 324754

index and errata. This raises several questions. The four mentioned Annian *auctores* treat pre-Roman Italy, the Golden Age, the foundation of Rome and its early times. All of them, Myrsilius excluded, display deep anti-hellenistic sentiments. Yet, without Berosus included, the possible meanings of those texts could drastically change. There is no way for the reader to know, as a synoptic reading with the *Defloratio* would immediately suggest, that when Myrsilius is mentioning the Etruscan god Janus, it is actually about Noah, and obviously, the latter is not even mentioned in the index.

Yet this book should not be considered by itself. The 1588 edition is part of a collection of octavos printed together and sold separately by the two Gilles with Charron during January of the same year: five books, all concerning Roman antiquities.[135] The focus of these prints are the works of the papal historian and antiquarian Onofrio Panvinio, hence his three main works concerning Roman antiquities: the *Reipublicae Romanae commentariorum libri tres*, the *Imperium Romanum* and the *Civitas Romana*.[136]

Consequently, two smaller booklets of ancient sources, the mentioned *Sexti Iulii Frontini De Coloniis*, containing the Annian *auctores*, and the *Origo Gentis Romanae*, were produced as a frame for the main publications, sold separately and possibly bound together by the owner, allowing him to follow Panvinio's antiquarian explanations with the edited sources he quoted at hand.[137] The *Origo* was totally new to the French public. As the title suggests, the *Origo*, like the four pseudo-authors, also discusses pre-Roman and early Roman Italy. This combination of authoritative modern authors with ancient sources might have provided a new reading for Annian texts. In fact, they must have been considered to be closely related to other euhemeristic ancient material like the newly discovered *Origo*, which presented the deeds of Janus and Saturnus in Italy

135 Cf. Parente, "Il 'Liber Antiquitatum Biblicarum'" 160.

136 Panvinio Onofrio, *Imperium Romanum* (Paris, Gilles Gilles – Nicolas II Gilles: 1588); Idem, *Reipublicae Romanae commentariorum libri tres recogniti* (Paris, Gilles Gilles – Nicolas II Gilles: 1588); Idem, *Civitas Romana* (Paris, Gilles Gilles – Nicolas II Gilles: 1588). Onofrio Panvinio owned at least three copies of three different editions of Annius' antiquities, with and without commentaries. He was critical about Annius' Roman annals by Cato, Fabius Pictor and Semprenius, but he considered them nonetheless a corruption of authentic texts not to be rejected. Ferray Louis J., *Onofrio Panvinio et les antiquités romaines* (Rome: 1996) 69–70, 225–227; Stenhouse, "Reading Inscriptions and Writing Ancient History: Historical Scholarship in the Late Renaissance"; Bauer S., *The Invention of Papal History: Onofrio Panvinio between Renaissance and Catholic Reform* (Oxford: 2020) 50–61.

137 *Origo gentis Romanae et de aquaeductibus urbis Romae libri duo* (Paris, Gilles Gilles – Nicolas II Gilles: 1588). The exemplar preserved in the Bibliothèque Municipale de Lyon (324754), is a huge sammelband of all these publications.

as well. Thanks to a new context of originally unrelated texts and completely separated from Annius of Viterbo, the pseudo-authors were strengthened and continued their *Eigenleben*. Ironically, the *Origo* has long been debated by modern philologists, some of whom believe it to be a fifteenth-century forgery itself.[138]

Gilles Gilles and Nicolas II Gilles's reforgery seems to be a catholic publication in the tense climate of Paris in 1588. A reconfirmation of Papal Roman authority through ancient history, in a city soon to be controlled by the Catholic League.[139] Thus, four Annian pseudo-authors still play a minor role in politically-charged editing at the end of the century.

Parisian printers were not the only ones still employing parts of Annius' *Antiquities*. In Basel in 1590, the typographer Konrad Waldkirch printed two interesting volumes of the *Antiquae Historiae ex XXVII authoribus contextae Libri VI* [Fig. 4.8].[140] During the preceding years, Waldkirch commonly printed Calvinist theology-related books, such as the German translation of the *Traité de l'Église* by Philippe Duplessis-Mornay and a German report of the colloquy of Montbéliard.[141] The *Antiquae Historiae* is something peculiar amongst his publications. What is even stranger is that an anonymous typographer in Lyon reprinted the very same books.[142] The first volume, *Antiquae Historiae*, is dated 1591 and, oddly, the *pars altera*, the *Historiae Antiquae*, is dated one year earlier, 1590. A closer analysis reveals that the Lyon and Basel books are identical small duodecimo volumes. They have the same paratextual and textual material, the same font, the same initial letters, the same woodcuts, the same paginations and signature marks. The only difference lies in the frontispiece: the two Lyon volumes have a straight line instead of the typographer's name, and the first

138 Momigliano A., "Some Observations on the 'Origo Gentis Romanae'", *Journal of Roman Studies* 48:1–2 (1958) 56–73.

139 There is another hypothesis. For C. Schiano, behind the publication of Onofrio Panvinio there is the Calvinist philologist Johannes Opsopoeus, at the time member of the humanist circle of the royal librarian Jacques-August de Thou. In this case, the publication may be comprehended as part of Henri III claims during the War of the Three Henrys. It's unknown if Opsopoeus also edited the Annian pseudo sources. Schiano C., *Il secolo della Sibilla: Momenti della tradizione cinquecentesca degli "Oracoli Sibillini"* (Bari: 2005), 53–54.

140 Godefroy Denis, *Antiquae Historiae ex XXVII authoribus contextae Libri VI* (Basel, Konrad Waldkirch: 1590); Idem, *Historiae Antiquae pars altera* (Basel, Konrad Waldkirch: 1590).

141 Bèze Théodore de, *Gruendlicher gegenbericht auff die zu Tuebingen außgangene schrifften des Muempelgartischen gespraechs halben welches im 1586* (Basel, Konrad Waldkirch: 1588); Mornay Philippe de, *Bestendiger bericht von der Kirchen darinn die hauptstueck darueber man heuttigs tags streittig erleuttert werden* (Basel, Konrad Waldkirch: 1589).

142 Godefroy Denis, *Antiquae Historiae ex XXVII authoribus contextae Libri VI* (Lyon, s.n.: 1591); Idem, *Historiae Antiquae pars altera* (Lyon, s.n.: 1590).

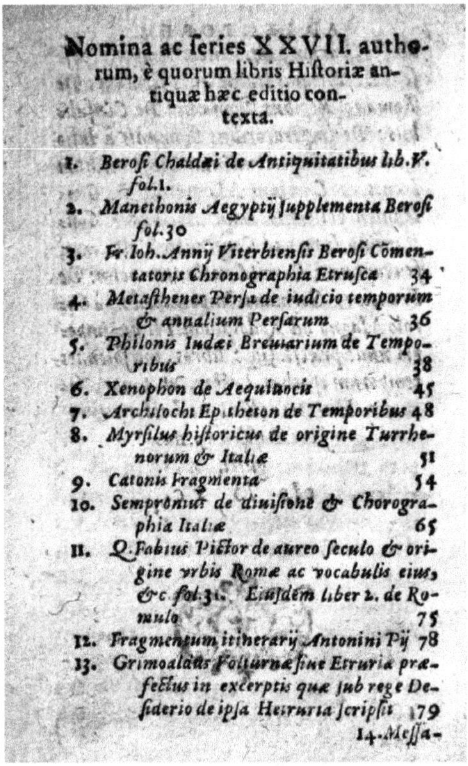
Nomina ac ſeries XXVII. authorum, è quorum libris Hiſtoriæ antiquæ hæc editio contexta.

1. *Beroſi Chaldæi de Antiquitatibus lib. V. fol. 1.*
2. *Manethonis Aegyptij ſupplementa Beroſi fol. 30*
3. *Fr. Ioh. Annij Viterbienſis Beroſi Cōmentatoris Chronographia Etruſca* 34
4. *Metaſthenes Perſa de iudicio temporum & annalium Perſarum* 36
5. *Philonis Iudæi Breuiarium de Temporibus* 38
6. *Xenophon de Aequiuocis* 45
7. *Archilochi Epitheton de Temporibus* 48
8. *Myrſilus hiſtoricus de origine Turrhenorum & Italiæ* 51
9. *Catonis Fragmenta* 54
10. *Sempronius de diuiſione & Chorographia Italiæ* 65
11. *Q. Fabius Pictor de aureo ſeculo & origine vrbis Romæ ac vocabulis eius, &c. fol. 31. Eiuſdem liber 2. de Romulo* 75
12. *Fragmentum itinerarij Antonini Pij* 78
13. *Grimoaldus Folturnæ ſiue Etruriæ præfectus in excerptis quæ ſub rege Deſiderio de ipſa Hetruria ſcripſit* 79

14. *Meſſa-*

FIGURE 4.8
Antiquae Historiae ex XXVII authoribus contextae Libri VI (Lyon [Basel], s.n. [Konrad Waldkirch]: 1591) [7r]
PRIVATE COLLECTION

tome a false date of printing stating 1591 in Roman numbers. A comparison of the paper would confirm this statement. Therefore, what has been thought to be another Lyonese Annian edition, should be considered a Basel one. What makes this statement even more complicated is that these two volumes are usually catalogued as a single book due to being normally bound together in a sammelband. Yet, they must have been sold separately. Even if the edition is clearly from Basel and not Lyon, the author of the *Historiae Antiquae* is French: the Huguenot jurist Denis Godefroy.

In 1590 Godefroy had to escape the Pays de Gex where he was *juge mage* for the Genevois. The army of the Duc of Savoy sacked the town and his library as well, and Godefroy found shelter in Basel where he taught Roman law during one year.[143] From the dedicatory epistle of the *Antiquae Historiae*, we know that Godefroy had already been offered the role of professor in history of law in Strasbourg, where he taught already in 1591. The letter is pledged to three Polish noblemen of the Ostrorog family, who were coming to study at the

143 Godefroy-Ménilglaise D.C., *Les savants Godefroy* (Paris: 1873) 21–63.

University of Strasbourg, sent by their educator and Godefroy's friend Andrea Lescinius from Baranavichy.[144] Thus, this small volume is conceived as a historical manual, 'historiae antiquae legendae novam methodum ac formam' [...], for future students.[145] This is again confirmed by a successive reedition in an octavo format in Strasburg by the publisher and typographer Lazarus Zetzner, when the Huguenot jurist was teaching there.[146]

Denis Godefroy was already famed for his 1583 edition of the *Corpus Iuris civilis*, reprinted and re-edited several times during his life and after. Accordingly, he was a careful philologist deeply interested in the history of law. The *Antiquae Historiae* is like an experimental methodological tool for the study of the past, comprising two separate volumes divided into six sections or books. They both include an index, and the first tome contains the already mentioned dedicatory epistle and a preface. The six books' organisation reflects Godefroy's conception of this new method in the study of history. In fact, the articulation does not refer to the common model of the four monarchies or the six ages, but to six epochs. These six periods are defined by their main political entities: pre-Roman Italy, Monarchic Rome, Roman Republic, from Julius Caesar to Charlemagne, from the Empire of Constantinople to the Ottoman Empire, from Charlemagne to the Emperor Rudolph II. It is a new disposition of time reminiscent of Jean Bodin's human history in the *Methodus*.[147] For Godefroy, history must be understood universally as a concatenation of causal events and their effects, as an alternation of statehood powers and not as the story of a single man, a single war or a particular event: empires fall and other empires come.[148]

As Godefroy explains in his preface, a historian must learn which events to extrapolate in order to show the causality of power alternation through analysis and demonstration. To do so, original sources are needed. In the *Antiquae Historiae* he chose to interlink twenty-seven main authorities in order to allow the reader to follow the *filum historiarum*.[149] The main problem and interest is that the first thirteen authors and texts are entirely Annian material.[150] Aside from Berosus and all the other Annian pseudo-authors, Godefroy inserted Annius' Etruscan chronography and the *Decretum Desiderii* and Annius'

144 *Antiquae Historiae ex XXVII authoribus contextae Libri VI*, fols. a–a 4 r.

145 Ibidem, fol. a 2 r.

146 Godefroy Denis, *Antiquae Historiae ex XXVII authoribus contextae Libri VI* (Strasbourg, Lazarus Zetzner: 1604).

147 Bodin J., *Methodus ad facilem historiarum cognitionem*, ed. S. Miglietti (Pisa: 2013).

148 *Antiquae Historiae*, fol. a 5.

149 Ibidem, fols. a 4 v.–a 5.

150 Ibidem, 1–81.

epigraphical forgery concerning the Lombard King Desiderius. This suggests that Godefroy's and Waldkirch's basis was Jean Temporal's *Berosi Chaldaei Sacerdotis* or even Badius' *Antiquitatum Variarum*. These older editions were clearly still viable and used. However, the textual disposition chosen by Godefroy was entirely new, responding to his own conception of chronology. Otherwise, the proximity of the three chroniclers, priests and public notaries Berosus, Manetho and Metasthenes is maintained. Interestingly, together with the antiquities, Godefroy chose to insert the *Origo gentis romanae*, thus confirming the proximity of these sources for the readers of the time.

Being perceived as ambiguous sources, the presence of Berosus, Manetho, Metasthenes and other authors from the *Antiquities* is explained by Godefroy in the above-mentioned preface. Even if the Huguenot jurist was a friend to some of the most prominent scholars of his time, like Isaac Casaubon and even Berosus' most virulent critic, Joseph Scaliger, he does not agree with them and states that he has another opinion. For Godefroy, Berosus, Manetho, and Metasthenes are still a way to access the most ancient possible archives, the royal libraries of the first monarchies of the world, and they deserve to be studied.[151]

We can understand Godefroy's work as a philo-imperial historical manual for students, where new methods for universal history are deeply intermingled with Annius' forgery. This is also employed by the Huguenot jurist to renew the *translatio imperii* concept. In fact, the last entries of the second volume of the *Historiae* are written by Godefroy himself, and they concern the reign of Emperor Maximilian II and Rudolph II.[152] In its style, the sobriety of these texts is curiously reminiscent of Berosus' description of Assyrian Kings and other Kingdoms. This edition also displays how, still at the beginning of the seventeenth century, the *Antiquities*, even if debated, were used and accepted. They were still trustworthy sources for many scholars interested in historical writing. Even if Godefroy's and Waldkirch's *Antiquae Historiae* was not printed in France, the false place of printing in Lyon was possibly thought to favour its circulation inside the Kingdom.

In 1604, the same year as Godefroy reprinted *Antiquae Historiae* in Strasbourg, another book containing Annius' texts was published in Paris.[153] No pseudo-authors, no chronography. There, just Annius of Viterbo's commentary

151 Ibidem, a 5 v.

152 *Historiae Antiquae pars altera* 638–639.

153 *Caii Valerii Catullii, Albii Tibullii, Sexti Aurelii Propertii opera omnia qui extant* (Paris, Marc Orry: 1604); *Caii Valerii Catullii, Albii Tibullii, Sexti Aurelii Propertii opera omnia qui extant* (Paris, Claude Morel: 1604).

to Propertius can be found, alongside many other commentators of the same elegy. This is not a compendium of ancient sources or a historical manual, but a complete and expensive folio-format *opera omnia* of Latin poets: Catullus, Tibullus and Propertius. It was printed as a collaboration between two Parisian typographers and publishers, Marc Orry and Claude Morel. Thus, it exists in two variants having the frontispiece as their only difference: one with Orry's device, the other with Morel's.

The *opera omnia* of the three Latin poets is accompanied by commentaries from authoritative scholars. This lets us infer that Annius' interpretation of Vertumnus as Janus and Noah was still credited. In order to understand the Dominican text a reader must have known or have read the other pseudo-authors. In fact, they are frequently quoted in Annius' commentary.[154] Yet, fatefully, his commentary to the elegy 4.2 is printed just before Joseph Scaliger's.[155] However, that's not surprising. Even if the interpretation of the poem differed from forger to critic, Scaliger accepted an Annian emendation to this very same elegy.[156]

Nevertheless, printing Annius' texts together with refutations of it was not uncommon. A re-editing of Gryphius' 1552–1560 version of Annian pseudo-authors along with the non-Annian pseudo-Philo was printed in Heidelberg in 1599.[157] The texts are followed by the *Censura* of Gaspar Barreiros, giving the reader the choice of accepting the authors as authentic or spurious and, accordingly, Annius of Viterbo as a scholar, a forgerer or a fool.

4 Conclusion

This is merely an introduction to some editions of the *Antiquities*, their reforging, their contingencies, their meaning and their readers. All of the above-mentioned volumes still need further study and must be widely compared with other European editions and their manuscript reception. The reforgeries elaborated by editors and typographers during the sixteenth century played an active and vital role in the acceptance, survival and defense of Annius' *Antiquities*. In fact, French typographers and booksellers repurposed

154 Ibidem, 805–812.

155 Ibidem, 812.

156 An emendation that will be transmitted even to Lachmann, Fumagalli, "Un falso tardo-quattrocentesco" 354.

157 Parente, "Il 'Liber antiquitatum biblicarum'" 172; Lehr, *Was nach den Sintflut* 367.

Annius' material for their own commercial or ideological reasons, often working closely together with religious authorities and university professors.

As Stephens has pointed out, 'the collection was constantly involved in the ongoing imperial rivalry between France and Spain [...] Seething political rivalries thus made the *Antiquities* immensely popular with propagandists and their printers'.[158] This is especially true for the first Parisian reforgeries, such as the ones edited by Geoffroy Tory and by Josse Badius. If the early Parisian editions show an indirect patronage of the French court, it is harder to demonstrate how the Lyonnaise editions from the middle of the sixteenth century were involved in active political propaganda. However, it is interesting to remark that the *Antiquities* could still have had a political role even after the end of the Italian Wars. As the Gilles and Godefroy reforgeries reveal, reediting and republishing Annius' material may still have had a Catholic or reformed ideological value during the French Wars of Religion, despite being criticised by a large majority of European scholars.

Moreover, Annian reforgeries display the multiple possible uses of the *Antiquities* during the Renaissance. If, in the early sixteenth century, the *Antiquities* were a fundamental source for theological studies and historiographical works concerning sacred and human history, from Johann Sichard to Denis Godefroy, they increasingly became a methodological and instrumental source for ancient history and thus ancient constitutions and state organisations. This gives rise to some unsettling considerations insofar as these texts were not simple antiquarian curiosities, but they were actively used to conceive and teach history of law and political history in order to construct political projects. This tendency appears clearly when one looks at the editions that have been considered here, and the suspicion becomes even stronger when confronted with the various handwritten marginalia left by Renaissance readers. That means that during the second half of the sixteenth century they were still not only an object of nationalistic propaganda, but also a valid reference for many. Considering the extensiveness of Annius' French editions, it should come as no surprise that Jean Bodin, for example, took his interest in the Sanhedrin from Annius' authors and commentaries.[159]

The performance of Annius' *Antiquities* through their editorial reforgeries illustrates well that one of the key factors for the longevity of this literary forgery was its early separation from its real author and the successive *Eigenleben* of the pseudo-ancient authorities. In the long run, this was possible only thanks to editorial reception and manipulation. Each successive edition separated

158 Stephens, "Discovering the Past" 81.

159 Grafton, "Annius of Viterbo as a Student of the Jews" 169.

Annius and his creation further. For every erudite wanting to debunk the fraud, it would have first of all been necessary to bind together once again the first editor and forger with his forgeries. Despite the enormous bibliography dedicated to Annius' *Antiquities*, the 'ingrata materia' of their reception, as Parente defined it, still needs to be studied in depth. Especially when considering that every single Annian source and commentary may have taken its own path in the hands of its readers, editors and printers.

Bibliography

Abélard J., *Les Illustrations de Gaule et singularités de Troye de Jean Lemaire de Belges: Études des éditions, genèse de l'oeuvre* (Geneva: 1976).

Annius of Viterbo, *De Futuris Christianorum triumphis in Saracenos* (Paris, Etienne Jehannot: 1495).

Annius of Viterbo, *Commentaria fratris Ioannis Annii Viterbensis ordinis predicatorum Theologiae professoris super opera diversorum auctorum de Antiquitatibus loquentium* (Rome, Eucharius Silber: 1498).

Annius of Viterbo, *Antiquitatum Variarium Volumina XVII* (Paris, Josse Badius – Jean Petit: 1512).

Annius of Viterbo, *Antiquitatum Variarium Volumina XVII* (Paris, Josse Badius – Jean Petit: 1515).

Annius of Viterbo, *Antiquitatum Variarum autores* (Lyon, Sebastian Gryphius: 1552).

Antoninus Pius, *Itinerarium Provinciarium Antonini* (Paris, Henri I Estienne: 1512).

Asher R.E., *National Myths in Renaissance France: Francus, Samothes and the Druids* (Edinburgh: 1993).

Auctores Vetustissimi Nuper in lucem editi (Venice, Bernardino de Vitali: 1498).

Baffioni G., "Notarella Anniana", *Studi Urbinati* 1 (1978) 61–74.

Baffioni G. – Mattiangeli P., *Annio da Viterbo: Documenti e ricerche* (Rome: 1981).

Bauer S., *The Invention of Papal History: Onofrio Panvino between Renaissance and Catholic Reform* (Oxford: 2020).

Berosi sacerdotis chaldaici, antiquitatum libri quinque (Antwerp, Johannes Steels: 1545).

Berosus babillonicus de antiquitatibus Seu defloratio berosi Caldaica Cum figuris et ipsius eleganti vita Libris Geneseos perutilis (Paris, Jean de Gourmont: 1509).

Berosus babilonicus. De his quae praecesserunt inundationem terrarum (Paris, Marnef: 1510).

Bèze Théodore de, *Gruendlicher gegenbericht auff die zu Tuebingen außgangene schrifften des Muempelgartischen gespraechs halben welches im 1586* (Basel, Konrad Waldkirch: 1588).

Bibliothecae historicae libri XVII (Lyon, Sebastian Gryphius: 1552).
Biondi A., "Annio da Viterbo e un aspetto dell'orientalismo di Guillaume Postel", in Donattini M. (ed.), *Umanisti, eretici, streghe: Saggi di storia moderna* (Modena: 2008) 217–235.
Bodin J., *Methodus ad facilem historiarum cognitionem*, ed. S. Miglietti (Pisa: 2013).
Caii Valerii Catullii, Albii Tibullii, Sexti Aurelii Propertii opera omnia qui extant (Paris, Marc Orry: 1604).
Caii Valerii Catullii, Albii Tibullii, Sexti Aurelii Propertii opera omnia qui extant (Paris, Claude Morel: 1604).
Callard C. – Crouzet-Pavane É. – Tallon A. (eds.), *La politique de l'histoire en Italie* (Paris: 2014).
Chartier R., *The Author's Hand and the Printer's Mind: Transformations of the Written Word in Early Modern Europe* (Cambridge: 2014).
Clark F., *The First Pagan Historian: The Fortunes of a Fraud from Antiquity to the Enlightenment* (Oxford: 2020).
Collins A., "Renaissance Epigraphy and its Legitimizing Potential: Annius of Viterbo, Etruscan Inscriptions and the Origins of Civilization", in Cooley A. (ed.) *The Afterlife of Inscriptions*: *Bulletin of the Institute of Classical Studies. Supplement* 75 (2000) 57–76.
Crahay R., "Réflexions sur le faux historique: le cas d'Annius de Viterbe", *Bulletin de la Classe des lettres et des sciences morales et politiques* 69 (1983) 241–267.
Crinitus Petrus, *De honesta disciplina libri XXV; de poetis Latinis liber V; et poematum liber II; cum indicibus* (Paris, Josse Badius – Jean Petit: 1508).
De bello Troiano historia: Declamationes tres fere argumenti (Lyon, Sebastian Gryphius: 1552).
De magistratibus sacerdotiisque Romanorum libellus (Lyon, Thibaud Payen: 1551).
De situ et memorabilibus orbis capitula pomponii melae de situ orbis libri tres (Basel, Robert Winter: 1536).
De urbis Romae regionibus et locis libellus (Basel, Thomas I Platter: 1538).
Dubois C.G., *Celtes et Gaulois aux XVI*ᵉ *siècle: Le développement littéraire d'un mythe nationaliste* (Paris: 1972).
Farenga P., "Le edizioni di Eucario Silber", in Chiabò M. – Maddalo S. – Miglio M. – Oliva A.M., *Roma di fronte all'Europa al tempo di Alessandro VI* (Rome: 2001).
Febvre L. – Martin H.J., *L'apparition du livre* (Paris: 1958).
Ferno M. – Campano G., *Opera Omnia* (Rome, Eucharius Silber: 1495).
Ferrary Louis J., *Onofrio Panvino et les antiquités romaines* (Rome: 1996).
Ferraù G., "Riflessioni teoriche e prassi storiografica in Annio da Viterbo", in Canfora D. – Chiabò M. – de Nichilo M. (eds.), *Principato ecclesiastico e riuso dei classici: Gli umanisti e Alessandro VI* (Bari-Monte Sant'Angelo: 2002) 151–193.

Ferraù G., "Nota sulla 'filologia' di Annio da Viterbo", in De Nichilo M. – Distaso G. – Iurilli A. (eds.), *Confini dell'umanesimo letterario: Studi in onore di Francesco Tateo* 2 (Rome: 2003) 631–647.

Flavii Iosephii hebraei antiquitatum iudaicarum libri XX (Cologne, Eucharius Cervicornus: 1534).

Flavii Iosephii hebraei, historiographi clarissimus, opera (Cologne, Eucharius Cervicornus: 1524).

Fragmenta Vetustissimorum Autorum (Basel, Johannes Bebel: 1530).

Fubini R., *Storiografia dell'Umanesimo in Italia: Da Leonardo Bruni ad Annio da Viterbo* (Rome: 2003).

Fumagalli E., "Un falso tardoquattrocentesco: lo pseudo-Catone di Annio da Viterbo", in Avesani E. – Ferrari M. – Foffano T. – Frasso G., Sottili A. (eds.), *Vestigia: Studi in onore di Giuseppe Billanovich* (Rome: 1984) 337–363.

Gabriel A., *The Library of Jean Grolier: A Preliminary Catalogue* (New York: 1971).

Godefroy Denis, *Antiquae Historiae ex XXVII authoribus contextae Libri VI* (Basel, Konrad Waldkirch: 1590).

Godefroy Denis, *Antiquae Historiae ex XXVII authoribus contextae Libri VI* (Lyon, s.n.: 1591).

Godefroy Denis, *Antiquae Historiae ex XXVII authoribus contextae Libri VI* (Strasbourg, Lazarus Zetzner: 1604).

Godefroy Denis, *Historiae Antiquae pars altera* (Basel, Konrad Waldkirch: 1590).

Godefroy Denis, *Historiae Antiquae pars altera* (Lyon, s.n.: 1590).

Godefroy-Ménilglaise D.C., *Les savants Godefroy* (Paris: 1873).

Goez W., "Die Anfange der historischen Methoden-Reflexion in der italienischen Renaissance und ihre Aufnahme in der Geschichtsschreibung des deutschen Humanismus," *Archiv fur Kulturgeschichte* 56 (1974) 25–48.

Goez W., "Die Anfänge der historischen Methoden-Reflexion im italienischen Humanismus", in Heinen H. (ed.), *Geschichte in der Gegenwart: Festschrift fuer Kurt Kluxen* (Paderborn: 1972) 3–21.

Grafton A., *Forgers and Critics: Creativity and Duplicity in Western Scholarship* (Princeton: 1990).

Grafton A., *Joseph Scaliger: I: Textual Criticism and Exegesis* (Oxford: 1983).

Grafton A., "Traditions of Invention and Inventions of Traditions in Renaissance Europe: The strange case of Annius of Viterbo", in Blair A. – Grafton A. (eds.) *The Transmission of Culture in Early Modern Europe* (Pennsylvania University Press: 1990).

Grafton A., *Joseph Scaliger: II: Historical Chronology* (Oxford: 1993).

Grafton A., *What was History? The Art of History in Early Modern Europe* (Cambridge: 2007).

Guenée B., *Histoire et culture dans l'occident medieval* (Paris: 1980).
Havens E. (ed.), *Fakes, Lies, and Forgeries: Rare Books and Manuscripts from the Arthur and Janet Freeman Bibliotheca Fictiva Collection* (Baltimore: 2014).
Historiae Romanae autores varii (Paris, Sebastian Gryphius: 1552).
Huppert G., *The Idea of Perfect History: Historical Erudition and Historical Philosophy in Renaissance France* (Urbana: 1970).
Jacks P., *The Antiquarian and the Myth of Antiquity: The Origins of Rome in Renaissance Thought* (Cambridge: 1993).
Jimenes R. (ed.), *Geoffroy Tory de Bourges: Humanisme et arts du livre à la Renaissance* (Bourges: 2019).
Jung M.R., *Hercule dans la literature française du XVIe siècle* (Geneva: 1966).
Kisch G., *Johannes Sichardus als Basler Rechtshistoriker* (Basel: 1952).
Lehr T., *Was nach den Sintflut wirklich geschah: Die Antiquitates des Annius von Viterbo und ihre Rezeption in Deutschland im 16. Jahrhundert* (Lausanne: 2012).
Ligota C.R., "Annius of Viterbo and Historical Method", *Journal of the Warburg and Courtauld Institutes*, 50 (1987) 44–56.
Marcocci G., "Contro i falsari: Gaspar Barreiros Censore di Annio da Viterbo", *Rinascimento* 50 (2010) 343–359.
Martin H.J. – Chartier R., (eds.), *Histoire de l'édition française: Tome 1. Le Livre conquérant, du Moyen Âge au milieu du XVIIe siècle* (Paris: 1989).
Merula Gaudenzio, *De Gallorum Cisalpinorum antiquitate ac origine* (Lyon, Sebastian Gryphe: 1538).
Momigliano A., "Some Observations on the 'Origo gentis romanae'", *Journal of Roman Studies* 48:1–2 (1958) 56–73.
Mornay Philippe de, *Bestendiger bericht von der Kirchen darinn die hauptstueck darueber man heuttigs tags streittig erleuttert werden* (Basel, Konrad Waldkirch: 1589).
Moulin Charles du, *Traicté de l'origine, progres et excellence du royaume* (Paris, Nicolas Edoard: 1561).
Mouren R. (ed.), *Quid novi? Sébastien Gryphe à l'occasion du 450e anniversaire de sa mort, Actes du colloque 23 au 25 novembre 2006* (Lyon: 2008).
O'Connell S.D., "Fashioning Noah: How a Forger Turned an Etruscan God into a Biblical Figure", in Stephens W. – Havens E.A. (eds.), *Literary Forgery in Early Modern Europe 1450–1800* (Baltimore: 2018) 135–146.
Olivé M.M., "El prefacio de las *Antiquitates* de Juan Annio de Viterbo: opotunidad e intencion politica", in J.M. Maestre (ed.), *Humanismo y Pervivencia del Mundo Clásico. V. Homenaje al profesor Juan Gil* (Madrid: 2015).
Origo gentis Romanae et de aquaeductibus urbis Romae libri duo (Paris, Gilles Gilles – Nicolas II Gilles: 1588).
Panvino Onofrio, *Civitas Romana* (Paris, Gilles Gilles – Nicolas II Gilles: 1588).

Panvino Onofrio, *Imperium Romanum* (Paris, Gilles Gilles – Nicolas II Gilles: 1588).

Panvino Onofrio, *Reipublicae Romanae commentariorum libri tres recogniti* (Paris, Gilles Gilles – Nicolas II Gilles: 1588).

Parente F., "Il 'Liber Antiquitatum Biblicarum' e I falsi di Annio da Viterbo", in *Paideia Cristiana: Studi in onore di Mario Naldini* (Rome: 1994) 153–172.

Pinzi C., "Carlo VIII a Viterbo", *Bollettino Storico Archeologico Viterbese* (Viterbo: 1908) 25–39.

Pocock J.G.A., *The Ancient Constitution and the Feudal Law: A Study of English Historical Thought in the Seventeenth Century* (Cambridge: 2009).

Polyhistor (Lyon, Sebastian Gryphius: 1538).

Prosperi V., "Veri falsi antichi moderni: le antiquitates di Annio da Viterbo e le Cronache troiane di Ditti Cretese e Darete Frigio", in Martínez J. – Velázquez I., (eds.), *De Falsa et Vera Historia Estudios sobre pseudoepígrafos y falsificaciones textuales antiguas – Studies on Pseudepigrapha and Ancient Text Forgeries* (Madrid: 2017).

Quétif Jacques – Échard Jacques, *Scriptores Ordinis Prædicatorum recensiti* [...] *tomus secundus* (Paris, J.B. Christophe Ballard – Nicoles Simart: 1721).

Renouard P., *Répertoire des imprimeurs parisiens: Libraires, fondeurs de caractères et correcteurs d'imprimerie depuis l'introduction de l'Imprimerie à Paris (1470) jusqu'à la fin deu XVIe siècle* (Paris: 1965).

Renouard P., *Bibliographie des impressions et des œuvres Josse Badius Ascensius, imprimeur et humaniste, 1462–1535* (Paris: 1908).

Rothstein M., "The Reception of Annius of Viterbo's Forgeries: The Antiquities in Renaissance France", *Renaissance Quarterly* 71:2 (2018).

Schiano C., *Il secolo della Sibilla: Momenti della tradizione cinquecentesca degli "Oracoli Sibillini"* (Bari: 2005).

Schnapp J.E., *Prophetie de fin du monde et peur des Turcs: Othoman, Antichrist, Apocalypse* (Paris: 2017).

Schoysman A., "Jean Lemaire de Belges et Josse Badius", *Le Moyen Age* CXII, 3 (2006) 575–584.

Sexti Iulii Frontini De Coloniis (Paris, Gilles Gilles – Nicolas II Gilles: 1588).

Silvio Piccolomini Enea (Pius II), *Cosmographia in Asiae et Europae eleganti descriptione* (Paris, Henri I Estienne: 1509).

Stenhouse W., "Reading Inscriptions and Writing Ancient History: Historical Scholarship in the Late Renaissance", *Bulletin of the Institute of Classical Studies. Supplement* 86 (2005).

Stephens W., "When Pope Noah Ruled the Etruscans: Annius of Viterbo and His Forged *Antiquities*", *Italian Issue Supplement: Studia Humanitatis: Essays in Honor of Salvatore Camporeale* 119:1 (2004) 201–223.

Stephens W., "Complex Pseudonymity: Annius of Viterbo's Multiple Persona Disorder", *MLN* 126 (2011) 689–708.

Stephens W. – Havens E.A. (eds.), *Literary Forgery in Early Modern Europe 1450–1800* (Baltimore: 2018).

Stephens W.E., *Berosus Chaldaeus: Counterfeit and Fictive Editors of the Early Sixteenth Century*, (Ph.D. dissertation, Cornell University: 1979).

Stephens W., *Giants in those Days: Folklore, Ancient History and Nationalism* (Lincoln NE – London: 1989).

Tigerstedt E.N., "Ioannes Annius and *Graecia mendax*", in Henderson C. (ed.), *Classical, Medieval and Renaissance Studies in Honor of Berthold Louis Ullman*, 2 vols. (Rome: 1964) 2:293–310.

Topographia antiquae Romae (Lyon, Sebastian Gryphius: 1534).

Tory Geoffroy, *Champfleury* (Paris, Geoffroy Tory – Gilles Gourmont: 1529).

Vasoli C., *I miti e gli astri* (Naples: 1977).

Vervliet H.D., *Post-Incunabula en Hun Uitgevers in de Lage Landen/Post-Incunabula and Their Publishers in the Low Countries* (New York: 1978).

Weiss R., "Traccia per una biografia di Annio da Viterbo", *Italia medioevale e umanistica* 5 (1962) 425–441.

Weiss R., "An Unknown Epigraphic Tract by Annius of Viterbo", in Brand C. – Foster K. – Limentani U. (eds.), *Italian Studies Presented to E. R. Vincent* (Cambridge: 1962) 101–120.

White P., *Jodocus Badius Ascensius. Commentary, Commerce and Print in the Renaissance* (Oxford: 2013).

Xenophontis opera in hoc volumine impressa (Milan? Venice?, Alessandro Minuziano? Guillaume Le Signerre? Bernardino de Vitali?: 1501–1502).

CHAPTER 5

Prenatal Prophecies and Linguistic Ciphers: A Russian Political Forgery Devoted to the Autocratic Evil of Ivan the Terrible

Brian J. Boeck

1 Introducing the Text

A strange, poorly studied early modern Russian text initiated a dissident literary discourse about tsar Ivan IV (aka Ivan the Terrible) and has indirectly shaped even modern historical representations of his reign. Although its testimony about early sixteenth-century events has been rejected by generations of scholars, this text provided the first unofficial Russian narrative about the violence and destruction that unfolded between *c.* 1565–1572. The text is not quite what it seems or what it purports to be. Even its name is deceptive. It is known to scholars by the title provided in some copies as the 'Extract about the Second Marriage of Vasilii III' (*Vypis' o vtorom Brake Vasiliia III*). I argue in this article that it most certainly was not written during the reign of Ivan's father, Vasilii III who reigned from 1505 to 1533. The *Vypis'* is actually a forgery that was created in the late 1580s or early 1590s. It was written by someone who was involved in Russian relations with Orthodox institutions under Ottoman rule and who was concerned about the fate of the ruling dynasty, which faced a crisis due to the fact that for the second time in recent memory a royal marriage did not result in a birth of an heir.

In manuscripts the text is entitled: Выпись из святогорьские грамоты что прислана к великому князю Василию Ивановичю о сочтении втораго брака и о разлучении перваго брака чадородиа ради. Творение Паисено, старца Серапонского [variant Ферапонтова] монастыря. This translates as 'Extract from the letter which was sent to the Grand Prince Vasilii Ivanovich about the contraction of a second marriage and the dissolution of a first marriage for the sake of child-bearing. The creation of Paisii, elder of the Serapon/Ferapontov monastery.' The text, henceforth the *Vypis'*, is extant in around twenty copies, most of which date to no earlier than the mid-seventeenth century, and which survive in miscellanies with varied contents. The earliest

 | DOI:10.1163/9789004106901_006

extant copy may date to the first or second decade of the seventeenth century.[1] The reference in the 'title' to the Athonite monk Paisii is an anachronism, since he was dead by the time of the events described in the text.

Before proceeding further, let us briefly characterise the text. Blending fact and fiction the text blames Ivan's evil tendencies on his father's violation of multiple interdictions against a divorce and second marriage by various international Orthodox learned and holy men. It invokes Muscovite imperial aspirations and dynastic mythologizing only to juxtapose them with a dire and dramatic, after-the-fact, 'prophecy' warning that the heir born of Vasilii's second marriage would visit destruction upon the Russian realm. One of its peculiar, distinguishing features is the inclusion of a number of odd sounding, non-Russian words, which have previously been considered meaningless. As I argue below they can be decoded and are very important for understanding and unraveling the forger's intentions. These were linguistic cyphers which were meant to lend authority to the literary forgery by the power of foreign knowledge and evocation of distant lands. These peculiar words serve as the forger's signature; they help to reveal the intellectual and cultural world of the text's creator and illuminate the context of the forgery's creation. Thus they emerge as an intellectual key for unlocking the mystery of this text.

Although the *Vypis'* is devoted to a series of Orthodox discussions that supposedly surrounded the divorce of tsar Vasilii III in 1525, none of these discussions can be confirmed by other sources.[2] The text cannot date to 1525, the year of Vasilii's divorce, because it contains a clear and compelling anachronism. It states unequivocally, but falsely, that Maxim the Greek (a monk and intellectual from Mt. Athos who came to Russia) was exiled to Tver', but in 1525 he was in fact sent for incarceration to the Iosifov monastery where he remained until he was summoned for a second trial in 1531. He was only sent to Tver' after a second trial. Thus the tract must date to after 1531, i.e. long after the issue of the second marriage was settled and after Ivan IV was born in August 1530. This is only the first example of the chronological slight of hand perpetrated by the author of *Vypis'*.

The *Vypis'* is a rhetorically complicated forgery that presents a rather simple narrative. Dramatic tension in the tract revolves around Grand Prince Vasilii's desire to divorce his barren first wife Solomonia in order to continue his dynastic line. When he announces his intention [*mysl'*] he faces an interdiction from

1 It is important to note that watermarks would exclude a sixteenth-century provenance. Zimin A.A., "Vypis' o vtorom brake Vasiliia III", *TODRL* 30 (1976) 135.

2 On the circumstances surrounding the marriage of Vasilii, see Nikitin A.L., *Osnovaniia russkoi istorii: mifologemy i fakty* (Moscow: 2001) 586–628.

Vassian Patrikeev a prominent courtier, who reminds him of New Testament and canonical pronouncements against divorce and invokes the possibility of divine retribution. Due to the bad council of a major villain (Metropolitan Daniil of Moscow) and a minor villain (a monk named Vassian Toporkov) this interdiction was ignored. Angered by opposition to his desire for a divorce, Vasilii orders his good advisor Patrikeev to be imprisoned along with Maxim the Greek and Maxim's associates. This unjust princely action is followed by a second interdiction from all four Orthodox patriarchs. One of them, Mark of Jerusalem, sternly prophesies that violation of the interdiction will not only result in the birth of an heir, but would also bring about divine retribution in the form of destruction of the realm. The narrative then shifts to discussions held at Mt. Athos (a very important Orthodox monastic center in Greece) about the tsar's predicament. Whether by design or by defect, the narrative abruptly ends, presenting a cliff hanger. Although the narrative lacks final resolution regarding the royal divorce, anyone familiar with the events of the reign of Ivan IV could conclude that the prophecy had indeed been fulfilled.

2 Historiography

The text has baffled scholars, who have alternated between ignoring it and grappling with its peculiarities. Although the tract has been discussed by scholars since the eighteenth century, there is no consensus about either its date or literary function. In the notes to his famous history published in 1817 Nikolai Karamzin provided a highly selective paraphrase of the *Vypis'* calling the text 'curious, but hardly reliable'. He also noted that it contained 'many strange expressions and made up words, which have never existed in our language'.[3] He mentioned it briefly a second time in connection to the trial of Maxim the Greek.[4]

For the next century it was only discussed in passing in larger studies devoted to Russian church history. In 1870 father Makarii proposed in passing that it was written 'during the reign of tsar Ivan the Terrible or even after his death'.[5] In 1900 it was briefly discussed again in E.E. Golubinskii's multi-volume history of the Russian church.[6] He suggested without extensive elaboration that

3 Karamzin N.M., *Istoriia gosudarstva Rossiiskogo*, vol. 7 (St. Petersburg: 1817) notes 277, 29–98.
4 Ibidem, note 343, 316.
5 Makarii, *Istoriia russkoi tserkvi*, vol. 6 (St. Petersburg: 1870) 173.
6 Golubinskii E.E., *Istoriia russkoi tserkvi*, vol. 2, pt. 1 (Moscow: 1900) 732–733.

it contained 'much that was undoubtedly false or awkwardly legendary' and proposed that it was written in the second half of the reign of Ivan IV.

The first study specifically dedicated to the text appeared only in the Soviet period. In a brief article published in 1928 Mikhail Tikhomirov called it one of 'the most curious monuments of the sixteenth century'.[7] He drew attention to the corrupt variant readings for a monastery named in the text's title and connected it to the monastic milieu on Mt. Athos. He determined that a number of names of the Metropolitan's associates and clerks appear to be authentic. He proposed that it dates to 1545–1547 and was written from memory by someone who had knowledge of the events surrounding the divorce of Vasilii. In a subsequent article, he confirmed the accuracy of its depiction of Vasilii III as a financial patron of not only Mt. Athos, but other Orthodox territories.

The most extensive study of the tract to date appeared in 1967. Sigurd Shmidt devoted a thirteen page article to interpreting the prophecy of Patriarch Mark and connecting it to specific events that occurred during Ivan's minority between the years 1530 and 1547.[8] He decoded references to heads being cut off and impalement as references to actual executions that took place in 1546–1547.[9] He proposed that some of the punishments in the prophecy were used against the arsonists who were blamed for the great fire in Moscow of 1547.[10] He concluded that the section of the tract containing the prophecy of patriarch Mark was written in spring or fall of 1547, relying on his inference about the fire for the date of the earliest date of composition.[11]

Shmidt's consideration of the text provided a mix of important insights and unsupported assertions. He succeeded in proving that the dramatic events of 1547 provide a compelling *terminus post quem* for the tract, but he did not pursue lines of inquiry that could link the prophecy to violent events of the *oprichnina*. His assertion that the first part of the tract was a pamphlet directed against the Glinskii family was not supported by extensive argumentation or mobilization of evidence. He also proposed that diplomatic sources could have been used to compile the tract without citing any specific texts.

In 1973 A.A. Zimin, one of the most prominent historians of early modern Russia, proposed that the tract could date to the late sixteenth or even early

7 Tikhomirov M.N., "K voprosu o Vypisi o vtorom brake tsaria Vasiliia III", in *Sbornik statei v chest' akad. A.I. Sobolevskogo* (Moscow: 1928) 91–98.

8 Shmidt S.O., "O vremeni sostavleniia "Vypisi" o vtorom brake Vasiliia III", in *Novoe o proshlom nashei strany: pamiati akademika M.N. Tikhomirova* (Moscow: 1967) 110–122.

9 Ibidem, 117.

10 Ibidem, 117, 119.

11 Ibidem, 119.

seventeenth century.[12] He disputed Shmidt's mid-sixteenth century date, arguing that the two-decade-old memories of Vasilii's reign were recent enough that the dates of key events would not have been confused. He drew attention to another anachronism, an important diplomatic event: the embassy of Ivan Andreevich Kolychev to Crimea departed before the issue of the second marriage arose.[13] On the basis of its interest in *oprichnina* (i.e. violence direct at parts of the tsar's realm) and prophecies he associated the text with other literary mystifications and works with an element of prediction or prophecy. These texts date to the late sixteenth and early seventeenth centuries. No extensive argumentation was provided to support this proposal either.

In a brief article published in 1998 Iankel' Solodkin proposed that the *Vypis'* was known or created in the western borderlands of the Muscovite state, in the city of Pskov in the late sixteenth century.[14] He pointed to a number of phrases about God punishing countries for the adultery of their leaders and references to cities consumed by fires. In his view these themes clearly resonate with the contents of the *Vypis'*. He noted that a letter to a priest named Ivan from Hegumen Kornilii of the Snetogorskii monastery in Pskov, who was active between 1587 and 1598, also invokes these general themes.[15] He also noted that one of the earliest copies of the *Vypis'* comes in a miscellany that can be associated with the city of Pskov. Therefore it seems very probable that the text was already in existence and was known in Pskov some time before the year 1598, when a new hegumen assumed office.

3 International Orthodoxy: The Date and Milieu of the Tract

As I argue below, the *Vypis'* is pervaded with highly specific references to international Orthodoxy that could only have been generated by someone who had a good understanding of Orthodox institutions outside of Russia as well as the rhetoric of Russian patronage of them. The pattern of references makes it probable that the author was connected in some way to the diplomatic chancery [*posol'skii prikaz*]. It seems highly probable that the author was either a clerk or one of the ecclesiastic or court officials who accompanied eastern Orthodox

12 Zimin A.A., "O metodike izucheniia povestvovatel'nykh istochnikov XVI v.", in *Istochnikovedenie otechestvennoi istorii* 1 (Moscow: 1973) 187–211.

13 Ibidem, 197.

14 Solodkin Ia.G., "K datirovke 'vypisi' o vtorom brake Vasiliia III" http://www.philosophy.nsc.ru/journals/humscience/2_98/11-SOLOD.HTM.

15 Serebrianskii N., *Ocherki po istorii monastyrskoi zhizni v Pskovskoi zemle* (Moscow: 1908) 491, 493, 529.

hierarchs on their journeys through Russia when they came to request alms from their Muscovite benefactors.

The author of the Tract displays a working understanding of the important financial support that the tsars provided to the Orthodox east. He possesses an accurate sense of the geography and recipients of tsarist financial support in the late sixteenth century.[16] He understands that Russian diplomats sometimes characterised this support as charity (*milostyni*) while at other times they presented it as bounty or reward for services or travel (*zhalovanie*).[17] He knows that Orthodox monks living under Ottoman rule were required to pay both ordinary (*dani*) and extraordinary (*okup*) levies to the Ottoman Sultan.[18] Even more crucial is the fact that the author knows the names and accurate genealogical relationships of three Ottoman sultans (Suleiman, Selim and Bayezid).[19] Needless to say the number of individuals in Russia with such knowledge was highly limited.

The author of the *Vypis'* also displays a keen understanding of the diplomatic rhetoric deployed in correspondence between Moscow and Orthodox eastern Christian lands. He is aware that Orthodox supplicants often emphasise the tsar's piety, insist that his power was inherited from his pious ancestors, and represent themselves to the tsar as his intercessors in prayer to God [*bogomoltsy*]. He is cognizant of the fact that recipients of Russian bounty often highlighted how the mercies that the tsar extended to monks in this world will be returned to him in the heavenly tsardom. He is informed that the patriarch of Constantinople should be officially addressed as the patriarch of new Rome. He knows that title 'despot' was formerly used to designate the rulers of Serbia. He knows that the Panteleimon monastery on Mt. Athos was founded and patronised by Russian tsars. He deploys particular phrasing about the Trinity which was occasionally used in letters to and from Orthodox institutions. Such examples indicate extensive knowledge, familiarity with diplomacy, and awareness of distant cultural relations, which take us into the realm of chancellery practice. More importantly, all of them can be found in

16 *Vypis'* 140.

17 Ibidem, 140, 145, 146. Both terms are interspersed throughout diplomatic record books. For publication of those books see footnote 25 below.

18 For more on payments to the Ottomans, see Papademetriou T., *Render unto the Sultan: Power, Authority, and the Greek Orthodox Church in the Early Ottoman Centuries* (Oxford: 2015) and Zachariadou E.A., *Deka Tourkika engrapha gia ten Megale Ekklesia: 1483–1567* (Athens: 1996).

19 *Vypis'* 147. The names of sultans appears to correlate with documents preserved in monastic archives on Mt. Athos. See Salakides G., *Sultansurkunden des Athos-Klosters Vatopedi aus der Zeit Bayezid II und Selim I* (Thessaloniki: 1995).

a section of a diplomatic record book for 1588–1594. I therefore posit that the author was connected with the field of Muscovite ecclesiastical diplomacy.

This hypothesis also makes it possible to propose a solution to one of the text's most enduring mysteries and linguistic cyphers – the curious case of the otherwise unknown and unaccounted for group of peoples, the Habiashis, Aruns, and Teflizes, who are described as threatening Mt. Athos in the last section of the text. In that section one monk confides to another:

> If not for the assistance that the Great Sovereign has provided us, his intercessors in prayers to God, grand prince Vasilii Ivanovich of all Russia, and necessities provided owing to his piety, and if not for his great sovereign reward to us to all holy monasteries [obiteli], on the Holy Mountain there would be in the monasteries very few monks. For due to the violence of the Muslim faith they would all be driven away by the Khabiashis [хабяшев/хабяжев] and Aruns [ароунов/ароутнов] and Teflizes [тефлизов] by the order of Suleiman Sultan, Selim Sultan's son, and Bayazit's grandson from their holy monasteries ...[20]

On one level the strange names in this passage function as markers of a foreign and exotic Orthodox world that was alien to most Russians. On another level they provide us with important clues about its creator, taking on the role of forensic evidence akin to intellectual fingerprints.

The three unusual names are more than just a meaningless mish-mash. They deploy terms related to peoples from different parts of the Ottoman Empire that could have been invented only by someone with substantive diplomatic knowledge. 'Habiashis' derives from the Ottoman word for Amharic populations, the Ethiopians, across the Red Sea whom the Ottomans were beginning to encounter after their conquest of Egypt and Hijaz after 1517. 'Habesha' is an Ottoman that comes from Arabic al-Habasha. The Aruns at first glance looks like a corrupted form of 'Arnut', the Ottoman term for Albanians. We will return to the etymology of this term and whether, in fact, it refers to Albanians shortly. The Teflizes appear to be referring to 'Teflisi', a Persian term for inhabitants of the city of Tblisi in modern Georgia. The mélange of exotic names provides a rather remarkable catalogue of peoples from the remote western, eastern, and southern parts of the Ottoman world. Although this decoding of the names demonstrates that the author of the text was familiar with the Ottoman world, his framing of an African, Christian population as a distinctly Muslim threat to Mt. Athos does not quite seem credible. Or does it?

20 *Vypis'* 147.

The mention of the Ethiopians in connection with Sultan Suleiman is very revealing if we contextualise it within the recent political developments in the Orthodox world, which threatened the long established status quo. This reference allows us to pinpoint a historic moment and a specific place in the Ottoman empire where Ethiopians could actually be perceived as dangerous rivals to Greek Orthodox monks. Under Ottoman Sultan Suleiman documents were issued (1534, 1547) that confirmed the right of the Ethiopian monks in Jerusalem to enter the Holy Sepulchre and to be the first to bring out the Holy fire during Easter (a great honor which was traditionally the privilege of the Greeks).[21] The very same documents make the Greek monks second, the Armenians third and the Georgians fourth in the order of precedence. According to European pilgrims, in the 1560s Greeks in Jerusalem continued to express resentment about this Ethiopian privilege.[22] At some point between 1614 and the 1640s the Ethiopians appear to have lost their privileged position.[23] If under Suleiman the Ottomans were capable of elevating the role of the Ethiopians at the Holy Sepulchre, they could at any time reassess the religious privileges of the Greeks in their empire. Therefore, the perceived threat to Mt. Athos could imminently become real. The anxiety that the Ottomans might at any moment arbitrarily expropriate and reassign key sacred sites is revealed in the hidden dialogue of the text.

It is curious that both the Ethiopians and Georgians make an appearance in the *Vypis'*. What about the Armenians? At first glance the Albanians appear to have usurped the place which by logic belongs to the Armenians if we position the names in dialogue with the power realignment introduced by the Ottomans in the Holy Sepulchre, but variant readings in the text suggest otherwise. The linguistic cypher provides a fascinating possibility. Two of the best manuscripts of the *Vypis'* transmit the reading '*ot ... aroutnov*' which literally means

---

21 Philippos A. (His Holiness, Ethiopian Archbishop), *Know Jerusalem* (Addis Ababa: 1972) 53–58.

22 Stoffregen Pedersen K., "The Qeddusan: The Ethiopian Christians in the Holy Land", in O'Mahony A. (ed.), *The Christian Heritage in the Holy Land* (London: 1995) 135. See also O'Mahony A., "Pilgrims, Politics, and Holy Places: The Ethiopian Community in Jerusalem until ca. 1650", in Levine L.I. (ed.), *Jerusalem: Its Sanctity and Centrality to Judaism, Christianity, and Islam* (New York: 1999) 476–477.

23 For 1614 see Hintlian K., "Travellers and Pilgrims in the Holy Land: The Armenian Patriarchate of Jerusalem in the 17th and 18th century [sic]", in O'Mahony A. – Gunner G. – Hintlian K. (eds.), *The Christian Heritage in the Holy Land* (London: 1995) 154, for 1640 Stoffregen Pedersen K., "The Qeddusan: The Ethiopian Christians in the Holy Land" 136–137 and Meinardus O., "The Copts in Jerusalem and the Question of the Holy Places", in O'Mahony A. – Gunner G. – Hintlian K. (eds.), *The Christian Heritage in the Holy Land* (London: 1995) 119.

'from the Aroutians'.[24] This is highly intriguing because in Armenian the word for resurrection is 'Harutyun'. This is auspiciously similar to the reading in the *Vypis'* and shares similar vowels and three consonants in the same sequence. I posit that it was known to the author on account of his extensive knowledge, but completely unintelligible to later copyists who generated corrupt versions of it. This deciphering of the term is even more intriguing when one takes into consideration that in Armenian the church of the Holy Sepulchre in Jerusalem is called 'Surp Harutyun'. So when he says 'the Aroutians' he is calling Armenian Christians 'Resurrectionists' in order to reveal his knowledge of a term derived from their own language.

Jerusalem, its Orthodox hierarchies, and Ottoman politics converge as a hot button issue not only for the author of *Vypis'* but also in Russian diplomacy. In this context it is also highly significant that the only other Russian texts that incorporate the Ottoman name for Ethiopians are diplomatic documents associated with the Holy Sepulchre in Jerusalem. In 1560 German the Patriarch of Jerusalem sent Ivan IV a letter in which he sought to leverage the sacred, symbolic and fundraising power of the Holy Sepulchre in obtaining donations from the tsar. Although the tsar had recently sent 500 rubles with his diplomatic representative, German hoped to solicit a new splendid headgear, a mitre that 'would be worn [by the Patriarch] when the holy liturgy is served, and when you are remembered for eternity, like many wear here at the Holy Sepulchre, the Ethiopians [хабезы], Armenians [армене], and others, since we are the only ones who don't have one'.[25] The patriarch was trying to leverage sanctity of Jerusalem and coerce the tsar into providing a costly gift by promising its visibility, enhanced international status of the Russian ruler, and the spiritual recompense through perpetual commemoration of the tsar in the place which was most holy to Christians. This once again draws our attention to the specific context of Jerusalem and the Holy Sepulcher and the inter-Christian competition for prestige that unfolded there.

Following the hypothesis that *Vypis'* was written by someone associated with ecclesiastical diplomacy in the late 1580s or early 1590s, it is even probable that the Patriarch's letter from 1560 would have been known then and there. In March of 1592 a letter from tsar Fedor to Sofronius the Patriarch of Jerusalem gratefully acknowledges his assistance in an unprecedented act, the creation of a Russian patriarchate. In accordance with established diplomatic practice, this occasion would have necessitated a search for a precedent in how the tsars had titled and addressed the patriarch in past correspondence. Previous

24 *Vypis'* 147.

25 Kashtanov S.M. (ed.), *Rossiia i grecheskii mir v XVI veke*, vol. 1 (Moscow: 2004) 258.

records must have also been consulted to determine what sort of diplomatic gifts would be appropriate to send to the patriarch of Jerusalem. It is no coincidence that the same general kind of gift was sent on both occasions. Listed first among gifts sent in 1592 for facilitating the creation of the patriarchate was a '*shapku sviatitel'skuiu sluzhebnuiu*', that is a mitre suitable for liturgical usage. This suggests a direct connection between past patronage and current awards.[26]

Let us sum up what we have learned from the linguistic cypher. The author of the after-the-fact prophecy about Vasilii's divorce directly linked it with Jerusalem and the person of the historical patriarch Mark of Jerusalem.

4 Making Sense of a Forged Prophecy

Now that we know that we are dealing with a forger who delighted in playing sophisticated linguistic games, we can decipher the 'many strange expressions and made up words' which have puzzled scholars since the nineteenth century as meaningful rather than meaningless.

The *Vypis'* impressively presents the antithesis of Ivan's positive, official image, during the reign of his son Fedor. In a larger study nearing completion I argue that it was still taboo to speak of Ivan's evils during the early years of Fedor's reign. The most damning words of the text are voiced by the historical patriarch Mark of Jerusalem. The author probably knew that Patriarch Mark III of Jerusalem died in 1503, two decades before the events which putatively provoked that prophecy, but he coopted the name of a venerable authority to communicate his most scathing message.

In Patriarch Mark's forged after-the-fact 'prophecy' Ivan IV is presented as a destroyer rather than a builder or conqueror. The prophecy addressed to Vasilii III reads:

> And if you thus enact that you cast away your first [wife] and for the sake of providing to yourself child-bearing, beware! Again, I say beware! Although God, the friend of humanity, will grant you child-bearing, so you will say to yourself: 'This is my heir, lord of our tsardom dominion'. But it will not be so. For adultery tsars are given offspring for the destruction of their tsardom. And you will think to yourself [this is the heir], but he will trample upon everything.
>
> The clans of Sarapadiians called Boyars, military commanders, and the tribes of Kalakovriches and all Urdiukeles [племени калаковрича и

26 Novikov Nikolai Ivanovich (ed.), *Drevniaia rossiiskaia vivliofika*, vol. 12 (Moscow, v tipografii Kompanii tipograficheskо: 1789) 387.

> всн урдюкеле], called Christians, will be oppressed in [martyrlike] passions/sufferings. But I say, he will despise all, the universal council, and take under his hand [i.e. subjugate] the Kelevdekerians [келевдекерии] and will be a robber of possessions belonging to others. The moth [*mol'*] will consume vestments [rizy], and by robbing the possessions of others he will annihilate his own. And your tsardom will become filled up with suffering and sorrow and those will be years of murders and tortures of the various Sarapadasian clans [Сарападасийских родов], and non-reprieve/lack of mercy towards Youths [variants: **and non-reprieve/ lack of mercy towards maidens**] some will be impaled and others will lose their heads [variants: **and others will be subjected to drowning in water and every kind of deadly torture**] and imprisonings without mercy and many towns will be violated by fire [variant: **and there will be great perversions and passions**].

It is important to note that the manuscript variations included in bold above are found in a group of manuscripts that in several other cases provide superior readings. If we consider these to be original, then several sharp statements about sexual depravity and violence directed against wider segments of society were edited out of the text very early in the history of its circulation in Russia. If we consider them to be additions, then they appear to enhance the text by alluding to evil actions that relate to Ivan's greatest crime, the sack of the prosperous city of Novgorod in 1570.

The 'prophecy' also contains several unusual, non-Russian words that appear to simulate an exotic language. The author partially decodes only two of these terms for his readers: 'urdiukele' as referring to Orthodox Christians and 'Sarapadasiiskii' to refer to boyars. Sigurd Shmidt proposed that the latter term relates in some way to the Biblical word 'Satrap'. The roles and responsibilities of satraps, as alluded to in chapter six of the Old Testament Book of Daniel, would appear to coincide with several offices primarily staffed by Boyars in Russia. The other terms have hitherto proven to be impervious to all efforts to decode them. Shmidt determined that they are not Greek, Albanian, Moldovan, Serbian or Turkish. My research suggests that they are not Armenian or Georgian either. I maintain, however, that they can be decoded not in reference to cognates from foreign languages but by using cultural information available in sixteenth-century Russia.

The author provides a clue by suggesting that 'Urdiukele' means Christians. Curiously the two related terms 'Kalakovriches' and 'Kelevdekerians' share the same, relatively rare for Russian k-l-k consonant sequence. Having first emphasised the suffering of all Christians, the author for some reason wanted to particularly emphasise the suffering of different kinds of followers of Christ.

He introduced some vowel variation and wove the modified word into his text in order to signify important variations on followers of the cross.

The author appears to have created an exotic term by drawing on the name of a real relic kept at the Trinity St. Sergius monastery. It is a large wooden, chancel cross that has multiple, intricate, finely executed panels carved into bone or walrus ivory. Called the 'Kilikeevskii cross' it was one of the relics which was brought to Ivan IV on the eve of his conquest of Kazan' in 1552, the first great victory which established Muscovy as empire.[27] Contemporary historians choose to interpret 'Kilikeevskii' as 'Cilician' referring to the region in Asia Minor, but the cross is clearly Russian not Byzantine or Armenian. I propose that the author used the term 'Kilikeevskii' to conjure up a 'foreign' word for a cross that simultaneously alludes to a wealthy and powerful monastery outside of Moscow. On this basis I propose that the two mysterious terms coined from this word provide opaque allusions to prominent monastic institutions and church hierarchs.

Since some of the most cryptic statements in the Tract pertain to Ivan's attacks on the church, it is likely that the subject was still considered sensitive enough that the author of the *Vypis'* preferred to encrypt his messages out of fear of persecution. The closest he comes to being specific is the line in the prophecy that Ivan will despise (or ignore) the universal church council (a rare and very important ecclesiastical event), which suggests unspecified transgressions of canon law or decisions made by the entire church hierarchy. Since Ivan's violations were plentiful, this could also be an allusion to his uncanonical fifth and sixth marriages, which came after a council granted him a special exception for his fourth marriage.[28]

The curious phrase that the 'moth will consume vestments [*rizy*]' appears spliced in between two related phrases about robbing. These phrases provide an echo of Christ's parable on stewardship in Luke 16:12, which rhetorically contrasts stewardship of the belongings of others with one's own. The insertion also appears to echo Christ's reference in Luke 12:33 to heavenly treasures which no thief can steal and no moth can destroy. Presented in connection with subjugation of Kelevdekerians, the reference which I interpret to mean church hierarchs, this could also allude to debates within the church about the appropriateness of acquisition of worldly wealth.

27 Nikolaeva T.V., *Drevnerusskaia melkaia plastika xi–xvi vekov* (Moscow: 1968) 378

28 For a definitive treatment of marriages see Martin, R.E., *A Bride for the Tsar: Bride-Shows and Marriage Politics in Early Modern Russia* (Ithaca: 2012).

A consideration of wisdom literature adds another layer of meaning to the deployment of the phrase the 'moth will consume vestments [*rizy*]'. An expression which roughly reads 'just as the moth consumes the vestment, so does sorrow consume the man' can be found in several old Russian compilations. One text in particular seems to have influenced our author. That text was the widely circulating supplication of Daniil the Prisoner, a twelfth-century, literary appeal to a ruler full of panegyric, allusions, admonitions, wise sayings, and ironic social commentary. The text contains similar phrasing: 'a moth destroys garments, and sorrow a man's mind'.[29] More importantly it insists that it is a prince's primary duty to protect his people from sorrow. In our 'prophecy' the very next sentence predicts that Ivan's realm will 'become filled up with suffering and sorrow'. Thus it becomes an inversion.

Intriguingly a variant reading in some manuscripts of Daniil the Prisoner might also provide the key for decoding the mysterious 'Sarapadasians' of our text. A rare interpolation reads: 'As a strong/hefty horse strikes at its master with its hoof, so does a rich boyar resent and wish evil to his prince'.[30] The very rare verb employed for striking is 'sarapat'. Sarapadasian clans could thus be interpreted as the proud, old boyars families who resented the rise of princely power.

The kinds of clothing being consumed by moths is also highly pertinent. By the sixteenth century the term '*rizy*' was most often used in relation to ecclesiastical vestments. An allusion to holy vestments that have lost their legitimate claimants or were unable to fulfill their intended function gains its power by drawing attention to absence. But it leaves it up to the reader to ponder the void. What exactly happened to those former wearers of those vestments? I would decode this phrase as an opaque reference to the murders of prominent church leaders such as bishops Pimen and Leonid of Novgorod and to Metropolitan Filipp of Moscow. This seemingly opaque reference to Ivan's most shocking victims confirms that the text was created before Filipp's rehabilitation under patriarch Iov in the late 1590s.[31] Prior to that point narrative caution prevailed.

The most successful forgeries are those which pass undetected because they speak to contemporary concerns. While I believe that it is possible to trace every action mentioned in the prophecy to specific events that unfolded

29 Isserlin E.M. (ed.), *Leksika i frazeologiia "Molenia" Daniila Zatochnika* (Leningrad: 1981) 176.

30 Ibidem, 110.

31 The first icon depicting Filipp dates to after 1595. See Putsko V., "Sviatitel' Filip, Mitropolit Moskovskii I vseia Rusi, v ikonopisi I litsevom shit'e xvii", *A'manakh Solovetskoe More* 6 (2007), http://www.solovki.info/?action=archive&id=383//.

between the years 1567 and 1570, I will not do so here. In a monograph in preparation I argue that another author working in the late 1590s already did this for us. He took the *Vypis'* at face value and penned a continuation-compilation which gathered evidence to demonstrate that numerous events of Ivan's reign confirmed the fulfillment of Patriarch Mark's prophecy. This unpublished text, which I call the *Tale of Persecutions* exhibits a deliberate selection bias in favor of events that resembled in essence the evil actions of Ivan and his father as they are presented in the *Vypis'*.

5 Conclusion

The central, after-the-fact, anti-divorce prophecy about Ivan IV that is embedded in the *Vypis'* adds little to our factual understanding of violence during Ivan's reign, but it tells us a great deal about the perceived limitations upon discussing it in the years immediately after Ivan's death in 1584. The author of the *Vypis'* was cautious enough to camouflage some of his most damning charges behind a group of puzzling words, foreign allusions and audacious claims by dead Orthodox authorities. Simultaneously, the author reveals that he was well informed about big-picture international Orthodox politics. Our author knew of recriminations between Ethiopians and Greek Orthodox monks that took place in Jerusalem, but nowhere else in the Orthodox world. His playful linguistic esoterica confirm his connection to the sphere of relations with the Orthodox east.

Bibliography

Golubinskii E.E., *Istoriia russkoi tserkvi*, vol. 2, pt. 1 (Moscow: 1900).

Hintlian K., "Travellers and Pilgrims in the Holy Land: The Armenian Patriarchate of Jerusalem in the 17th and 18th century [sic]", in O'Mahony A. – Gunner G. – Hintlian K. (eds.), *The Christian Heritage in the Holy Land* (London: 1995).

Isserlin E.M. (ed.), *Leksika i frazeologiia "Molenia" Daniila Zatochnika* (Leningrad: 1981).

Karamzin N.M., *Istoriia gosudarstva Rossiiskogo*, vol. 7 (St. Petersburg: 1817).

Kashtanov S.M. (ed.), *Rossiia i grecheskii mir v XVI veke*, vol. 1 (Moscow: 2004).

Levine L.I. (ed.), *Jerusalem: Its Sanctity and Centrality to Judaism, Christianity, and Islam* (New York: 1999).

Makarii, *Istoriia russkoi tserkvi*, vol. 6 (St. Petersburg: 1870).

Martin R.E., *A Bride for the Tsar: Bride-Shows and Marriage Politics in Early Modern Russia* (Ithaca: 2012).

Meinardus O., "The Copts in Jerusalem and the Question of the Holy Places", in O'Mahony A. – Gunner G. – Hintlian K. (eds.), *The Christian Heritage in the Holy Land* (London: 1995).

Nikitin A.L., *Osnovaniia russkoi istorii: mifologemy i fakty* (Moscow: 2001).

Nikolaeva T.V., *Drevnerusskuiu melkaia plastika xi–xvi vekov* (Moscow: 1968).

Novikov Nikolai Ivanovich (ed.), *Drevniaia rossiiskaia vivliofika*, vol. 12 (Moscow, v tipografii Kompanii tipograficheskо: 1789).

O'Mahony A. (ed.), *The Christian Heritage in the Holy Land* (London: 1995).

O'Mahony A., "Pilgrims, Politics, and Holy Places: The Ethiopian Community in Jerusalem until ca. 1650", in Levine L.I. (ed.), *Jerusalem: Its Sanctity and Centrality to Judaism, Christianity, and Islam* (New York: 1999).

Papademetriou T., *Render unto the Sultan: Power, Authority, and the Greek Orthodox Church in the early Ottoman Centuries* (Oxford: 2015).

Philippos A. (His Holiness, Ethiopian Archbishop), *Know Jerusalem* (Addis Ababa: 1972).

Putsko V., "Sviatitel' Filip, Mitropolit Moskovskii I vseia Rusi, v ikonopisi I litsevom shit'e xvii", *A'manakh Solovetskoe More* 6 (2007).

Salakides G., *Sultansurkunden des Athos-Klosters Vatopedi aus der Zeit Bayezid II und Selim I* (Thessaloniki: 1995).

Serebrianskii N., *Ocherki po istorii monastyrskoi zhizni v Pskovskoi zemle* (Moscow: 1908).

Shmidt S.O., "O vremeni sostavleniia "Vypisi" o vtorom brake Vasiliia III", in *Novoe o proshlom nashei strany: pamiati akademika M.N. Tikhomirova* (Moscow: 1967).

Solodkin Ia.G., "K datirovke 'vypisi' o vtorom brake Vasiliia III", http://www.philosophy.nsc.ru/journals/humscience/2_98/11-SOLOD.HTM.

Stoffregen Pedersen K., "The Qeddusan: The Ethiopian Christians in the Holy Land", in O'Mahony A. (ed.), *The Christian Heritage in the Holy Land* (London: 1995).

Tikhomirov M.N., "K voprosu o Vypisi o vtorom brake tsaria Vasiliia III", in *Sbornik statei v chest' akad. A. I. Sobolevskogo* (Moscow: 1928).

Zachariadou E.A., *Deka Tourkika engrapha gia ten Megale Ekklesia: 1483–1567* (Athens: 1996).

Zimin A.A., "O metodike izucheniia povestvovatel'nykh istochnikov XVI v.", in *Istochnikovedenie otechestvennoi istorii* 1 (Moscow: 1973).

Zimin A.A., "Vypis' o vtorom brake Vasiliia III", TODRL 30 (1976).

CHAPTER 6

Girolamo Baruffaldi as a Forger: The Case of Barbara Torelli

Camilla Russo

In the history of literary forgery in Italy, Girolamo Baruffaldi is probably one of the most representative figures. His production offers a veritable mine of case studies. He became famous for having convinced entire generations of scholars about the real existence of the *Iscrizione ferrarese*, an inscription supposedly placed on the ceiling vault above the main altar of Ferrara Cathedral, referring to the circumstances of the construction of the church. No one apart from Baruffaldi has ever seen the artefact. But the inscription was considered, until the twentieth century, to be one of the most ancient witnesses of the Italian vernacular, until it was finally recognised as a forgery by the scholar Angelo Monteverdi, who argued its implausibility with regard to language, metre and style.[1] Over the years, scholars attributed several other poetic fakes to Baruffaldi, most spread through the printed book *Rime scelte de' poeti ferraresi antichi, et moderni*, an anthology of verse by the most important poets from Ferrara published by Baruffaldi in 1713. In this chapter, I describe some characteristic aspects of Baruffaldi's *modus operandi*, by illustrating one case study still less investigated by scholars: the sonnet *Spenta è d'amor la face, il dardo è rotto*, falsely attributed to the Ferrarian noblewoman Barbara Torelli Strozzi. In the first section, I provide an overall presentation of the *Rime scelte*, particularly on why Baruffaldi decided to publish the anthology. In the second section, I describe the sonnet, pointing out the clues concerning its inauthenticity. In the third part, I introduce the supposed author, Barbara Torelli, trying to reconstruct her image among contemporaries, which played an essential role in creating the forgery. Following this I reconstruct the process of composition, considering the different versions provided by the forger, and discuss the critical debate around the text, from the eighteenth century until today. Finally, in the last section, I put forward an argument concerning the motives behind the forgery.

1 See Monteverdi A., "Lingua italiana e Iscrizione ferrarese", in Monteverdi A. (ed.), *Cento e Duecento* (Rome: 1971) 7–24; Monteverdi A., "Storia dell'Iscrizione ferrarese del 1135", in Monteverdi A. (ed.), *Cento e Duecento* (Rome: 1971) 25–95.

 | DOI:10.1163/9789004106901_007

The profile of Girolamo Baruffaldi is above all that of a scholar deeply rooted in the cultural life of his city, Ferrara, where he was born in 1675. After completing his studies in philosophy and law, he embarked on an ecclesiastical career. In 1711, however, he was forced to leave the city due to an accusation, probably unfounded, which led to his being banned from the papal states, which at that time included Ferrara, and he could only return there in 1713. In the following years, he obtained several literary awards: he was a member of the Arcadian colony of Ferrara, and in 1722 he attained a position at the city 'Studio' (the current university), holding the chair of eloquence from 1724 on. In the meantime, he was appointed archpriest in the locality of Cento, near Ferrara, and spent his last years there, passing away in 1755. Baruffaldi was a passionate bibliophile with multifaceted literary interests. This resulted in a prolific and varied production, ranging from sacred rhymes (*La via della croce*, 1723) to others of a playful and satirical character, also extending to theatre (such as the comedy *Il poeta*, of 1734) and the didactic genre, upon which he ventured with the poem *Il canapaio*, dated 1741. He was always a genuine lover of local history and literature: the first draft of the *Dissertatio de poetis ferrariensibus* (1698), later reworked in a second edition, never printed, dates back to the early years of his literary activity. This was followed by an *Istoria della città di Ferrara* (1700), the *Vite dei pittori e scultori ferraresi* (published posthumously in 1844), and, above all, the *Biblioteca degli scrittori ferraresi*, started in 1711 but never finished.[2]

The anthology of the *Rime scelte* was published in Ferrara in 1713 by the publisher Pomatelli. From the first pages onwards it exhibits a programmatic celebratory and promotional intent concerning the Ferrarian poetic tradition, evident already in the preface, entitled *Ragionamento*:

> Il fine, pertanto, che da noi s'è avuto nel tessere la raccolta presente non è stato già o di esporre il fiore delle rime ferraresi, o di solo trarre dall'oscurità certi antichi, e poco noti componimenti degni d'essere ravvivati [...]. Ma precisamente l'idea nostra sì è stata di compilare in uno tutta la serie de' Poeti volgari di questa Città, e mostrare come in Ferrara la Poesia sia nata, e quale in tutti i secoli si sia mantenuta.[3]
>
> (The aim, therefore, that we have had in weaving together the present collection has not been either to exhibit the flower of the Ferrara rhymes

2 A biography can be found in Amaturo R., *Baruffaldi, Girolamo*, in *Dizionario Biografico degli Italiani*, vol. 7 (Rome: 1970) 6–93

3 Baruffaldi Girolamo, *Ragionamento per introduzione alla presente raccolta*, in *Rime scelte de' poeti ferraresi antichi, e moderni. Aggiuntevi nel fine alcune brevi Notizie Istoriche intorno ad essi* (Ferrara, Bernardinus Pomatellus: 1713) [16].

> or to draw from the obscurity certain ancient and little-known compositions worthy of being revived [...]. But precisely, our idea was to compile in one place the whole series of vernacular poets of this city and show how Poetry was born in Ferrara and how it continued over the centuries.

The idea of a collection of Ferrara poets was based on the preliminary observation of the excellence and superiority of Ferrara in every artistic field, including and especially the poetic one: 'E ben si vede, se avvi genere alcuno di scienze, e precisamente di Poesia, che non abbia avuto il suo maggiore accrescimento in Ferrara' ('And it is clear that every kind of science, especially Poetry, has had its greatest growth in Ferrara.').[4]

In the exaltation of the city's poetic tradition, Baruffaldi assigns a prominent role to the flowering of poetry at the court of Ercole I and Ercole II d'Este. Among the Latin poets, he remembers, in particular, Tito Vespasiano Strozzi and his son Ercole; in the vernacular, Ariosto and Tasso. Finally, he arrives to the paradox of 'voler far Dante ferrarese' ('pretending to make Dante citizen of Ferrara'):[5] Baruffaldi refers to the testimony of Benvenuto da Imola, who had traced the origin of the Alighieri family to Ferrara, and that of Dante himself, who in *Paradiso* XV had made his ancestor Cacciaguida say that he had married a 'donzella ferrarese'.

From these premises, he presents the collection as a work long-awaited by local writers:

> Per tutti questi riflessi, sono parecchi anni che da i letterati ferraresi andavasi sospirando una universale raccolta delle rime di tutti i loro Poeti, così antichi, come moderni; essendo che egli è ben vero essere già de' migliori state pubblicate l'opere in separati volumi, ma non resta che degli altri ancora non fosse desiderabile vederne un saggio, tanto più che ne veggiamo taciuto il nome, e la memoria, in alcune raccolte universali, uscite anche frescamente alla luce.[6]
>
> (For all these reflections, for several years, the Ferrarian writers had been sighing for a universal collection of the rhymes of all their Poets, both ancient and modern; even if the works of the best have been published in separate volumes, it remains desirable to see a sample by the others as well, especially since we see their name and memory silenced in some universal collections, which have also recently been published.)

4 Ibidem, [7].
5 Ibidem, [6].
6 Ibidem, [12].

Already the last part of this speech, with the warning that the 'name and memory' of some of the anthologised poets had been 'silenced' in other collections printed up to that moment, could have aroused some suspicion about the authenticity of some of the texts gathered in the collection. As has been authoritatively demonstrated,[7] it contains several more or less apparent forgeries: the most sensational is perhaps that of the poet Anselmo da Ferrara, a ghost-name to which Baruffaldi gives body, but there is no lack of texts falsely attributed to real poets, especially from the early centuries, such as Gervasio Riccobaldo, Buonaccorso da Montemagno il Vecchio, Antonio Beccari, Filippo Brunelleschi, Leonello d'Este and others. Still, according to the anthologist, they derived from manuscripts conserved by him or kept in libraries that had since then become inaccessible. In any case, they were already impossible to identify by contemporary scholars. A clue pointing towards his guilt, in this sense, resonated moreover from the words with which Baruffaldi, towards the end of the *Ragionamento*, ensures us of the reliability of his sources, offering up a sort of *excusatio non petita*:

> Di quelle rime, le quali ci sono parute difficili da trovarsi, per maggiore informazion di chi legge, s'è dato conto nelle Annotazioni, indicando il luogo d'onde si sono cavate, per così levare ogni dubbio che si possano essere inventate, o involate ad altro Autore. A questo fine serve principalmente la prima Tavola posta al fine, ove si mettono sotto.[8]

> (To give the readers more information, an account has been provided in the *Annotazioni* of those poems which have resulted difficult to find. This section indicates where I took them from in order to remove any doubt that I may have invented them or stolen them from another author. It is the primary purpose of the *Table* placed at the end.)

Among the falsifications of the *Rime scelte*, there is the sonnet *Spenta è d'amor la face, il dardo è rotto*, ('The torch of Love is extinguished, his arrows are broken') which can be read on p. 55 of the collection, with the attribution to Barbara Torelli.

---

7 In addition to the essays cited, see Tissoni Benvenuti A., "Appunti sull'antologia dei poeti ferraresi di Girolamo Baruffaldi", *Giornale storico della letteratura italiana* 146 (1969) 18–48; Dionisotti C., "Appunti su antichi testi", *Italia medioevale e umanistica* 7 (1964) 77–131; Comboni A., *Un falsario al lavoro: Girolamo Baruffaldi*, in Peron G. – Andreose A. (eds.), *Contrafactum. Copia, imitazione, falso. Atti del XXXII Convegno interuniversitario, Bressanone / Brixen, 8–11 luglio 2004* (Padova: 2008) 205–213; Comboni A. – Russo C., "Per un archivio dei falsi letterari italiani. I testi dei primi secoli (secc. xii–xv)", *Filologia Italiana* 15 (2018) 27–76.

8 Baruffaldi, *Ragionamento* [21].

1 A Devoted Wife?

Barbara Torelli (or Torella, a common variant written in older documents) was born in the castle of Montechiarugolo, near Parma, but probably descended from Salinguerra III, who in 1309 held the lordship of Ferrara for a short period. She was a rather prominent figure in the Ferrarian literary society of the early sixteenth century. Friend of Isabella d'Este, and praised in the rhymes of several contemporary poets – including Ariosto himself – she became famous above all for her tormented marital story: after a turbulent marriage with the warlord Ercole Bentivoglio, she remarried, this time to the poet Ercole Strozzi, mostly known for his work in Latin and a prominent figure in the Este literary circle. But after a few months, Ercole was brutally murdered by a hitman, for reasons never fully understood, on the night between 5 and 6 June 1508. This was just thirteen days after their second, and first legitimate, child, Giulia, was born: their son Cesare was born in 1506. At dawn on 6 June 1508, the body was found near his house, with twenty-two stab wounds, his throat slashed, and his hair torn. In response to the dreadful murder, which remained unsolved, various hypotheses already flourished among contemporaries. For example, it may have been connected with the licentious conduct displayed by Strozzi, who had some success with women ('sempre a nuovi amori attendeva')[9] and who might have favored, with a passionate correspondence under a pseudonym, the affair of Lucrezia Borgia, the famous wife of Alfonso I, with Francesco Gonzaga or, according to others, with Pietro Bembo. There are those who suspected Lucrezia herself, a great friend of Strozzi's and dedicatee of many of his poems, perhaps jealous of his recent passion for Barbara, or simply anxious to keep her secret loves safe. But there were also those who pointed the finger at Duke Alfonso I, secretly in love with Barbara and eager to get rid of his uncomfortable rival.[10] However, the most accredited hypothesis has remained that of the economic motive, traced back to the legal dispute that arose between Giangaleazzo Sforza, brother-in-law of Ercole Bentivoglio, and the Strozzi, who demanded the return of the dowry from Torrelli's first marriage.[11] In any case, the murder caused a sensation among the poets of the Este circle, who dedicated numerous obituary verses to the victim. Many of them emphasise the widow's devotion to the deceased husband, so her marital fidelity, even after

9 Fòrnari Simone, *La spositione di M. Simone Fornari da Reggio sopra l'Orlando Furioso di L. Ariosto* (Florence, Lorenzo Torrentino: 1549) 691.

10 See also Giovio Paolo, *Elogia virorum literis illustrium* (Basel, Heinrich Petri: 1577) 104.

11 There is a summary of this in Catalano M., "La tragica morte di Ercole Strozzi e il sonetto di Barbara Torelli", *Archivum Romanicum* 10 (1926) 221–225.

her death, became a sort of leitmotif among contemporaries. For example, read Aldo Manuzio's epitaph:

> Sed mulierum quae est gloria et honos Barbara
> Taurclla coniux, quac picntissimo viro ct
> Una ut quiesceret ipsa, donec corporum
> Erit excitatio, sibi hoc viva posuit.[12]
>
> (However Barbara Torelli, who is the glory and honor of wives, who is the wife, the only one, of a man full of virtues, while she was still alive erected this monument, to sleep with him till the resurrection of the bodies.)

Equally representative are those of Pietro Bembo:

> Uxor honorata Manes dum conderet urna,
> Talia cum multis dicta dedit lacrymis:
> 'Non potui tecum dulcem consumere vitam:
> At iam adero amplexans te cinerem ipsa cinis'.[13]
>
> (While the wife buried the honorable ashes, she said these words, with many tears: 'I didn't consume my sweet life with you: but now I will be close to you who are ash, hugging you, being ash myself.')

It seems, moreover, that Bembo attributed to Torelli the merit of having encouraged Strozzi's growing interest in the vernacular, he having up to that moment only attended to composition in Latin: Barbara is probably to be identified as the 'so rare woman' who had inspired his poems in the vernacular ('Sì rara donna in vita al cor ti corse / per trarne fuor rime leggiadre et conte' ll. 3–4),[14] as celebrated in the *strambotto* composed in honor of Strozzi after his death, perhaps on the occasion of one of the anniversaries of the event.[15]

---

12 The epitaph is in the biography of Ercole Strozzi written by Lorenzo Strozzi. See Strozzi Lorenzo di Filippo, *Le vite degli uomini illustri della casa Strozzi. Commentario di Lorenzo di Filippo Strozzi ora interamente pubblicato, con un ragionamento inedito di Francesco Zeffi sopra la vita dell'autore*, ed. P. Stromboli (Florence: 1892) 79.

13 Bembi Pietro, *Carmina*, ed. R. Sodano (Turin: 1990) 55–56.

14 Bembo Pietro, *Le rime*, ed. A. Donnini (Rome: 2008).

15 Pignatti F., "Un madrigale sconosciuto di Ercole Strozzi", *Atti e Memorie dell'Arcadia* 7 (2018) 7–31: 19–20.

Words similar can also be read in Ariosto's epitaph, which explicitly mentions the funeral monument built by the widow, who had arranged to be buried there, when the time came, next to her husband:

> Qui patriae est olim iuvenis moderatus habenas,
> Quique senum subiit pondera pene puer;
> Quem molles elegi ostendunt, seu grandia mavis,
> Sive canenda lyra carmina quantus erat;
> Herculis hic Strozzae tegitur cinis: intulit uxor
> Barbara, Taurellae stemmate clara domus.
> Quale hoc cumque suo statuit sacrum aere sepulchrum,
> Iuncta ubi vult chari manibus esse viri.
>
> (One who a long time ago, when he was young, held the reins of the fatherland, and who bore burdens suitable for an older man, being only a boy; and whom gentle elegies laud, or his great deeds, if you prefer, or the many poems sung accompanied by the lyre. Here are buried the ashes of Ercole Strozzi. His wife buried him, Barbara, of the noble family of the Torelli. And in this place, she prepared for herself the holy grave in which she wanted to be joined, holding hands with the dear husband.)

In fact, we know that Torelli had stipulated, in 1509, a contract to this effect with the church of Santa Maria in Vado, to which she had granted two properties in exchange. It is, therefore, likely that this verse was also composed on the occasion of an anniversary rather than soon after the poet's death.

The cliché of the widow's marital fidelity, advocated by Strozzi's partners,[16] almost fueled the myth of a widowhood spent entirely in the memory of the second husband. Actually, we should not take it too literally. It seems that a few years later, in Venice, she was in love with an agent of the Gonzaga family, a certain Folenghino.[17] Furthermore, according to a source never yet used by scholars, Barbara also contracted a third marriage in 1525, of which Marin Sanudo's diaries give us news, reproducing the text of a letter received by the chronicler from his secretary in February of that year:

---

16 See also the epitaph composed by Ludovico Bigo Pittorio, in the name of the widow: 'Herculis hic Strozae dum conderet ossa mariti / Barbara, Taurellae gloria gentis, Ait: "Care vale coniunx, siqua prece fata moventur, claudet et haec cineres ocius urna meos"' (Pictorii Ferrariensis Lodovici Bigi, *In coelestes proceres hymnorum epitaphiorumque liber. Eiusdem epigrammaton libelli duo* (Ferrara, [n.p.]: 1514), fol. F8r).

17 Bellonci M., *Lucrezia Borgia. La sua vita, i suoi tempi* (Milan: 1947) 528.

> Come era sta de i fatti uno paro di noze di la signora Barbara Torella fo moier di missier Hercules Strozi ferarese, in missier Lazaro Doria genovese, et hozi la dieno sposar, et lei ha voluto l'orator nostro [Andrea Navaier] sia suo compare di l'anello; et per questo hozi si va su quel di Luca [Lucca] per far lo dimane el sposalicio, perché si l'havessono fatto qui in Pisa, Hariano pagato una grande gabella di la dotte, che si paga 10 per 100, però si va a concluder le noze fuora dil territorio fiorentino.[18]
>
> (Among the news there is the wedding between Barbara Torelli, the former wife of Ercole Strozzi of Ferrara, and Lazzaro Doria from Genoa. They will get married these days, and she wanted our orator [Andrea Navaier] as the witness. And for this reason today we go to Lucca to celebrate the wedding tomorrow because if they had celebrated it here in Pisa, they would have paid a large tax on the dowry, equal to ten percent, so they will celebrate the wedding outside the Florentine territory.)

Torelli must have been still alive in the summer of 1529, since that year she received two letters, now preserved in the State Archive of Florence, from Filippo Doria, both from Genoa, on 3 July and 14 August, and at least one from Lazzaro himself, dated 20 July in the locality of Nove (Treviso). From the last letter, we also learn that she was, on that date, in the Pisan area, more precisely in the locality of Lavaiano, where her husband sent the letter to her.[19] There is little information on the last years of her life: in the absence of further documentation, we can give credit to what is reported in the *Repertoire des Femmes Celebres*,[20] according to which Torelli spent her last years between Parma and Bologna, the city in which she dictated her will in November 1533.

2 The Sonnet

In the sonnet *Spenta è d'Amor la face, il dardo è rotto*, the poetess speaks in the person of Barbara Torelli, who mourns her murdered husband, employing, with a certain amount of originality, some of the most classic images of the poetry of death.

---

18 Sanudo Marin, *I diarii*, vol. XXXVII (Venice: 1893) 625.

19 Firenze, Archivio di Stato, Carte Strozziane, serie I, file 64, document n° 10, 13 and 180 (*Le Carte Strozziane del R. Archivio di Stato in Firenze. Inventario*, vol. I (Florence: 1884) 343).

20 Prudhomme L.M., *Répertoire universel, historique, biographique des femmes célèbres, mortes ou vivantes* [...], (Paris: 1826).

The first quatrain, which states, in a definite sense, the acknowledgement of the death of the relative, opens with the topical image, already used by Petrarch, but widespread in the gloomy poetry of the sixteenth and seventeenth centuries, of Love who remains with broken weapons after Death took away the loved one, crushing the plant under which the poetess used to find shelter. The second quatrain introduces a series of *impossibilia*. The first one consists of the desire to die with her husband. The meaning of the expression 'amor legò' ('love has bonded'), in l. 8, is controversial: it could indicate the couple's marriage or, as seems more likely, the birth of the daughter. As we shall see, its interpretation is crucial in the discussion of the composition of the forgery. Two more *impossibilia* take place in the first triplet: they consist respectively of the image of the loving fire ('foco') that defeats the ice ('freddo ghiaccio') of death (ll. 9–10) and of the desire to be able to bring the deceased back to life through kneading with tears ('rimpastar col pianto') the inert dust ('polve') of his ashes (ll. 10–11). After the miracle of Love's victory over Death, finally, in the last triplet, the poetess hopes to be able to show it off, bold and daring ('baldanzosa e ardita'), to the cruel monster ('mostro crudel') who was responsible for the crime.

A transcription of the text, taken from the edition of the *Rime scelte*, is provided below:

Spenta è d'Amor la face, il dardo è rotto,
E l'arco, e la faretra, e ogni sua possa,
Poi ch'ha Morte crudel la pianta scossa,
A la cui ombra, cheta io dormia sotto.

Deh perché non poss'io la breve fossa
Seco entrar dove hallo il destin condotto,
Colui che appena cinque giorni, et otto,
Amor legò prìa de la gran percossa?

Vorrei col foco mio quel freddo ghiaccio
Intepidire, e rimpastar col pianto
La polve, e ravvivarla a nuova vita:

E vorrei poscia baldanzosa, e ardita
Mostrarlo a lui, che ruppe il caro laccio,
E dirgli: Amor (mostro crudel) può tanto.[21]

---

21 Baruffaldi, *Rime scelte* 55 (the accent on the word 'perché', l. 5, has been added).

> (The torch of Love is extinguished, his arrow is broken, as well as his bow, his quiver, and all his power, since the cruel Death has crushed the plant in the shade of which I used to sleep. Oh, why can't I enter the tomb where fate has led him, who Love tied (i.e. to me) only five days and eight more before the blow [i.e. the murder]? If only I could warm that cold ice with my fire and knead with my tears his ashes, to make them live again. And then, victorious, I would like to show it [the miracle] to the murderer who broke up the dear tie and say to him: 'Love, cruel monster, can do such a thing'.)

The text takes up a usual series of images and expressions of the gloomy lyric of the sixteenth and seventeenth centuries. Particularly noteworthy is the image of kneading with tears ('rimpastar col pianto') the deceased's ashes to bring them back to life, which has a more modern and already eighteenth-century flavor and can be considered a strong, stylistic clue against the forger. Another proof is that sometimes the same elements of the poetry are reused in other compositions, included both in the *Rime scelte* and others works by Baruffaldi. As regards the latter case, we can see that the expression 'mostro crudel', used in the last line of the sonnet, recurs also in a line of his tragedy *Giocasta la Giovane*: 'Mostro crudel, guardami in volto e dimmi / se ti desta nel core alcun rimorso / del tuo delitto nel vedermi. Io sono / colei che tu tradisti' (l. 45). In other cases, an expression recurs in other sonnets of the anthology: for example, in a line of the sonnet *Cruda, in un'aura, in un sospir cangiato*, published in the *Rime scelte* and attributed – maybe falsely – to the poet Francesco Berni,[22] we read 'Spenta d'Amor la face avrei col fiato',[23] which recalls the *incipit* of the sonnet by Pseudo-Torelli, 'Spenta è d'amor la face'. Another case concerns the expression, in the *explicit* of our sonnet, 'Amor [...] può tanto', which recurs in the sonnet *O più d'altrui, che di te stessa amante*, attributed to the Ferrarian Battista Guarini: 'E se 'n duo cerchi angusti Amor può tanto'.[24]

Despite the question of the authenticity of the Berni sonnet, which is still controversial, for the one attributed to Guarini we can be sure Baruffaldi was not the forger since it had already appeared in the edition of his poetry published in Venice by Giovanni Battista Ciotti in 1598. Although one could imagine a mutual influence between these texts, coincidentally included in the *Rime scelte*, it seems much more probable that the one by Torelli is a fake,

22 Even if this text has not yet been studied, it seems significant that we can read it only from the anthology composed by Baruffaldi.

23 Baruffaldi, *Rime scelte* 347, l. 4.

24 Ibidem, 258, l. 10.

composed by Baruffaldi using elements taken from other texts, regardless of whether they were authentic or false themselves. The re-use of pre-existing materials is recurrent in the *Rime scelte*: it is recognisable, for example, in the false texts attributed to the poets Anselmo da Ferrara, definitely invented, and Gervasio Riccobaldo, a real poet who, however, never wrote the texts printed in the anthology. As demonstrated by Andrea Comboni, both the sonnets *Chi può aggiunger un dito a sua statura* and *Tinto di morte era tuo sancto viso* by Pseudo-Anselmo, and the sonnet *Io ho dottanza che la donna mia* by Pseudo-Riccobaldo, have been constructed starting from lines or single expressions used by Italian poets of the thirteenth century, like Guittone d'Arezzo and Giacomo da Lentini.[25] In both these cases, the anthology known as 'Giuntina di rime antiche', printed in Florence by the Giunta printer-family in 1527, which Baruffaldi knew well, played an important role.[26] Another example is the sonnet *Io sto alla signoria d'un tal Zitello*, also by Pseudo-Riccobaldo, whose source was no less than Petrarch's *Canzoniere*, from which Baruffaldi harvested several expressions.[27] Baruffaldi, who probably did not feel confident with the ancient style, recurred to these models to make his forgeries more realistic, according to a universal tendency well described by scholars.[28]

3 The Construction of the Imposture

Although hers was such a prominent figure in the literary circles of the Este court, that of Baruffaldi would be the first and only testimony of Barbara Torelli's poetic activity. The sonnet attributed to her is published, in the *Rime scelte*, after a series of four sonnets in the vernacular by Ercole Strozzi, to be precise *Trionfal, gloriosa, e lieta barca*; *Euro gentil, che gli aurei crespi nodi*; *O beato pensier, ch'a ogni tua voglia* and *Sonno, che gli Animali, Uomini e Dei*,[29] all dated to 1508, while the date 1509 appears next to that of Barbara. Baruffaldi presents the figure of the presumed author in the *Notizie istoriche*, the final

25 Comboni, *Un falsario al lavoro*. The sonnets referred to appear in Baruffaldi, *Rime scelte* 1, 2 and 3, respectively.

26 *Sonetti e canzoni di diversi antichi autori toscani in dieci libri raccolte* (Florence, Giunta: 1527).

27 For an exhaustive description of these cases see Comboni, *Un falsario al lavoro*.

28 See, for example, Grafton A., *Forgers and Critics Creativity and Duplicity in Western Scholarship* (Princeton NJ: 1990).

29 We know of only nine texts in the vernacular by Strozzi, who was mainly known for his Latin production. The sonnets are published in Vagni G., "Su un sonetto di Ercole Strozzi già attribuito a Baldassarre Castiglione", *Aevum* 85:3 (2011) 751–775.

section of the anthology, which contains brief presentations of the poets included in the collection:

> Barbara Torella Moglie d'Ercole Strozza, et origine della di lui morte, come Donna di rare bellezze, e d'alto sapere, e perciò pretesa da molti. Ne' funerali d'Ercole suo marito fatti l'anno 1509, e descritti da Celio Calcagnini, si legge un suo sonetto.[30]
>
> (Barbara Torelli, Wife of Ercole Strozzi, and the reason why he died, since she was a woman of rare beauty and very high knowledge, and therefore sought after by many. One of her sonnets can be read in the 'Funerals' of her husband Ercole, celebrated in 1509 and described by Celio Calcagnini.)

No reference to her appears, however, in the presentation of Ercole in the *Notizie istoriche*:

> Ercole Strozza figliuolo di Tito. Poeta celebre anch'esso. Fu amazzato l'anno 1508, essendo Giudice de' Savj, e fu seppellito con solenni esequie in S.[anta] M.[aria] in Vado.[31]
>
> (Ercole Strozzi son of Tito, also a famous poet. He was killed in the year 1508, being Judge 'de' Savj', and was buried with a solemn funeral in the church of Santa Maria in Vado.)

Nevertheless, the situation was quite different in the draft of the *Rime scelte*, drawn up in July 1712. It is contained in the ms. Cl. I 557 of the Ariostea Municipal Library of Ferrara, among a series of autograph papers called *Opistographa*, so entitled – by Baruffaldi himself – since they were written on the reverse of some papers already printed.[32] In the draft, the few notices about Barbara were initially included in her husband's presentation:

> 1508 Ercole Strozza figliuol di Tito: ambi di nobilissima stirpe, et <poeti> insigni nel poetar latino. Tito scrisse ancora qualche cosa in volgare. Sono

30 Baruffaldi, *Rime scelte* 326.

31 Ibidem, 573.

32 'Opistographa' is a Greek expression which means 'written on the reverse'. The series is divided into fascicles, or 'squarzi', the word preferred by Baruffaldi. The draft of the *Rime scelte* is in 'squarzo D'.

> famosi li suoi amori con la celebre Barbara Torelli che poi gli fu moglie, e per cui colpa, nata gelosia, fu fatto da un poderoso rivale ammazare l'anno 1508, essendo Giudice de' Savj. Il suo cadavero fu sepolto in Santa Maria in Vado con sontuosi funerali.[33]
>
> (Ercole Strozzi, son of Tito: both of noble lineage, and <poets> [canceled in course of writing], outstanding in poetry in Latin. Titus also wrote something in the vernacular. His love affairs with the famous Barbara Torelli, who was later his wife, are famous, and on account of her, having been born jealous, he was killed by a powerful man in 1508, while he was Judge 'de' Savj'. His body was buried in Santa Maria in Vado church, with sumptuous funerals.)

Only subsequently, after many pages, Barbara is also presented as an author:

> 1509 Barbara Torella, moglie di Ercole Strozza, et origine della di lui morte come donna di rare bellezze e d'alto sapere, e perciò pretesa da principi ancora. Ne' funerali di d'Ercole [sic] descritti da C.[elio] C.[alcagnini] che ms. [manoscritti] si conservano da G.[irolamo] B.[aruffaldi] si trova il saggio qui addotto.[34]
>
> (Barbara Torelli, wife of Ercole Strozzi, and the reason why he died, since she was a woman of rare beauty and high knowledge, and therefore demanded even by princes. In the 'Funerals' of Ercole, described by C.[elio] C.[alcagnini], which are kept in the manuscripts of G.[irolamo] B.[aruffaldi], you will find the sample presented here.)

It can be observed, in the first place, how in the passage from the draft to the printed version, the *Notizie istoriche* around Strozzi become more succinct, since Baruffaldi eliminates both the details of death and those, even rougher, of his loves with Barbara; she is no longer even mentioned in her husband's introduction. Furthermore, since in the *Rime scelte* Barbara's sonnet follows, as we have seen, Strozzi's texts, one would have expected that the *Notizie istoriche* on her would be found, in the draft, immediately after those concerning her husband; instead, they are separated by several pages and found among the notes concerning poets of the end of the sixteenth and the seventeenth centuries. This clue would suggest that Baruffaldi had the idea of

33 *Brevi annotazioni*, fol. 9r.

34 Ibidem, fol. 24r.

attributing a composition to her only at a later time: in this case, the drastic reduction, in the printed version of the *Rime scelte*, of the *Notizie istoriche* concerning Strozzi – in particular, that of his death caused by jealousy aroused by the woman – would have been the result of a redistribution of information, since those about Barbara could now be made use of in the construction of an autonomous poetic character.

As said, the witness of the *Rime scelte* constitutes the earliest evidence of the fact that Torelli also devoted herself to poetry. Baruffaldi himself does not mention her among the Ferrarian poets counted in the first draft of the *Dissertatio de poetis Ferrariensibus* of 1698 – a treatise on the birth of poetry in Ferrara which already contains, *in nuce*, many of the reflections then developed in the *Rime scelte* – nor in the main text of the *Biblioteca degli scrittori ferraresi cronologicamente descritta*, which remained only in a handwritten copy in the ms. Cl. I 594 of the Ariostea Municipal Library of Ferrara, with the date of 1711.[35] There he speaks extensively of Ercole Strozzi, but only names Barbara to insist on the fact that the couple were legally married at the time of the murder:

> … gli autori tutti concordano che la Torella fosse veramente sua moglie da pochi giorni, ma poiché vive ancora l'opinione che foss'ella unicamente sua amasia, per ribatterla porterò qui in primo luogo il testimonio della sua medaglia, battuta in que' giorni, con da una parte la di lui faccia coronata di lauro […] e dall'altra il volto parimenti della Torella, giovane di bell'aspetto, colle trecce bizzarramente composte, con intorno queste parole: Barbara Taurella ux. […] Per quello spirito vaticinante che si suppone ne' poeti, egli affrettò gli sponsali con Barbara nel tempo stesso che assunse il carico di giudice de' Savi […].[36]

> (… all the authors agree that Torelli was really his wife for a few days, but since many still think she was only his mistress, to contradict this opinion I will bring here in the first place the proof of his medal, produced in those days, with on one side his face crowned with laurel, and on the other the face of Torelli, a handsome young girl, with bizarrely composed braids, with these words around them: 'Barbara Taurella ux.' […] For that

35 Baruffaldi Girolamo, *Dissertatio de poetis ferrariensibus* […] (Ferrara, [n.p.]: 1698); Baruffaldi Girolamo, *Biblioteca degli scrittori ferraresi cronologicamente descritta* […], mdccxi, *con osservazioni opportune sopra le loro opere così stampate come manoscritte*, Ferrara, Biblioteca Comunale Ariostea, ms. Cl. I 594.

36 Baruffaldi, *Biblioteca*, quoted from Tissoni Benvenuti, "Appunti" 44.

prophetic spirit that is expected in poets, he hastened his marriage with Barbara when he took on the role of Giudice de' Savi [Judge of the Wise].)

Some information on Barbara's poetic activity is instead added in a note affixed, at a later time, on the verso side of the same page of the manuscript:

> La Barbara Torella di cui ragionavamo come di leggiadro spirito ch'ella era, poetava gentilmente et oltre la Partenia, favola pastorale lodata dall'Ingegneri, p. 61 della Poes. Rappresent., si leggono diverse rime, e fra di esse sono in morte del marito, ch'io ho in un ms. antico con altre. Il Crescimbeni la crede mantovana.[37]
>
> (The Barbara Torelli who we discussed as the graceful spirit that she was, sweetly composed in addition the *Partenia*, a pastoral fable praised by Ingegneri, on p. 61 of his work entitled 'On Representative Poetry'. You can read several stanzas, and among them are those about the death of her husband, which I have in an ancient ms. along with others. Crescimbeni believes her to be Mantuan.)

First of all, this testimony is uncertain because we do not know its exact date; since he had to add a note, however, it seems evident that Baruffaldi was unaware of any poetic production by Torelli when he wrote his *Biblioteca* in a clean copy in 1711. Above all, the information reported in Ingegneri's note is incorrect because it does not refer to the widow of Ercole Strozzi, but to the Barbara Torelli born, even if in the same family – that of the counts of Montechiarugolo – many decades later (i.e. in 1546), and who married the knight Giovanni Paolo Benedetti, from Parma, from whom she became widowed in 1592. Torelli Benedetti was also known in literary society, but with a more active role: her cousin was Pomponio Torelli, founder of the Accademia degli Innominati, with which she maintained assiduous contacts; in addition to the pastoral fable entitled *Partenia*, she composed several other poems in the vernacular that are handed down mainly in manuscripts or appear in contemporary collections of poetry.[38]

---

37 Ibidem, 45.

38 See Sampson L., *Torelli Benedetti, Barbara*, in *Dizionario Biografico degli Italiani*, vol. 26 (Turin: 2019) (https://www.treccani.it/enciclopedia/barbara-torelli-benedetti_%28Dizionario-Biografico%29/).

On the other hand, the news reported by Baruffaldi does not seem precisely first-hand, but exhibits a clear dependence, as recently noted by the scholar Tissoni Benvenuti, on Crescimbeni's comments:

> Barbara Torelli, la cui favola Pastorale intitolata 'La Partenia' vien lodata da Angelo Ingegneri [riferimento in nota a 'Poes[ia]. Rappres[entativa]. pag. 61'], può esser, che sia della stessa casa d'Ippolita Taurella Mantovana, che fu moglie di Baldassarre Castiglioni e Poetessa latina assai celebre, un'elegia della quale, scritta al Marito, è inserita tra gli Opuscoli di Paolo Colomesio, il quale riporta anche il suo Epitaffio, che è il seguente [...]. Favella di Barbara anche Muzio Manfredi che la chiama Barbara Torelli Benedetti.[39]

> (Barbara Torelli, whose pastoral fable entitled *La Partenia* is praised by Angelo Ingegneri [reference in the note to the work 'Poesia Rappresentativa' (On Representative Poetry) p. 61'], could be from the same lineage as Ippolita Taurella Mantovana, who was the wife of Baldassarre Castiglioni and a very famous Latin poetess, one of whose elegies, written to her husband, is included among the Opuscoli by Paolo Colomesio, who also reports her Epitaph [...]. Barbara is also spoken of by Muzio Manfredi, who calls her Barbara Torelli Benedetti.)

The information reported by Crescimbeni, which Baruffaldi takes up, including the reference to the work by Ingegneri, were already in themselves vague and uncertain, potentially referring to both Torelli Strozzi and Torelli Benedetti: they, therefore, constituted an ideal canvas for the construction of the poetic figure of Torelli Strozzi, attributing to her a real literary work, composed by an author whose homonymy could have easily gone unnoticed.

Finally, we can read additional information on the alleged poetess in the second edition of the *Dissertatio de poetis Ferrariensibus*, which has remained unedited in the papers of the ms. Antonelli 602 of the Ariostea Municipal Library of Ferrara:

> 29. *De Barbara Taurella.* Barbara Taurella vidua honestissima amore Herculis Strozzae capta, cum par et nobilitas, et pulchritudo, et omnigena virtus esset, musis quoque se dedit. *Partheniam*, Pastoralem comediam,

39 Crescimbeni Giovanni Mario, *Comentarj del canonico Gio. Mario Crescimbeni custode d'Arcadia, intorno alla sua Istoria della volgar poesia*, vol. 4 (Rome, Antonio de' Rossia alla Piazza di Ceri: 1711) 86.

scripsit, ac nonnulla epigrammata italica, inter quorum illuum eminet in obitu Herculis sponsi sui, eum quo vix tres decim dies coniugali nodo convixit. Marito tumulum construxit, ut ex epitaphio per Thebaldeum:

Herculis hic Strozzae Tumulus, quem condidit Uxor
Moerens, Taurellae Barbara Gentis honos.
Plus dederit quamvis non hac Mausole meretur
Plus tua, fortuna haec, non pietate minor.

Epitaphium quoque Aldi, ac nummisma, uxoris nomine adnotato obice occurrunt. Obiit florente adhuc aetate.[40]

(29. About Barbara Torelli. Barbara Torelli, the most honest widow, having fallen in love with Ercole Strozzi, at one time a girl full of nobleness, beauty, and every virtue, also devoted herself to the Muses (i.e. poetry). She wrote the *Partenia*, a pastoral comedy, and some epigrams in the Italian vernacular, among which the one on the death of her husband Ercole, with whom she lived, joined by the conjugal knot, for thirteen days, stands out. She had a sepulchre erected for her husband, as one can read in the epitaph by Tebaldeo: 'This is the sepulcher of Ercole Strozzi, which the sad wife Barbara, the honor of the Torelli family, has erected. This destiny has given to him more than yours, although he did not deserve this death, giving him not less piety than you'.

Also, an epitaph by Aldo [Manuzio] exists, and a coin with the name of the wife. He died in the prime of his life.)

This second edition of the *Dissertatio*, significantly different from that printed in 1698, is not dated. Therefore, it is impossible to establish its relative chronology in relation to the *Rime scelte*, which as we have seen represented a sort of continuation of that work. In any case, the reference to the quotes by Tebaldeo[41] – unpublished until now – and Manuzio, are particularly interesting because they tell us Baruffaldi was aware of these sources, which probably had inspired the theme of the sonnet.

To summarise the information gathered so far on the elaboration of the forgery, we see that Baruffaldi seems to start talking about the poetic activity of Barbara Torelli first in the *Biblioteca*, in 1711, confusing her (perhaps

40 Ferrara, Biblioteca Comunale Ariostea, ms. Cl. I 594, p. 14. Only the first part of this quote is also in Tissoni Benvenuti, "Appunti" 45), ending with the word 'convixi'.

41 See the previous footnote.

intentionally?) with Barbara Torelli Benedetti and mentioning the existence of other rhymes preserved in one of his manuscripts. The posteriority of the note in relation to the main text in the *Biblioteca*, does not, however, allow us to exclude the possibility that Baruffaldi added it while he was already writing the *Opistographa*. There we find the first organic construction of the poetic character of Barbara Torelli, previously mentioned only as of the wife of Strozzi, then presented in turn as a poetess. The second *Dissertatio*, perhaps posterior, replicates the content of the sonnet, in particular the mention of the *coniugali nodo*, which, at the time of the murder, tied the couple for only thirteen days, and adds a quote from the obituary verse by Tebaldeo and mentions one by Aldo Manuzio. As already observed by Tissoni Benvenuti, however, here Baruffaldi becomes more cautious, keeping the source silent and avoiding compromising himself as the owner of the phantom manuscript. In the meantime, he probably had the opportunity to learn more about Torelli, as can be seen from the allusion to the epitaphs of Tebaldeo and Aldo.

4 The Critical Debate

Perhaps due to the particular fascination exercised by the figure of Barbara Torelli, combined with the undisputed expressive value of the sonnet published in her name by Baruffaldi, no one ever seriously questioned its authenticity until the early twentieth century. The information reported in the *Rime scelte* was reproduced, without further verification, by several Ferrarian scholars: Ferrante Borsetti, in the *Historia almi Ferrariae Gymnasii* of 1735, defines Torelli's work as noble poetry ('poetria nobilissima'), probably taking up the news from Baruffaldi that one of her sonnets can be read 'in descriptione eiusdem [of Strozzi] Funerum, facta for Celium Calcagninum nostrum anno 1509' ('in the description of Strozzi's funeral monument, provided by our Celio Calcagnini in 1509').[42] The name of Torelli also appears, a few years later, in the *Storia e ragione di ogni poesia* by Francesco Saverio Quadrio, which initially mentions her as Strozzi's wife, alluding to their marriage which lasted only thirteen days, but seeming to confuse her with Barbara Torelli Benedetti.[43] Finally, the sonnet could also be read, with another likewise attributed to the widow Strozzi, in two eighteenth-century anthologies handed down in the mss. Cl. I

42 Borsetti Ferranti Bolani Ferrante, *Historia almi Ferrariae gymnasii* (Ferrara, Bernardinus Pomatellus: 1735) ii, 140.

43 Quadrio Francesco Saverio, *Della storia e ragione d'ogni poesia* (Bologna, Ferdinando Pisarri: 1739–1752) ii, 376, 383; v, 406.

565 and Antonelli 202, both of the Ariostea Municipal Library of Ferrara. The first codex was copied by Vincenzo Faustini, a Ferrarian erudite of that time; here, the sonnet appears together with other poetic texts of authors of the Este circle. Girolamo Baruffaldi junior, son of our forger, copied the second codex. He claims to have copied it from a manuscript of rhymes owned in Ferrara by a certain Antonio Schincaglia, which no one has ever been able to identify. Although it was prepared by Faustini, the ms. Cl. I. 565 is also probably connected to Baruffaldi's circle, because Faustini himself also intervened in the ms. Antonelli, by copying there a third sonnet attributed to Torelli – although perhaps, in this case, referring to the widow of the knight Benedetti. Equally compromised by the proximity to the forger's environment seems to be the witness of Giannantonio Liberati: in his *Memorie storiche de' poeti parmigiani defunti*, handwritten on the papers of the ms. 396 of the Palatine Library of Parma, he dwells at length on the figure of Barbara Torelli, trying to demonstrate, with an articulate yet weak genealogical reasoning, the Parmesan origin of the woman. At one point, he also speaks of the sonnet in question, and more generally of Torelli's alleged poetic production:

> Alcuni vi furono che giudicarono il famoso sonetto che noi trasponiamo [*Spenta d'amor la face, il dardo è rotto*] per esemplare fatica d'altro poeta, affermando non avere giamai vedute altre rime di Barbara; ma noi possiamo ben assicurare il nostro lettore che un altro di lei sonetto leggevasi nel codice Rebuschiano sullo stesso soggetto, del quale siamo molto pentiti non averne ricercata copia quando viveva ancora il nostro carissimo Signor dottore.[44]
>
> (Some judged the famous sonnet that we transpose [*Spenta d'amor la face, il dardo è rotto*] as the work of another poet, stating that they have never seen any other rhymes by Barbara; but we can reasonably assure our reader that another sonnet of hers was recorded in the Rebuschian codex on the same subject, of which we are very sorry not to have made a copy when our dearest doctor still lived.)

There is also no trace of the Rebuschian codex, as was the case also with the one supposedly owned by Antonio Schincaglia. We learn about the Schincaglia manuscript thanks to Girolamo Baruffaldi junior. As for Giannantonio Liberati, who affirms to have seen the Rebuschian manuscript, he was the son of

44 Liberati G., *Memorie storiche de' poeti parmigiani defunti*, quoted from Tissoni Benvenuti, "Appunti" 43.

Isabella Clementini in Liberati who had been a correspondent for Baruffaldi, as well as the dedicatee of the didactic poem *Il canapaio*. Thus, the proximity to the forger's environment would, in any case, make it difficult to accept the manuscripts as a sure testimony antecedent to and independent of the *Rime scelte*. Not to mention that, through the insistence with which Liberati himself tries to convince readers of the existence of other poems by Torelli, he involuntarily confirms that a particular atmosphere of suspicion surrounded the text. Thus, these suspicious testimonies suggest that Baruffaldi involved his associates in the composition of the forgery, be it as deliberate accomplices, as is the case with his son Girolamo junior, or as naive dupes, as maybe was the case with Liberati.

Once again, Torelli's is not the only such case in the *Rime scelte*, and reveals a *modus operandi* characteristic of his other forgeries. Another example is in the diptych between Buonaccorso da Montemagno il Vecchio and Antonio Beccari. Both the first sonnet, *Giù per quell'onda, che ancor fuma, e stride*, attributed to Buonaccorso, and the responsive one, *Stato foss'io su quelle rive infide*, attributed to Beccari, are inventions of Baruffaldi. However, the sonnets were published for the first time in 1709 by a friend of Baruffaldi, Agostino Gobbi, in the anthology *Scelta di sonetti, e canzoni de' più eccellenti Rimatori d'ogni Secolo*. Here the role played by Baruffaldi is evident in the note appended to the texts, in which Gobbi reveals that the texts are derived 'Da un M.S. antico del Dottor Baruffaldi' ('from an ancient manuscript owned by Baruffaldi'), who also appears in the thanks at the end of the volume.[45]

After the death of Baruffaldi, scholars rarely if ever questioned the authenticity of the text, instead discussing the origin, Parma or Ferrara, of Barbara Torelli. For example, the erudite Ireneo Affò writes,[46] in a letter to Girolamo Tiraboschi in June 1778,[47] that Liberati tended to be too broad when it came to attributing some of the authors cited to Parma.[48] Despite this, in the fourth

45 The false diptych is presented in Comboni – Russo, "Per un archivio dei falsi letterari italiani" 43, 47, 49, 51, 55–56.

46 Ireneo Affò (1741–1797) was an art and literary historian from Busseto (Parma). He is famous especially for the work *Memorie degli scrittori e letterati parmigiani*, in five volumes, printed in Parma from 1789 to 1797 (cf. *Dizionario Biografico degli Italiani*, at the link https://www.treccani.it/enciclopedia/ireneo-affo_(Dizionario-Biografico)).

47 Girolamo Tiraboschi (1731–1794), one of the most important literary historians of the Italian tradition, wrote a famous *Storia della letteratura italiana* in ten volumes, published between 1772 and 1782 (cf. *Dizionario Biografico degli Italiani*, at the link https://www.treccani.it/enciclopedia/girolamo-tiraboschi_(Dizionario-Biografico)).

48 '[Col Liberati] non siamo né in riga, né in ispazio, perch'egli è molto facile a battezzar Parmigiani anche quegli che sono certamente estranei' (*Lettere di Girolamo Tiraboschi al padre Ireneo Affò, tratte da' codd. della Biblioteca Estense di Modena e della Palatina di Parma*, part I (Modena: 1894), 110, note 1).

volume of his *Memorie degli scrittori e letterati parmigiani*, he fully accepts the 'Scrittori ferraresi' testimony, limiting himself to underlining the chronological order mistake made by Quadrio.[49] Even Girolamo Tiraboschi, in his *Storia della letteratura italiana*, grants full authority to the Archpriest of Cento, i.e. Baruffaldi, stating that:

> Barbara Torella moglie di Ercole Strozzi fu essa pur coltivatrice della volgar poesia, e nella morte del suo infelice marito, con cui non era vissuta che pochi giorni, scrisse un elegante sonetto, che si ha alle stampe nella Raccolta dei Poeti ferraresi, e altrove.[50]

> (Barbara Torelli, the wife of Ercole Strozzi, was also a cultivator of poetry in the vernacular, and upon the death of her unhappy husband, with whom she had only lived for a few days, she wrote an elegant sonnet, which is printed in the 'Raccolta dei Poeti ferraresi', and elsewhere.)

In his *Memorie istoriche di letterati ferraresi*, which came out posthumously in 1777, Giannandrea Barotti seems more cautious: he expresses skepticism about several pieces of information reported by Baruffaldi in the *Rime scelte* and the second draft of the *Dissertatio*, in particular, the one according to which Strozzi was one of the judges 'de' Savi' at the time of his death – as we today know, he had by that time been out of the office for two years already – and about the hypothesis that the jealousies aroused by Barbara would have been the main cause of the death of Ercole. Barotti also expresses some reservations on the content of the sonnet, although he does not explicitly question its authenticity.[51] He observes that Giulia, the orphan, was only ten in 1518, when Torelli was carrying out, as we understand from a letter from Pietro Bembo, marriage negotiations: he concludes that she would have had to be born well before those thirteen days ('cinque giorni, e otto') in which, according to the interpretation provided by Baruffaldi himself in the *Dissertatio* – cited by Barotti – the entire duration of their marriage lasted. Today we know that the objection is unfounded because the date corresponded, as we will see later, to the birth of Giulia herself. We must, therefore, conclude that the negotiations carried out in pursuing her interests had started well in advance! In any case,

49 Affò Ireneo, *Memorie degli scrittori e letterati parmigiani raccolte dal padre Ireneo Affò minor osservante Bibliotecario di S.A.R.* [...], vol. 4 (Parma, Stamperia Reale: 1793) 297.

50 Tiraboschi Girolamo, *Storia della letteratura italiana*, 13 vols. (Modena, Società Tipografica: 1772–1782) VI:ii, 908.

51 Barotti Giannandrea, *Memorie istoriche di letterati ferraresi. Opera postuma di Giannandrea Barotti*, I (Ferrara, Stamperia Camerale: 1777) 179–203.

these reservations, moreover expressed by an intellectual who had had ample access to Baruffaldi's drafts,[52] lead one to ask whether the sonnet was truly universally accepted by all as a work of Torelli.

It continued, in any case, to be considered as authentic throughout the nineteenth century. A real watershed, for the question of attribution was indeed represented by the position of the poet Giosuè Carducci: he not only did not doubt the authenticity of the sonnet but even described it, with a judgment that would remain famous, as one of the very few beautiful poems that Italian women have ever written ('fra le pochissime belle poesie che abbiano mai scritto le donne italiane').[53] In this period, the text had been anthologised in numerous *Parnasi* of Italian poetry, and even in the manuals used by schools, such as that of Francesco Torraca of 1911.[54] The first suspicions concerning the poem's authenticity were advanced only in 1919, and almost *en passant*, by Giulio Bertoni, who after having praised them, a few years earlier, as proof of Barbara Torelli's 'very high talent' and 'great nobility' in poetry ('elevatissimo ingegno' and 'grande nobiltà di sentire'),[55] now no longer considered the sonnet authentic.[56] Bertoni did not provide argumentation for this radical change of opinion, but rather expressed his opinion in a rather curt way. The following year, however, a study by Michele Catalano would be released, dedicated to the literary environment of the court of Alfonso I, which offered an overall review of the data in question. He argues based on the two surely indisputable facts, already mentioned several times here: that no other compositions of Barbara have reached us – despite her having been, as we have seen, a rather prominent figure in the poetic scene of her time – and, more importantly, that in the many praises bestowed upon her by her contemporaries, there is no mention of her poetic skills. Having called into question the attribution, however, Catalano at first does not consider the thesis that it was a forgery, proposing instead that the sonnet be attributed to Ludovico Ariosto, a partner of Strozzi, who would have composed and disseminated it in the name of the widow to pay homage to the memory of his deceased friend.[57]

52 This is affirmed by his son Lorenzo Barotti, in the introduction of the posthumous work Barotti L., *Ai lettori*, in *Memorie istoriche di letterati ferraresi. Opera postuma di Giannandrea Barotti*, i [Ferrara: 1777] v–viii [v–vi].

53 Carducci G., *Delle poesie latine edite ed inedite di Ludovico Ariosto* (Bologna: 1936) 194.

54 Torraca F., *Manuale della letteratura italiana. Sec. xvi* (Florence: 1911) 232.

55 Bertoni G., *La Biblioteca Estense e la coltura ferrarese ai tempi del duca Ercole I (1471–1505)* (Turin: 1903) 169.

56 Bertoni G., *L'*Orlando Furioso *e la Rinascenza a Ferrara* (Modena: 1919) 308.

57 Catalano M., *Lucrezia Borgia, duchessa di Ferrara. Con nuovi documenti, note critiche un ritratto inedito* (Ferrara: 1920).

This thesis initially exercised a certain charm, and it was taken into consideration by Giuseppe Fatini,[58] who in 1924 published the text among the dubious rhymes of the author of *Orlando Furioso*.[59] Nevertheless, in two subsequent essays, Catalano retraced his steps. He starts from the observation that the source cited by Baruffaldi – the alleged *Descrizione dei funerali di Ercole Strozzi* written by Celio Calcagnini – was untraceable, nor was it possible to identify it with the funeral oration composed by Calcagnini for the first anniversary of Strozzi's death, and published by Aldo Manuzio among the Latin works of the Strozzi.[60] He also realised that the date of May 24, which corresponds to the thirteen days before the murder, could not be identified with that of the marriage between the two, as the expression 'amor legò' would suggest: in fact the wedding had already been celebrated on September 25 of the previous year. However still Catalano did not question Baruffaldi's good faith, believing that he, in turn, must have obtained the information from his source. He, therefore, considered the hypothesis that, like other contemporary scholars, Baruffaldi had been misled by the homonymy with Barbara Torelli Benedetti. Finally, he came across a letter in which Barbara Torelli Strozzi writes to the Marquis of Mantua, Francesco Gonzaga, that thirteen days before her husband's murder, an unfortunate daughter was born to her ('hora de tredici dì inanti che lui [Ercole Strozzi] manchasse, naque una sgratiata figliolina').[61] Therefore, the expression 'amor legò' must necessarily refer to her birth. Catalano concluded that the attribution should no longer be questioned and that the sonnet should be returned by right to Barbara. In an attempt to further strengthen this hypothesis, he searched for other poetic proofs of Torelli, coming across the testimonies of Faustini and Liberati, and subjecting them to scrutiny. Despite the unavailability of the manuscript sources cited by the two scholars, Catalano believed he could attribute to Torelli at least the sonnet *Nel tetto umile ove pien d'aspri affanni*. This is his final conclusion:

> Il rinvenimento dei codici Schincaglia e Rebuschi, da me inutilmente ricercati a Ferrara e a Parma, darebbe forse dati più sicuri che risolverebbero in modo definitivo l'attribuzione del sonetto. Ma, non ostante la mancanza dei due codici, le notizie che di essi si posseggono, congiunte

58 Ariosto Ludovico, *Lirica*, ed. G. Fatini (Bari: 1924) 261.

59 Fatini G., "Su la fortuna e l'autenticità delle liriche di L. Ariosto", *Giornale Storico della Letteratura Italiana*, Supplement 22–23 (1924) 133–296.

60 *Oratio tumultuaria habita in funere Herculis Strozzae*, in *Strozii poetae pater et filius* (Venice, Aldo Manutio: 1513), fol. 148–152.

61 Catalano, "La tragica morte" 232.

> ai nuovi elementi interpretativi della poesia, inducono a prestare fede alla tradizione che vuole la Strozzi autrice del sonetto.[62]
>
> (The discovery of the Schincaglia and Rebuschian manuscripts, sought in vain by me in Ferrara and Parma, would perhaps give more certain data that would definitively resolve the attribution of the sonnet. However, despite the lack of the two manuscripts, the information we possess about them, combined with the new interpretative elements of the poem, leads us to believe in the attribution to Strozzi's widow.)

The hypothesis remained in vogue for almost forty years, probably also thanks to the eagerness, displayed by publishers and anthologists, to welcome into their poetic collections such an early example of female poetry, linked to a rough outline of a story that had involved some of the most prominent personalities of the Este society of the time: Ariosto, Lucrezia Borgia and Pietro Bembo himself.

The question was reopened only in 1969, when Antonia Tissoni Benvenuti published, in the *Giornale storico della letteratura italiana*, an essay dedicated to an overall review of the forgeries – confirmed or still dubious – present in the anthology of the *Rime scelte*.[63]

Tissoni Benvenuti starts from the works of Catalano, verifying, in particular, the stability of the two main arguments put forward by him in favor of the sonnet's authenticity, namely the presence of other rhymes attributable to Torelli Strozzi and the coincidence of Giulia's date of birth. In addition to the scarcely reliable character of the testimonies of Faustini and Liberati – probably contaminated, as we have seen, by the proximity to the forger's environment – it is above all the unavailability of the Schincaglia and Rebuschian manuscripts that cast doubt on the first argument. She also rejects the attribution to Torelli of the sonnet *Nel tetto umile ove pien d'aspri affanni*, handed down together with *Spent'è d'amor la face* in the anthologies copied by Baruffaldi junior and Liberati, which is of significantly lower quality than ours. As for the coincidence of Giulia's date of birth, to which the words 'amor legò' should refer, Tissoni Benvenuti notes that this expression, admissible if anything for a firstborn, would have been excessive for a couple in which both had children from previous ties, and one with each other as well. Therefore, it should be interpreted as a reference to marriage, especially since in his drafts, particularly in the *Biblioteca*, Baruffaldi lays great emphasis on demonstrating that the two

62 Catalano, "La tragica morte" 235.

63 Tissoni Benvenuti, "Appunti".

were officially married at the time of the murder. Therefore, she deduces that one of the motivations that led him to falsify the sonnet must have been a desire to fabricate evidence to substantiate what he was saying.

An important incentive would also have come from the work of Crescimbeni, and from the desire to demonstrate, almost in an exercise of one-upmanship, that he was better informed than him. We saw this in the *addendum* inserted, later on, in the draft of the *Biblioteca*, which clearly shows its dependence on the *Comentarj*. Last but not least, the fact that the forger assumes an increasingly cautious – but also suspicious – attitude in giving news of the sources from which the text derived, first affirming, in the *Biblioteca*, that he possesses a handwritten copy, to then deciding to omit the compromising detail in the *Dissertatio*. In conclusion, Tissoni Benvenuti points out the proximity of the sonnet to another composition indeed composed by him, *Al sepolcro del divino Ariosto*, recited in March 1707, on the occasion of an 'adunanza' ('assembly') of the Accademia degli Intrepidi.[64] In addition to the 'civic pride' motive, therefore, Tissoni Benvenuti identifies the main reason for the imposture as demonstrating the marriage: so, once he discovered the date of birth of the daughter of the couple, he would have decided to use it to fabricate the proof that he lacked, also adding, in this way, a poetic composition of prestige to his collection.[65]

The work of Tissoni Benvenuti represents a turning point in the discussion on the authenticity of the text, allowing a first reconstruction of the process of composition and pointing out the main clues against the forger: the absence of previous witnesses, not only of the sonnet but also of possible poetic activity of Torelli – a figure who is anything but obscure, as we have seen, in the literary society of her time – and the suspicious character of some witnesses, like the ones of the Rebuschian and Schincaglia manuscripts. We can add some elements to this. First of all, the sonnet has been constructed starting from pre-existent materials, derived from both other works of Baruffaldi and other texts, of authentic or dubious authenticity. Furthermore, the quote of the epitaph by Tebaldeo and Bembo allows us to hypothesise that obituary verses like these, composed by such famous poets, have played a role in inspiring Baruffaldi to attribute to Barbara Torelli a sonnet entirely focusing on a wife's devotion to her dead husband.

The less convincing part of the work by Tissoni Benvenuti is that concerning the motives of the forger. As already stated, Tissoni Benvenuti argues that

64 Tissoni Benvenuti, "Appunti" 46, n. 1.
65 Ibidem.

Baruffaldi may have produced the forgery to fabricate proof of the marriage. Even if Baruffaldi was motivated, in this case, by a moral scruple – after all he was a priest – his principal reason must have been another. It seems probable that he was interested most of all in the possibility of inserting the composition of a woman in the *Rime scelte*, thus backdating the beginnings of female poetry in Ferrara by several decades. As we have seen, Baruffaldi was obsessed by records: in the *Ragionamento introduttivo* he assumes that poetry itself was born in Ferrara, and he tries to demonstrate it by counterfeiting the *Iscrizione ferrarese*, presented as the first example of poetic use of an Italian vernacular, as well as several poems assigned to the first centuries of Italian literature. At the same time, he shows a certain interest in female poetry: in the *Ragionamento* he enhances the role of the 'Donne Ferraresi [che] esercitarono la Poesia' ('Ferrarian women who practiced poetry'), while not sparing the reader the usual paternalistic touches. He observes that although it is always necessary to tolerate every defect in women ('tollerabile [...] ogni neo'), there is no need to do it in the case of the poetesses of Ferrara, as most of these 'poetarono di buon gusto' ('were very good at composing poetry'). Furthermore, they serve to increase the honor of the noble art of Poetry ('servono per degno ornamento dell'Opere, accrescendo onore alla nobilissima arte Poetica').[66] In the anthology of the *Rime scelte* there are in total seven Ferrarian poetesses, all real people, even if not all the texts attributed to them by Baruffaldi are surely authentic: Caterina Vegri, Aurelia Roverbella – or Roverella–, Orsina and Barbara Cavalletta, Benedetta Gamberini and Matilde Bentivoglio Calcagnini. If we exclude Caterina Vegri, who lived in the fifteenth century but was *sui generis*, since she wrote only spiritual poems, the first poetess in chronological order is Aurelia Roverbella – or Roverella – whose production originates from after the middle of the sixteenth century. Thus, Baruffaldi did not miss the opportunity to anticipate the birth of a female poetic tradition in Ferrara, by attributing a sonnet to a poetess like Barbara Torelli. She had a perfect pedigree: she was part of the prestigious cultural circle of the Este family and had a troubled marital past, which involved a famous Latin poet of Ariosto's time. It seems probable that he knew her story, also through the obituary verses which circulated at that time and which he quotes, including the detail of the thirteen days, probably misunderstood by the forger as referring to the marriage.

Another element that has not entered the discussion until now is the particular interest Baruffaldi had in the genealogy of the Torelli family, as evidenced by the fact that he composed a biography of Salinguerra Torelli.

66 Baruffaldi, *Rime scelte*, [15].

The work is probably lost for good, but we know about its existence through its being mentioned by Mazzucchelli in his *Scrittori d'Italia* as well as in the *Opere postume dell'arciprete Baruffaldi*, published in 1786 by the publisher Pomatelli of Ferrara.[67]

5 Conclusions

In this chapter, I have presented a representative and less investigated case study within the Italian tradition of forgeries, the sonnet *Spenta è d'amor la face, il dardo è rotto*, published by Girolamo Baruffaldi in the *Rime scelte* under the name of Barbara Torelli Strozzi. After an initial focus on the anthology, a profile of the presumed author and an analysis of the sonnet were presented. The following sections reconstruct the process of composition and the ensuing critical debates, with a final discussion of the motives of the forger. The principal aim of Baruffaldi was to promote the primacy of Ferrarian poetry in the Italian tradition, this time with regard to female production, contributing to a purpose that underlies the entire anthology. The analysis of the sonnet allows us to identify, in addition to the ones already identified by scholars, some further clues which expose the forger, and to recognise, at the same time, some habits characteristic of his *modus operandi*. I refer in particular to the re-use of others materials, from his or others' works, and to the involvement of other scholars. Through the production of new data, I demonstrate how the legend of the devotion of Ercole Strozzi's widow, not to be taken literally but fueled by the epitaphs composed by other famous poets of the time – such as Bembo, Tebaldeo and Ariosto – might have played a principle role in the composition of the forgery.

More problematic, relying on the data presented, is to establish precisely when Baruffaldi composed the forgery. The progressive increase of documentary evidence, starting with the draft of the *Rime scelte* in the *Opistographa* up to the citation of the epitaphs of Tebaldeo and Manuzio in the second edition of the *Dissertatio*, suggests that Baruffaldi might have discovered the figure of Barbara Torelli during his research on Ercole Strozzi, while he was working

67 *Gli scrittori d'Italia, cioè Notizie storiche, e critiche intorno alle vite, e agli scritti dei letterati italiani del conte Giammaria Mazzuchelli bresciano*, vol. II:i (Breschia, Giambatista Bossini: 1758) 493 (n° clx); *Rime serie, e giocose. Opere postume dell'arciprete Baruffaldi*, 3 vols. (Ferrara, Francesco Pomatelli: 1786–1787) I:80; the work, listed in the *Registro di tutte le opere* [...] *del dott. Girolamo Baruffaldi*, would have been in the volume entitled *Notizie d'Uomini Illustri* (n° 169).

on7he *Rime scelte*: his interest probably gradually increased to the point of inserting her into the collection with an independent voice.

In any case, the sonnet continued to enjoy a great success and to be republished in the numerous Italian *Parnasi* of the eighteenth and nineteenth centuries and many of the anthologies of our days. As Amedeo Quondam – who does not discuss the authenticity of the sonnet – has shown, its degree of diffusion in the anthologies of the twentieth century is perhaps the highest among the texts attributable to Petrarchism.[68] Moreover, it has also found wide acceptance in various works of Italian literature of the second half of the twentieth century, while it has been cited, even recently, in the comments of modern critical editions. It can therefore be considered a long-lasting forgery, which has been able to exercise an undisputed fascination upon the imagination of contemporaries and later readers.

Bibliography

Affò Ireneo, *Memorie degli scrittori e letterati parmigiani raccolte dal padre Ireneo Affò minor osservante Bibliotecario di S. A. R.* […], vol. 4 (Parma, Stamperia Reale: 1793).

Amaturo R., *Baruffaldi, Girolamo*, in *Dizionario Biografico degli Italiani*, vol. 7 (Rome: 1970) 6–9.

Ariosto Ludovico, *Lirica*, ed. G. Fatini (Bari: 1924).

Barotti Giannandrea, *Memorie istoriche di letterati ferraresi. Opera postuma di Giannandrea Barotti*, I (Ferrara, Stamperia Camerale: 1777).

Barotti Lorenzo, *Ai lettori*, in *Memorie istoriche di letterati ferraresi. Opera postuma di Giannandrea Barotti*, vol. 1 (Ferrara, Gli Eredi di Guiseppe Rinaldi: 1777).

Baruffaldi Girolamo, *Dissertatio de poetis ferrariensibus* […] (Ferrara, [n.p.]: 1698).

Baruffaldi Girolamo, *Ragionamento per introduzione alla presente raccolta*, in *Rime scelte de' poeti ferraresi antichi, e moderni. Aggiuntevi nel fine alcune brevi Notizie Istoriche intorno ad essi* (Ferrara, Bernardinus Pomatellus: 1713).

Baruffaldi Girolamo, *Giocasta la Giovane. Tragedia di scena mutabile del dottor Girolamo Baruffaldi ferrarese* (Venice, Girolamo Maranti Impressor Vescovile e del Sant' Ufizio: 1727).

Bellonci M., *Lucrezia Borgia. La sua vita, i suoi tempi* (Milan: 1947).

Bembo Pietro, *Carmina*, ed. R. Sodano (Turin: 1990).

Bembo Pietro, *Le rime*, ed. A. Donnini (Rome: 2008).

68 Quondam A., *Petrarchismo mediato: Per una critica della forma 'antologia'. Livelli d'uso nel sistema linguistico del petrarchismo* (Rome: 1974) 153.

Bertoni G., *La Biblioteca Estense e la coltura ferrarese ai tempi del duca Ercole I (1471–1505)* (Turin: 1903).
Bertoni G., *L'Orlando Furioso e la Rinascenza a Ferrara* (Modena: 1919).
Borsetti Ferranti Bolani Ferrante, *Historia almi Ferrariae gymnasii* (Ferrara, Bernardinus Pomatellus: 1735).
Boscolo Marchi M., *La cattedrale di Ferrara in età medievale* (Rome: 2016).
Carducci G., *Delle poesie latine edite ed inedite di Ludovico Ariosto* (Bologna: 1936).
Caro Annibal, *Amori pastorali*, ed. E. Garavelli (Manziana: 2002).
Le Carte Strozziane del R. Archivio di Stato in Firenze. Inventario, vol. 1 (Florence: 1884).
Catalano M., "La tragica morte di Ercole Strozzi e il sonetto di Barbara Torelli", *Archivum Romanicum* 10 (1926) 221–225.
Catalano M., *Lucrezia Borgia, duchessa di Ferrara. Con nuovi documenti, note critiche e un ritratto inedito* (Ferrara: 1920).
Comboni A., *Un falsario al lavoro: Girolamo Baruffaldi*, in Peron G. – Andreose A. (eds.), *Contrafactum. Copia, imitazione, falso. Atti del XXXII Convegno interuniversitario, Bressanone / Brixen, 8–11 Iuglio 2004* (Padova: 2008) 205–213.
Comboni A. – Russo C., "Per un archivio dei falsi letterari italiani. I testi dei primi secoli (secc. XII–XV)", *Filologia Italiana* 15 (2018) 27–76.
Cox V., *Lyric Poetry by Women of the Italian Renaissance* (Baltimore: 2013).
Crescimbeni Giovanni Mario, *Comentarj del canonico Gio. Mario Crescimbeni custode d'Arcadia, intorno alla sua Istoria della volgar poesia*, vol. 4 (Rome, Antonio de' Rossi alla Piazza di Ceri: 1711).
Crescimbeni Giovanni Mario, *La bellezza della volgar poesia* (Rome, Antonio de' Rossi alla Piazza di Ceri: 1712).
Damaschino Primo (Annibale Adami), *La spada d'Orione stellata nel cielo di Marte cioè il valore militare de' più Celebri Guerrieri de' nostri secoli*, Parte prima (Rome, [n.p.]: 1689).
Dionisotti C., "Appunti su antichi testi", *Italia medioevale e umanistica* 7 (1964) 77–131.
Fatini G., "Su la fortuna e l'autenticità delle liriche di L. Ariosto", *Giornale Storico della Letteratura Italiana, Supplement* 22–23 (1924) 133–296.
Filippi Marco, *Vita di Santa Caterina vergine e martire* (Venice, Guerra: 1592).
Fòrnari Simon, *La spositione di M. Simon Fornari da Reggio sopra l'Orlando Furioso di L. Ariosto* (Florence, Lorenzo Torrentino: 1549).
Giovio Paolo, *Elogia virorum literis illustrium* (Basel, Heinrich Petri: 1577).
Grafton A., *Forgers and Critics: Creativity and Duplicity in Western Scholarship* (Princeton NJ: 1990).
Lettere di Girolamo Tiraboschi al padre Ireneo Affò, tratte da' codd. della Biblioteca Estense di Modena e della Palatina di Parma, vol. 1 (Modena: 1894).
Monteverdi A., "Lingua italiana e Iscrizione ferrarese", in Monteverdi A. (ed.), *Cento e Duecento* (Rome: 1971) 7–24.

Monteverdi A., "Storia dell'Iscrizione ferrarese del 1135", in Monteverdi A. (ed.), *Cento e Duecento* (Rome: 1971) 25–95.

Muscetta C. – Ponchiroli D., *Parnaso italiano. Poesia del Quattrocento e del Cinquecento* (Turin: 1959).

Opere minori in verso e in prosa di Lodovico Ariosto, ordinate e annotate per cura di Filippo Luigi Polidori, vol. I (Florence: 1894).

Oratio tumultuaria habita in funere Herculis Strozzae, in *Strozii poetae pater et filius* (Venice, Aldo Manutio: 1513).

Petronio G., *La letteratura italiana. La civiltà della corte* (Milan: 1995).

Pictorii Ferrariensis Lodovici Bigi, *In coelestes proceres hymnorum epitaphiorumque liber. Eiusdem epigrammaton libelli duo* (Ferrara, [n.p.]: 1514).

Pignatti F., "Un madrigale sconosciuto di Ercole Strozzi", *Atti e Memorie dell'Arcadia* 7 (2018) 7–31.

Prose sacre di Anton Maria Salvini lettore di lettere greche nello Studio Fiorentino e Accademico della Crusca (Florence, Gio: Gaetano Tartini e Santi Franchi: 1716).

Prudhomme L.M., *Répertoire universel, historique, biographique des femmes célèbres, mortes ou vivantes* […] (Paris: 1826).

Quadrio Francesco Saverio, *Della storia e ragione d'ogni poesia*, 4 vols. (Bologna, Ferdinando Pisarri: 1739–1752).

Quondam A., *Petrarchismo mediato. Per una critica della forma antologia. Livelli d'uso nel sistema linguistico del petrarchismo* (Rome: 1974).

Rime serie, e giocose. Opere postume dell'arciprete Baruffaldi, 3 vols. (Ferrara, Francesco Pomatelli: 1786–1787).

Sampson L., *Torelli Benedetti, Barbara, in Dizionario Biografico degli Italiani*, vol. 26 (Turin: 2019).

Sanudo Marin, *I diarii*, vol. XXXVII (Venice: 1893).

Sapegno N., *Scrittori d'Italia. Secoli XVI–XVIII* (Florence: 1950).

Gli scrittori d'Italia, cioè Notizie storiche, e critiche intorno alle vite, e agli scritti dei letterati italiani del conte Giammaria Mazzuchelli bresciano, vol. II:i (Brescia, Giambatista Bossini: 1758).

Sonetti e canzoni di diversi antichi autori toscani in dieci libri raccolte (Florence, Giunta: 1527).

Strozii poetae pater et filius (Venice, [n.p.]: 1513).

Strozzi, Lorenzo di Filippo, *Le vite degli uomini illustri della casa Strozzi. Commentario di Lorenzo di Filippo Strozzi ora interamente pubblicato, con un ragionamento inedito di Francesco Zeffi sopra la vita dell'autore* ed. P. Stromboli (Florence: 1892).

Tartaro A. – Tateo F., *Il Quattrocento. L'età dell'Umanesimo, in La letteratura italiana. Storia e testi*, vol. III:1 (Rome – Bari: 1972).

Tiraboschi Girolamo, *Storia della letteratura italiana*, 13 vols. (Modena, Società Tipografica: 1772–1782).

Tissoni Benvenuti A., "Appunti sull'antologia dei poeti ferraresi di Girolamo Baruffaldi", *Giornale storico della letteratura italiana* 146 (1969) 18–48.
Torraca F., *Manuale della letteratura italiana. Sec. XVI* (Florence: 1911).
Vagni G., "Su un sonetto di Ercole Strozzi già attribuito a Baldassarre Castiglione", *Aevum* 85:3 (2011) 751–775.
Volume primo de' Baccanali di Girolamo Baruffaldi, seconda edizione (Bologna, Lelio dalla Volpe: 1758).

CHAPTER 7

The Deceptive Power of a Monogram: Appropriating Dürer's Identity in the Sixteenth and Early Seventeenth Centuries

Ksenija Tschetschik-Hammerl

Putting a signature on a document can generally be interpreted in the framework of speech act theory as *performative*.[1] John Austin defines the term *performative* as follows: 'The name is derived, of course, from "perform", the usual verb with the noun "action": it indicates that the issuing of the utterance is the performing of an action – it is not normally thought of as just saying something'.[2] Whereas in the legal context as well as in some other aspects of ordinary life a signature indeed fulfils the performance of authorisation or authentication, the performative capacity of signatures in art can be much more diverse and complex.

Several comprehensive studies in the last decades have examined the wide range of signatures deployed by western artists from the Middle Ages to the Early Modern period and have shown that the function of signatures within various artistic practices goes beyond a mere statement of authorship.[3]

1 I am very grateful to my doctoral supervisors Professor Bettina Uppenkamp and Professor Horst Bredekamp with whom I could discuss various aspects of this topic. If not otherwise indicated, the translations of quotations in English are mine.

2 Austin J.L., *How To Do Things With Words: The William James Lectures Delivered at Harvard University in 1955* (Oxford: 1962) 6. Austin focuses mainly on spoken utterances. Nevertheless, he casually refers to signatures as performatives without dealing with them thoroughly. See Austin, *How To Do Things With Words* 62. On signatures generally, see Macho Th., "Handschrift – Schriftbild: Anmerkungen zu einer Geschichte der Unterschrift", in Grube G. – Kogge W. – Krämer S. (eds.), *Schrift: Kulturtechnik zwischen Auge, Hand und Maschine* (Munich: 2005) 413–422; Fraenkel B., "La signature: du signe à l'acte", *Sociétés & Représentations* 25.1 (2008) 13–23.

3 On the functioning of signatures in the Middle Ages, see Białostocki J., "Begegnung mit dem Ich in der Kunst", *Artibus et Historiae* 1:1 (1980) 25–45; Claussen P.C., "Früher Künstlerstolz: Mittelalterliche Signaturen als Quelle der Kunstsoziologie", in Clausberg K. (ed.), *Bauwerk und Bildwerk im Hochmittelalter: Anschauliche Beiträge zur Kultur- und Sozialgeschichte* (Giessen: 1981) 7–34; Dietl A., *Die Sprache der Signatur: Die mittelalterlichen Künstlerinschriften Italiens* (Florence: 2009); Bredekamp H., *Image Acts: A Systematic Approach to Visual Agency*, trans., ed. and adapted E. Clegg (Berlin: 2018) 45–62. An illuminating and methodically innovative study on signatures deployed by several prominent European artists from the Early Modern

 | DOI:10.1163/9789004106901_008

By putting a signature on their artworks artists also conferred on these objects their attitudes, ambitions and art-theoretical reflections. Of particular interest for this essay is one remarkable category of identity marks, which is most elusive and indeed seems to contradict the very notion of the signature as a vehicle of additional information within an artwork. Several Renaissance artists deployed signatures that seem to have been intended either to withhold information or even to mislead. This category of signatures has been defined in literature as 'unexpected' ('imprévue'), 'illusionistic', 'hidden' or 'encrypted' ('versteckt', 'rébus').[4] Certainly one has to be cautious when assessing the legibility of encrypted signatures from earlier times.[5] Nevertheless several Renaissance artists evidently intended to complicate their signature's legibility, either to stress particular visual qualities of their works or to allude to their exceptional artistic or social standing.[6] As an example, the Italian artist Jacopo Ligozzi, who in the late sixteenth century was active as painter and natural history illustrator at the Medici court in Florence, once hid his tiny monogram in the shade of a large caterpillar depicted as a part of his portrayal of a spurge.[7]

period offers Gludovatz K., *Fährten legen – Spuren lesen: Die Künstlersignatur als poetische Referenz* (Munich: 2011). On the role of signatures in the work and career of Artemisia Gentileschi, see Mann W.J., "Identity Signs: Meanings and Methods in Artemisia Gentileschi's signatures", *Renaissance Studies* 23:1 (2009) 71–107.

4 For the 'imprévue' and the 'rébus' signatures, see Perrot F., "La signature imprévue", *Revue de L'Art* 26 (1974) 33–39; Lebensztejn J.-C., "Esquisse d'une typologie", *Revue de L'Art* 26 (1974) 48–56, Gandelman C., "The Semiotics of Signatures in Painting: A Peircian Analysis", *American Journal of Semiotics* 3:3 (1985) 83–86. For 'Versteckte Signaturen' ('hidden signatures'), see Burg T., *Die Signatur: Formen und Funktionen vom Mittelalter bis zum 17. Jahrhundert* (Munster: 2007) 367–377. Burg sees 'hidden signatures' as a sub-category within 'illusionistic signatures'.

5 This is in particular true for self-portraits that artists occasionally inserted in the visual narratives of their works as substitutes of their signatures. Those self-representations could have been easily recognised by artist's acquaintances during his or her lifetime but are much harder to identify for us today. For self-representations as signatures, see Stoichita V.I., *The Self-Aware Image: An Insight into Early Modern Meta-Painting*, trans. A.-M. Glasheen (Cambridge: 1997) 198–267; Burg, *Die Signatur* 377–388.

6 The Dutch landscape artist Herri met de Bles inserted a small figure of an owl in his pictures as his identity mark. His biographer Karel van Mander defined the function of this mark as follows: 'This was the master of the owl who put into all his works a little owl, which is sometimes so hidden away that people allow each other a lot of time to look for it wagering that they will not find it anyway and thus pass their time, looking for the owl.' See Mander Karel van, *The Lives of the Illustrious Netherlandish and German Painters from the First Edition of the 'Schilder-boeck' (1603–1604)*, ed. H. Miedema, vol. 1 (Doornspijk: 1994) 137. Also see Burg, *Die Signatur* 424–426.

7 Jacopo Ligozzi, *Spurge* (*Euphorbia dendroides L.*), 1587. Bodycolours on paper, 67 × 45 cm. Florence, Gabinetto dei Disegni e delle Stampe delle Gallerie degli Uffizi, inv. 1956 O, see Faietti M., "Dentro alle 'cose di natura': Lo sguardo di Jacopo", in Cecchi A. – Conigliello L. –

The artist seems to have foreseen a surprising moment of discovery of his monogram which thus functions as secondary evidence of his artistic virtuosity. Patricia Rubin describes the functioning of 'an extremely coy form of inscription' Titian employed in the series of pictures he made for the *Camerino* of the Duke Alfonso d'Este as follows: '[…] and Titian's slight signatures added but one more detail for close inspection, sudden discovery and amused delight'.[8]

Unfortunately, scholars and connoisseurs of art have so far gained little insight from dealing with the dubious monograms that can be found on various objects of art from the sixteenth and seventeenth centuries and can be mistaken for the authentic 'AD'-signs of the Nuremberg painter and engraver Albrecht Dürer (1471–1528). The deceptive potential of those signatures predisposed them to place such monograms alongside a range of falsified 'AD's. Indeed, many falsified monograms were later added to genuine or non-genuine works of the Nuremberg artist by other hands and were most likely often meant to increase the market value of the objects they were set on.[9] However, as I am going to argue in this essay on selected examples, potentially deceptive 'AD'-marks from the sixteenth and early seventeenth centuries were not always necessarily forgeries. Indeed, a more nuanced approach to the imitation of Dürer's monogram in the Early Modern period can contribute to our understanding of the meta-pictorial functioning of hidden or encrypted signatures.

The German art historian Hans Kauffmann was the first scholar who considered the practice of imitating of Dürer's monograms as part of the phenomenon of Dürer's increased reception at different places in Europe around 1600,

---

Faietti M. (eds.), *Jacopo Ligozzi, 'pittore universalissimo'*, exh. cat. Florence, Palazzo Pitti, Galleria Palatina (Florence – Livorno: 2014) 39–45, fig. 1 and fig. 5 (detail of the monogram), 40–44.

8 Rubin P., "Signposts of Invention: Artists' Signatures in Italian Renaissance Art", *Art History* 29:4 (2006) 564.

9 See Meder J., *Die Handzeichnung: Ihre Technik und Entwicklung* (Vienna: 1919) 693; Tietze H., *Genuine and False: Copies, Imitations, Forgeries* (London: 1948) 13. Otto Kurz summarised about all kinds of deceptive 'AD's: 'Dürer's popular monogram was freely employed to stamp as an original by his hand any work which was supposed to represent his style. […] This degradation of a signature to a mere trade-mark is a rather unimaginative kind of fraud.' See Kurz O., *Fakes: A Handbook for Collectors and Students* (New Haven: 1948) 33. Lisa Oehler studied the 'AD'-monograms on works of Dürer's contemporaries, mainly the Nuremberg artist's disciples. Oehler proposed to view these falsified monograms as a visual sign of the follower's tribute to the master. Nevertheless, Oehler's stylistic attributions need a re-assessment. See Oehler L., "Das Dürermonogramm auf Werken der Dürerzeit", *Städel-Jahrbuch* 3 (1971) 79–108; Oehler L., "Das Dürermonogramm auf Werken der Dürerschule", *Städel-Jahrbuch* 4 (1973) 36–80.

a period which is often named the *Dürer-Renaissance*.[10] Kauffmann's observation remained, however, literally only a remark and has barely been pursued further in subsequent studies. Although the growing scholarly interest in the social, economic and art-theoretical foundations for Dürer's popularity among artists and collectors in the Early Modern period, and in particular during the *Dürer-Renaissance*, has resulted in a number of comprehensive studies and exhibitions on this subject, the issue of the deceptive 'AD'-monograms has either remained neglected or has only been vaguely linked to artists' commercial strategies.[11] Not denying the fact that commercial success had a strong impact on artistic strategies of self-promotion in the Early Modern period, for which Dürer himself offers an example, I will argue in what follows that imitations of Dürer's monograms often had a more subtle objective than just to serve as a means of commercial fraud. Moreover, to regard imitations of Dürer's monograms merely as more or less malevolently intended forgeries ignores that in the Early Modern period the act of deception enjoyed a rather positive reputation.[12]

10 Kauffmann H., "Dürer in der Kunst und im Kunsturteil um 1600", *Anzeiger des Germanischen Nationalmuseums in Nürnberg* (1954) 30–31.

11 The term *Dürer-Renaissance* describes the huge popularity among collectors, mostly in German speaking regions around 1600, and the tendency among artists in the same time period to imitate Dürer's works. For the first mentioning of the term, see Tietze H. – Tietze-Conrat E., *Kritisches Verzeichnis der Werke Albrecht Dürers*, vol. 2 (Basel – Leipzig: 1928–1938) 256–260; see also more recently Bartrum G., "The Dürer Renaissance, c. 1570–c. 1630", in Bartrum G. (ed.), *Albrecht Dürer and His Legacy: The Graphic Work of a Renaissance Artist*, exh. cat. London, The British Museum (London: 2002) 266–267. Gustav Glück, who wrote one of the first articles on Dürer's imitations from the sixteenth and the seventeenth centuries, did not differentiate between imitations and forgeries and was inclined to use the last term for works bearing a 'false' Dürer-monogram. See Glück G., "Fälschungen auf Dürers Namen", *Jahrbuch der Kunsthistorischen Sammlungen des Allerhöchsten Kaiserhauses* 28 (1909/1910) 1–27. Joseph L. Koerner defines a range of possibilities for which the imitations of Dürer monograms could have been aimed: 'Spurious Dürer monograms, for their part, can mean many things: that a work pretends to be by Dürer, that it is copied from him, that it comes from his shop, that it pays homage to him, that it has been attributed to him by some collectors.' See Koerner J.L., "Albrecht Dürer: A Sixteenth-Century *Influenza*", in Bartrum G. (ed.), *Albrecht Dürer and His Legacy* 27. Andrea Bubenik in her book on Dürer's reception also acknowledges: 'The Dürer monogram could also be used by artists as a sign of respect or homage.' The art historian does however not elaborate on this subject. See Bubenik A., *Reframing Albrecht Dürer: The Appropriation of Art, 1528–1700* (Farnham – Burlington: 2013) 82. Anja Grebe in her book on Dürer's reception through several centuries interprets all kinds of imitations, including monograms, from the perspective of commercial interests of artists or collectors, see Grebe A., *Dürer: Die Geschichte seines Ruhms* (Petersberg: 2013).

12 For the appreciation of illusion in the Renaissance and Baroque art theory and practice, see Brusati C., *Artifice and Illusion: The Art and Writing of Samuel van Hoogstraten* (Chicago – London: 1995).

In this chapter I will show that by deploying monograms that could be misattributed to Dürer artists did in fact not intend to obscure their identities, but, on the contrary, strove to strengthen the esteem of their artworks by employing the performative capacities of deceptive monograms. The scope of artists who designed their monograms imitating Dürer's famous identity sign is quite broad.[13] This study will focus on monograming practices of the artists Albrecht Altdorfer, Heinrich Aldegrever, Hans Hoffmann and Ambrosius Bosschaert the Elder. It is the first time this selection of artists is brought together and I will show that these four very different artists can indeed be united by the principle that they all often or occasionally risked to deceive their viewers through their monograms. The discussion of monograming practices as strategies of self-fashioning by Albrecht Altdorfer and Heinrich Aldegrever will be followed by an examination of the interplay between the imitation of Dürer's sign and the illusionistic depiction of nature in the work of Hans Hoffmann and Ambrosius Bosschaert. To begin with, it is important to make a short introduction into the question of how Dürer's monograms could have become a powerful source of imitation for other artists.

1 Dürer's Monograms as a Source of Inspiration

Albrecht Dürer belongs to those early modern artists who signed all sorts of creative outputs very frequently. This remarkable consistency is rooted in Dürer's early engagement with printmaking, since it was exactly in this innovative artistic technology that the pioneer printmakers started, by the second half of the fifteenth century, to use their signatures and monograms as a kind of trademark.[14] Dependent upon the commercial success of their printed images, the artists could have them sold far away from their hometowns, where the catchy monograms had to serve for the potential buyers as guarantors of authorship and quality.[15] However, in contrast with his older colleagues who

13 The artists who are known to have imitated Dürer's monogram are the Augsburg sculptor Hans Daucher (1485–1538), the Nuremberg sculptor Georg Schweiger (1613–1690), the Riva-born medallist Antonio Abondio (1538–1591), the Dutch sculptor Adrian de Vries (1556–1626), the two Italian engravers from Mantua Adamo Scultori (*c.* 1530–1587) and Andrea Andreani (1558/59–1629). I am very grateful to Barbara Furlotti for drawing my attention to Adamo Scultori.

14 On the usage of monograms and dates in early prints, see Burg, *Die Signatur* 456–473; Landau D. – Parshall P., *The Renaissance Print, 1470–1550* (New Haven – London: 1994) 46–50.

15 For the commercial purpose of monograms in printed images, see Koerner J.L., *The Moment of Self-Portraiture in German Renaissance Art* (Chicago – London: 1993) 203–223. More specific on Dürer's entrepreneurship, see Schmid W., "Dürer's Enterprise: Market

specialised in printmaking, like for instance Martin Schongauer, Dürer was not content with restricting a monogram's purpose to a simple declaration of authorship.[16] As the art historian Philipp Fehl has brilliantly demonstrated, the Nuremberg artist endowed his monogram with characteristics of an encrypted and lively self:

> In his prints Dürer never shows himself fully identifiable as a person. He is there in the effigy of his signatures only, but the signature has a life of its own and claims a place in the world of his prints in which the present and the contemplated past are joined, [...]. As is well known, Dürer's famous combination of the letters 'A' and 'D' also is a pun on his name. The A in the construction with a horizontal beam represents a door, or Thür, Thürer, Dürer.[17]

Indeed, from around 1500, Dürer started to integrate his monograms in the visual narrative of his printed compositions not only spatially, but occasionally even emotionally. In the woodcut *The Adoration of the Shepherds* from the series *Small Woodcut Passion*, for instance, Dürer reversed the letter 'D' into the direction of the Christ Child, thus emphasizing the focus of the composition, but also creating an impression that his monogram joins the shepherds in their veneration of the Nativity scene.[18] In the image *The Kiss of Judas* from the same printed series, Dürer's monogram can be found in the lower right corner of the composition.[19] The monogram looks like it was collapsed on its side and appears as if it is shaken in the face of the turbulent and violent atmosphere of the represented event. In his prints Dürer's monograms thus seem to fulfil

Area – Market Potential – Product Range", in North M. (ed.), *Economic History and the Arts* (Cologne: 1996) 27–47.

16 For the signing practices of the painter and engraver Martin Schongauer, see Naß M., "Stellung und Bedeutung des Monogramms Martin Schongauers in der Graphik des 15. Jahrhunderts", in Krohm H. – Nicolaisen J. (eds.), *Martin Schongauer: Druckgraphik im Berliner Kupferstichkabinett* (Berlin: 1991) 48–62.

17 Fehl Ph., "Dürer's Literal Presence in his Pictures: Reflections on his Signatures in the Small Woodcut Passion", in Winner M. (ed.), *Der Künstler über sich in seinem Werk* (Weinheim: 1992) 192.

18 Albrecht Dürer, *The Adoration of the Shepherds* (*The Small Passion*, 5), *c.* 1510. Woodcut, 12.7 × 9.8 cm, see Schoch R. – Mende M.– Scherbaum A. (eds.), *Albrecht Dürer: Das druckgraphische Werk*, vol. 2 (Munich: 2001–2004) no. 190, 293–294. For the interpretation of the 'AD'-monogram, see Fehl, "Dürer's Literal Presence" 197.

19 Albrecht Dürer, *The Kiss of Judas* (*The Small Passion*, 11), *c.* 1509. Woodcut, 12.8 × 9.8 cm, see Schoch – Mende – Scherbaum, *Albrecht Dürer*, vol. 2 no. 197, 304–305. For the interpretation of the 'AD'-monogram, see Fehl, "Dürer's Literal Presence" 198.

several purposes at once. On the one hand, they are intended to intensify the visual effect of the compositions. 'They are, again and again, of the salt that gives the stories their taste, [...]' as Philipp Fehl elegantly puts it.[20] On the other hand, they also secure the permanent presence of the artist's self within his creations. Dürer was indeed exceptionally concerned with the preservation of his image in the historical memory and continuously worked on forming his own posthumous image throughout his various self-portraits, inscriptions and other written documents. Joseph Leo Koerner, analysing Dürer's earliest self-portrait, in which the artist, as an older man, identified himself as a thirteen-year old boy, noticed:

> Before passing his youthful portrait on to us, the aging Dürer remembers it in the inscription he composes. Image and word represent the confrontation of future with past such as shall be replayed in countless acts of 'gedächtnus'.[21]

Perhaps in particular because of his confrontation with the medium of printmaking and the conditions of its trade, Dürer was remarkably aware of the fact that the audiences for his works were to surpass Nuremberg and his own times. His frequent deployment of the 'AD'-sign on his works and in particular on his drawings can be regarded as an essential part of his strategy to create a powerful doppelgänger of himself which could sustain a vivid impact on future beholders, even in the artist's absence.

2 Self-Fashioning Through Confusion

Already during Albrecht Dürer's lifetime several artists started to imitate the 'AD'-monogram in order to fashion their own artistic reputation by referring to a renowned colleague. Albrecht Altdorfer (*c.* 1480–1538) was one of the first artists who designed his own identity sign with a strong reference to Dürer's monogram and also seems to have sought to induce a deceptive effect. The artist was only slightly younger than Albrecht Dürer and, during his career, advanced to a highly respectable public position as artist and political figure in his native Regensburg. Altdorfer frequently signed his prints and drawings with a characteristic monogram comprising two capital letters 'A'. As Christopher Wood

---

20 Fehl, "Dürer's Literal Presence" 197.

21 Koerner, *The Moment of Self-Portraiture* 44. See also Albrecht Dürer, *Self-Portrait*, 1484. Silverpoint on prepared paper, 27.3 × 19.5 cm. Vienna, Albertina Museum.

rightly observes: 'Altdorfer's monogram itself, with its A nested within a larger A, directly emulated Dürer's'.[22] Dürer's early printed images like, for example, his woodcut series *Apocalypse* became widely known and highly esteemed shortly after they were initially issued in 1498; thus it is hardly surprising that Altdorfer should have had an interest to refer in his works to the authority of his Nuremberg colleague.[23] A particular variation of the 'AA'-monogram, however, which can be found on three early drawings by Altdorfer, further suggests that the Regensburg artist conspicuously explored the power of his works to invoke the illusion of Dürer's authorship. The three early drawings *Two Women Holding a Basket with Fruits*, *Samson and Delilah* and *Witches Sabbath* feature a very particular type of the artist's monogram; within the inner 'A' of the 'AA'-sign one may also distinguish a tiny curl, likely identifiable as letters 'O' or 'D' [Figs. 7.1–7.2].[24]

Karl Oettinger has argued that the enclosed sign constituted an 'O', explaining this with Altdorfer's supposed intention to fashion himself in the Italian manner as 'Alberto Altdorfio'.[25] Even though Altdorfer's interest in contemporary Italian printmaking is evident by his works, it still appears very unlikely that he should have abbreviated his fictionally Italianated name to his monogram.[26] In another interpretation it has been argued that the tiny curl does indeed

22 Wood Ch.S., *Albrecht Altdorfer and the Origins of Landscape* (London: 1993) 79.

23 For the innovative character of Dürer's *Apocalypse* and its early popularity, see Krüger P., "Die Apokalypse", in Schoch – Mende – Scherbaum, *Albrecht Dürer*, vol. 2, 59–105. On Dürer's early fame, see Białostocki J., *Dürer and his Critics. 1500–1971: Chapters in the History of Ideas Including a Collection of Texts* (Baden-Baden: 1986); more recently Grebe, *Dürer* 25–169.

24 Albrecht Altdorfer, *Samson and Delilah*, 1506. Pen and ink, heightened with white, on brown prepared paper, 17.1 × 12.2 cm. New York, The Metropolitan Museum of Art; *Witches Sabbath*, 1506. Pen and black ink, heightened with white, on brick red prepared paper, 17.9 × 12.4 cm. Paris, Musée du Louvre, Département des Arts graphiques. See Mielke H. (ed.), *Albrecht Altdorfer: Zeichnungen, Deckfarbenmalerei, Druckgraphik*, exh. cat. Berlin, Kupferstichkabinett; Museen der Stadt Regensburg (Berlin: 1988) no. 2, 28–29; Grollemundl H. – Savatier Sjöholm O. – Lepape S. (eds.), *Albrecht Altdorfer: Maître de la Renaissance allemande*, exh. cat. Paris, Musée du Louvre (Paris: 2020) no. 15a, 80–81.

25 Oettinger K., *Datum und Signatur bei Wolf Huber und Albrecht Altdorfer, zur Beschriftungskritik der Donauschulzeichnungen*, Erlangen Forschungen 8 (Erlangen: 1957) 47–48.

26 The impact of the Italian engravings, in particular *nielli* as well as engravings from the workshop of Andrea Mantegna, on Altdorfer's graphic style and compositions has often been outlined in the scholarship. The drawing *Two Women Holding a Basket with Fruits* points to Altdorfer's knowledge of Peregrino da Cesena's *Allegory of Abundance*, 1490–*c.* 1520. Engraving printed from a plate engraved in the *niello* manner, 4.1 × 2.8 cm. London, The British Museum, see Bushart M., "Intermedialität um 1500: Wechselwirkungen zwischen Druckgraphik und Malerei in der Kunst der Dürerzeit", in Fajt J. – Jaeger S. (eds.), *Das Expressive in der Kunst 1500–1550: Albrecht Altdorfer und seine Zeitgenossen* (Berlin – Munich: 2018) 49–50. The parallel hatchings on the Berlin drawing also remind

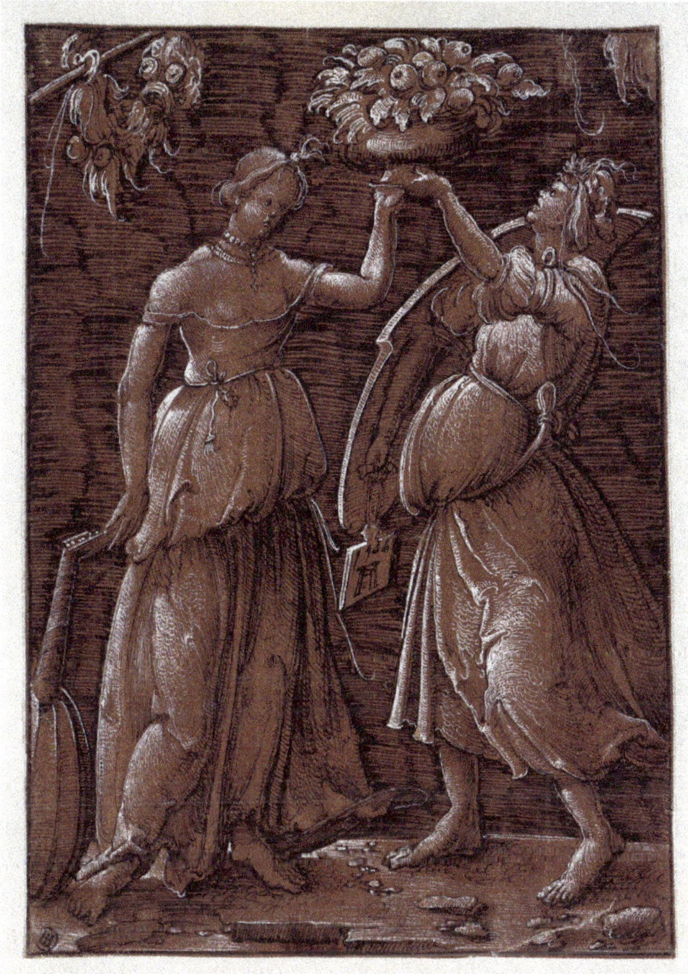

FIGURE 7.1 Albrecht Altdorfer, *Two Women Holding a Basket with Fruits*, 1506. Pen and ink, heightened with white, on red-brown prepared paper, 17.3 × 12.3 cm
BERLIN, STAATLICHE MUSEEN, KUPFERSTICHKABINETT. IMAGE BPK / KUPFERSTICHKABINETT, SMB / JÖRG P. ANDERS

form a 'D', and thus a reference to Dürer, but that it was just a later addition to Altdorfer's three drawings by collectors or art dealers.[27] This hypothesis builds

of the engraving *Four Muses Dancing* from Andrea Mantegna's workshop, after 1497, see Grollemund – Savatier Sjöholm – Lepape, *Albrecht Altdorfer* no. 4b, 54.

27 In a recent exhibition catalogue on Altdorfer we find the following remark in the entry to Altdorfer's Berlin drawing *Two Women Holding a Basket with Fruits* (here named as

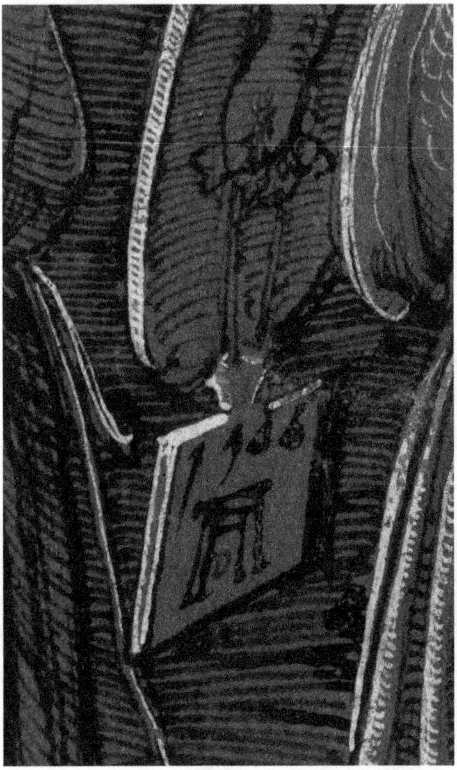

FIGURE 7.2
Albrecht Altdorfer, detail with the artist's monogram of *Two Women Holding a Basket with Fruits*, 1506
BERLIN, STAATLICHE MUSEEN, KUPFERSTICHKABINETT.
IMAGE BPK / KUPFERSTICHKABINETT, SMB / JÖRG P. ANDERS

on the fact that many drawings by Dürer's contemporaries had been posthumously initialled with false 'AD's. Nevertheless, the monograms on Altdorfer's three drawings reveal no traces of deploying a different ink from the rest of the composition.[28] Furthermore, the tiny size of the included curl makes it hard to believe that any artistically unsolidified hand of a collector dared to execute

Allegory with Euterpe and Victoria) 'ein "D" zwischen den Schenkeln des "A" von späterer Hand' ('a "D" within the limbs of the 'A' is by later hand'). The author, however, gives no explanation to this assertion. See Roller S. – Sander J. (eds.), *Fantastische Welten: Albrecht Altdorfer und das Expressive in der Kunst um 1500*, exh. cat. Frankfurt am Main, Städel Museum and Liebieghaus Skulpturensammlung; Vienna, Kunsthistorisches Museum (Frankfurt am Main – Munich: 2014) no. 95, 175.

28 Hans Mielke remarked on the Berlin drawing: 'Eingehende Betrachtung des Originals, auch bei beträchtlicher Vergrößerung, spricht für den eigenhändigen Eintrag des Kringels durch den Zeichner' ('Thorough examination of the original, even by employing considerable magnification, points to the execution of the curl by the artist himself'). See Mielke, *Albrecht Altdorfer: Zeichnungen* no. 5, 32. My own study of the original drawing in Berlin also led me to the conclusion that the curl, or a letter 'D' as I interpret it, has been drawn by the same hand as the whole drawing.

it. Instead, Altdorfer was evidently very fond of tiny elements, as his drawings reveal. Moreover, in the Berlin drawing *Two Women Holding a Basket with Fruits* we also find a quite explicit reference to Dürer in the shape of the fictional squarish tablet with handle inscribed with a monogram. Such fictional supports of monograms were widely used by Dürer himself in his printed images.[29] Therefore, I am inclined to assume that Altdorfer included the tiny 'D's in the three variants of his monograms with the deliberate intention to confer them with a deceptive potential. Altdorfer's reference to Dürer in his monograms can be generally understood as a reflection on the origin of his style, since the Regensburg artist was apparently influenced by Dürer's vivid and highly innovative graphic language.[30] However, Altdorfer not only strove to be compared with Dürer, as his drawings with tiny 'D's imply, he overtly intended to cause a confusion of attribution. Several other ways in which the Regensburg artist employed his monograms also support the impression that the artist, through the signing of his works, sought to induce the effect of visual uncertainty. Altdorfer often obscured his monograms by putting them in deep shadow on printed images or by executing them in a very loose manner on several of his drawings, as if intending to provoke the beholder to doubt his or her vision and subsequently to draw a closer look on Altdorfer's works.[31]

Another example of an early imitation of Dürer's monogram can be found in the oeuvre of the German printmaker Heinrich Aldegrever (*c.* 1502–1555/1561). He was born in the Westphalian Paderborn and was active in the neighbouring

29 Lisa Pon observes that Marcantonio Raimondi used the image of a blank tablet with handle as reference to Dürer. See Pon L., *Raphael, Dürer, and Marcantonio Raimondi: Copying and the Italian Renaissance Print* (New Haven – London: 2004) 70–72.

30 For Altdorfer's dependence on Dürer's style and personality, see Wood Ch.S., *Albrecht Altdorfer* 70–71; Bushart M., *Sehen und Erkennen: Albrecht Altdorfers religiöse Bilder* (Munich – Berlin: 2004) 57–73; Messling G., "Anarchist und Apelles? Altdorfer und der deutsche Humansimus", in Roller – Sander, *Fantastische Welten* 22.

31 For obscured 'AA'-monograms on engravings, see *Venus with Two Putti*, *c.* 1512–1515. Engraving, 6 × 3.5 cm; *Pyramus and Thisbe*, *c.* 1515–1518. Engraving, 6.2 × 4.1 cm. both in London, The British Museum. For loose 'AA'-monograms that are almost undistinguishable from meaningless loops and other curls within Altdorfer's drawings, see *Wild Man Carrying an Uprooted Tree*, 1508. Pen and black ink, heightened with white, on red-brown prepared paper. London, British Museum, in Grollemund – Savatier Sjöholm – Lepape, *Albrecht Altdorfer* no. 16b, 82–83; *St Nicholas of Bari Rebuking the Tempest*, 1508. Pen and brown ink, heightened with white, on brick-red prepared paper, 19.2 × 14.7 cm. Oxford, Ashmolean Museum, in Mielke, *Albrecht Altdorfer. Zeichnungen* no. 21, 54–55. For the connection between Altdorfer's monograms and his graphic style, see Tschetschik-Hammerl K., "Das Dürer-Monogramm als Gegenstand der Nachahmung im 16. und frühen 17. Jahrhundert", in Dressen A. – Gramatzki S. – Knoblich B. (eds.), *Original – Kopie – Fälschung II*, kunsttexte.de 3 (2018) 11–13.

Soest. Despite assertions by some earlier art-historians there is no evidence that the artist either visited Dürer in his Nuremberg workshop or met the master on some other occasion.[32] Similar to Hoffmann and Altdorfer, he was instead acquainted with Dürer through the master's works. Aldegrever diligently studied Dürer's printed images, which, as in Altdorfer's case, were easily accessible to him, and subsequently produced engravings of his own, which show a varying dependence on Dürer's compositions. Like several other printmakers of his generation, by-named in art-historical literature as the *Kleinmeister* (Little Masters), he also specialised in engravings of very small dimensions that were appreciated by art lovers of his time as items worthy to collect. Though small and often densely crowded, Aldegrever's engravings always feature the artist's monogram. Following Dürer's model, he experimented with various ways to imbed his monogram in the visual narrative of his compositions, like inscribing it on fictional tablets or stones. But the strongest reference to Dürer in Aldegrever's prints is ensured by the design of his monogram, comprising a capital 'A' enclosing a 'G' which looks very much like a 'D'. Indeed, the similarity of Aldegrever's monogram with Dürer's signature is so strikingly illusive that it can easily provoke a confusion. The deceptive power of Aldegrever's monograms has been conventionally explained as a means to increase the market value of the artist's prints.[33] A closer look at his printed images reveals, however, an artistic personality who not only creatively interpreted Dürer's visual inventions but also developed many printed series illustrating quite unconventional allegorical and biblical subjects. His works were obviously valued for their own sake, since they often served as models for other printmakers. As has

32 The early scholarship on Aldegrever was eagerly interested in emphasising his connection to Dürer, see Tross L., "Aldegrever, Maler und Kupferstecher in der Stadt Soest", *Westphalia: Zeitschrift für Geschichte und Alterthumskunde Westphalens und Rheinlands* 3 (1826) 4–7; Gehrken F.J., "Heinrich Aldegrever, Goldschmied, Maler, Kupferstecher und Prägschneider: Biographisch und kunsthistorisch", *Westfälische Zeitschrift: Zeitschrift für vaterländische Geschichte und Altertmskunde* 4.5 (1841) 145–165; Zschelletzschky H., *Das graphische Werk Heinrich Aldegrevers: Ein Beitrag zu seinem Stil im Rahmen der deutschen Stilentwicklung* (Strasbourg: 1933) 23–25. The consensus of the recent scholarship is that there is no evidence that Aldegrever could have been either Dürer's assistant or have visited Nuremberg, see "Introduction", Bevers H. – Mielke U. – Wiebel Ch. (eds.), *Heinrich Aldegrever, The New Hollstein: German Engravings, Etchings and Woodcuts, 1400–1700*, 3 (Rotterdam: 1998) 11–12; Knauer M., *Dürers unfolgsame Erben: Bildstrategien in den Kupferstichen der deutschen Kleinmeister* (Petersberg: 2013) 42.

33 For a commercial interpretation of Aldegrever's monograms, see Knauer M., "Kupferstiche der deutschen Kleinmeister: Zur Erforschung eines Bildmediums in einer Epoche kulturellen Umbruchs", Möseneder K. (ed.), *Zwischen Dürer und Raffael: Graphikserien Nürnberger Kleinmeister* (Petersberg: 2010) 14; Grebe, *Dürer* 198.

been stated: 'The copies of Aldegrever's prints are witness to the fact that his art must have caught the mood of the moment'.[34]

Moreover, Aldegrever's early *Self-Portrait* from 1530 presents the Westphalian printmaker as an exceptionally self-conscious artist who was obviously interested in the dissemination of his countenance through the replicated medium of engraving [Fig. 7.3].

In this *Self-Portrait* he immortalised himself as an elegantly dressed young man with a slightly enlarged eye, which is typical for artist's self-portraits and hints to Aldegrever's intense self-observation in the mirror. To ensure that his portrait would always be rightly associated with his name even beyond German-speaking regions Aldegrever accompanied his self-image with a large fictional tablet inscribed in Latin:

> ALDEGREVERS HEC EST PRAESENS PICTORIS IMAGO / HENRICI PROPRIAE QVAM GENVERE MANVS / ANNO SVE AETATIS XXVIII
>
> The present image is of the painter Aldegrever, done by Heinrich's own hand, when he was twenty-eight years of age.[35]

In the lower part of his *Self-Portrait* the artist placed a second spacious inscription plate symmetrically, which gives the exact date the engraving was produced: 'ANNO DOMINI MDXXX' ('In the year of our Lord 1530'). Besides two elaborate inscriptions, Aldegrever also included in his ambitious image his large monogram, indicating thereby that this sign should be regarded as an essential element of his artistic identity. Inscribed on a Baroque cartouche one recognises a familiar 'A' with an enclosed 'G', which, due to the tiny gap in its structure, barely escapes to be mistaken for a 'D'. Combined with very ambiguous monograms, Aldegrever's prints could have induced misattribution to Dürer as much as they unmasked the identity of their true author. In other words, Aldegrever's images as well as his monograms were designed by the artist to deceive but were at the same time self-exposing. Through potential confusion with Dürer, the artist sought to showcase himself as equal to the

34 Bevers – Mielke – Wiebel, *Heinrich Aldegrever* 15.

35 Although Aldegrever identifies himself in the inscription as a 'painter' it is not known that he ever engaged himself with this artistic medium. See Heyder M., "Aldegrever (Trippenmeker), Heinrich", in Meissner G. – Beyer A. – Savoy B. – Tegethoff W. (eds.), *Allgemeines Künstlerlexikon (AKL): Die bildenden Künstler aller Zeiten und Völker*, vol. 2 (Munich – Leipzig: 1992) 184–188.

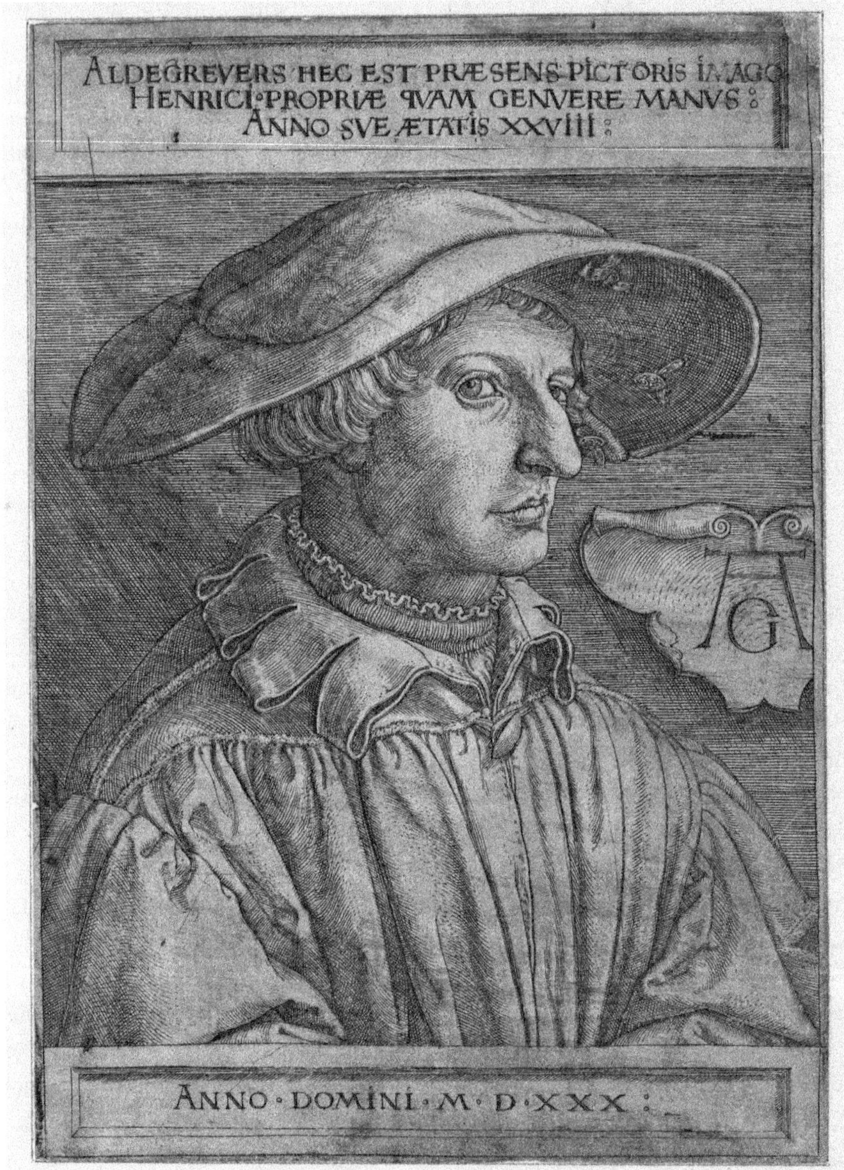

FIGURE 7.3 Heinrich Aldegrever, *Self-Portrait at Age Twenty-Eight*, 1530. Engraving, 14.7 × 10.5 cm
NEW YORK, THE METROPOLITAN MUSEUM OF ART, HARRIS BRISBANE DICK FUND, 1917

more famous colleague while at the same time retaining his own autonomy, as his *Self-Portrait* from 1530 makes evident.[36]

3 The Symbiosis of Imitative Practices

Among the artists discussed in this study Hans Hoffmann (*c.* 1548–1591) is the only one who is regarded by scholarship as a proponent of the so-called *Dürer-Renaissance*. Although the artist had an impressive career and advanced to the position of painter at the court of the enigmatic Emperor Rudolf II who reigned in Prague, Hoffmann has been predominantly remembered as a most prominent imitator of Dürer's works.[37] Shortly after Hoffmann's death the Nuremberg writing master and biographer of local artists, Andreas Gulden, praised Hoffmann for his ability to imitate Dürer's works and remarked that the artist had 'copied after Albrecht Dürer so diligently that many of his works were sold as Dürer's originals' ('copierte den Albrecht Dürer so fleissig nach, dass viel seiner Arbeit für die Dürerischen Orginalien verhandelt worden').[38] Gulden's remark is an early written testimony of Hoffmann's success as a deceptive imitator as well as evidence that it was widely known among the artist's contemporaries that he was capable of producing works remarkably similar to those by his compatriot. In the sixteenth century it was regarded as a proof of artistic virtuosity when an artist managed to fool the collectors' eye and intellect, as several episodes narrated by the influential artists' biographers Giorgio Vasari and Karel van Mander indicate.[39] Nevertheless Hans Hoffmann has remained a very controversial figure in the modern art-historical literature

36 Just seven years later Aldegrever produced his second and also very ambitious self-portrait, see Heinrich Aldegrever, *Self-Portrait*, 1537. Engraving, 19.8 × 12.8 cm, see Bevers – Mielke – Wiebel, *Heinrich Aldegrever* no. 189, 164–165.

37 DaCosta Kaufmann Th., *The School of Prague: Painting at the Court of Rudolf II* (Chicago – London: 1988) 215–217.

38 Neudörfer Johann – Gulden Andreas, *Des Johann Neudörfer Schreib- und Rechenmeisters zu Nürnberg Nachrichten von Künstlern und Werkleuten daselbst aus dem Jahre 1547 nebst der Fortsetzung des Andreas Gulden*, ed. G.W.K. Lochner, Quellenschriften für Kunstgeschichte und Kunsttechnik des Mittelalters und der Renaissance, 10 (Vienna: 1875) 198.

39 For van Mander's anecdote about the Dutch engraver Hendrick Goltzius, who successfully deceived art collectors and buyers by offering them a supposedly rediscovered engraving by Albrecht Dürer which, in fact, was Goltzius' own creation, see Mander, *The Lives* 397. Goltzius indeed produced a print in the manner of Albrecht Dürer as a part of his series *Meisterstiche*, see Hendrick Goltzius, *Circumcision*. 1594. Engraving, 46.4 × 35.1 cm. For Vasari's anecdotes on deceitful imitations, see Lenain T., *Art Forgery: The History of a Modern Obsession* (London: 2011) 179–198.

since, compared to other artists, like for example Altdorfer and Aldegrever, imitations of Dürer's works made up a very substantial part of Hoffmann's artistic output. Furthermore, Hoffmann did not design his own monogram as a reference to Dürer's but instead alternatingly signed his works with his own initials and with Dürer's monogram. By the first half of the twentieth century art-historians saw Hoffmann mainly as an early case of art forgery.[40] In recent scholarship the ambiguous character of Hoffmann's signing practices has been taken into account and a more differentiated attitude towards the artist has come to prevail. It has been suggested that he produced works for various collectors and that he occasionally created forgeries signed with false monograms on behalf of the Nuremberg merchant Willibald Imhoff the Elder and his heirs, whose exceptionally rich collection at the end of the sixteenth century contained a great number of Dürer's drawings and prints.[41] The problem with this assumption is that there is no written evidence that Hoffmann was ever paid by Willibald Imhoff for any work.[42] According to Willibald's eldest son, Hans Imhoff, Hoffmann was a friend of his father and the family.[43] Indeed, two

40 Thausing M., *Dürer: Geschichte seines Lebens und seiner Kunst* (Leipzig: 1876) 141–142; Peltzer R.A., "Hoffmann, Hans", in Thieme U. – Becker F. (eds.), *Allgemeines Lexikon der bildenden Künstler von der Antike bis zur Gegenwart*, vol. 17 (Leipzig: 1924) 257–258; Tietze – Tietze-Conrat, *Kritisches Verzeichnis* 256–260.

41 It has often been assumed that by coping works by Dürer and signing them with false 'AD's Hoffmann may have provided the Imhoff-family with a kind of ersatz in case the originals would once have to be sold. See Pilz K., "Hans Hoffmann: Ein Nürnberger Dürer-Nachahmer aus der 2. Hälfte des 16. Jahrhunderts", *Mitteilungen des Vereins für Geschichte der Stadt Nürnberg* 51 (1962) 243–245; Budde H., *Die Kunstsammlung des Nürnberger Patriziers Willibald Imhoff unter besonderer Berücksichtigung der Werke Albrecht Dürers* (Munster: 1996); Bubenik, *Reframing* 47–49, 105. Anja Grebe explains different signatures on Hoffmann's works with his adjustment to the different demands of his Nuremberg commissioners, see Grebe, *Dürer* 191–193. In my earlier article on Hoffmann's monograms I did also support this assumption, which now, because of a thorough study of Hoffmann's artistic practices, I see more sceptically. See Tschetschik K., "Monogramme Albrecht Dürers auf den Zeichnungen des Nürnberger Künstlers Hans Hoffmann: Fälschung oder Täuschung?", in Münch B.U. – Tacke A. – Herzog M. – Heudecker S. (eds.), *Fälschung – Plagiat – Kopie: Künstlerische Praktiken in der Vormoderne*. Kunsthistorisches Forum Irrsee, 1 (Petersberg: 2014) 41–51.

42 Willibald Imhoff the Elder meticulously made notes on his expenses in his account book ('Unkostpuch'), however no mentioning of payments to an artist can be found there, see Imhoff W., "Unkostpuch meyner haushaltunkostpuch nach volendung des ersten, so 18 jar lang geweret hott, angefangen a di 13 Junyo 1564. Gott der Herr verleyhe syn gotlichen segen. Per Wiliboldt Imhoff, Nürnberg (Nürnberg, Stadtbibliothek, Amb. 64 4)", in Pohl H. (ed.), *Willibald Imhoff, Enkel und Erbe Willibald Pirckheimers*, Quellen zur Geschichte und Kultur der Stadt Nürnberg, 24 (Nuremberg: 1992) 91–279.

43 Imhoff Hans, *Theatrum virtutis honoris oder Tugendbüchlein* (Nuremberg, Paul Kauffmann: 1606) 94.

drawn portraits of Willibald Imhoff the Elder by the hand of Hans Hoffmann evoke an impression of familiarity between the artist and his subject and support the assumption of friendship.[44]

Moreover, judging from the visual evidence of the works which Hoffmann produced during his frequent visits to the Imhoff family collection from 1574 to 1583 it seems very likely that the artist used his access to the collection primarily for study purposes.[45] Analysing the scope of Hoffmann's early drawings, many of which are housed today in The Collection of Prints and Drawings at The Museum of Fine Arts in Budapest, one can observe that they rarely look like finished works. Most probably, these pieces, among which are a number of copies after Dürer's drawings, have been produced by the artist as a stock of working material and thus rather testify to Hoffmann's learning process than to any commercial strategy. We find among them close copies as well as copies that strongly differ from Dürer's originals. Some of these variations look very much like experimental re-imaginations of motives by Dürer in differing techniques.[46] Hoffmann's learning process can thus be described in the following way: he appropriated a wide range of drawing techniques from Dürer's originals either by closely copying them or by varying some of their characteristics. Subsequently, he applied the techniques learnt in that way to completely new subjects. The artist, for instance, showed a particular interest in Dürer's natural studies and copied the master's *Stag Beetle* at least two times. Although he deliberately introduced some changes in these copies, he also

---

44 Hans Hoffmann, *Portrait of Willibald Imhoff the Elder*, 1508 (corrected to 1580). Pen and black ink on paper. 13.1 × 11.1 cm and *Portrait of Willibald Imhoff the Elder*. Grey washes and white gouache on blue paper, 32.4 × 35. both in holdings of Budapest, Museum of Fine Arts, 149 and 374, see Bodnár S., "Hans Hoffmanns Zeichnungen in Budapest", *Acta historiae artium Academiae Scientiarum Hungaricae* 32 (1986) no. 36–37, 110–111, Bodnár S., *German Drawings of the Fifteenth and Sixteenth Centuries in Museum of Fine Arts, Budapest* (Budapest: 2020) no. 246, 215, no. 247, 215–216.

45 The time-period during which Hoffmann had access to Imhoff's collection stems from the dates on his copies after Dürer's drawings. For the earliest date, see *Stag Beetle*. 1574. Watercolour and Gouache on paper, 9.7 × 9.4 cm. Budapest, Museum of Fine Arts, 184; for the latest date, see *Dead Blue Roller*. 1583. Watercolour and gouache on paper, 29.2 × 16.9 cm. Cleveland, Museum of Art, Dudley P. Allen Fund 1946.217, see for both studies Koreny F., *Albrecht Dürer und die Tier- und Pflanzenstudien der Renaissance* (Munich: 1985) no. 37, 122; fig. 11.1, 56.

46 For example, Hoffmann tried to translate Dürer's silverpoint drawing *Portrait of Endres Dürer* into a pen-and-ink drawing heightened with white on grey prepared paper. See Hans Hoffmann, *Portrait of Endres Dürer*. Pen and black ink, heightened white on grey prepared paper, 24.1 × 20.2 cm. Budapest, Museum of Fine Arts, 143, see Bodnár, "Hans Hoffmanns Zeichnungen" 90, Bodnár, *German Drawings* no. 215, 192; Albrecht Dürer, *Portrait of Endres Dürer*, 1514. Silverpoint on bluish-white prepared paper, 29.6 × 21 cm. Vienna, Albertina, 3137, see Koschatzky W. – Strobl A., *Die Dürer Zeichnungen der Albertina* (Salzburg: 1971) 306–307.

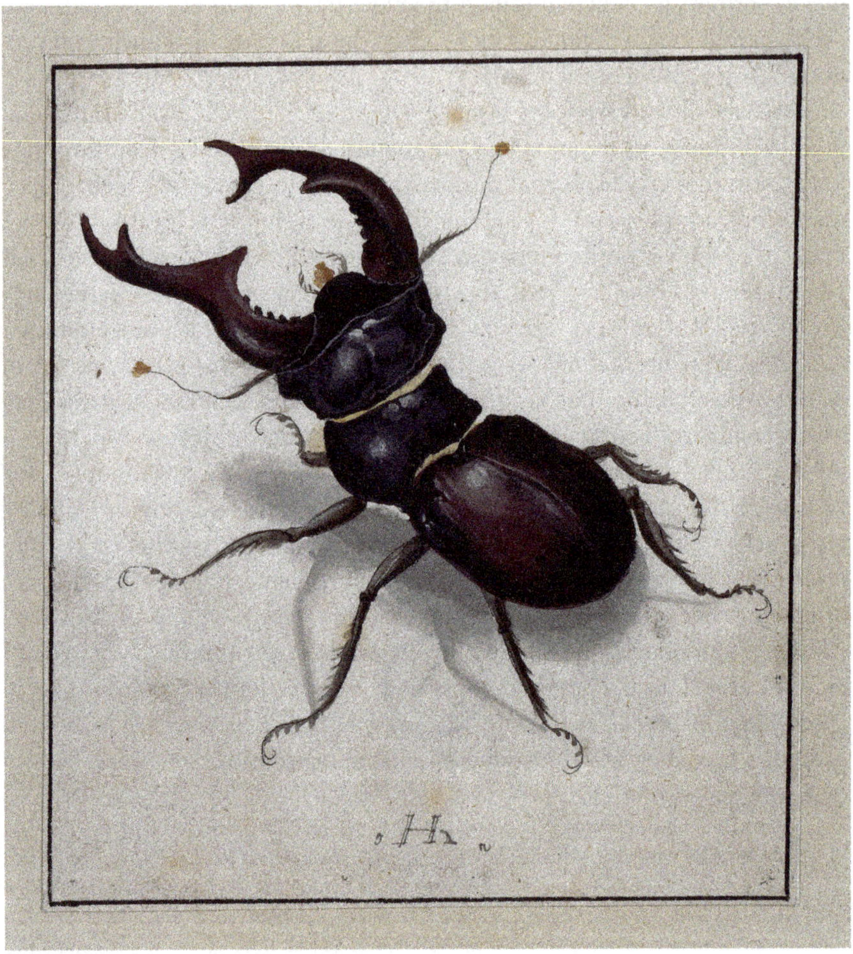

FIGURE 7.4 Hans Hoffmann, *Stag Beetle*, reversed copy after Dürer, *c.* 1574. Watercolour and gouache on paper, 11.4 × 10.3 cm
BERLIN, STAATLICHE MUSEEN, KUPFERSTICHKABINETT. IMAGE BPK / KUPFERSTICHKABINETT, SMB / JÖRG P. ANDERS

tried to render Dürer's miniature painting technique most carefully. The two copies after Dürer's *Stag Beetle* known today carry Hoffmann's own initials 'Hh' [Fig. 7.4].[47]

47 For Albrecht Dürer's *Stag Beetle* dated 1505 and Hans Hoffmann's copies after this study, see Koreny, *Albrecht Dürer* no. 36–37, 120–123.

Following Dürer's example, Hoffmann also executed a group of studies with insects and other small animals.[48] Hoffmann's nature studies testify to his outstanding ability to observe nature as well as to his utmost interest in evoking an illusionistic effect.

Although Hans Hoffmann claimed authorship on his works from the very beginning of his artistic career and sometimes put his own monogram consisting of the capital 'H' and the small 'h' fused together even on unfinished or apparently immature works, he also occasionally signed his drawings with spurious Dürer-signatures.[49] Most of these works are close copies after originals by Albrecht Dürer, like *Dead Blue Roller* or *Wing of a Blue Roller*.[50] Szilvia Bodnár, one of the first and few experts to closely study Hoffmann's works, has noticed that Hoffmann's usage of false 'AD'-monograms rather resembles a play with different identities ('Rollenspiel') because the artist continuously seems to disclose his ability to fake Dürer's works.[51] Hoffmann's copies after Dürer's drawings known today indeed reveal that the artist often made several copies after the same subject and signed them with Dürer's initials as often as with his own. Considering Hoffmann's almost obsessive studiousness and his particular interest in the depiction of natural subjects as trompe-l'oeil I dare further to suggest that Hoffmann's deployment of the deceptive 'AD's is related to his ambition to fashion himself as a highly accomplished illustrator of nature.

48 Hans Hoffmann, *Green Grasshopper*. Gouache on parchment, 5.5 × 7.8 cm. Budapest, Museum of Fine Arts, 180, see Bodnár, "Hans Hoffmanns Zeichnungen" no. 20, 101, Bodnár, *German Drawings* no. 231, 205; idem, *Cross Spider*, signed 'Aug 30/ 1578'. Watercolours and Gouache on paper, 5.5 × 4.4 cm. Budapest, Museum of Fine Arts, 175, see Bodnár, "Hans Hoffmanns Zeichnungen" no. 23, 102, Bodnár, *German Drawings* no. 234, 205; idem, *Dragonfly*, 1577. Watercolours on paper, 8.1 × 7.8 cm. Budapest, Museum of Fine Arts, see Bodnár, "Hans Hoffmanns Zeichnungen" no. 21, 101, Bodnár, *German Drawings* no. 232, 205; idem, *Grasshopper and a Fly*. Watercolours and gouache on paper, 5.9 × 9.8 cm; idem, *Goldfinch*. Watercolours and Gouache on paper, 12.1 × 11.2 cm. Berlin, Staatliche Museen zu Berlin, Kupferstichkabinett, see Pilz, "Hans Hoffmann" no. 34, 266, no. 35, 266.

49 For example, Hoffmann signed his very early and still very immature *Portrait of Barbara Möringer*. 1573. Oil on wood, 82.6 × 68.2 cm. Kronach, Franconian Gallery, Branch Museum of the Bayerisches Nationalmuseum, R 1034, see Weniger M., *Zweigmuseum des Bayerischen Nationalmuseums Festung Rosenberg Kronach* (Petersberg: 2014) no. 83, 222–223. The tiny abbreviation 'Hh' can be easily found to the left of the woman's figure almost touching the lower edge of the picture-frame.

50 For 'AD'-signed copies after *Dead Blue Roller*, see Koreny, *Albrecht Dürer* fig. 11.2 56, no. 12, 58–59; respectively for *Wing of a Blue Roller*, see Koreny, *Albrecht Dürer* no. 23, 86–87, no. 24, 88–89. It is important to note that Hoffmann, as evidenced by his copies after Dürer's *Stag Beetle* or his former Bremen copy after the *Hare*, quite often signed his close imitations also with his monogram 'Hh'.

51 Bodnár, "Hans Hoffmanns Zeichnungen" 84.

Several nature studies of Hoffmann's own invention are known which also claim Dürer's authorship.[52] The study of the *Hare,* which is held today in the collection of the Kupferstichkabinett in Berlin, is of a formidable size and shows a prominently placed 'AD'-sign and the date '1528' [Fig. 7.5].

The study reveals the distinct characteristics of Hoffmann's painting manner, like an outstanding diligence in the depiction of the animal's fur and other tiny details.[53] The *Hare* is executed on vellum with watercolours and gouache laid down opaque and in multiple layers. Although of a quite different appearance, the motive of a single crouching hare from Hoffmann's study is reminiscent of Dürer's nowadays famous watercolour drawing *Hare* from the Albertina Museum in Vienna [Fig. 7.6].[54]

Hoffmann studied Dürer's original drawing during his visits to the art collection of Willibald Imhoff, as is testified by at least one copy after it which is known today. The remarkably close copy, which, until World War II, was housed in the Kunsthalle in Bremen, presents Hoffmann's familiar 'Hh'-monogram and the date '1582' above the elongated ears of the hare.[55] In contrast to this close copy, Hoffmann's study from Berlin is not a copy at all. Some scholars speculated that the Berlin *Hare* could be a copy after some, today lost, original

52 The following natural studies by Hans Hoffmann seem to be his own inventions and bear Dürer's monograms: *Two Squirrels*, signed '1512 / AD'. Gouache and watercolours on parchment, 26 × 25.1 cm. Private collection; *Four Feathers*, signed '1512 / AD'. Present whereabouts unknown; *Wing of a Blue Roller*, distantly refers to Dürer's study of same subject matter, signed '15 AD 24'. Watercolours and gouache on parchment, 18.9 × 23.9 cm. New York, Ian Woodner Collection, see Koreny, *Albrecht Dürer* no. 28, 96; fig. 25.1, 90; no. 25, 90–91.

53 For further arguments for the attribution of this study to Hans Hoffmann, see Koreny, *Albrecht Dürer* no. 52, 154–155. For a detailed discussion on the differences between Dürer's depiction of the hare's fur and Hoffmann's respectively, see Leonhard K., "Hans Hoffmanns Hase", in Felfe R. – Saß M. (eds.), *Naturalismen: Kunst, Wissenschaft und Ästhetik*, Naturbilder/Images of Nature 9 (Berlin – Boston: 2019) 33–48.

54 For the provenance and early reception of Dürer's *Hare*, see Mende M., "Hoffmanns Dürer-Hasen", in Zettl L. (ed.), *Der Hase wird 500: 1502–2002 Beiträge zu Albrecht Dürer und seinem Hasen* (Nuremberg: 2002) 16–21; Metzger C., "Lieben, Lächeln und Sich erinnern: Albrecht Dürers Hase", in Schröder K.A. (ed.), *Die Gründung der Albertina – zwischen Dürer und Napoleon. 100 Meisterwerke der Sammlung*, exh. cat. Albertina Museum Vienna (Ostfildern: 2014) 49–56.

55 Hans Hoffmann, *Hare* (after Dürer), 1582. Watercolours and gouache, 21.6 × 18.3 cm. formerly Bremen, Kunsthalle, today in private collection, see Röver-Kann A. – Miller M. (eds.), *Dürer-Zeit: Die Geschichte der Dürer-Sammlung in der Kunsthalle Bremen*, exh. cat. Kunsthalle Bremen (Munich: 2012) no. 54, 172–173.

by Dürer.[56] Fritz Koreny dismissed this assumption, detecting several characteristics of the Berlin piece which would be very untypical for Dürer.[57] I would add to Koreny's argumentation that the Berlin *Hare* can neither be regarded as completely independent of the Viennese original nor is it simply a variation. Hoffmann's study is rather the result of a deliberate transformation by the artist, who tried thereby to surpass the original. Beyond enlarging the study's measurements, Hoffmann sought to make the animal look more vivid and appealing than Dürer's prototype. He presented the hare in a provoking close-up en-face with disproportionately enlarged head and eyes. The animal is also shown casting a contrasting shadow to the side. Thus, Hoffmann's *Hare* might be interpreted as a product of an imagined contest between the younger artist and his older colleague in order to prove that he was not merely the master's equal, but could even outdo him. Hoffmann expressed his ambitions most conspicuously in the form of the false Dürer signature which he placed beneath the animal figure. Whereas Dürer's original is dated '1502', Hoffmann put a much later date on his study. He dated his version of the *Hare*, quite impertinently, with the year of Dürer's death '1528'. But exactly this date can provide a link to the actual year the study could have been produced. By permuting the last digits '2' and '8' of '1528' we easily obtain the date '1582' and thus also the year in which Hoffmann produced his close copy after Dürer's *Hare* mentioned above. It is possible that the Berlin *Hare* was executed in 1582 as a part of a series of works in which the artist experimented with transformation of different visual characteristics of Dürer's study. Hoffmann's painting *Hare among other plants* from a private collection is also dated with '1582' and includes the figure of the hare, which is an imitation after Dürer's *Hare*.[58] Thus, the falsified date '1528' on Hoffmann's study from Berlin claims Dürer's authorship, but at the same time, it playfully points to the personality of the copyist and stages him as a follower of the artist who took up the baton after the master's death. Comparing the faked 'AD'-monogram on Hoffmann's *Hare* from Berlin with the artist's own signatures on several of his drawings, we can also trace striking similarities in handwriting. In particular, characteristic scribbles

56 Bock E., *Die deutschen Meister: Beschreibendes Verzeichnis sämtlicher Zeichnungen mit 193 Lichtdrucktafeln*, Die Zeichnungen Alter Meister im Kupferstichkabinett, im Auftrage des Generaldirektors, ed. M.J. Friedländer, vol. 1 (Berlin: 1921) no. 1271, 47.

57 Koreny, *Albrecht Dürer* 154.

58 Hoffmann's *Hare among other plants* from a private collection is an opulant composition in watercolours and gouache on vellum which is signed with 'Hh'-monogram and date '1582'. See Koreny, *Albrecht Dürer* no. 47, 144–145.

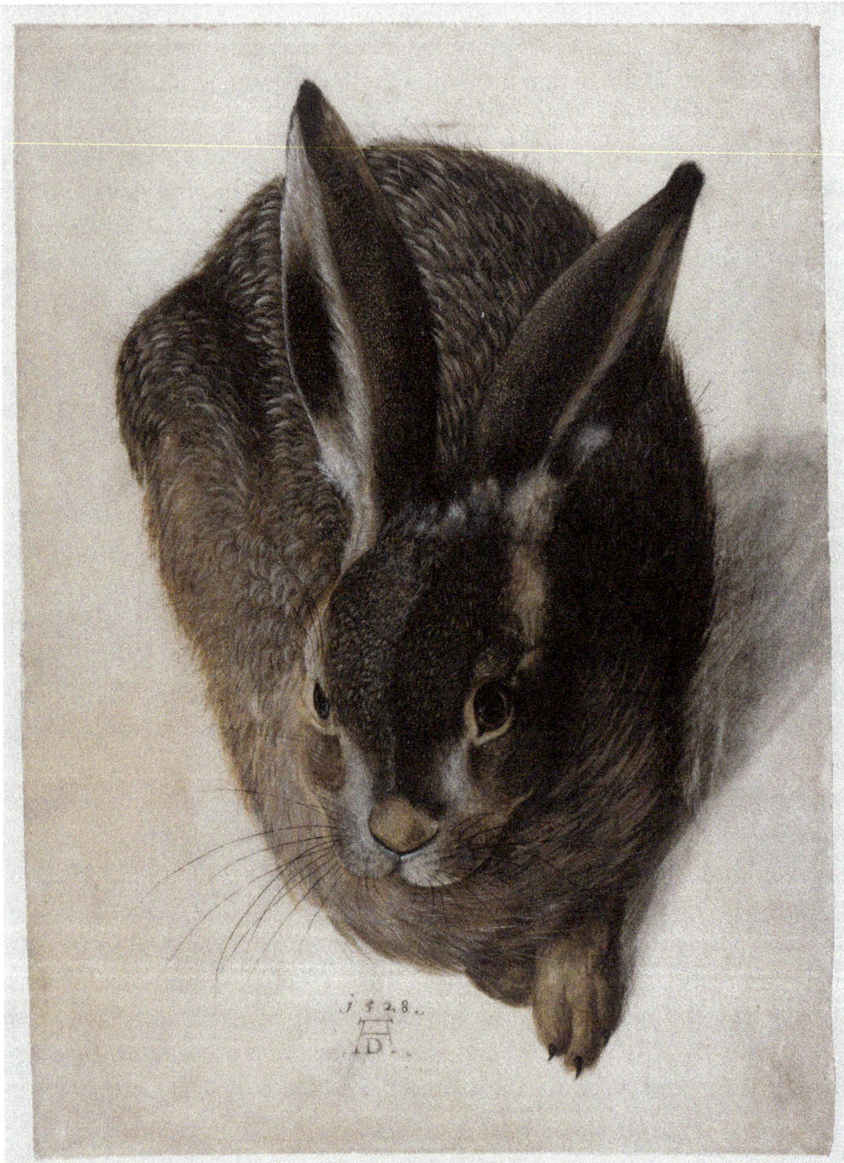

FIGURE 7.5 Hans Hoffmann, *Hare*, signed with faked monogram 'AD' and date '1528'. Watercolour and gouache on vellum, 35.5 × 26 cm
BERLIN, STAATLICHE MUSEEN, KUPFERSTICHKABINETT. IMAGE BPK / KUPFERSTICHKABINETT, SMB / JÖRG P. ANDERS

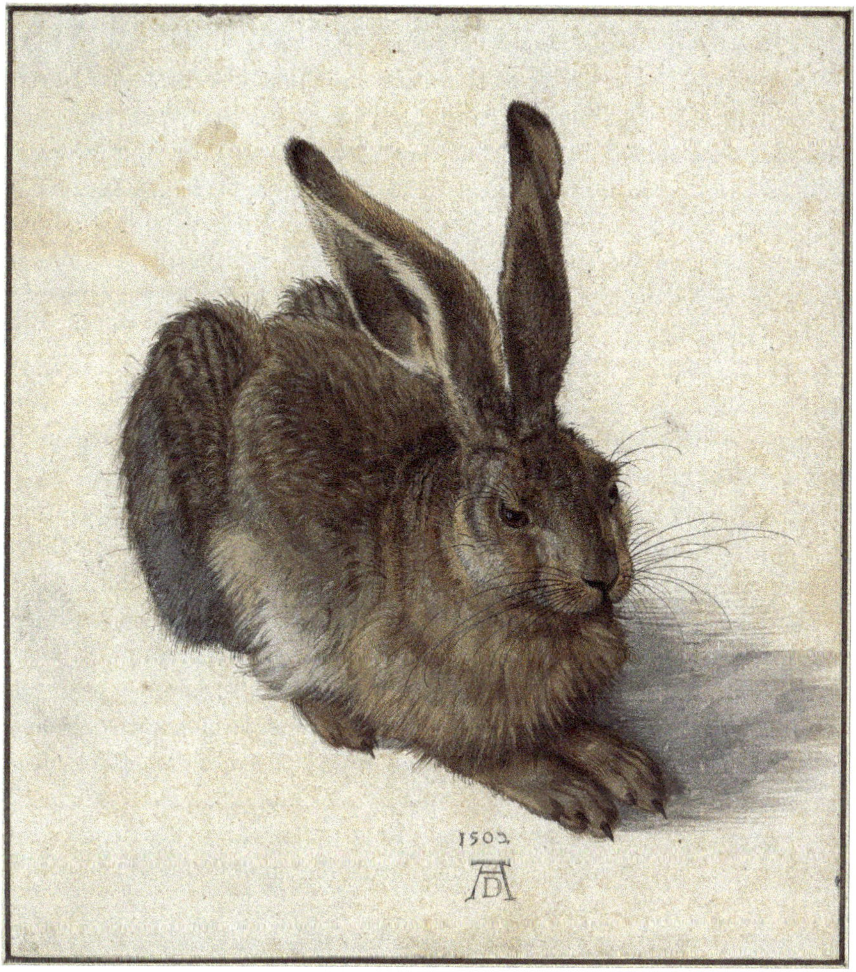

FIGURE 7.6 Albrecht Dürer, *Hare*, 1502. Watercolours and gouache on paper, 25 × 22.5 cm
VIENNA, ALBERTINA MUSEUM. IMAGE © ALBERTINA, WIEN

emerge, flanking both artist's own initials as well as his faked 'AD'-signs.[59] The 'AD'-signature on Hoffmann's Berlin *Hare* seems to have been designed to showcase the artist as Dürer's equal by exposing the viewer to the risk of confusion. By combining the deceptive signature with a vividly and richly detailed

59 For flanking scribbles, see Hoffmann, *Dragonfly*, 1577 (see also here footnote no. 48); idem, *Lion*, copy after Dürer, 1577. Watercolours and Gouache on vellum, 17.2 × 27.7 cm. Nuremberg, Germanisches Nationalmuseum, see Koreny, *Albrecht Dürer* no. 59, 172–173.

natural study, Hoffmann also seems to have intended to strengthen the claim of his *Hare* to appear as a powerful illusion of nature.

Another artist who, like Hans Hoffmann, combined the illusion of Dürer's authorship with the illusion of natural representation was Ambrosius Bosschaert the Elder (1573–1621). The Dutch artist was a painter and art dealer, who, escaping Spanish rule, came with his family from his native Antwerp to Middelburg and who was later active in cities like Amsterdam, Utrecht and Breda.[60] Alongside Jan Brueghel the Elder, Bosschaert is regarded as an originator of the independent flower still-life painting.[61] In the early seventeenth century paintings like Bosschaert's *Bouquet of Flowers in a Niche*, today in the Princely Collections of Liechtenstein, were considered highly innovative. At the time, the idea that, beside historical and mythological narratives, a mere arrangement of natural and artisanal objects might constitute the single subject matter of a panel painting was still very new [Fig. 7.7].[62]

Thus, Bosschaert would have felt the need to imbed his innovative paintings into an established and highly esteemed artistic tradition, which, for the Dutch painter, was embodied by Albrecht Dürer and his monogram. In his *Bouquet of Flowers in a Niche* one recognises, in the lower left of the composition, inscribed on the protruding edge of the niche, the artist's monogram 'AB'. Ingvar Bergström, an eminent expert in the history of still-life painting, observed: 'Bosschaert's "AB" was almost certainly based on Dürer's well-known "AD", and, in spite of all their differences, both he and Dürer shared a common worship of nature: *Natura sola magistra*'.[63] It is worth to look more closely at Bosschaert's relationship to the Nuremberg artist. At a quick glance Bosschaert's initials might be mistaken for Dürer's, since the design of the capital 'A', which

60 For Bosschaert's biography, workshop and catalogue of his works, see Bol L.J., *The Bosschaert Dynasty: Painters of Flowers and Fruit*, trans. A.M. de Bruins-Cousins (Leigh-on-Sea: 1960); for a more recent biography of the artist, see Meijer F.G., "Bosschaert Ambrosius, d.Ä.", in Meissner – Beyer – Savoy – Tegethoff, *Allgemeines Künstlerlexikon*, vol. 13, 200–201.

61 On the origins of early flower still-life paintings, see Bergström I., *Dutch Still-Life Painting in the Seventeenth Century*, trans. Ch. Hedström – G. Taylor (London: 1956) 12–14, 42–97; Segal S., "Introduction", in Segal S. (ed.), *Flowers and Nature: Netherlandish Flower Painting of Four Centuries*, exh. cat. Osaka, Nabio Museum of Art; Tokyo, Station Gallery (Amstelveen: 1990) 13–72; Clippel K. – Linden D., "The Genesis of the Netherlandish Flower Piece", *Simiolus* 38:1–2 (2015–2016) 73–86.

62 First published by Bol, *The Bosschaert Dynasty* no. 34, 21/22, 29, 65; more recently published in Schröder K.A. (ed.), *Von Rubens bis Makart: Die fürstlichen Sammlungen Liechtenstein*, exh. cat. Albertina Museum Vienna (Vienna – Cologne: 2019) no. 19, 105–107.

63 Bergström, *Dutch Still-Life Painting* 67. Hans Kauffmann also mentions Bosschaert's monogram as an example of '[Verkleidung] des eigenen Monogramms in die Form des Dürermonogramms' ('disguise of the artist's own monogram in the shape of Dürer's monogram'), see Kauffmann, "Dürer in der Kunst und im Kunsturteil" 31.

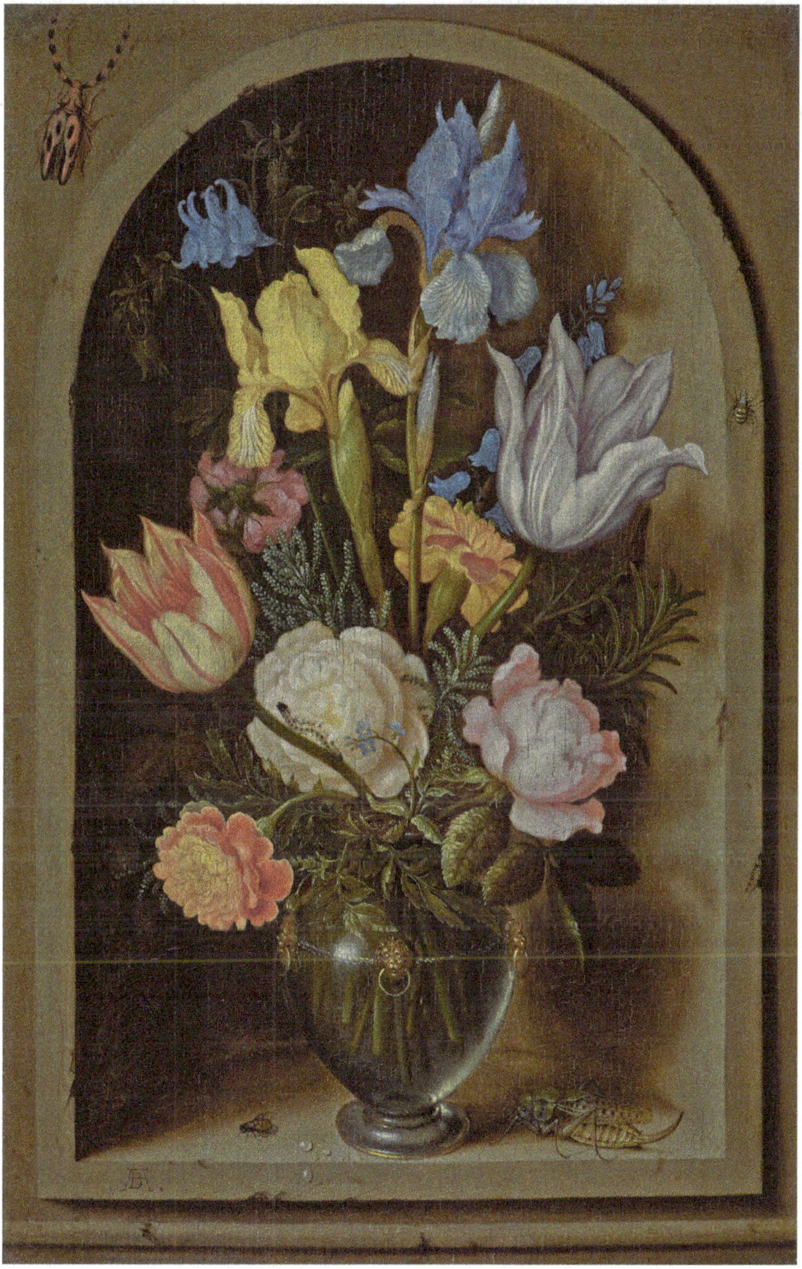

FIGURE 7.7 Ambrosius Bosschaert the Elder, *Bouquet of Flowers in a Niche*, c. 1616–1619. Oil on wood, 35 × 23 cm
VIENNA – VADUZ, LIECHTENSTEIN THE PRINCELY COLLECTIONS. IMAGE LIECHTENSTEIN, THE PRINCELY COLLECTIONS, VADUZ-VIENNA / SCALA, FLORENCE

accommodates in its arc a capital 'B', resembles once again the familiar sign of Dürer. We notice furthermore that the inscribed 'B' is split by the crossbeam of the 'A' precisely in the middle, so that, as a result, the lower part of the 'B' resembles the shape of a 'D'. In fact, Bosschaert's monogram can be read as if it was built upon Dürer's sign, since the German artist's 'AD' appears as if it had been simply complemented by the still-life painter with a smaller additional roundness of a 'D' to form his 'AB'. The Dutch artist's eagerness to refer in his flower piece to Dürer's authority might appear surprising. Beyond some nature studies, like the above-mentioned Viennese *Hare*, it is not known that Dürer ever produced any kind of still-life paintings. Moreover, it is not certain that Bosschaert ever could have had a chance to see any genuine natural study by Dürer's hand. As an art dealer, the painter from Middelburg was rather acquainted with Dürer's prints as well as confronted with the high regard for the Nuremberg master among the art collectors in the Dutch Republic. Dürer was hugely venerated in the Low Countries, which the artist had experienced himself during his famous voyage to the Netherlands in 1520–1521.[64] Around 1600 his reputation had still not faded away, as can be seen in Karel van Mander's almost mythological account of Dürer's life in his *Schilder-Boeck*, an influential compendium of artist's biographies, first published in 1604.[65]

Beyond establishing the reference to Dürer's authority, Bosschaert's monogram has clearly been designed by the artist to fulfil a performative effect. The striking similarity with the famous 'AD'-monogram should have induced the viewers, for example of the *Bouquet of Flowers in a Niche*, to take a closer look at the intriguing signature. A careful observation, of course, dismisses any conjectures about Dürer's authorship of this painting. On the other hand,

64 On Dürer's popularity in the Netherlands of the sixteenth century, see Held J.S., *Dürers Wirkung auf die niederländische Kunst seiner Zeit* (s'Gravenhage: 1930); Fircks J., "Zwischen Nürnberg und Antwerpen: Zur wechselseitigen Wahrnehmung deutscher und niederländischer Künstler in der Dürerzeit", in Borchert T.-H. (ed.), *Van Eyck bis Dürer: Altniederländische Meister und die Malerei in Mitteleuropa*, exh. cat. Bruges, Groeningenmuseum (Bruges: 2010) 82–93; Eichberger D., "Dürer and the Netherlands: Patterns of Exchange and Mutual Admiration", in Silver L. – Smith J.C. (eds.), *The Essential Dürer* (Philadelphia: 2010) 149–165; Grebe, *Dürer* 199–201. For a detailed analysis of the Dutch artist's, Jan Gossaert's, expanding of Dürer's models, see Silver L., "Dürer and Gossaert", Foister S. – Brink P. (eds.), *Dürer's Journeys: Travels of a Renaissance Artist*, exh. cat. London, The National Gallery (New Haven – London: 2021) 103–115. It is important to note that Jan Gossaert, like later Ambrosius Bosschaert, was active in Middelburg. On the popularity of Dürer's painting *Saint Jerome* (1521) among Dutch artists, see Harth A. – Martens M.P.J., "Albrecht Dürer's Iconic Image of Saint Jerome: Making, Meaning and Reception", in Foister – Brink (eds.), *Dürer's Journeys* 253–265.

65 See Mander, *The Lives* 89–98.

a closer look at the panel truly reveals Bosschaert's outstanding illusionistic capacity. Even at a very short distance the smooth surface prevents any traces of brushstrokes to become visible. Instead, the beholder can marvel at the tiny eyes of a glossy fly, the shining pearls of water and the notches on the protruding edge of the stone niche. All these elements appear exceptionally real. Thus, Bosschaert's imitation of the 'AD'-monogram not only inscribes his innovative painting subject in the genealogy of artistic tradition of his time, but also performs an important role in creating a specific visual experience of his illusionistic *Bouquets*.

4 Conclusion: Deceptive Hidden Monograms

The cases of imitation of the 'AD'-monogram discussed in this essay have emphasised the significance of signatures as a means of artistic self-reflection and self-representation. Through imitating Dürer's identity sign several artists sought to fashion their own reputation by referring to the venerated artistic authority. But the most remarkable characteristic of these imitative practices is the creation of a deceptive capacity, which transforms mere references to challenging and even risky ventures to prove individual artistic skill and talent. On the one hand, artists applied deception to seek the comparison with the acclaimed master; on the other hand, and arguably even more striking, they apparently sought to employ the deceptive power of their monograms to enhance particular visual qualities of their works.

In conclusion, I am going to present one further argument that the usage of deceptive 'AD'-monograms was interrelated with the broader category of elusive signatures. As at least one work by Hans Hoffmann suggests, the artist sought to delineate his ambitions as a painter of illusionistic depictions of nature not only with risky forgeries of Dürer monograms. One very particular monogram can be discovered in Hoffmann's *Thistle with Robin Perching on a Pine-Stump*, today in the graphics collection of Germanisches Nationalmuseum in Nuremberg [Fig. 7.8].

The composition, consisting of some ordinary natural species, reveals – typically for Hoffmann – a diligent execution with tiny brush, gouache and watercolours on a large piece of vellum. For a long time this work, though definitely recognised as Hoffmann's, has been regarded as one which the artist had left unsigned.[66] A close examination of the composition revealed however,

---

66 Hoffmann's *Thistle with Robin Perching on a Pine-Stump* originates from the collection of Nuremberg merchant and art collector Paulus Praun and is mentioned in the

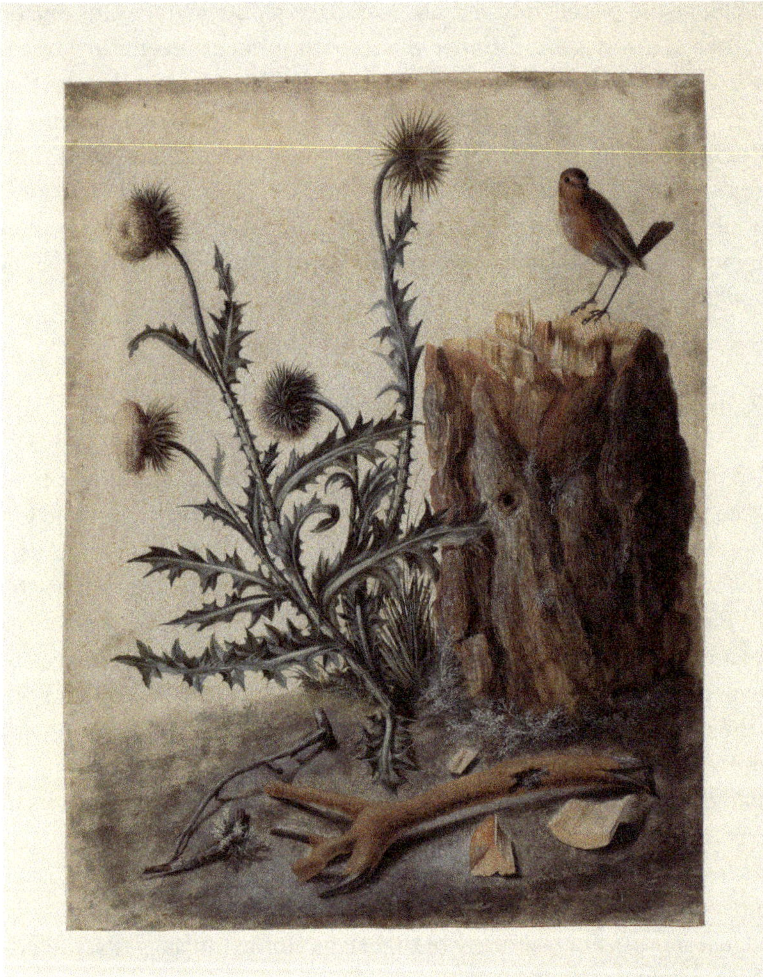

FIGURE 7.8 Hans Hoffmann, *Thistle with Robin Perching on a Pine-Stump*, *c.* 1582–1585. Watercolours and gouache on vellum, 46.4 × 35.8 cm
NUREMBERG, GERMANISCHES NATIONALMUSEUM, IMAGE © GERMANISCHES NATIONALMUSEUM, FOTO: MONICA RUNGE

earliest inventories of the collection from 1616 and 1719, see Achilles-Syndram K. (ed.), *Die Kunstsammlung des Paulus Praun: Die Inventare von 1616 und 1719*, Quellen zur Geschichte und Kultur der Stadt Nürnberg 25 (Nuremberg: 1994) no. 87; no. 134. It has been also mentioned in the inventory of the Praun family collection composed by Christoph Gottlieb von Murr, see Murr Christoph Gottlieb von (ed.), *Description du Cabinet de Monsieur Paul de Praun à Nuremberg* (Nuremberg, Jean Théophile Schneider: 1797) 17. Most recently published as unsigned work of Hans Hoffmann by Koreny, *Albrecht Dürer* no. 51, 152–153; Achilles-Syndram K. – Schoch R. (ed.), *Kunst des Sammelns: Das Praunsche Kabinett. Meisterwerke von Dürer bis Carracci*, exh. cat. Nuremberg, Germanisches Nationalmuseum (Nuremberg: 1994) no. 72, 208–209.

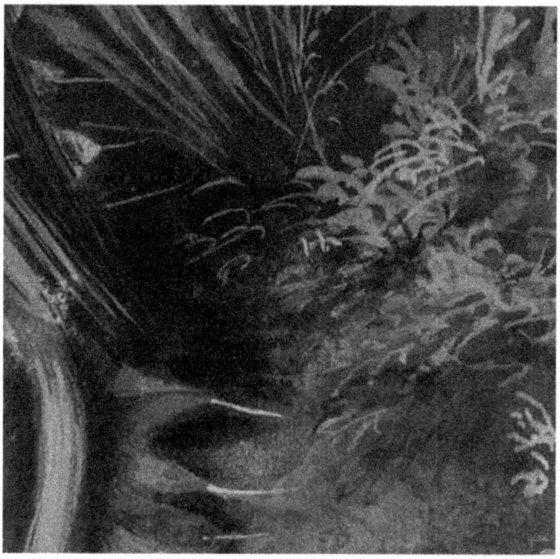

FIGURE 7.9
Hans Hoffmann, detail with the hidden 'Hh'-monogram of *Thistle with Robin Perching on a Pine-Stump*, c. 1582–1585
NUREMBERG, GERMANISCHES NATIONALMUSEUM, IMAGE © GERMANISCHES NATIONALMUSEUM, FOTO: MONICA RUNGE

that it contains a clandestine signature. Investigating the picture surface with a magnifying glass I could detect beneath the old pine-stump, among multiple lichens rendered with white and curled brush-lines Hoffmann's miniature monogram [Fig. 7.9]. The shape of this monogram resembles Hoffmann's 'Hh' on his Berlin *Stag Beetle* [see Fig. 7.4, p. 182].

The hidden monogram on Hoffmann's composition from Nuremberg thus oscillates between the representation of an object and legibility as a monogram. Like his colleagues Bosschaert and Ligozzi, Hoffmann apparently expected that his viewers, inspired by the naturalism of his *Thistle with Robin*, would take a closer look at the painting and subsequently would discover the clandestine monogram. Similarly, as the artist manoeuvred, with his faked 'AD's, dangerously close at the edge of being confused with Dürer, he also risked that his hidden monogram would be left undetected forever. The performance of deception can easily fail its purpose.

Bibliography

Achilles-Syndram K. – Schoch R. (ed.), *Kunst des Sammelns: Das Praunsche Kabinett. Meisterwerke von Dürer bis Carracci*, exh. cat. Nuremberg, Germanisches Nationalmuseum (Nuremberg: 1994).

Achilles-Syndram K. (ed.), *Die Kunstsammlung des Paulus Praun: Die Inventare von 1616 und 1719*, Quellen zur Geschichte und Kultur der Stadt Nürnberg 25 (Nuremberg: 1994).

Austin J.L., *How To Do Things With Words: The William James Lectures Delivered at Harvard University in 1955* (Oxford: 1962).

Bartrum G. (ed.), *Albrecht Dürer and his Legacy: The Graphic Work of a Renaissance Artist*, exh. cat. London, The British Museum (London: 2002).

Bergström I., *Dutch Still-Life Painting in the Seventeenth Century*, trans. Ch. Hedström – G. Taylor (London: 1956).

Bevers H. – Mielke U. – Wiebel Ch. (eds.), *Heinrich Aldegrever, The New Hollstein: German Engravings, Etchings and Woodcuts, 1400–1700*, 3 (Rotterdam: 1998).

Białostocki J., "Begegnung mit dem Ich in der Kunst", *Artibus et Historiae* 1:1 (1980) 25–45.

Białostocki J., *Dürer and his Critics. 1500–1971: Chapters in the History of Ideas Including a Collection of Texts* (Baden-Baden: 1986).

Bock E., *Die deutschen Meister: Beschreibendes Verzeichnis sämtlicher Zeichnungen mit 193 Lichtdrucktafeln*, Die Zeichnungen Alter Meister im Kupferstichkabinett, im Auftrage des Generaldirektors, ed. M.J. Friedländer, 2 vols. (Berlin: 1921).

Bodnár S., *German Drawings of the Fifteenth and Sixteenth Centuries in Museum of Fine Arts, Budapest* (Budapest: 2020).

Bodnár S., "Hans Hoffmanns Zeichnungen in Budapest", *Acta historiae artium Academiae Scientiarum Hungaricae* 32 (1986) 73–121.

Bol L.J., *The Bosschaert Dynasty: Painters of Flowers and Fruit*, trans. A.M. de Bruins-Cousins (Leigh-on-Sea: 1960).

Bredekamp H., *Image Acts: A Systematic Approach to Visual Agency*, trans., ed. and adapted E. Clegg (Berlin: 2018).

Brusati C., *Artifice and Illusion: The Art and Writing of Samuel van Hoogstraten* (Chicago – London: 1995).

Bubenik A., *Reframing Albrecht Dürer: The Appropriation of Art, 1528–1700* (Farnham – Burlington: 2013).

Budde H., *Die Kunstsammlung des Nürnberger Patriziers Willibald Imhoff unter besonderer Berücksichtigung der Werke Albrecht Dürers* (Munster: 1996).

Burg T., *Die Signatur: Formen und Funktionen vom Mittelalter bis zum 17. Jahrhundert* (Munster: 2007).

Bushart M., "Intermedialität um 1500: Wechselwirkungen zwischen Druckgraphik und Malerei in der Kunst der Dürerzeit", in Fajt J. – Jaeger S. (eds.), *Das Expressive in der Kunst 1500–1550: Albrecht Altdorfer und seine Zeitgenossen* (Berlin – Munich: 2018) 43–53.

Bushart M., *Sehen und Erkennen: Albrecht Altdorfers religiöse Bilder* (Munich – Berlin: 2004).

Claussen P.C., "Früher Künstlerstolz: Mittelalterliche Signaturen als Quelle der Kunstsoziologie", in Clausberg K. (ed.), *Bauwerk und Bildwerk im Hochmittelalter: Anschauliche Beiträge zur Kultur- und Sozialgeschichte* (Giessen: 1981) 7–34.

Clippel K. – Linden D., "The Genesis of the Netherlandish Flower Piece", *Simiolus* 38:1–2 (2015–2016) 73–86.

DaCosta Kaufmann Th., *The School of Prague: Painting at the Court of Rudolf II* (Chicago – London: 1988).

Dietl A., *Die Sprache der Signatur: Die mittelalterlichen Künstlerinschriften Italiens* (Florence: 2009).

Eichberger D., "Dürer and the Netherlands: Patterns of Exchange and Mutual Admiration", in Silver L. – Smith J.C. (eds.), *The Essential Dürer* (Philadelphia: 2010) 149–165.

Faietti M., "Dentro alle 'cose di natura': Lo sguardo di Jacopo", in Cecchi A. – Conigliello L. – Faietti M. (eds.), *Jacopo Ligozzi, 'pittore universalissimo'*, exh. cat. Florence, Palazzo Pitti, Galleria Palatina (Florence – Livorno: 2014) 39–45.

Fehl Ph., "Dürer's Literal Presence in His Pictures: Reflections on His Signatures in the Small Woodcut Passion", in Winner M. (ed.), *Der Künstler über sich in seinem Werk* (Weinheim: 1992) 191–244.

Fircks J., "Zwischen Nürnberg und Antwerpen. Zur wechselseitigen Wahrnehmung deutscher und niederländischer Künstler in der Dürerzeit", in Borchert T.-H. (ed.), *Van Eyck bis Dürer: Altniederländische Meister und die Malerei in Mitteleuropa*, exh. cat. Bruges, Groeningenmuseum (Bruges: 2010) 82–93.

Fraenkel B., "La signature: du signe à l'acte", *Sociétés & Représentations* 25.1 (2008) 13–23.

Gandelman C., "The Semiotics of Signatures in Painting: A Peircian Analysis", *American Journal of Semiotics* 3:3 (1985) 73–108.

Gehrken F.J., "Heinrich Aldegrever, Goldschmied, Maler, Kupferstecher und Prägschneider. Biographisch und kunsthistorisch", *Westfälische Zeitschrift: Zeitschrift für vaterländische Geschichte und Altertmskunde* 4.5 (1841) 145–165.

Glück G., "Fälschungen auf Dürers Namen", *Jahrbuch der Kunsthistorischen Sammlungen des Allerhöchsten Kaiserhauses* 28 (1909/1910) 1–27.

Gludovatz K., *Fährten legen – Spuren lesen: Die Kunstlersignatur als poetische Referenz* (Munich: 2011).

Grebe A., *Dürer. Die Geschichte seines Ruhms* (Petersberg: 2013).

Grollemund H. – Savatier Sjöholm O. – Lepape S. (eds.), *Albrecht Altdorfer: Maître de la Renaissance allemande*, exh. cat. Paris, Musée du Louvre (Paris: 2020).

Harth A. – Martens M.P.J., "Albrecht Dürer's Iconic Image of Saint Jerome: Making, Meaning and Reception", in Foister S. – Brink P. (eds.), *Dürer's Journeys. Travels of a Renaissance Artist*, exh. cat. London, The National Gallery (New Haven – London: 2021) 253–265.

Held J.S., *Dürers Wirkung auf die niederländische Kunst seiner Zeit* (s'Gravenhage: 1930).

Imhoff Hans, *Theatrum virtutis honoris oder Tugendbüchlein* (Nuremberg, Paul Kauffmann: 1606).

Imhoff W., "Unkostpuch meyner haushaltunkostpuch nach volendung des ersten, so 18 jar lang geweret hott, angefangen a di 13 Junyo 1564. Gott der Herr verleyhe syn gotlichen segen. Per Wiliboldt Imhoff, Nürnberg (Nürnberg, Stadtbibliothek, Amb. 64 4)", in Pohl H. (ed.), *Willibald Imhoff, Enkel und Erbe Willibald Pirckheimers,* Quellen zur Geschichte und Kultur der Stadt Nürnberg, 24 (Nuremberg: 1992) 91–279.

Kauffmann H., "Dürer in der Kunst und im Kunsturteil um 1600", *Anzeiger des Germanischen Nationalmuseums in Nürnberg* (1954) 18–60.

Knauer M., "Kupferstiche der deutschen Kleinmeister. Zur Erforschung eines Bildmediums in einer Epoche kulturellen Umbruchs", in Möseneder K. (ed.), *Zwischen Dürer und Raffael: Graphikserien Nürnberger Kleinmeister* (Petersberg: 2010) 9–16.

Knauer M., *Dürers unfolgsame Erben: Bildstrategien in den Kupferstichen der deutschen Kleinmeister* (Petersberg: 2013).

Koerner J.L., "Albrecht Dürer: A Sixteenth-Century *Influenza*", in Bartrum G. (ed.), *Albrecht Dürer and his Legacy: The Graphik Work of a Renaissance Artist*, exh. cat. London, The British Museum (London: 2002) 18–38.

Koerner J.L., *The Moment of Self-Portraiture in German Renaissance Art* (Chicago – London: 1993).

Koreny F., *Albrecht Dürer und die Tier- und Pflanzenstudien der Renaissance* (Munich: 1985).

Koschatzky W. – Strobl A., *Die Dürer Zeichnungen der Albertina* (Salzburg: 1971).

Kurz O., *Fakes: A Handbook for Collectors and Students* (New Haven: 1948).

Landau D. – Parshall P., *The Renaissance Print, 1470–1550* (New Haven – London: 1994).

Lebensztejn J.-C., "Esquisse d'une typologie", *Revue de L'Art* 26 (1974) 48–56.

Lenain T., *Art Forgery: The History of a Modern Obsession* (London: 2011).

Leonhard K., "Hans Hoffmanns Hase", in Felfe R. – Saß M. (eds.), *Naturalismen: Kunst, Wissenschaft und Ästhetik*, Naturbilder/Images of Nature 9 (Berlin – Boston: 2019) 33–48.

Macho Th., "Handschrift – Schriftbild: Anmerkungen zu einer Geschichte der Unterschrift", in Grube G. – Kogge W. – Krämer S. (eds.), *Schrift: Kulturtechnik zwischen Auge, Hand und Maschine* (Munich: 2005) 413–422.

Mander Karel van, *The Lives of the Illustrious Netherlandish and German Painters From the First Edition of the 'Schilder-boeck' (1603–1604)*, ed. H. Miedema, 6 vols. (Doornspijk: 1994).

Mann W.J., "Identity Signs: Meanings and Methods in Artemisia Gentileschi's signatures", *Renaissance Studies* 23:1 (2009) 71–107.

Meder J., *Die Handzeichnung: Ihre Technik und Entwicklung* (Vienna: 1919).

Meissner G. – Beyer A. – Savoy B. – Tegethoff W. (eds.), *Allgemeines Künstlerlexikon (AKL): Die bildenden Künstler aller Zeiten und Völker*, 99 vols. (Munich – Leipzig: 1991–2017).

Mende M., "Hoffmanns Dürer-Hasen", in Zettl L. (ed.), *Der Hase wird 500: 1502–2002 Beiträge zu Albrecht Dürer und seinem Hasen* (Nuremberg: 2002) 16–21.

Messling G., "Anarchist und Apelles? Altdorfer und der deutsche Humansimus", in Roller S. – Sander J. (eds.), *Fantastische Welten: Albrecht Altdorfer und das Expressive in der Kunst um 1500*, exh. cat. Frankfurt am Main, Städel Museum; Vienna, Kunsthistorisches Museum (Frankfurt am Main – Munich: 2014) 21–25.

Metzger C., "Lieben, Lächeln und Sich erinnern: Albrecht Dürers Hase", in Schröder K.A. (ed.), *Die Gründung der Albertina – zwischen Dürer und Napoleon: 100 Meisterwerke der Sammlung*, exh. cat. Albertina Museum Vienna (Ostfildern: 2014) 49–56.

Mielke H. (ed.), *Albrecht Altdorfer: Zeichnungen, Deckfarbenmalerei, Druckgraphik*, exh. cat. Berlin, Kupferstichkabinett; Museen der Stadt Regensburg (Berlin: 1988).

Murr Christoph Gottlieb van (ed.), *Description du Cabinet de Monsieur Paul de Praun à Nuremberg* (Nuremberg, Jean Théophile Schneider: 1797).

Naß M., "Stellung und Bedeutung des Monogramms Martin Schongauers in der Graphik des 15. Jahrhunderts", in Krohm H. – Nicolaisen J. (eds.), *Martin Schongauer: Druckgraphik im Berliner Kupferstichkabinett* (Berlin: 1991) 48–62.

Neudörfer Johann – Gulden Andreas, *Des Johann Neudörfer Schreib- und Rechenmeisters zu Nürnberg Nachrichten von Künstlern und Werkleuten daselbst aus dem Jahre 1547 nebst der Fortsetzung des Andreas Gulden*, ed. G.W.K. Lochner, Quellenschriften für Kunstgeschichte und Kunsttechnik des Mittelalters und der Renaissance, 10 (Vienna: 1875).

Oehler L., "Das Dürermonogramm auf Werken der Dürerzeit", *Städel-Jahrbuch* 3 (1971) 79–108.

Oehler L., "Das Dürermonogramm auf Werken der Dürerschule", *Städel-Jahrbuch* 4 (1973) 36–80.

Oettinger K., *Datum und Signatur bei Wolf Huber und Albrecht Altdorfer, zur Beschriftungskritik der Donauschulzeichnungen*, Erlangen Forschungen 8 (Erlangen: 1957).

Perrot F., "La signature imprévue", *Revue de L'Art* 26 (1974) 33–39.

Pilz K., "Hans Hoffmann: Ein Nürnberger Dürer-Nachahmer aus der 2. Hälfte des 16. Jahrhunderts", *Mitteilungen des Vereins für Geschichte der Stadt Nürnberg* 51 (1962) 236–271.

Pon L., *Raphael, Dürer, and Marcantonio Raimondi: Copying and the Italian Renaissance Print* (New Haven – London: 2004).

Roller S. – Sander J. (eds.), *Fantastische Welten: Albrecht Altdorfer und das Expressive in der Kunst um 1500*, exh. cat. Frankfurt am Main, Städel Museum; Vienna, Kunsthistorisches Museum (Frankfurt am Main – Munich: 2014).

Röver-Kann A. – Von Miller M. (eds.), *Dürer-Zeit: Die Geschichte der Dürer-Sammlung in der Kunsthalle Bremen*, exh. cat. Kunsthalle Bremen (Munich: 2012).

Rubin P., "Signposts of Invention: Artists' Signatures in Italian Renaissance Art", *Art History* 29:4 (2006) 563–599.

Schmid W., "Dürer's Enterprise: Market Area – Market Potential – Product Range", in North M. (ed.), *Economic History and the Arts* (Cologne: 1996) 27–47.

Schoch R. – Mende M. – Scherbaum A. (eds.), *Albrecht Dürer: Das druckgraphische Werk*, 3 vols. (Munich: 2001–2004).

Schröder K.A. (ed.), *Von Rubens bis Makart: Die fürstlichen Sammlungen Liechtenstein*, exh. cat. Albertina Museum Vienna (Vienna – Cologne: 2019).

Segal S. (ed.), *Flowers and Nature: Netherlandish Flower Painting of Four Centuries*, exh. cat. Osaka, Nabio Museum of Art; Tokyo, Station Gallery (Amstelveen: 1990).

Silver L., "Dürer and Gossaert", in Foister S. – Brink P. (eds.), *Dürer's Journeys: Travels of a Renaissance Artist*, exh. cat. London, The National Gallery (New Haven – London: 2021) 103–115.

Stoichita V.I., *The Self-Aware Image: An Insight into Early Modern Meta-Painting*, trans. A.-M. Glasheen (Cambridge: 1997).

Thausing M., *Dürer: Geschichte seines Lebens und seiner Kunst* (Leipzig: 1876).

Thieme U. – Becker F. (eds.), *Allgemeines Lexikon der bildenden Künstler von der Antike bis zur Gegenwart*, 37 vols. (Leipzig: 1907–1950).

Tietze H. – Tietze-Conrat E., *Kritisches Verzeichnis der Werke Albrecht Dürers*, 2 vols. (Basel – Leipzig: 1928–1938).

Tietze H., *Genuine and False: Copies, Imitations, Forgeries* (London: 1948).

Tross L., "Aldegrever, Maler und Kupferstecher in der Stadt Soest", *Westphalia: Zeitschrift für Geschichte und Alterthumskunde Westphalens und Rheinlands* 3 (1826) 4–7.

Tschetschik K., "Monogramme Albrecht Dürers auf den Zeichnungen des Nürnberger Künstlers Hans Hoffmann: Fälschung oder Täuschung?", in Münch B.U. – Tacke A. – Herzog M. – Heudecker S. (eds.), *Fälschung – Plagiat – Kopie: Künstlerische Praktiken in der Vormoderne*. Kunsthistorisches Forum Irrsee, 1 (Petersberg: 2014) 41–51.

Tschetschik-Hammerl K., "Das Dürer-Monogramm als Gegenstand der Nachahmung im 16. und frühen 17. Jahrhundert", in Dressen A. – Gramatzki S. – Knoblich B. (eds.), *Original – Kopie – Fälschung II*, kunsttexte.de 3 (2018) 1–31.

Weniger M., *Zweigmuseum des Bayerischen Nationalmuseums Festung Rosenberg Kronach* (Petersberg: 2014).

Wood Ch.S., *Albrecht Altdorfer and the Origins of Landscape* (London: 1993).

Zschelletzschky H., *Das graphische Werk Heinrich Aldegrevers: Ein Beitrag zu seinem Stil im Rahmen der deutschen Stilentwicklung* (Strasbourg: 1933).

CHAPTER 8

Mind Your *U*'s and *V*'s!: Counterfeiting Newspapers in Civil War Britain

Laurent Curelly

The British Civil Wars, which began as a standoff between King Charles I and his Parliament and culminated in the public execution of the Stuart king and the establishment of a republic, were accompanied by a print revolution that caused a flurry of pamphlets and newspapers to roll off the country's presses. The staggering growth of cheap print that characterised such unsettled decades as the 1640s and 1650s was made possible by the weakening and the eventual collapse of monarchical order. Not only were the king's authority and legitimacy contested but political, social and religious norms were hotly debated, and frequently challenged, by pamphleteers of all stripes and of all persuasions. Newspapers were central to the development of cheap print as they sought to satisfy an ever-growing number of readers' appetite for news and, more often than not, by joining the fray, they shaped public opinion and contributed to the expansion of a budding public sphere. Pamphlets in general, and so-called newsbooks in particular, were used as 'paper bullets', some of which were especially destructive, as they strengthened partisanship and helped to carry polemic further afield. Forgers of existing newspapers were not long before trying their luck on the thriving news market.

Early modern British journalism is now well-documented. A fair number of general studies are available to modern-day scholars, so that Civil War periodicals have lost much of their eerie unfamiliarity and have become scientific objects that are investigated from various perspectives.[1] Studies have been

1 See for instance Cotton A.N.B., *London Newsbooks in the Civil War: Their Political Attitudes and Sources of Information* (Ph.D. dissertation, University of Oxford: 1971); Frank J., *The Beginnings of the English Newspaper, 1620–1660* (Cambridge MA: 1961); Raymond J., *The Invention of the Newspaper – English Newsbooks, 1641–1649* (Oxford: 1996); see also Nelson C. – Seccombe M., *British Newspapers and Periodicals, 1641–1700: A Short-Title Catalogue of Serials Printed in England, Scotland, Ireland, and British America* (New York: 1987). Lately, historians and literary scholars have especially developed an interest in news networks across Europe and have attempted to map out these networks. See for example Raymond J. (ed.), *News Networks in Seventeenth-Century Britain and Europe* (London – New York: 2006); Raymond J. – Moxham N. (eds.), *News Networks in Early Modern Europe* (Leiden – Boston: 2016); Ryan Y.,

 | DOI:10.1163/9789004106901_009

published that deal with one aspect or another of English newsbooks, with a focus on one particular newspaper or on one specific type of periodicals, such as royalist newspapers, also known as mercuries.[2] However, counterfeiting, a significant aspect of the Civil War press, has not attracted much attention thus far, apart from occasional mentions in general studies of the early modern English press and a seminal article by Jason Peacey that centres on *Mercurius Pragmaticus*,[3] a newspaper that was regarded by contemporary journalists as an index and a model of royalist journalism. Even less attention has been paid to what instances of counterfeiting reveal about forgery as an economic and socio-cultural practice. By describing various examples of newspaper counterfeiting this essay aims to contribute to the history of literary forgery.

It will investigate both mercury-type newspapers and diurnal-type newsbooks. Two forms of journalism coexisted during the Civil Wars: the 'diurnal' type was of an informative, if potentially combative, nature while the 'mercury' type was of a sardonic nature and sported satire as a badge of authority.[4] There could be some overlap between these generic categories, and a diurnal could contribute to polemic or spark controversy just as a mercury did. 'Mercuries' were by no means the preserve of English royalists but they were clearly not the format that their parliamentarian rivals favoured. Investigating royalist weeklies is especially rewarding as most of these writings were highly charged pieces of polemic – not dissimilar to pamphlets – penned by authors who made a point of lampooning their political opponents. If royalist authors were especially expert at spicing up their news with satirical content, some of their adversaries took up the gauntlet and responded to the attacks in the same vein.

Networks, Maps and Readers: Foreign News Reporting in London Newsbooks, 1645–1649 (Ph.D. dissertation, Queen Mary University of London: 2019).

2 See for instance Curelly L., *An Anatomy of an English Radical Newspaper – The Moderate (1648–9)* (Newcastle-upon-Tyne: 2017); Macadam A.E.J., *Mercurius Britanicus: Journalism and Politics in the English Civil War* (Ph.D. dissertation, University of Sussex: 2005); McElligott J., *Royalism, Print and Censorship in Revolutionary England* (Woodbridge: 2007); Peacey J., "The Management of Civil War Newspapers: Auteurs, Entrepreneurs and Editorial Control", *Seventeenth Century* 21:1 (2006) 99–127.

3 Peacey J., "'The counterfeit silly curr': Money, Politics, and the Forging of Royalist Newspapers during the Civil War", *Huntington Library Quarterly* 67:1 (2004) 27–58.

4 Both diurnal-type newsbooks and mercury-type newspapers were weekly publications. Originally, diurnals published the proceedings of the House of Commons day by day, but their format evolved and became more complex and diverse as time went by. Mercuries took their name from the Roman god of commerce, who was also the messenger of the gods in the Roman Pantheon; many of them had titles beginning with 'Mercurius'.

This chapter will primarily concentrate on both mercuries written by royalist authors and, to a lesser extent, by their parliamentarian counterparts, and on diurnals, typically penned by parliamentarian writers. In the abovementioned essay Jason Peacey explores the issue of newspaper counterfeiting and seeks to uncover the forgers' reasons for hijacking this title. He especially points out that the various issues of *Mercurius Pragmaticus*, original and counterfeit, reflected their authors' diverging approaches to political circumstances. Peacey certainly has a point when he argues that loyalism to the king was by no means monolithic and that different brands of royalism coexisted at particular times during the Civil Wars. However, it will be argued that political differences should not be played up and that the economic factor may have been as much of an incentive for counterfeiters as political differences. Forgery in the seventeenth-century news market may well have been favoured by commercial interests rather than political concerns.

In addition, this thesis challenges the assumption that the eighteenth century was a defining period in Britain for practices of literary forgery that involved self-reflection.[5] Such practices, I argue, chimed with, and may even have been precipitated by, the emergence of a public sphere that was facilitated by the development of cheap print at a time of political crisis.[6] News writing, of which counterfeiting was a feature, was primarily shaped by political partisanship but it was part and parcel of a vibrant economic print market that impacted on its forms as well as on its actors. The 'commodification of culture' that, according to Hammond,[7] characterised post-Restoration Britain may well have been anticipated by the penetration of cheap print in the 1640s and the 1650s – after all, books began to be advertised in newspapers, and the fact that newspapers are not canonical literary artefacts does not make much difference.

By 'counterfeiting' here is meant the fraudulent appropriation of another author's work in order to pass it off as one's own. There is no question, as will be evidenced further down, that counterfeiting was perceived as a theft. On

5 See Baines P., *The House of Forgery in Eighteenth-Century Britain* (Aldershot: 1999) chap. 1.

6 Similarly, Jürgen Habermas's claim that the public sphere as a social space of media communication developed in eighteenth-century Europe should be qualified as it ignores the proliferation of cheap print in the British Civil Wars and its political ramifications. See Habermas J., *The Structural Transformation of the Public Sphere* (1962), trans. Thomas Burger and Frederick Lawrence (Cambridge: 1989).

7 Hammond B.S., "Plagiarism: Hammond versus Ricks", in Kewes P. (ed.), *Plagiarism in Early Modern England* 52. The word 'plagiarism' as used in this book should be taken with a pinch of salt and cannot quite be equated with 'forgery', which implies the appropriation of a commodity, in the case of this study a newspaper, but not the actual copying of it. See Marantz Cohen P., "The Meanings of Forgery", *Southwest Review* 97:1 (2012) 12–25.

that account, it was deemed morally wrong. Counterfeiting newspapers did not imply actual copying. What was involved in all cases was not so much the content of the newspapers as their very titles. On several occasions, authors complained that their titles had been counterfeited, that is to say stolen and appropriated, by an unscrupulous rival so that, when this occurred, readers were faced with two, sometimes three, competing issues of the same weekly. I would suggest that the perception of journalistic counterfeiting as 'a moral crime against authorship because it threatens literary livelihoods'[8] developed during the Civil Wars, primarily as a result of the expansion of cheap print and contemporaries' increased awareness of its significance.

This chapter will focus on various instances of newspaper forgery in Civil War Britain. It will investigate these cases by examining textual evidence. It will first show how counterfeiting, though not necessarily counterfeiters, can be identified. It will then concentrate on the way newsbook authors responded to their newspapers being forged and to counterfeiting as a practice. Last, it will consider the forgers' possible motives and cast light on what this reveals about forgery as a socio-cultural fact with reference to the news trade.

1 Identifying Counterfeiting

Pinpointing forgery is not too much of a challenge. When several competing issues of a newsbook appeared at a specific time, the odds are high that one or more of them were counterfeits. This typically led authors to remark, and often complain, that they had been robbed of their titles, even if forgers themselves lamented, disingenuously it must be said, that their newspapers had been faked. Authors were fully aware, sometimes even before counterfeit issues were published, that rivals had poached on their home turf, and they frequently settled scores with them in subsequent newspaper issues.

If identifying cases of forgery is clearly not a mind-boggling problem, telling counterfeit issues from original newsbooks is more problematic for twenty-first century students of early modern journalism, but even for contemporary readers, it may have been something of a challenge. For modern-day scholars, this requires a form of forensic investigation that looks for intra-, inter- and paratextual clues that seventeenth-century readers did not necessarily have access to. The devil lies in the details, and so does the identification of forgery, as will be shown.

---

8 Hammond, "Plagiarism: Hammond versus Ricks" 52.

A clue that is helpful to us but that British Civil War readers could not rely on are the compulsive seventeenth-century collector George Thomason's handwritten annotations on some newspaper issues. Thus, Thomason must have had a hunch that a counterfeit 'Kingdomes Weekly Intelligencer', a long-standing parliamentarian newsbook, was being printed and sold as he wrote 'different from ye former' on his copies of two successive issues.[9] What must have caught his attention was a somewhat altered layout as the original title featured numbered news items while counterfeit copies had none of that numbering. It is unknown whether, initially, contemporary readers were fooled by such a trick and whether, with the next three issues, they realised that a different 'Kingdomes Weekly Intelligencer' had been published, which they were willing to adopt anyway as if it had been the original title and although they knew it to be forged. Not all issues had an imprint but some issues of 'Kingdomes Weekly Intelligencer' did. The original title was printed by George Bishop and Robert White, whose names will come back later, while the counterfeit newspaper came off Robert Austin and Andrew Coe's presses.[10] The counterfeiters only signed what was to be their last issue, both in an attempt to claim authority for their title and to comply with the recent 'Ordinance for the Regulation of Printing'. The ordinance had been passed by Parliament the week before due to 'the great late abuses and frequent disorders in Printing many false, **forged**, scandalous, seditious, libellous, and unlicensed Papers, Pamphlets, and Books'.[11] It tightened regulations as it imposed pre-publication

9 These are "THE KINGDOMES VVeekly Intelligencer: SENT ABROAD To prevent mis-information" no. 21 (23–30 May 1643) and no. 22 (30 May–6 June 1643). For the sake of clarity, I will retain the original spelling as well as capitalisation for all newspapers in the footnotes but I will use the generic title in the text (unless I deem it necessary to stick to the original format). Spelling, capitalisation as well as typeface are distinguishing features that help to recognise forged issues. Italics, albeit not in this instance, are also significant details for characterisation, which is why, contrary to standard academic usage, newspaper titles will be given in inverted commas rather than italics, some titles being partly or wholly italicised, or not italicised at all. The counterfeit title ran for four weeks altogether.

10 In the former case, the imprint said: 'Printed **by** G. Bishop and R. White' while in the latter case it said: 'Printed **for** R. Austin and A. Coe' (bold type is mine). The former were printers while the latter were likely to have been publishers or booksellers. Although Nelson and Seccombe point to this difference in their catalogue of seventeenth-century English newspapers, they include only one Publisher-Printer index, as if the ones could not clearly be distinguished from the others. See Nelson C. – Seccombe M., *British Newspapers and Periodicals* 705–724. Despite its fuzziness, I shall retain this distinction for clarity's sake.

11 "An Ordinance for the Regulation of Printing", in Firth C.H. – Rait R.S. (eds.), *Acts and Ordinances of the Interregnum, 1642–1660* (London: 1911) 184–186. The ordinance is dated 14 June 1643. Bold letters are mine.

licensing, thus making it compulsory for titles to be entered into the Stationers' Company's register and for the printer's name to be mentioned. The forgers of the 'Kingdomes Weekly Intelligencer' were thus forced out of the market, and the next issues of the original newsbook were 'Licenced and Entred into the Hall book according to order', and duly included the two printers' names.[12]

Thomason's comments also identified original and counterfeit issues of 'Mercurius Britanicus', a long-lived parliamentarian mercury. It, and such like periodicals, were characterised by their hybrid quality, half-newspapers because of their seriality and periodicity, and half-pamphlets because of the polemic they carried. For three weeks in the spring of 1644, 'Mercurius Britanicus' was counterfeited, which prompted Thomason to write 'ye true one' and 'ye counterfairt' [sic] or 'the false one' on the copies he had bought.[13] As for the previous example, the forgery stemmed from a rivalry between printers, Robert White and George Bishop again, who were business partners but then fell out and split up, the one and the other collaborating with different authors to produce their own versions of 'Mercurius Britanicus'. It was White, rather than Bishop, who printed the issues immediately before the forgery and those that followed it. Does this mean that White's newspaper was 'ye true one'? This is what Thomason seems to have believed, but then again, he called the next issue printed by White 'the false one'. The fact is that he must have been confused by two competing issues that were almost identical, barring the content, however strongly the authors claimed that their own version was authentic. Confusing it must have been indeed, since the original and counterfeit issues were dressed in similar garb. Apart from the imprint, however, there is one detail that marked them out, although this very detail makes it impossible to decide which was the original title and which was the forged one. Punctuation comes into play here: while the full title of this newspaper as printed by White was '*Mercurius Britanicus*. Communicating the affaires of great BRITAINE', the rival title was '*Mercurius Britanicus*: Communicating the affaires of great BRITAINE'[14] – one had a full stop whereas the other had a colon [Figs. 8.1–8.2].

I would argue that, although Civil War weeklies were hastily produced and sometimes had a sloppy appearance, this detail was no mere coincidence. It was an identity marker that ensured that newspapers were identifiable after

12 See for example "THE KINGDOMES VVeekly Intelligencer: SENT ABROAD To prevent mis-information" no. 25 (4–11 July 1643) 200.

13 Respectively '*Mercurius Britanicus*' no. 27 (11–18 March 1644) for the first annotation and no. 28 (18–25 March 1644) for the last two.

14 Bold type is mine.

all, although readers – Thomason was one of them – may have been taken in by copies that looked like two peas in a pod, unless they had a keen eye for forensic detail. Of course, such a detail did not escape the authors' notice. This case shows that authentic and forged newspapers almost developed in tandem, and that counterfeiting may well have encouraged further counterfeiting. It also shows that some titles became authoritative, hence worth forging – the layout of the newspapers helped titles to be identified, and this is what forgers had a vested interest in retaining first, although they did not necessarily imitate it slavishly.

Precisely, variations in the layout of a newspaper title-page and/or title – in particular punctuation, capitalisation and italicisation – occurred, which makes it possible to identify cases of forgery but does not always help to tell original titles from forged copies. Two examples will illustrate this point. First, 'A Perfect Diurnall of the Passages in Parliament', an established parliamentarian newspaper, was counterfeited on several occasions, with as many as three forged copies for a single week. Some of them were laid out in much the same way, except for the publishers' names, whose spelling was altered, to the extent that, in one of the issues, the publishers included this expanded colophon: 'Printed for Walt. Cook and ROBERT WOOD, to prevent all false Copies, under their Names, 1642'.[15] In some of the counterfeit issues, the publisher's name 'Wood' was altered to 'Woody', and in one of them, it became 'Woodner'.[16] The publishers' warning was meant to inform readers of the forgery and perhaps deter the counterfeiters from appropriating their very names, but it only had limited effect when it came to the title itself.

To add insult to injury, the original diurnal had to contend with a forged title that departed from the original template. It thus came into its own and seems to have acquired as much authority as the initial newspaper. The counterfeiter made a point of marking his publication out from that of his rival by altering the layout: he introduced pagination, he changed the typeface of the title as he removed the italics from the word 'Parliament' and used lower case instead of capital letters, and, more significantly, he added a woodcut representing Parliament in session as well as fancy letters at the beginning of each entry. As a selling point, he included this notice: 'More fully and exactly taken than any other printed Copies as you will finde upon Comparing, &c'.[17] No doubt

15 "A Perfect Diurnall OF THE PASSAGES IN *PARLIAMENT*" no. 23 (14–21 November 1642).

16 See for instance the various avatars of no.14 as listed in the appendix. The spelling 'Woody' was then used consistently by counterfeiters; 'Woodner' was a one-off.

17 "A Perfect Diurnall OF THE PASSAGES In Parliament" no. 14 (12–19 September 1642) 1.

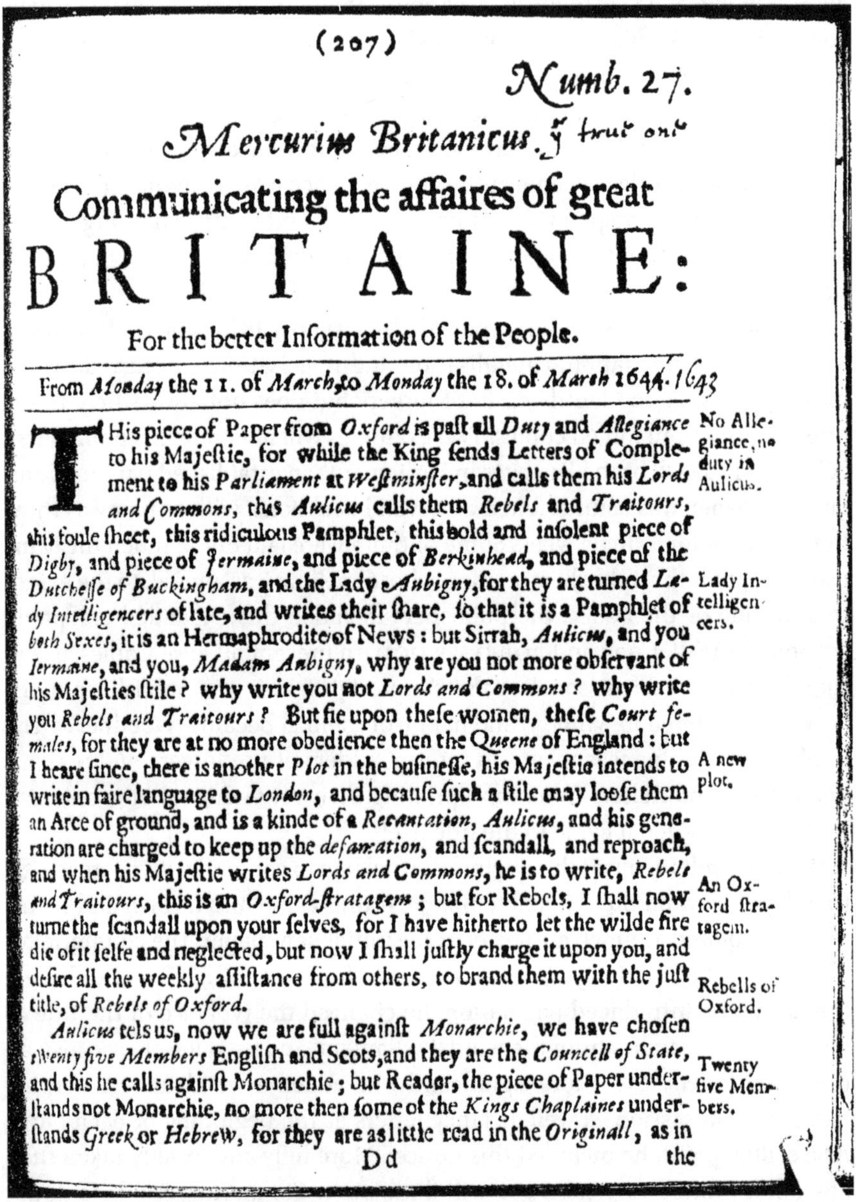

(207)

Numb. 27.

Mercurius Britanicus.

Communicating the affaires of great

BRITAINE:

For the better Information of the People.

From Monday the 11. of March, to Monday the 18. of March 1644. 1643

THis piece of Paper from Oxford is paſt all Duty and Allegiance to his Majeſtie, for while the King ſends Letters of Complement to his Parliament at Weſtminſter, and calls them his Lords and Commons, this Aulicus calls them Rebels and Traitours, this foule ſheet, this ridiculous Pamphlet, this bold and inſolent piece of Digby, and piece of Jermaine, and piece of Berkinhead, and piece of the Dutcheſſe of Buckingham, and the Lady Aubigny, for they are turned Lady Intelligencers of late, and writes their ſhare, ſo that it is a Pamphlet of both Sexes, it is an Hermaphrodite of News: but Sirrah, Aulicus, and you Jermaine, and you, Madam Aubigny, why are you not more obſervant of his Majeſties ſtile? why write you not Lords and Commons? why write you Rebels and Traitours? But fie upon theſe women, theſe Court females, for they are at no more obedience then the Queene of England: but I heare ſince, there is another Plot in the buſineſſe, his Majeſtie intends to write in faire language to London, and becauſe ſuch a ſtile may looſe them an Acre of ground, and is a kinde of a Recantation, Aulicus, and his generation are charged to keep up the defamation, and ſcandall, and reproach, and when his Majeſtie writes Lords and Commons, he is to write, Rebels and Traitours, this is an Oxford-ſtratagem; but for Rebels, I ſhall now turne the ſcandall upon your ſelves, for I have hitherto let the wilde fire die of it ſelfe and neglected, but now I ſhall juſtly charge it upon you, and deſire all the weekly aſſiſtance from others, to brand them with the juſt title, of Rebels of Oxford.

No Allegiance, no duty in Aulicus.

Lady Intelligencers.

A new plot.

An Oxford ſtratagem.

Rebells of Oxford.

Aulicus tels us, now we are full againſt Monarchie, we have choſen twenty five Members Engliſh and Scots, and they are the Councell of State, and this he calls againſt Monarchie; but Reader, the piece of Paper underſtands not Monarchie, no more then ſome of the Kings Chaplaines underſtands Greek or Hebrew, for they are as little read in the Originall, as in the

Twenty five Members.

Dd

FIGURE 8.1 *Mercurius Britanicus, communicating the affaires of great Britaine for the better information of the people* no. 27 (11–18 March 1644), London: Printed by G. Bishop and R. White, title page. Images produced by ProQuest as part of *Early English Books Online*. www.proquest.com

© BRITISH LIBRARY BOARD, THOMASON COLLECTION, E.37(27)

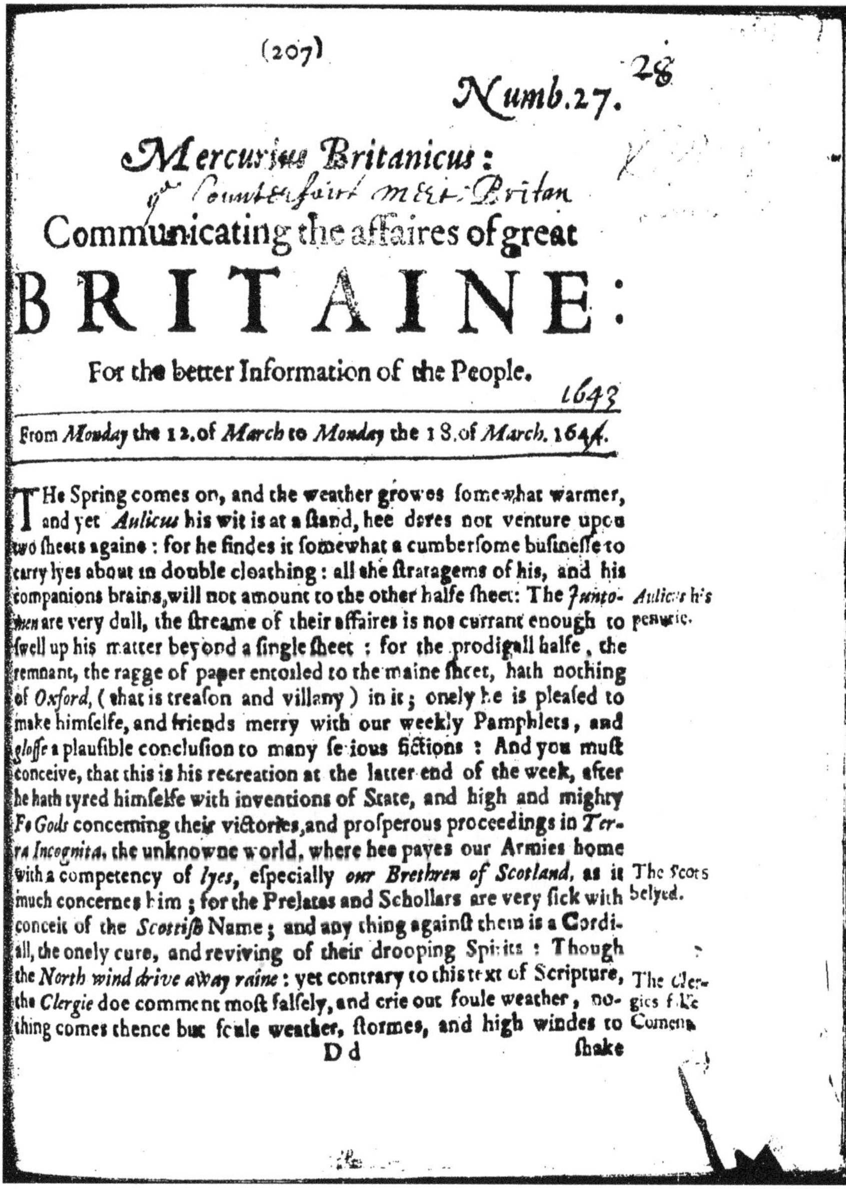

(207)

28

Numb. 27.

Mercurius Britanicus:

y^e Counterfeit merc: Britan

Communicating the affaires of great

BRITAINE:

For the better Information of the People.

1643

From *Monday* the 12. of *March* to *Monday* the 18. of *March*. 1644.

THe Spring comes on, and the weather growes somewhat warmer, and yet *Aulicus* his wit is at a stand, hee dares not venture upon two sheets againe: for he findes it somewhat a cumbersome businesse to carry lyes about in double cloathing: all the stratagems of his, and his companions brains, will not amount to the other halfe sheet: The *Junto-men* are very dull, the streame of their affaires is not currant enough to swell up his matter beyond a single sheet: for the prodigall halfe, the remnant, the ragge of paper entoiled to the maine sheet, hath nothing of *Oxford*, (that is treason and villany) in it; onely he is pleased to make himselfe, and friends merry with our weekly Pamphlets, and *glosse* a plausible conclusion to many serious fictions: And you must conceive, that this is his recreation at the latter end of the week, after he hath tyred himselfe with inventions of State, and high and mighty *Fo Gods* concerning their victories, and prosperous proceedings in *Terra Incognita*, the unknowne world, where hee payes our Armies home with a competency of *lyes*, especially *our Brethren of Scotland*, as it much concernes him; for the Prelates and Schollars are very sick with conceit of the *Scottish* Name; and any thing against them is a Cordiall, the onely cure, and reviving of their drooping Spirits: Though the *North wind drive away raine*: yet contrary to this text of Scripture, the *Clergie* doe comment most falsely, and crie out foule weather, nothing comes thence but foule weather, stormes, and high windes to

Aulicus his penurie.

The Scots belyed.

The Clergies false Comment

Dd shake

FIGURE 8.2 *Mercurius Britanicus, communicating the affaires of great Britaine for the better information of the people* no. 27 (11–18 March 1644), London: Printed by G. Bishop and R. White, title page. Images produced by ProQuest as part of *Early English Books Online*. www.proquest.com
© BRITISH LIBRARY BOARD, THOMASON COLLECTION, E. 37(28)

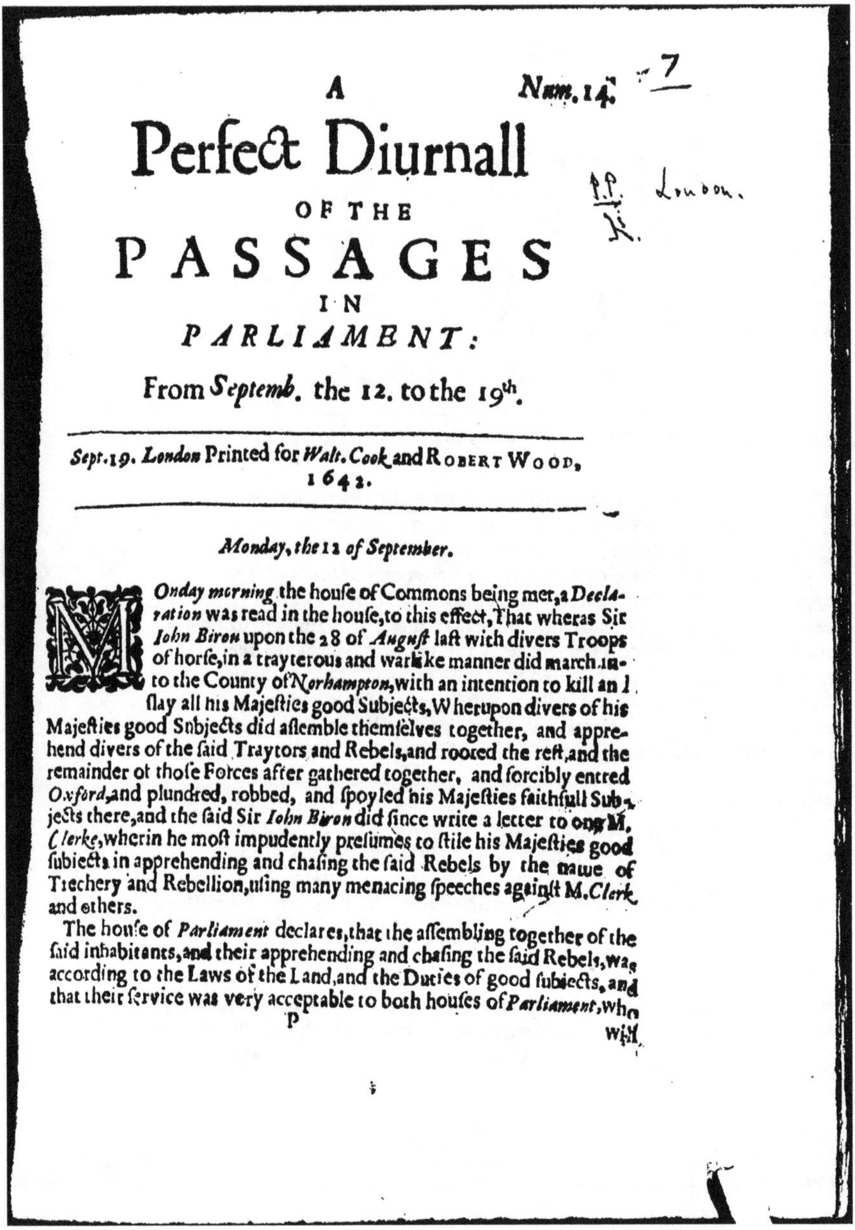

A

Num. 14.

Perfect Diurnall

OF THE

PASSAGES

IN

PARLIAMENT:

From *Septemb.* the 12. to the 19th.

Sept. 19. *London* Printed for *Walt. Cook* and ROBERT WOOD, 1642.

Monday, the 12 of September.

M*Onday morning* the houſe of Commons being met, a *Declaration* was read in the houſe, to this effect, That whereas Sir *John Biron* upon the 28 of *Auguſt* laſt with divers Troops of horſe, in a trayterous and warlike manner did march into the County of *Northampton*, with an intention to kill and ſlay all his Majeſties good Subjects, Whereupon divers of his Majeſties good Subjects did aſſemble themſelves together, and apprehend divers of the ſaid Traytors and Rebels, and rooted the reſt, and the remainder of thoſe Forces after gathered together, and forcibly entred *Oxford*, and plundred, robbed, and ſpoyled his Majeſties faithfull Subjects there, and the ſaid Sir *John Biron* did ſince write a letter to one M. *Clerke*, wherin he moſt impudently preſumes to ſtile his Majeſties good ſubjects in apprehending and chaſing the ſaid Rebels by the name of Trechery and Rebellion, uſing many menacing ſpeeches againſt M. *Clerk* and others.

The houſe of *Parliament* declares, that the aſſembling together of the ſaid inhabitants, and their apprehending and chaſing the ſaid Rebels, was according to the Laws of the Land, and the Duties of good ſubjects, and that their ſervice was very acceptable to both houſes of *Parliament*, who

P will

FIGURE 8.3 *A Perfect Diurnall of the Passages in Parliament* no. 14 (12–19 September 1642), London: Printed for Robert Wood, title page. Images produced by ProQuest as part of *Early English Books Online*. www.proquest.com

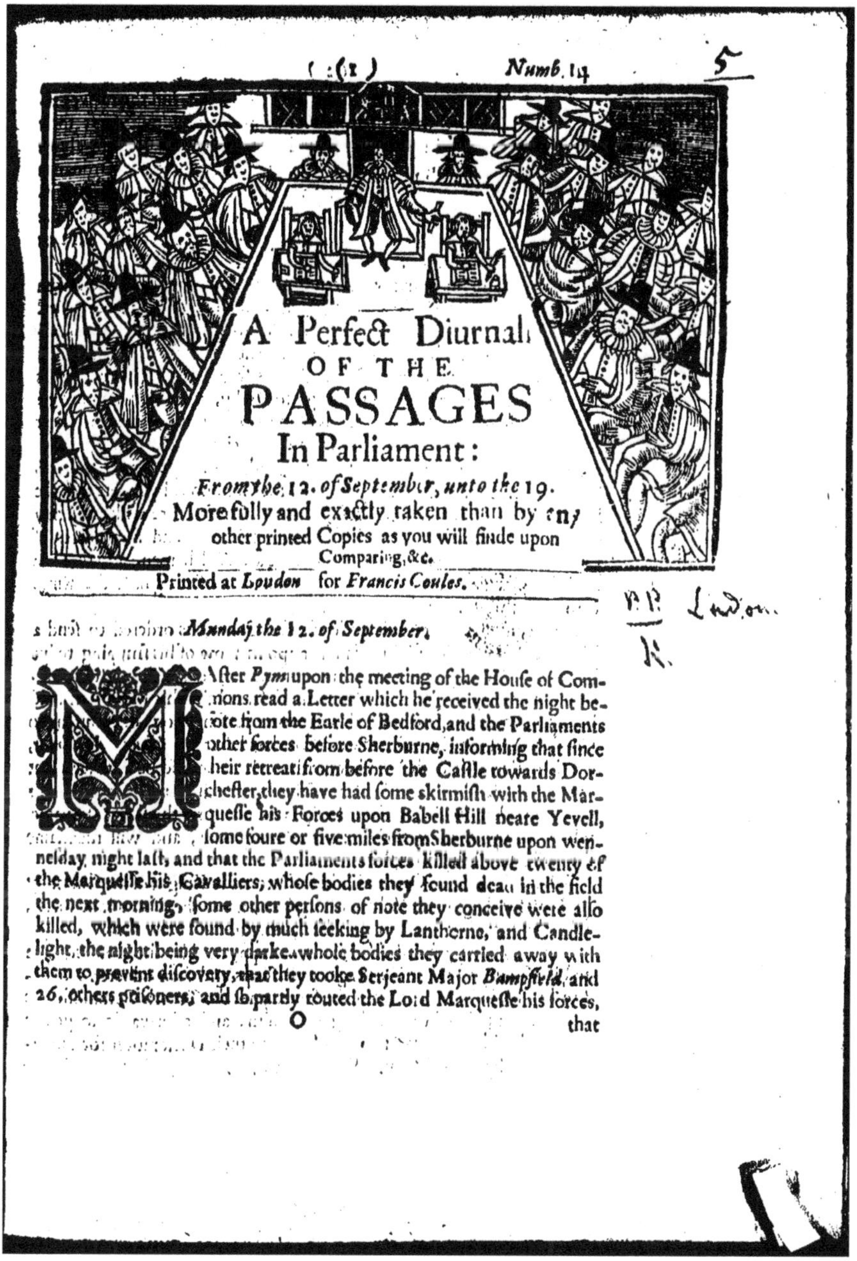

(1) *Numb.* 14

A Perfect Diurnall OF THE PASSAGES In Parliament:

From the 12. *of September, unto the* 19.

More fully and exactly taken than by any other printed Copies as you will finde upon Comparing, &c.

Printed at *Loudon* for *Francis Coules.*

Munday the 12. *of September.*

After *Pym* upon the meeting of the House of Commons read a Letter which he received the night before from the Earle of Bedford, and the Parliaments other forces before Sherburne, informing that since their retreat from before the Castle towards Dorchester, they have had some skirmish with the Marquesse his Forces upon Babell Hill neare Yevell, some foure or five miles from Sherburne upon wednesday night last, and that the Parliaments forces killed above twenty of the Marquesse his Cavalliers, whose bodies they found dead in the field the next morning, some other persons of note they conceive were also killed, which were found by much seeking by Lantherne, and Candle-light, the night being very darke, whole bodies they carried away with them to prevent discovery, that they tooke Serjeant Major *Bampfield*, and 26. others prisoners, and so partly routed the Lord Marquesse his forces, that

FIGURE 8.4 *A Perfect Diurnall of the Passages in Parliament* no. 14 (12–19 September 1642), London: Printed for Francis Coules, title page. Images produced by ProQuest as part of *Early English Books Online*. www.proquest.com

the woodcut was meant to bring added value to the publication, as was the author's claim that his newspaper was thorough and accurate, in other words, that the news in it could be trusted [Figs. 8.3–8.4].

The irony of it was that this counterfeit was forged in its turn, with the same woodcut as in the rival newspaper but without fancy letters and with the word 'Parliament' capitalised anew.[18] The forgery seems to have been committed by Walter Cook and Robert Wood, who had been deprived of their original title. It was common for printers to borrow and counterfeit their competitors' type.[19] This makes it very difficult to decide with any degree of accuracy where many of these periodicals were actually printed, considering that some printers were also publishers and booksellers. The imprints, where they exist, are not always clear, not to mention the fact that they may have been faked. The counterfeiting was taken seriously enough by the author, and possibly the publishers, of this counterfeit 'Perfect Diurnall' for them to include this warning: 'Courteous Reader, take heed of a false & counterfeited Diurnall which is this day printed & fashioned with such a modell like this, by a company of Grub street mercenary fellowes; let this note be your informer to distinguish them hereafter, by the Printers names & the Bookseller, who are here nominated' – 'Perfect Diurnall' issues were 'now printed by I. Okes and F. Leach, and [...] to be sold by Francis Coles in the Old Baily'. This was accompanied, as in previous issues, by a note that said that the news 'was collected by the same hand that formerly drew up the copy for William Cooke in Furnivals Inne'.[20] Interestingly, the forger felt the need to include this comment on an alleged genealogical relation of his copies to the original title, although readers would probably have been hard put to ascertain this lineage. His remark hints at a cutthroat news environment in which, notwithstanding his hyperbolic words, cheating seemed to be the norm.

Another example of counterfeiting worth mentioning because of variations in typeface concerned the long-lasting royalist mercury 'Mercurius Pragmaticus' that was printed in the heyday of royalist journalism towards the end of the 1640s. The letters 'U' included in the title came in various type fonts. It would be tedious to list all the combinations here, all the more so as these combinations sometimes occurred haphazardly. The original version, authored by Marchamont Nedham, alternated a serified 'U', a Roman 'U' and a Roman 'V' – thus, the title of the first issue was 'MERCURIUS PRAGMATICVS' – but

18 "A Perfect Diurnall OF THE PASSAGES In PARLIAMENT" no. 28 (19–26 December 1642).

19 See Potter L., *Secret Rites and Secret Writing: Royalist Literature 1641–1660* (Cambridge: 1989) 14.

20 "A Perfect Diurnall OF THE PASSAGES In Parliament" no. 28 (19–26 December 1642).

counterfeits often, albeit not always, departed from the original format. The various authors of 'Mercurius Pragmaticus' literally minded their U's and their V's, as the title of this chapter suggests.[21] Interestingly, the counterfeiters made little effort to conceal the forgery; on the contrary, it seems that they intended to draw potential readers' attention to the fact that the counterfeit publications were actually different from the existing title, probably in an attempt to impart different identities to their incarnations of 'Mercurius Pragmaticus', which they may have assumed would supplant the original mercury in the end. They supposed that readers would recognise their versions just by looking at the type fonts used in the title [Figs. 8.5–8.7].

In addition, one of the counterfeit versions of 'Mercurius Pragmaticus' in early 1649 included an opening poem, as did most mercuries as of 1647, but one that was markedly, and blatantly, different from the standard format: it comprised five six-line stanzas instead of the usual four four-line stanzas.[22]

'Mercurius Pragmaticus' was a title that had acquired authority, which made it worth forging. Why it became authoritative in the first place is anybody's guess. Perhaps this was due to its author's identity. Although newsbooks were published anonymously, authors were known by the printers they collaborated with and probably by their rivals. The London news market was certainly flourishing but it was rather compact, and authors were likely to rub shoulders with other news writers as they took their books of news to print. Forging a title but introducing variations possibly helped to deflect readers' attention from the original newspaper so as to lure them to the forged title. Commercial gain was certainly of the essence.

Telling forged newspaper issues from original ones unambiguously is difficult, not because forgers made much attempt to conceal their theft, but because we only have circumstantial evidence – Thomason's comments are not absolutely reliable, typeface fluctuated, and authors' words could not always be taken at face value. The news trade was characterised by instantaneity and by dynamic forces that make the forensic reconstruction of these forgery cases difficult. Obviously, forgers did not intend to provide identical copies. They dressed their newspapers in borrowed garb but added their personal touch to them. In other words, they gave their counterfeit titles enough of a twist to

21 An example of such variations is number 19 (1–8 August 1648): while the original title was 'MERCURIUS PRAGMATICVS', the counterfeit issue for that week was 'MERCVRIVS PRAGMATICVS'. It continued in this vein for two weeks. Another example is no. 23 (5–12 September 1648): the original, i.e. the title that was counterfeited as well as the initial 'Pragmaticus', was the same as above while the forged title was 'Mercurius PRAGMATICUS', with a different typeface.

22 "MERCVRIVS PRAGMATICUS" no. 41 (9–16 January 1649).

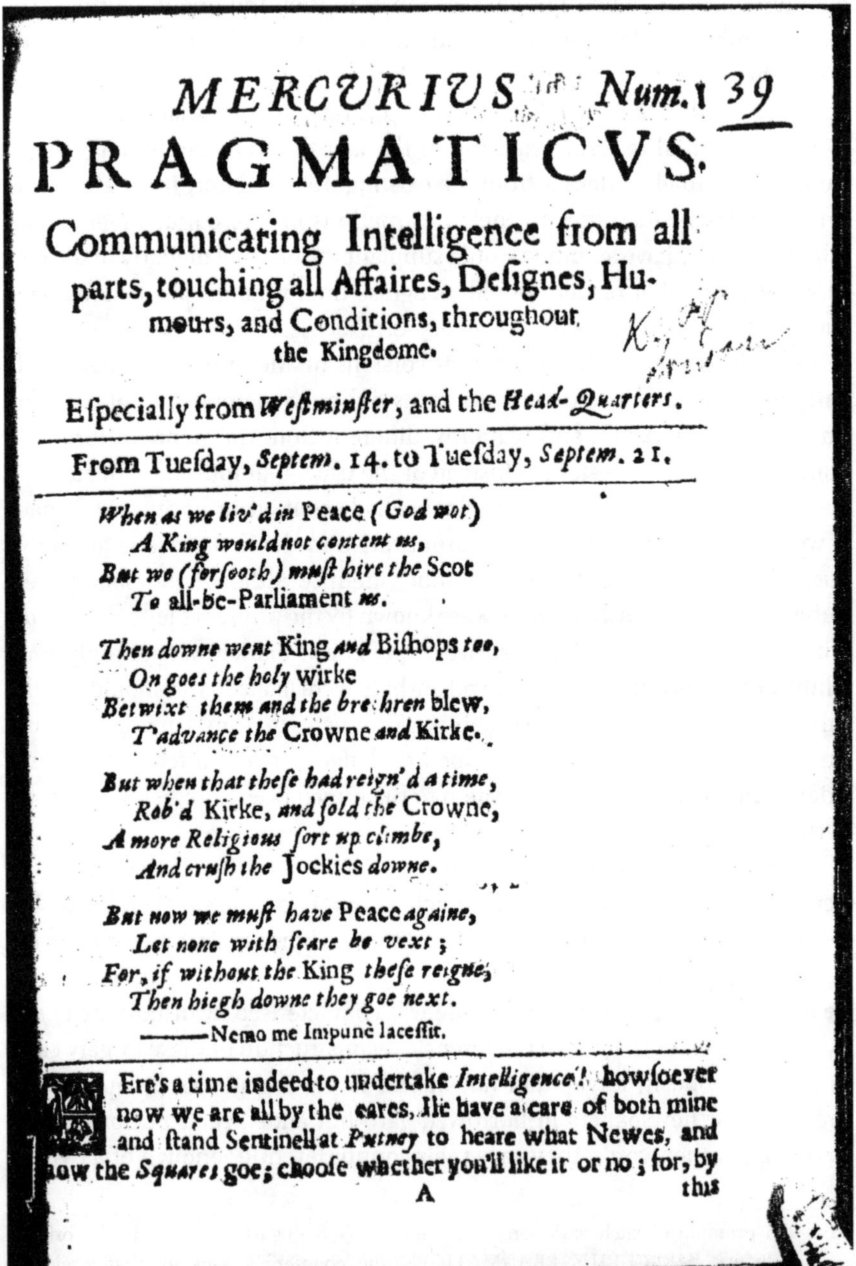

MERCVRIUS Num. 1 39

PRAGMATICVS.

Communicating Intelligence from all parts, touching all Affaires, Designes, Humours, and Conditions, throughout the Kingdome.

Especially from *Westminster*, and the *Head-Quarters*.

From Tuesday, *Septem.* 14. to Tuesday, *Septem.* 21.

When as we liv'd in Peace *(God wot)*
A King would not content us,
But we (forsooth) must hire the Scot
To all-be-Parliament *us.*

Then downe went King *and* Bishops *too,*
On goes the holy wirke
Betwixt them and the brethren blew,
T'advance the Crowne *and* Kirke.

But when that these had reign'd a time,
Rob'd Kirke, *and sold the* Crowne,
A more Religious sort up climbe,
And crush the Jockies *downe.*

But now we must have Peace *againe,*
Let none with feare be vext;
For, if without the King *these reigne,*
Then hiegh downe they goe next.

——Nemo me Impunè lacessit.

HEre's a time indeed to undertake *Intelligence*! howsoever now we are all by the eares, Ile have a care of both mine and stand Sentinell at *Putney* to heare what Newes, and how the *Squares* goe; choose whether you'll like it or no; for, by

A thus

FIGURE 8.5 *Mercurius Pragmaticus* no. 1 (14–21 September 1647), title page.
Images produced by ProQuest as part of *Early English Books Online*.
www.proquest.com

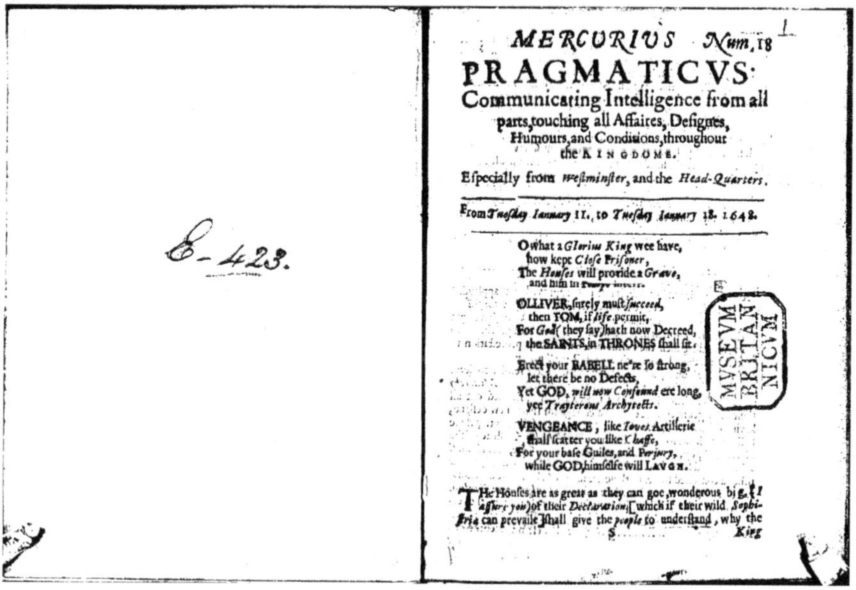

E-423.

MERCURIUS Num. 18
PRAGMATICVS:
Communicating Intelligence from all parts, touching all Affaires, Designes, Humours, and Conditions, throughout the KINGDOME.
Especially from *Westminster*, and the *Head-Quarters*.

From *Tuesday January* 11. to *Tuesday January* 18. 1648.

O what a *Glorius King* wee have,
how kept *Close Prisoner*,
The *Houses* will provide a *Grave*,
and him in [illegible] interr.

OLLIVER, surely must *succeed*,
then TOM, if *life* permit,
For *God* (they say) hath now Decreed,
the SAINTS, in THRONES shall sit.

Erect your BABELL ne're so strong,
let there be no Defects,
Yet GOD, *will now Confound* ere long,
yee *Trayterous Archytects*.

VENGEANCE, like *Joves* Artillerie
shall scatter you like *Chaffe*,
For your base Guiles, and *Perjury*,
while GOD himselfe will LAUGH.

THe Houses are as great as they can goe, wonderous big (*I assure you*) of their *Declaration*, [which if their wild *Sophistria* can prevaile] shall give the *people* to understand, why the *King*

FIGURE 8.6 *Mercurius Pragmaticus* no. 18 (11–18 January 1648), title page. Images produced by ProQuest as part of *Early English Books Online*. www.proquest.com
© BRITISH LIBRARY BOARD, THOMASON COLLECTION, E.423(2)

make them look like the original titles on which they were modelled but reasonably different in outlook so that readers could recognise them. The appropriation of titles thus allowed for a certain degree of cosmetic change. What seems to have mattered to forgers was to hijack the titles that they believed carried enough authority for them to carve out a place for themselves in the highly competitive news business. Thus, counterfeiters' intentions may help us to get a clearer view of newspaper forgery in Civil War Britain. Counterfeiting was cause for concern to authors who, as a result, were deprived of their livelihoods. Unsurprisingly, some of them responded to their titles being counterfeited and even inveighed against forgery as an established practice. Their reactions will be discussed next.

2 Responses to Counterfeiting

Authors typically fulminated against those who poached their titles. This form of commercial rivalry was often perceived by authors as underpinning bitter

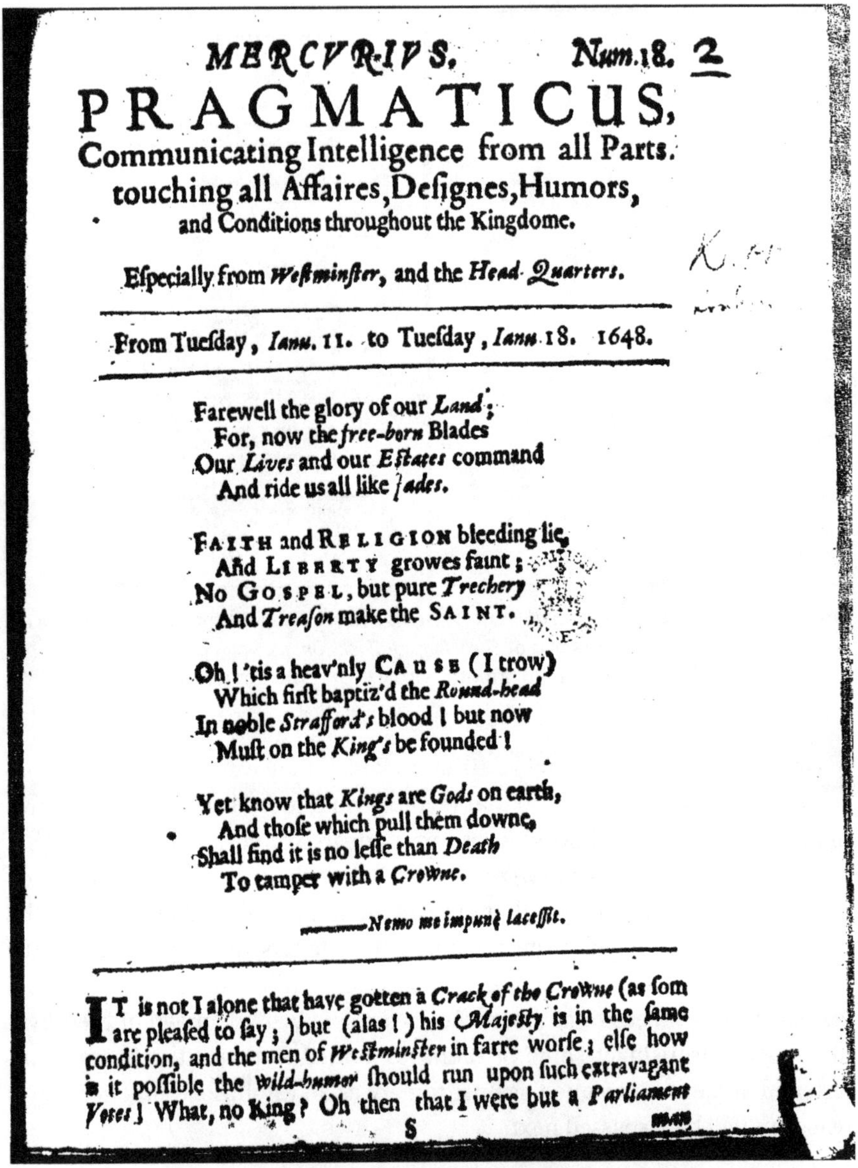

MERCURIUS. Num. 18. 2

PRAGMATICUS,

Communicating Intelligence from all Parts.
touching all Affaires, Designes, Humors,
and Conditions throughout the Kingdome.

Especially from *Westminster*, and the *Head-Quarters*.

From Tuesday, *Janu.* 11. to Tuesday, *Janu.* 18. 1648.

Farewell the glory of our *Land*;
For, now the *free-born* Blades
Our *Lives* and our *Estates* command
And ride us all like *Jades*.

FAITH and RELIGION bleeding lie,
And LIBERTY growes faint;
No GOSPEL, but pure *Trechery*
And *Treason* make the SAINT.

Oh! 'tis a heav'nly CAUSE (I trow)
Which first baptiz'd the *Round-head*
In noble *Strafford's* blood! but now
Must on the *King's* be founded!

Yet know that *Kings* are *Gods* on earth,
And those which pull them downe,
Shall find it is no lesse than *Death*
To tamper with a *Crowne*.

——*Nemo me impunè lacessit.*

IT is not I alone that have gotten a *Crack of the Crowne* (as som are pleased to say;) but (alas!) his *Majesty* is in the same condition, and the men of *Westminster* in farre worse; else how is it possible the *Wild-humor* should run upon such extravagant *Votes*! What, no King? Oh then that I were but a *Parliament* man

S

FIGURE 8.7 *Mercurius Pragmaticus* no. 18 (11–18 January 1648), title page. Images produced by ProQuest as part of *Early English Books Online*. www.proquest.com
© BRITISH LIBRARY BOARD, THOMASON COLLECTION, E.423(1)

personal conflicts, which were expressed in acrimonious language. For example, the author of the genuine 'Mercurius Britanicus' complained about his title being forged by an impostor who 'walks the streets, as if he would outface me in my owne likenesse' and came to the conclusion that 'these are the Arts, and tricks, and whimsies, that the Malignants practice to silence me, or betray me, because I speak home, as well as abroad'.[23] To the author as to the publisher, Robert White, the publication of this counterfeit was nothing but an act of disloyalty committed by ill-meaning royalists ('Malignants') towards Parliament, as if 'Britanicus' had been hijacked by a royalist fifth column. England's divisions were epitomised in this commercial dispute.[24] The author of the forged mercury as well as the publisher, George Bishop, responded on a more personal note by denouncing the supposedly roguish behaviour of the true 'Britanicus' who acted 'on purpose out of malice to the said Bishop' and 'more out of a desire of gain, than sincerity of heart'.[25]

Such disputes sometimes degenerated into all-out rhetorical war, occasionally compounded by sarcastic comments, as in this warning by the author of the revived royalist mercury 'Mercurius Elencticus': 'I am still noy'd with a Counterfeit. [...] Yet I will let him alone (this weeke) to try if hee will desist without more a doe: which if hee will not, let him looke (the next weeke) I shall proclaime open-warre against him'.[26] There is some irony indeed that, at a time when the royalists were at a low ebb – even though the Commonwealth was faced with growing opposition – royalist news writers should have lashed out at one another rather than stand as one. Personal rivalries and commercial stakes, it seems, mattered as much to them as political allegiance. Of course, by 1649, the republic was still the prime target of their satire but internal divisions certainly did not help the royalist cause to recover and thrive. Similarly, the author of a counterfeit 'Mercurius Melancholicus' expressed his frustration at being allegedly dispossessed of his title with this threat: 'You or I sir must yeild' to which the author of another counterfeit version replied: 'You or I Sir must supersede'.[27] The author of the original newspaper was concerned that

23 "*Mercurius Britanicus*. Communicating the affaires of great BRITAINE" no. 28 (18–25 March 1644) 215.

24 For the political implications of this rivalry see further down.

25 "*Mercurius Britanicus*: Communicating the affaires of great BRITAINE" no. 28 (18–25 March 1644) 215; no. 29 (25 March–1 April 1644) 223.

26 "*Mercurius Elencticus*." no. 4, revived title (14–21 May 1649) 25.

27 "*Mercurius Melancholicus*: OR, NEWES FROM WESTMINSTER, and other Parts" no. 4 (17–24 September 1647) title page; "*Mercurius Melancholicus* OR, NEWES FROM WESTMINSTER, and other Parts" no. 4 (17–24 September 1647) title page. These two issues were quite similar, the latter actually being a shortened version of the former that included stylistic variations. The former issue was clearly plundered for content.

his title had been forged, including the adorned masthead 'to make him shew and sell the better'; he dismissed his rival's copy as 'adulterate, bastard, and not the lawfully begotten of his owne Genius', and urged his readers not to spare the forger, 'that if the Hypocrite presumes in his borrowed garbe, once more to kisse your hand, that you would returne him another with your foot'.[28] The message was conveyed metaphorically, but its implications were clear: the author of 'Mercurius Melancholicus' had been robbed of his work, and readers were invited not to purchase the other version of the mercury.

News writers felt it was necessary to inform their readers of forgeries taking place, as they were the ones who bought newspapers and greatly contributed to their success and longevity. This may explain why authors commonly encouraged them to arbitrate between original newspapers and counterfeits. The author of the royalist periodical 'Mercurius Pragmaticus', for instance, asked them repeatedly to 'kick away the Counterfeit silly Curre'.[29]

Whether readers were baffled by such disputes is unknown, but political opponents clearly rejoiced over them and delighted in counting points, as did the author of the antiroyalist 'Mercurius Anti-Pragmaticus' who made fun of 'Mercurius Pragmaticus' being counterfeited:

> But alas! Alas for Pragmaticus, for the poore man is in great perplexity. […] You must know that his trade had like to have been spoiled the last week save one, a fellow having laid a plot to undoe him, put forth a booke in his name, which so tickled the itching fancies of the Royall partie, that they swore it was Pragmaticus his Master-piece, when alas the poor soule had no hand in it.[30]

Of course, the author of 'Mercurius Anti-Pragmaticus' only pretended to sympathise with his usurped royalist rival. Irony was a staple of mercury writing, allowing authors to impart further mordancy to their satire and defeat their

---

28 "*Mercurius Melancholicus*: Or, NEWES FROM Westminster, and other Parts" no. 4 (18–25 September 1647) 19. The original title was published on Saturdays while the two counterfeit versions came out the day before. The author insisted that 'Saturday (and none other) [is] the day when [Melancholicus] walks abroad, and takes the ayre'.

29 "MERCVRIVS PRAGMATICUS" no. 8 (2–7 November 1647). See also: 'Reader, there came forth a Counterfeit Rascall last week, with an Impudent Preface; prethee kick him aside, if he peep abroad', in "MERCURIUS PRAGMATICVS" no. 21 (15–22 August 1648); and 'Prethee Reader, kick away the silly Counterfeit', in "MERCURIUS PRAGMATICVS" no. 22 (22–29 August 1648). Despite variations in the fonts used in the title, these issues were Nedham's, as can be ascertained by the poems in them, which he reprinted in his collection during the Restoration.

30 "MERCURIUS ANTI-PRAGMATICVS" no. 19 (27 January–3 February 1648) 2.

adversaries on the news stage. However, in tis tit-for-tat rhetorical war, they needed robust opponents to legitimise their own writing. This is why the revived 'Mercurius Brittanicus' – with a slightly different spelling from the older title – became involved in a wrangle between two competing authors of 'Mercurius Pragmaticus', debasing the one and advertising the other as the only rival worth attacking:

> I espied two Pamphleteers: The one intituled *Mercurius Pragmaticus*, the other *Mercurius Pragmaticus* for King *Charles* the second. The latter pretendeth propriety to act this part upon that Stage, and under that notion: but indeed he saith he slept the last Quarter, (I took him for one of the 7 sleepers) the other who intituleth himself *Mercurius Pragmaticus* is but legitimate, and a Basterd according to his Brothers testimony, His own testimony gives him to be one of the infernall crue, a railing impudent fellow […], I shall not be carefull to answer him, but returne to him that pretendeth himself Champion of *Charles the second*.[31]

The author of '*Mercurius Pragmaticus*, (For King Charles II.)' was none other but Marchamont Nedham, the seasoned news writer who had not only penned the royalist periodical 'Mercurius Pragmaticus' but who, a little over a year before, had authored the parliamentarian newsbook 'Mercurius Britanicus' itself, which was coming back onto the stage with a vengeance, but without Nedham this time. By promising to joust with Nedham's 'Pragmaticus' rather than with a counterfeit title, the author of 'Mercurius Brittanicus' credentialed his political rival and legitimised him as a worthy adversary. And by conferring authority on Nedham's title, he fashioned his own mercury as an authoritative publication. Some newsmongers thus saw counterfeit papers as illegitimate publications that they had better ignore, as did the author of 'Mercurius Brittanicus' who preferred to aim his satire at an authentic, rather than forged, enemy newspaper.

It was not so much authors as titles that carried authority. If news writers were especially ticklish about being robbed of their papers, it was because the forgers deprived them of a good that had value attached to its name. Counterfeiting was perceived as a wrongful practice, hence for example this censorious judgment passed by the author of the short-lived 'Metropolitan

31 "*Mercurius Brittanicus. Communicating Intelligence from all parts, and touching and handling the Humors and Conceits of MERCVRIVS PRAGMATICVS*" no. 1 (24 April–4 May 1649) 1.

Nuncio' regarding the confusion 'Mercurius Pragmaticus' was in because of the publication of competing versions:

> I wonder that old birds should be catch'd with chaffe, and wise men deceived with fooles: that Truth must stand at the dose and a lyer be welcom'd in, and that honest men should suffer their pockets to be prick'd by such pilfering knaves, who hath noting [sic] to live upon but what they filch from others pennes.[32]

News writers generally saw forgery of their titles not only as a personal offence but, just as importantly, as a practice that violated the ethos of truthfulness that mattered so much to them. They may occasionally have breached it themselves but this did not prevent them from taking offence at their newspapers being forged, and also at the very act of counterfeiting other authors' titles. Their response was probably – mainly? – prompted by commercial interests but this is not incompatible with the fact that they regarded forgery as a breach of ethics, in addition to being a threat to their trade.

Authors often responded to counterfeiting by highlighting their attachment to truth. This is, for instance, what the author of a new 'Perfect Diurnall' did after the passing of the 1643 'Ordinance for the Regulation of Printing', addressing his readers thus:

> However you have formerly been abused with many false and truthlesse Informations, through the publishing in Print of sundry Fictions, unlicensed Diurnals, and such like Passages, to the great scandal of the Parliament, and prejudice of the kingdom [...] you may henceforth expect from this Relator to be informed only of such things as are of Credit.[33]

That this comment was motivated by political imperatives as a result of which unlicensed titles were forced out of the market does not make the author's regard for truth any less real. 'Grub street mercenary fellowes',[34] that is to say newspaper counterfeiters, were undesirable not only because they deprived authors of their publications but also because they were likely to provide false news, sometimes referred to as 'forgeries'. Such indignation at fake news and forged titles was voiced by parliamentarian authors, as in 'A Perfect Diurnall',

32 "THE *Metropolitan Nuncio*" no. 3 (6–13 June 1649) not paginated.

33 "A Perfect Diurnall OF SOME PASSAGES IN PARLIAMENT, And from other parts of this Kingdom" no. 1 (26 June–3 July 1643) 1.

34 "A Perfect Diurnall OF THE PASSAGES In Parliament" no. 28 (19–26 December 1642).

and royalist writers alike. It may have been induced by seventeenth-century satirists' common portrayal of newsbook writers as purveyors of fake news. The author of 'Mercurius Elencticus', for instance, included this programmatic statement in the first issue of his newspaper: 'Room for another Mercury, one I'le warrant you that was better bred than to tell Lyes [...] my heart is honest, and my Intelligence true'.[35] Admittedly, authors' minds cannot be fathomed and their sincerity of heart cannot be proved, but it may be argued that telling the truth was not merely a commercial argument; it was seen as integral to the ethos of Civil War journalism, even though perceptions of truth varied according to partisan affiliation.

It was common for newspapers to claim that they would provide true news in order to 'undeceive' their readers, as they would put it. To be sure, the large number of counterfeit titles may not suggest any strong attachment to an ethos of truthfulness, but newspaper authors typically boasted that their news was true, and there is no reason to believe that they were disingenuous about the aim they were pursuing. However, Civil War weeklies served a propagandistic purpose that made tampering with the news a political necessity. This does not mean, though, that the news was fake; it is just that the reporting was sometimes biased. Authors condemned forgery as immoral possibly because it involved something more mundane – a commercial pursuit – than the purveying of true news as underpinning the ethics of journalism. Being chiefly driven by economic imperatives, counterfeiting was clearly perceived as an improper practice by the authors themselves who sometimes behaved like fraudsters although they claimed to be above the fray.

In addition to incriminating forgers and accusing them of illicit and immoral behaviour, some authors, especially authors of mercuries, responded to counterfeiting by denouncing their rivals' supposed lack of talent as writers. These authors commonly added accusations of stylistic impropriety to the charges of immorality that they heaped on counterfeiters. A case in point is the author of the counterfeit 'Mercurius Pragmaticus, (For King Charles II)' who cast aspersions on the author of the original version, Nedham, in these words: 'with nonscence [sic] hee crams his barren-witted Pamphlet full of bombast stuffe, and for the better sale of it, tis?' He dismissed him as a hack writer lacking wit, 'so undeserving a varlet' that by mentioning him, he 'undervalued [his] pen'.[36] One year and a half before, Nedham as the established author of 'Mercurius Pragmaticus' had reviled his usurper as a 'silly Pamphleteer' who 'boasts himselfe to be Pragmaticus, and dresses himself in the same garb, according to his

35 "*Mercurius Elencticus.*" no. 1 (29 October–5 November 1647) 1.

36 "*Mercurius Pragmaticus,* (For King Charles II)" no. 4 (8–15 May 1649), not paginated.

weake indeavour, but comes farre short, either of an Ape or a Monkey, in the art of imitation'.[37] Counterfeiters and their victims alike commonly pointed to their rivals' presumed stylistic shortcomings and literary incompetence, and their satire drew upon much the same *topoi* as those that they used for their political opponents.

This disdainful appreciation of their rivals' writing also concerned the poetic fragments that were so characteristic of Civil War mercuries as of the autumn of 1647. News writers denigrated forgers' poetry, much as they did their political adversaries' verse. For instance, the author of the royalist 'Mercurius Melancholicus' intimated that one of his counterfeiters was a poetaster as this address to the reader suggests: '[The Melancholicus] which came forth last Munday, was a counterfeit also, his small-beere Rimes savouring more of Arcadia, then Parnassus, more of a Sheppard then a Poet: but if I heare him creak again, Ile break his Pipe'.[38] He conveniently contrasted pastoral poetry as inspired by Arcadian shepherds with the more solemn poetry associated with Apollo in Parnassus. This hierarchy of poetic genres was irrelevant, anyway, as the poetry included in mercuries was primarily of a satirical nature, but it helped him to satirise his rival without naming him precisely. He very probably believed him to have been Samuel Sheppard, the long-running author of the royalist newspaper 'Mercurius Elencticus', hence the pun on his name. There is no knowing for sure whether he had identified the forger of his title correctly or whether he meant to ruin Sheppard's reputation so as to outsell him. Be it as it may, it seems that, as a rule, authors accused those of their rivals who had forged their titles of literary incompetence so as to smear them and increase their own sales in the process.

It should be stressed that responses to counterfeiting had more to do with issues relating to property and commerce than with political issues. Authors occasionally claimed that forgers betrayed the cause that they defended in their original titles and that counterfeiting was a counter-productive practice, but such comments on forgers' political impropriety were few and far between.[39] Authors' motives for usurping their rivals' titles will be addressed next.

37 "MERCVRIVS PRAGMATICUS" no. 12 (30 November–7 December 1647), not paginated.

38 "*Mercurius Melancholicus*. OR, NEWES FROM WESTMINSTER, and other parts" no. 51 (7–14 August 1648).

39 See for example "*Mercurius Britanicus* Communicating the affaires of great BRITAINE" no. 29 (25 March–1 April 1644) 224: 'counterfeiting and betraying the Cause by their Intelligence'; "*Mercurius Elencticus*." no. 3, revived title (7–14 May 1649) 18: 'I cannot but resent an injury foule enough, not so much in respect of myself, as the advancement of that Cause wee both so fairly pretend to, which by this meanes must suffer detriment or scandal'.

3 Laying Bare the Counterfeiters' Motives

Identifying the reasons why forgers stole newspaper titles is not quite simple. It was common for mercury writers to accuse usurpers of depriving them of their livelihoods or of making profit on their backs. Thus, the author of one of the versions of 'Mercurius Pragmaticus for King Charles II' claimed that the alleged counterfeiter of his periodical was driven by greed:

> I would have him to know, that I perceive his beggarly, lowsy drift, which is to buy my wit, and sell it agayne when he hath transcribed it, with his trayterous Pen, and make himself a Broaker of my Genius, to finger up some beggarly pence.[40]

In the same vein, the author of the competing version rejoiced about Commonwealth authorities' resolve to crack down on owners of underground presses and seize their equipment, while bragging about having a portable press that allowed him to escape censors. This measure, he argued, would rid him of counterfeiters, so that, ultimately, he would 'be left upon the stage [...] and not be troubled with those Billowes and unlegitimate varlets who write for gayne more then loyalty'.[41] There was clearly some money to be made from news writing but how much cannot be determined with any certainty. Only wild guesses can be made about print-runs, not to mention the fact that writing a royalist newspaper when Parliament got the upper hand, let alone when the Commonwealth was established, was a precarious business, considering that authors were chased continuously, though not necessarily successfully. It is very likely that forgers would really have deprived their victims of a living, or at least that they might have made a dent in their revenue, had they carried their enterprise through. Some did carry it through.

Financial gain, I would argue, was the driving force behind counterfeiting. We may also consider political rivalry as a cause, but cases where this is explicit are few. I have described elsewhere the birth of the radical newspaper 'The Moderate'.[42] Its author initially forged John Dillingham's established weekly 'The Moderate Intelligencer'. There was very little difference between the two publications. The counterfeiter, presumably Gilbert Mabbott, was reprimanded

40 "*Mercurius Pragmaticus, (For King Charles II)*" no. 4 (8–15 May 1649), not paginated. Again, the generic, rather than formatted, title is given in the text, as it refers to all the existing versions. The citation, as is the case here, makes it clear which version it was. It is difficult to decide who counterfeited whom, though.

41 "*Mercurius Pragmaticus, for King Charles II*" no. 6 (22–29 May 1649), not paginated.

42 Curelly L., *An Anatomy of an English Radical Newspaper*.

by the House of Lords and commanded to change his title. He complied with the order by omitting 'Intelligencer' from the title. He retained the original format as well as some of the content of 'The Moderate Intelligencer', but as the political situation came to a head during the summer of 1648, he developed his own editorial line that marked 'The Moderate' out from its sibling. The newspaper came into its own as it began to support the Independent faction in Parliament and the New Model Army while Dillingham tended to side with the Presbyterians. It acquired a distinct radical quality as time went by and came to back the Levellers against Army Grandees, and then against Commonwealth authorities, although it was by no means a Leveller organ. The newsbook's line was probably in tune with the author's political options but it is likely that he capitalised on the evolving circumstances to carve out a niche for himself as a newsmonger. 'The Moderate' was born as a counterfeit of a newspaper that expressed a mainstream political position and generally went with the tide, but it soon became a publication which advanced a radical agenda. Counterfeiting here was motivated by economic, rather than political, reasons unless one posits that, right from the outset, Mabbott intended to steal his rival's paper to tailor it to his political views – but this is clearly not what the first few issues show.

True, an example does not make a rule. Perhaps one should look at other cases. The various versions of 'A Perfect Diurnall' do not reflect any diverging political opinions. They mostly include factual reportage. The editorial process is limited to the arrangement of the news on the page, and the inclusion of various textual layers makes it difficult to distinguish between original material and the author's additions. They are few editorial comments, except perhaps in the authorised version of the newspaper after the passing of the 1643 licensing law. The writer steps forward, and his comments convey a sense of partisanship in favour of Parliament, unsurprisingly for a diurnal that was sanctioned by Parliament. By then, 'A Perfect Diurnall' was no longer counterfeited. The diurnal 'The Kingdomes Weekly Intelligencer' came to be forged in its turn. Both the original title and counterfeit issues included editorial comments that demonised royalists and praised the parliamentarian army, but these do not betray any dissenting opinions among authors. Again, commercial gain, rather than political motives, seems to account for the forgeries.

Some historians of the Civil War press have claimed that diurnals were typically drab publications, rather than political fora. This is debatable as even diurnals became politically charged publications, some of which, for instance, included fully-fledged editorials. As state censorship was strengthened their authors were under licensers' scrutiny and departed little from the official line.

So should one look to mercuries instead for cases of forgery that were politically motivated?

Quite expectedly, both the original and the counterfeit versions of the parliamentarian mercury 'Mercurius Britanicus' refuted the royalist mercury 'Mercurius Aulicus' and, more generally, lambasted the royalists. Both of them supported the Anglo-Scottish alliance as enshrined in the Solemn League and Covenant, the deal brokered by the English and the Scottish Parliaments whereby the Scots would assist the parliamentarian army in return for the establishment of a national Presbyterian Church in England. In addition, both of them adopted an anti-episcopal line. Although the author of one of the versions, the one that was ultimately printed by Robert White, accuses the counterfeiter of his title of betraying Parliament's cause, his words should definitely not be taken at face value as there is little by way of political expression that distinguishes the two incarnations of the paper. The author of the original version argues that 'after so many Malignant experiments to betray Britanicus, this, the mock-Britanicus, the counterfeit Britanicus, the Bishops Britanicus, is not the least, but the grandest, the supreamest, the Oxfordest stratagem'.[43] In much the same vein, his rival calls him a schemer and a pretender. True, the original author's invective 'Bishops Britanicus' – with a pun on the name of the printer of the counterfeit title and on the dignitaries of the Church of England – reflects his anti-episcopal stance, but his rival made use of much the same rhetoric with reference to the English episcopate.

Should one turn to royalist mercuries for politically motivated counterfeiting, then? There may have been various brands of royalism but the difficulty in assessing their impact on forgery lies in the fact that royalist authors' opinions evolved over time and that news writers did not uphold consistent views of contemporary actors or debates. Much of their writing was opportunistic. For example, the author of the revived version of 'Mercurius Elencticus' took pains to distance himself from a counterfeit that had barged onto the market:

> Gentlemen, the last week I was anticipated, and you abused by a Counterfeit, which after it usurps my Title stiles itself: For King Charles II – I truly honour every Man, who really intends the service of his Majesty.

43 "Mercurius Britanicus Communicating the affaires of great BRITAINE" no. 29 (25 March–1 April 1644) 223. 'Oxfordest' is a reference to the King and his Court in exile in Oxford and to Oxford University scholars who, by and large, supported the King.

> But when, under that Attracting pretence, another man is Robbed of his Fancy (bee it never so meane;) besides that it is Felony, it savours house-height of Malice or Mercerariness. [...] I cannot but resent an injury foule enough, not so much in respect of myself, as the advancement of that Cause wee both so fairly pretend to, which by this meanes must suffer detriment or scandal.[44]

It is not so much his rival's political options that he finds fault with as the very act of counterfeiting an established newspaper. Arguably, a close examination of the content of the two versions does not reveal any significant political differences between them. The Levellers, a radical group that called for a more democratic form of government based on popular sovereignty, were depicted in much the same way. And yet, there was enough in Leveller thought that might have antagonised royalist authors in other circumstances than the spring of 1649 when the Levellers were hell-bent on attacking the Commonwealth government.

Both the authors of 'Mercurius Elencticus' and 'Mercurius Elencticus for King Charls II' showed half-hearted support for the Levellers. They pretended to throw in their lot with them as they praised John Lilburne, one of their leaders, for his bravery and encouraged them to fight against the ruling oligarchy. But one should not be mistaken by this show of sympathy. The third draft of the Levellers' constitutional text *The Agreement of the People*, published in May 1649, elicited mockery and disapproval from one of the authors:

> John Lilburne feares not these Thunder-bolts of Tyrannie, who to let them see how little hee values [the people's] votes, this day published a paper styled an agreement of the People of England, with a Declaration and a Preparative (before they purge) wherein hee prescribes them what government hee will have; which is every way so absolute, that hee counts it damnation for any wilfully to dissent, and not to joyne with him in the firme and spedy establishment thereof.[45]

Such an assertion of popular sovereignty as is expressed in *The Agreement of the People* cannot have been but anathema to defenders of the Stuart monarchy. The rival newspaper's author did not champion the cause of the radicals either, and his encouragement of the Levellers is mitigated by tongue-in-cheek humour, as this comment on Leveller-inspired mutinies in the Army testifies:

44 "*Mercurius Elencticus.*" no. 1, revived title (24 April–1 May 1649) 2.
45 "*Mercurius Elencticus.*" no. 2, revived title (1–8 May 1649) 11.

> Wel play'd Levellers, down with them States-men of war, now boyes or never for God and King Charls his sake fight lustily, we'l have a reserve for you in a corder, shall lend ye a back-blow upon a pinch without doubt.[46]

There may not have been straightforward animosity on his part towards the Levellers but there is no question that he wished to rid England of them in the end. He delighted in playing them off against Commonwealth authorities, as is shown in the epigram that rounds off the issue: 'And as their discord with their daies increase, / Charls, by Heavens power, shall consummate our peace'.[47] Thus, he hoped to capitalise on divisions within the various factions that had initially backed Parliament against the royalists. And these divisions were many.

The case of 'Mercurius Pragmaticus' is slightly more difficult to apprehend in that it was originally authored by Marchamont Nedham, who switched political allegiance on several occasions as he wrote both in support of Parliament and in support of the King over less than ten years. His political views changed over time. Jason Peacey argues that the various editions of 'Mercurius Pragmaticus' mirrored factional tensions within the royalist camp and insists that Nedham's version of the newspaper revealed his hostility towards the Scots and the notion of a Presbyterian church settlement as well as his sympathy for Lilburne, although he was averse to the Levellers' ideas.[48] But then Peacey admits that, in the spring of 1649, 'the prevailing mood [...] acknowledged the usefulness of the Levellers'.[49] The Levellers seem to have been convenient allies for the royalists at that particular time.

Peacey's contention that 'the complex history of *Pragmaticus* reflected the machinations of royalist factions, whose grandees sought to secure control of powerful propaganda weapons with which to fight their battles against one another as much as against Parliament'[50] is certainly compelling, but I would argue that it needs qualifying. First, royalist news writers defended the same cause, and even though their perception of the Civil Wars changed over time, expressing occasional sympathy for actors of the opposite side was mostly a means to an end. Second, mercuries were hybrid literary formats, of which irony and satire were staple ingredients, so that the degree of seriousness with which they described their political opponents cannot always be measured with utmost precision. Last, there is enough rhetorical evidence in the

46 "Mercurius Elencticus, (FOR KING CHARLS II.)" no. 2 (7–14 May 1649), not paginated.

47 Ibidem.

48 Peacey, "Money, Politics, and the Forging of Royalist Newspapers" 41–42.

49 Ibidem, 45.

50 Peacey, "Money, Politics, and the Forging of Royalist Newspapers" 48.

newspapers to support the conclusion that many counterfeiting ventures were driven by commercial motivations at least as much as they were caused by political dissent.

4 Conclusion

It is hoped that this survey of newsbook counterfeiting in Britain in the 1640s will offer new perspectives on the history of forgery. First, it shows that this practice affected the whole of the news market throughout the Civil War period. It concerned both diurnals and mercuries, but in the case of the former, disputes came to be solved by political authorities as these papers came under the scrutiny of state censors. And when this monitoring did not take place successfully, it was strengthened by Parliament, so that the forgery of such a periodical as 'A Perfect Diurnall', for instance, ceased in July 1643 with the passing of the 'Ordinance for the Regulation of Printing'. As mercuries were underground publications – at least royalist mercuries – they could not be controlled as effectively as the parliamentarian press, even though there were lapses in state censorship. In this relatively unconstrained environment, despite successful press seizures, counterfeiters were free to step onto the news stage.

Second, this study of counterfeiting suggests that news writing was an author's individual pursuit rather than a collective enterprise, although it was common for writers to team up with printers. Many authors' identity is elusive, and attribution can mostly be done on the basis of external rather than internal evidence. Counterfeiters' identity is even more mysterious since newsbooks never featured their authors' names; again, it was not so much the authors that mattered to readers as the very titles. Titles, with their reputation attached to them, were potentially profitable commercial products. They had – were born with or acquired – a distinct identity in terms of format and layout which made them recognisable by readers. When a counterfeiter hijacked a title, he did so for his own benefit but he did not necessarily try to conceal the theft. He pretended that his paper was genuine but he often imparted a different identity to his publication that was reflected in format, including typeface, layout and sometimes content. Most cases of forgery testify to the forgers' typographic appropriation and partial rebranding of newspapers. The changes introduced by counterfeiters, from typography to editorial bias, reflected various forms of forgery and appropriation: some authors did their best to conceal the theft, but introduced minor, if visible, variations so that their publications could eventually be recognised and they could claim authority for the titles, while a news writer like Mabbott, the presumed author of 'The Moderate', whose attempt to counterfeit Dillingham's 'Moderate Intelligencer' was thwarted, issued a publication that came to feature a wholly different political line from his rival's. It seems that forgers entered the volatile Civil War news market more or less tentatively and stepped on other news writers' toes; some counterfeiters turned out to be unsuccessful while others were victorious enough for their newsbooks to have gained as much authenticity as the original titles. In that case, readers would probably have been at a loss to tell the original publication from the forged incarnation(s), and students of the seventeenth-century British press happen to be just as confused as contemporary readers must have been.

Last, it seems that commercial gain was counterfeiters' main, albeit not single, motivation. Different avatars of the same newsbook may occasionally have conveyed their authors' conflicting political views, but this was far from being the norm. Much more trivially perhaps, forgers were lured by the commercial appeal of established, or promising, titles. This is not to say that journalism was an exceptionally lucrative trade but it was a business out of which authors could make a living, at least when a newspaper survived its first issues. The news market was undeniably unpredictable but successful entrepreneurs, including forgers, could nonetheless earn a profit from their sales. The fact that these publications prospered at a time of crisis, when news had acquired both a political and a commercial value, and gained popularity and authority as sources of information, certainly accounts for the steady growth of newspaper forgery as a socio-cultural practice in mid-seventeenth-century Britain. In addition to their being fora of expression, Civil War newsbooks should therefore be seen as fully-fledged products with physical characteristics of their own. Considering them as such was certainly one of the keys to success for authors of original as well as forged newspaper issues, which is why many counterfeiters minded their U's and their V's.

Appendix: List of Newspaper Incarnations Mentioned in This Chapter

Parliamentarian Newsbooks

A Perfect Diurnall

The following four entries are the various versions of A Perfect Diurnall no. 14 (12–19 September 1642).

A Perfect Diurnall OF THE PASSAGES In Parliament: From the twelfth of September to the nineteenth. Sept. 19. Printed for Wall: Cook and Rob: Woodner. 1642.

A Perfect Diurnall OF THE PASSAGES In Parliament: from Sept. 12. to the 19th. Sept. 19. London Printed for Walt. Cook and Robert Wood, 1642.

A Perfect Diurnall OF THE PASSAGES In Parliament: From the 12. of September, to the 19. Of the said moneth. Sept. 19. London Printed for Walt. Cook and Robert Woody. 1642.
A Perfect Diurnall OF THE PASSAGES In Parliament: From the 12. of September, unto the 19. More fully and exactly taken than any other printed Copies as you will finde upon Comparing, &c. Printed at London for Francis Coules.
A Perfect Diurnall OF THE PASSAGES IN *PARLIAMENT* no. 23 (14–21 November 1642)
A Perfect Diurnall OF THE PASSAGES In PARLIAMENT no. 28 (19–26 December 1642)
A Perfect Diurnall OF THE PASSAGES In Parliament no. 28 (19–26 December 1642)

Mercurius Anti-Pragmaticus
MERCURIUS ANTI-PRAGMATICVS no. 19 (27 January–3 February 1648)

Mercurius Britanicus
Mercurius Britanicus. Communicating the affaires of great BRITAINE no. 27 (11–18 March 1644)
Mercurius Britanicus: Communicating the affaires of great BRITAINE no. 27 (11–18 March 1644)
Mercurius Britanicus. Communicating the affaires of great BRITAINE no. 28 (18–25 March 1644)
Mercurius Britanicus: Communicating the affaires of great BRITAINE no. 28 (18–25 March 1644)
Mercurius Britanicus: Communicating the affaires of great BRITAINE no. 29 (25 March–1 April 1644)
Mercurius Britanicus Communicating the affaires of great BRITAINE no. 29 (25 March–1 April 1644)

Mercurius Brittanicus
Mercurius Brittanicus. Communicating Intelligence from all parts, and touching and handling the Humors and Conceits of MERCVRIVS PRAGMATICVS no. 1 (24 April–4 May 1649)

The Kingdomes Weekly Intelligencer
THE KINGDOMES VVeekly Intelligencer: SENT ABROAD To prevent mis-information no. 21 (23–30 May 1643)
THE KINGDOMES VVeekly Intelligencer: SENT ABROAD To prevent mis-information no. 22 (30 May–6 June 1643).
THE KINGDOMES VVeekly Intelligencer: SENT ABROAD To prevent mis-information no. 25 (4–11 July 1643)

The Metropolitan Nuncio

THE *Metropolitan Nuncio* no. 3 (6–13 June 1649)

Royalist Mercuries

Mercurius Elencticus

Mercurius Elencticus. no. 1 (29 October–5 November 1647)
Mercurius Elencticus. no. 1, revived title (24 April–1 May 1649)
Mercurius Elencticus. no. 2, revived title (1–8 May 1649)
Mercurius Elencticus. no. 3, revived title (7–14 May 1649)
Mercurius Elencticus. no. 4, revived title (14–21 May 1649)

Mercurius Elencticus, For King Charls II

Mercurius Elencticus, (FOR KING CHARLS II.) no. 2 (7–14 May 1649)

Mercurius Melancholicus

Mercurius Melancholicus: OR, NEWES FROM WESTMINSTER, and other Parts no. 4 (17–24 September 1647)
Mercurius Melancholicus OR, NEWES FROM WESTMINSTER, and other Parts no. 4 (17–24 September 1647)
Mercurius Melancholicus. OR, NEWES FROM WESTMINSTER, and other parts no. 51 (7–14 August 1648)

Mercurius Pragmaticus

MERCURIUS PRAGMATICVS no. 1 (14–21 September 1647)
MERCVRIVS PRAGMATICUS no. 8 (2–7 November 1647)
MERCVRIVS PRAGMATICUS no. 12 (30 November–7 December 1647)
MERCVRIVS PRAGMATICVS no. 19 (1–8 August 1648)
MERCURIUS PRAGMATICVS no. 21 (15–22 August 1648)
MERCURIUS PRAGMATICVS no. 22 (22–29 August 1648)
MERCVRIVS PRAGMATICVS no. 23 (5–12 September 1648)
Mercurius PRAGMATICUS no. 23 (5–12 September 1648)
MERCVRIVS PRAGMATICUS no. 41 (9–16 January 1649)

Mercurius Pragmaticus, For King Charles II

Mercurius Pragmaticus, (For King Charles II) no. 4 (8–15 May 1649)
Mercurius Pragmaticus, (For King Charles II) no. 4 (8–15 May 1649)
Mercurius Pragmaticus, for King Charles II no. 6 (22–29 May 1649)

Bibliography

Baines P., *The House of Forgery in Eighteenth-Century Britain* (Aldershot: 1999).

Cotton A.N.B., *London Newsbooks in the Civil War: Their Political Attitudes and Sources of Information* (Ph.D. dissertation, University of Oxford: 1971).

Curelly L., *An Anatomy of an English Radical Newspaper – The Moderate (1648–9)* (Newcastle-upon-Tyne: 2017).

Firth C.H. – Rait R.S. (eds.), *Acts and Ordinances of the Interregnum, 1642–1660* (London: 1911).

Frank J., *The Beginnings of the English Newspaper, 1620–1660* (Cambridge MA: 1961).

Habermas J., *The Structural Transformation of the Public Sphere: An Inquiry into a Category of Bourgeois Society*, trans. T. Burger (Cambridge: 1989).

Hammond B.S., "Plagiarism: Hammond versus Ricks", in Kewes P. (ed.), *Plagiarism in Early Modern England* (Basingstoke – New York: 2002) 41–55.

Macadam A.E.J., *Mercurius Britanicus: Journalism and Politics in the English Civil War* (Ph.D. dissertation, University of Sussex: 2005).

Marantz Cohen P., "The Meanings of Forgery", *Southwest Review* 97: 1 (2012) 12–25.

McElligott J., *Royalism, Print and Censorship in Revolutionary England* (Woodbridge: 2007).

Nelson C. – Seccombe M., *British Newspapers and Periodicals, 1641–1700: A Short-Title Catalogue of Serials Printed in England, Scotland, Ireland, and British America* (New York: 1987).

Peacey J., "'The counterfeit silly curr': Money, Politics, and the Forging of Royalist Newspapers during the English Civil War", *Huntington Library Quarterly* 67:1 (2004) 27–57.

Peacey J., "The Management of Civil War Newspapers: Auteurs, Entrepreneurs and Editorial Control", *Seventeenth Century* 21:1 (2006) 99–127.

Potter L., *Secret Rites and Secret Writing: Royalist Literature 1641–1660* (Cambridge: 1989).

Raymond J., *The Invention of the Newspaper – English Newsbooks, 1641–1649* (Oxford: 1996).

Raymond J. (ed.), *News Networks in Seventeenth-Century Britain and Europe* (London – New York: 2006).

Raymond J. – Moxham N. (eds.), *News Networks in Early Modern Europe* (Leiden – Boston: 2016).

Ryan Y., *Networks, Maps and Readers: Foreign News Reporting in London Newsbooks, 1645–1649* (Ph.D. dissertation, Queen Mary University of London: 2019).

CHAPTER 9

The Theatre of Forgery: Curzio Inghirami (Volterra, 1614–1655) and Giorgio Grognet de Vassé (Malta, 1774–1862)

Ingrid Rowland

The ancient Greeks, Romans, and Etruscans seem to have enjoyed great freedom to invent patriotic myths – among them Hesiod, Euripides, Plato, Virgil, Ovid – but the development of academic disciplines in the Early Modern era discouraged the varieties of creative exuberance by which ancient Greek poets, for example, attempted to explain how the impressive surviving monuments of their Bronze Age came into being. Early modern and modern scholars have hewed to other standards, piecing together the relatively well-documented past of great cities like Athens, Rome, Palmyra or Syracuse to the satisfaction of these cities' later residents. Minuscule cities like Chiusi are sometimes lucky enough to have a hero like Lars Porsenna to provide a focus for local patriotic pride. But where textual records are scanty and surviving monuments are tantalisingly impressive, the more imaginative citizens of places like Viterbo, Volterra, and Malta, rich in ruins and poor in testimonia, have been tempted to resort to fiction, like the *Res Gestae of King Porsenna* composed around 1458 by an ambitious Florentine cleric to provide a rousing foundation story for Montepulciano (only to have his chronicle promptly plagiarised by a humanist from Siena), or the twentieth-century novel *Nifur, La Splendida Etrusca*, which provided a new view of life in Porsenna's Chiusi in the 1980s, or Valerio Massimo Manfredi's Etruscan-themed horror story, *Chimaira* of 2001, which sets its action in Volterra.[1] For some ingenious spirits, however, fiction has

1 For the *Gesta Porsennae Regis*, see Rowland I.D, "L'*Historia Porsennae* e la conoscenza degli Etruschi nel Rinascimento", *Studi Umanistici Piceni/Res Publica Litterarum* 9 (1989) 185–193; ibid, "Due 'traduzioni' rinascimentali dell'*Historia Porsennae*", in Prete S. (ed.), *Protrepticon: Studi in memoria di Giovannangiola Secchi Tarugi* (Milan: 1989) 125–133; ibid, "Il mito di Porsenna: leggenda e realtà", in Rotondi Secchi Tarugi L. (ed.), *Il Mito nel Rinascimento* (Milan: 1993) 391–407; ibid, "Pio II, l'urbanistica e gli esordi dell'etruscologia: osservazioni intorno ai manoscritti delle *Gesta Porsemnae Regis*", in Nevola F. (ed.), *Pio II Piccolomini. Il papa del Rinascimento a Siena, Atti del covegno internazionale (Siena, 5–7 maggio 2005)* (Colle Val d'Elsa: 2009) 167–178. For *Chimaira*, see Manfredi V.M., *Chimaira* (Milan: 2001). I picked up *Nifur, la splendida etrusca* at the newsstand of the Chiusi train station, probably around

 | DOI:10.1163/9789004106901_010

afforded an insufficient tribute to past greatness: nothing will do but History. If that history must be fabricated, so be it; the sixteenth-century philosopher Giordano Bruno already furnished a useful guiding principle for such mighty efforts in his dialogue *On the Heroic Frenzies* of 1585: 'se non è vero, è molto ben trovato' ('If it's not true, it ought to be').[2]

The founding father of early modern patriotic forgery was the ingenious Giovanni Nanni (1438–1502; [Fig. 9.1]), a Dominican friar of Viterbo and a charismatic preacher who had retired to his native city after becoming a vocal convert to the doctrine of the Immaculate Conception of the Virgin Mary, a position to which his fellow Dominicans were adamantly opposed.[3] Upon his return home in the early 1490s, the city council of Viterbo engaged Nanni, still a formidable public speaker, to deliver a series of lectures on local history. These presentations began to include a series of remarkable new discoveries, some of them contained in a series of hitherto lost or unknown texts preserved in two manuscripts that he happened to have in his possession, but also including archaeological artefacts that ranged in date from the primeval era of Isis and Osiris up to the putative foundation of Viterbo in AD 776.[4] In 1498, under the more ancient-sounding name Iohannes Annius, he published an edition of these newly available ancient texts together with his own commentaries, as well as a collection of 'forty Annian questions', a back-and-forth exchange of questions and answers that delved more deeply into the significance of his discoveries and their implications for Viterbo's illustrious place in universal history. The book was an international sensation, reprinted in Paris, pirated in Venice, destined to exert an insidious influence on classical scholarship for generations. By the time of its first edition, Annius had found employment in the Vatican as Master of the Sacred Palace, the theologian who examined all the sermons delivered before the Pope – in his case, Alexander VI Borgia, for

1987, but can find no bibliographic information about the book on the Web and no longer have it on hand. I do remember that the Etruscan names were fanciful rather than accurate.

2 Bruno Giordano, *De gli eroici furori* (London: John Charlewood, 1585), cited from Bruno Giordano, *Giordano Bruno on the Heroic Frenzies*, ed. E. Canone, trans. I.D. Rowland (Toronto: 2014) 300–301. Bruno's interlocutors are discussing love and physics rather than history and forgery, but the phrase has become proverbial in contemporary Italian.

3 Fumagalli E., "Aneddoti della vita di Annio da Viterbo, O.P., I: Annio e la vittoria dei genovesi sui sforzeschi, II: Annio e la disputa sull'Immacolata Concezione", *Archivum Fratrum Praedicatorum* 50 (1980) 167–199.

4 Stephens W.E., *Giants in Those Days: Folklore, Ancient History and Nationalism* (Lincoln NE: 1989); Grafton A., *Forgers and Critics: Creativity and Duplicity in Western Scholarship* (Princeton NJ: 1990); Rowland I.D., "Annius of Viterbo (1432/7–1502) and the Beginnings of Urban History", in *Acta ad archaeologiam et artiam historiam pertinentia* (Theme Number: "From Site to Sight: The Transformation of Place in Art and Literature") 26 (N.S. 12) (2013) 13–30.

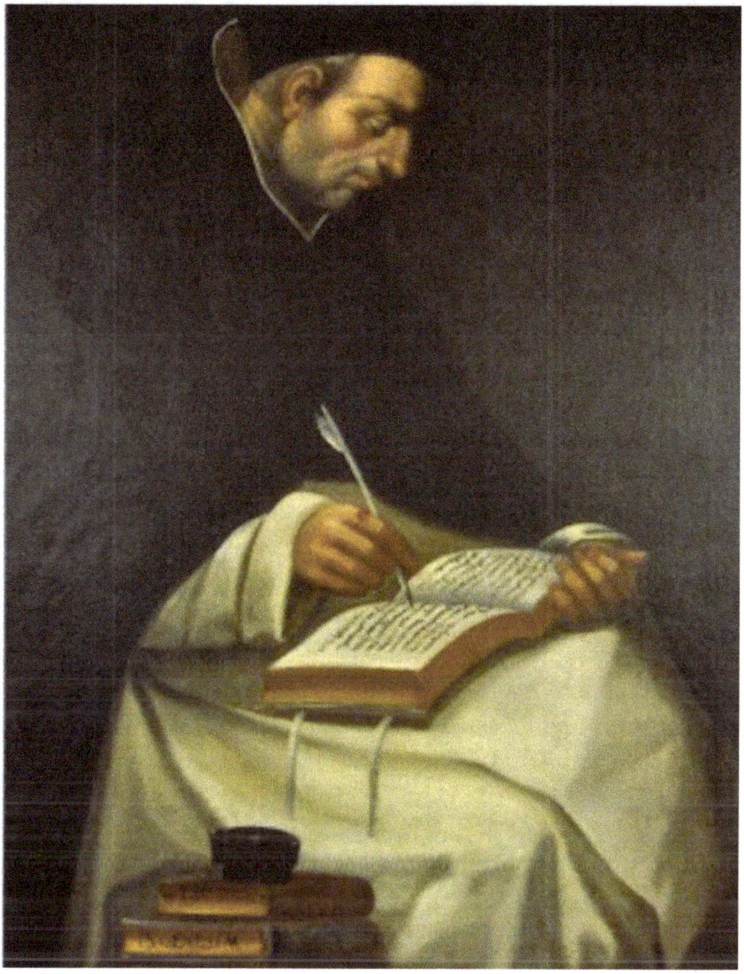

FIGURE 9.1 Anonymous painter, Giovanni Nanni (Annius) of Viterbo
VITERBO, MUSEO COMUNALE. AUTHOR'S PHOTO

whom Annius had previously concocted flattering stories about the pontiff's Egyptian ancestry.[5]

Passionately defended and passionately attacked in his own lifetime, Annius was unmasked as a forger shortly after his death in 1502, but his fictions were so extensive, and so initially convincing, that they left a stubborn legacy in subsequent scholarship, not least because they were mixed in with a great many

5 Curran B., *The Egyptian Renaissance: The Afterlife of Ancient Egypt in Early Modern Italy* (Chicago: 2007) 107–131.

genuine insights, including his unprecedented ability to read the Etruscan alphabet correctly.[6] A fascinating story can be put together from his texts, his artefacts, and his legacy, but inevitably we are missing an essential aspect of what made him so persuasive to his contemporaries in the first place: namely, his abilities as a public performer. He was, after all, a lifelong member of the Order of Preachers, founded by the future saint Dominic Guzmán in 1206 and approved by Pope Innocent II in 1216 to preach the Gospel to schismatics and infidels. Dominican friars preached the Gospel through homilies and sacred orations, but they were also instrumental in the development of medieval sacred theatre.[7] Furthermore, the Dominican education that Annius had received on entering the order refined his skills not only in public preaching and performance, but also in the rigorous techniques of scholastic argumentation. He could entertain multitudes – he famously stopped an incipient riot in Genoa – and he could stand his ground in sophisticated scholarly debate.[8]

The life of an itinerant preacher had also taught Annius to be adaptable, as when he changed his mind about the Immaculate Conception, and when he made a quick, clever response to the sudden emergence of a genuine archaeological discovery entirely beyond his control. One fall day in 1494, on a rabbit hunt near Viterbo (conveniently near the castle of his latest mistress Giulia Farnese), Pope Alexander VI was delighted when one of the rabbits jumped down a hole that turned out to be the entrance to an Etruscan tomb, hollowed out of the local volcanic tuff and still filled with inscribed sarcophagi. The sarcophagi were quickly transported to Viterbo itself, where the Pope, his entourage, and the good people of Viterbo waited eagerly to hear how their city's renowned expert on Etruria would interpret their meaning. It took Annius a month to compose a suitable treatise, the *Borgiana lucubratio* ('Borgian Study'), in which he connected the inscriptions to the visit of Isis to the wedding party of Viterbo's fifth Etruscan king, Iasius Ianigena.[9] His learned conversation on the spur of the moment must have been impressive as well, for the pope

6 Rowland I.D., "Annius of Viterbo and the Beginning of Etruscan Studies", in Bell S. and Carpino A. (eds.), *A Companion to the Etruscans* (Chichester, West Sussex: 2016) 433–445.

7 In Tuscany, *rappresentazioni sacre* began in earnest in Florence with the Confraternity of St. John the Evangelist at the beginning of the fifteenth century, encouraged, according to their own tradition, by the Dominican Archbishop Antonino; Evangelista A., "L'attività spettacolare della Compagnia di San Giovanni Evangelista nel Conquecento", *Medioevo e Rinascimento* 18/15 (2004) 299–366; Toschi P., *L'antico teatro religioso italiano* (Matera: 1966).

8 Zarri G., "Dallo scisma all'apogeo della Chiesa; i Domenicani tra I secoli XV e XVII", in Festa G. – Rainini M. (eds.), *L'Ordine dei Predicatori, I Domenicani: storia, figure e istituzioni (1216–2016)* (Bari – Rome: 2016) 30–57.

9 Danielsson O., *Etruskische Inschriften in Handschriftlicher Überlieferung*, Skrifter utgivna av K. Humanistiska Vetenskaps-Samfund i Uppsala 25:3 (Uppsala: 1928).

subsequently promoted him to the lofty post of Master of the Sacred Palace in Rome, the third highest position, at the time, in the entire Dominican hierarchy.[10] For this most versatile of practitioners, forgery was eminently, therefore, a performing art. Forgery would be no less theatrical an undertaking for one of the friar's most colourful successors: Curzio Inghirami of Volterra, who tried his hand at comedy before becoming the chief defender of his native city's illustrious ancient past.

1 Curzio Inghirami: Dramatist, Forger and Conceptual Artist

Curzio Inghirami composed his first comedy in the aftermath of plague. The outbreak that ravaged Italy in 1630 was not as severe as the Black Death of 1348, but its toll was grim enough: Florence lost 12% of its population in the space of a year, but in Padua mortality reached 61%.[11] Alessandro Manzoni's influential novel *I promessi sposi* of 1827 (first translated into English as *The Betrothed* in 1828) paints a vivid picture of the plague's dire effects in Milan, which lost a third of its residents: the overburdened *lazzaretto*, or plague hospital, the common graves, the bonfires of victims' personal effects, the violent eruptions of mass hysteria.[12] In the Grand Duchy of Tuscany, an efficient, centralised bureaucracy in Florence imposed stringent measures on the entire territory, and for the Tuscan city of Volterra, on its rugged hilltop thirty kilometers from the sea, containment meant two years of virtual isolation from the rest of the world in 1630 and 1631.[13] Isolation, however, was never complete; Volterrans, rich and poor, still died in staggering numbers.[14] By January 1632, when the

10 Walsh R., "Master of the Sacred Palace", in *Catholic Encyclopedia*, 10 (New York: 1913): https://en.wikisource.org/wiki/Catholic_Encyclopedia_(1913)/Master_of_the_Sacred_Palace.

11 Alfani G., "Plague in seventeenth-century Europe and the decline of Italy: an epidemiological hypothesis", *European Review of Economic History* 17:4 (November 2013) 408–430.

12 Both Manzoni's novel *I promessi sposi* (1827) and his nonfiction essay *Storia della Colonna Infame*, which appeared as a historical appendix to the definitive edition of *I promessi sposi* in 1840 focus on the plague of 1630 and the mass hysteria about 'untori'; see Manzoni A., *La peste a Milano. Storia della Colonna Infame. I Promessi Sposi (capitoli 31, 32, 34)*, with a preface by Piero Gibellini and a comment by Mino Martinazzoli (Brescia: 2020).

13 Cipolla C.M., *Cristofano and the Plague: A Study in the History of Public Health in the Age of Galileo* (London: 1973); Henderson J., *Florence Under Siege: Surviving Plague in an Early Modern City* (New Haven: 2019).

14 Good archival evidence for deaths in Volterra begins only in the 1670s, but the death toll within the Inghirami family shows how gravely the plague affected the city despite all the preventive measures undertaken by the Grand Duchy of Tuscany.

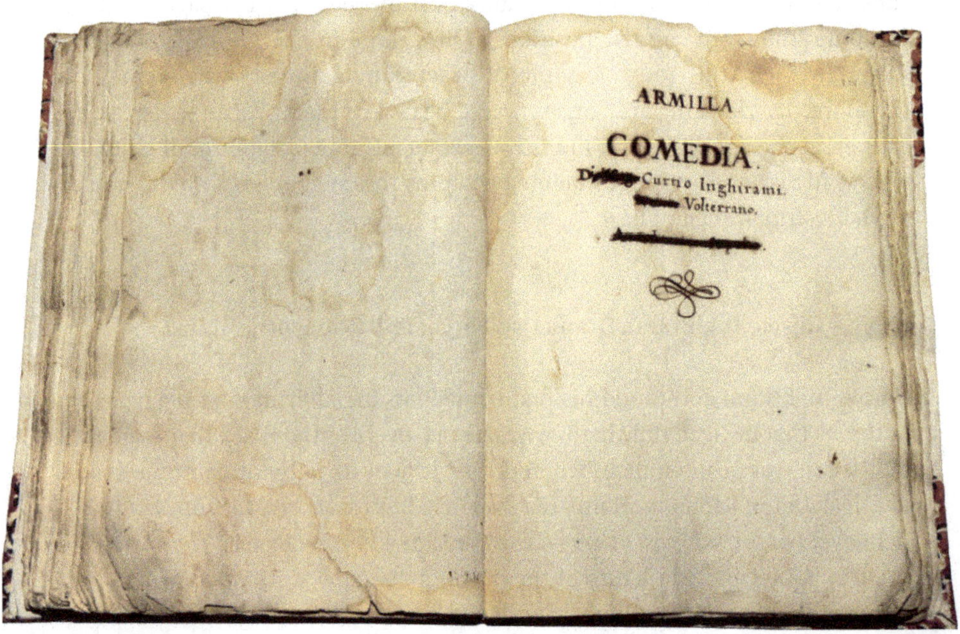

FIGURE 9.2 Curzio Inghirami, *Armilla*, 1634. Volterra, Biblioteca Comunale Guarnacci, Archivio Maffei, MS IV.53.4.6, Inv. 5883

pestilence had begun to abate, they revolted against their Florentine sanitary commissioner, Luigi Capponi, who had forbidden religious processions as a health hazard.[15] He had also forbidden theatre, a tradition nearly as vibrant in Volterra as it was in contemporary London. As with London in plague years, all the normal forms of social engagement had been shut down in the normally bustling piazzas of the city and in the villages and villas of the surrounding countryside.

This was the traumatic background against which nineteen-year-old Curzio Inghirami handed over the manuscript of *Armilla* [Fig. 9.2] to the scrutiny of the Inquisition in June 1634. The eldest son of a local landed aristocrat, Curzio had lost both parents and several relatives to the recent plague.[16] Since 1631, he and his younger sister Lucrezia had been brought up by their paternal grandmother, much of the time in their isolated country villa, Scornello, rather than in their palazzo inside the plague-ridden city. Two of his surviving uncles acted as the young orphans' official guardians.

---

15 Bacci R. – Trentini S., *Sette Secoli di Solidarietà: La Compagnia della Misericordia di Volterra* (Volterra: 2006) 14.

16 Males are mentioned more frequently than females in the Inghirami family trees preserved in the Archivio di Stato in Volterra. It is therefore much easier to arrive at the death toll from plague among Curzio's male relatives than among the women in his family.

Tellingly, many of the characters in *Armilla* are young men wandering far from home, and Armilla herself is a motherless maiden. Despite an intricate, outrageous comic plot that involves Armilla's beloved disguising himself in turn as a girl, a manservant and a Turkish galley slave, and a brief threat of Armilla's making an incestuous marriage, the Inquisitor restricted his comments on the play to a few marginal injunctions to 'Moderate yourself', and proclaimed the work suitable for publication on 13 June 1634. By 30 June, the Inquisition had issued an imprimatur, allowing Curzio to print the text, but *Armilla* was never published during its author's own lifetime.[17]

This silence may have been imposed by Curzio's uncle, Cavaliere Giulio Inghirami, Postmaster General of the Grand Duchy of Tuscany, who had other plans for his enterprising nephew than writing comedies. Curzio was already preparing himself reluctantly to study law at the University of Florence (where his uncle Cavaliere Giulio lived), but late in November of 1634, his life took a surprising turn. He and his sister had decided to go fishing one splendid morning in the river below their villa. As they made their way down the steep hillside toward the River Cecina in the company of a manservant, Curzio amused himself by throwing rocks, when one of his projectiles, a hard brown clod of earth, suddenly broke apart to reveal that it was really a capsule with a hollow interior, with two sheets of discoloured paper curled up inside. The outermost sheet bore an inscription that looked rather like the word 'Pisa' written backwards, but the other contained a remarkable Latin text [Fig. 9.3]:

> In the year of the prophesied King of the Jews, 1624, one thousand five hundred ninety-first from his Crucifixion:
>
> *A Dog shall come who shall serve out his term of indenture faithfully and freely for nine years, and more. The Wolf is the mother of the Lamb. The Lamb shall love the Dog. A Pig shall come forth from the horde of Pigs and shall devour the work of the Dog. Beware, beware, beware.*
>
> *Prospero of Fiesole, resident of this colony, Guardian of the Citadel, Prophesied the year after Catilina's death. You have discovered the treasure. Mark the spot, and go away.*[18]

17 Curzio's two surviving comedies, *Armilla* and *L'Amico Infido*, edited by Simone Migliorini and the present author, are in press with the Accademia dei Sepolti, the Volterran academy of which Curzio himself was Consul from some time in the 1640s until his death in 1655; the relevant papers have disappeared from the archives of the Sepolti and probably did so long ago.

18 Curzio Inghirami, *Antiquitatum Ethruscarum Fragmenta* (Frankfurt, [n.p.]: 1637), †2ii verso. See also Rowland I.D, *The Scarith of Scornello: A Tale of Renaissance Forgery* (Chicago: 2004) 6, 130. At the time I wrote the book, I hadn't yet realised that Curzio was an orphan when he discovered the Etruscan Antiquities.

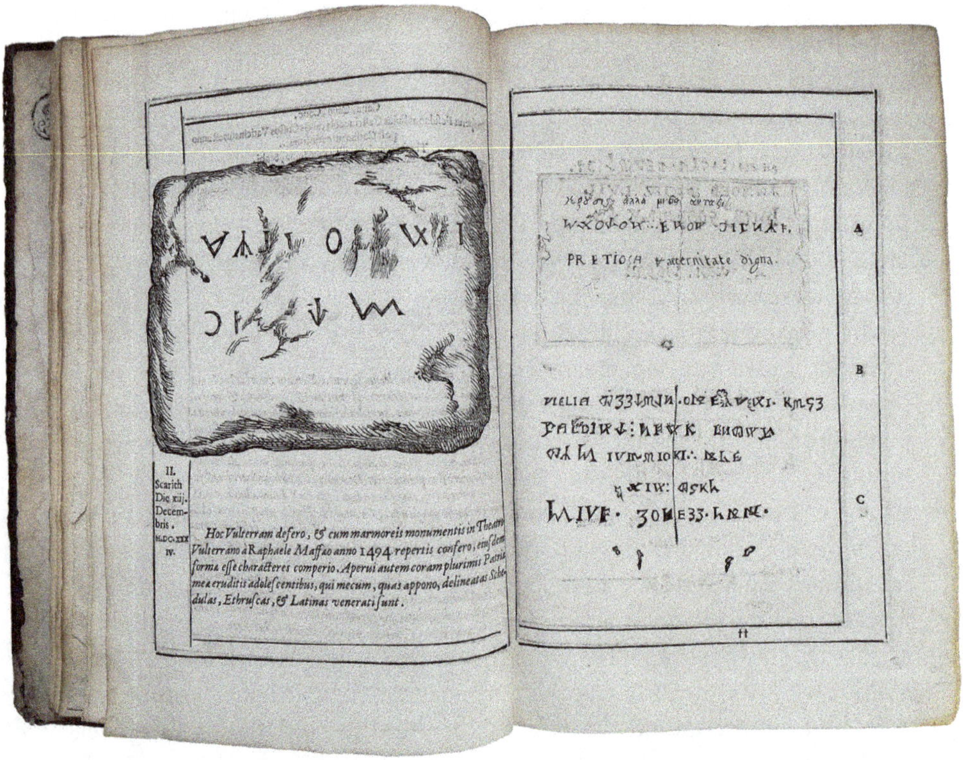

FIGURE 9.3 The first scarith. Curzio Inghirami, *Antiquitatum Ethruscarum Fragmenta*, †† 2ii verso
IMAGE PROVIDED BY SOKOL BOOKS

As Curzio would later report (with a certain laconic flair), 'I read it over, and I marveled; I marked the spot'. He also, if briefly, obeyed Prospero of Fiesole's warning to go away, but curiosity quickly overtook any fear of some ancient Etruscan curse. One day later, he had returned to the site to see what else he could find, and before long he, the local parish priest and a group of workmen from the Inghirami villa had amassed a whole pile of capsules full of papers, some with handwritten texts in Latin and some, excitingly, written in Etruscan script.[19] He would learn from the buried texts that the capsules themselves were called *scarith* and that Prospero of Fiesole had been a student priest in Volterra in the year 63 BCE. Unfortunately, 63 was also the year when Lucius Sergius Catilina, unsuccessful rival of Cicero for the Roman consulship in 64, had retreated to Tuscany to recruit a band of rebels against the Republic,

19 Rowland, *The Scarith of Scornello* 3–22.

only to be vanquished when Cicero unleashed the legions of the Roman army against the traitor. As Cicero's troops moved northward, Prospero, as he diligently reported for posterity, had been detailed to guard a fortress at Scornello (coincidentally the future site of Curzio Inghirami's country house), an outpost of Etruscan Volterra a few Roman miles south of the mother city's lofty citadel, with a panoramic view to the south. Sensing the impending end of his whole culture, the novice priest had enclosed all the important Etruscan records he could find inside protective scarith, and buried them next to the fort along with his 'dear household gods', one of which, made of battered tin [Fig. 9.4], Curzio was lucky enough to find, along with an ancient bronze lamp. Modern hindsight can identify the 'lamp' as an Iron Age Etruscan safety pin, or fibula, showing that there were genuine Etruscan artefacts at Scornello. The household god, on the other hand, with its tunic and his long sword (a weapon unknown in ancient Etruria), looks like a well-used toy soldier with an 'Etruscan' inscription added to his skirt.

The scarith rapidly became a sensation, not least because of Curzio's skill at presenting them to the public. He began with the citizens of Volterra and the local gentlemen's academy, the *Sepolti*, 'buried' to worldly concerns in their pursuit of philosophy. Whether or not people believed that the scarith were genuine, they all agreed that Curzio himself was a charming young man. The physical presence of the scarith themselves gave his presentations an added shiver of excitement.

To certify the authenticity of his nephew's discovery, Cavaliere Giulio decided to seek an official affidavit from the police. The investigation, which involved two officials from Florence, took place in May and June of 1635, alternating days of interviews with days spent observing Curzio and his team of workmen in the field. Thirteen new scarith emerged during their tour, two of them pulled from the soil by one of the inspectors. This first-hand experience only reinforced their general impression from examining the site that the artefacts had been buried for a long time and were very, very old.[20] A second investigation produced similar results.[21] Just one year after submitting *Armilla* to the censors, the aspiring playwright had become Volterra's semi-official 'Defender of the Etruscan Antiquities'.

20 Fiore C., "'Parmi di andare peregrinando dolcissimamente per quell'Etruria': Scoperte antiquarie e natura nell'Etruria di Curzio Inghirami e Athanasius Kircher", *Storia dell'Arte* 33 (2012) 53–81: esp. 55–58; Rowland, *The Scarith of Scornello* 145–146.

21 Rowland, *The Scarith of Scornello* 37.

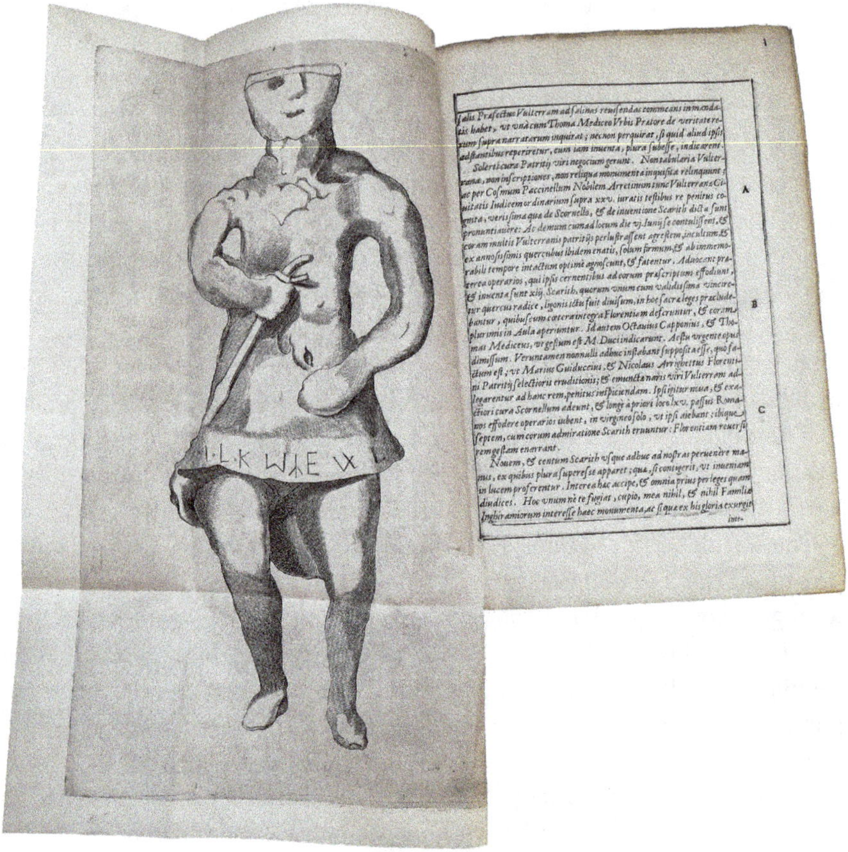

FIGURE 9.4 The 'dear household god' of Prospero of Fiesole. Curzio Inghirami, *Antiquitatum Ethruscarum Fragmenta* (Frankfurt [Florence], [n.p.]: 1637) unpaginated insert
IMAGE PROVIDED BY SOKOL BOOKS

Cavaliere Giulio began to arrange further presentations of the scarith at the Grand Duchy of Tuscany's two universities, Florence and Pisa. At the University of Pisa, Curzio met his first serious opposition in the person of Paganino Gaudenzio, the Swiss-born Professor of Humane Letters, who objected to the fact that the scarith texts were written on paper, noting that two ancient authors, Livy and Dionysius of Halicarnassus, reported instead that the Etruscans had written their books on bolts of linen.[22] Curzio replied that the phrase 'linen books' (*libri lintei*) simply meant linen rag paper, but Gaudenzio, undaunted,

22 The *libri lintei* mentioned by Livy and Dionysius were ancient books preserved in the temple of Juno Moneta in Rome; see Ogilvie R.M., "Livy, Licinius Macer and the Libri Lintei", *Journal of Roman Studies* 48:1/2 (1958) 40–46.

committed his thoughts to an essay, *De Charta exercitatio*, 'On Paper', which received its imprimatur in September 1636.[23] Gaudenzio held off publication temporarily, under pressure from Grand Duke Ferdinand II, who was scarcely older than Curzio and greatly impressed by both his young subject and the scarith's revelations about the glories of Etruscan – that is, Tuscan – history. The Grand Duke undoubtedly helped sponsor the printed edition of the scarith texts, *Antiquitatum Ethruscarum Fragmenta* [Fig. 9.5] which became available shortly after Curzio's public demonstrations in Florence and Pisa, an expensive illustrated folio volume bearing a false Frankfurt imprint and the date 1637, 'or, in Etruscan, MMMMCCCCXCV'. In fact, the book had been printed in Florence late in 1636.[24]

Publication brought the scarith to international attention, but the considerable beauties of the printed *Antiquitatum Ethruscarum Fragmenta* proved far less persuasive as a medium than the engaging presence of Curzio himself. Initially, Inghirami had decided to 'let readers judge for themselves' as they looked over Prospero of Fiesole's texts, but eventually he was forced to respond more directly to his critics.[25] In 1637, Vicente Nogueira, a Rome-based Portuguese scholar, sent a series of objections to his old friend, Cavaliere Giulio Inghirami, and shortly afterwards Curzio wrote: 'After I learned that the Lord Cavaliere told you that I would reply to your doubts, to avoid exhibiting bad manners I have decided to send you these few lines'.[26] Nogueira complained to his patron, the powerful cardinal Giulio Sacchetti, that Curzio had exhibited 'a certain sourness of tone in his responses': the pressures on the young Defender of the Etruscan Antiquities were beginning to tell.[27] Nogueira was certain that the scarith were fakes, but hesitated openly to identify Curzio as their creator. Cavaliere Giulio took offence nonetheless, accusing his old friend of treachery and breaking off their friendship.[28] The enmity of this eminent Tuscan put

23 Rowland, *The Scarith of Scornello* 62–70.

24 Ibidem, 38.

25 Curzio Inghirami to [Vicente Nogueira], 13 October 1637, Biblioteca Comunale di Volterra, Archivio Maffei MS 200, unpaginated: 'ho fatto proposito di non rispondere à qual si sia, che opponesse a queste scritture, poiché professando di darle al mondo pure, e nel modo, che li ho trovate, ho gusto, che ognuno ne faccia qual giuditio che gli parrà' ('I've made it my policy not to reply to just anyone who opposes these writings, because in deciding to give them to the world in their pure state, and in the form in which I found them, I'd like for everyone to make whatever assessment of them that they prefer').

26 Ibidem.

27 For the 'sourness of tone' see Rowland, *The Scarith of Scornello* 71.

28 Ibidem, 58.

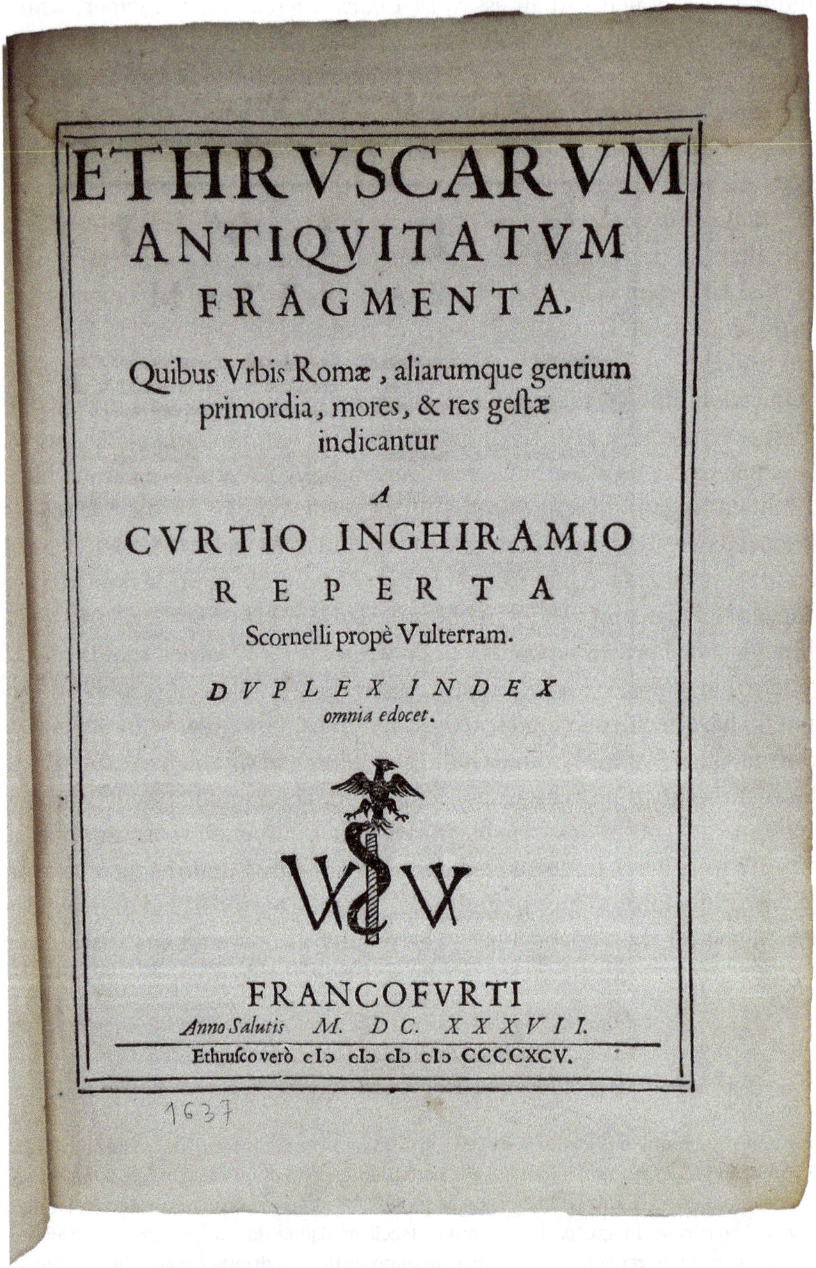

ETHRVSCARVM
ANTIQVITATVM
FRAGMENTA.

Quibus Vrbis Romæ, aliarumque gentium
primordia, mores, & res gestæ
indicantur

A

CVRTIO INGHIRAMIO
REPERTA
Scornelli propè Vulterram.

DVPLEX INDEX
omnia edocet.

FRANCOFVRTI
Anno Salutis M. DC. XXXVII.
Ethrusco verò cIↄ cIↄ cIↄ cIↄ CCCCXCV.

1637

FIGURE 9.5 Curzio Inghirami, *Antiquitatum Ethruscarum Fragmenta* (Frankfurt [Florence], [n.p.]: 1637)
IMAGE PROVIDED BY SOKOL BOOKS

Nogueira in a potentially dangerous position. Portugal was on the brink of a revolt against Spanish rule, and his real job in Rome was to spy on the Vatican for the side of the rebels. Rather than call any more attention to himself, he retreated into silence.[29]

In 1639, Paganino Gaudenzio issued his own printed attack on the Etruscan Antiquities, incorporating *De Charta*, in which he decried the scarith texts as 'not ancient records, but rather deceptions, invented to play with simple mortals'.[30] Like Nogueira, he stopped short of naming Curzio as the forger because of implicit threats from the Grand Duke and Cavaliere Giulio to end his employment at Pisa if he persisted in attacking the Grand Duchy's grand Etruscan heritage.[31] Gaudenzio therefore published the book in Protestant Amsterdam, far away from Tuscan censors.

In 1640, Leone Allacci, a Greek-born scriptor in the Vatican Library, launched what would become the definitive attack against the Etruscan Antiquities, identifying Curzio Inghirami as their creator without the slightest hesitation.[32] His *Animadversiones in antiquitatum etruscarum fragmenta ab Inghiramio edita*, published in Paris, drove home his argument with scathing wit as well as impeccable scholarship. Yet Curzio, undaunted, invited Allacci to Volterra, where they debated before the Academy of the Sepolti, and apparently both participants enjoyed the experience a great deal.[33] At some point in their acquaintance, Allacci, alone among all of Curzio's critics, seems to have understood an essential truth about the saga of Prospero of Fiesole: it comprised the next step, after *Armilla*, in Inghirami's development as a comic writer.

When Curzio and Lucrezia Inghirami first handled a scarith on the banks of the River Cecina, their manservant reported that they were bent over a bundle laughing.[34] It is difficult to imagine that the writer of *Armilla* wrote prophecies like 'The Pig shall come forth from the horde of pigs and shall devour the work of the Dog' with a straight face. As writers, both Allacci and Curzio delighted in heaping up piles of rhetoric to a humorous extreme. Here, for example, is *Armilla*'s bombastic Captain Aristofano trading insults with his gluttonous servant Trana:

29 Rowland, *The Scarith of Scornello* 57–58.

30 Gaudenzio Paganino, *Ad antiquitates etruscas quae Volaterrae nuper dederunt observationes* (Amsterdam, Joannes Jansonius: 1639) A2.

31 Rowland, *The Scarith of Scornello* 67.

32 Ibidem, 74–82.

33 Ibidem, 82–94.

34 Ibidem, 3.

Captain: Whoever refuses my friendship proves himself my enemy: and now, if I can't live content, let all order be banished, let confusion reign over all, cast to the Furies, to the devils, let my rage be unleashed.
Trana: But tell me, Signor Captain, how long do you plan to wait before we eat? By now …
Captain: A month, a year, a century, an eternity, and what will you say? While my heart seethes like an inferno of wrath, 'I want to eat!'
Trana: How will you live without eating?
Captain: What eating? What eating? My life is here, in this sword and in my victories. And you, craven rogue, it's a marvel that after spending so much time with me, not a bit of my valor has rubbed off on you.
Trana: And none of my hunger has rubbed off on you.
Captain: It's there all right, but Trana, it's time to put away these trifles. Be a hero and imitate my actions: run, fly, pounce, feint, join, resist; collide, shove, deflect, stab, slice, thrust, withdraw; charge, attack, assault, damage, injure, demolish, shatter.
Trana: En garde! Oh dear!
Captain: Persist, attack, stand your ground; never fear, never flee, and let your ferocious heart make you breathe forth fury. Trana, I want you to make those people regret ever having offended Captain Aristofano. Come on, have a lion's heart and fear no one.
Trana: I'm afraid of myself, not anyone else.
Captain: You great coward, for once put this pusillanimity of yours behind you, and in the presence of this glorious Champion, this mighty terror of the entire universe, brighten up, get mean, and get moving! Step lively, run, knock, smite, smite again and beat down that door, and speak, cry, shout that Meandro, Cammillo and all the rest of them should come out and fight, whether they're ten, twenty, a hundred, a thousand, ten thousand, an army, four armies, a thousand armies, the entire world, no matter their numbers, I'll trounce them all![35]

And here is Allacci making fun of Curzio's 'Etruscan' vocabulary:

I've long since developed a callus on my stomach from prolonged contact, but certainly not to the point where I'd not prefer to drink bilge rather than to hear words at which I recoil just as I would from a snake. Are these portents of words or monsters: Scarith, Caris, Mor, Turg, Asgaria, Vlerda, Dorchethes, Lartes, Saph, Roith, Ochincres, Brocon,

35 Inghirami Curzio, *Armilla*, Act 5, Scene 1.

> Spugi, Barconictus, Ancironae, Schilia, Cronuethia, Schesia, Procravia, Ocalia, Dantelia, Bentia, Porachal, Balth, Rebalth, Rurerebalth, Vosgaria, Onebrae, Enebrae, Inurnes.[36]

Curzio's fellow citizens, on the other hand, regarded their scarith with rever ence, none more fervently than his best friend, Raffaele Maffei, an upstanding Volterran thirteen years older than Curzio himself.[37] For Maffei, who rose to become one of the most important officials in Volterra, the Etruscan Antiquities were sacrosanct. Ironically, then, Curzio became locked into the position of defending his work as if it were genuine, constrained to continue creating scarith (or at least creating their 'transcribed' texts) to round out Volterra's ancient history and to defend his creations in scholarly essays. Eventually he gathered the essays into a fat book, *Discourse on the Oppositions made to the Etruscan Antiquities*, published in 1645 by Amadore Massi, official printer to the Grand Duke of Tuscany, the same printer who had made his debut in Florence nine years earlier with the anonymous publication of that false product of the Frankfurt press, *Antiquitatum Ethruscarum Fragmenta*.[38]

At the same time, Curzio penned another comedy, *L'Amico Infido*, which features, amid a host of other characters, a pedant who comes to Volterra in search of his errant former pupil, eager to see the Etruscan Antiquities as a sidelight to his mission:

> I could not neglect searching for him in this most ancient and venerable city, which was once the capital of all Etruria. And if I should fail to find him, at least I shall spend a few days here to see the remarkable texts that I hear have just been discovered in a certain Villa nearby. I have been given to understand that in them are contained the ancient traditions of all Europe, hitherto unknown to us.[39]

A far more polished drama than *Armilla*, *L'Amico Infido* weaves an intricate plot that rises to a climax worthy of a Rossini opera, with the entire cast onstage talking simultaneously in the final act before exiting en masse to an offstage

---

36 Rowland, *The Scarith of Scornello* 77.

37 The most complete treatment of Maffei's life is Cinci A., *Storia volterrana del provveditore Raffaello Maffei* (Volterra: 1887).

38 Inghirami Curzio, *Discorso sopra l'opposizioni fatte all'Antichità Toscane* (Florence, Amadore Massi and Lorenzo Landi: 1645).

39 Inghirami Curzio, *L'Amico Infido*, Volterra, Biblioteca Comunale, Archivio Maffei, MS IV.53.4.14, Inv. 5891.

wedding banquet. Sadly, a rat has eaten a corner of the sole surviving manuscript, but virtually all of the dialogue can be reconstructed nonetheless.[40] Curzio also tried his hand at a different kind of forgery, this time based not on objects, but on non-objects: he produced a history of medieval Volterra, *Extract of the Chamber of Volterra*, that cites a lengthy series of documents from the city archives for its information. The documents themselves, however, have never been found. It seems likely that they never existed in the first place.[41]

Curzio's comedies, the story he spun from the scarith and his putative history of Volterra, like Curzio's own life, spent on the razor's edge between scholarly fame and scholarly opprobrium, challenged the intricate strictures of seventeenth-century society in a small Tuscan city through a combination of humor and wild fantasy that left his contemporaries entirely confused. They never knew whether to regard him with pride or with shame. His portrait in Giuseppe Allegrini's *Series of Portraits of Illustrious Tuscans with Historical Praises of the Same* (*Serie di ritratti d'uomini illustri toscani con gli elogi storici dei medesimi*) of 1766–1778 [Fig. 9.6] describes him as 'Illustrious Volterran Patrician and Man of Letters, and Extremely Meritorious Subject of his Fatherland', but the records of the Accademia dei Sepolti from the time of his presidency have been deliberately removed.[42] Centuries before the term was coined in the twentieth century, Curzio Inghirami was a conceptual artist operating in what he and his own contemporaries called the theatre of the world, striking a unique, elusive balance between life and art.

2 Giorgio Grognet de Vassé and the Spirals of Atlantis

The Maltese architect and antiquarian Giorgio Grognet de Vassé [Fig. 9.7] harbored a deep faith in the significance of his native land that links him to the similar convictions of Annius for Viterbo and Curzio Inghirami for Volterra. In his own case, he believed, nay, knew implicitly, that his native Malta had provided the real inspiration for Plato's Atlantis. He was certain, as well, that inspiration from Atlantis lay behind the achievements of the Etruscans. Grognet's patriotic enthusiasm, like that of his predecessors, drove him to archaeological forgery, although, as shall be seen below, he delegated the

40 Inghirami, *L'Amico Infido*, Act 4, Scene 5.

41 Solaini E., "Il falso 'Estratto del Camerotto di Volterra'", *Rassegna Volterrana* 1:1 (January 1924) 17–19.

42 Allegrini Giuseppe, *Serie di ritratti d'uomini illustri toscani con gli elogi storici dei medesimi*, Vol. 3 (Florence, Appresso Giuseppe Allegrini: 1770) 128.

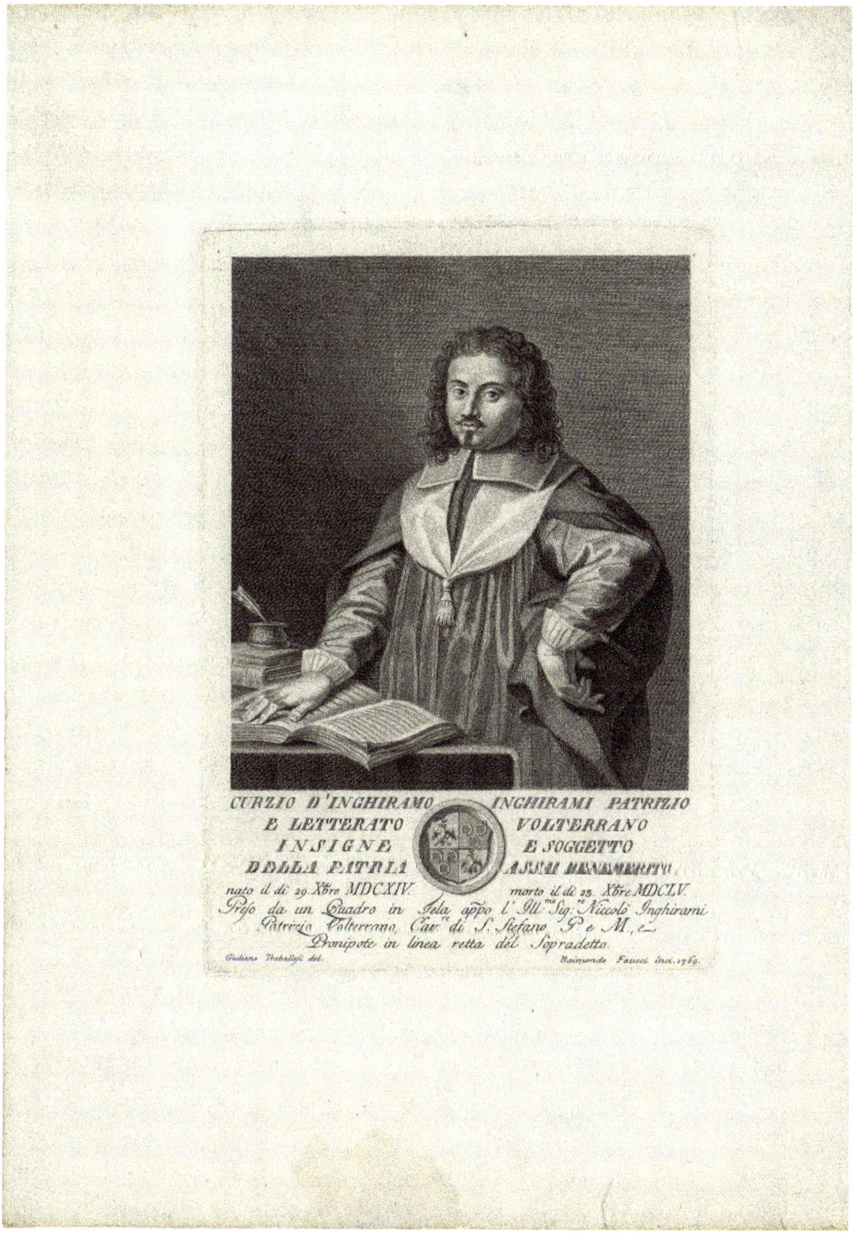

FIGURE 9.6 Portrait of Curzio Inghirami, from Giuseppe Allegrini, *Serie di ritratti d'uomini illustri toscani con gli elogi storici dei medesimi*, Vol. 3 (Florence, Giuseppe Allegrini: 1770) 128

first public presentation of his momentous 'discovery' to a Parisian colleague, the Marquis Agricol-Joseph-François-Xavier-Pierre-Esprit-Simon-Paul-Antoine Fortia d'Urban, taking advantage of the latter's social connections in the French capital. Grognet himself had long since returned to Malta after a life story that reads more like a picaresque novel.

Born into an aristocratic Maltese family in 1774, Grognet was sent to Italy in 1788, at the age of fourteen, to study at the fashionable new Seminario Tuscolano in Frascati, just outside Rome. His parents hoped that the seminary would prepare young Giorgio for a glittering career in the Church, but instead he fell in love with the ideals of the Enlightenment and the French Revolution, and with the monumental remains of an ancient stone wall outside Frascati that reminded him of the enigmatic remains of Malta's Neolithic temples.[43]

Before graduating in 1895, he took minor orders, the first step toward ordination as a priest. To keep peace with his wealthy family on his return to Malta, he took a position as a *chierico*, a cleric who had not yet taken priestly vows.[44] In 1797, however, the Abbé Grognet and several other young Maltese idealists slipped aboard a French Republican warship docked in the Grand Harbor of Malta and set sail for Corfu to enlist in Napoleon's army. By 1802, frustrated by his failure to rise beyond the rank of lieutenant, Grognet bribed his way into a position with Napoleon's Corps of Engineers, which brought him to Paris before dispatching him to Italy.[45] Grognet's surviving drawings from this period include the design for a bridge in La Spezia as well as architectural plans and gouache paintings. In late 1813, as Napoleon's empire crumbled, Grognet resigned from the French Army and settled in Rome, where he struggled to survive as a freelance draftsman, aspiring antiquarian and architect. His admission to the prestigious Accademia Archeologica del Campidoglio suggests

43 Schiavone M.J., "Grognet de Vassé, Giorgio", in *Dictionary of Maltese Biographies, Vol. 2, G–Z*, (Pietà: 2009) 989–990; Cutajar D., "The Architect-Engineer Giorgio Grognet (1774–1862): Paradigm of an Early Romantic Intellectual", *Times of Malta*, 25 April 1980 and 26 April 1980, accessed 22 August 2019, https://www.academia.edu/38328843/D.Cutajar_1980_Georgio_Grognet.pdf?source+swp_share, 1. The Seminario was organised in 1770 as a direct dependency of the Bishopric of Frascati by Henry Benedict Stuart, the brother of Bonnie Prince Charlie and son of the Old Pretender, taking over the spaces and role of the Jesuit seminary of Frascati just before the Order's suppression in 1773. "Progetti: IV Centenario della basilica cattedrale tuscolana", Scuola SCIC Rocca di Papa Istituto Suore di Carità Immacolata Concezione di Ivrea, accessed 20 August 2019, http://www.scuola-scic-roccadipapa.com/index.php?option=com_content&view=article&id=4&catid=18&Itemid=138.

44 Cutajar, "Giorgio Grognet" 4–6.

45 Ibidem, 6.

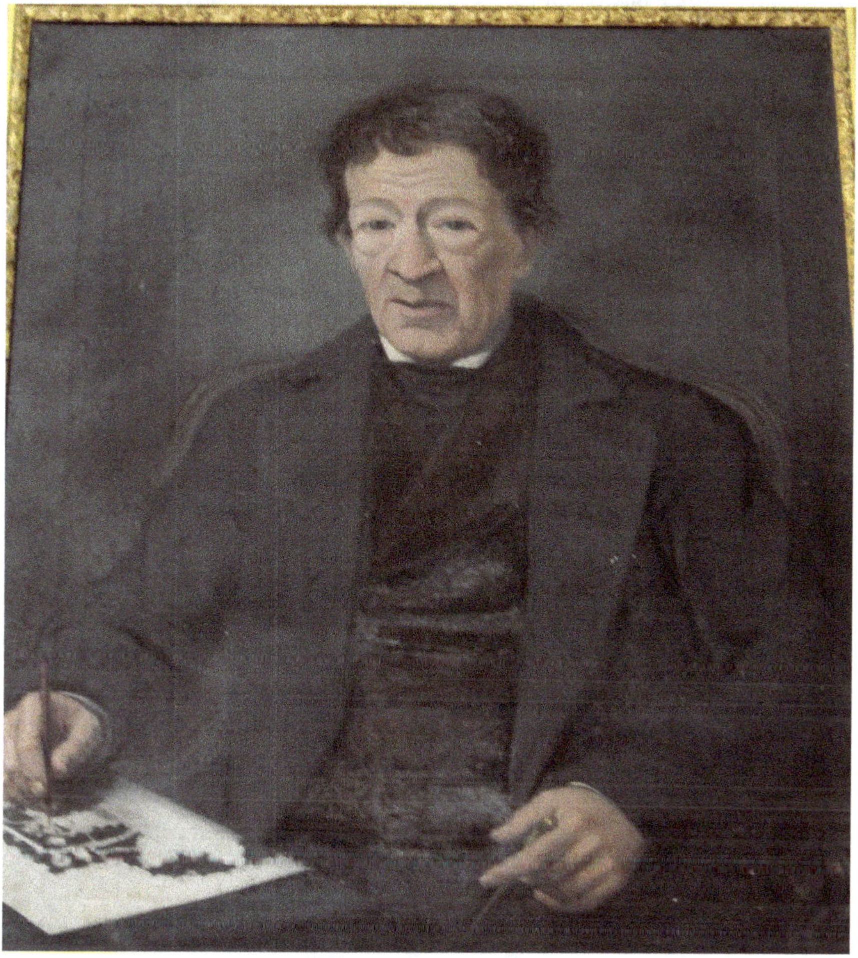

FIGURE 9.7 Anonymous, Portrait of Giorgio Grognet de Vassé, *c.* 1862. Mosta, Basilica of the Assumption of Our Lady
AUTHOR'S PHOTO

some degree of success, but in 1816 or 1817 he returned again to Malta and his elderly parents.[46]

At some point during his Roman sojourn, or perhaps earlier in Paris, Grognet had befriended a wealthy French mathematician, antiquarian and author, the Marquis Agricol-Joseph-François-Xavier-Pierre-Esprit-Simon-Paul-Antoine Fortia d'Urban (1756–1843), who had already published several volumes on the earliest history of the Celts (and by extension the French), *Memoirs Useful for*

46 Cutajar, "Giorgio Grognet" 4–6.

the History of the Terrestrial Globe Before the Flood of Ogyges, in which both Malta and Atlantis played a significant role.[47]

The ninth volume of this work, *History and Theory of the Flood of Ogyges, or Noah, and the Submersion of Atlantis*, identified both Plato's Atlantis and Homer's Ogygia with the Maltese island of Gozo, using a comparison between the masonry of the Neolithic temple complex at Ġgantija with structures 'en Sicile, en Etrurie, en Ecosse, en Basse-Bretagne et en Danemarck'.[48] Both Ġgantija and the temples of Ħaġar Qim on Malta's main island had already captured the interest of seventeenth-century writers like Giovanni Francesco Abela and Athanasius Kircher, but had attracted particular international attention after the Maltese Islands became an area of interest to Napoleon and the British Navy.[49] Inspired by Fortia d'Urban's theories, Grognet had begun to formulate his own ideas about the significance of Malta's megalithic structures and stone carvings. In their massive forms and recurring spiral designs, he saw the traces of lost Atlantis, with the circular harbor and circular walls so vividly described in Plato's dialogues *Timaeus* and *Critias*.[50]

Between 1820 and 1822, Grognet also made friends with another French antiquarian, Louis Domeny di Rienzi, who had stopped in Malta after traveling the Mediterranean in search of antiquities. Somewhere in North Africa, Rienzi had picked up a stone inscribed in both Greek and Punic; during his stay in Malta, he ordered translations of its texts into Italian (Malta's lingua franca), which suggests that he was a man of limited education. A local merchant was able to translate the ancient Greek; for the Phoenician, he asked an erudite local scholar, Giuseppe Cannolo.[51] When Rienzi left Malta for France

---

47 Ganado A., "Bibliographical notes on Melitensia–2", *Melita Historica* 14:1 (2004) 67–94: 76.

48 Fortia D'urban A.-J.-F.-X.-P.-E.-S.-P.-A., *Mémoires pour servir à l'Histoire Ancienne du Globe Terrestre*, vol. 9, *Histoire et Théorie du Déluge d'Ogygès ou de Noé, et de la Submersion de l'Atlantide* (Paris: 1809) 275. Fortia d'Urban devotes respectful but skeptical attention to Olof Rudbeck's identification of Atlantis with Sweden, scoffing at the idea an ideal city could ever be located in a region that was buried for half the year under ice.

49 Trump D.H., *Malta: Prehistory and Temples* (Santa Venera: 2002) 6–9.

50 See Rowland I.D., "The Atlantic Visions of Giorgio Grognet de Vassé (1774–1862)", in Cochran Anderson J. – Dow D.N. (eds.), *Visualizing the Past in Italian Renaissance Art: Studies in Honor of Brian A. Curran*, Brill's Studies on Art, Art History and Intellectual History (Leiden: 2021) 81–108: esp. 81–84.

51 Ganado A., "The Talents of Giuseppe Cannolo (1756–1845): An Appreciation", in Vella C. (ed.), *Proceedings of History Week 2009* (Santa Venera: 2012) 28–35: 30–31; Said I., "Giuseppe Cannolo: Il-ġenju eċċentriku traduttur u l-interpretu tal-iskjavi", *L'Aċċent, Maltese Language Magazine* 13 (2015) 40–44.

in 1822, he entrusted his bilingual stone to Grognet, who sent on a drawing of the object to his friend Fortia d'Urban.[52]

In 1826, a Maltese priest, Don Giuseppe Felice Galea, discovered another Punic inscription as he dug one day in his garden in Città Vecchia (today's Mdina).[53] When he showed his discovery to Grognet, the architect could see that the text distinctly bore the word 'Atlantis'. Both Galea and Grognet wrote to Fortia d'Urban about the exciting discovery, which Fortia d'Urban in turn announced to the Asiatic Society.[54]

The second discovery he announced that day involved a manuscript, as Fortia d'Urban explained to his audience:

> Today I come to speak to you about a work in which the author, born in Cyrene, reports that he has copied a *History of Libya*, written by Aristippus of Cyrene, about four hundred years before our [Christian] era. Here is the translation I have made of that work, with the greatest care. We shall find a series of events that will certainly seem strange to us, but it is precisely because of this that they should excite our curiosity. The author, Eumalos of Cyrene, after having spoken in his first five books about Libya and Atlas, the ancient king of that region, to which he gave the name Atlantis, writes what you are about to hear in his sixth book.[55]

This sixth book of Eumalos declared that Atlantis was situated, like Malta, in the center of the Mediterranean, and therefore corroborated the reference to Atlantis on Don Galea's Punic inscription. Fortia d'Urban had never seen the manuscript of the Eumalos text himself. His own translation into French was based on an Italian translation of the text made by none other than Grognet, who had seen the Greek manuscript in Malta at the house of Louis Domeny de Rienzi.[56] In fact, no one but Grognet and Rienzi can be said ever to have seen the manuscript of Eumalos of Cyrene; Fortia d'Urban told his Parisian listeners that the original had been lost at sea shortly after its discovery. Fortia d'Urban's

---

52 Ganado, "Giuseppe Cannolo" 30.

53 Ibidem, 30.

54 Ganado, "Bibliographical Notes" 76–77; Colavito J., "Eumalos of Cyrene on Atlantis", accessed 19 August 2019, http://www.jasoncolavito.com/eumalos-on-atlantis-hoax.html. Fortia d'Urban published his discourse, and I have made my own translation of the text, which differs somewhat from Colavito's. See also Franke T.C, "The Atlantis-Malta Hoax of Fortia d'Urban and Grognet from 1828", 7–10 November 2013, accessed 19 August 2019: https://www.atlantis-scout.de/atlantis-malta-hoax.htm.

55 Fortia D'urban A.-J.-F.-X.-P.-E.-S.-P.-A., *Discours composé pour la Société asiatique par M. le marquis de Fortia d'Urban, séance du 4 février 1828* (Paris: n.d.) 1–2.

56 Ganado, "Giuseppe Cannolo" 30–33.

address to the Asiatic Society raised both interest and skepticism, beginning with Louis Domeny de Rienzi himself.[57] In a letter to Fortia d'Urban published in 1832, Rienzi reported that he himself, along with his mentor Andreas Ariston, had discovered the Eumalos manuscript on the Tunisian island of Djerba in 1807 and that he had written to Grognet about the discovery in 1822. According to Rienzi, Grognet had given Fortia d'Urban a garbled account of the manuscript's discovery, and could not possibly have spent enough time with the text to have translated the sixth book:

> You, Monsieur, have translated M. Grognet's putative Italian translation of the sixth book. I myself have translated part of the original Greek, to which I have added a commentary. But the shipwreck that has swallowed up all my possessions and my writings, the fruit of more than twenty voyages and labors (more than twelve to the Orient), and the little Memory that remains to me, cannot reassure me that any part of the translation of the sixth book that has been addressed to you by M. Grognet is exact.[58]

'I believe', Rienzi concluded, 'that most of the sixth book has been fabricated by him. [...] To sum up, M. Grognet seems to me to have played the role of minor-league Annius of Viterbo, who himself forged the very books he attributed to the ancients'.[59] Of course, Rienzi's story of a papyrus manuscript that gets lost in a shipwreck suggests that he, too, belonged to the club.

The eminent German scholar August Böckh attacked both the Atlantis inscription and Eumalos text in a lecture delivered in Berlin in 1832, published the following year in an English periodical, *The Philological Museum*.[60] There Böckh reports that Fortia d'Urban and Grognet had already tried to pass off another forged Phoenician inscription in 1824, although without any mention of Atlantis; this may be the inscription that Rienzi discovered in 1819 and passed on to Grognet in 1822. Böckh then proceeds to demolish the authenticity of their more recent finds with all the tools of modern German philology. But then he had his own personal interest in rooting out spurious Atlantic

57 Domeny De Rienzi L., *Question importante de Manuscrits et Inscriptions Antiques, Réponse à M. le Marquis de Fortia d'Urban* (Paris: 1832).

58 Ibidem, 5.

59 Ibidem, 5, 7.

60 Böckh A., "De titulis quibusdam suppositis Augusti Boeckhii prolusion academica", *The Philological Museum* 2 (1833) 457–467.

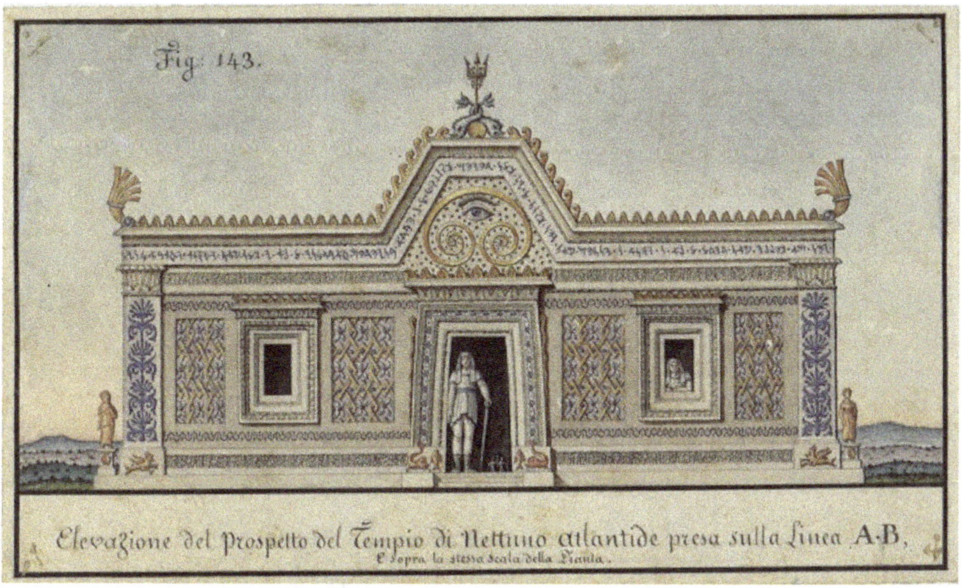

FIGURE 9.8 Giorgio Grognet de Vassé, Atlantic temple, *c.* 1854
COURTESY NATIONAL LIBRARY, MALTA

artefacts, for, as he wrote to his friend Alexander von Humboldt in 1833, 'when it comes to Atlantis, I can't entirely convince myself that it is all Plato's fiction'.[61]

As Grognet tried to promote these dubious antiquarian efforts through Fortia d'Urban, he set up an office in Valletta, the capital of Malta, as an architect and civil engineer.[62] Some of his projects seemed as extreme as his ideas about Atlantis, such as digging a tunnel under the English Channel to connect Britain and France.[63] He also continued gathering evidence for a monumental publication on Atlantis, amassing an impressive body of illustrations, including reconstructions of 'Atlantic' architecture [Fig. 9.8].

In Paris, Grognet had seen an ancient Greek marble relief (*c.* 560 BCE) discovered on the island of Samothrace, one of the cult centers for the Kabeiroi, a Greek mystery cult about which contemporary scholars know very little and

61 Humboldt A.V. – Böckh A., *Alexander von Humboldt/August Böckh/Briefwechsel*, ed. Werther R. – Knobloch E., Beiträge zur Alexander von Humboldt Forschung (Berlin: 2011) 33:61, cited in Franke, "The Atlantis-Malta Hoax".

62 Cutajar, "Giorgio Grognet" 7.

63 Anonymous, "Giorgio Grognet de Vassé", *L'Arte* (1863) 2–4: 4.

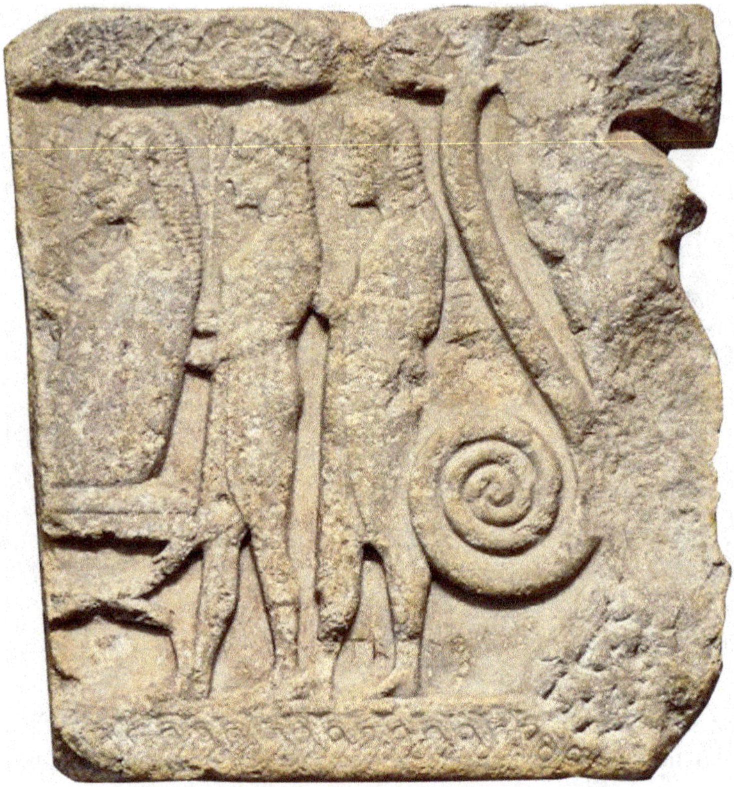

FIGURE 9.9 Greek relief sculpture from the island of Samothrace showing Agamemnon, Talthybius and Epeius, *c.* 560 BCE, Paris, Louvre. PHOTO: MARIE-LAN NGUYEN, 2007, WIKIMEDIA COMMONS, LICENSED UNDER CREATIVE COMMONS ATTRIBUTION-SHARE ALIKE 4.0 INTERNATIONAL LICENSE, https://creativecommons.org/licenses/by-sa/4.0/deed.en

about which less was known in Grognet's own time.[64] The piece had been brought to the Louvre in 1816 [Fig. 9.9], and depicts the Greek king Agamemnon, the herald Talthybius and Epeius, the builder of the Trojan Horse, standing next to an immense conspicuous spiral.[65] Grognet, who remembered the conspicuous spirals on Malta's Neolithic temples, decided that what he called the 'famous Kabiric spiral' was one more legacy to the Greeks from the people of Atlantis, 'from whom they took all their civilization, and all their knowledge'.[66]

64 Hemberg B., *Die Kabiren* (Uppsala: 1950); Rice D.G. – Stambaugh J., *Sources for the Study of Greek Religion, Corrected Edition* (Atlanta: 2009) 158–162; Beekes R.S.P. "The Origin of the Kabeiroi", *Mnemosyne*, 4th Series, 57:4 (2004) 465–477.

65 Comte De Clarac F., *Description des antiques du Musée National du Louvre* (Paris: 1848) 218.

66 Grognet De Vassé G., *Compendio ossia Epilogo anticipato di un Opera Estesa sulla precisa Situazione della Sommersa Isola Atlantide* (Malta: 1854) 21–22.

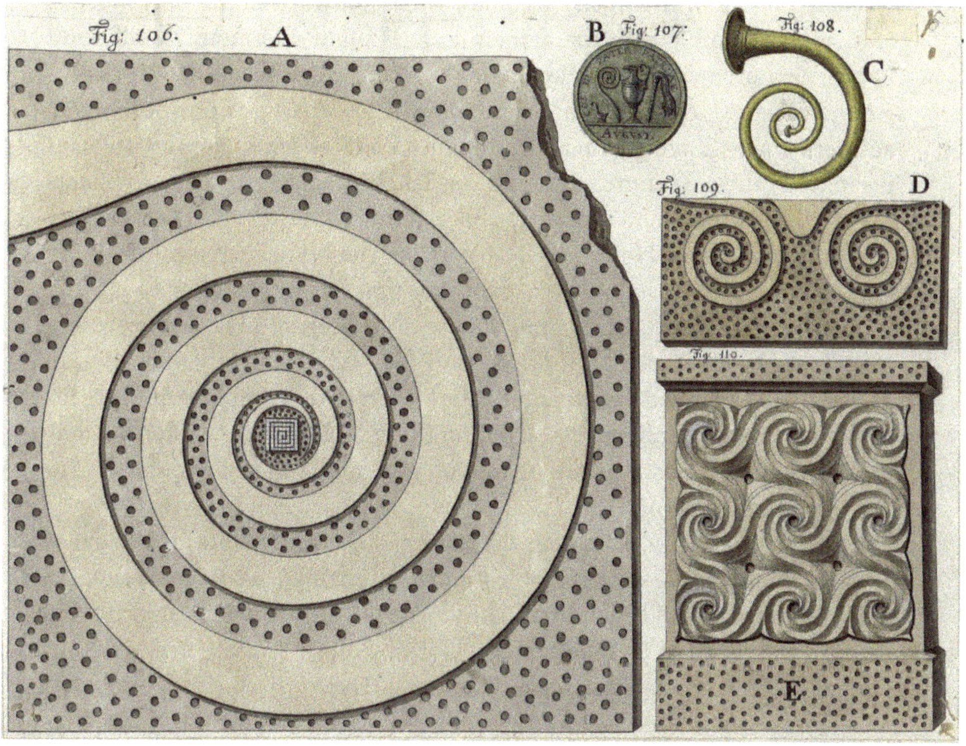

FIGURE 9.10 Giorgio Grognet de Vassé, Spiral motifs on Neolithic temples in Malta, *c.* 1854, watercolour, Valetta, National Library MS 615, Figs. 106-110
PHOTO: COURTESY OF NATIONAL LIBRARY, MALTA

In his travels around the Mediterranean, he gathered all the evidence of spirals he could find, from coins, statues, tombs, temples, vase paintings and Ionic columns [Fig. 9.10], and traced them all back to Plato's great lost city – and to Malta. Visitors to the islands often dropped by his studio on Kingsway (the former Strada Reale) to see his maps of the Mediterranean before the sinking of Atlantis and his lively gouache paintings of stone walls, ruins, spiral carvings and hitherto unknown Atlantic architecture. Today, those drawings provide the most directly eloquent testimony to his lifelong project: the grand books he intended to write never quite materialised in the way that Fortia d'Urban's many volumes had done. But Grognet had another spectacular strategy in reserve to promote his Atlantic vision.

In 1832, he received a commission to design the replacement for a small sixteenth-century parish church in Mosta, a village on Malta's main island. For the modest settlement, he drew up plans for a huge domed church in Neoclassical style, inspired by the Pantheon in Rome. Maltese churches, like Gothic cathedrals, are community projects, created by the collective will of ordinary people with ordinary incomes. Their construction is a slow process, and, as with Gothic cathedrals, their scale is often enormously ambitious: imposing church domes still dominate the Maltese landscape. Grognet's project, however, was truly exceptional, not only for its departure from the Baroque aesthetic that still prevails in Malta, but also for its sheer immensity. The cornerstone of the new church at Mosta was laid in 1833, but all the participants expected construction to take years, if not decades. As Grognet's huge circular structure rose above Mosta's modest horizon, the original sixteenth-century church continued to function, at the same time providing a handy scaffold for work on the dome. During building season, Grognet lived in Mosta, in a townhouse he had designed; for the rest of the year, he and his family lived in Valletta, where he tried to start an Atlantic Society with scant success.[67] Like his Mosta neighbors, he offered his labour for the church virtually without charge, and therefore opened a private school of 'Civil and Military Architecture' to earn some added money.[68]

In 1857, twenty-four years after the setting of the cornerstone, the dome of Grognet's new Pantheon closed over Tommaso Dingli's Renaissance church. In 1860, the same teams began to dismantle Dingli's structure and carry it away through the doors of its replacement, block by block. In 1862, nearly ninety, Grognet died and was interred in the church. The Mosta Rotunda [Fig. 9.11] was finally consecrated eighteen years later, in 1880, almost fifty years after work began. For many decades, Grognet's dome, built of Maltese limestone rather than Roman concrete, would rank, at 39.6 meters, as the third largest unsupported span in the world, after the Pantheon and St. Peter's in Rome.[69] It looms above the low buildings of Mosta and remains one of the islands' most conspicuous landmarks.

As his Pantheon rose over Mosta, Grognet continued his antiquarian researches on Atlantis, but aside from his splendid gouaches of Cyclopean walls and Kabiric spirals, he produced only a small summary of his Atlantic

67 Anonymous, "Villa Grognet", *Times of Malta*, 7 April 2012, accessed 19 August 2019: https://timesofmalta.com/articles/view/Villa-Grognet.414368.

68 Cutajar, "Giorgio Grognet" 8; Bianco L., "Building Science and Professional Ethics in Nineteenth-century Ecclesiastical Architecture in Malta", *Terra Sebus. Acta Musei Sabesiensis* 10 (2018) 413–424; Bianco L., "The Realisation of the Rotunda of Mosta, Malta: Grognet, Fergusson, and the Episcopal Objection", *European Journal of Science and Theology* 14:4 (2018) 203–213; Macgill T., *A Hand-Book, or Guide, for Strangers Visiting Malta* (Malta: 1839) 126: 'the lower orders [...] work gratis, on Sundays and on other church holydays'.

69 This classification scheme leaves out Brunelleschi's octagonal dome for Santa Maria del Fiore, evidently to Mosta's advantage.

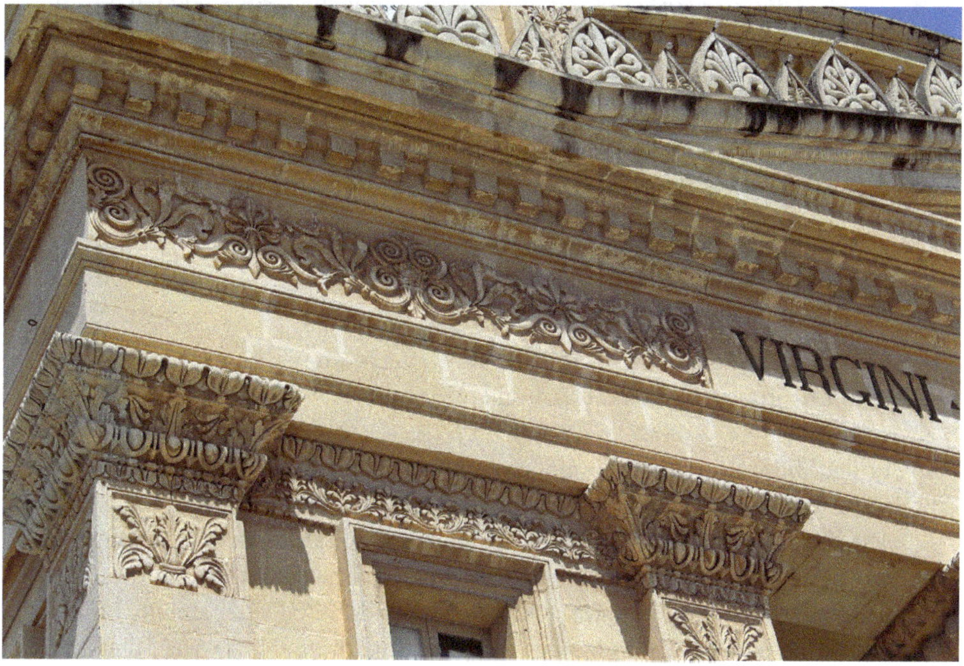

FIGURE 9.11 Mosta Dome, "Atlantic" detailing. Mosta, Malta, 1862
AUTHOR'S PHOTO

theories, a book published in 1854, when the author was eighty.[70] In 1863, *L'Arte*, a Maltese 'Patriotic Bimonthly', paid homage to his lifelong struggle on behalf of his Malta's Atlantic heritage. His final appearance on the world's stage was a tragic performance, at least in the eyes of *L'Arte*'s anonymous correspondent:

> Not long ago, a decrepit old man could be seen, slow and sickly, dragging his emaciated steps among us, shrouded already in the pallor of death. His merits, his virtues, had not been enough to save him from the shipwreck of dire poverty! A sterile admiration could only insult his privation; friendship alone was unstinting in its compassion. On the edge of the grave he cursed celebrity, yet he loved humankind, he loved knowledge, and turned his thoughts to Art, and to his ungrateful native land.
>
> A foreigner, visiting these islands of ours, is taken by the guide to contemplate our Pantheon at Mosta. The bold concept of that structure, the majesty of the forms, the vastness, the harmony of the parts surprise him: he asks about the mighty talent that germinated the magnificent idea

70 Grognet De Vassé, *Compendio, ossia epilogo anticipato.*

> [...] and in a corner of the sumptuous Temple his gaze is pointed toward a tomb. After a life spent in combating every Trial a man could undergo, he sleeps, obliged to content himself with widespread fame, spurned by Fortune, which, moreover, he had despised. There, beneath a humble slab of stone, rest the ashes of the illustrious architect GIORGIO GROGNET DE VASSÉ; there his weary bones were placed on September 8, 1862.[71]

This anonymous writer offers two aphorisms, neither a particular source of solace:

> The Olympus of genius will always be the insane asylum.
> Destitution is often the pedestal of glory.[72]

In fact, however, Grognet's monumental Pantheon provides a lasting testament to his belief in Malta's Atlantic origins, in the most durable of materials. The church of Mosta is a veritable symphony of spirals, from the spiraling coffers of its main dome and all the minor domes of the colossal structure, to the detailing of its Ionic columns, palmette antefixes, spiral and palmette friezes, and spiral-patterned wooden doors. By creating the solid, modern, Christian successor to the most ancient buildings in Europe, the Neolithic temples of Malta, and designing his own neo-Atlantic temple on the basis of what he saw as the most powerful of all primordial decorative motifs, he inserted the Kabeiric spiral into the great flow of history, creating his own evidence for its enduring significance. Rather than taking a turn on the stage of the 'theatre of the world', he carved his greatest performance from the Rock of Ages.

Bibliography

Alfani G., "Plague in seventeenth-century Europe and the decline of Italy: an epidemiological hypothesis", *European Review of Economic History* 17:4 (November 2013) 408–430.

Allegrini Giuseppe, *Serie di ritratti d'uomini illustri toscani con gli elogi storici dei medesimi*, Vol. 3 (Florence, Giuseppe Allegrini: 1770).

Anonymous, "Giorgio Grognet de Vassé", *L'Arte* (1863) 2–4.

Anonymous, "Villa Grognet", *Times of Malta*, 7 April 2012, accessed 19 August 2019: https://timesofmalta.com/articles/view/Villa-Grognet.414368.

71 Anonymous, "Giorgio Grognet de Vassé" 4.

72 Ibidem, 3–4.

Bacci R. – Trentini S., *Sette Secoli di Solidarietà: La Compagnia della Misericordia di Volterra* (Volterra: 2006).

Beekes R.S.P., "The Origin of the Kabeiroi", *Mnemosyne*, 4th Series, 57:4 (2004) 465–477.

Bianco L., "Building Science and Professional Ethics in Nineteenth-century Ecclesiastical Architecture in Malta", *Terra Scbus. Acta Musei Sabesiensis* 10 (2018) 413–424.

Bianco L., "The Realisation of the Rotunda of Mosta, Malta: Grognet, Fergusson, and the Episcopal Objection", *European Journal of Science and Theology* 14:4 (2018) 203–213.

Bruno Giordano, *De gli eroici furori* (London: John Charlewood, 1585).

Bruno Giordano, *Giordano Bruno on the Heroic Frenzies*, ed. E. Canone, trans. I.D. Rowland (Toronto: 2014).

Böckh A., "De titulis quibusdam suppositis Augusti Boeckhii prolusion academica", *The Philological Museum* 2 (1833) 457–467.

Cinci A., *Storia volterrana del provveditore Raffaello Maffei* (Volterra: 1887).

Cipolla C.M., *Cristofano and the Plague: A Study in the History of Public Health in the Age of Galileo* (London: 1973).

Colavito J., "Eumalos of Cyrene on Atlantis", accessed 19 August 2019, http://www.jasoncolavito.com/eumalos-on-atlantis-hoax.html.

Comte De Clarac F., *Description des antiques du Musée National du Louvre* (Paris: 1848).

Curran B., *The Egyptian Renaissance: The Afterlife of Ancient Egypt in Early Modern Italy* (Chicago: 2007) 107–131.

Cutajar D., "The Architect-Engineer Giorgio Grognet (1774–1862): Paradigm of an Early Romantic Intellectual", *Times of Malta*, 25 April 1980 and 26 April 1980, accessed 22 August 2019, https://www.academia.edu/38328843/D.Cutajar_1980_Georgio_Grognet.pdf?source+swp_share.

Danielsson O., *Etruskische Inschriften in Handschriftlicher Überlieferung*, Skrifter utgivna av K. Humanistiska Vetenskaps-Samfund i Uppsala 25:3 (Uppsala: 1928).

Domeny De Rienzi L., *Question importante de Manuscrits et Inscriptions Antiques, Réponse à M. le Marquis de Fortia d'Urban* (Paris: 1832).

Evangelista A., "L'attività spettacolare della Compagnia di San Giovanni Evangelista nel Conquecento", *Medioevo e Rinascimento* 18/15 (2004) 299–366.

Fiore C., "'Parmi di andare peregrinando dolcissimamente per quell'Etruria': Scoperte antiquarie e natura nell'Etruria di Curzio Inghirami e Athanasius Kircher", *Storia dell'Arte* 33 (2012) 53–81.

Fortia D'urban A.-J.-F.-X.-P.-E.-S.-P.-A., *Mémoires pour servir à l'Histoire Ancienne du Globe Terrestre, vol. 9, Histoire et Théorie du Déluge d'Ogygès ou de Noé, et de la Submersion de l'Atlantide* (Paris: 1809).

Fortia D'urban A.-J.-F.-X.-P.-E.-S.-P.-A., *Discours composé pour la Société asiatique par M. le marquis de Fortia d'Urban, séance du 4 février 1828* (Paris: n.d.).

Franke T.C., "The Atlantis-Malta Hoax of Fortia d'Urban and Grognet from 1828", 7–10 November 2013, accessed 19 August 2019: https://www.atlantis-scout.de/atlantis-malta-hoax.htm.

Fumagalli E., "Aneddoti della vita di Annio da Viterbo, O.P., I: Annio e la vittoria dei genovesi sui sforzeschi, II: Annio e la disputa sull'Immacolata Concezione", *Archivum Fratrum Predicatorum* 50 (1980) 167–199.

Ganado A., "Bibliographical notes on Melitensia–2", *Melita Historica* 14:1 (2004) 67–94.

Ganado A., "The Talents of Giuseppe Cannolo (1756–1845): An Appreciation", in Vella C. (ed.), *Proceedings of History Week 2009* (Santa Venera: 2012) 28–35.

Gaudenzio Paganino, *Ad antiquitates etruscas quae Volaterrae nuper dederunt observationes* (Amsterdam, Joannes Jansonius: 1639).

Grafton A., *Forgers and Critics: Creativity and Duplicity in Western Scholarship* (Princeton NJ: 1990).

Grognet De Vassé G., *Compendio ossia Epilogo anticipato di un Opera Estesa sulla precisa Situazione della Sommersa Isola Atlantide* (Malta: 1854).

Hemberg B., *Die Kabiren* (Uppsala: 1950).

Henderson J., *Florence Under Siege: Surviving Plague in an Early Modern City* (New Haven: 2019).

Humboldt A.V. – Böckh A., *Alexander von Humboldt/August Böckh/Briefwechsel*, ed. Werther R. – Knobloch E., Beiträge zur Alexander von Humboldt Forschung (Berlin: 2011).

Inghirami Curzio, *Antiquitatum Ethruscarum Fragmenta* (Frankfurt [Florence], [n.p.]: 1637).

Inghirami Curzio, *Discorso sopra l'opposizioni fatte all'Antichità Toscane* (Florence, Amadore Massi and Lorenzo Landi: 1645).

Inghirami Curzio, *Armilla and L'Amico Infido*, ed. S. Migliorini – I.D. Rowland (Volterra: forthcoming).

Macgill T., *A Hand-Book, or Guide, for Strangers Visiting Malta* (Malta: 1839).

Manfredi V.M., *Chimaira* (Milan: 2001).

Manzoni A., *La peste a Milano. Storia della Colonna Infame. I Promessi Sposi* (*capitoli 31, 32, 34*), with a preface by Piero Gibellini and a comment by Mino Martinazzoli (Brescia: 2020).

Ogilvie R.M., "Livy, Licinius Macer and the Libri Lintei", *Journal of Roman Studies* 48:1/2 (1958) 40–46.

"Progetti: IV Centenario della basilica cattedrale tuscolana", Scuola SCIC Rocca di Papa Istituto Suore di Carità Immacolata Concezione di Ivrea, accessed 20 August 2019, http://www.scuola-scic-roccadipapa.com/index.php?option=com_content&view=article& id=4&catid=18&Itemid=138.

Rice D.G. – Stambaugh J., *Sources for the Study of Greek Religion, Corrected Edition* (Atlanta: 2009) 158–162.

Rowland I.D., "Due 'traduzioni' rinascimentali dell'*Historia Porsennae*", in Prete S. (ed.), *Protrepticon: Studi in memoria di Giovannangiola Secchi Tarugi* (Milan: 1989) 125–133.

Rowland I.D., "L'*Historia Porsennae* e la conoscenza degli Etruschi nel Rinascimento", *Studi Umanistici Piceni/Res Publica Litterarum* 9 (1989) 185–193.

Rowland I.D., "Il mito di Porsenna: leggenda e realtà", in Rotondi Secchi Tarugi L. (ed.), *Il Mito nel Rinascimento* (Milan: 1993) 391–407.

Rowland I.D., "Pio II, l'urbanistica e gli esordi dell'etruscologia: osservazioni intorno ai manoscritti delle *Gesta Porsemnae Regis*", in Nevola F. (ed.), *Pio II Piccolomini. Il papa del Rinascimento a Siena, Atti del covegno internazionale (Siena, 5–7 maggio 2005)* (Colle Val d'Elsa: 2009) 167–178.

Rowland I., *The Scarith of Scornello: A Tale of Renaissance Forgery* (Chicago: 2004).

Rowland I.D., "Annius of Viterbo (1432/7–1502) and the Beginnings of Urban History", in *Acta ad archaeologiam et artiam historiam pertinentia* (Theme Number: "From Site to Sight: The Transformation of Place in Art and Literature") 26 (N.S. 12) (2013) 13–30.

Rowland I.D., "Annius of Viterbo and the Beginning of Etruscan Studies", in Bell S. and Carpino A. (eds.), *A Companion to the Etruscans* (Chichester, West Sussex: 2016) 433–445.

Rowland I.D., "The Atlantic Visions of Giorgio Grognet de Vassé (1774–1862)", in Cochran Anderson J. – Dow D.N. (eds.), *Visualizing the Past in Italian Renaissance Art: Studies in Honor of Brian A. Curran*, Brill's Studies on Art, Art History, and Intellectual History (Leiden: 2021) 81–108.

Said I., "Giuseppe Cannolo: Il-ġenju eċċentriku traduttur u l-interpretu tal-iskjavi", *L'Aċċent, Maltese Language Magazine* 13 (2015) 40–44.

Schiavone M.J., "Grognet de Vassé, Giorgio", in *Dictionary of Maltese Biographies, Vol. 2, G–Z*, (Pietà: 2009) 989–990.

Solaini E., "Il falso 'Estratto del Camerotto di Volterra'", *Rassegna Volterrana* 1:1 (January 1924) 17–19.

Stephens W.E., *Giants in Those Days: Folklore, Ancient History and Nationalism* (Lincoln NE: 1989).

Toschi P., *L'antico teatro religioso italiano* (Matera: 1966).

Trump D.H., *Malta: Prehistory and Temples* (Santa Venera: 2002).

Walsh R., "Master of the Sacred Palace", in *Catholic Encyclopedia*, 10 (New York: 1913): https://en.wikisource.org/wiki/Catholic_Encyclopedia_(1913)/Master_of_the_Sacred_Palace.

Zarri G., "Dallo scisma all'apogeo della Chiesa; i Domenicani tra I secoli XV e XVII", in Festa G. – Rainini M. (eds.), *L'Ordine dei Predicatori, I Domenicani: storia, figure e istituzioni (1216–2016)* (Bari – Rome: 2016) 30–57.

CHAPTER 10

Sailing and Sinking on the Sea of Forgery: The Tradition of Fake Sagas in Seventeenth- and Eighteenth-Century Sweden and Denmark

Philip Lavender

Ships and sea journeys appear not infrequently in both forgeries and the lengthier performances which forgeries find themselves embedded in. Helen Hughes' contribution to this volume shows how in the late eighteenth century forgers were deported from the British Isles on ships and even continued plying their trade, producing new forgeries while on the high seas. Patricia Pires Boulhosa's contribution too shows how certain Icelanders may have invented an agreement concerning the sending of six ships (presumably loaded with goods) to Iceland annually, in order then to complain that the provision had not been met and affirm on those grounds that the Icelanders could continue to trade freely with merchants of any nation. Sailing and sea travel involve distances and transnational movements which, particularly in the Early Modern period, could readily serve as justifications for forgers. When forgery in the antiquarian mode is under consideration, the sudden appearance of documents from the distant past can be explained if they have been squirrelled away in an archive on some distant shore in the interim. Likewise the hazards of sea travel can explain the loss of an original document, when merely a recent copy (much easier to produce) survives.[1] In this chapter I thus look at the ways in which seafaring and forgery interact in the context of (pseudo-)Icelandic sagas and their rediscovery in the seventeenth and eighteenth centuries.

The Icelandic sagas – to provide some background – is the designation given to prose narratives which flourished in medieval Iceland. The earliest were written down in the twelfth century, though they may have circulated in somewhat similar oral forms prior to that time. Iceland had submitted to missionary efforts in the year 1000, so the sagas are the product of a Christian society, but many of them hark back to the pre-Christian period, in particular the settlement period of Iceland (870–930) and beyond to the legendary

1 See also Ingrid Rowland's contribution in this volume in which we learn of a manuscript of Eumalos of Cyrene, contributing to the identification of Malta as Atlantis, which Fortia d'Urban claimed to have been lost at sea.

or 'pre-historical' period and events that took place in mainland Scandinavia during that time. Other sagas have little to do with anything historical or even pseudo-historical, 'saga' being the term applied to any reasonably lengthy prose narrative. They are anonymous and represent a significant body of highly developed vernacular literature which surfaced at a time when other parts of Europe were still producing many texts in Latin. When people talk of sagas, they are often referring to *medieval* prose narratives, but sagas continued to be written and copied in Iceland up to the start of the twentieth century. In fact, the seventeenth century saw something of a renaissance in saga-copying as antiquarian scholars in Denmark and Sweden realised that these works contained a wealth of material about the early history of Scandinavia which could be used for political propagandistic purposes.[2] Stretching the limits of interpretation allowed for nationalistic aims to be met by these texts, but where this was not enough, scholars were not necessarily averse to forging new sagas to bolster their theories and impartial scribes were not averse to forging sagas which they could sell to antiquarians who would happily pay for texts which supported their convictions. It is to this milieu in late seventeenth- and early eighteenth-century Scandinavia that this chapter looks.

An additional aim of this chapter, beyond considering the maritime vicissitudes undergone by forgeries of this type, is to see how several particular cases of saga forgery can be seen as more than just isolated examples. The few articles which exist on the topic of saga forgery typically focus on one or two examples and treat them as case studies, sometimes considering them in relation to the particular authentic sagas which served as inspiration and source material. To a certain extent this is perfectly reasonable: how can a group of shadowy and presumably unconnected individuals be said to form part of a tradition? But if we have learnt anything from the pioneering work of Anthony Grafton it is that, despite its elusiveness, forgery is perfectly capable of responding to previous scholarship, among which we may also include preexisting forgeries.[3] This responsiveness can surely be considered part of the essence of a tradition. Since forgeries imitating and thus inspired by Old Norse-Icelandic sagas have never been studied as a tradition in their own right I attempt to do so here

---

2 See Springborg P., "Antiqvæ Historiæ Lepores – om renæssancen i den islandske håndskriftsproduktion i 1600-tallet", *Gardar: Årsbok för Samfundet Sverige-Island i Lund-Malmö* 8 (1977) 53–89. Also Skovgaard-Petersen K., "The Literary Feud between Denmark and Sweden in the Sixteenth and Seventeenth Centuries and the Development of Danish Historical Scholarship", in Brink J.R. – Gentrup W.F. (eds.), *Renaissance Culture in Context: Theory and Practice* (Aldershot: 1993) 114–120.

3 Grafton A., *Forgers and Critics, New Edition: Creativity and Duplicity in Western Scholarship* (Princeton – Oxford: 2019).

by looking at four main examples: *Hjalmars och Hramers saga, Krembres saga Gautakonungs och Augis Konungs i Uppsala, Hafgeirs saga Flateyings* and its companion piece *Þjóstólfs saga hamramma*. The discussion takes us from the 1690s all the way up to the 1990s (with some tangents into the distant past), revealing along the way the long lives of such works. This longue durée confounds any simplistic notion of exposure followed by oblivion and thus taps into the more variegated performance which is forgery.

1 Crossing the Sea to Wendland: *Hjalmars och Hramers saga*

Fragmentum Mscr Runici [...], i.e. 'Fragment of a runic manuscript', is an abbreviated form of the title given on the first page of a dissertation submitted by one Lucas Halpap to the University of Uppsala in 1690. On the second page a more user-friendly title, *Hialmars och Ramers Saga* (hereafter *Hjalmars saga*), was provided. In a note to the reader preceding the text Halpap explains: 'I procured this same manuscript for myself some months ago at a price worthy of contempt from a certain farmer, who admitted that he had previously had many more leaves of the same work, but these he had put to other uses, and he had deprived this extremely fine creation of its greater and better part'.[4] Following this introduction the remaining text appears in both original form and facing-page Swedish translation, and it immediately becomes clear why the fragment caused such a stir, living up to the promise of its title. This is because it is not written in the Roman alphabet but rather in runes. The runic alphabet or futhark was used for inscriptions, principally surviving in stone, wood or metal, across a large swath of Northern Europe, first appearing in the second century AD and continuing through the Viking Age into the medieval period. While they are not uncommon as marginalia in manuscripts, nor as standalone elements embedded in text written in the Roman alphabet or as ciphers, there are very few coherent texts of any significant length which are written in runes. The only one known at the time was the so-called 'Codex Runicus', but even this was not ancient, principally containing medieval law-codes and believed to have been written in Southern Sweden (Denmark at the time) around 1300–1350.

4 The quote appears on an unnumbered page, under the heading 'Benevolo Lectori S', and starts with the words 'Nam hoc ipsum ...' (translation my own). Transcriptions and translations of the introductory material, along with a transcription of the text and an English translation, can be viewed in a recent digital edition: Lavender P., *Hjalmars & Hramers saga: A Digital Edition & Translation* at https://hjalmars-saga.dh.gu.se/index.html.

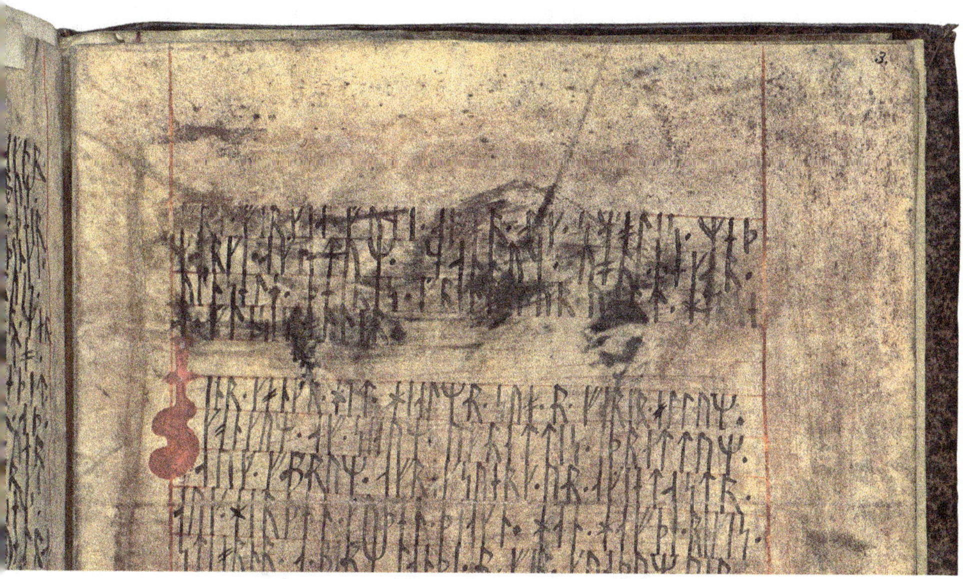

FIGURE 10.1 Detail of first full page from MS V. r. 1 a, Royal Library (Kungliga Biblioteket), Stockholm, containing the start of *Hjalmars saga och Hramers*. On the top line, from the middle to the penultimate word, the runes spell out 'abor auk samolis' (Abor and Zamolxis)

The date of the events described in the saga itself was a point of discussion, but a sense of the great age was given by the first few fragmentary lines which told of how 'from Greece Abor and Samolis came with many excellent men' [Fig. 10.1].[5] Contemporary learned readers would have recognised these names as slight modifications of the Abaris and Salmoxis mentioned in Book IV of Herodotus' *Histories*, the former a Hyperborean and the latter a Scythian deity (or alternately escaped Pythagorean slave).[6] Herodotus had been rediscovered and experienced an upsurge of interest during the Renaissance, with 44 editions appearing between the 1502 *editio princeps* and 1700.[7] When not branded the 'father of lies', he was generally known as the 'father of history', so any story including characters mentioned by him must of necessity be of extreme antiquity. In Sweden many classical sources had also recently been used by Olof Rudbeck to back up his theories that Sweden was Plato's Atlantis and the ancient Swedes were identical with the Hyperboreans (or 'Yfwerborne', i.e. 'High-Born', as he interpreted the word). Against this background, three years

5 See pp. 4–5 in Halpap's dissertation. All translations are my own.

6 See Herodotus, *Histories*, 4 vols., ed. A.D. Godley (London – New York – Cambridge MA: 1924–1950) II 235, 295 (IV:36, IV:94–96). Note that Olof Rudbeck had argued that Hyperborean was the designation which the ancient Greeks used to refer to the ancient Swedes.

7 See Habaj M., "Herodotus' Renaissance Return to Western-European Culture", *Studia Antiqua et Archaeologica* 22:1 (2016) 83–94.

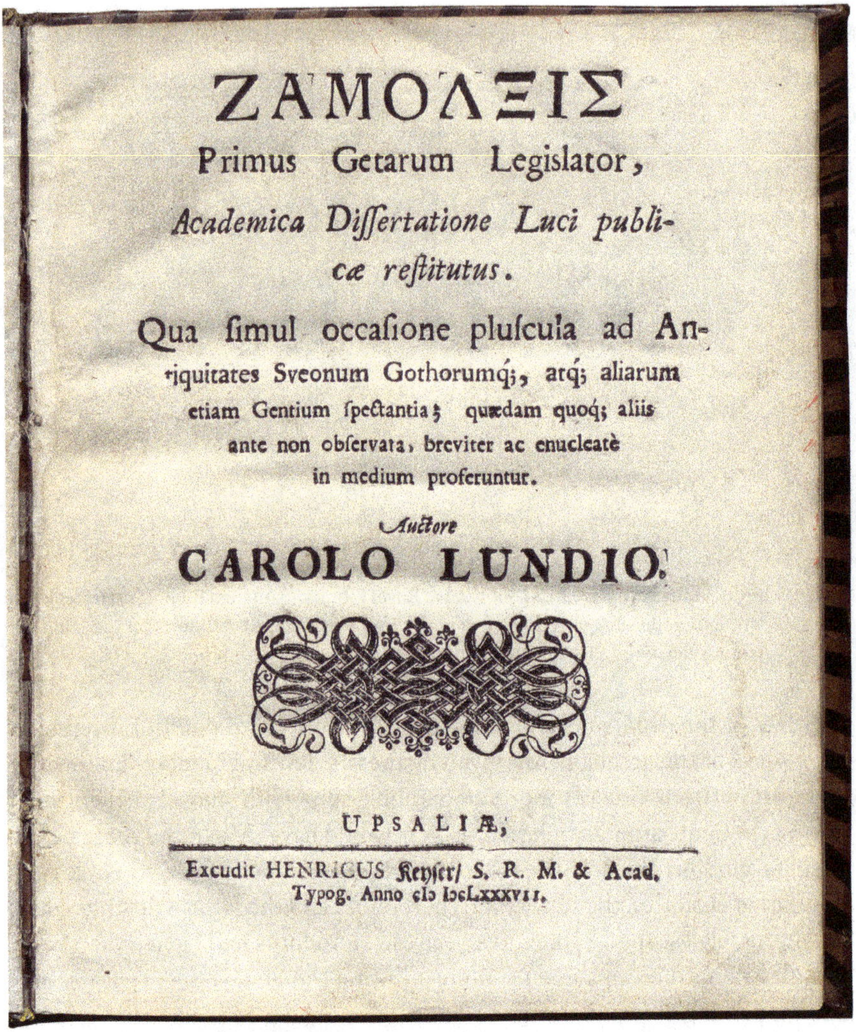
ΖΑΜΟΛΞΙΣ

Primus Getarum Legislator,

Academica Diſſertatione Luci publi-
cæ reſtitutus.

Qua ſimul occaſione pluſcula ad An-
tiquitates Sveonum Gothorumq́;, atq́; aliarum
etiam Gentium ſpectantia; quædam quoq́; aliis
ante non obſervata, breviter ac enucleatè
in medium proferuntur.

Auctore

CAROLO LUNDIO.

UPSALIÆ,

Excudit HENRICUS Keyſer/ S. R. M. & Acad.
Typog. Anno cIↄ IↄcLXXXVII.

FIGURE 10.2 Title page from Carl Lundius, *Zamolxis primus Getarum legislator* (Uppsala, Henricus Keyser: 1687)
IMAGE PROVIDED BY UPPSALA UNIVERSITY LIBRARY AND BASED ON THEIR EXEMPLAR

prior to 1690, a Rudbeckian dissertation had appeared at Uppsala, precisely on the subject of Salmoxis and his having been involved in the earliest laws of the ancient Swedes, at that time considered to be the Goths. The thesis was written by Carl Lundius (1638–1715) and entitled 'Zamolxis primus Getarum legislator' ('Zamolxis, first lawmaker of the Goths') [Fig. 10.2]. This meant that the ancient Hyperborean was very fresh in the minds of the academic elite of Sweden at the time.

As mentioned, the text which Halpap presented is fragmentary, so one is led to believe that part of the narrative – that explaining what led up to Abor and Samolis coming from Greece – is missing at the start. Nevertheless, the plot of the surviving (and legible) section of the saga has little to do with Herodotean characters and is as follows. A king named Hjalmar is introduced along with his sworn brother, Hramer. They set out on an expedition to Bjarmaland, where Hjalmar becomes king and marries the daughter of the vanquished ruler. The couple have two children, one a daughter named Heidil. Heidil grows up and attracts various suitors, but is ultimately married to Hramer. Another suitor, Ulfr, is unhappy about this, but regardless Hramer and Heidil leave to establish themselves on an island. At this point the reader is made aware that there is yet more damage to the source manuscript, but when the narrative is taken up once more, Ulfr has attacked Hramer and Heidil's home. Hramer manages to escape and returns to Hjalmar. The sworn brothers thus make preparations and end up meeting Ulfr in a sea-battle, during which Hjalmar is killed and Hramer is captured. The story ends with Ulfr, at this late point in the tale, revealed as being hostile to the local religion, putting the pagan priests to flight. In the final lines we are told that the fleeing priests eventually sought out the home of a man named Hröðr in 'Vin(d)land', and the narrator informs us that Hröðr was his father.

The story of what happened after the publication of the thesis involves almost as many twists and turns as the narrative itself and is helpfully summarised by Vilhelm Gödel in an article published in 1896.[8] In brief, Johan Hadorph (1630–1693), who was the National Antiquarian at the time, made contact with Halpap in order to get hold of the sensational manuscript for the College of Antiquities. The manuscript was not, however, forthcoming, and by 1692 it seems that Halpap had left the country, having relocated to Stade (near Bremen), and, according to his stepfather in Stockholm, had taken the manuscript with him. Hadorph did not give up, however, and eventually it seems that Halpap was prevailed upon to contact his stepfather and ask him to dig up the manuscript (which it now seems was among his books in Stockholm) and hand it over to the Archive of Antiquities.[9] Thus finally, in 1694, the manuscript could be seen by the National Antiquarian, but unfortunately this was no longer Hadorph, who had died in 1693. The new Antiquarian was Johan Peringskiöld (1654–1720) who thus worked on a new edition of the text, which appeared

8 Gödel V., "Hjalmars och Hramers saga: Ett litterärt falsarium från 1690", *Svenska fornminnesförenings tidskrift* 9 (1896) 137–154.

9 The College of Antiquities (Antikvitetskollegiet) became the Archive of Antiquities (Antikvitetsarkivet) in 1692.

in 1701. This edition, with the title 'Historia Hialmari regis Biarmlandiæ atque Thulemarkiæ', presented a facsimile of the runes followed by a transliteration of them and, on a facing page, translations into both Swedish and Latin. Just two years later Peringskiöld's text was republished in England as part of the first volume of George Hicke's monumental *Linguarum veterum septentrionalium thesaurus grammatico-criticus et archæologicus* (1703). Besides the parchment manuscript which had arrived at the Archive of Antiquities, and which today is kept at the Kungliga Bibliotek in Stockholm, at least three other paper manuscripts are found in Swedish collections, but they all seem to be based on either Halpap's or Peringskiöld's editions.[10] This flurry of activity provoked discussion and those who were not predisposed to accept Rudbeck's ideas that the ancient Swedes were Hyperboreans naturally looked on the work with suspicion. Nevertheless, a full scholarly refutation of the work's authenticity did not appear until 1774 when Carl Gustaf Nordin published a dissertation, once again in Uppsala, with the title *Monumenta suiogothica vetustioris aevi falso meritoque suspecta* ('Swedo-Gothic Monuments of the most ancient age and rightly suspected of being fake').[11]

Following Nordin's dissertation, the case on *Hjalmars saga* can in some ways be seen as closed. The Rudbeckian zeitgeist had passed and so the constellation of elements found in the saga was no longer credible historically and thus could only be interpreted as the brainchild of a specific intellectual moment (approximately 1680–1700). Nordin had rejected the saga's authenticity principally on the basis of text-internal clues, among which were the many obvious borrowings from recent editions of sagas. To this Gödel added a critique of the saga's formal and material aspects: the ink seems young, the forger has not bothered to write out a full text under the purposefully besmirched patches and the runes do not match what we know about the development of the script. Gödel's aforementioned article neatly summarises the whole affair, and exonerates both Halpap and the farmer of blame. He believes Halpap was too young and inexperienced to have pulled off the hoax and the real culprit must be Lundius, especially since the fragment seems to provide proof for his dissertation on Salmoxis/Zamolxis. A general desire to produce ancient texts where none existed for the Swedish people and to prove that ancient Swedes

10 Busch K., *Großmachtstatus und Sagainterpretation. Die schwedischen Vorzeitsagaeditionen des 17. und 18. Jahrhunderts* (Ph.D. dissertation, Friedrich-Alexander-Universität Erlangen-Nürnberg: 2002) 217–218.

11 The discussion of *Hjalmars saga* makes up chapter 2 of the dissertation.

had been the inventors of runes would also have contributed, according to Gödel. Apart from Nils Ahnlund's ideas that a rogue named Nils Rabenius might have disguised himself as the farmer in question in order to pass the forged manuscript off to an unsuspecting Halpap, no alternative theories have been presented, and none besides Gödel's Lundius-theory has gained any traction.[12]

In the present chapter I want to take up a slightly different question concerning the saga, namely how were the readers and audience who were presented with the saga in 1690 expected to understand the history behind this marvellous runic manuscript? As already mentioned, the author states in the final lines that he is the son of the man (Hröðr) who took in the exiled pagan priests once they had arrived in 'Vin(d)land'. Thus presumably this runic manuscript, or its antigraph (perhaps with several intermediates), had been written in 'Vin(d)land' and at some point made the return journey across the sea to Sweden in order to end up in the farm where Halpap supposedly found it. We can take this in two stages, first by considering the 'Vin(d)land' origin and then by looking at the rustic discovery of manuscript fragments.

In Halpap's text the destination of the exiled pagan priests is given in runes (ᚢᛁᚿᛚᛆᚿᚦ) and presented in the Swedish translation as 'Vindland'. The manuscript which later turned up, as well as Peringskiöld's facsimile, also present the runes as in Halpap's text, but in Peringskiöld's transliteration we read 'Vinland', with 'Vinland' in the Swedish translation and 'Vinlandiam' (acc.) in the Latin. This region is not mentioned previously in the saga, so no clues as to its location can be gleaned through comparison, and the variation between 'Vindland' and 'Vinland' (the latter the more literal transliteration of the runes) leads to some ambiguity. 'Vínland' ('Wine-land') in the Old Norse sagas is well known as being the term used to refer to the parts of the North-American continent to which Icelandic and Greenlandic seafarers sailed around the year 1000. It seems unlikely, however, that any reference is intended here to transatlantic voyages. Rather, if we look at Olof Verelius' edition of *Hervarar saga*, which had been published in 1672 and which was essential reading for all Rudbeckians and Gothicists, we can see the most likely reference. There we read of how the King of Garðaríki (approx. Russia) married his daughter, Sifka, to King Heiðrekr, and as part of the dowry the latter received 'Vindland'.[13] The Swedish translation presents this as 'Wenden' and an explanatory note at the end of the chapter explains that 'Vindlandia or Venden is used here for the kingdom

12 See Ahnlund N., *Nils Rabenius (1648–1717)* (Stockholm: 1927) 150–151. Busch, *Großmachtstatus und Sagainterpretation*, subscribes to the Lundius theory (215).

13 Verelius Olof (ed.), *Hervarar saga på gammal götska* (Uppsala, Henricus Curio: 1672) 137.

which belonged to Russia' (my translation). The reference is clearly to the land inhabited by the Wends (also approximately equivalent to Pomerania), a Slavic people who lived in the north of modern-day Germany and Poland along the coast of the Baltic Sea.[14] The reference in *Hjalmars saga* should also be understood in this sense.

But what does Vindland/Wendland have to do with ancient Swedish antiquities? The southern coast of the Baltic Sea had long been an area of Nordic expansion. Ancient Sweden, for example, was seen as having at regular intervals spewed out migrations of people into the adjoining southern territories. Some may have occurred and others were more fanciful and lacked proof, but it was the early modern Swedish imagination of such connections which is most likely to have influenced *Hjalmars saga*. The turning point in this regard is Gustav Vasa's decision to declare himself, in addition to King of the Swedes and Goths, King of the Wends (or 'Rex Vandalorum' in Latin) from around 1540 onwards. This was apparently a tit-for-tat move inspired by the Danish king's self-promotion as King of the Goths (since he owned Gotland), but it remained part of the official Swedish royal title until 1973. As Sweden moved into its 'Stormaktstiden' ('The Era of Great Power', 1611–1721) expansion into the areas south of the Baltic Sea could be supported by the idea that there was some natural historical claim to overlordship of those regions since time immemorial.

Thus during the seventeenth century there was a great deal of back and forth across the Baltic Sea, much of it concerned with military campaigns during the Thirty Years War (1618–1648) and the Second Northern War (1655–1660). As Swedish troops marauded around Vindland/Pomerania ideas of ancestral entitlement to the region circulated at the same time as the then-accepted practice of the gathering of war loot was carried out. In his monograph on the subject ('Literary War Loot from the Era of Great Power') Otto Walde describes in detail how Sweden's inferior libraries came to be stocked during the seventeenth century thanks to a certified effort to procure book collections and archives in the wake of conflicts such as the Battle of Prague (1648) and the occupation of Warsaw (1655). Large numbers of books and manuscripts, in particular from Poland, made their way into Swedish collections, often 'strongly motivated by the intimate connection between both lands' history'.[15] One outstanding example is the Codex Argenteus, a sixth-century manuscript containing a Gothic-language Bible translation. This treasure arrived in Uppsala University

14 Later Eric Julius Biörner is of a similar opinion. See Biörner Eric Julius, *Inledning til de yfwerborne Göters gamla Häfder* (Stockholm, J.L. Horn: 1738) 48.

15 Walde O., *Storhetstidens litterära krigsbyten: En kulturhistorisk-bibliografisk studie* (Uppsala – Stockholm: 1916–1918) I:23 (my translation).

Library in 1669 after various wanderings following on from its removal from the imperial library in Prague in 1648. An edition was published in Stockholm in 1671 and it inspired both scholars and forgers.[16] Since the Gothic language was imagined as that spoken by the ancient ancestors of the Swedes, the return of such an ancient text in a strange alphabet (the Gothic alphabet) from south of the Baltic Sea could have surely set inquisitive minds to thinking. If ancient works of the Goths could return, why not ancient works from other groups of emigrants, such as the Wends/Vandals?

While the vast majority of the books plundered during military encounters ended up in institutional libraries or the private collections of aristocrats, the final destinations of many remain unknown. It is unlikely that they would have ended up in humble farmhouses in Sweden, but not impossible that unassuming fragments could have gone astray in the tumult of war. The point being made, however, is merely that the concept of manuscripts from Wendland being present in Sweden would have been extremely familiar with learned people in the seventeenth century, enough so that this vector of transmission could have been a credible one to hint at in a forged text.

Moving on to the finding of fragments of manuscript in a farm, the most obvious point of reference in the northern world is Árni Magnússon (1663–1730), an avid manuscript collector who after studying at Copenhagen University was made Secretary of the Danish Royal Archives in 1697 and Professor at the university in 1701. Árni's manuscript collection still exists today, partly in Copenhagen and partly in Reykjavik, and, as the foremost of its kind, it stands as a testament to his tenacity. He acquired many works through his network of Icelandic connections and during his travels around the country as part of a royal commission sent by the Danish king in the years 1702–1712. A look at his correspondence reveals his dedication, as in the following passage:

> I am enquiring as far and wide as possible about such old documents, as well as single leaves from old Icelandic vellum books; should you have or be able to procure in your neighbourhood more of the like, I ask you not to begrudge me their loan, at the very least, if they cannot otherwise be parted with.[17]

---

16 See Johansson J.V., "De Rudbeckianska förfalskningar i Codex Argenteus", *Nordisk tidskrift för bok- och biblioteksväsen* 42 (1955) 12–27. Johansson see modifications made to Codex Argenteus as stemming from Carl Lundius, whom he also believes was responsible for *Hjalmars saga*.

17 This translation is taken from Svanhildur Óskarsdóttir, "Manuscripts on the Brain: Árni Magnússon, Collector", in Driscoll M.J. – Svanhildur Óskarsdóttir (eds.), *66 Manuscripts from the Arnamagnæan Collection* (Copenhagen: 2015) 9–37: 9. The original can be found

It should be noted that 'neighbourhood' here does not refer to part of a town – there were no towns in Iceland until much later – but rather to a rural district of scattered farms. Árni's letter is from 1704, but Halpap's introduction reveals that 15 years earlier the dream of finding textual antiquities in unsuspecting rustic locales already existed. I have quoted above the vague reference to 'a certain farmer' which Halpap gave in his introductory address to the reader. Halpap is not more explicit in his published dissertation, but Gödel provides more information on this shadowy individual when he quotes a letter, undersigned by Hadorph, from Antikvitetskollegiet and written either late 1691 or early 1692. In said letter, Halpap's discovery is referred to as having been 'found two years ago in Rasbo parish in a farmer's house'.[18] Rasbo lies just a few kilometres north-east of Uppsala and thus close to what many considered to be the heartland of the ancient Swedes.

The search for antiquities in rural Sweden long preceded Árni Magnússon's Icelandic efforts and Halpap's dissertation, however. A pioneer was Johannes Bureus (1568–1652) of whom it has been said that he was 'the first person in Sweden to dedicate himself to tracking down and studying monuments and literary remains from times past'.[19] Bureus is most known for his work with runes, and as Matthew Norris has pointed out, during his travels around the Swedish countryside 'old books existed in rumour more often than in reality'.[20] Nevertheless, when Bureus was made National Antiquarian (predecessor to Hadorph and Peringskiöld) in 1630, one of the mandates which was drawn up, and passed on to his assistants Axehielm and Aschaneus, was to 'seek out and collect [...] old runic writings, whether in books or on stones, both fragmentary as well as whole'.[21] Manuscripts came to light, for example that of the medieval *Konunga- och höfdinga styrelse*, which Bureus published in 1634, albeit in this case the most likely place of origin was Vadstena Abbey, not a rural farmhouse.[22] Those who followed in Bureus' footsteps also found (or claimed to have found) new fragments, such as that containing *Annotationes ex scriptis Karoli episcopi Arosiensis excerptae* ('Notes copied out of the writings of Karl,

in Árni Magnússon, *Arne Magnussons private brevveksling*, ed. K. Kålund (Copenhagen: 1920) 271–272.

18 Gödel, "Hjalmars och Hramers saga" 140 (my translation).

19 Vennberg E., "Johan Bure", in *Svenskt biografiskt lexikon* (https://sok.riksarkivet.se/sbl/artikel/17156) (my translation).

20 Norris M., *A Pilgrimage to the Past: Johannes Bureus and the Rise of Swedish Antiquarian Scholarship, 1600–1650* (Lund: 2016) 330.

21 Norris, *A Pilgrimage to the Past* 364. The original Swedish text is reproduced in Schück H., *Kgl. vitterhets historie och antikvitets akademien, dess förhistoria och historia I* (Stockholm: 1932) 140.

22 Schück, *Kgl. vitterhets historie* [...] *I* 86.

Bishop of Västerås'). This parchment leaf was apparently found by Olof Verelius slotted into a manuscript belonging to Olof Rudbeck and subsequently published in 1678, but Henrik Janson has convincingly argued that the leaf is a forgery and its supposed discovery an invention.[23] It seems that while significant finds in surprisingly humble settings might not have been particularly common, the dream of encountering a fragment or a manuscript containing long-lost information was very present in the minds of Swedish antiquarians in the seventeenth century.

Thus as a background to the sparse information which Halpap's text and account of its discovery provides, we can draw on these two major concepts of how ancient writings might make themselves available to hungry Swedish antiquarians. For the most part these concepts should be seen as discrete – manuscripts and fragments would either be war booty (ending up in institutional or aristocratic libraries) or surface unexpectedly in a rustic farmhouse. But by eliciting both of them Halpap – and presumably those who supported him – provides a surplus of potential avenues of transmission. Thus we can trace an ephemeral, if somewhat artificial, itinerary which goes as follows. Ancient pagan priests sailing south across the Baltic Sea to Vindland, a manuscript brought back again, perhaps as war-plunder, ending up in the hands of a rank-and-file soldier, only to be stashed away in a humble farmhouse. As unlikely as this story is – and it is improbable that Halpap and his colleagues intended a coherent trajectory to be drawn up out of the barest of hints – these movements not only present a conception of Swedish history, both ancient and more recent, involving expansion and domination, but also provide a neat rationale for why such a fabulous object had remained out of sight for centuries only to suddenly appear again at the end of the seventeenth century. The ensuing celebrity surrounding the case of this runic manuscript has ensured that *Hjalmars saga* has received more attention than any other forged saga.[24] But in the next two sections we cast our gaze upon later saga forgeries which are much less well known.

---

23 Janson H., "Äkta förfalskning åter bevismaterial: Annotationes ex scriptis Karoli", *Scandia: Tidskrift för historisk forskning* 67 (2001) 41–60. See also Sävborg D., "Några anmärkningar om *Annotationes ex scriptis Karoli* och dess källor", *Historisk tidskrift* 137 (2017) 64–79.

24 See, for example, Havens E.A., "Babelic Confusion: Literary Forgery and the Bibliotheca Fictiva", in Stephens W. – Havens E.A. (eds.), *Literary Forgery in Early Modern Europe, 1450–1800* (Baltimore: 2018) 33–73. Havens says 'this vogue [for spectacular ancient discoveries] also extended to the manuscript tradition, perhaps nowhere more imaginatively than in the late-seventeenth-century invention of the ancient Icelandic Hjálmar saga' (53).

2 The Practicality of Sinking in the Baltic Sea: *Krembres saga*

Peter Erasmus Müller (1776–1834), a Danish scholar who was Bishop of Zealand in the last few years of his life, published between 1817 and 1820 a three-volume work entitled *Sagabibliothek*. This eminently usable work included plot summaries of a large number of Old Norse-Icelandic sagas accompanied by additional details and observations. While the first volume focused on sagas set in Iceland, the second looked back to legendary Scandinavian history prior to the settlement of Iceland around AD 870 and covered the genre commonly known as *fornaldarsögur* ('sagas of ancient times'). While the works which represent the generic core are discussed early on, towards the end of the volume a number of minor, dubious or peripheral examples are briefly discussed. *Hjalmars saga* is one of these, 'whose language displays such clear evidence of forgery'.[25] A work named 'Krembre saga' is presented immediately after, its entry beginning with the words 'This made-up saga …'.[26] This section focusses on this lesser-known sibling of and successor to *Hjalmars saga*, in which we see awareness of *Hjalmar saga*'s appearance and subsequent reception, albeit seemingly put to the use of mocking Rudbeckian apologists rather than bolstering them.

The mysterious *Konungs Krembres i Giötaland och Konungs Augis i Upsala saga* ('The Saga of King Krembre in Götaland and King Augis in Uppsala'), to use its full name, tells of events (of dubious historicity) in ancient Scandinavia and continental Europe and has been roundly branded a forgery (or something of the kind). It exists in six manuscripts dating from the eighteenth century, two of which contain a Swedish-language text which claims, in a brief introduction, to be a translation from the original Old Norse [Fig. 10.3].[27] A third manuscript, kept at the Royal Library in Stockholm, includes the text in both Swedish and Icelandic (Old Norse), while the three remaining manuscripts are of a slightly later date and are found in the collections of the Royal Library in Copenhagen.[28] They contain both the Icelandic text and Danish translations of the saga. The introductory notes accompanying the saga in two of the Swedish manuscripts are signed by Nils Hufwedsson Dal (1690–1740), a scholar associated with the Swedish Archive of Antiquities between 1717 and 1729. His proximity, as the only named individual to appear in close connection with the

25 Müller P.E., *Sagabibliothek*, 3 vols. (Copenhagen: 1817–1820) II 667 (my translation).

26 Ibidem, II 667 (my translation).

27 These are Säfstaholmssamlingen I Papp 3 (National Archive in Stockholm) and V 138 b (Uppsala University Library).

28 These are, respectively, Papp. fol. nr 98, NKS 1211 fol., NKS 1212 fol. and Thott 1776 4to.

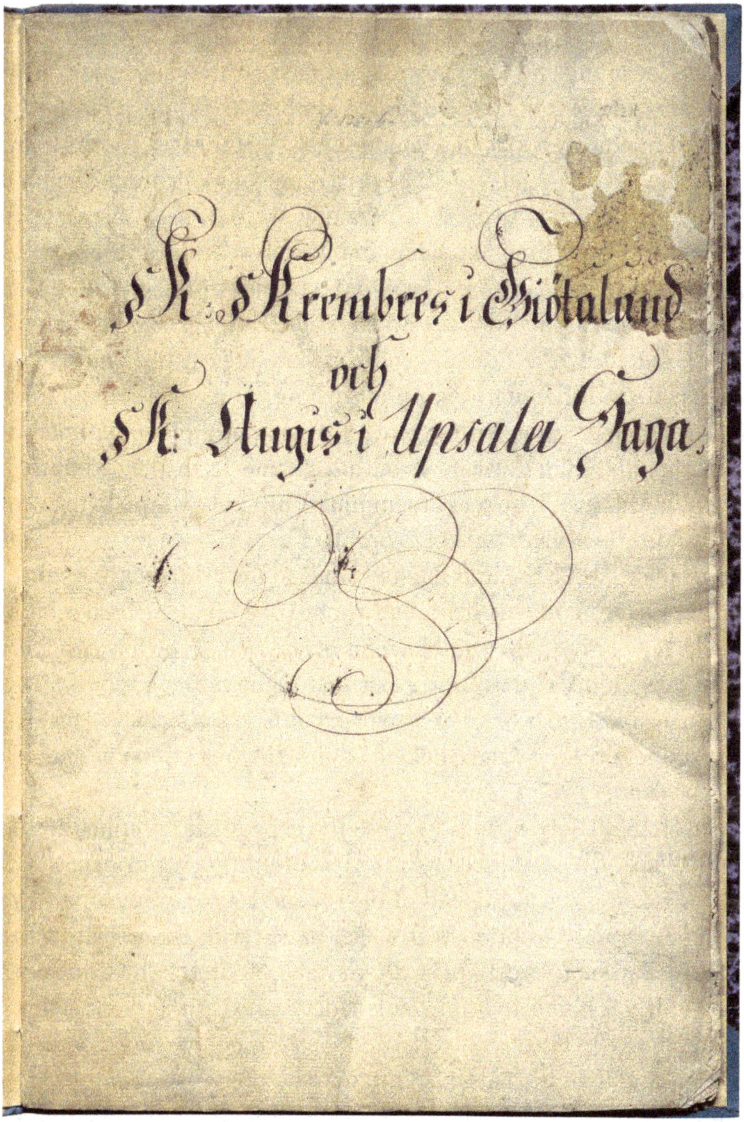

FIGURE 10.3 Title page, showing the start of *Krembres saga*, from MS V 138 b, Uppsala University Library (early eighteenth century). The introduction concerning the origins of the 'translation' begins on the following leaf.
IMAGE PROVIDED BY UPPSALA UNIVERSITY LIBRARY

saga, has led to his falling under suspicion of being its author, and I will provide further evidence in favour of this interpretation here.

The Swedish, Icelandic and Danish texts of the saga show no major divergences when presenting the story of King Krembre. Thus the plot can be divided into two main parts, followed and brought together by a shorter third and final act. The first part tells of the aging King Krembre from Småland (southern Sweden). He wants to die in a blaze of glory, thus he gathers a huge army, launches his ships from Simrishamn and travels south over the sea and through Europe, finally crossing the Alps. On the far side of the mountains he comes, inevitably, into conflict with the Romans and, although successful until that point, is defeated by the Roman generals, Mari and Kattil). The second part of the saga tells of King Augis in Uppsala, whose people will suffer a great famine. His desperate solution is to execute a portion of the population, but when a woman named Hilder Þisa hears of this, she mocks the king's strategy. When he learns of this insult, he seeks to humiliate her, but ends up being won over by her wisdom. She solves the king's problem by advising him to send off some of his people to settle the uninhabited lands to the north, and he subsequently marries this woman who has greatly impressed him. The final section of the saga tells how Fridulf, the son of Krembre and one of the few survivors of the Roman expedition, comes to Uppsala and requests the hand of Signy, daughter of Augis and Hilder Þisa. He is refused at first, but achieves his aim after fighting a duel on King Augis' behalf against the objectionable berserk Östein Hjässaklyfware ('Skull-Cleaver').

This 'saga' is immediately curious because the expedition described in the first part bears a strong resemblance to historical events known from classical sources to have taken place at the end of the second century BC, namely the Cimbrian migration and Cimbrian War which ended with the defeat of the Cimbrians at the Battle of Vercellae (northern Italy) in 101 BC. The Cimbrians seem to have left their homeland in what is today Danish Jutland and, after a lengthy decade-long trip through Central and Western Europe, been defeated by Gaius Marius and Quintus Lutatius Catulus, who thus correspond to Mari and Kattil from the saga. While Old Norse sagas do exist which recount battles and events from the classical world – for example, *Trojumanna saga* ('The Saga of the Trojans') and *Rómverja saga* ('The Saga of the Romans') – they tend to be based on continental and classical texts which circulated widely in medieval Europe.[29] No comparable source existed with regard to the Cimbrian migrations. Information on these mass movements of people was briefly touched

29 The two named sagas are based primarily on Dares Phrygius' *De Excidio Troiae* and a mixture of Sallust's *Bellum Iugurthinum* and *Coniuratio Catiliniae* along with Lucan's

upon in a number of classical sources, the earliest being Posidonius of Rhodes' writings (non-extant, but used by Strabo in his *Geography*), while Marius' life and battles are told in Sallust's *Bellum Jugurthinum* and Plutarch's *Parallel Lives*.[30] Yet none of these gave an extensive and coherent account of the migration from the Cimbrian perspective, as is found in *Krembres saga*.

In fact, such accounts were only composed in the Early Modern period when German and Danish historians invented historical traditions as part of the nation-building one-upmanship which was becoming popular at the time. Johannes Aventinus (1477–1534) was one such writer, who explained that the Cimbrians were Germans and gave a lengthy account of their war with the Romans in his *Bayrische Chronik* (written in the 1520s and 1530s, first published in 1554). In Denmark, Cimbrian heritage was asserted as a refutation to Johannes Magnus' pro-Swedish assertion in *Historia de omnibus Gothorum Sveorumque regibus* (1554) that Denmark was basically a penal colony for exiles from the Gothic realm.[31] Erasmus Lætus (1526–1582) explained in his *Res Danicae* (1574) that the Cimbrians and Danes had merged at some point in the past and had gone on their migration due to Gothic aggression. Niels Pedersen (d. 1579) in *Cimbrorum et Gothorum origines, migrationes, bella, atqve coloniæ* (first published 1695) [Fig. 10.4] simply saw the Cimbrians as the ancient ancestors of the Danes, and Carl Christoffer Lyschander (1558–1623/4) in *Synopsis historiarum danicarum* (1622), drawing on Pedersen's work,[32] traced their ancestry through the Cimbrians back to Adam. Both Pedersen and Lyschander made the Goths offshoots of the Cimbrians and described fake sources to back up their claims. The ball was now back in the Swedes' court and the appearance of a counter-refutation, such as *Krembres saga*, would have been welcomed by certain Swedish scholars.

Research on *Krembres saga* has been limited, in part because it never successfully captivated scholars in the way that *Hjalmars saga* did. While the latter had been edited twice and appeared in print editions three times within fifteen years after its appearance in 1690 (the 'original' manuscript, as we have

---

Pharsalia, respectively. See Jensen J.-L. (ed.), *Trojumanna saga: The Dares Phrygius Version* (Copenhagen: 1981); Þorbjörg Helgadóttir (ed.), *Rómverja saga* (Reykjavik: 2010).

30 On the classical literary accounts of the Cimbrian migration see Demougeot E., "L'invasion des Cimbres-Teutons-Ambrons et les Romains", *Latomus* 37 (1978) 910–938. The section of Livy's *History of Rome* which covered the period of the Cimbrian Wars is no longer extant.

31 The early modern development of a Danish-Cimbrian historiography has been studied by Skovgaard-Petersen K., "Peace-Loving Yet Powerful – Depictions of the Cimbrians in Early Modern Danish Historiography" (forthcoming). I draw on her work in this paragraph.

32 Though Pedersen's work was unpublished at this time, it circulated and was available in manuscript form.

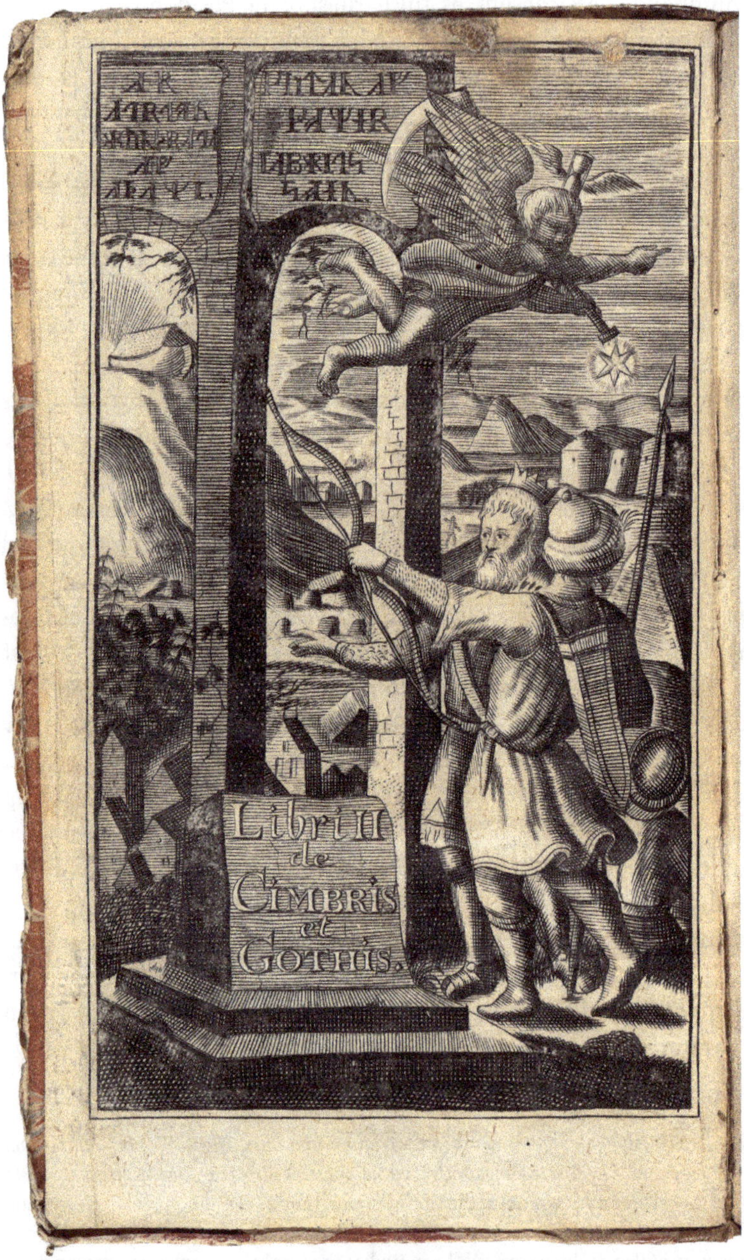

FIGURE 10.4 Frontispiece from Niels Pedersen, *Cimbrorum et Gothorum origines, migrationes, bella, atqve coloniæ, libris duobus* (Leipzig, Johann Melchior Liebe: 1695)

IMAGE PROVIDED BY LUND UNIVERSITY LIBRARY

seen, only surfacing after the first edition), *Krembres saga* existed exclusively in manuscript form for close to two centuries, with a more widely accessible print edition only appearing in 1902. The failure (if we see it as such) to make it into print is surely connected to the lack of success in convincing its readers of its authenticity, these doubts being as old as the saga itself. The closing words of Nils Hufwedsson Dal's introduction, for example, state that he 'leaves it now to the reader's own judgement whether it should be considered authentic or not, given that both the chronology and style in this saga seem to me to be suspicious'.[33] Are these frank and genuine doubts or are we witnessing a double-bluff of kinds, the forger himself inserting comments of this type to deflect accusations of forgery?

Letters exchanged in 1756 between Sven Lagerbring (1707–1787) and Jakob Langebek (1710–1775), important Swedish respectively Danish learned antiquarians, represent some of the earliest evidence of scholarly interaction with *Krembres saga*. Lagerbring had come across the saga in the library of Baron Gustaf Bonde (1682–1764) in Stockholm and wanted to know if his Danish colleague had ever heard of it, particularly since he himself was 'inclined to believe that the whole story has been flung together by Dal'.[34] Langebek's reply gets straight to the point:

> As far as *Krembres saga* is concerned, I cannot deny that I consider it so suspicious both in terms of content and its circumstances that I would immediately declare it a recently-composed fable and a kind of public deception, of which this is not the first example from the hand of certain producers of antiquities.[35]

Lagerbring, already 'inclined' to do so, seems to have gratefully accepted Langebek's conclusion, stating later in his *Swea Rikes Historia* that the theory that the Cimbrian migrations set out from Simrishamn (or Cimbershamn) – a theory which is given literary form in *Krembres saga* – is based on a vague similarity in names and 'seems to have been put forward solely to amuse children and puerile hunters of antiquities'.[36]

---

33 Bygdén L., "Konung Krembres i Giötaland och Konung Augis i Uppsala saga", *Samlaren* 23 (1902) 83–107: 90 (my translation).

34 Lagerbring Sven, *Bref 1746–1787, Sven Lagerbring, Skrifter och brev*, ed. L. Weibull (Lund: 1907) 117 (my translation).

35 Langebek Jakob, *Breve fra Jakob Langebek udgivne af Det Kongelige Danske Selskab for Fædrelandets Historie og Sprog*, ed. H.Fr. Rørdam (Copenhagen: 1895) 237 (my translation).

36 Lagerbring Sven, *Swea Rikes Historia ifrån de äldsta tider til de närwarande: Första Delen som innefattar Rikets öde, ifrån des början til år 1060* (Stockholm, Carl Stolpe: 1769) 570 (my translation).

Slightly earlier Baron Gustaf Bonde, the owner of the manuscript of *Krembres saga* referred to by Lagerbring, also partially reveals in print his stance with regard to the saga. He was responsible for a regnal list inserted (without attribution) as explanatory material at the start of Eric Julius Biörner's *Nordiska kämpa dater* (1737), a pioneering collection of legendary Icelandic sagas in Old Norse with accompanying Latin and Swedish translations. The introduction to the regnal list clearly makes use of information found only in *Krembres saga*, making it the first independent witness to the saga's existence, and thus Bonde must have had a certain amount of faith in the saga's reliability as a historical source. This faith does not appear to have remained fully intact as can be seen in his later notes to the first volume of Olof von Dalin's *Svea Rikes Historia* (1747) – not to be confused with Lagerbring's similarly-named work – which appeared as an appendix to Dalin's posthumously-published *Witterhets-Arbeten* (1767). Bonde refers to *Krembres saga* in relation to the story of Hildur (i.e. Hilder Þisa) and says that wise women were subsequently named after her 'as long as this *Saga of King Kremb*[*r*]*e* is reliable'.[37] If Bonde then believed the saga to be completely reliable, he probably would not have included this comment and phrased it in this way. If even Bonde, who had presumably paid good money for his manuscript, harboured niggling doubts, then it is unsurprising that the wider scholarly community had not received it in a more positive manner.

If the eighteenth-century for the most part looked upon *Krembres saga* with scepticism, nineteenth- and twentieth-century scholars have shared their predecessors' concerns about its authenticity while providing alternative perspectives regarding the intentions of the saga's originator. Peter Erasmus Müller's entry in his *Sagabibliothek* has already been mentioned. Leonard Bygdén, the scholar who published most on *Krembres saga* (including a text), aired the idea that Nils Hufwedsson Dal may be not only its translator but its author although 'at the present time no definitive judgement can be laid down on the matter'.[38] Even if the author cannot be conclusively identified, Bygdén is in no doubt that the work is born of the seventeenth and eighteenth centuries' antiquarian imaginary and it is therein that its interest can be located. But is it a forgery? Bygdén, taking into account more than one work of the type, responds in the negative: 'they can nevertheless not easily be defined as forgeries'.[39] His hesitancy is based in a concept of authorial intention, given that while there may have been a secondary motive to hoodwink, the primary motive was, in his

37 Bonde Gustaf, "Anmärkningar wid första delen af Swea Rikes Historia jämte Påminnelser wid samma anmärkningar", in Olof von Dalin, *Witterhets-Arbeten, i bunden och obunden Skrifart*, vol. 3 (Stockholm, Carl Stolpe: 1767) 459–508: 498 (my translation).

38 Bygdén, "Konung Krembres" 86 (my translation).

39 Ibidem, 87 (my translation).

opinion, to mould national historical material into a saga format. The word that he prefers for such activity is 'mystification'. Gun Nilsson, writing half a century later, feels that Dal is almost certainly the author of the saga and also briefly discusses the motive behind it, saying that 'it is most tempting to believe that it is a stylish attempt at playing with the rudbeckians'.[40] She does not, however, settle on a specific term to define the nature of this apparent hoax. It is only Samuel E. Bring, in the entry on Nils Hufwedsson Dal from *Svenskt biografiskt lexikon*, who vaunts the possibility that 'Dal bought the manuscript in good faith in Copenhagen'.[41]

It is worth taking a moment to consider the applicability of the term 'mystification' when discussing *Krembres saga*. Julia Abramson, in her monograph *Learning from Lying: Paradoxes of the Literary Mystification*, gives an account of how literary mystifications first surfaced, at least under that name, in Paris in the 1750s. She explains how mystification lies somewhere between forgery and fiction on a spectrum: like forgery it is intended to deceive by means of imitation, but unlike forgery it is not meant to deceive permanently, but rather to come to light after a short amount of time and even includes hints at its deceptive nature so that the initiated may see through the ruse (i.e. academic insider jokes).[42] Abramson explains moreover how demystification is an integral part of mystification, since the latter must be 'accompanied or followed by the author's willing public revelation of his identity', making the mystifier into 'a real source to confirm the insight of those who recognize it as a trick'.[43] Abramson's definition does not, thus, fit easily with *Krembres saga*. For one thing, it would make Dal a mystifier *avant la lettre*, beating the French *philosophes* to the punchline. This is not impossible, but more problematic is that, to our knowledge, Dal never came forth and revealed *Krembres saga* as a hoax. Abramson's definition, it must be conceded, involves a static intention on the part of the mystifier, who sets out to mystify and always plans to demystify. No room is left for changed intentions: what happens if a lucrative payout comes

40 Nilsson G., "Den isländska litteraturen i stormaktstidens Sverige", *Scripta Islandica* 5 (1954) 19–41: 39–40 (my translation).

41 Bring S.E., "Nils Hufwedsson Dal", in *Svenskt biografiskt lexikon* (https://sok.riksarkivet.se/sbl/artikel/15837) (my translation).

42 For the problems associated with considering forgery as involving an intent to permanently deceive, and thus using this as the basis for creating a distinction between forgery and mystification, see the introduction to this volume.

43 Abramson J.L., *Learning from Lying: Paradoxes of the Literary Mystification* (Newark: 2005) 16.

between the producer of the hoax and its revelation?[44] Mystification, it seems, may not be as cut and dry as Abramson suggests, but abiding by her rather prescriptive requirements we must conclude that *Krembres saga* is no simple example of that practice.

One important part of Abramson's definition, however, are the telltale signs secreted in the text by the mystifier, and it is worth asking the question of whether such are present in *Krembres saga* or its paratext, Dal's introduction. In the case of the latter, the answer is a resounding yes. For example, there we are informed of the Icelander, one 'Torleik Jonson', who had to sell off his manuscripts in order to cover the costs of his journey back to Iceland so that he could deal with a family emergency. Dal was able to take his pick – among which was the manuscript containing *Krembres saga* – and, we are told, 'Mr Torfæus bought most of the remaining ones'.[45] 'Torfæus' is without doubt the renowned Icelandic historian and antiquarian Þormóður Torfason (1636–1719) also commonly called Thormod Torfæus. But the problem is that Dal made his trip to Copenhagen in 1722, apparently the first and last time that he went there,[46] and by then Torfæus had already been dead for three years, so it simply cannot be the case that he purchased the remaining manuscripts belonging to Torleik Jonson.[47]

This is not the only problem with Dal's introductory comments. He also mentions that the original manuscript containing *Krembres saga*, the one which was lost when the ship carrying it sunk near Gotland, had been sent to 'Hr Salan', who apparently had also given him the money with which to buy the manuscript.[48] The Salan brothers, Jonas (1664–1706), Petter (1671–97) and

44 For an interesting example of how motives can shift, see the statement regarding the forgery of ancient Etruscan scarith in Rowland I., *The Scarith of Scornello: A Tale of Renaissance Forgery* (Chicago: 2004): 'what started as the prank of two giggling teenagers ended up as Europe's antiquarian sensation' (130).

45 Bygdén, "Konung Krembres" 89 (my translation).

46 Bring, "Nils Hufwedsson Dal". The trip was funded by a stipendium, and Dal was required to gather descriptions of books held by Danish antiquarians for the Uppsala librarian, Erik Benzelius. Even if Dal had made another earlier trip to Copenhagen, one which has failed to be recorded for posterity, it is highly unlikely that he would have come into contact with important scholars and book collectors.

47 It should be noted that I have been unable to find any record of a Torleik Jonson (presumably Þorleikur Jónsson) who fits the dates. The same can be said for similar names, Þorleifur Jónsson and Þorlákur Jónsson. Torfæus' library is, moreover, fairly well catalogued and no sign of these putative manuscripts can be traced. See Kålund K., *Arne Magnussons i AM. 435 a–b 4° indeholdte Håndskriftfortegnelse med to Tillæg* (Copenhagen: 1909).

48 Bygdén, "Konung Krembres" 90.

Nicolaus (1667–1717), are well known for their involvement in saga-editing and book-collecting.[49] All three of the antiquarian-minded Salan brothers were, however, long dead by 1722.[50]

These incongruities, both that concerning Torfæus and that with regard to 'Hr Salan', can be explained in more ways than one. Perhaps the comments should lead us to imagine that Dal had made a trip to Copenhagen prior to 1722. This is, however, highly unlikely, if for no other reason than that the Great Northern War would have made travel between Sweden and Denmark extremely difficult between 1700 and 1721. The alternative explanation is that these allusions to well-known antiquarians are merely made up. Either Dal simply wanted to give the impression of a trip prior to 1719 (when Torfæus died), counting on whoever read the introduction not being sufficiently familiar with his early life but recognising the names of Salan and Torfæus and thus getting an impression of a date in the early 1710s or thereabouts. Or perhaps he wanted the recipient to imagine that this trip actually did take place in 1722 and the incongruous names are thus inserted as 'ironic clues' of the type described by Abramson when defining literary mystifications.[51] The latter seems most likely to me, with Dal winking at a group of anti-Rudbeckians, who saw the incongruity and laughed at the gullibility of those who were duped, principally Gustaf Bonde. But in either case Dal was indeed consciously trying to mislead in his preface and is thus most likely also to have been the author of the forgery. Dal, as far as we know, never openly revealed his deception, so the saga is no clear-cut mystification, but rather lies somewhere in the grey area between mystification and forgery.

Taking this assessment as our new point of departure, it is worthwhile considering to what extent Dal was influenced by *Hjalmars saga*, the clear predecessor of his creation. The previously-described misgivings aired by various scholars in the eighteenth century are surely, at least in part, a result of *Krembres saga* having been produced in the wake of *Hjalmars saga*. While the nail in the coffin of the latter saga was not to be hammered in until Carl Gustaf Nordin's

49 For more on their manuscript collection see Grape A., "Om bröderna Salan och deras handskriftssamling", *Nordisk tidskrift för bok- och biblioteksväsen* 1 (1914) 207–238. One more brother, Johan (1670–1739), chose a different, non-academic path in life.

50 Note that Gödel makes the mistake in his catalogue of the Old Norse manuscripts in Kungliga Biblioteket of assuming that the 'Hr Salan' referred to was Petter. Gödel V., *Katalog öfver Kongl. bibliotekets fornisländska och fornnorska handskrifter* (Stockholm: 1897–1900) 226.

51 It might also be argued that Dal simply made clumsy mistakes and mentioned individuals who were dead. This, however, seems extremely unlikely, since Dal was well informed of important Icelanders (such as Torfæus) and published a biographical summary of several of them in 1724.

thesis appeared in Uppsala in 1774, we know that doubts were raised about *Hjalmars saga*'s authenticity as early as 1701, when Otto Sperling (1634–1715), the German-Danish scholar and at that time professor, wrote in a letter that it was an old piece of parchment which had been covered in runes and smoked and dirtied to make it look old.[52] Biörner responded to and refuted Sperling's claims and it is into this context of heightened awareness that *Krembres saga* took the stage.[53] It is, in fact, a key point to note when considering *Krembres saga* just how much it stands in the shadow of its forerunner, *Hjalmars saga*. This, both in as much as its reception was predetermined along lines laid out by *Hjalmars saga*'s own reception and in terms of how it was perceived as an inferior follow-up. An example of this opinion from a later scholar is Gun Nilsson's remarks, with regard to *Krembres saga*, that 'a forgery on the level of *Hjalmars och Ramers saga* it is not, however'.[54]

Regardless of its relative quality, the author of *Krembres saga* seems to have learnt from Halpap's predicament. Halpap left the door open for demands for the original to be presented, something which Dal knew only too well since he worked at the Archive of Antiquities and had written a biographical sketch of Johan Hadorph.[55] Sperling's just-mentioned critique of *Hjalmars saga* took aim at the unconvincing material aspects of the manuscript which was conjured up in response to Hadorph's demands. Thus Dal, smartly, claimed that his putative original had gone down off the coast of Gotland in a shipwreck. Langebek found this all too convenient and, without even having seen the saga, commented that it was inconceivable that 'such a curious man [should] be so careless as to let such a rare and unique original set out to sea and himself carry a copy or translation by land'.[56] Consequently Langebek drily notes that 'there have been many learned shipwrecks, such as that which swallowed the original of *Krembres saga* off the coast of Gotland, in the world. One deems various learned conflagrations to be suspicious'.[57] A questionable shipwreck was preferable, however, to a suspicious manuscript which could be scrutinised at length.

It is possible that Dal, in telling of the manuscript's loss at sea, was influenced by previous stories of manuscripts going astray during sea voyages. The obvious tale which may have played a role is that of Hannes Þorleifsson, whose

52 Gödel, "Hjalmars och Hramers saga" 144.

53 Biörner Eric Julius, *Cogitationes critico philologicæ de orthographia linguæ svio gothicæ tam runica quam vulgari* (Stockholm, L. Salvius: 1742).

54 Nilsson, "Den isländska litteraturen" 40 (my translation).

55 Dal Nils Hufwedsson, *Specimen biographicum de antiquariis Sveciæ* (Stockholm, Henricus C. Merckell: 1724).

56 Langebek, *Breve fra Jakob Langebek* 238 (my translation).

57 Ibidem, 239 (my translation).

ship sank off Norway in 1682 with a trove of Icelandic manuscripts. Jonas Rugman (Jón Jónsson in Icelandic) too, whose boat, headed for Copenhagen, ended up in Sweden in 1658, delivering Icelandic manuscripts into Swedish hands, may have been in Dal's mind. The ship did not sink, although at least one scholar has suggested that it was forced to deviate from its course due to inclement weather, but the manuscripts never reached their intended destination.[58] Dal was definitely familiar with Rugman's story since he recounts it in his brief work on Icelandic scholars, *Islandorum, in rem antiquarium Releciæ, merita, seculi septimi decimi spatio posteriore* ('The good deeds of Icelanders in the matter of Swedish antiquities in the later part of the seventeenth century'), now our principle source on the matter.[59]

Krembres saga may not, ultimately, have been a great success in a general sense, failing to convince many of its authenticity, but it seems unlikely that it was originally intended to dupe a broad spectrum of readers. The way it was presented, moreover, shows that its author had taken a considered approach to the best ways to introduce a forged saga into circulation and learnt from previous attempts. In the following section we turn our gaze to Copenhagen, where the final copies of *Krembres saga* were made and perhaps influenced new attempts at fabrication.

3 The Long Journey Home?: *Hafgeirs saga Flateyings* and *Þjóstólfs saga hamramma*

The youngest manuscripts of *Krembres saga* seem to be the three Danish ones: only one of these, the Danish translation found in Thott 1776 4to, can be securely dated, namely to 1757, thanks to the inclusion of this information by the Icelandic scribe Jón Marteinsson (1711–1771). The others would seem to have been produced around the same time or afterwards, the saga having made its way to Copenhagen as a result of Lagerbring and Langebek's correspondence from 1756. Jón Marteinsson was one of several scribes working in Copenhagen in the third quarter of the eighteenth century, and we may imagine that there was a fair amount of contact between the educated and close-knit Icelandic scribal community present in the city at the time. Jón seems to have principally copied for Jakob Langebek, but many of the manuscripts in his hand passed into the collection of Peter Friderich Suhm (1728–1798), Langebek's protegé

58 Heimir Pálsson, *Örlagasaga Eyfirðings: Jonas Rugman – Fyrsti íslenski stúdentinn í Uppsölum. Málsvörn menningaröreiga* (Reykjavik: 2017): 24. See also Busch, *Großmachtstatus und Sagainterpretation* 16.

59 See Dal, *Specimen biographicum* N2v.

who bought around 40 manuscripts from the auction of his mentor's library.[60] While Langebek's manuscripts would have passed into Suhm's possession after the former's death in 1775, Suhm and his scribes probably had easy access to Langebek's collection in the preceding decades, and it is perfectly feasible that they would have been well acquainted with the curiosity that was the forged work named *Krembres saga*. It may also have been the case that this saga – presumably copied so that proof existed of its fraudulent nature – inspired the next attempts at producing a saga-imitation which would fool book-collectors in the city.

The two sagas which surfaced at this time and which would eventually come under suspicion of being less than authentic are named *Hafgeirs saga Flateyings* and *Þjóstólfs saga hamramma*. They exist today in manuscripts housed in two institutions, namely the Arnamagnæan Collection in Reykjavík and the National Library of Iceland, also in Reykjavik. *Hafgeirs saga* exists in a single witness, bearing the shelfmark KB Add. 6 fol., while *Þjóstólfs saga* is found in three, the oldest being KB Add. 376 4to. Despite their present home, KB Add 6 fol. and KB Add. 376 4to, both of which only contain a single (forged) saga, first turned up in Denmark. The former tells the story of a young nordic prince (Fenesius), sent away by his father to protect him from a hostile mother, who encounters and defeats giants before himself being defeated in battle. His son (Hafgeir) must take up the gauntlet, avenging his father and accidentally discovering Iceland in the process. The latter saga describes the adventures of a young Icelander (Þjóstólfr), believed to be a layabout by some, but who proves that he possesses prodigious strength when he travels out to the royal courts of Norway and Denmark. He returns to Iceland to marry, but after the death of his wife ends his days far from home in Constantinople. These two sagas have been the subject of two scholarly articles by Peter Jorgensen, but have otherwise attracted little attention.[61] Jorgensen gives the subtitles 'An

60 See Kålund K., *Katalog over de oldnordiske-islandske håndskrifter i det store kongelige bibliotek* (Copenhagen: 1900) L. The c. 3000 manuscripts making up Suhm's library, including the 40 which had previously been owned by Langebek, were transferred to the Royal Library in Copenhagen in 1796. On Suhm's influence from Langebek see Rørdam E., "Suhm, Peter Frederik", in Bricka C.F. (ed.), *Dansk biografisk leksikon*, 19 vols. (Copenhagen: 1887–1905) XVI 558–570: Langebek is said to be one of the 'men who […] had a great influence on the direction which Suhm's studies took and to whom he attached himself with great devotion' (560; my translation).

61 Jorgensen P., "*Hafgeirs saga Flateyings*: An Eighteenth-Century Forgery", *Journal of English and Germanic Philology* 76 (1977) 155–164. Jorgensen P., "*Þjóstólfs saga hamramma*: The Case for Forgery", *Gripla* 3 (1979) 96–103. See also, however, Schlitz S.A., *The Copenhagen Sagas* (Ph.D. dissertation, University of Georgia: 2003), a doctoral dissertation with Jorgensen as supervisor.

Eighteenth-Century Forgery' to his first article and 'The Case for Forgery' to the second article, revealing clearly in what direction his thoughts are tending.

Jorgensen's arguments in the first article are grounded in a stylistic assessment of *Hafgeirs saga*. He identifies it as roughly fitting the genre of legendary sagas which were first popular in the fourteenth century. Romantic elements also point to the literature of, at earliest, the late middle ages, while the verses in the saga are confused and match no known type of poetry from the middle ages or postmedieval period in Iceland. The orthography contains some archaic forms, but not used consistently enough to suggest that they are an accurate reproduction of forms from an older manuscript, and a number of more recent vocabulary items appear which belie any argument for great age. The core of Jorgensen's accusation of forgery rests upon a note on a flyleaf of KB Add. 6 fol., written in the same hand as the rest of the manuscript, which claims that the text was copied from a twelfth-century vellum exemplar. The stylistic analysis, as seen, refutes the possibility of a twelfth-century origin for the text, hence Jorgensen argues that the flyleaf note proves that *Hafgeirs saga* was either a forgery or the product of a naïve/confused scribe.[62] After identifying the scribe as the Icelander Þorlákur Magnússon Ísfiord (*c.* 1748–1781), who carried out copying work during a five-year stay in Copenhagen (1771–1776), Jorgensen concludes 'there is also no doubt that Ísfiord was not a naïve scribe'.[63] Beyond this, Jorgensen also presents something of a character assassination of Ísfiord, accusing him of adopting pseudonyms and pilfering leaves from manuscripts, presumably because if he can be shown to be not just knowledgeable but also of dubious moral character, this would support the accusation that he is a forger.[64]

In the second article by Jorgensen a similar line of argumentation is upheld as regards the text of *Þjóstólfs saga* in KB Add. 376 4to, but in this case we are on shakier ground. As Jorgensen shows, stylistically, orthographically and lexically, *Þjóstólfs saga* cannot be a faithful copy of a medieval saga. Jorgensen, once again identifies the scribe, in this case Þorleifur Arason Adeldahl (b. *c.* 1749).[65] He was a student and scribe in Copenhagen in the period 1771–1774, characterised as having 'a quick, sharp mind' and being 'an accomplished scribe', that

62 A number of additional points are added to support this, for example the seemingly fallacious inclusion of lacunae in the transcription and the improbability of a twelfth-century manuscript turning up in Copenhagen in the 1770s and not causing a stir.

63 Jorgensen, "*Hafgeirs saga*" 159.

64 It is also said that Ísfiord typically included information on his sources on title pages, not flyleaves, and thus the latter usage might suggest tergiversation.

65 Schlitz gives his cognomen as Adaldahl, and Aðaldal is another alternative which appears in discussions of this scribe.

is to say, no mere dupe.[66] He is also shown to have come into contact with a number of manuscripts which either subsequently went missing or are now missing leaves, hence he may have been involved in disreputable activities. So far, so similar. The big difference is that KB Add. 376 4to contains no note, such as that on the flyleaf of KB Add. fol. 6, which explicitly makes a claim for the saga to have a medieval origin. Without such a note, it is hard to prove that there was any clear deception: writing sagas which imitated or pastiched the style of older ones was by no means uncommon in eighteenth-century Iceland. Jorgensen's defence here suggests that a lie of omission can be as misleading as an overtly false statement. The vast majority of Adeldahl's manuscripts include mention of the source and of his role as scribe, and by leaving out such information it may be that he wanted the reader to assume a medieval source and at the same time avoid attaching his name to something of dubious authenticity. The argumentation is at times circumstantial and overstated, but cannot be categorically refuted.

Having proved that *Hafgeirs saga* was a forgery and Ísfiord its originator/perpetrator (and attempted to prove the same for *Þjóstólfs saga* and Þorleifur Arason Adeldahl), all that remains for Jorgensen to do is to provide a motive. He does so, albeit not explicitly, by showing that both manuscripts came to form part of the collection of Bernhard Møllman (1702–1778) 'university professor, royal historiographer and head librarian of the Royal Library in Copenhagen'.[67] Møllman is portrayed as aging, half-blind, 'having a soft spot in his heart for needy students' and thus an easy target for a scam.[68] One is left to infer that Ísfiord and Adeldahl's motives were primarily financial.

The major difference between these two sagas and the previous two discussed in this chapter are that *Hafgeirs saga* and *Þjóstólfs saga* are rather more convincing. That is not to say that these sagas are particularly outstanding works of literature, but rather that in their mediocrity and avoidance of grand rewritings of Scandinavian prehistory they are perfectly attuned to a number of late-medieval or post-reformation Icelandic sagas. It is this familiarity, perhaps born of the authors being well-read in sagas of this type, which probably allowed them to fly under the radar for so long. Konrad Maurer, writing in the nineteenth century, does not mention them in his groundbreaking article on Icelandic 'apocrypha',[69] and Kristian Kålund's catalogue of the Danish Royal Library, published in 1900, includes entries for both KB Add. 6 fol. and

66 Jorgensen, "*Þjóstólfs saga*" 97–98.
67 Jorgensen, "*Hafgeirs saga*" 163.
68 Jorgensen, "*Þjóstólfs saga*" 102.
69 Maurer K., "Über isländische Apokrypha", *Germania* 13 (1868) 59–76.

KB Add. 376 4to but barely mentions their dubious authenticity.[70] No outright accusation of forgery surfaced until that presented by Jorgensen. I am only aware of one subsequent (unpublished) refutation, although that involves Shaun F.D. Hughes critiquing Jorgensen's intolerance for post-medieval saga-tradition and elevation of certain concepts of historicity and authenticity rather than disputing whether anyone was misled, purposefully or not, by these sagas.[71]

While some parts of Jorgensen's arguments are more convincing than others, and his prejudices may be less palatable to a more recent audience, it is not my intention here to refute or confirm his analysis. I subscribe, on the whole, to the assessment that neither *Hafgeirs saga* nor *Þjóstólfs saga* have a claim to being a product of the Middle Ages, but I want to look at a more recent stage in the lengthy performance surrounding these works which have been accused of being forgeries. This most recent chapter in the lives of these potential forgeries involves Jonas Rugman's fateful journey from Iceland to Denmark, with manuscripts in tow, being carried out in reverse. This played out at the end of the twentieth century, in the two decades after these two sagas were 'exposed'.

Following Iceland's achieving of full independence in 1944, a process was initiated whereby many Icelandic manuscripts which had ended up in Danish collections would be returned to their place of origin. After a long period of negotiation, the first two manuscripts were sent back in 1971, and it was decided that a statement would be made by these being two of the most historically significant and valuable manuscripts kept in Denmark: Flateyjarbók (containing sagas of Norwegian kings among other things) and Codex Regius (containing the *Poetic Edda*). Interestingly enough, despite the Danish authorities having originally intended to send the manuscripts by plane, the Icelandic minister for education, Gylfi Þ. Gíslason, asked for them to be sent by boat, and thus it was that they were transported by and sailed into Reykjavik harbour on the Danish ship, Vædderen (i.e. the Ram), on the 21st April, the first week of Icelandic summer.[72] The choice to send these manuscripts by boat seems

70 Kålund, *Katalog over* [...] *det store kongelige bibliotek* 427, 446. Under Kålund's entry for Add. fol. 6 mention is made of the fact that the scribe claims that the saga was copied from a manuscript 'exarata seculo XII' and this is followed by a '(!)', which presumably suggests surprise and perhaps also disbelief.

71 This critique was presented as a paper entitled "'The Never-Ending Story': Saga-Writing from Ari Þorgilsson to Bergsveinn Birgisson" as part of the series "Miðaldastofa" at the National University of Iceland in the Spring of 2018. I am grateful to Hughes for sharing his lecture notes with me.

72 Sigrún Davíðsdóttir, *Håndskriftsagens saga i politisk belysning*, trans. Kim Lembek (Odense: 1999) 365–367.

to take on a symbolic significance when one considers the various sea-lanes which these and similar manuscripts had traversed since their original departure from Iceland.

Following this momentous occasion a panel was set up to assess the holdings of Danish repositories, such as the Arnamagnæan Collection and the Royal Library, and decide which items should be considered Icelandic cultural patrimony and thus sent back to Iceland. The panel was called the 'Deleudvalg' ('Sharing-Committee') and was made up of two Danes and two Icelanders.[73] As part of this process various lists were drawn up, among which we find 'Udleveringsliste nr. 9' ('Repatriation List, no. 9'), which includes 34 items all from the Royal Library's additamenta collection.[74] On this list, finalised on the 10th December 1981 and signed by all four members of the board, we find both KB Add. 6 fol. containing *Hafgeirs saga* and KB Add. 376 4to containing *Þjóstólfs saga hamramma*. The board-members agreed unanimously that *Þjóstólfs saga* was Icelandic cultural patrimony, while *Hafgeirs saga* received three votes for and one against.[75] The decision concerning which manuscripts were to be returned was based on a definition of Icelandic cultural patrimony which was voted into Danish law in 1965 and reads as follows:

> Manuscripts are considered Icelandic cultural patrimony if the artefact is known or with fair certainty can be assumed to have been authored or translated by an Icelander and moreover for the most part deals with Iceland and Icelandic matters or belongs to late-medieval Icelandic fictional literature. These criteria are valid regardless of whether the manuscript is the original copy or a later one.[76]

---

73 For more information see Sigrún Davíðsdóttir, *Håndskriftsagens saga* 368–370.

74 These manuscripts had been transferred to the Royal Library from the University Library's (Universitetsbibliotek) additamenta in 1938. List 9 can be found in the unedited archives of the Arnamagnæan Commission in Copenhagen, in the "Forhandlingsprotokol for Deleudvalget vedrørende islandske håndskrifter i Danmark", vol. IV, pp. 624–625.

75 The people voting were Jónas Kristjánsson (Foreman of the Icelandic Manuscript Institute), Ole Widding (Dictionary editor), Magnús Már Lárusson (Rector of the University of Iceland) and Christian Westergård-Nielsen (Professor at Aarhus University).

76 The legal amendment can be read online at https://www.retsinformation.dk/eli/lta/1965/194 (§1 stk. 3). The translation is my own. Note that in the ninth meeting of the Deleudvalget (26th–31st May 1974) various additional considerations regarding this formulation were raised. See "Forhandlingsprotokol for Deleudvalget vedrørende islandske håndskrifter i Danmark", vol. I, pp. 70–76. See also Sigrún Davíðsdóttir, *Håndskriftsagens saga* 372.

Thus for a manuscript to be considered Icelandic cultural patrimony it had to fulfill two requirements relating to both the individual involved in its production and its content. Based on Jorgensen's scribal identifications of Ísfiord and Adeldahl, it is clear that both manuscripts were 'written [...] by an Icelander', and so both naturally meet the first criterion. The second criterion is more complex. The narrative of *Þjóstólfs saga* does play out to a large degree in Iceland and the hero is Icelandic, thus it is fair to say that the requirement is met. *Hafgeirs saga*, on the other hand, has only a limited connection to Iceland. It is hard to reconcile Hafgeir's single winter spent on Flatey, as described in one chapter out of fourteen, as leading to the saga 'for the most part' dealing with Icelandic subject matter. I would argue, moreover, that it can hardly be called 'late-medieval Icelandic fictional literature', since the eighteenth-century date of composition lies well outside of the board's definition of late-medieval, which ended in 1550 in the most generous appraisal.[77] Thus since it does not fulfill both requirements, an argument could be made that *Hafgeirs saga* should not have been repatriated to Iceland (although I do not advocate any new action).

It seems we must accept that *Hafgeirs saga* is not a cherished work, and it is most likely that no great amount of time was expended on deciding where it should go. Although the meeting took place in 1981, one might suspect that the members of the board were unaware of Jorgensen's research. This cannot, however, be the case, since at least one of the four members of the 'Deleudvalg' was well informed of the claims concerning *Þjóstólfs saga* and presumably also those about *Hafgeirs saga*. That member was Jónas Kristjánsson, who was the editor of *Gripla*, the journal in which Jorgensen published his article on *Þjóstólfs saga* and who is explicitly thanked by Jorgensen in the first footnote in said article. Jónas Kristjánsson at least, it would seem, voted for *Þjóstólfs saga*'s return to Iceland knowing full well that it was not an authentic piece of late-medieval Icelandic fiction and likewise did so also in the case of *Hafgeirs saga*. In any case, nobody objected, and the two manuscripts containing the sagas were transported to Iceland in 1997 (this time by plane), and now reside at the Arnamagnæan Collection in Reykjavik. The fact that they were repatriated makes them officially Icelandic cultural patrimony. The Danish legal definition makes it clear that a manuscript written by an Icelander writing about Icelandic matters was to be considered as such, and whether it was a forgery or not had no relevance in that determination! It seems thus, strange as it

77 See Christian Westergård-Nielsen's discussion of this matter in vol. 1, p. 70 of the "Forhandlingsprotokol for Deleudvalget".

may sound, that these sagas performed as authentic texts during the repatriation process.

4 Conclusion

All of the forged sagas discussed here involve sea journeys: pagan priests sailing south to Wendland in *Hjalmars saga*, King Krembre leading the Cimbrians once again south across the Baltic Sea in *Krembres saga*, Hafgeir unintentionally sailing to a soon-to-be discovered Iceland in *Hafgeirs saga* and Þjóstólfr sailing from Iceland to visit royal courts in Norway and Denmark in *Þjóstólfs saga*. Sailing also plays a role in the wider performance of forgery surrounding these works: one can surmise that *Hjalmars saga*, if written south of the Baltic, must have come by boat back to Sweden at some point; the original text of *Krembres saga* is said to have been lost in a shipwreck off the coast of Gotland; *Hafgeirs saga* and *Þjóstólfs saga* were repatriated to Iceland as part of a process which was initiated with a symbolic sea-journey involving manuscript treasures entering Reykjavik harbour on an early summer's day. The sea and travel across it is thematically ubiquitous in sagas, authentic as well as forged. But it also plays a significant role in the transnational circulation of both genuine and fabricated sagas in the Early Modern period. The expanding international market for antiquities and the journeys that it entailed sent texts down new sea-lanes and raised new possibilities for forgers to take advantage of these vectors of transmission in formulating stories of discovery and disappearance.

In this chapter I have shown how these diverse sagas, despite previously being treated individually and described, for the most part, as isolated cases of forgery, can be seen to form a loose tradition. *Hjalmars saga* stands at the head of this tradition, though it too may have been a response, in part, to fabricated texts included in Danish accounts of the ancient Cimbrians, such as the fake runic sources mentioned by both Niels Pedersen and Carl Christoffer Lyschander. *Krembres saga* was not successful in the same way as *Hjalmars saga*, but this may in part be due to different aims and in part due to scholars having been put on their guard by *Hjalmars saga*. It seems likely, moreover, that its author, most likely Nils Hufwedsson Dal, had identified problems with Halpap's modus operandi and thus 'sank' his original manuscript to avoid being forced to offer it up for scrutiny. Copies of *Krembres saga*, in turn, made it into libraries in Copenhagen in the 1750s, where they would have been available to and a potential inspiration for Þorlákur Magnússon Ísfiord and Þorleifur Arason Adeldahl, the scribes (and authors?) of *Hafgeirs saga* and *Þjóstólfs saga* in the 1770s. While these accounts focus on the late seventeenth and eighteenth centuries, the stories stretch both back in time all the way to Herodotus' days and forward to 1997 when *Hafgeirs saga* and *Þjóstólfs saga* were repatriated to Iceland. Thus we can see how forgery challenges oversimplified ideas of chronology and is often in excess of any simple narrative which presents a forged item as made, exposed and then forgotten.

Bibliography

Abramson J.L., *Learning from Lying: Paradoxes of the Literary Mystification* (Newark: 2005).

Ahnlund N., *Nils Rabenius (1648–1717)* (Stockholm: 1927).

Árni Magnússon, *Arne Magnussons private brevveksling*, ed. K. Kålund (Copenhagen: 1920).

Biörner Eric Julius, *Cogitationes critico philologicæ de orthographia linguæ svio gothicæ tam runica quam vulgari* (Stockholm, L. Salvius: 1742).

Biörner Eric Julius, *Nordiska kämpa dater* (Stockholm, Joh. L. Horrn: 1737).

Biörner Eric Julius, *Inledning til de yfwerborne Göters gamla Häfder* (Stockholm, J.L. Horn: 1738).

Bonde Gustaf, "Anmärkningar wid första delen af Swea Rikes Historia jämte Påminnelser wid samma anmärkningar", in Olof von Dalin, *Witterhets-Arbeten, i bunden och obunden Skrifart*, vol. 3 (Stockholm, Carl Stolpe: 1767) 459–508.

Bring S.E., "Nils Hufwedsson Dal", in *Svenskt biografiskt lexikon* (https://sok.riksarkivet.se/sbl/artikel/15837).

Busch K., *Großmachtstatus und Sagainterpretation. Die schwedischen Vorzeitsagaeditionen des 17. und 18. Jahrhunderts* (Ph.D. dissertation, Friedrich-Alexander-Universität Erlangen-Nürnberg: 2002).

Bygdén L., "Konung Krembres i Giötaland och Konung Augis i Uppsala saga", *Samlaren* 23 (1902) 83–107.

Dal Nils Hufwedsson, *Specimen biographicum de antiquariis Sveciæ* (Stockholm, Henricus C. Merckell: 1724).

Demougeot E., "L'invasion des Cimbres-Teutons-Ambrons et les Romains", *Latomus* 37 (1978) 910–938.

Grafton A., *Forgers and Critics, New Edition: Creativity and Duplicity in Western Scholarship* (Princeton – Oxford: 2019).

Grape A., "Om bröderna Salan och deras handskriftssamling", *Nordisk tidskrift för bok- och biblioteksväsen* 1 (1914) 207–238.

Gödel V., "Hjalmars och Hramers saga: Ett litterärt falsarium från 1690", *Svenska fornminnesförenings tidskrift* 9 (1896) 137–154.

Gödel V., *Katalog öfver Kongl. bibliotekets fornisländska och fornnorska handskrifter* (Stockholm: 1897–1900).
Habaj M., "Herodotus' Renaissance Return to Western-European Culture", *Studia Antiqua et Archaeologica* 22:1 (2016) 83–94.
Havens E.A., "Babelic Confusion: Literary Forgery and the Bibliotheca Fictiva", in Stephens W. – Havens E.A. (eds.), *Literary Forgery in Early Modern Europe, 1450–1800* (Baltimore: 2018) 33–73.
Heimir Pálsson, *Örlagasaga Eyfirðings: Jonas Rugman – Fyrsti íslenski stúdentinn í Uppsölum. Málsvörn menningaröreiga* (Reykjavik: 2017).
Herodotus, *Histories*, 4 vols., ed. A.D. Godley (London – New York – Cambridge MA: 1924–1950).
Hickes George, *Linguarum veterum septentrionalium thesaurus grammatico-criticus et archæologicus*, 2 vols (Oxford, Theatro Sheldoniano: 1703–1705).
Hughes S.F.D., "'The Never-Ending Story': Saga-Writing from Ari Þorgilsson to Bergsveinn Birgisson" (unpublished lecture-notes).
Janson H., "Äkta förfalskning åter bevismaterial: Annotationes ex scriptis Karoli", *Scandia: Tidskrift för historisk forskning* 67 (2001) 41–60.
Jensen J.-L. (ed.), *Trojumanna saga: The Dares Phrygius Version* (Copenhagen: 1981).
Johansson J.V., "De Rudbeckianska förfalskningar i Codex Argenteus", *Nordisk tidskrift för bok- och biblioteksväsen* 42 (1955) 12–27.
Jorgensen P., "*Hafgeirs saga Flateyings*: An Eighteenth-Century Forgery", *Journal of English and Germanic Philology* 76 (1977) 155–164.
Jorgensen P., "*Þjóstólfs saga hamramma*: The Case for Forgery", *Gripla* 3 (1979) 96–103.
Kålund K., *Katalog over de oldnordiske-islandske håndskrifter i det store kongelige bibliotek* (Copenhagen: 1900).
Kålund K., *Arne Magnussons i AM. 435 a–b 4° indeholdte Håndskriftfortegnelse med to Tillæg* (Copenhagen: 1909).
Lagerbring Sven, *Swea Rikes Historia ifrån de äldsta tider til de närwarande: Första Delen som innefattar Rikets öde, ifrån des början til år 1060* (Stockholm, Carl Stolpe: 1769).
Lagerbring Sven, *Bref 1746–1787, Sven Lagerbring, Skrifter och brev*, ed. L. Weibull (Lund: 1907).
Langebek Jakob, *Breve fra Jakob Langebek udgivne af Det Kongelige Danske Selskab for Fædrelandets Historie og Sprog*, ed. H. Fr. Rørdam (Copenhagen: 1895).
Lavender P., *Hjalmars & Hramers saga: A Digital Edition & Translation* at https://hjalmars-saga.dh.gu.se/index.html.
Lundius Carl, *Zamolxis primus Getarum legislator* (Uppsala, Henricus Keyser: 1690).
Lyschander Carl Christoffer, *Synopsis historiarum danicarum* (Copenhagen, Henrich Waldkirch: 1622).
Maurer K., "Über isländische Apokrypha", *Germania* 13 (1868) 59–76.
Müller P.E., *Sagabibliothek*, 3 vols. (Copenhagen: 1817–1820).

Nilsson G., "Den isländska litteraturen i stormaktstidens Sverige", *Scripta Islandica* 5 (1954) 19–41.

Nordin Carl Gustaf, *Monumenta suiogothica vetustioris aevi falso meritoque suspecta* (Uppsala, Edmannianis: 1773–1774).

Norris M., *A Pilgrimage to the Past: Johannes Bureus and the Rise of Swedish Antiquarian Scholarship, 1600–1650* (Lund: 2016).

Pedersen Niels, *Cimbrorum et Gothorum origines, migrationes, bella, atqve coloniæ* (Leipzig, Johann Melchior Lieben: 1695).

Rowland I., *The Scarith of Scornello: A Tale of Renaissance Forgery* (Chicago: 2004).

Rowland I.D., "The Theatre of Forgery: Curzio Inghirami (Volterra, 1614–1655) and Giorgio Grognet de Vassé (Malta, 1774–1862)", in Lavender P. – Amundsen Bergström M. (eds.), *The Performance of Forgery* (Leiden: 2022) 235–265.

Rørdam E., "Suhm, Peter Frederik", in Bricka C.F. (ed.), *Dansk biografisk leksikon*, 19 vols. (Copenhagen: 1887–1905) XVI 558–570.

Schlitz S.A., *The Copenhagen Sagas* (Ph.D. dissertation, University of Georgia: 2003).

Schück H., *Kgl. vitterhets historie och antikvitets akademien, dess förhistoria och historia I* (Stockholm: 1932).

Sigrún Davíðsdóttir, *Håndskriftsagens saga i politisk belysning*, trans. Kim Lembek (Odense: 1999).

Skovgaard-Petersen K., "The Literary Feud between Denmark and Sweden in the Sixteenth and Seventeenth Centuries and the Development of Danish Historical Scholarship", in Brink J.R. – Gentrup W.F. (eds.), *Renaissance Culture in Context: Theory and Practice* (Aldershot: 1993) 114–120.

Skovgaard-Petersen K., "Peace-Loving Yet Powerful – Depictions of the Cimbrians in Early Modern Danish Historiography" (unpublished).

Springborg P., "Antiqvæ Historiæ Lepores – om renæssancen i den islandske håndskriftsproduktion i 1600-tallet", *Gardar: Årsbok för Samfundet Sverige-Island i Lund-Malmö* 8 (1977) 53–89.

Svanhildur Óskarsdóttir, "Manuscripts on the Brain: Árni Magnússon, Collector", in Driscoll M.J. – Svanhildur Óskarsdóttir (eds.), *66 Manuscripts from the Arnamagnæan Collection* (Copenhagen: 2015) 9–37.

Sävborg D., "Några anmärkningar om *Annotationes ex scriptis Karoli* och dess källor", *Historisk tidskrift* 137 (2017) 64–79.

Vennberg E., "Johan Bure", in *Svenskt biografiskt lexikon* (https://sok.riksarkivet.se/sbl/artikel/17156).

Verelius Olof (ed.), *Hervarar saga på gammal götska* (Uppsala, Henricus Curio: 1672).

Walde O., *Storhetstidens litterära krigsbyten: En kulturhistorisk-bibliografisk studie* (Uppsala – Stockholm: 1916–1918).

Þorbjörg Helgadóttir (ed.), *Rómverja saga* (Reykjavik: 2010).

CHAPTER 11

Of Theatrical Illusion and Fake Advertisements: George Bickham the Younger, Samuel Foote and the Great Bottle Hoax of 1749

Jacqueline Hylkema

On 11 January 1749, the *General Advertiser*, a popular local newspaper, published an advertisement to announce that next Monday evening, the New Theatre at London's Haymarket would present:

> a person who performs the several most surprising Things following, viz. first, he takes a common Walking Cane from any of the spectators, and thereon plays the Music of every Instrument now in use, and likewise Sings to surprising perfection. Secondly, he presents you with a common wine bottle, which any of the spectators may first examine; this bottle is placed on a Table in the middle of the Stage, and he (without any Equivocation) goes into it in Sight of all the Spectators, and sings in it; during his stay in the bottle any person may handle it, and see plainly that it does not exceed a common Tavern Bottle.[1]

Obviously, it would be impossible for a man to fit into a wine bottle – let alone sing in it – but the advertisement was republished several times in the week to come.[2] It proved to be particularly effective: by Monday, the advertisement had become the talk of London and the New Theatre sold out that evening. When the stage remained empty, the audience realised that the advertisement had been a hoax and as the *General Advertiser* reported the next day, it:

> immediately grew Outrageous and in a Quarter of an Hour's Time broke to Pieces all the Boxes, Benches, Scenes, and every Thing that was in their Power to destroy, leaving only the Shell of the House remaining – Surely this will deter any one from venturing to impose on the Public, in the like manner for the future.[3]

1 "General Advertiser" (11 January 1749) 13.
2 Namely on 12–14 and 16 January 1749.
3 "General Advertiser" (17 January 1749) 1.

 | DOI:10.1163/9789004106901_012

Over the next few weeks, this report would be followed by a number of pamphlets and prints on the Great Bottle Hoax, as the event became commonly known. This was hardly unusual: the eighteenth century was rife with forgeries, hoaxes and other kinds of fakery, to the extent that it is often referred to as the 'the Age of Forgery', and the exposure of these deceptions usually resulted in abundant public debate. These debates usually focused on the victims' gullibility and their lack of reason, and the commentaries on the events at the New Theatre were no exception to this. In the satirical print *An Apology to the Town, for Himself and the Bottle*, published by the London print seller Bispham Dickinson on 7 February 1749, the fictitious hoaxer boasts that his trick has exposed the public's

> reigning Taste and Want of Wit
> Your Taste that still 'gainst Reason flies
> To Grasp Impossibilities
> And void of Sense, to all that's new
> Impatient flies: or False or New;
> Each foreign Gazette now compleat
> With Pride reveals the glorious Cheat.

The audience's lack of 'solid judgement' and consequent national shame is repeated in several of the prints that Dickinson published in the wake of the hoax. *The Magician, or Bottle Cungerer/English Credulity; or, Ye're all Bottled*, which appeared on 5 March 1749, shows how Satan seduces the Haymarket audience with a small bottle, to the acute embarrassment of Britannia. The opening lines of the verse read: 'With grief, resentment and averted eyes, Britannia droops to see her sons (once wise so fam'd for arms, for conduct so renown'd with every virtue, every glory crown'd) now sink ignoble, and to nothing fall; obedient marching forth at Folly's call'.

George Bickham the Younger weighed in on the bottle debate with the satirical engraving *The Bottle Conjurer, from Head to Foot without Equivocation* [Fig. 11.1], published on 24 January 1749.[4] The son of the well-known engraver and publisher George Bickham the Elder, Bickham (as I will refer to him here) was one of England's first satirical printmakers and a major presence in the London print trade. According to Timothy Clayton, the 'vibrant, energetic, and enigmatic' Bickham 'often sailed close to the wind in matters of piracy,

4 This contribution elaborates on my brief discussion of Bickham's print in Hylkema J., "The Pleasure of Being Deceived: Spectatorship in the Arts and Other Deceptions in Eighteenth-Century England", *De Achttiende Eeuw* 46:1 (2014) 49–69.

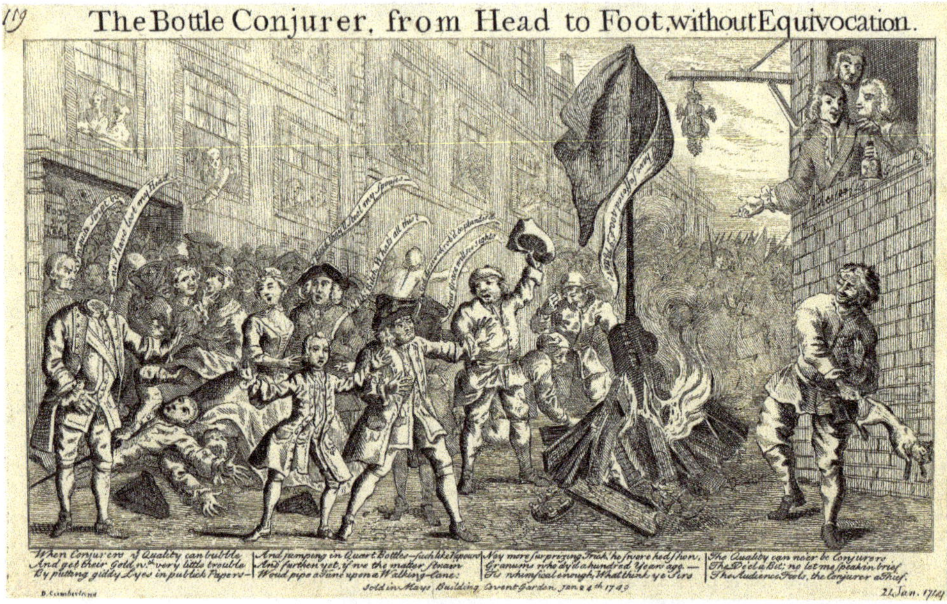

FIGURE 11.1 George Bickham the Younger, *The Bottle Conjurer, from Head to Foot, without Equivocation*, 1749. Engraving. London, British Museum

obscenity, and political acceptability, but he was easily the most talented political satirist of his period'.[5] In this contribution, I want to propose that Bickham's take on the great Bottle Hoax moves away from political commentary and far beyond simple Schadenfreude at the audience's gullibility. Instead, this image provides a sustained comparison between the Great Bottle Hoax and the nature of illusionist art, in particular the stage of Samuel Foote, the manager of the unfortunate New Theatre.

Samuel Foote [Fig. 11.2] was a well-known actor and playwright and like his friend David Garrick, he had been trained by Charles Macklin, whose school of acting focused on making the audience believe that they were witnessing an actual event rather than a performance. The success of Macklin, Garrick and Foote was a crucial part of a debate on the boundaries between artistic illusion and deception on the London stage in the 1740s and, particularly, how its audiences should respond to these. Bickham's *The Bottle Conjurer* is part of this discourse and explores it on different levels. It introduces the subject of

5 Clayton T., 'George Bickham', in *Oxford Dictionary of National Biography* (Oxford: 2004).

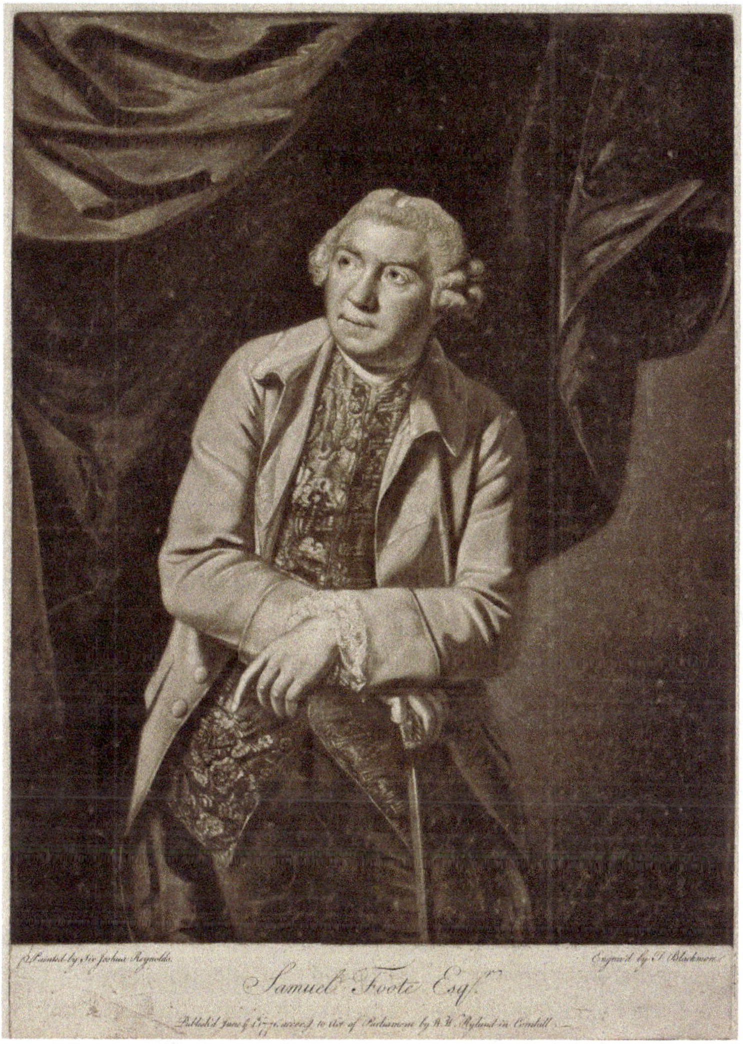

FIGURE 11.2 Thomas Blackmore, *Samuel Foote Esqr*, 1771. Mezzotint after Sir Joshua Reynolds. London, British Museum

deception in a comparison of the advertisement placed by the hoaxer, whom he explicitly identifies, and the one used by Foote for a former production at the New Theatre. More importantly, Foote's approach to theatre, and acting in particular, was rooted in seventeenth-century notions of illusionism, and Bickham engages with this discourse to elaborate on the boundaries between Foote's deceit on the stage of the New Theatre and the Great Bottle Hoaxer, particularly in terms of how these related to the respective audiences.

Bickham's print was published on 24 January 1749, when the identity of the hoaxer was still hotly debated. Foote was an obvious suspect as he was known for his eccentric productions and pranks.[6] On 18 January, he and John Potter, the owner of the New Theatre, both placed advertisements in the *General Advertiser* to protest their innocence. Potter explained that when he was approached to let his theatre, he really had believed that something along the lines of the advertisement 'would be exhibited, to the Satisfaction of the Spectators'.[7] Foote, however, wrote that he had suspected that 'a Fraud on the Public was intended', and had advised Potter 'on No Account to open his Doors'.[8]

So, who was the elusive 'Bottleman'? Potter wrote in his advertisement that he had been a man of 'genteel appearance' and had given his name as William Nicholls.[9] But Nicholls was never found and the mystery sparked a number of satirical prints and pamphlets which presented themselves as by 'the bottle conjurer': the author of *An Apology to the Town, for Himself and the Bottle* presented himself as a Mr J. Nick'All ('Mr P-tt-r was mistaken in the name'). Other satires offered the perspective of the fictitious performer: in the pamphlet *A Modest Apology* (1749) the conjurer explained that his intention had been to jump into 'a very, very large *Bottle*' but had been too frightened by the audience to appear on stage.[10]

Bickham's *The Bottle Conjurer* was entirely serious in his attempt to identify the culprit, and it is likely that his identification is correct. His print shows the audience building a bonfire in the street with the remains of the theatre they have just destroyed. The crowd is observed by three men in the window of the public house on the right-hand side of the image – the one at the front faces the viewer and proudly points at the riot below him. In his other hand he is clasping a small bottle with a tiny man inside. A name is written on the window sill immediately below him: 'Chesterfield'. This identifies him as Philip Stanhope, the Earl of Chesterfield, who remains the main suspect behind the hoax until this day. Stanhope allegedly betted William Bentinck, the Duke of

---

6 During S., *Modern Enchantments: The Cultural Power of Secular Magic* (Cambridge: 2009) 96. During gives two examples of these pranks in his brief but excellent discussion of the Great Bottle Hoax. The second of these is a distinctly Jonsonian episode in which Foote 'persuaded an heiress to marry a friend by having an actor pass himself off as a real magician and tell her fortune in his friend's favor'.

7 "General Advertiser" (18 January 1749) 1.

8 Ibidem, 2.

9 Ibidem, 1.

10 *A Modest Apology for the Man in the Bottle. By Himself.* Published anonymously (London, J. Freeman: 1749) 22.

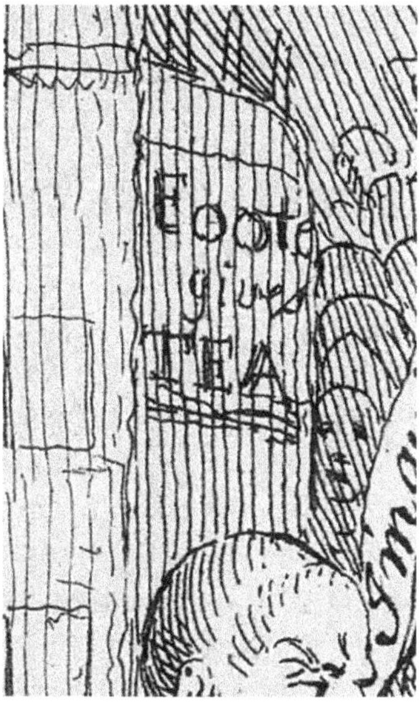

FIGURE 11.3
George Bickham the Younger, *The Bottle Conjurer, from Head to Foot, without Equivocation*, 1749. Engraving. London, British Museum. Detail, left part of the image

Portland, that he could 'find fools enough in London to fill a playhouse and pay handsomely for the privilege of being there'.[11] In the opening lines of the accompanying text, Bickham refers to Stanhope's motif, money, and the method he used in his deception:

> When Conjurers of Quality can bubble
> And get their Gold with very little trouble
> By putting giddy Lyes in publick Papers

The remark is significant as it is referring to the medium in which Stanhope presented his deception, the theatre section of 'publick Papers', in which the audience might reasonably have expected to find advertisements of actual productions. He elaborates on this with a small billboard next to the entrance of the theatre, which reads 'Foote Gives Tea' [Fig. 11.3]. This is not the title of a play but a reference to the way in which Foote used to advertise his own productions. In 1737, two satirical plays by Henry Fielding, Foote's predecessor as manager of the New Theatre, had been the direct cause of the introduction of the Licensing Act, which among other things stipulated that dramatic productions staged in London would be restricted to two patented playhouses,

11 Walsh W.S., *Handy-book of Literary Curiosities* (Philadelphia: 1893) 476.

the Royal Theatres in Drury Lane and Covent Garden.[12] In order to dodge the act, Foote presented his productions as 'tea parties' – once at the theatre, the audience would be served tea, along with a dramatic performance. Ian Kelly, notes that Foote had cards printed to publicise his events:

> Mr Foote's compliments to his friends and the public, and hopes for the honour of their Drinking Tea with him at the Little Theatre in the Haymarket, every morning at playhouse prices.[13]

Advertisements for the events gave even less information: an announcement in the theatre section of the *General Advertiser* on 15 December 1747 simply mentions that for 'positively the last Time', 'Mr Foote Gives Tea' at the Theatre Royal in Covent Garden and then gives the prices for the tickets to the event.[14] The tea parties appear to have been reprised briefly in 1748, but had most definitely ended long before January 1749.

Bickham's print rearranges time but with a very specific aim: the inclusion of Foote's billboard creates a deliberate juxtaposition between Stanhope and Foote, and their respective deceptions. Stanhope's 'giddy Lyes' were presented as an authentic advertisement in a publication that would be expected to publish facts and truths. The advertisements for Foote's tea parties, published in the same newspaper, were strictly speaking not at all deceitful. Of course, everyone realised that Foote was trying to get around the Licensing Act – and his production did attract attention from the authorities – but every single word in the advertisement was true: tea was served.[15]

However, this is not to say that the performance that came with the tea itself was entirely free from deception. In fact, Foote's production very much focused on the subject of theatrical deception and a debate that went back to the seventeenth century. The final act of William Shakespeare's *The Winter's Tale* (1611) offers a good starting point for a brief introduction to this debate. When King Leontes is presented with a statue of his long-dead wife Hermione, it is so deceptively realistic that it seems to be alive. 'See, my lord', Leontes mutters to his courtiers, 'Would you not deem it breathed? and that those veins Did verily

12 Donohue J., "Introduction: The Theatre from 1660 to 1800", in Donahue J. (ed.), *The Cambridge History of British Theatre: Volume 2, 1660–1895* (Cambridge: 2004) 1–52: 22–23.

13 Quoted in Kelly I., *Mr Foote's Other Leg: Comedy, Tragedy and Murder in Georgian London* (London: 2012) 120.

14 "General Advertiser" no. 15 (December 1747) 2.

15 Kelly, *Mr Foote's Other Leg* 120.

bear blood?'.[16] One of them replies, 'The fixture of her eye has motion in't, As if we are mocked with Art'.[17] According to the courtiers, the statue was made by 'that rare Italian master Giulio Romano', who in fact had been a painter but was indeed well-known for his ability to create deceptively realistic art.[18] In *The Lives of the Artists* (1550), Giorgio Vasari describes Romano's fresco of Cupid and Psyche in the Palazzo Te as 'seeming to be alive (so strong is the relief), they deceive the human eye with a most pleasing illusion'.[19]

The notion that a visual work of art could be so realistic that its beholder could, however briefly, be mocked by it and experience it as real was to become a major theme in early modern art. Most seventeenth-century art theorists wrote about artistic illusionism and the technical mastery required. In *Painting Illustrated in Three Dialogues* (1685), William Aglionby for instance writes about the crucial role of colours in painting: 'Tis they that must deceive the Eye, to the degree, to make Flesh appear warm and soft, and to give an Air of Life, so as his Picture may seem almost to Breathe and Move'.[20] Samuel van Hoogstraten – a formidable illusionist painter – notes in his *Inleyding tot de Hooge Schoole der Schilderkonst* (1678) that '[w]ant een volmaekte Schildery is als een spiegel van de Natuer, die de dingen, die niet er zijn, doet schijnen te zijn, en op een geoorlofde vermakelijke en prijslijke wijze bedriegt' ('the perfect painting is a mirror of nature, that makes things that are not there appear as if they are, and as such is deceptive in a permissible, entertaining and praiseworthy manner').[21] Like Shakespeare, Van Hoogstraten saw a clear connection between the theatre and illusionist painting – as Thijs Weststeijn notes, he would train the pupils in his studio in play-acting, with texts written by himself.[22]

Performance definitely was a major factor in the creation of illusion. Richard Burbage, one of Shakespeare's principal actors, was known for his ability to transform into his character on stage and make his audience believe that he was

16 Shakespeare William, *The Winter's Tale*, ed. J. Pitcher, Bloomsbury Arden Shakespeare, third series (London: 2010), v.3.64–65.

17 Ibidem, v.3.67–68.

18 Ibidem, v.2.70–73.

19 Vasari Giorgio, *The Lives of the Most Eminent Painters, Sculptors and Architects*, Volume VI, trans. G. du C. De Vere (London: 1913) 155. For a discussion of Shakespeare's possible sources on Giulio Romano, see Gombrich E.H., "'That Rare Italian Master …' Giulio Romano, Court Architect, Painter and Impresario", in D. Chambers – J. Martineau (eds.), *Splendours of the Gonzaga* (London: 1981) 77–85.

20 Aglionby William, *Painting Illustrated in Three Dialogues* (London, Printed by John Gain for the author: 1685) 17.

21 Hoogstraten Samuel van, *Inleyding tot de hooge schoole der schilderkonst: anders de zichtbaere werelt* (Rotterdam, François van Hoogstraten: 1678) 25. My translation.

22 Weststeijn T., "The Sublime and the 'Beholder's Share': Junius, Rubens, Rembrandt", *Journal of Historians of Netherlandish Art* 8:2 (Summer 2016) [16].

Hamlet, Lear, Prospero and Leontes. The poet and dramatist Richard Flecknoe said of Burbage that he had been able to completely transform himself into his part and 'never assumed himself again until the play was done'.[23] An anonymous funeral elegy for Burbage noted that his performances had been

> Soe livly, that Spectators, and the rest
> Of his sad Crew, whilst he but seem'd to bleed,
> Amazed, thought even then hee dyed in deed.[24]

Burbage's well-known ability to convince the audience that they were witnessing the character, rather than an actor playing the character would have added another dimension to the final act of *The Winter's Tale* and Leontes' remarks about how realistic the statue is. 'Chide me, dear stone, that I may say indeed Thou art Hermione – or rather, thou art she'.[25] In Leontes' eyes, the statue crosses its representation boundary and becomes Hermione, in much the same way as Burbage became Leontes in the eyes of the audience when the play was first performed at the Globe in 1611.

While artistic illusionism continued to play a key part in European drama until well into the eighteenth century, it seems to have made a relatively quick exit from the English stage. The theatre of the Restoration was, as Robert Leach writes, more pictorial and its acting style focused 'on "showing" not "being", so as to complete the stage picture rather than embody the character's life. [...] This kind of performance, to be successful, had to *demonstrate* emotion, never "live" it'.[26] The risk of falling victim to theatrical illusion was further reduced by the audience's close proximity to the stage, the common practice of actors to fall out of character as soon as they finished their lines, and repeated interchanges, scripted as well as spontaneous, between actors and members of the audience.[27]

The resistance against theatrical illusionism only grew in the eighteenth century. As Matthew Craske points out, 'the intellectual culture of the Enlightenment was both preoccupied and deeply distrustful of optical deception and, in particular, anything which smacked of a magician's tricks. [...] To be enlightened was to show the capacity to transcend the alluring deceit of surface

23 Cited in Leach R., *An Illustrated History of British Theatre and Performance. Volume One – From the Romans to the Enlightenment* (Abingdon – New York: 2019) 181.

24 Cited in Foakes R.A., "Shakespeare's Elizabethan Stages", in Bate J. – Jackson R. (eds.), *Shakespeare: An Illustrated Stage History* (Oxford: 1996) 14.

25 Shakespeare, *The Winter's Tale*, V.3.23–25.

26 Leach, *An Illustrated History* 336.

27 Ibidem, 463–464.

appearances'.[28] This also applied to theatre audiences: in 1746, Pierre-Antoine de la Place, Shakespeare's first French translator, observed in his *Le Théâtre Anglois* (1746), that English intellectuals, 'naturellement melancoliques, sont moins disposes que d'autres a se preter a l'illusion. La constant etude du vrai rend souvent le Coeur indocile & rebelle a la vraisemblance' ('melancholic by nature, are less disposed than others to submit themselves to illusion. The constant study of truth often renders the heart unyielding and rebellious to verisimilitude').[29]

But this attitude was beginning to change: on the evening of 14 February 1741, one single performance had reintroduced realistic acting on the London stage. For his interpretation of the role of Shylock in Shakespeare's *The Merchant of Venice*, Charles Macklin had decided not to play the role for comic effect, as had become usual, but restored Shakespeare's original text and researched every aspect of Shylock's character in detail.[30] His aim in this was for his character to appear 'natural', the word commonly used for a representation that appears so realistic that it could deceive the spectator into thinking that she or he was looking at the original rather than its representation.[31] On opening night, he became Shylock in an approach that was, as Ian Kelly writes, 'new and daringly radical'.[32] And it was shocking: Kelly describes how the performances drew gasps from the audience, as they realised that this was 'affectingly "real"'.[33]

However new and radical it may have seemed to its audiences, Macklin's performance as Shylock implicitly entailed a revival of the acting style so closely associated with Burbage and the illusionist effect described in *The Winter's Tale*, and it made Macklin the godfather, as Kelly observes, of a new wave of realistic actors.[34] Macklin was also an acting coach and his first two students were David Garrick and Samuel Foote, both in their early twenties. Garrick made his debut in October 1741 and became a superstar overnight. It is impossible to overestimate the impact that Garrick was to have on the London stage – as Peter Holland observes, 'for English theatre, the mid-18th century

28 Craske M., *Art in Europe, 1700–1830: A History of the Visual Arts in an Era of Unprecedented Urban Economic Growth* (Oxford: 1997) 145–146.

29 Place Pierre-Antoine de la, *Le Théâtre Anglois*, Tome I (London, [n.p.], 1746) xxxix. My translation.

30 Appleton W.W., *Charles Macklin: An Actor's Life* (Cambridge MA: 1960) 46.

31 Lovejoy A.O., *Essays in the History of Ideas* (Baltimore – London: 1948) 70.

32 Kelly, *Mr Foote's Other Leg* 92.

33 Ibidem, 92.

34 Ibidem, 90.

cannot be called anything other than the Age of Garrick'.[35] Foote's career never became anywhere near as stellar as his friend's, even though he had already been famous when first discovered by Macklin. During a brief spell at Fleet Prison, for debts he had run up while a student at Oxford, he had published two bestselling pamphlets on the recent murder of his uncle. Once out of prison, Foote's literary fame and great wit instantly made him a celebrity – Samuel Johnson called him 'irresistible'.[36]

Foote's first performance was a failure – he had been terribly miscast as Othello – but he soon found theatrical success in other ways. One of these was *A Treatise on the Passions, so Far as They Regard the Stage* (1747) a book in which he elaborates on Macklin's approach to natural acting, particularly in terms of how various emotions are performed. Much of the book is taken up by comparisons of the acting styles of contemporary actors. Foote's highest praise is reserved for Macklin and Garrick, both of whom perform roles in such a way that they become real in the eyes of the audience. Foote particularly praises Garrick's interpretation of King Lear, in which 'the Passions of Joy, Tenderness, Grief and Shame, are blended together in so masterly a Manner, that the Imitation would do Honour to the Pencil of a *Rubens* or an *Angelo*'. By comparing the quality of imitation in Garrick's theatrical performance to the work of Rubens and Michelangelo, both known for their illusionist mastery, Foote – like Shakespeare in *The Winter's Tale* – places his illusionist stage explicitly in the tradition of the artistic illusionism of the sixteenth and seventeenth centuries.

In 1747 Foote also launched the production that was to become known as *Mr Foote Gives Tea* and would cement his association with natural acting and theatrical illusion. In his first few years on the stage, it had become obvious that Foote not only had a great talent for comedy but also was a highly accomplished mimic. Ian Kelly quotes a contemporary who remarked that while doing an impression, Foote 'seemed to confirm us in the opinion that he was not an actor, but the real person he represented'.[37] Foote decided to elaborate on this talent in a one-man show initially called *Diversions of the Morning*, which was performed at the New Theatre, at 11 o'clock in the morning, and offered the audience hot chocolate.[38] The production became hugely successful and was soon moved to six o'clock in the evening – which allowed Foote to serve tea rather

35 Holland P., "The Age of Garrick", in Bate J. – Jackson R. (eds.), *Shakespeare. An Illustrated Stage History* (Oxford: 1996) 69.

36 Kelly, *Mr Foote's Other Leg* 8.

37 Ibidem, 112.

38 Ibidem, 117.

than chocolate and led him to abandon the initial title of his production and simply advertise it as a tea party.[39] After dozens of performances at Haymarket, *Foote Gives Tea* moved to the Royal Theatre at Covent Garden, where it ran even longer. Foote's tea party parodied the theatrical world and commented on specific acting styles by imitating the performances of well-known colleagues. He especially made fun of the old declamatory style but implicitly contrasted this with the effect of his own natural style, becoming the person he represented in the eyes of his audience. If Foote's *Treatise on the Passions, so Far as They Regard the Stage* was the handbook on illusionist acting, his tea parties were the masterclasses.

Pictorial illusion had fared rather better in England than its theatrical counterpart, in the sense that deceptive realism in painting continued to be appreciated there after the Restoration. Samuel van Hoogstraten produced some of his finest illusionist works while living in London in the 1660s. These included so-called 'deceptions', images in which everyday objects, like letter racks, were rendered as realistically as possible in order to fool the viewer into thinking that he or she was looking at the objects themselves, rather than a representation. In print, a variation on this genre was found in the so-called medley print, or 'deceptio visus', which appeared to show a scattered collection of prints from different genres, ingeniously stacked on top of each other. George Bickham's father, a master of the genre, made a particularly well executed medley print to use as his trade card.

Bickham also created visual deceptions, for instance in the medley print *The Champion; or Evening Advertiser by Capt Hercules Vinegar, of Pall-mall* (1740) [Fig. 11.4] a political satire on Robert Walpole's government. The print shows a collection of paper objects, including playing cards, satirical prints, a portrait, an article seemingly torn from a newspaper, a portrait of Walpole, and a letter addressed to Bickham himself. At the top of the image, Bickham created a spoof of the masthead of the satirical magazine *The Champion, or the Evening Advertiser* leaving the name of its author, Captain Hercules Vinegar, Henry Fielding's pen name, clearly visible. An advertisement for the print, published in the *Daily Post* on 26 September 1740, explicitly refers to the print as a 'Deceptio Visus' and Bickham certainly sets out to deceive his viewers.[40] In order to make the objects in his stack appear as realistic as possible, Bickham added shading, tears and stains and the newspaper masthead shows the lettering, in reverse, on the other side of the sheet shining through. The effect

39 Kelly, *Mr Foote's Other Leg* 121.
40 "Daily Post" (26 September 1740) 2.

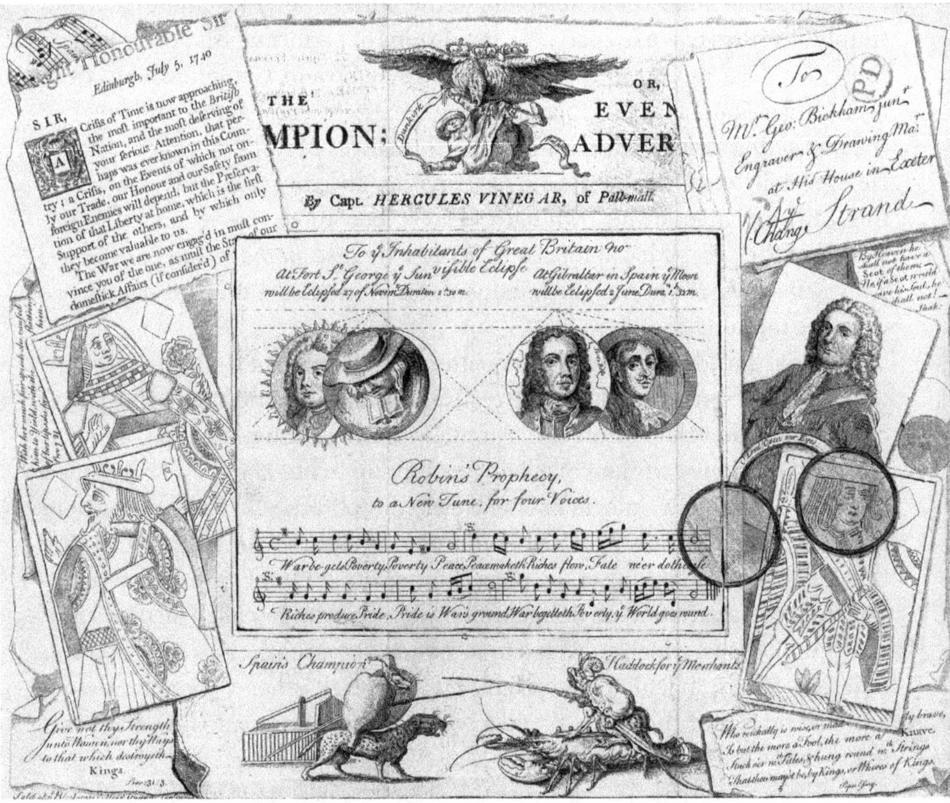

FIGURE 11.4 George Bickham the Younger, *The Champion; or Evening Advertiser by Capt Hercules Vinegar, of Pall-mall*, 1740. Engraving. London, British Museum

is exactly that described by Van Hoogstraten: 'a mirror of nature, that makes things that are not there appear as if they are'.[41]

Like Foote, Bickham was well aware of the historical roots of his artistic deception. In the final stage of his career, he revealed a distinct interest in the artists associated with seventeenth-century visual illusionism: between 1761 and 1763, he exhibited several prints after Rubens and, especially, Rembrandt with the Free Society of Artists.[42] He must also have been familiar with the

41 Hoogstraten, *Inleyding tot de Hooge Schoole* 25.

42 Graves A., *The Society of Artists of Great Britain, 1760–1791, the Free Society of Artists, 1761–1783: a complete dictionary of contributors and their work from the foundation of the societies to 1791* (London: 1907) 32–33.

seventeenth-century tradition in which the artistic illusions on the canvases and screens of Europe were compared with practices of actual deception. In *The Winter's Tale* for instance, the audience believes, like King Leontes and his courtiers, that Romano's statue is so lifelike that it seems to breathe. But not all is as it seems: this is not a deceptively realistic representation of King Leontes' dead wife but his wife – who is very much alive – pretending to be a statue. The statue is a hoax, masterly executed by Queen Hermione and her loyal servant Paulina. As such Shakespeare is bringing together two kinds of deceit: the actual deception of the hoax and illusionist art that transcends its representational frame and deceives the spectator into believing, however briefly, that they are looking at a living person rather than a statue or that they are witnessing an actual event rather than a play with Richard Burbage, performed on the stage of the Globe.

It must be noted that comparisons between artistic illusions and actual deception continued to be made in the eighteenth century: for instance, in 1720 the South Sea Bubble resulted in the publication of a number of medley prints in which printmakers compared their own illusions as well as the responses of their viewers to the deceptions of the South Sea Company and the gullibility of those who had invested in it.[43] However, for his reflection on the Great Bottle Hoax and how it compared to Samuel Foote's illusionistic theatre, Bickham turned to a very specific seventeenth-century motif: the mountebank.

By the early seventeenth century, the mountebank's reputation had become so associated with all kinds of deception – including fabricated identities and fake potions, that it had become synonymous with fakery.[44] All over Europe, paintings and prints were published depicting mountebanks and emphasising the deceptive nature of his profession. Bickham's father also added to the discourse, with his undated broadside *The High German Doctor and the English Fool*, which parodies the speeches that mountebanks would make on their raised stages. Many of these images also reflected on the nature of the mountebank's audience and their readiness to believe his lies – Jan van de Velde II underlines this sentiment in his undated engraving *The Quack*

---

43 See Cao M.M., "Trompe L'oeil and Financial Risk in the Age of Paper", *Grey Room* 78 (2020) 6–33, and Goldring T., "The Greater Fool: Paper, Illusion, and Time in Representations of the South Sea Bubble", *Eighteenth-Century Studies* 54:1 (2020) 53–75.

44 See Hylkema J., "The Artist and the Mountebank: Rochester's Alexander Bendo and the Dynamics of Forgery and Illusion in 17th-Century Art", in Becker D. – Fischer A. – Schmitz Y. (eds.), *Faking, Forging, Counterfeiting: Discredited Practices at the Margins of Mimesis* (Bielefeld: 2018) 59–76.

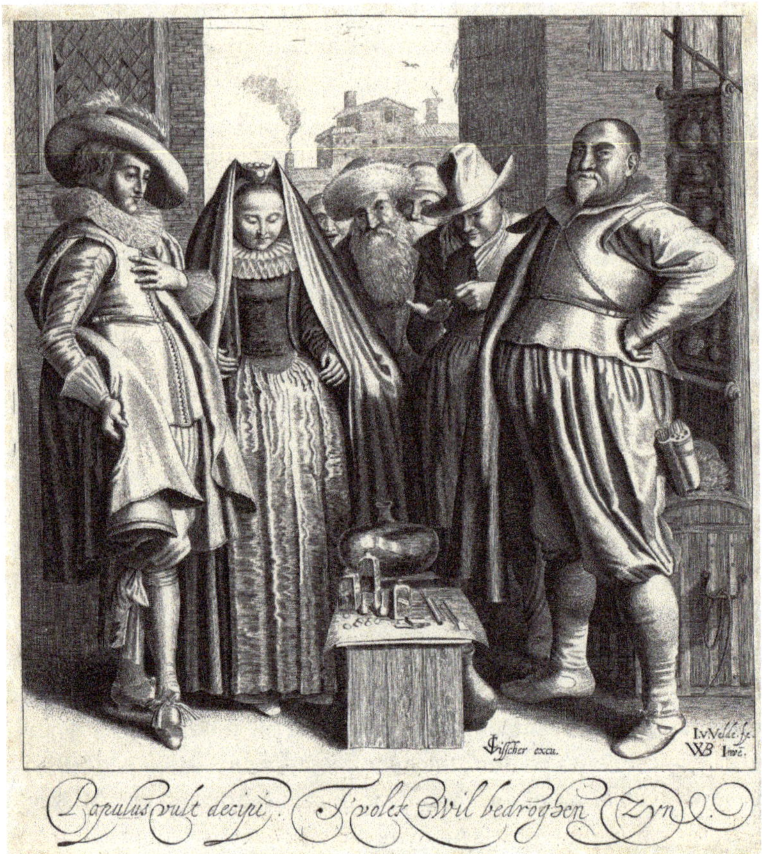

FIGURE 11.5 Jan van de Velde II, *Populus vult decipi – T'volck wil bedroghen zyn* (*People want to be conned* (*The Quack*)), c. 1630. Engraving after Willem Pieterszoon Buytewech. Amsterdam, Rijksmuseum
IMAGE © RIJKSMUSEUM

(ca. 1630) [Fig. 11.5] by adding a variation on the first part of the well-known motto 'mundus vult decipi, ergo dicipiatur' in Latin and Dutch. 'Populus vult decipi' – if the people want to be deceived, it only serves them right, Van de Velde implies, when they are.

The raised stage, the deceptive claims and the presence of an audience made mountebanks an ideal device to hold up a mirror to audiences and spectators. Ben Jonson's *Volpone* (1606) offered an implicit comparison between the gullible audience of a mountebank, Volpone in disguise, and the audience watching Burbage in the role. Volpone, the scene implies, is deceiving his audience on stage into believing that he is Scoto of Mantua, in much the same way

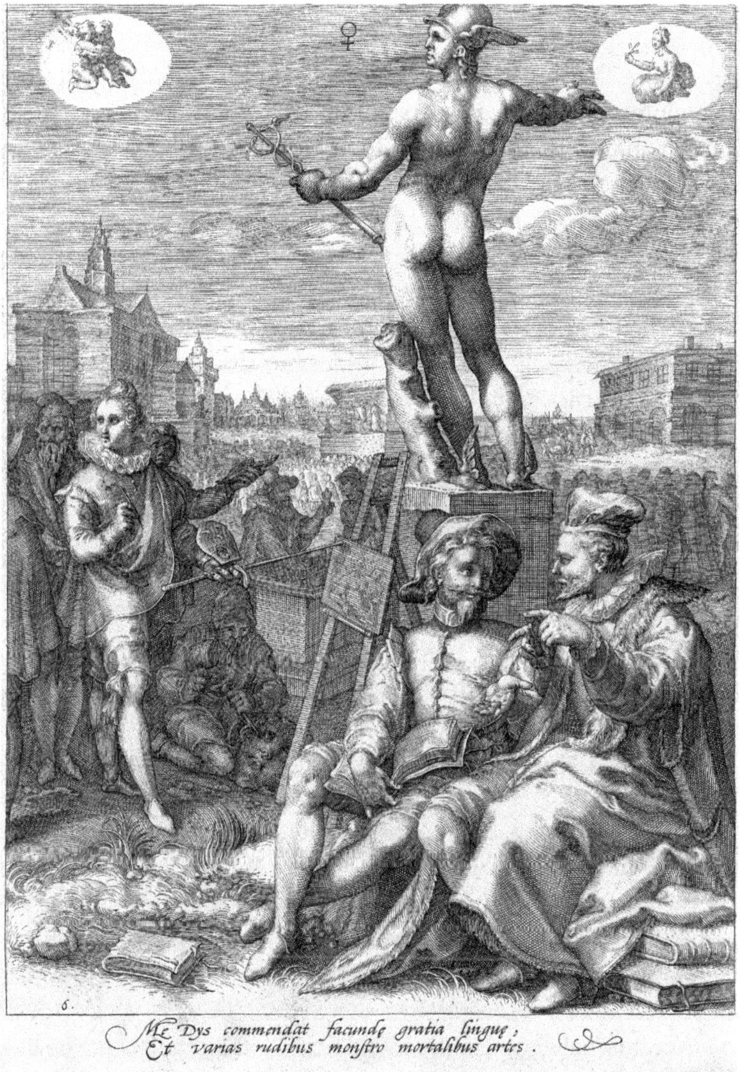

FIGURE 11.6 Jan Saenredam, 'The Children of Mercury', *c.* 1596, engraving after Hendrick Goltzius. Amsterdam, Rijksmuseum
IMAGE © RIJKSMUSEUM

that Burbage makes his audience in the theatre believe, however temporarily, that he is Volpone. A drawing made by Hendrick Goltzius, whose work was also popular in England, explicitly compares the mountebank with a range of artists, including a painter, sculptor and actors on the stage. As the motto to Jan Saenredam's engraving of the image [Fig. 11.6] emphasises, these all persuade their respective audiences of their 'artes' – which in Latin refers to arts as well as tricks.[45]

Gerard Dou's *The Quack* (1652) [Fig. 11.7] makes the comparison between artists and mountebanks even more explicit – and personal. The painting shows a mountebank on a raised stage, holding up a bottle of what he claims is medicine. The small crowd that has gathered around the mountebank includes a peasant, a poacher, a prostitute, a kitchen maid and school boys and to his right, Dou has inserted his own likeness, leaning out of his studio's window while still holding his palette. The composition establishes a comparison between the two men and their respective deceptions. Dou was celebrated all over Europe for his remarkably realistic technique and the illusions it created – in 1662, the Dutch poet Dirk Traudenius remarked of Dou's paintings that 'here it is not paint that lies on the panel, but life and spirit'.[46] In *The Quack*, Dou invites his audience to reflect on how he manages to achieve this illusion: the gleaming seal of the mountebank's diploma looks as if it were made of real wax and the tapestry on his table looks so realistic that the viewer wants to reach out and stroke it. Meeting his viewer's eye, Dou appears to say 'I am deceiving you, just like the mountebank deceives his audience'.

By 1749, Bickham had already published a number of prints on quackery in contemporary London, such as *Dr Rock's Political Speech to the Mob in Covent-Garden* (1743), *The Cats Paw* (1746) and *Quackery Unmask'd, or, Empiricism Display'd* (1748). In terms of their composition, these prints do include some of the elements of traditional mountebank satires, such as Dr Rock's impromptu raised stage, his attentive audience, and the medication he is holding up in his left hand, and all contain references to the gullibility of the audiences in the images. However, none of these prints include any comparison between illusion in the arts and the alleged deceptions of the infamous medicine vendor Richard Rock and the highly controversial physician Thomas Thompson. But Bickham's *The Bottle Conjurer, from Head to Foot without Equivocation* fits remarkably well in the tradition of Goltzius and Dou: the billboard on the left of the image identifies the New Theatre explicitly as the stage of Foote's masterclasses in artistic illusionism, whereas the representation of Stanhope contains strong references to seventeenth-century quack images. The window sill of the public house provides him with a raised stage and he is

45 'Me dys commendat facunde gratia lingue, Et varias rudibus monstro mortalibus artes' – 'the grace of my eloquent tongue recommends me to the gods, and I show the crude mortals various arts' (my translation).

46 Traudenius Dirk, *Rijmbundel* (Amsterdam, Gerrit van Goedesberg: 1662) 17.

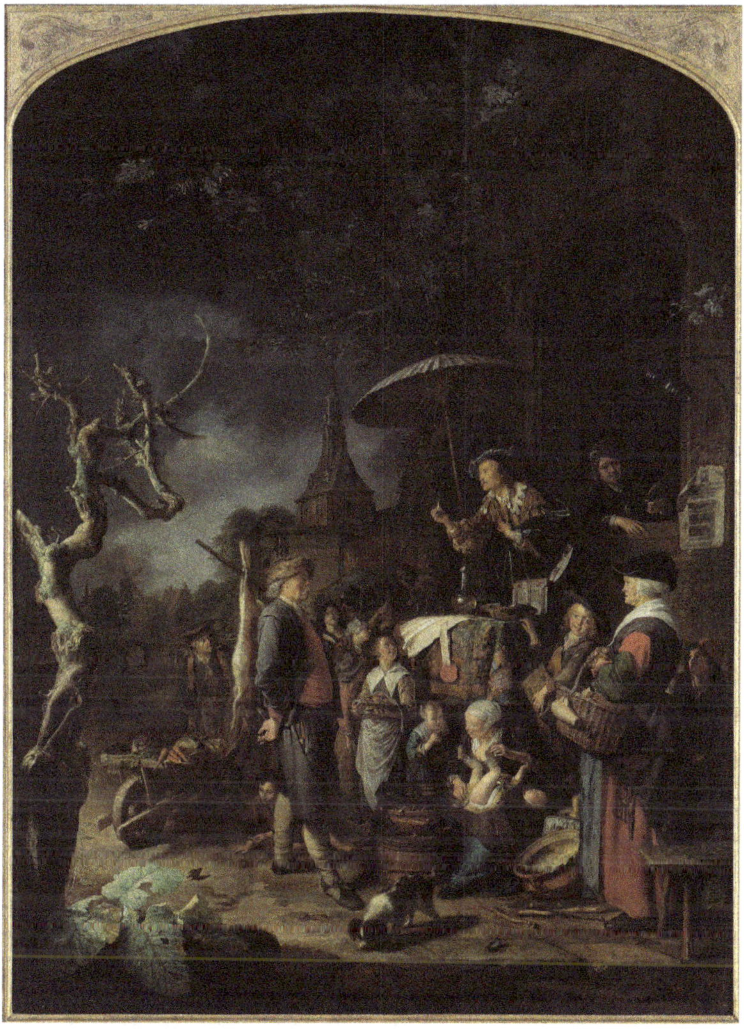

FIGURE 11.7 Gerard Dou, *The Quack*, 1652. Oil on panel. Rotterdam, Museum Boijmans Van Beuningen
IMAGE © STICHTING MUSEUM BOIJMANS VAN BEUNINGEN

holding up his bottle in the same fashion as the mountebanks in the images by Dou, Goltzius and many others.

Casting Stanhope in the role of mountebank and juxtaposing his deception with *Foote Gives Tea*, a production so focused on the creation of theatrical illusionism, provides a deeper dimension to Bickham's first comparison of the two advertisements and allows him to elaborate on the seventeenth-century debate on the nature of artistic deceit and how it compares to actual deception.

However, even though the print includes the same key players – illusionist art, actual deception and an audience – as found in the images by Goltzius, Dou and others, Bickham develops all three in radically different ways. Like Dou's *The Quack*, Bickham's image places its emphasis on the actual deceiver, 'the bottle conjurer'. It is important to note that Dou's image does not condemn the mountebank in any way: as in all seventeenth-century mountebank images, it is implied that his gullible audience is simply asking for it – mundus vult decipi, ergo dicipiatur. This is clearly different in Bickham's image: however gullible the audience at the New Theatre may have been, Bickham still holds Stanhope responsible for the deception and its disastrous consequences. The seventeenth-century mountebank tradition always depicts the audience while it watches the mountebank and becomes convinced by his lies but Bickham chooses to depict the effect of the deception. Even though he includes a number of comical elements, such as a man literally losing his head, his representation of the mob is explicit about the savagery of the riot: people are trampled and the banner on top of the fire spells out the extent of John Potter's financial ruin.

But the image's most radical departure from the traditional comparison between artistic illusion and actual deception is found in its most subtle element, Foote's billboard. Dou's painting is first and foremost a celebration of his own mastery and reflects that the seventeenth-century discourse on illusionist art had very much focused on the artist and the technical brilliance that was required to create an illusionary effect. In the eighteenth century however, this emphasis shifted to the spectator and his experience of the deception. The French art theorist Roger de Piles wrote at the beginning of the eighteenth century, that '[l]'a Peinture, dont l'essence est de surprendre les yeux & de les tromper' ('the essence of art is to catch the eyes unaware and deceive them') and the best paintings manage to be so forceful and realistic in their imitation that the spectator is fooled into wanting to 'entrer en conversation avec les figures qu' elle représente' ('have a conversation with the figures they represent').[47] When the spectator finds out that he has been deceived, De Piles observes, it is the surprise of the discovery that gives the spectator pleasure.[48] In England this shift towards the spectator also marked the first beginnings of a resistance towards illusionist art. In *The Theory of Painting* (1715), Jonathan Richardson chides the 'ill Connoisseur' who imagines a painting to be good

47 Piles Roger de, *Cours De Peinture Par Principes, Par M. De Piles* (1708; Amsterdam – Leipzig, Arkstée & Merkus: 1766) 13 and 4. My translations.

48 Ibidem, 3.

simply 'because a Piece of Lace, or Brocade, a Fly, a Flower, a Wrinkle, a Wart, is highly finish'd, and (if you please) Natural, and well in its Kind'.[49]

The Bottle Conjurer follows this turn to the audience, in the sense that it does not consider, let alone celebrate, Foote's artistic abilities but instead focuses on the audience's response to illusionist theatre. As Pierre-Antoine La Place would note in 1746, the English resistance to illusionist art was extended to the theatre, rendering the English 'Coeur indocile & rebelle a la vraisemblance' ('heart unyielding and rebellious to verisimilitude').[50] At that time, many hearts had been won over by the reintroduction of natural acting by Macklin and, particularly Garrick, but not everyone agreed. A clear example of the debate about natural acting and how audiences should respond to it is found in the introduction to *A Guide to the Stage, or Select Instructions and Precedents from the best Authorities towards Forming a Polite Audience* (1751), in which the anonymous author notes

> We daily see and hear injudicious applause, laborious attention, rustic laughter, and inelegant tears, with other errors no less gross than obvious. There are even some who wilfully forget themselves, see and hear Romeo and Juliet in person, are at Denmark or Mantua, without once dreaming of Drury-Lane or Garrick.[51]

The author firmly rejects the experience of a performance as an actual event and argues that those who allow themselves to be carried away by the illusion simply lack judgement and sophistication. The remedy for this 'impolite' behaviour is for the audience to remain firmly aware of the stage's representational frame and remember throughout that this *is* David Garrick playing Romeo on the Drury Lane stage, rather than Romeo himself. Sophisticated spectators never forget the representational nature of the scene before them, however natural the acting may seem.

To be seduced by theatrical illusion, or not – that was the question for London's theatregoers in the 1740s and Samuel Foote tackled it head-on in his

---

49 Richardson Jonathan, *An Essay on the Theory of Painting. By Mr. Richardson. The Second Edition, Enlarg'd, and Corrected* (London, Printed for A.C. and sold by A. Bettesworth: 1725) vi.

50 Place, *Le Théâtre Anglois* xxxix. The full quote reads: 'Les Anglais, naturellement melancoliques, sont moins disposes que d'autres a se preter a l'illusion. La constant etude du vrai rend souvent le Coeur indocile & rebelle a la vraisemblance'. My translation.

51 *A Guide to the Stage: or, Select Instructions and Precedents from the best Authorities towards Forming A Polite Audience; With Some Account of the Players, &c.* Published anonymously (London, D. Job and R. Baldwin: 1751) B.

tea party productions by demonstrating the different approaches to acting and their respective effect. As such, *Foote Gives Tea* was part of the debate about illusionism in the theatre and this is the main reason why Bickham chose to pit this production against Stanhope's hoax. As *A Treatise on the Passions, so Far as They Regard the Stage* shows, Foote clearly perceived his illusionist theatre as rooted in Shakespeare's writing and the visual tradition of the sixteenth and seventeenth centuries. His is a stage on which the actor feels emotions and lives the part to the extent that it will appear real to the audience. Or as Mirzoza, the heroine of *Les Bijoux Indiscrets* (1748) by Foote's friend Denis Diderot, puts it 'La perfection d'un spectacle consiste dans l'imitation si exacte d'une action, que le spectateur, trompé sans interruption, s'imagine assister à l'action même' ('The perfection of a performance lies in imitating an event so precisely that the spectator, deceived without interruption, imagines himself to be present at the event itself').[52]

This kind of performance is a kind of deception and the seventeenth-century mountebank vehicle enables Bickham to evoke the question of whether this is, to use Van Hoogstraten's phrase, permissible. Van Hoogstraten and many other seventeenth-century art theorists would have argued that it was. As the art theorist Charles-Alphonse Dufresnoy, points out in *De Arte Graphica* (1668), the experience of artistic illusion is a process, in which the art is first explicitly offered as a representation. As a result of the process of illusion, caused by the mastery of the creator, 'the art and effort of the work will be concealed: the greatest art, indeed, is to seem quite artless'.[53] In other words, the work is not offered as a deception – the shift from encountering a painting to the experiencing of it as that which it represents, happens in the viewing process. This is a crucial notion in Bickham's image: Foote's deceptions took place in a theatre, and were offered as theatrical performances. Bickham was not the only one to remark on this in the debate on the Great Bottle Hoax: the anonymous author of the pamphlet *A Letter to the Town, Concerning the Man and the Bottle* (1749) wonders why the audience at Haymarket became so furious when the theatre is where one goes to be deceived.[54]

The other crucial factor in the early modern acceptance of artistic deceit is found in its temporal nature. When the illusion ends, the representational frame is restored: the viewer realises that it is only a painting and is left with

52 Hobson M., *The Object of Art: The Theory of Illusion in Eighteenth-Century France* (Cambridge: 1982) 150. My translation.

53 Dufresnoy Charles-Alphonse, *De Arte Graphica*, ed. and trans. C. Allen – Y. Haskell – F. Muecke, Travaux Du Grand Siècle 24 (Geneva: 2005) 205.

54 *A Letter to the Town, Concerning the Man and the Bottle*. Published anonymously (London, W. Reeve and A. Dodd: 1749) 10.

admiration for the painter. There is no lasting effect, nor any damage. Whether the same applied to the theatre of Macklin, Garrick and Foote was very much part of the debate on illusionist theatre in the 1740s. The author of *A Guide to the Stage* believed that being seduced into experiencing a performance as an actual event was harmful, in the sense that it caused embarrassment to oneself as well as others. Foote clearly disagreed that the experience of theatrical illusion was incompatible with judgement. Even though he does not pay much attention to the audience in his *Treatise on the Passions*, he does make it clear in the book's foreword that he is offering his ideas on 'natural' acting to his readers in order to make them understand what makes a performance so convincing that audiences will forget that they are in the theatre. Foote emphasises that theatrical illusion is an emotional process: if the actor's emotions are credible and realistic, the audience will empathise and see Lear or Hamlet before them, rather than Garrick. This does not mean that Foote has no time for notions like taste and judgement – on the contrary.[55] Foote firmly believes in the development of taste and judgement, but in the theatre, these can be overruled by the spectator's emotional response. When the performance is over, the audience can be 'rationally pleased' by their emotional response to the performance and discuss it with others in terms of which aspects of the performance created this effect.[56] In his juxtaposition of Foote's production and the Great Bottle Hoax, Bickham seems to side with Van Hoogstraten, Dufresnoy and Foote: the audiences that were seduced by the realism of Foote's illusions may have shed a few inelegant tears, but these were soon dried after his performance finished. And more importantly, the theatre was left standing.

The Great Bottle Hoax would be used well into the 1820s to denote gullibility and stupidity in satirical prints but then, like most exposed hoaxes, it quietly slipped away into obscurity and would only sometimes resurface as a literary anecdote. Bickham's print has also largely been forgotten, even though it goes far beyond the 'seek the bottleman' discussions that appeared in the aftermath of the hoax. It engages with a major debate about the theatre at the start of the Age of Garrick and in its elaboration on the mountebank motif, the print connects this discussion to the discourse on artistic illusionism in seventeenth-century paintings, prints, plays and art theory. Bickham's print, however, is in line with the discourse's eighteenth-century turn to the audience

55 Foote Samuel, *A Treatise on the Passions, so Far as They Regard the Stage; with a Critical Enquiry into the Theatrical Merit of Mr. G-k, Mr. Q-n, and Mr. B-y. The First Considered in the Part of Lear, the Two Last Opposed in Othello* (London, C. Corbet: 1747) 8–9.

56 Ibidem, 9.

and contrasts the respective deceptions of Foote and Stanhope on an ethical point. Foote and Stanhope may both have managed to persuade their respective audiences of a deception, but one was offered within an appropriate artistic context, the theatre, and gave its audience pleasure, whereas the other presented its 'giddy Lyes' outside that context and brought nothing but misery. As such, Bickham's image presents a continuation of the tradition that artistic deceit is permissible but parts ways with Goltzius and Dou in its unequivocal condemnation of its mountebank, Stanhope.

Bibliography

Aglionby William, *Painting Illustrated in Three Dialogues* (London, Printed by John Gain for the author: 1685).

Appleton W.W., *Charles Macklin: An Actor's Life* (Cambridge MA: 1960).

Cao M.M., "Trompe L'oeil and Financial Risk in the Age of Paper", *Grey Room* 78 (2020) 6–33.

Clayton T., "George Bickham", in *Oxford Dictionary of National Biography* (Oxford: 2004).

Craske M., *Art in Europe, 1700–1830: A History of the Visual Arts in an Era of Unprecedented Urban Economic Growth* (Oxford: 1997).

"Daily Post" (London), 26 September 1740, *17th–18th Century Burney Collection Newspapers*.

Donohue J., "Introduction: The Theatre from 1660 to 1800", in J. Donahue (ed.), *The Cambridge History of British Theatre: Volume 2, 1660–1895* (Cambridge: 2004) 1–52.

Dufresnoy Charles-Alphonse, *De Arte Graphica*, ed. and trans. C. Allen – Y. Haskell – F. Muecke, Travaux Du Grand Siècle 24 (Geneva: 2005).

During S., *Modern Enchantments: The Cultural Power of Secular Magic* (Cambridge: 2009).

Foakes R.A., "Shakespeare's Elizabethan Stages", in Bate J. – Jackson R. (eds.), *Shakespeare: An Illustrated Stage History* (Oxford: 1996).

Foote Samuel, *A Treatise on the Passions, so Far as They Regard the Stage; with a Critical Enquiry into the Theatrical Merit of Mr. G-k, Mr. Q-n, and Mr. B-y. The First Considered in the Part of Lear, the Two Last Opposed in Othello* (London, C. Corbet: 1747).

"General Advertiser" (London), 15 December 1747, *17th–18th Century Burney Collection Newspapers*.

"General Advertiser" (London), 11 January 1749, *17th–18th Century Burney Collection Newspapers*.

"General Advertiser" (London), 17 January 1749, *17th–18th Century Burney Collection Newspapers*.

"General Advertiser" (London), 18 January, 1749, *17th–18th Century Burney Collection Newspapers*.

Goldring T., "The Greater Fool: Paper, Illusion, and Time in Representations of the South Sea Bubble", *Eighteenth-Century Studies* 54:1 (2020) 53–75.

Gombrich E.H., "'That Rare Italian Master ...' Giulio Romano, Court Architect, Painter and Impresario", in D. Chambers – J. Martineau (eds.), *Splendours of the Gonzaga* (London: 1981) 77–85.

Graves A., *The Society of Artists of Great Britain, 1760–1791, the Free Society of Artists, 1761–1783: a complete dictionary of contributors and their work from the foundation of the societies to 1791* (London: 1907).

A Guide to the Stage: or, Select Instructions and Precedents from the best Authorities towards Forming A Polite Audience; With Some Account of the Players, &c. Published anonymously (London, D. Job and R. Baldwin: 1751).

Hobson M., *The Object of Art: The Theory of Illusion in Eighteenth-Century France* (Cambridge: 1982).

Holland P., "The Age of Garrick", in Bate J. – Jackson R. (eds.), *Shakespeare. An Illustrated Stage History* (Oxford: 1996).

Hoogstraten Samuel van, *Inleyding tot de hooge schoole der schilderkonst: anders de zichtbaere werelt* (Rotterdam, François van Hoogstraten: 1678).

Hylkema J., "The Pleasure of Being Deceived: Spectatorship in the Arts and Other Deceptions in Eighteenth-Century England", *De Achttiende Eeuw* 46:1 (2014) 49–69.

Hylkema J., "The Artist and the Mountebank: Rochester's Alexander Bendo and the Dynamics of Forgery and Illusion in 17th-Century Art", in Becker D. – Fischer A. – Schmitz Y. (eds.), *Faking, Forging, Counterfeiting: Discredited Practices at the Margins of Mimesis* (Bielefeld: 2018) 59–76.

Jonson Ben, *Volpone in The Alchemist and Other Plays*, ed. G. Campbell (Oxford: 1998).

Kelly I., *Mr Foote's Other Leg: Comedy, Tragedy and Murder in Georgian London* (London: 2012).

Leach R., *An Illustrated History of British Theatre and Performance. Volume One – From the Romans to the Enlightenment* (Abingdon – New York: 2019).

A Letter to the Town, Concerning the Man and the Bottle. Published anonymously (London, W. Reeve and A. Dodd: 1749).

Lockwood T., "Fielding and the Licensing Act", *Huntington Library Quarterly* 50:4 (1987) 379–393.

Lovejoy A.O., *Essays in the History of Ideas* (Baltimore – London: 1948).

Lynch J., *Deception and Detection in Eighteenth-Century Britain* (Aldershot: 2008).

A Modest Apology for the Man in the Bottle. By Himself. Published anonymously (London, J. Freeman: 1749).

Nick-all J. (pseudonym), *An Apology to the Town, for himself and the Bottle* (London, B. Dickinson: 1749).

Piles Roger de, *Cours De Peinture Par Principes, Par M. De Piles* (1708; Amsterdam – Leipzig, Arkstée & Merkus: 1766).

Place Pierre-Antoine de la, *Le Théâtre Anglois*, Tome I (London, [n.p.], 1746).

Richardson Jonathan, *An Essay on the Theory of Painting. By Mr. Richardson. The Second Edition, Enlarg'd, and Corrected* (London, Printed for A.C. and sold by A. Bettesworth: 1725).

Shakespeare William, *The Winter's Tale*, ed. J. Pitcher, Bloomsbury Arden Shakespeare, third series (London: 2010).

Traudenius Dirk, *Rijmbundel* (Amsterdam, Gerrit van Goedesberg: 1662).

Vasari Giorgio, *The Lives of the Most Eminent Painters, Sculptors and Architects*, Volume VI, trans. G. du C. De Vere (London: 1913).

Walsh W.S., *Handy-book of Literary Curiosities* (Philadelphia: 1893).

Weststeijn T., "The Sublime and the 'Beholder's Share': Junius, Rubens, Rembrandt", *Journal of Historians of Netherlandish Art* 8:2 (Summer 2016) [no page numbers].

CHAPTER 12

Counterfeiting Coins and Convict Transportation from England to Australia in the Eighteenth Century

Helen Hughes

> It has been said that 'a coin is a metallic record of the environment in which it was issued, reflecting the ethics, sociology, and economics of its time'. If this be true of coins, then it is doubly so in regard to commemorative medals.
>
> W.J. MIRA

•••

> In criminology as in economics there is scarcely a more powerful word than 'capital'.
>
> PETER LINEBAUGH

1 Origins

All art histories require an origin. National art histories are no different.[1] In order to take a coherent shape and character, each national art history must identify a point and place in time from which the rest evolves, or can be said to be history. Typically, national histories of Australian art identify either one of two dates as their year one: 1770, the year Captain Cook 'discovered' the eastern coast of the continent we now call Australia; or 1788, the year Governor Arthur Phillip arrived with the First Fleet to establish the penal colony of

1 The author wishes to acknowledge the research assistance of Dr Julia Lomas; the specialist advice on numismatics given by Peter Lane and Sim Comfort; colleagues Philip Brophy and Zoë de Luca, who proofread this chapter; and editors Matilda Amundsen Bergström and Philip Lavender.

 | DOI:10.1163/9789004106901_013

New South Wales. (And this despite the fact that the various colonies were not federated as an Australian nation until 1901.) In recent decades, in step with an increasingly widespread acknowledgement of Indigenous sovereignty and custodianship prior to colonisation, a significant effort has been made to push the origin back some 60,000 years as a result of important attempts to decolonise the discipline and recognise the long history of Indigenous artistic practice on this continent. Of course, there is no one inaugural date but many, each generating its own canon and mode of historiography.

In the more typical, Anglocentric treatment of 1788 as a kind of year one of Australian art, there is one artwork that clearly stands out as being the 'first' and which is commonly referred to as such. It is a silver medal made on board the convict transport the *Charlotte*, one of the eleven ships comprising the First Fleet which sailed from England to establish the first penal colony of New South Wales in Australia, arriving in January 1788. *The Charlotte Medal*, as the artwork has come to be known, is believed to have been engraved in the six days that the fleet was anchored at Botany Bay, before sailing up the coast to Sydney Cove for disembarkation on more prosperous land – the unceded, custodial land of the Gadigal people of the Eora nation. The medal is therefore synchronous with the moment of invasion, which is celebrated/mourned on the 26th of January each year since 1788, and thus synonymous with the origins of settler Australian art history.[2]

As a prospective origin for Australian art history, *The Charlotte Medal* is a provocative one. First of all, its presumptive artist was no hero in the national imagination – no Jacques-Louis David parading an icon of political martyr Marat through the streets of revolutionary Paris.[3] Quite the opposite: its artist was a convict, a genre of Australian pioneer that was feverishly repressed in the

2 *The Charlotte Medal* had existed in relative obscurity for some 220 years until it was sold at auction in 2008 by a Melbourne dentist and numismatic collector John Chapman to the Australian National Maritime Museum for 750,000 AUD. Perhaps on account of its only recent unearthing, *The Charlotte Medal* has not been included in the major historical surveys of Australian art – such as Bernard Smith and Alwynne Wheeler's 1988 *The Art of the First Fleet*, or Smith's canonical *Place, Taste, and Tradition: Australian Art since 1788* of 1945, both of which focus on drawings made by convicts and naval draughtsmen in the early years of settlement. The only major historical survey to properly install *The Charlotte Medal* at the beginning of settler-colonial Australian art is Lesley Carlisle's *Australian Commemorative Medals and Medalets from 1788* of 1983, which may point to a disciplinary blindspot in art history that has resulted in the marginalisation of numismatics and the decorative arts.

3 Art historian Zoë de Luca also refers to this essay in her analysis of colonial Australian art in her as yet unpublished Ph.D. thesis in Art History & Communication studies at McGill University, Montreal, as well as in her unpublished manuscript *Methodology for a Move. From Canon to Port: Returning European Vision with Richard Bell's* ... no tin shack ... (*2019*) from 2021.

national consciousness for well over a century.[4] Moreover, the medal's artist, Thomas Barrett, was not just your humdrum pickpocket (though he was that, too). Rather, he was a convict who had participated in a serious act of mutiny and who had racked up not one, nor two, but three death sentences during his short life. Secondly, *The Charlotte Medal* is comparable in shape, size, medium, and skillset with a coin, and was in fact made by a convict artist who participated in the forgery racket – specifically, the racket of 'coining' (counterfeiting coins). Barrett was discovered spending forged coins on board the *Charlotte* just a few months prior to producing *The Charlotte Medal*. Yet where his 'queer coins' were intended for circulation and exchange, the medal was, we shall see, a personal memento. All of which leads to the third key point: that *The Charlotte Medal*, as the first colonial Australian artwork, inaugurates a particular entanglement between early settler art in Australia and the crime of forgery in England. As we shall see, a large proportion of early settler art in Australia was made by convicted forgers. Ironically, or perhaps appositely for the antipodes, what was a crime in England became the basis for Western art on the Australian continent. On first impression, this entanglement is suggestive because forgery – a crime that pivots around binaries of original and copy, legitimate and illegitimate – resonates loudly throughout many aspects of colonial Australian history and national identity, and especially so in the settler tradition of Australian art history, where anxieties over cultural authenticity and originality have been dominant for decades.[5]

Unlike in modern Australia, however, in eighteenth-century England forgery strongly connoted a gallows death, as an 1819 satirical banknote by George Cruickshank makes clear [Fig. 12.1]. It is this historical entanglement, between forgery and capital punishment, that I attend to in this essay in an effort to unspool the legal context that troubles as it originates the canon of Australian art.[6] A closer look at the criminal context of forgery in colonial Australian

4 For a useful introduction to this phenomenon known as 'the convict stain', see Frost L., "The Politics of Writing Convict Lives: Academic Research, State Archives, and Family History", *Life Writing* 8:1 (2011) 19–33.

5 See, for example: chapter one of McLean I., *White Aborigines: Identity Politics in Australian Art* (Cambridge: 1998) 1–16; Taylor P., *POPISM*, exhibition catalogue (Melbourne: 1982); Taylor P., "Popism: The Art of White Aborigines", *Flash Art* 112 (1983) 48–50; Foss P., "Theatrum Nondum Cogitorium", *The Foreign Bodies Papers* (Sydney: 1981) 15–38; Smith T., "The Provincialism Problem", *Artforum* 13:1 (1974) 54–59; and Butler R., "Introduction", in *What is Appropriation? An Anthology of Critical Writings on Australian Art in the '80s and '90s* (Sydney – Brisbane: 1996) 13–48.

6 To clarify my use of terminology, I use the English term Australia (from the Latin terms *terra Australis*, southern land), and the dates 1770 and 1788, to refer to the settler-colony nation of Australia (not the continent it has only recently come to describe) and its art histories.

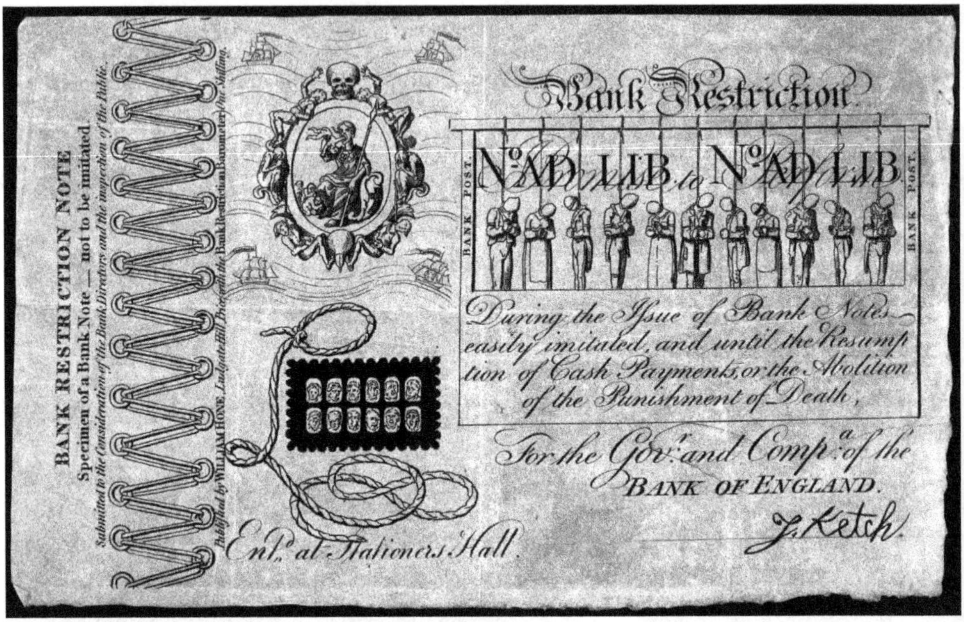

FIGURE 12.1 George Cruickshank, *Bank Restriction Note*, 1819. Etching on paper, 124 × 195 mm
IMAGE © BRITISH MUSEUM

art complements the aesthetic and cultural frameworks of forgery that have dominated settler Australian art history to date by revealing legal anxieties over the very conception of an origin as being fixed, legible, and determinant. As Sara Malton shows in her analysis of forgery plots in nineteenth-century English novels, the crime of forgery is best understood as a twin of bastardy – the begetting of illegitimate children.[7] She reminds us that eighteenth-century forgery law did not merely persecute forgers of financial instruments, like banknotes and coins, but forgers of birth certificates, wills, marriage documents, and powers of attorney, too.[8] Thus, forgery in eighteenth-century England is equally concerned with capital as it is with personal identity and patrilineal structures of inheritance – all of which is crucial for understanding the origins of settler Australian art as premised upon the illegal British invasion and occupation of sovereign Aboriginal land.

Lastly, awareness of the changing nature of money in eighteenth-century England, the likes of which facilitated widespread acts of forgery, allows us to

7 Malton S., *Forgery in Nineteenth-Century Literature and Culture: Fictions of Finance from Dickens to Wilde* (London: 2009) 6.
8 Ibidem, 6.

recast the origins of settler Australian art historiography. As we shall see, the eighteenth-century English economy was increasingly dependent on credit and paper notes that were materially – and seemingly magically – removed from metallurgic value. In step with this shift, Malton writes, economic relationships came to be marked by their intangibility and anonymity, as financial transactions became an increasingly 'remote' or 'distant' phenomenon.[9] Following the Financial Revolution in England, capital began to circulate in a vast network that was increasingly global in scope. This roaming, transnational, financial framework is useful for glimpsing what is, ultimately, a more useful method for historicising Australian art of this period than the prevailing national frameworks.

2 Thomas Barrett and *The Charlotte Medal*

In September 1782, a twenty-six-year-old Englishman named Thomas Barrett (born *c.* 1758) was tried before Justice Ashhurst at Justice Hall in the Old Bailey in London for stealing a silver watch, a steel chain, a watch key, a hook, two shirts, and one shift from a woman named Ann Milton on 20 July 1782.[10] With the British court system then in the full grips of the Bloody Code, Barrett was found guilty of this petty crime and sentenced to death.[11] In a display of patrimony that was not uncommon amongst British judges of the eighteenth century, however, Barrett's sentence was duly commuted to transportation for life (that is, fourteen years).[12] At this point in time, a sentence of transportation meant being shipped as a convict to a penal colony in America. For Barrett, it would be the colony of Virginia. So, in March 1784, he left Dover as a prisoner on the *Mercury* on the transatlantic voyage to Virginia, where, as Philip McCouat has explained, convicts could expect: 'to be marched to the auction block, still in chains, and auctioned off, usually as field workers on plantations.

9 Malton, *Forgery in Nineteenth-Century Literature and Culture* 4.

10 Hosty K., "The Charlotte Medal", *Signals Journal* 84 (2008) 12.

11 The Bloody Code is the retrospective nomenclature used to describe this period of British criminal legal history, which saw the profound reification of property as against the devaluation of human life – namely, the proliferation of death penalty.

12 Hay D., "Property, Authority, and the Criminal Law", in Hay D. – Linebaugh P. – Rule J. – Thompson E.P. – Winslow C. (eds.), *Albion's Fatal Tree: Crime and Society in Eighteenth-Century England* (New York: 1975) 17–63.

Their status hover[ing] somewhere above slaves and below white servants'.[13] Some resistance to this fate could thus be expected.

On the morning of 8 April 1784, due west of St Mary's on the West India Rocks (nearby the Scilly Islands southwest of Cornwall) and just days into the journey, a large group of convicts mutinied with the assistance of the first mate of the ship, who supplied them with a 'brace of pistols and two blunderbusses'.[14] Ultimately overpowering the captain and crew after an hour-long struggle, during which three crewmates were mortally wounded, the convicts proceeded to load the captain and remaining crew up with iron manacles and head towards Torbay, on the south-west coast of England. Fifty-five convicts were recaptured several days later by the *Helena* as they were rowing to land. Some of the convicts made it to Devon, while others, including Barrett, made it significantly further – as far as Plymouth, Bristol, and London – before they, too, were recaptured. The convicts deemed most responsible for the mutiny, including Barrett, were summonsed before a court at the Old Bailey. Barrett was again sentenced to death, but again reprieved – this time on account of his having supposedly 'intervened to save the life of the *Mercury*'s steward, and prevented another mutineer from cutting off the captain's ear with scissors'.[15] He was held in a prison hulk, the *Dunkirk*, on the Thames until a suitable arrangement could be determined.

Just a few years on from Barrett's original trial and sentencing in 1782, the American Revolutionary War (1775–1783) in the American colonies was escalating. At its outset, England was obliged to halt sending its convicts to the New World, and instead warehoused them in prison hulks anchored along the Thames, as well as at Portsmouth, Plymouth, Cork, and Dublin.[16] It was not until August 1786 that the British Government settled on the idea of establishing a penal colony at Botany Bay on the south-east coast of Australia – it having been claimed for the British Crown by Cook in 1770 – that a destination for these convicts was properly tabled. Thus, in March 1787, Barrett boarded the two-decked, three-masted, barque the *Charlotte*, which was one of eleven ships comprising the First Fleet – three store ships, six convict ships (of which the *Charlotte* was one), and two war ships responsible for escorting the fleet

13 McCouat P., "Colonial Artist, Thief, Forger and Mutineer: Thomas Barrett's Amazing Career", *Journal of Art in Society* (2015), http://www.artinsociety.com/colonial-artist-thief-forger-and-mutineer-thomas-barretts-amazing-career.html/.

14 Cuneen M., "The Mercury Mutineers: Biographical Analyses of Early Australian Convicts", *People Australia, National Centre of Biography* (Canberra: 2021), https://peopleaustralia.anu.edu.au/essay/24/text38996.

15 Hosty, "The Charlotte Medal" 12.

16 Ibidem, 11.

(H.M.S. *Sirius* and H.M.S. *Supply*). In embarking on this voyage, Barrett became one of over 700 first-generation convicts to be sent to the new penal colony under the authority of Governor Phillip.[17]

The journey of the First Fleet from Spithead, where all eleven ships were assembled in May 1787, to Botany Bay took over eight months, including stopo vers in Tenerife, Rio De Janeiro, and Cape Town in order for the ships to resupply and rest their crews.[18] To the incredulity of the *Charlotte*'s officials, in Rio de Janeiro Barrett was discovered trying to buy food using forged coins, which he is believed to have somehow struck while aboard the ship. The Surgeon General of the First Fleet, John White, who travelled with Barrett on board the *Charlotte*, describes the revelation in his journal entry of 5 August 1787:

> This morning a boat came along side, in which were three Portugueze and six slaves, from whom we purchased some oranges, plantains, and bread. In trafficking with these people, we discovered that one Thomas Barret, a convict, had, with great ingenuity and address, passed some quarter dollars which he, assisted by two others, had coined out of old buckles, buttons belonging to the marines, and pewter spoons, during their passage from Teneriffe.[19]

As Kieran Hosty has noted, it would have been immensely difficult forging these coins at sea with minimal light under deck, against the rocking waves, without access to tools, nor forge, nor dies.[20] Moreover, and as Sim Comfort pointed out when reading a draft of this paper, Barrett would not have had access to a flame to melt these items down below deck (though the cook would have in the kitchen).[21] He could have struck coins if he had the dies; but it is more likely that he smuggled the readymade coins on board.

There are a handful of other contenders who may have engraved the medal, including a jeweller named John Penny who travelled as a convict on the *Friendship*.[22] It is also possible that one of the First Fleet sailors engraved the

---

17 Bateson C., *The Convict Ships* (Sydney – London: 1974) 115.

18 Ibidem, 114–115.

19 White John, *Journal of a Voyage to New South Wales with Sixty-five Plates of Non descript Animals Birds Lizards Serpents curious Cones of Trees and other Natural Productions* (London, J. Debrett Piccadilly: 1790) 70.

20 Hosty, "The Charlotte Medal" 12.

21 Sim Comfort, email to the author, September 6, 2021.

22 See Shofield A. – Fahy K., *Australian Jewellery: Late Nineteenth and Early Twentieth Century* (Balmain: 1990) 10; and Field M., "Introduction", in Field M. – Millett T. (eds.), *Convict Love Tokens: The Leaden Hearts Convicts Left Behind* (Adelaide: 1998) 1–4:3. Aboard the First Fleet there were several other possible candidates as makers of *The Charlotte Medal*. In

medal, as they would all have had access to medicinal silver crockery as well as strong needles for repairing clothes and sailcloth. Though Hosty, a curator at the National Maritime Museum which acquired the medal in 2008, notes that several inaccurate aspects of the depiction of the *Charlotte* suggest a landsman's eye, not a sailor's.[23] For now, at least, the Maritime Museum along with a host of Australian numismatists, including leading authorities Leslie Carlisle and Peter Lane, accredit it to Barrett.[24]

Whether Barrett made the forged coins or simply spent them is in some ways besides the point as English criminal law at this time did not discriminate between makers and spenders or 'utterers' of counterfeit coins – both acts were considered forgery under the same criminal statute. That forgery should have occurred on board the *Charlotte* is not surprising given that the crime ran rampant in eighteenth-century England. Indeed, Randall McGowan has described forgery as '*the* quintessential offense of the long eighteenth century'.[25] Once the penal colonies of New South Wales and Van Diemen's Land (modern-day Tasmania) were established in Australia, forgery quickly emerged there too as one of the main criminal offences (alongside theft, drunkenness, and absconding).[26]

Forgery crimes proliferated in eighteenth-century England in part due to the rapid transition that the English economy was undertaking away from a system based on an inherent metallurgic worth (i.e. that of tin, copper, silver, or gold) to a 'fiduciary' system based on trust and the exchange of paper instruments (such as cheques, promissory notes, wills, deeds, and bonds), which were more easily forged than metal coins.[27] This transition from a metallic to a paper economy also led to a change in profile of the criminal forger. Acts

---

addition to a journeyman watchmaker, and a watch case and watch chain maker, there was a jeweller named John Penny that both Shofield, Fahy and Field each believe is responsible for *The Charlotte Medal*. Coincidentally, Penny was one of the mutineers that acted alongside Barrett en route to Virginia on the *Mercury*. However, he travelled to New South Wales on the *Friendship*, where he is less likely to have encountered John White.

23 Hosty, "The Charlotte Medal" 12.

24 Lane P., "Australia's First Medallion: Silver Charlotte Metal", *Collectables Trader* (2008); and Carlisle L., *Australian Commemorative Medals and Medalets from 1788* (New South Wales: 1983) 1.

25 McGowan R., "Making the 'Bloody Code?' Forgery Legislation in Eighteenth-Century England", in Landau N. (ed.), *Law, Crime and English Society* (Cambridge: 2002) 119. Emphasis added.

26 Hackforth-Jones J., *The Convict Artists* (Melbourne – Sydney: 1977) 10.

27 See Baines P., *The House of Forgery in Eighteenth-Century Britain* (Vermont: 1999) 12; see also chapter one, "Clipped Coins", of Caffenezis C.G., *Clipped Coins, Abused Words, and Civil Governments: John Locke's Philosophy of Money* (New York: 1989).

of coin clipping and counterfeiting were typically undertaken by members of the working-class who had skills in metalwork and access to the relevant materials, tools, and machinery, and who, by defrauding banks, could be said to distribute financial loss across society.[28] The proliferation of paper instruments, by contrast, led to the rise of the white collar forger who defrauded his or her associates by forging their signatures on promissory notes, deeds, wills, or bonds. This white-collar expression of forgery has led Paul Baines to label their crime 'bourgeois' in the sense that it defrauded individuals, and often those who were already well-known to the forger.[29] Across the arc of the long eighteenth century, then, forgery crimes went from posing a threat to the sovereignty of money (and thereby the state), to posing a threat to the concept of personal identity itself.[30] This destabilisation of identity was at the root of the acute moral panic that forgery induced in the English population during the eighteenth century, and forms part of the historical backdrop against which so many forgers were convicted and sentenced either to death or transportation.[31]

This genealogical framework of forgery is also useful for understanding why nineteenth-century Australian settlers tried, from shame, to destroy evidence of their convict ancestors; and why, much later around the bicentennial, settlers tried – this time from white guilt – to invent some.[32] To further think genealogy and coins together here, just briefly, it is also interesting to consider the colonial term 'currency', which described non-official, illegitimate currencies circulating in the colonial economy, and quickly became slang to describe native-born white Australians. This was against the term 'sterling', which referred to the official British denomination used in the colonies, and also to British-born settlers. 'Currency', of course, flipped from being pejorative to a strategic political form of self-identification for native-born whites by the mid-nineteenth century.[33]

Summoned to defend the authority of the economy, which was becoming increasingly reliant on credit, English criminal law made forgery a capital offence in the 1690s, around the time that the Bank of England was established

28 Baines, *House of Forgery* 22.

29 Ibidem, 22.

30 Ibidem, 14.

31 McGowan R., "Forgers and Forgery: Severity and Social Identity in Eighteenth-Century England", in Lemings, D. – Walker, C. (eds.), *Moral Panics, the Media, and the Law in Early Modern England* (London: 2009) 157–175.

32 Barnwell A., "Convict Shame to Convict Chic: Intergenerational Memory and Family Histories", *Memory Studies* 12:4 (August 2019) 398–411.

33 Molony J.N., *The Native Born: The First White Australians* (Melbourne: 2000) 25–26.

in 1694. The wide-reaching 1729 Forgery Statute, which has been described as 'sweeping and general, rather than narrow and specific', expanded the range of forgery offences that were punishable by death even further.[34] McGowan has noted that, by some estimates, forgery accounted for a third of all capital legislation in this period.[35] V.A.C. Gatrell writes that a full 'fifth of English executions between 1805 and 1818 were for forgery, and mostly brought by the Bank of England for forgery of banknotes'.[36] Of course, death sentences also applied to cases of theft where the stolen goods in question were valued at or above 40 shillings. But juries famously intervened in many such cases: *viz.*, the phenomenon of juries deliberately undervaluing stolen goods to avoid sending defendants to the gallows.[37] Such clemency was impossible to exercise in forgery cases, however, given that the value of forgeries was determined by the highly specific paper instruments or coins in evidence on trial. The inflexibility of the application of the death penalty in forgery cases thus led to a number of high-profile executions (including that of the clergyman William Dodd, who was hanged in 1777) and thus public outrage over this particularly, and indiscriminately, bloodthirsty statute.

Death sentences for forgery cases could be, and often were, however, commuted to transportation for life. Thus, many forgers were transported to the penal colonies in Australia. Here, convicts readily found work as artists – whether that entailed working in public postings for the government, or working as indentured servants privately for individuals. Working-class convict forgers often built artistic practices on the basis of their practical experience (i.e. as chinaware painters, or coach and chaise painters, such as Joseph Lycett). Middle- and upper-class convicts developed artistic careers on account of the more ornamental educations they had enjoyed, which may have included an introduction to drawing and painting (consider here the convict artist Thomas Griffiths Wainewright, who had studied at the Royal Academy). Skills in mimesis and reproduction (requisite for both forgery and much art of this period) may also have been a contributing factor towards an artistic practice in the colonies. Thus, what was a crime in England became a foundation stone for Western art on the Australian continent – appositely referred to by Europeans

34 McGowan R., "From Pillory to Gallows: The Punishment of Forgery in the Age of the Financial Revolution", *Past & Present* 165 (1999) 109.

35 McGowan, "Making the 'Bloody Code'" 119.

36 Gatrell V.A.C., *The Hanging Tree: Execution and the English People 1770–1868* (Oxford: 1994) 188, cited in Malton *Forgery in Nineteenth-Century Literature and Culture* 2.

37 Hay, "Property, Authority, and the Criminal Law" 17–63.

as 'the Antipodes' (from *anti-* meaning opposite and *podes* meaning foot), that foreign and backwards landmass located at the opposite end of the earth.

3 Forgery and Colonial Australian Art

As for the origins of settler-colonial Australian art, most of it was made by convicts. Jocelyn Hackforth-Jones, in what remains the only major overview of the convict art of Australia, asserts that the

> history of art in New South Wales and Van Diemen's Land during the first half century of settlement is essentially the history of convict art. The convicts were the only coherent group of artists to record the appearance, growth and progress of the two colonies from settlement to civilisation.[38]

The distinguished historian of Australian art, Ian McLean, concurs: 'Most colonial artists – or at least those employed to provide the cultural capital of the colony – were convicts'.[39] But it was not just convict artists generally, but convicted forger artists specifically who were undertaking this work. As we shall see, most of the convict art made in the penal colonies in the early decades of settlement was by forgers.

Consider the following. During the period of convict transportation, the artists Thomas Watling, Joseph Lycett, Francis Greenway, Thomas Griffiths Wainewright, George Edward Peacock, Joseph Backler, Knud Bull, Jacob Josephson, and James Walsh were all transported to the penal colonies for forging notes, cheques, or legal documents. Richard Read Senior was found guilty of uttering forged five-pound notes, which is a different offense to forging the notes himself, though it fell under the same criminal act (the 1729 Forgery Statute). John William Lancashire was transported for an unspecified crime, but soon after arriving in Sydney in 1798 was tried for forgery – so it is possible that his original conviction was for forgery too. Likewise, William Buelow Gould was transported for theft in 1827, but in 1839 was sentenced to three years at the Port Macquarie penal settlement for forgery. Charles Henry Theodore Costantini was transported for larceny, but later claimed his original conviction was for forgery; recent research by Andrew Morris supports the

38 Hackforth-Jones, *The Convict Artists* 10.

39 McLean I., "Convict Art and Cultural Capital: The Case of Thomas Watling", unpublished conference paper for "Colonial Places, Convict Spaces: Penal Transportation in Global Context, c. 1600–1940" (Leicester: 1999).

theory that Costantini was involved in the forgery racket.[40] And as we have seen, Barrett was initially transported to the colonies in America for theft, then to New South Wales for mutiny, but was discovered spending bad coins aboard the *Charlotte* during the stopover in Rio de Janeiro. By contrast, there is but a small handful of other significant convict artists who fall outside the forgery category. These include Thomas Bock (convicted for administering an abortifacient to a young woman whom he had impregnated), Charles Rodius (theft), John Eyre (housebreaking), William Dowling (an Irish rebel and political prisoner), Walter Preston (highway robbery), and Fred Strange (theft); and a smaller handful still whose crimes are unspecified: William Harrison Craig, T.R. Brown (who is presumed to be a convict, though precious little is known about him), and Philip Slaeger.

If we broaden our art-historical lens to consider numismatic objects like *The Charlotte Medal*, which are often excluded from art historical accounts, we see, further, that the convicted coin forger William Henshall was transported to Sydney during the Macquarie era (1810–1821), and was here compelled to manufacture the first official Australian currency – the Holey Dollar and Dump.[41] The Irish engraver and freemason Samuel Clayton was convicted of forgery and transported to New South Wales in 1816, where he subsequently enjoyed a successful career as a portrait painter, engraver, and silversmith, also being responsible for engraving the first Australian banknote.[42] The Birmingham engraver and talented die-sinker James Grove was discovered in 1802 to have engraved a set of plates for counterfeit Bank of England notes. He was arrested, and sent to Newgate before being sentenced to death at the Warwick Assizes in March 1802. His sentence was commuted to transportation, and in April 1803 he left for New South Wales on the H.M.S. *Calcutta* where, amongst many other remarkable achievements during his life in the colony, he cut stamps for the issue of government bills.[43] Thus, we may say with some confidence that the majority of convict artists working in the early years of settlement were convicted of, or closely connected to, forgery crimes – forgery being the defining crime of eighteenth-century English life, and thus also that of early colonial

40 Morris A., "Charles Henry Theodore Costantini: Convict, Surgeon, Artist, and Forger", *Australiana* 25:3 (2002).

41 Lane P. – Fleig P., "William Henshall: Maker of Holy Dollars and Dumps", *Journal of the Numismatic Association of Australia* 15 (2004) 1–30.

42 Smith M., *Samuel Clayton: Forger, Freemason, Freeman* (Melbourne: 2017).

43 Earnshaw J., "Grove, James (1769–1810)", *Australian Dictionary of Biography, National Centre of Biography, Australian National University*, https://adb.anu.edu.au/biography/grove-james-2132/text2705.

Australia. In empirical terms, then, settler Australian art was, right from its inception, inextricably entwined with the crime of forgery.

As there were no prison buildings extant in New South Wales at the moment of British invasion, convicts were not imprisoned, as such, but made to work: either as indentured labourers on public works (i.e. clearing roads, constructing buildings) or they were assigned as servants to individuals, who paid for their upkeep in exchange for the free labour provided by the government (i.e. by the convict). For example, the aforementioned Watling, often referred to as the first professional artist to arrive in Sydney, was assigned as a convict servant to Surgeon General John White in an arrangement that saw Watling produce hundreds of drawings for White, over 500 of which are now held in the British Museum. But before he encountered Watling, who arrived in New South Wales in 1792, White appears to have put Barrett to work as an indentured artist on the *Charlotte*. For reasons that remain unknown to us, White believed that Barrett had forged the counterfeit coins on board the *Charlotte* (as opposed to having smuggled them aboard) and was thoroughly impressed with his achievement, as White's oft-cited 5 August journal entry explains:

> The impression, milling, character, in a word, the whole was so inimitably executed that had their metal been a little better the fraud, I am convinced, would have passed undetected. A strict and careful search was made for the apparatus wherewith this was done, but in vain; not the smallest trace or vestige of any thing of the kind was to be found among them. How they managed this business without discovery, or how they could effect it at all, is a matter of inexpressible surprise to me, as they never were suffered to come near a fire and a centinel was constantly placed over their apartments. Besides, hardly ten minutes ever elapsed, without an officer of some degree or other going down among them. The adroitness, therefore, with which they must have managed, in order to complete a business that required so complicated a process, gave me a high opinion of their ingenuity, cunning, caution, and address; and I could not help wishing that these qualities had been employed to more laudable purposes.[44]

In desiring employment of Barrett's skills in metal work and mimesis towards 'more laudable purposes', White's journal reflection is indicative of the extractive attitude of the colonial project more broadly, which saw convict labour (like sovereign Aboriginal land) as a natural resource to be exploited to the

44 White, *Journal of a Voyage* 70–71.

most productive ends. Indeed, the settler-colonial nation of Australia was in large part built on the skilled labour of the approximately 163,000 convicts transported there over the almost century-long period of transportation (1778–1868). Quickly after the forgery incident in Rio de Janeiro, White conjured a 'more laudable' exercise for Barrett's skills. To wit, White commissioned Barrett to engrave a silver medal that would commemorate the landing of the First Fleet at its destination in Botany Bay in January 1778.

It is important to note here, as Australian numismatist Peter Lane stated in a 2008 article, that while casting and striking (the techniques used to counterfeit coins) and engraving (that used on *The Charlotte Medal*) are different skillsets, many silversmiths possessed both. And it is possible that Barrett, though precious little is known about his life prior to his first conviction, was a silversmith in possession of these skills. A few weeks before the Ann Milton theft, writes Lane,

> a Thomas Barrett got off a charge at the Old Bailey for stealing a silver waiter, two silver sauce spoons, a silver wine strainer and a silver stand. If this was the same man, and if in fact he did steal the goods and was a silversmith, he could have easily melted them down and made other objects from them thus hiding their [stolen] identity.[45]

While there is no maker's mark or signature that links *The Charlotte Medal* incontrovertibly to Barrett, a range of curators and numismatists have attributed the work to Barrett based on the following factors [Fig. 12.2].[46] First, White exalts Barrett's silversmithing talent in his journal entry. Secondly, White and Barrett were both stowed on the *Charlotte*, and the occupants of this ship had a considerable amount of time to kill during the six days spent at anchorage at Botany Bay, before the Fleet moved up the coast to Port Jackson – precisely the window of time to which the medal is dated. John Chapman, the medal's erstwhile owner, surmised that: 'The work must have been completed prior to disembarkation, because there would have been no time allowed for such frivolity while the new settlement was being established'.[47] Thirdly, the medium of *The Charlotte Medal* is silver, of a kind used in the production of surgical kidney dishes, which White would certainly have had amongst his medical

45 Lane P., "Australia's First Medallion".

46 Carlisle L., *Australian Commemorative Medals* 1.

47 Chapman J., "The Solution of the Charlotte Enigma", *Journal of the Numismatic Association of Australia* 9 (1998) 29.

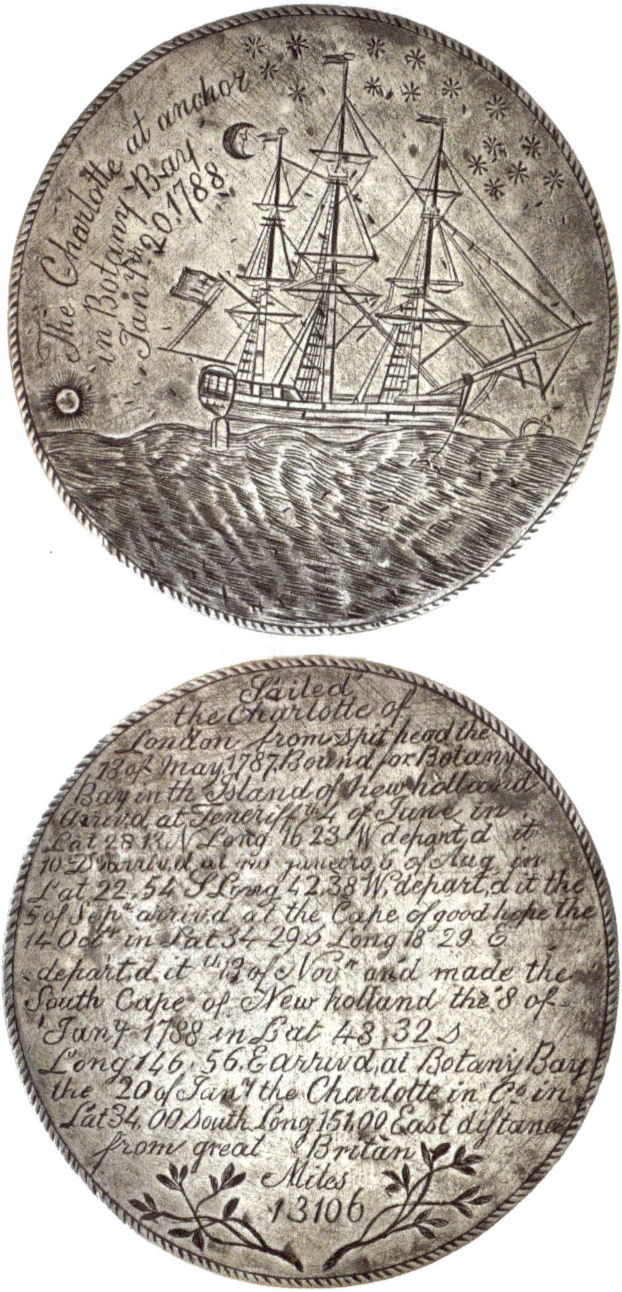

FIGURE 12.2 Thomas Barrett, *The Charlotte Medal*, 1788. Silver, 74 mm (diameter). Sydney, Australian National Maritime Museum Collection purchased with the assistance of the Australian Government through the National Cultural Heritage Account
IMAGE ©AUSTRALIAN NATIONAL MARITIME MUSEUM COLLECTION

possessions on board the *Charlotte* as Surgeon General and could have given to Barrett.

That the medal was made on water, not on land, is of further significance to the question of national Australian art history. As Lane remarked in an email to me, it is technically inaccurate to describe *The Charlotte Medal* as the 'first' colonial artwork because it was made in the days *prior* to disembarkation at Sydney Cove – that is, invasion proper.[48] However, Ian McLean would posit that the medal's waterbirth is precisely what makes it 'Australian'. In his book *White Aborigines: Identity Politics in Australian Art*, McLean convincingly argues that non-Indigenous Australian cultural identity is born of ocean, not of land: its identity is 'founded in negativity rather than positivity, in migration rather than indigeneity'.[49]

The medal itself is 74 mm wide. It is hand-engraved, as opposed to cast or struck from a die, meaning that the medal is a singular, not multiple, object. The obverse depicts the *Charlotte* at anchor in swelling water engraved with a steady hatching technique. The sun is shown low in the sky, just above the horizon in the left, while a waxing, crescent moon embellished with a face sits further up. In the upper right is a scattering of sixteen ornamental stars – none of which resemble known constellations.[50] Chapman interprets this combination of imagery as simply denoting the passing of time.[51] The ship itself is conveyed with basic accuracy, though (likely due to the small amount of space in which the scene can unfold) the decks of the *Charlotte* are shown as empty – this despite the fact that they would have been 'woefully overcrowded', packed full, as they were, with livestock alongside the various human cargo.[52] To the left of this scene, in an elegant cursive script, the following caption is given: 'The Charlotte at anchor in Botany Bay Jany. th 20, 1788'.

Small enough to fit in the palm of one's hand, *The Charlotte Medal* nevertheless opens onto the vast expanse of Empire in the form of a description of the nautical route of the ship's journey – the path taken from Spithead to Botany Bay. In this way, the medal very much figures forth the ontology of a coin,

48 Lane P., email to the author, 10 June 2021.

49 McLean, *White Aborigines* 7.

50 Hosty has argued that the while the ship is a 'fair representation of its type,' aspects of its depiction 'suggest a landsman's and not a sailor's eye' – most noticeably, the fact that the anchor defies gravity, the ship rides to a considerable swell despite it being sheltered while anchored at Botany Bay, and the fact that the stars eschew any identifiable constellations. Hosty, "The Charlotte Medal" 13–14.

51 Chapman, "The Enigma" 29.

52 Bateson, *The Convict Ships* 98.

which is defined by its circulation, travel, and trade. Besides a minor botanical embellishment, the reverse side is text only, being inscribed:

> Sailed the Charlotte of London from Spit Head the 13 of May 1787. Bound for Botany Bay in the Island of New Holland arriv'd at Teneriff the 4th June in Lat 28.13N Long 42.38 W depart'd it 10 arriv'd at Rio Janeiro 6 of Aug in Lat 22.54 S Long 42.38 W depart'd it the 5 Sept arriv'd at the Cape of Good Hope for 14 Octr in Lat 34.29 Lon S 18.29 E depart'd it the 13 of Novr and made the South Cape of New Holland the 8 of Jany 1788 in Lat 43.32 S Long 146.56E arrived Botany Bay the 20 Jany the Charlotte in Co in Lat 34.00 South Long 151.00 East distance from Great Britain miles 13106.

The inscription's enumeration of longitudinal and latitudinal coordinates dissects the globe into a knowable, mappable entity. 'Bound for Botany Bay', a phrase enshrined in so many popular convict ballads of the period, implies a sense of destination and destiny: in White's case, an intrepid new horizon; for those of the convicts who sung the ballads, the dire fate of exile and social death.[53] The final phrase of the inscription, 'distance from Great Britain miles 13106', locks the two sites – Great Britain and New South Wales – into imperial union, synthesising the opposing hemispheres in a manner befitting a two-sided coin.

Another version of *The Charlotte Medal* was discovered in the early 1940s during the renovation of a house in Camden Town, New South Wales, which is believed to have been engraved by the same hand [Fig. 12.3].[54] Made from a disk of inferior-quality copper metal, just a millimetre thick, the copper version is a much-battered specimen replete with holes. It is almost half the size of the silver version at 47 mm in diameter, and contains an abbreviated inscription of the nautical route: 'Holland Jany/ th 8. 1788 in Lat 43.32/S Long 146.56 E arriv'd/ at Botany Bay th 20 of Jany/ in Lat 34. South/ Long 151 East Distance/

53 Anderson H., *Farewell to Judges and Juries: The Broadside Ballad and Convict Transportation to Australia, 1788–1868* (Melbourne: 2000).

54 In her study of drawings from the First Fleet, Louise Anemaat has explained that exchanging and copying was '[t]he common practice before mechanical reproduction.' Not considered an intellectual property breach as it may be today, copying was then considered a valid way of circulating imagery, of 'responding to the fascination of the new,' and of servicing the desire of collectors for new knowledge. Copies also, at their most basic level, functioned as an insurance against loss. As the bronze *Charlotte Medal* shows us, this was true for metal objects as well as works on paper. Aneemat L., *Natural Curiosity: Unseen Art of the First Fleet* (Sydney: 2014) 15–16.

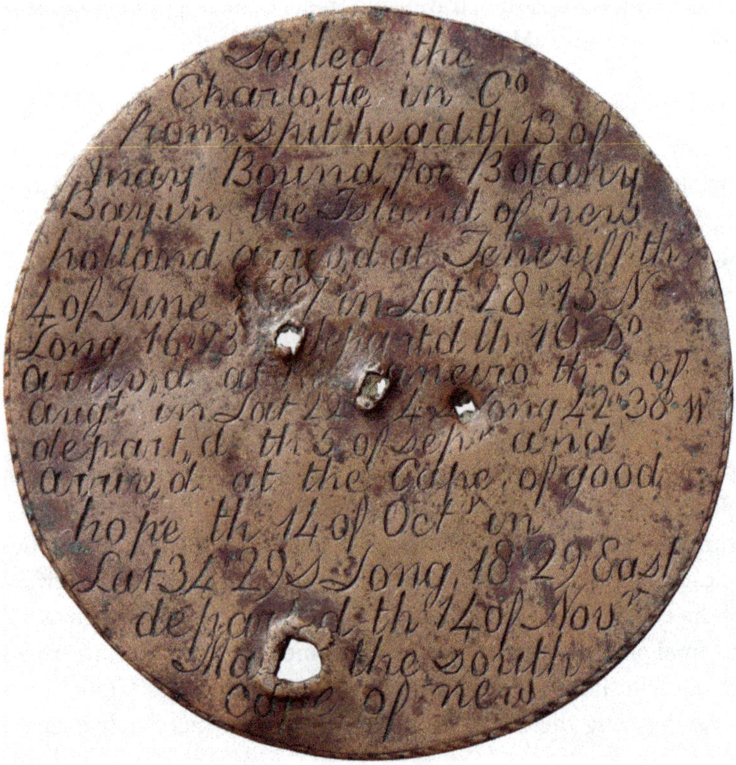

FIGURE 12.3 *Copper Charlotte Medal*, 1788. Copper, 47 mm (diameter)
PRIVATE COLLECTION. IMAGE © NATIONAL MUSEUM OF AUSTRALIA

from great Britain Miles/ 13106/ WB' (including a minor error in transcription, which suggests that the copper medal postdates the accurate inscription of the silver medal). Beneath this inscription, we see the same ornamental stars, and similarly anthropomorphised sun and moon as found on the silver *Charlotte Medal*.[55] The discovery of the copper version is important because it helps situate the original silver *Charlotte Medal* amongst the broader visual culture of exonumia (numismatic objects other than coins and paper money, such as medals and tokens) from which it originated, including convict love tokens,

55 Chapman, "The Enigma" 28. Chapman suggests that the owner of the medal was one William Broughton, a storekeeper and magistrate, who was, at the time of the medal's engraving, John White's personal servant on the voyage of the *Charlotte*. Moreover, Broughton's property, Lachlan Vale in Appin, was located just 15 kilometres north of Camden Town, where the copper medal was later discovered. See also Lane, "Australia's First Medallion".

maritime engraved coins, and counterfeit coins. This is the broader context to which this paper now turns.

4 Convict Love Tokens and Maritime Engraved Coins

Numismatics (the study of currency including coins and medals) is a useful framework to rub against the grain of national art history, for currency is typically imprinted with a royal subject, head of state, or coat of arms. In their circulation across borders, however, coins also map transnational networks of exchange. As we shall see, numismatic objects routinely evade national borders or, in the case of forgeries, undermine state sovereignty and economics. They can even, in some cases, notionally cheat a death sentence. The evasive, escapist quality of coins and other forms of exonumia, such as love tokens and maritime engraved coins, helps us understand how these numismatic objects can be said to transgress as much as affirm national authority. Like the two sides of a coin, in fact, the difference between transgression and affirmation can appear random or arbitrary.

Convict love tokens are a form of convict folk art typically made by refashioning King George III Cartwheel pennies. Such love tokens are readily comparable in size, medium, and technique to both *Charlotte* medals, and particularly the copper version. The making of love tokens was a noted part of convict life, both on land and sea. Hosty notes that Barrett 'would no doubt have observed, and possibly taken part in, the manufacture of [...] "love tokens"' during his time imprisoned on the hulks'.[56] Arthur Griffiths in his *Chronicle of Newgate* made mention of inmates of that infamous London prison 'grinding the impressions of penny-pieces, then pricking figures or words on them to give to their friends as memorials'.[57] In a footnote, Griffiths further explains:

> These Newgate tokens were circular thin pieces of metal of various sizes. The initials or the names of a loving pair were punched upon them, together with a heart or some symbol of affection; sometimes with a motto, such as 'True for ever', 'Love for life'. The greatest value was attached to these tokens by the criminal classes. Those at large constantly wore them round their necks, and treated them as amulets to preserve them from danger and detection.[58]

56 Hosty, "The Charlotte Medal" 12.
57 Griffiths A., *The Chronicles of Newgate* (London: 1896) 414.
58 Ibidem, 414.

Accordingly, *The Charlotte Medal* should be understood as emerging from a larger numismatic culture that includes convict love tokens, as well as coin currency and its forgery. Indeed, it seems plausible that, during his time on board the *Charlotte* or awaiting transportation on the *Dunkirk*, Barrett was involved in the production of all three 'metallic records' as Mira would call them: medals, counterfeit coins, and convict love tokens.

During the Georgian period, English men and women across the class spectrum were obsessed with mementoes, keepsakes, and trinkets.[59] Seamen regularly made or commissioned mementos very similar to convict love tokens as gifts for their loved ones in advance of long and potentially dangerous voyages. In so doing, they often borrowed stock phrases and symbols – such as 'when this you see, remember me', or pictures of arrow-struck love hearts and entwined hands. These inscriptions were typically accompanied by the name or initials of the departing person and the year of departure. Like *The Charlotte Medal*, these maritime mementoes are coin-sized; and like the *Medal*, they are commemorative in nature – though highly personalised, as against the imperial grandeur of the arrival of the First Fleet at Botany Bay in 1788. But unlike *The Charlotte Medal*, which so clearly narrates the nautical route to Australia and was thus indisputably produced there, convict love tokens were made hastily while awaiting transportation.[60] They were given to their intended recipient prior to the convict's departure and thus did not undertake the voyage themselves. This particular object history of love tokens has led to their other, mournful moniker: 'the leaden hearts the convicts left behind'.[61]

Convict love tokens differ from maritime 'forget-me-nots' in several ways. First, the text and iconography of love tokens often betrays the condition of incarceration. Thus, to the end of the phrase 'when this you see, remember me' is added 'until I get my liberty'. Convict love tokens also often feature imagery of shackles, prison walls, and barred windows. Secondly, instead of ornately carved brooches or tokens made of 'more noble metals',[62] modes familiar to the love tokens of seafarers, convicts often favoured King George III Cartwheel

59 Tindal C. – Greiner A. – Hallam D., "Harnessing the Powers of Elemental Analysis to Determine the Manufacture and Use of Convict Love Tokens – A Case Study", *AICCM Bulletin* 36:1 (2015) 45.

60 Sim Comfort, a numismatist and collector of British naval medals, hypothesises that 'blank' love tokens for seafarers were available for on-the-spot engravings at the jeweller shops, which could typically be found at major ports. He suggests that the engraved love token might be the closest thing to an engagement ring that a sailor's sweetheart would ever receive. Comfort S., *Forget Me Not: A Study of Naval and Maritime Engraved Coins and Plate (1745 to 1918)* (London: 2004) IX.

61 Field M. – Millett T. (eds.), *Convict Love Tokens*.

62 Tindal – Greiner – Hallam, "Harnessing the Powers" 45.

pennies as the basis of their mementoes. Made of soft and malleable copper, which was easy to engrave, as well as possessing a relatively large face suitable for inscription (just over 40 mm in diameter), Cartwheel pennies were appropriated by convicts, one or both of their faces smoothed back, then inscribed with text and/or an image. Because King George III pennies were cumbersome on account of their size and weight, they were considered inconvenient and 'hard on the pocket' by both shopkeepers and consumers.[63] Being so unpopular, they were more readily available for appropriation in the manufacture of convict love tokens.

There was also something appropriately iconoclastic about convicts engraving pennies, a process that necessarily entailed the defacing of the image of either King George III (obverse) or Britannia with her shield, trident, and olive branch (reverse). In this way, convict love tokens can be said to 'amount to an iconoclastic degradation of the royal image and a bastardizing usurpation of royal authority' in much the same way forged coins do.[64] Curiously, the same can be said of the first official Australian coin currency, the Holey Dollar and Dump [Fig. 12.4], which, we recall, was minted by the convicted coin forger William Henshall in New South Wales under Governor Macquarie. The Holey Dollar and Dump was made from the silver Spanish dollar, which was in the early nineteenth century the most common coin used for international trade. Macquarie minted 80,000 new coins from 40,000 Spanish *reales* by having Henshall punch a hole out of their centre (the dump, valued at fifteen pence), and retaining their perimeter (the dollar, valued at five shillings). Both the dollar and dump were then counterstruck with their new values and royal allegiances right over the top of the Spanish coin design, which featured the profile of King Charles IV of Spain on the obverse and the crowned Spanish coat of arms on the reverse, which remained partially visible beneath.[65] In a brazen move, then, settler Australian currency is inaugurated by a form of iconoclasm, in a manner not dissimilar to that of convict love tokens. The motivations for this act of iconoclasm highlight the rudimentary and provisional dimension of the fledging Colony of New South Wales at the time, not unlike the way convicts made do with whatever materials could be found at hand in prison or on the hulks.

---

63 Tindal – Greiner – Hallam, "Harnessing the Powers" 46.

64 Neill M., "Bastardy, Counterfeiting, and Misogyny in *The Revenger's Tragedy*", *Studies in English Literature* 36 (1996) 401; cited in Malton S., *False Economies: Forgery and Other Illegitimate Issue, 1837–1895* (Ph.D. dissertation, University of Toronto: 2004) 7.

65 Lane – Fleig, "William Henshall" 20–23.

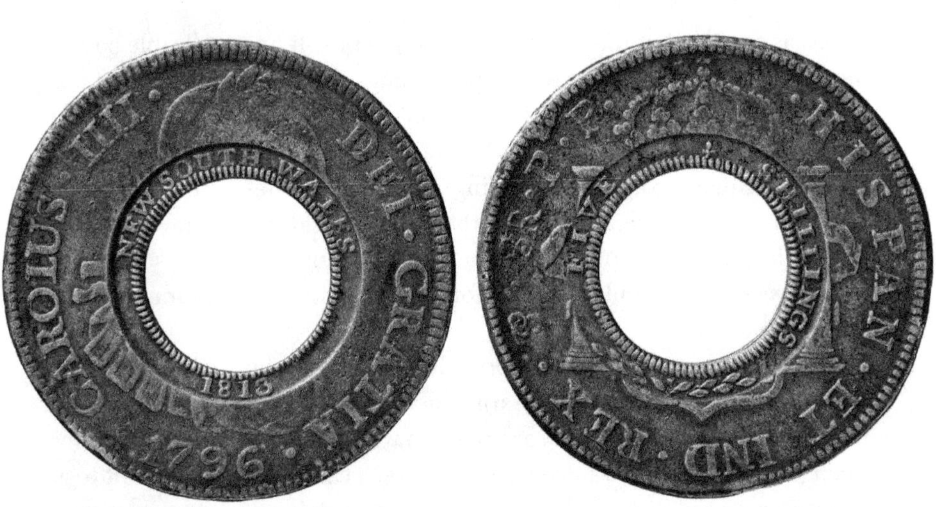

FIGURE 12.4 Holey Dollar and Dump, 1813. Silver, 41 mm (diameter)
IMAGE © NATIONAL MUSEUM OF AUSTRALIA

The images and texts inscribed on convict love tokens are also clearly related to the techniques of scrimshaw – the art of the mariner, made of carved and inked whalebone. But, as Hamish Maxwell-Stewart and James Bradley have argued, the tokens are even more closely related to the words, phrases, and images found on convict tattoos, which are themselves a significant feature of the visual culture produced by and on the bodies of convicts transported to Australia.[66] As with love tokens, convict tattoos are significant because they represent some of the only examples of the convict 'voice from below' – convicts being a class that left behind few first-hand accounts of their lives whether in the form of letters or biographies, but whose lives were, by contrast, thoroughly documented by mechanisms from 'above', such as the exhaustive convict musters or 'black books' in which detailed accounts of convict tattoos were recorded, along with an inventory of other physical characteristics, including eye colour, hair colour, complexion, deformities, or scarring.[67] Simon Barnard puts the figure of tattooed convicts arriving in Australia as high as thirty-seven per cent of all male convicts, and fifteen per cent of all female convicts.[68] It is not just text and iconography that passes between love tokens and tattoos, but

66 Maxwell-Stewart H. – Bradley J., "Convict Tattoos: Tales of Freedom and Coercion", in Field M. – Millett T. (eds.), *Convict Love Tokens: The Leaden Hearts Convicts Left Behind* (Adelaide: 1998) 47–52.

67 Frost L. – Maxwell-Stewart H. (eds.), *Chain Letters: Narrating Convict Lives* (Melbourne: 2001).

68 Barnard S., *Convict Tattoos: Marked Men and Women of Australia* (Melbourne: 2016) 1.

technique too: one of the main inscriptive techniques for love tokens was stippling (i.e. small indented dots), a method shared with stick-and-poke tattoos. This link between *The Charlotte Medal*, convict love tokens, and convict tattoos is significant because it shows that the first colonial artwork emerged from a set of convict folk traditions that were directly and indirectly critical of the state. By defacing and reinscribing coins or inking the body, convicts carved out minor pockets of agency and self-determination.

Common subject matter across *The Charlotte Medal*, recorded convict tattoos, and convict love tokens can also be observed. A brief sketch of their relationship is helpful for understanding the fine line that convict artists constantly traversed: between artist and criminal, self-expression and extracted labour. Barnard notes that '[a]pproximately one per cent of tattooed male convicts bore a tattoo of a vessel of some kind: brigs, boats, cutters, sloops, ships and fishing smack'.[69] Some of these men were tattooed with very specific ships: Charles Deverall, a brig named *Badger*; Henry Orme, a ship labelled *Moffat* (he was transported on the *Moffatt*); and the indent for Joseph Sutcliff notes that he was tattooed with 'a bust of the *Prince Regent*', again the ship on which he was transported.[70] At least three love tokens in the National Museum of Australia in Canberra feature three-masted ships that relate to the *Charlotte*'s depiction by Barrett. An 1839 love token issued by convict John Bloxidge, transported to New South Wales in 1840, features a man standing on the shore with a three-masted ship in the background [Fig. 12.5].[71]

The obverse of an 1831 token issued by John Woodfield sports a similar pictorial schema: a man on the shore looking out to a three-masted ship, inscribed in elegant cursive: 'Randall Woodfield. / Ships Cooper. / 1831' [Fig. 12.6]. The reverse depicts a man in striped pants, his left wrist chained to the wall, against the background of an impenetrable brick wall punctuated by two barred windows. Its caption suggests the convict's identity: 'John Woodfield, Aged 19'. The two sides of the coin presumably link/separate father and son at the moment just prior to the son's transportation to the other side of the world.

A third example, issued by William Brain in 1838, unlike the aforementioned, is entirely stippled like a tattoo [Fig. 12.7]. Its obverse shows a convict in the foreground, 'slanged' (that is, chained) wrists to ankles, and a three-masted ship in the background. In the sky are birds, an ornamental sun with face, a

---

69 Ibidem, 98.

70 Ibidem, 98–99.

71 The obverse reads: 'JO[H?]N / BLOXIDGE / AD 18. [15?] YS 1839 / REMMEMBER ME / WHEN FAR AWAY'.

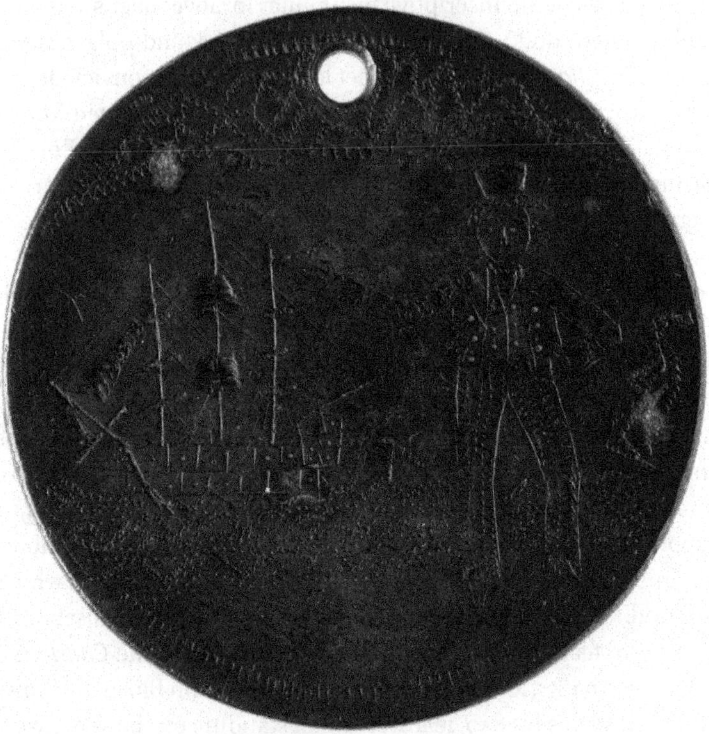

FIGURE 12.5 Convict love token from John Bloxidge, 1839. Metal (non-specific), 36 mm (diameter)

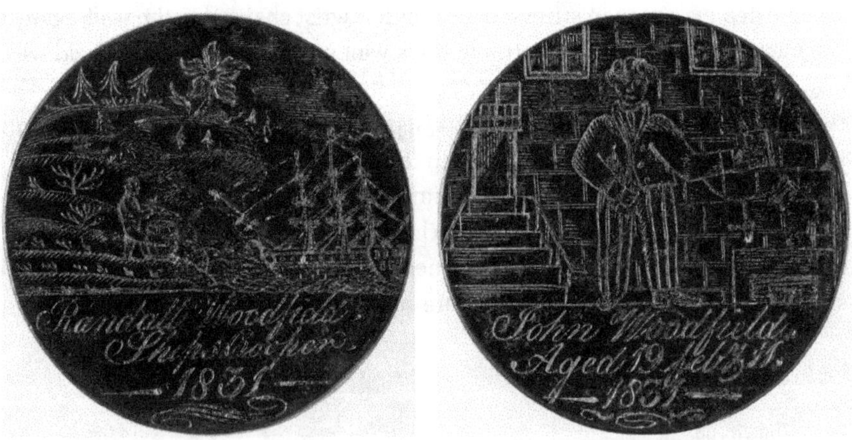

FIGURE 12.6 Convict love token from John Woodfield, 1831. Metal (non-specific), 35 mm (diameter)

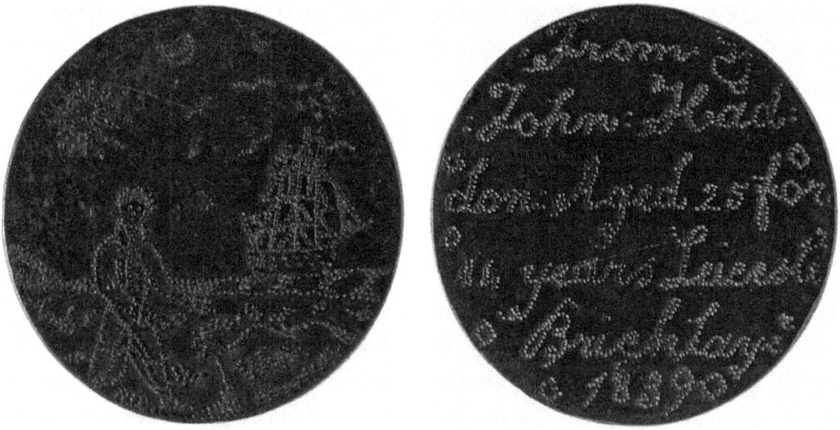

FIGURE 12.7 Convict love token from William Brain, 1838. Metal (non-specific), 36 mm (diameter)
CANBERRA, NATIONAL MUSEUM OF AUSTRALIA. IMAGE © NATIONAL MUSEUM OF AUSTRALIA

crescent moon, and a cluster of seven stars (likely referring to the Pleiades, or seven sisters).[72]

A love token dated 1787, held in the private collection of Sim Comfort in London, is even more revealing for our purposes [Fig. 12.8]. Made of copper and 30 mm in diameter, it depicts a view of an armed ship, inscribed above '*THE*SEARRUS*' and below '1787' – presumably referring to H.M.S. *Sirius*, one of the two royal naval escorts of the First Fleet that left England for Botany Bay in 1787.[73] On the other side, we see a man and woman taking tea, seated at a table, beneath a heart crossed with two arrows and dangling, noticeably, from a chain (a motif that, Comfort notes, does not appear in other maritime engraved coins), and two birds in the sky. In the exergue beneath this scene is inscribed the initials '*I*R*'.[74]

While the *Searrus* engraved coin seems to have been executed in a looser hand and perhaps more speedily than *The Charlotte Medal*, Peter Lane and Timothy Millett note, in a short entry on this object in the 1998 book *Convict Love Tokens*, that the *Searrus* token closely relates in style to *The Charlotte Medal* (whose exact significance was, in 1998, still somewhat unknown):

72 Beneath this imagery is a stone inscribed 'Wm Brain.' The reverse bears a familiar sentiment: 'When this you / see think of / me when I / am far away / Wm BRAIN / aut 21 1838 / AGED 21'.

73 See Comfort, *Forget Me Not* 97–99.

74 Ibidem, 98.

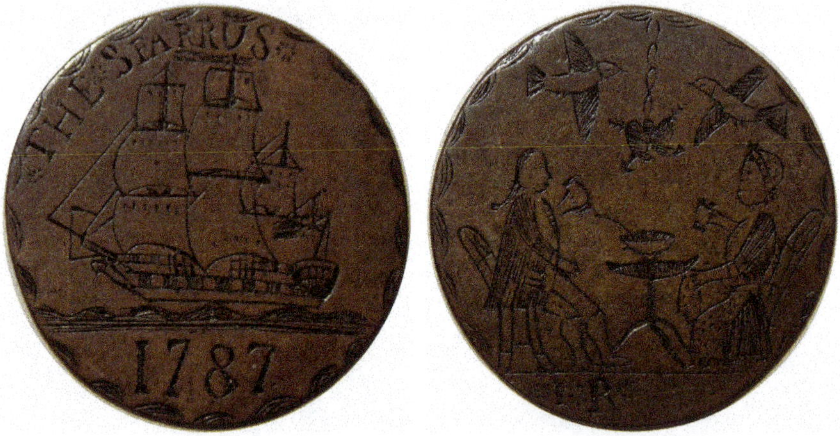

FIGURE 12.8 Convict love token depicting the *Searrus*, 1787. Copper, 30 mm (diameter)
LONDON, SIM COMFORT COLLECTION. IMAGE © SIM COMFORT ASSOCIATES

> An item in the Millford Haven Collection [of British naval medals, published in 1919] depicts the *Charlotte*, also from the First Fleet. The engraved presentation of the *Charlotte* is in many ways similar to the engraved view of the *Searrus*, with the same primitive rendering of the ship's hull, a similar rendering of the stern of both ships, and several other similar details. One in particular is the use of a number of short lines arranged in a circular/radiant patterns to represent stars.[75]

Lane and Millett suggest both works were done by the same hand.[76] Comfort, in his 2004 book *Forget Me Not*, concurs, and supposes the *Searrus* medal may have been made for Ino (John) Rowley, a freeman on board the *Sirius* (a vessel that did not transport convicts) who worked as a sawyer on Norfolk Island briefly, before returning to England on the *Waaksameid* from Port Jackson in 1791.[77]

As Millett, the collector who amassed some 307 examples of convict love tokens, has observed in his study of the genre, the givers of convict love tokens (i.e. those whose names or initials are inscribed on the token itself) were not

75 Millett T. – Lane P., "Known Convict Love Tokens", in Field M. – Millett T. (eds.), *Convict Love Tokens: The Leaden Hearts Convicts Left Behind* (Adelaide: 1998) 75–114: 77. See also Mountbatten L.A., *British Naval Medals* (1919).

76 Ibidem, 77.

77 Comfort, *Forget Me Not* 98.

always one and the same with the maker.[78] This fact should become self-evident when one compares the high rates of illiteracy amongst convicts – many simply signed their names with a cross – with the detailed inscriptions born by the love tokens.[79] Thus, it may not have been, for example, John Woodfield, John Bloxidge, nor William Brain who made the tokens they gifted their loved ones. More likely, Millett suggests, convicts commissioned love tokens by other resident inmates who possessed the requisite skills in metal engraving – perhaps trading tobacco for a token.[80] Such an explanation would also account for the fact that several love tokens inscribed with different names or initials may betray the same maker's hand.[81] As Millett explains, the convicts with skills in metalwork required to make love tokens were, principally, coin and banknote forgers – what he refers to as the '"unofficial" craftsmen' of the prisons.[82] Thus, forgers not only populate the origins of colonial Australian art as indentured labourers on shore in the colonies; they are also responsible for much of its immediate prehistory, in the form of love tokens, made either on the hulks or on land in prisons back in England.

From this brief comparison of *The Charlotte Medal* with other maritime engraved coins and convict love tokens, we see that Barrett's depiction of the *Charlotte* on the silver medal is closely related to the expressive convict tradition of depicting one's vessel of transportation on love tokens as well as in tattoos.[83] While the medal was, one presumes, on some level extracted from Barrett by White, given the power imbalance between them and White's subsequent deployment of Watling as an artist in servitude, the medal's cousins – in love tokens and tattoos – preserve a powerful form of convict self-imaging and self-determination. That, like the *Charlotte Medal*, it was forgers who were most responsible for producing love tokens, and that the love tokens (like Macquarie and Henshall's Holey Dollar and Dump) represent an iconoclastic defacing of royal authority, is crucial: for it shows that forged coins and exonumia made from defaced coins both undermine state sovereignty and its economy in different ways. Ironically, the artwork that can be said to inaugurate settler Australian art comes from this distinctly iconoclastic tradition. As emblematised by these numismatic objects, the earliest colonial artworks can thus be seen to transgress as much as affirm national borders.

78 Millett sold his collection to the National Museum of Australia in 2008.

79 Millett, "Leaden Hearts" 16.

80 Ibidem, 17.

81 Ibidem, 17.

82 Ibidem, 17.

83 For further on the matter of tokens portraying and naming prison hulks, see Millett, "Leaden Hearts" 21.

5 Capital and Capital Punishment

In the opening lines of *Forget Me Not: A Study of Naval and Maritime Engraved Coins and Plate* (*1745 to 1981*), Comfort compares the mariner's art of scrimshaw to maritime engraved coins, lamenting the paucity of terminology to describe the latter. He writes:

> The Americans have this wonderful vocabulary that relates to scrimshaw. The person executing the artwork is a scrimshander and scrimming is sometimes used as a verb for creating scrimshaw.
>
> What you can say about engraved coins is fairly limited. The object is an engraved coin or engraved piece of plate, the action of creating an image is called engraving and the person engraving it is the engraver.[84]

The verb to engrave (to incise or carve) is, naturally, related to the noun grave ('excavation in earth for the reception of a dead body'), derived from the Old English *graef* (trench, cave, ditch), and the Old High German *grab* (grave, tomb). It is to this etymology that I turn in this chapter's conclusion, where I shall suggest that the descriptor 'engraved coin' is, even if only accidentally, apposite for capturing the almost magical relationship between coins and death. Money's chthonic association becomes useful shorthand for understanding capitalism's entanglement with capital punishment (or the commuted death sentence of transportation), and thus the historical entanglement between forgery and capital punishment. Following this line of thinking, this chapter attempts to locate *The Charlotte Medal* and its convict forger artist at the nexus of capital and capital punishment in Britain during the long eighteenth century, which is also to say at the inauguration of settler Australian art history.

The Charlotte Medal, convict love tokens, and forged coins are all metallic records of the legal and penal contexts of eighteenth-century England – characterised by the so-called great crime wave and resultant overcrowded prisons, and by the public spectacle of the gallows and the spectre of transportation (either to the colonies in America or Australia). While transportation was considered less severe than a death sentence, it entailed a very real form of social death for the transported. Indeed, Tom Gretton has likened convict love tokens to 'tiny gravestones' – inscribed with what were, effectively, a convict's 'last words in the world they knew'.[85] In his essay "Last Dying Speech

84 Comfort, *Forget Me Not* v.

85 Gretton T., "Last Dying Speech and Confession", in Field M. – Millett T. (eds.), *Convict Love Tokens: The Leaden Hearts Convicts Left Behind* (Adelaide: 1998) 39–46: 39.

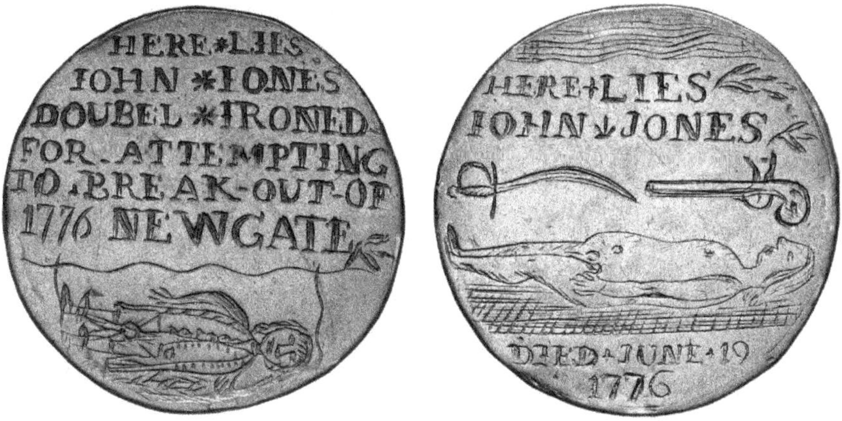

FIGURE 12.9 Convict love token from John Jones, 1776. Metal (non-specific)
SYDNEY, TIMOTHY MILLETT COLLECTION. IMAGE © TIMOTHY MILLETT

and Confession", Gretton reads the love tokens as emerging from a poor and working urban culture whose subjects were the primary consumers of popular broadsides that commemorated prisoners' last words prior to their execution, namely: *The Ordinary of Newgate* and the *Newgate Calendar* that replaced it in 1783 (the printed matter famously depicted in the execution scene of Hogarth's *Idle and Industrious Apprentice* series).

As we have already seen, the prevalence of sailing ship imagery on love tokens relates to the visual culture of mariners and their practice of making mementoes for loved ones. These, too, Gretton notes, had an epitaphic quality: for sea voyages in the eighteenth century were often months long and dangerous, and were considered by seamen and their loved ones to be closer in nature to a 'provisional death' than a mere separation.[86] For the families of both seamen on the eve of voyage and convicts on the eve of transportation, love tokens were a material 'trace of vanishing human beings'.[87] One striking convict token referred to by Gretton literalises the relationship between imprisonment and death [Fig. 12.9]. The obverse is inscribed 'HERE*LIES/JOHN*JONES/ DOUBLE*IRONED/ FOR ATTEMPTING/ TO BREAK-OUT-OF/ 1776 NEWGATE', and shows the convict chained to the floor of his cell beneath a wavy line, which, perhaps inadvertently, connotes burial. The reverse reads 'HERE+LIES/ JOHN*JONES', under which a cutlass and pistol is depicted. At the base of the image, Jones's dead and naked body lies primed on a slab,

86 Ibidem, 44.
87 Ibidem, 46.

as if about to be dissected by surgeons, as was often the fate for executed criminals.[88]

While we have established that *The Charlotte Medal* is not a love token (in that it was not an expression of affection, nor a 'leaden heart' that stayed behind), we can glimpse in it a kind of death. On 17 February 1788, just weeks after disembarking the *Charlotte* at Sydney Cove, Barrett, along with three other convicts was caught stealing 'pease and beef' from the government store. Minor by today's standards, then it was a serious crime, as food during the first months and years of settlement was a scarce resource and starvation posed a serious risk for all – not least convicts, who, save for the Indigenous population, were at the bottom of the imperial pecking order. One of the convicted men (the youngest, named John Ryan) was sentenced to 300 lashes for his part in the crime. The remaining three (Barrett, Henry Lavell or Lovell, and Joseph Hall) were each sentenced to death that evening. There was not a willing executioner amongst the Marines who had been marshalled to oversee the hanging. The young convict named Ryan was duly pressured by threat of death to assume the role of 'Jack Ketch', to which he eventually acquiesced.[89] The two others besides Barrett, Lavell and Hall, were given twenty-four hours' reprieve at the final moment. But not Barrett. Arthur Bowes Smyth noted in his journal that Barrett 'was hung on the arm of a tree [...] turn'd off exactly a quarter after six hour, in sight of all the convicts male and female'.[90] Lieutenant Ralph Clark, also in the crowd, supposed Barrett thought the marines were calling his bluff, and were only intending to scare him. Clark wrote of the execution:

> Barret and he mounted the Ladder – from his going I dont think that he had the least thought that was to Suffer but when the Provos Martial put a handkerchiff a bout his head he turned as white as a sheet – when Soon after the Ladder was puld from under him and he Lanched into the other world without a gron[91]

---

88 Linebaugh P., "The Tyburn Riot Against the Surgeons", in Hay D. – Linebaugh P. – Rule J. – Thompson E.P. – Winslow C. (eds.), *Albion's Fatal Tree: Crime and Society in Eighteenth-Century England* (New York: 1975) 65–118.

89 Jack Ketch was a prolific English executioner under King Charles II, and subsequently become a synonym for executioners/execution more generally.

90 Bowes-Smyth Arthur, *Journal of a Voyage from Portsmouth to New South Wales and China – in the Lady Penrhyn, Merchantman – William Cropton Sever, Commander by Arthur Bowes Smyth, Surgeon – 1787–1788–1789* (c. 1790) 107.

91 Ralph Clark cited in Gillen M., *The Founders of Australia: A Biographical Dictionary of the First Fleet* (Sydney: 1989) 25.

As with everyone else in the fledging colony, White, too, was present, recording the event in his journal as follows:

> They were, about six o'clock the same evening, taken to the fatal tree, where Barrett was launched into eternity, after having confessed to the Rev. Mr. Johnson, who attended him, that he was guilty of the crime, and had long merited the ignominious death which he was about to suffer, and to which he said he had been brought by bad company and evil example.[92]

Barrett was thus both the maker of the first colonial artwork and the victim of the first colonial execution – a coincidence that is frequently noted by commentators, but rarely theorised. The death that we glimpse in *The Charlotte Medal* relates both to the social death suffered by convicts upon their transportation, the threat of a gallows death that so often haunted their lives (many convicts only narrowly avoided death sentences themselves), and the execution of its maker, Barrett.

Through an analysis of *The Charlotte Medal*'s proximity to forged coins, we saw that the first colonial artwork must be understood in relation to eighteenth-century English capitalism and its undermining by forgers. From our brief sketch of eighteenth-century forgery law and the sad fate of Barrett in New South Wales, we saw that *The Charlotte Medal* must also be understood in relation to capital punishment – the two of which were, as Peter Linebaugh has argued, inextricably entwined in eighteenth-century England, where various enclosures of common land, the criminalisation of perquisites and customary rights, amidst a rapidly expanding suite of property laws (many of which were encompassed by Waltham's Black Act of 1723) led to the widespread criminalisation, imprisonment, and, in thousands of instances, public execution of England's working poor.[93] Put another way, capitalism and capital punishment developed hand in hand in eighteenth-century England, each one relying upon the other: 'the organised death of living labour (capital punishment) and the oppression of the living by dead labour (the punishment of capital)', writes Linebaugh, were intimately entangled.[94] But it was the crime of forgery, as Sara Malton has argued, that was 'situated at the *centre* of debates about the stability of the capitalist system and the validity of capital punishment' – because

92 White, *Journal of a Voyage to New South Wales*.

93 Linebaugh P., *The London Hanged: Crime and Civil Society in the Eighteenth Century* (London: 2003).

94 Ibidem, 1.

forgery crimes revealed key vulnerabilities in the state and its economy, and because forgery convictions claimed so many lives (including the seemingly less expendable lives of middle- and ruling-class forgers).[95]

The Charlotte Medal is part of a broader numismatic order comprising maritime engraved coins, convict love tokens, and counterfeit coins – all of which index, in one way or another, death, whether provisional (seafaring), social (transportation), or a state-sanctioned (execution). Thus, if *The Charlotte Medal* can be seen as a kind of origin for settler-colonial Australian art, it can also be seen as a tombstone – a birth that is simultaneously a kind of death. Of course, deaths inaugurate many new aesthetic and political regimes. In his famous essay "Painting in the Year Two", American art historian T.J. Clark famously selected Jacques-Louis David's portrait of the slain French revolutionary Jean-Paul Marat (*La Mort du Marat*, 1793) as his 'candidate for the beginning of modernism'.[96] Unlike the martyred death of Marat, rendered iconic by David and marched through the streets of Paris, however, the death that haunts *The Charlotte Medal* is effaced, utterly spectral to the object, if not totally invisible. This is a condition that is mirrored in the near-total invisibility of convicts throughout early works of Australian art history – convicts rarely appear in oil paintings, even those made by convicts themselves – and is emblematic of the relative expendability of convict life in the colonial regime.[97]

In the explicit connection between the dead body and the coin or exonumia, we might, finally, recall the funerary ritual of placing a coin in the mouth or over the eyes of a deceased person. Dating at least as far back as classical antiquity, this was a custom sometimes known as 'Charon's obol' or *viaticum* (meaning provisioning for a journey, from the Latin *via* meaning road or way). In classical tradition, the coin or token (the obol) is given as a payment or bribe to the ferryman (Charon) to ensure safe passage over the river Styx or Acheron – that is from the world of the living to the afterlife. But, as Susan Stevens explains, *viaticum*:

95 Malton, *False Economies* 6. Emphasis added. Forgery was a capital offence from the 1690s until the 1832 Forgery Act and Coinage Offences Act, which abolished the death sentence for forgery offences.

96 Clark T.J., "Painting in the Year Two", *Representations* 47 (1994) 13.

97 Some exceptions to this rule include John Glover, *My Harvest Home*, 1835, Tasmania Museum and Art Gallery, Hobert; Knud Bull, *The Wreck of the 'George III'*, 1850, National Gallery of Australia, Canberra; and Francis Greenway, *Untitled* [*Scene Inside Newgate*], 1812 and *The Mock Trial*, 1812, Mitchell Library, State Library of New South Wales, Sydney. Bull and Greenway were both convicts themselves.

> has an interesting and suggestive later history, since it carries into Christian Latin a meaning of nourishment for the soul during its journey after death. *Viaticum* is the eucharist, the *communion Dei* which was placed in the mouth of the faithful at the moment of death to provide for the soul in its passage to eternal life. This Christian deathbed rite has been thought by some to replace the classical 'Charon's obol'.[98]

Stevens explains that the mouth was considered the portal from whence the soul escaped the body, hence the placement of the coin in this opening. While this practice was geographically widespread, ranging from West Africa across Europe and up to northern England, what was common about this funerary ritual was the unanimously low value of the coin, which was symbolic of the 'poverty of death'.[99] In these rituals, the fungible coin comes to represent death as the great equaliser. Interestingly, the convict love token plays a related role to the *viaticum* or eucharist. As Gretton suggests, then the convict love token 'replaces both the body and the voice of the convict' at the moment of its departure, and in this light too 'comes to resemble a communion wafer'.[100]

The obol, *viaticum*, and, by extension, convict love token is an object of exchange – one that marks and makes tangible the passage or transition from one world to the next; from the realm of the living to the realm of the dead. The water-born *Charlotte Medal* – as with its cousins in coins, maritime exonumia, and convict love tokens – may also be understood as a metallic record of the intermediary and liminal passage between life and death (whether provisional, social, or state-sanctioned), between Old England and the penal colony. In this way, *The Charlotte Medal* is a slippery object with which to inaugurate a national art-historical canon. But in fact, it figures forth *precisely* the interdependencies and far-flung connections, the exploitations and extractions, as well as augurs the utterly devastating consequences of invasion that we know follow January 20th 1788 – all of which must be understood as foundational to the tradition. As we have seen, forgery is also foundational to this history. For forgers, like Barrett, were the makers of these liminal and intermediary metallic records, and frequent passengers between worlds too.

98 Stevens S., "Charon's Obol and Other Coins in Ancient Funerary Practice", *Phoenix* 45:3 (1991) 220–221.

99 Stevens, "Charon's Obol" 219.

100 Gretton, "Last Dying Speech" 43–44.

Bibliography

Anderson H., *Farewell to Judges and Juries: The Broadside Ballad and Convict Transportation to Australia, 1788–1868* (Melbourne: 2000).

Aneemat L., *Natural Curiosity: Unseen Art of the First Fleet* (Sydney: 2014).

Baines P., *The House of Forgery in Eighteenth-Century Britain* (Vermont: 1999).

Barnard S., *Convict Tattoos: Marked Men and Women of Australia* (Melbourne: 2016).

Barnwell A., "Convict Shame to Convict Chic: Intergenerational Memory and Family Histories", *Memory Studies* 12:4 (August 2019) 398–411.

Bateson C., *The Convict Ships* (Sydney – London: 1974).

Bowes-Smyth Arthur, *Journal of a Voyage from Portsmouth to New South Wales and China – in the Lady Penrhyn, Merchantman – William Cropton Sever, Commander by Arthur Bowes Smyth, Surgeon – 1787–1788–1789* (c. 1790).

Butler R., *What is Appropriation? An Anthology of Critical Writings on Australian Art in the '80s and '90s* (Sydney – Brisbane: 1996).

Caffentzis C.G., *Clipped Coins, Abused Words, and Civil Governments: John Locke's Philosophy of Money* (New York: 1989).

Carlisle L., *Australian Commemorative Medals and Medalets from 1788* (New South Wales: 1983).

Chapman J., "The Solution of the Charlotte Enigma", *Journal of the Numismatic Association of Australia* 9 (1998) 28–33.

Clark T.J., "Painting in the Year Two", *Representations* 47 (1994) 13–63.

Comfort S., *Forget Me Not: A Study of Naval and Maritime Engraved Coins and Plate (1745 to 1918)* (London: 2004).

Cunneen M., "The Mercury Mutineers: Biographical Analyses of Early Australian Convicts", *People Australia, National Centre of Biography* (Canberra: 2021).

Field M., "Introduction", in Field M. – Millett T. (eds.), *Convict Love Tokens: The Leaden Hearts Convicts Left Behind* (Adelaide: 1998) 1–4.

Field M. – Millet T. (eds.), *Convict Love Tokens: The Leaden Hearts Convicts Left Behind* (Adelaide: 1998).

Foss P., "Theatrum Nondum Cogitorium", *The Foreign Bodies Papers* (Sydney: 1981) 15–38.

Frost L., "The Politics of Writing Convict Lives: Academic Research, State Archives, and Family History", *Life Writing* 8:1 (2011) 19–33.

Frost L. – Maxwell-Stewart H. (eds.), *Chain Letters: Narrating Convict Lives* (Melbourne: 2001).

Gatrell V.A.C., *The Hanging Tree: Execution and the English People 1770–1868* (Oxford: 1994).

Gillen M., *The Founders of Australia: A Biographical Dictionary of the First Fleet* (Sydney: 1989).
Gretton T., "Last Dying Speech and Confession", in Field M. – Millett T. (eds.), *Convict Love Tokens: The Leaden Hearts Convicts Left Behind* (Adelaide: 1998) 39–46.
Griffiths A., *The Chronicles of Newgate* (London: 1896).
Hackforth-Jones J., *The Convict Artists* (Melbourne – Sydney: 1977).
Hay D. – Linebaugh P. – Rule J. – Thompson E.P. – Winslow C. (eds.), *Albion's Fatal Tree: Crime and Society in Eighteenth-Century England* (New York: 1975).
Hosty K., "The Charlotte Medal", *Signals Journal* 84 (2008) 10–15.
Lane P., "Australia's First Medallion: Silver Charlotte Metal", *Collectables Trader* (2008).
Lane P. – Fleig P., "William Henshall: Maker of Holy Dollars and Dumps", *Journal of the Numismatic Association of Australia* 15 (2004) 1–30.
Linebaugh P., *The London Hanged: Crime and Civil Society in the Eighteenth Century* (London: 2003).
Malton S., *False Economies: Forgery and Other Illegitimate Issue, 1837–1895* (Ph.D. dissertation, University of Toronto: 2004).
Malton S., *Forgery in Nineteenth-Century Literature and Culture: Fictions of Finance from Dickens to Wilde* (London: 2009).
Maxwell-Stewart H. – Bradley J., "Convict Tattoos: Tales of Freedom and Coercion'", in Field M. – Millett T. (eds.), *Convict Love Tokens: The Leaden Hearts Convicts Left Behind* (Adelaide: 1998) 47–52.
McCouat P., "Colonial Artist, Thief, Forger and Mutineer: Thomas Barrett's Amazing Career", *Journal of Art in Society* (2015).
McGowan R., "Making the 'Bloody Code?' Forgery Legislation in Eighteenth-Century England", in Landau N. (ed.), *Law, Crime and English Society* (Cambridge: 2002) 117–138.
McLean I., *White Aborigines: Identity Politics in Australian Art* (Cambridge: 1998).
McLean I., "Convict Art and Cultural Capital: The Case of Thomas Watling", conference paper for "Colonial Places, Convict Spaces: Penal Transportation in Global Context, c. 1600–1940" (Leicester: 1999).
Millett T. – Lane P., "Known Convict Love Tokens", in Field M. – Millett T. (eds.), *Convict Love Tokens: The Leaden Hearts Convicts Left Behind* (Adelaide: 1998) 75–114.
Molony J.N., *The Native Born: The First White Australians* (Melbourne: 2000).
Morris A., "Charles Henry Theodore Constantini: Convict, Surgeon, Artist, and Forger", *Australiana* 25:3 (2003).
Mountbatten L.A., *British Naval Medals* (London: 1919).

Neill M., "Bastardy, Counterfeiting, and Misogyny in *The Revenger's Tragedy*", *Studies in English Literature* 36 (1996) 397–416.

Shofield A. – Fahy K., *Australian Jewellery: Late Nineteenth and Early Twentieth Century* (Balmain: 1990).

Smith B., *Place, Taste and Tradition: A Study of Australian Art since 1788* (Melbourne: 1945).

Smith M., *Samuel Clayton: Forger, Freemason, Freeman* (Melbourne: 2017).

Smith T., "The Provincialism Problem", *Artforum* 13:1 (1974) 54–59.

Stevens S., "Charon's Obol and Other Coins in Ancient Funerary Practice", *Phoenix* 45:3 (1991) 220–221.

Taylor P., *POPISM* (Melbourne: 1982).

Taylor P., "Popism: The Art of White Aborigines", *Flash Art* 112 (1983) 48–50.

Tindal C. – Greiner A. – Hallam D., "Harnessing the Powers of Elemental Analysis to Determine the Manufacture and Use of Convict Love Tokens – A Case Study", *AICCM Bulletin* 36:1 (2015) 44–55.

Index Nominum

www.ingramcontent.com/pod-product-compliance
Lightning Source LLC
Chambersburg PA
CBHW071326230926
51849CB00002B/327
9789004449480